1 MONTH OF
FREE
READING

at
www.ForgottenBooks.com

By purchasing this book you are eligible for one month membership to ForgottenBooks.com, giving you unlimited access to our entire collection of over 1,000,000 titles via our web site and mobile apps.

To claim your free month visit:
www.forgottenbooks.com/free914114

ISBN 978-0-266-94806-3
PIBN 10914114

(B. A. I. 125.)

U. S. DEPARTMENT OF AGRICULTURE.

FIFTEENTH ANNUAL REPORT

OF THE

U. S.

BUREAU OF ANIMAL INDUSTRY

FOR

THE YEAR 1898.

o

WASHINGTON:
GOVERNMENT PRINTING OFFICE.
1899.

101100

[Public—No. 15.]

AN ACT providing for the public printing and binding and the distribution of public
documents.

Sec. 73. Extra copies of documents and reports shall be printed promptly when
the same shall be ready for publication, and shall be bound in paper or cloth, as
directed by the Joint Committee on Printing, and shall be the number following,
in addition to the usual number.

Of the Report of the Bureau of Animal Industry, 30,000 copies, of which 7,000
shall be for the Senate, 14,000 for the House, and 9,000 for distribution by the
Agricultural Department.

Approved, January 12, 1895.

2

LETTER OF TRANSMITTAL.

U. S. DEPARTMENT OF AGRICULTURE,
BUREAU OF ANIMAL INDUSTRY,·
Washington, D. C., May 8, 1899.

SIR: I have the honor to submit herewith the Fifteenth Annual Report of the Bureau of Animal Industry, prepared in accordance with the organic act of the Bureau, and recommend that it be forwarded to the Public Printer for printing.

The table of contents shows over fifty leading titles. This variety of subjects ought to make the volume valuable in some particulars to all stock raisers. •

Respectfully,

D. E. SALMON,
Chief of Bureau of Animal Industry.

Hon. JAMES WILSON,
Secretary.

CONTENTS.

	Page.
Report of the Chief of the Bureau	11
Blackleg in the United States and the distribution of vaccine by the Bureau of Animal Industry. By V. A. Nörgaard	27
Report upon experimental exports of butter, 1897. By Henry E. Alvord	83
Breeds of dairy cattle. By Henry E. Alvord	137
Fifty dairy rules	201
Meat and milk inspection in Shanghai. By W. J. Blackwood, U. S. N	205
Agriculture and dairying in Scotland. By John C. Higgins	213
The vitality and retention of virulence of certain pathogenic bacteria in milk and its products. By Charles F. Dawson	224
Colored spots in cheese. By R. A. Pearson	229
The serum treatment for swine plague and hog cholera. By E. A. de Schweinitz	235
Experiments in "stamping out" hog cholera in Page County, Iowa	249
The enzymes, or soluble ferments, of the hog cholera germ. By E. A. de Schweinitz	266
The production of immunity in guinea pigs from hog cholera by the use of blood serum from immunified animals. By E. A. de Schweinitz	269
Inoculation to produce immunity from Texas fever in Northern cattle. By E. C. Schroeder	273
Investigations concerning tuberculosis and glanders:	
Some results in the treatment of tuberculosis with antituberculosis serum. By E. A. de Schweinitz	289
The composition of the tuberculosis and glanders bacilli. By E. A. de Schweinitz and Marion Dorset	295
Notes upon the fats contained in the tuberculosis bacilli. By E. A. de Schweinitz and Marion Dorset	301
The mineral constituents of the tubercle bacilli. By E. A. de Schweinitz and Marion Dorset	302
Some products of the tuberculosis bacillus and the treatment of experimental tuberculosis with antitoxic serum. By E. A. de Schweinitz	305
The attenuated bacillus tuberculosis: Its use in producing immunity from tuberculosis in guinea pigs. By E. A. de Schweinitz	318
A new stain for bacillus tuberculosis. By Marion Dorset	326
Asthenia (going light) in fowls. By Charles F. Dawson	329
Laboratory methods for the diagnosis of certain microorganismal diseases. By Charles F. Dawson	335
Breeding zebroids	369
The military administration of Germany in its relation to national horse breeding	372
The cattle industry of Colorado, Wyoming, and Nevada, and the sheep industry of Colorado in 1897. By John T. McNeely	377
A cattle disease in Marshall County, Kansas	382
A cattle disease in Uruguay. By Albert W. Swalm	385
The cattle tick and tuberculosis in New South Wales. By George S. Baker	386

	Page.
Preliminary catalogue of plants poisonous to stock. By V. K. Chesnut....	387
Feeding wild plants to sheep. By S. B. Nelson	421
Cooperation between the experiment station veterinarian and the local veterinarian. By A. W. Bitting	426
Contagious diseases of animals in European countries	428
American animals and animal productions in Great Britain. By W. H. Wray	440
Some agricultural experiment station work:	
The feeding of lambs. By James Wilson and C. F. Curtiss	463
Further experiments in feeding lambs. By James W. Wilson and C. F. Curtiss	466
Feeding range lambs. By C. F. Curtiss and James W. Wilson	469
Feeding for mutton in South Dakota. By E. C. Chilcott and E. A. Burnett	471
Larkspur poisoning of sheep. By E. V. Wilcox	473
Tuberculosis in Kansas. By N. S. Mayo	479
Transmission of Texas fever. By N. S. Mayo	481
Experiment with blood serum as a preventive and cure for Texas fever. By J. C. Robert	482
Steer-feeding experiments to ascertain the comparative value of corn and red and white Kafir corn. By C. C. Georgeson	483
Feeding sheaf wheat to steers. By H. T. French	486
Texas itch in Kansas. By N. S. Mayo	488
Dehorning cattle. By Gilbert M. Gowell and Fremont L. Russell	489
Dehorning cattle. By. F. Wm. Rane	491
Milking scrub cows	491
Wheat in the sheaf and chopped wheat for pigs. By H. T. French	494
Feeding sheaf wheat to hogs. By H. T. French	495
Corn, cowpeas, and wheat bran for fattening pigs. By J. F. Duggar	496
Hog cholera in Iowa. By W. B. Niles	500
Peanuts, cowpeas, and sweet potatoes as food for hogs. By J. F. Duggar	501
Gape disease of young poultry in Kentucky. By H. Garman	504
Experiments in egg production. By James Dryden	506
Food value of California eggs. By M. E. Jaffa	510
Draft upon horses	511
Feeding value of potatoes	511
Extracts from consular reports:	
Animal products in South Africa	512
Trichinæ: German inspection of American hog products	516
American hams in Germany	519
Horses, cattle, etc., in Switzerland	520
Animals and animal products in Malta	520
Butter in Paraguay	521
American butter in Japan	521
Sheep and wool in Cape Colony	522
Somali, or black-head, sheep	522
Prices in Cape Colony	523
Imports of hides and skins from Calcutta	523
Extracts from correspondence	524
Movement of farm animals	550
Range or average price of farm animals at Chicago	579
Imports and exports of animals and animal products 1897 and 1898	581
Numbers and values of farm animals, 1897 and 1898	597
State live stock sanitary boards, secretaries of State boards of health, etc	603
Rules and regulations of the Bureau of Animal Industry	605

ILLUSTRATIONS.

PLATES.

Page

Frontispiece. Duchess of Smithfield 4256.
PLATE I. Map indicating the geographic distribution of blackleg in United
    States 33
    II. Section of muscle from a blackleg swelling......................... 49
    III. College creamery, Iowa State Agricultural College................ 83
    IV. Hog cholera germs 235
    V. Hog cholera and swine plague cultures 235
    VI. Crystalline substance isolated from artificial liquid cultures..... 305
    VII. Section of liver showing necrosis produced by crystalline sub-
        stance isolated from artificial cultures 305
    VIII. Bacterium astheniæ 334
    IX. Organisms causing anthrax, malignant edema, and Texas fever.. 356
    X. Organisms causing tuberculosis, blackleg, tetanus, actinomycosis,
        glanders, and swine plague.. 358
    XI. Bacilli of hog cholera... 360
    XII. Cecum of turkey affected with entero-hepatitis 362
    XIII. Bacterium sanguinarium causing infectious leukæmia in fowls—
        Entero-hepatitis in turkeys 364
    XIV. Nodular tæniasis in fowls—Roup................................... 366
    XV. Nodular disease in sheep... 368
    XVI. Zebroid Lordello, out of the mare Stael by the zebra Canon. One
        year old when photographed.. 369
    XVII. Zebroid Ménélick, out of the mare Ella by the zebra Canon. Three
        months old when photographed...................................... 369
    XVIII. Artillery shaft horse Fregatte 376
    XIX. Artillery fore horse Gertrude 376
    XX. Heavy riding horse Stroich... 376
    XXI. Lancers horse Nelson 376
    XXII. Hussars horse Schnucke 376
    XXIII. Delphinium menziesii 473
    XXIV. Delphinium menziesii 473
    XXV. Delphinium scopulorum.. 473

FIGURES.

Fig. 1. Vaccinating outfit 63
    2. Hypodermic syringe 67
    3. A vaccinating chute.. 72
    4. Barber pasteurizing and cooling apparatus......................... 115
    5. Cross section of heater for Barber apparatus...................... 115
    6. Bair cooler.. 115

                                                                                    Page.
Fig. 7. The De Laval pasteurizing and cooling apparatus.......................   116
      8. Cross section of heater for the De Laval pasteurizing apparatus,
             with connecting pipes   117
      9. Elevation of disk cooler, with section through the two upper disks.   118
     10. Diagram of butter prices (wholesale) in London and New York for
             the year 1897   135
     11. Ayrshire bull John Webb 5180..   145
     12. Ayrshire cow Red Rose 5566..   145
     13. Brown Swiss bull Gibbo 720...   147
     14. Brown Swiss cow Brienzi 168..   147
     15. Devon bull Fine Boy of Pound 6185...   149
     16. Devon cow Miss T 9605...   149
     17. Dutch Belted bull Duke of Ralph 255   151
     18. Dutch Belted cow Lady Aldine 124   151
     19. Guernsey bull Sheet Anchor 3934..   153
     20. Guernsey cow Fantine 2d 3730..   153
     21. Holstein-Freisian bull De Brave Hendrik 230 H.-F. H. B.............   157
     22. Holstein-Freisian cow Jamaica 1336 H. H. B. and calf   157
     23. Jersey bull Pedro 3187...   163
     24. Jersey cow Brown Bessie 74997...   163
     25. Normandy bull Americain 2..   167
     26. Normandy cow Amie 8...   167
     27. Polled Durham bull Young Hamilton 49......................................   169
     28. Polled Durham cow Daisy 2   169
     29. Red Polled bull Dobin 3462   171
     30. Red Polled cow Beauty 5th 2629   171
     31. Shorthorn bull Baron Cruickshank 106296   173
     32. Shorthorn cow Kitty Clay 4th...   173
     33. Simmenthal bull Segg 1   175
     34. Simmenthal cow Jungferli 7..   175
     35. Diagram of cow showing points   185
     36. Map of Page County, Iowa   253
     37. Ratio of white to red blood corpuscles   273
     38. Fly amanita (Amanita muscaria)   394
     39. False hellebore (Veratrum viride)   396
     40. Lily of the valley (Convallaria majalis)   396
     41. Slender nettle (Urtica gracilis)   397
     42. Pokeweed (Phytolacca decandra)...   398
     43. Corn cockle (Agrostemma githago)   399
     44. Aconite (Aconitum columbianum)   399
     45. Dwarf larkspur (Delphinium tricorne)   400
     46. Cursed crowfoot (Ranunculus sceleratus)   401
     47. Mandrake (Podophyllum peltatum)..   402
     48. Black cherry (Prunus serotina)   403
     49. Stemless loco weed (Aragallus lambertii)...................................   403
     50. Woolly loco weed (Astragalus molissimus)   404
     51. Rattlebox (Crotalaria sagittalis)...   405
     52. Caper spurge (Euphorbia lathyris)   406
     53. Snow on the mountain (Euphorbia marginata)   406
     54. Castor-oil plant (Ricinus communis)...   407
     55. Red buckeye (Æsculus pavia)   407
     56. Water hemlock (Cicuta maculata)..   408
     57. Oregon water hemlock (Cicuta vagans)......................................   400

Page.

Fig. 58. Poison hemlock (*Conium maculatum*) 409
59. Narrow-leaf laurel (*Kalmia angustifolia*) 410
60. Broad-leaf laurel (*Kalmia latifolia*) 410
61. Branch ivy (*Leucothoë catesbœi*) 411
62. Stagger bush (*Pieris mariana*) 412
63. Great laurel (*Rhododendron maximum*) 412
64. Milkweed (*Asclepias eriocarpa*) 413
65. Jimson weed (*Datura stramonium*) 414
66. Bittersweet (*Solanum dulcamara*) 415
67. Black nightshade (*Solanum nigrum*) 415
68. Spreading nightshade (*Solanum triflorum*) 416
69. Sneezeweed (*Helenium autumnale*) 417

FIFTEENTH ANNUAL REPORT OF THE BUREAU OF ANIMAL INDUSTRY.

REPORT OF THE CHIEF OF THE BUREAU.

MEAT INSPECTION.

The increase of work in connection with meat inspection was very large during the year and required the appointment of a large number of employees. These were obtained upon certification by the Civil Service Commission, and have proved, as in the previous year, to be competent and satisfactory. Although the Bureau force of employees is enlarged from year to year, as the appropriations for the inspection work will permit, the efficiency of the employees is also increased through the examination by the Civil Service Commission, and the Bureau is thus enabled to maintain a thorough system of inspection.

A reference to the tables giving the number of animals inspected this year and for 1897 shows that the number has been greatly increased; yet it is still true that the appropriation for this Bureau is not sufficient to permit of the inspection of all meat entering into interstate commerce, although the law contemplates that all should be inspected. It is true, however, this year as last, that all of the beef exported to Europe and the greater part of the pork and other meat products exported have been inspected in accordance with the law.

During the year meat inspection has been in operation at 135 abattoirs, as against 128 for the previous year, and in 35 cities, as against 33 in 1897.

The table following gives the number of inspections of animals before slaughter, made either in the stock yards or at the abattoirs, and shows the number inspected for official abattoirs and the number of inspections of animals for abattoirs in other cities and miscellaneous buyers; also the number condemned on this inspection at

11

abattoirs and the number rejected in the stock yards. The number of rejected animals slaughtered and the number of these condemned will be found in the table of postmortem inspections.

Antemortem inspection.

Kind of animal.	For official abattoirs in cities where inspections were made.	For abattoirs in other cities and miscellaneous buyers.	Total inspections.	Condemned at abattoirs.	Rejected in stock yards.
Cattle	4,552,919	4,675,318	9,228,237	104	27,491
Sheep	5,706,092	4,322,195	10,028,287	741	9,501
Calves	241,092	227,107	468,199	67	2,439
Hogs	20,713,863	10,896,812	31,610,675	9,679	66,061
Total	31,213,966	20,121,432	51,335,398	10,591	105,585

A comparison with the figures for 1897 shows a gain for 1898 of 1,178,212 cattle, 1,983,932 sheep, 19,216 calves, and 6,043,931 hogs—a total gain of 9,025,291 animals. This is an increase over 1896 of 15,417,919 animals. The number of condemned animals at abattoirs was 3,275 fewer than in 1897, and the number rejected in stock yards was 27,247 greater.

The number of animals inspected at time of slaughter and the number of carcasses and parts of carcasses condemned are given in the following table:

Postmortem inspection.

Kind of animal.	Number of inspections.			Carcasses condemned.			Parts of carcasses condemned at abattoirs.
	For abattoirs.	Animals rejected in stock yards.	Total.	For abattoirs.	Animals rejected in stock yards.	Total.	
Cattle	4,418,738	14,143	4,433,181	6,900	3,118	10,018	12,591
Sheep	5,496,904	4,753	5,501,657	2,606	961	3,567	237
Calves	244,330	825	245,155	203	138	344	52
Hogs	20,893,199	43,641	20,936,840	a 69,652	7,927	77,579	b 35,250
Total	31,053,171	63,662	31,116,833	79,364	12,144	91,508	48,180

a Includes 19,978 condemned on microscopic examination.
b Includes 5,902 condemned on microscopic examination.

In addition to the above, there were killed by city inspectors 1,785 cattle, 1,509 sheep, 192 calves, and 14,698 hogs which had been rejected in the stock yards by officers of the Bureau of Animal Industry.

The meat-inspection tag or brand was placed on 14,815,753 quarters and 968,014 pieces of beef, 5,448,477 carcasses of sheep, 217,010 carcasses of calves, 680,876 carcasses of hogs, and 394,563 sacks of pork.

The meat-inspection stamp was affixed to 4,433,569 packages of beef products, 5,163 packages of mutton, and 10,145,048 packages of hog products, of which 374,131 contained microscopically examined pork.

The number of cars sealed containing inspected meat for shipment to packing houses and other places was 18,631.

There were issued 35,267 certificates for meat products which had received the ordinary inspection. These covered exports comprising 1,256,716 quarters, 67,120 pieces, and 735,814 packages of beef, weighing 339,650,091 pounds; 5,163 packages of mutton, weighing 324,996 pounds; 39,212 hog carcasses; and 653,564 packages of pork, weighing 244,956,482 pounds.

The cost of this work was $409,138.09, which makes an average of 0.8 cent for each of the 51,335,398 antemortem inspections, besides covering all the subsequent work of postmortem inspection, tagging, stamping, etc.

The cost of inspection has been growing gradually less year by year. The average cost per head was 4.75 cents in 1893, 1.75 cents in 1894, 1.1 cents in 1895, 0.95 cent in 1896, and 0.91 cent in 1897.

For the purpose of comparison, the following table is given:

Number of animals inspected before slaughter for abattoirs having inspection, 1891–1898.

Fiscal year.	Cattle.	Calves.	Sheep.	Hogs.	Total.
1891	83,891				83,891
1892	3,167,009	59,089	583,361		3,809,459
1893	3,922,174	92,947	870,512		4,885,633
1894	3,862,111	96,331	1,020,764	7,964,850	12,944,056
1895	3,752,111	109,041	1,344,031	13,576,917	18,783,000
1896	4,050,011	213,575	4,710,190	14,301,963	23,275,739
1897	4,289,058	259,930	5,179,643	16,813,181	26,541,812
1898	4,552,919	241,092	5,706,092	20,713,863	31,213,966

MICROSCOPIC INSPECTION OF PORK.

The number of samples of pork examined was 2,802,846, of which 1,927,838 were from carcasses and 875,008 from pieces. The following table shows that better results are obtained by making the inspection in the carcass than when samples from cured meat are examined:

Comparison of inspections from carcasses and from pieces.

Samples.	From carcasses.		From pieces.	
	Number.	Per cent.	Number.	Per cent.
Class A	1,892,131	98.148	864,042	98.747
Class B	15,729	0.816	5,064	0.579
Class C	19,978	1.036	5,902	0.674
Total	1,927,838	100	875,008	100

The samples of pork submitted for microscopic examination were classified as follows: Class A, samples in which no sign of trichinæ, living or dead, or calcified cysts are found; Class B, samples in which degenerate trichinæ cysts are found, but in which the body of the parasite is not recognizable; Class C, samples in which recognizable bodies, living or dead, of trichinæ are found. All hogs belonging to the latter class must be condemned and disposed of according to section 20 of the regulations dated June 14, 1895.

The number of certificates issued for microscopically examined pork was 20,158, covering shipments aggregating 373,366 packages, weighing 120,271,659 pounds. Of this quantity, 698 packages, weighing 161,303 pounds, were exported to countries not exacting a certificate of microscopic inspection.

The cost of microscopic inspection was $171,040.94, an average per specimen examined of 6.1 cents, or an average of 0.142 cent for each pound exported.

This cost per pound for the inspection of pork shows a remarkable reduction from the cost in 1897, when it was 0.256 cent. The cost in 1896 was 0.264 cent; in 1895, 0.2 cent; in 1894, 0.248 cent.

The number of samples examined increased 49 per cent over last year, the expense increased 53 per cent, and the exports increased 176 per cent.

The following table shows the exports of microscopically inspected pork for the fiscal years 1892 to 1898, inclusive:

Exports of microscopically inspected pork, 1892–1898.

Fiscal year.	To countries requiring inspection.	To countries not requiring inspection.	Total.
	Pounds.	*Pounds.*	*Pounds.*
1892	22,025,698	16,127,176	38,152,874
1893	8,059,758	12,617,652	20,677,410
1894	18,845,119	16,592,818	35,437,937
1895	39,355,230	5,739,368	45,094,598
1896	21,497,321	1,403,559	22,900,880
1897	42,570,572	1,001,783	43,572,355
1898	120,110,356	161,303	120,271,659

INSPECTION OF VESSELS AND EXPORT ANIMALS.

The following table shows for the fiscal year 1898 the number of inspections of domestic and Canadian cattle and sheep for export, the number rejected, the number of American cattle tagged, and the number of each exported; also the number of horses, mules, and hogs exported under the supervision of the Bureau inspectors. For comparison the statistics for the fiscal year 1897 are included.

Number of inspections, exportations, etc., of American and Canadian live stock for the fiscal years 1897 and 1898.

Kind of animal.	American.				Canadian.		
	Number of inspections.	Number rejected.	Number tagged.	Number exported.	Number inspected.	Number rejected.	Number exported.
1898.							
Cattle	859,346	1,438	418,694	a 400,512	19,397	5	19,398
Sheep	297,719	180	....	b 147,907	29,497	38	29,459
Horses	....	....	....	29,576	....	....	3,955
Mules	....	....	....	221	....	....	....
Hogs	....	....	....	599	....	....	....
1897.							
Cattle	845,116	1,565	410,279	c 399,554	13,136	12	13,124
Sheep	348,108	189	....	d 184,596	23,289	72	23,217
Horses	....	....	....	22,623	....	....	6,185
Mules	....	....	....	100	....	....	....
Hogs	....	....	....	....	....	....	....

a Includes 15,929 exported from Chicago by way of Canadian ports.
b Includes 5,172 exported from Chicago by way of Canadian ports.
c Includes 5,501 shipped from Chicago by way of Montreal.
d Includes 2,231 shipped from Chicago by way of Montreal.

The number of certificates issued for exported cattle was 1,616, as against 1,563 for 1897. The number of clearances of vessels carrying live stock was 971, as against 954 in 1897.

The following table gives the number of cattle and sheep inspected at time of landing by the inspectors of the Bureau stationed in Great Britain, with the number and percentage lost in transit:

Number and percentage of cattle and sheep inspected by Bureau inspectors in Great Britain and number and percentage lost in transit.

From—	Cattle.			Sheep.		
	Landed.	Lost in transit.		Landed.	Lost in transit.	
	Number.	Number.	Per cent.	Number.	Number.	Per cent.
United States	381,420	851	0.22	151,863	1,224	0.8
Canada	17,164	56	.32	27,912	394	1.39
Total	398,584	907	.23	179,775	1,618	0.89

This table shows an increase of 20,898 cattle and a decrease of 9,408 sheep when compared with the report for 1897. The number of head of cattle lost in transit in 1897 was 2,323, or 0.61 per cent, as against 907 head, or 0.23 per cent, for this year. The number of sheep lost in transit in 1897 was 2,676, or 1.39 per cent, as against 1,618, or 0.89 per cent, for this year.

The cost of the inspection of export animals, the supervision of Southern cattle transportation, and the inspection of animals imported from Mexico was $101,210.55. It is estimated that half of this expense is on account of the export inspection, and, with this as a basis, the cost of inspecting the 548,419 domestic cattle and sheep exported was $50,605.28, or 9.2 cents per head. The number of inspections made on these animals in this country was 1,157,065, and in Great Britain 533,283, making a total of 1,690,348, the average cost of each inspection being 2.99 cents.

Following is a statement showing the inspection of domestic cattle and sheep for export and the number exported for 1898 and previous years:

Inspections and exports of domestic cattle and sheep, 1893 to 1898, inclusive.

Fiscal year.	Cattle.				Sheep.		
	Number of inspections.	Number rejected.	Number tagged.	Number exported.	Number of inspections.	Number rejected.	Number exported.
1898...............	859,346	1,438	418,694	400,512	297,719	180	147,907
1897...............	845,116	1,565	410,379	390,554	348,108	189	184,596
1896...............	815,882	1,303	377,639	365,345	733,657	898	422,608
1895...............	657,756	1,060	324,339	324,299	704,044	179	350,808
1894...............	725,243	184	360,580	363,535	135,780	....	85,809
1893...............	611,542	292	280,570	289,240	....	....	....

SOUTHERN CATTLE INSPECTION.

During the quarantine season of 1897 there were received and yarded in the quarantine divisions of the various stock yards 35,317 cars, containing 972,224 cattle; the number of cars cleaned and disinfected was 35,280.

In the noninfected area in Texas 225,096 cattle were inspected for the identification of brands prior to removal to other States for grazing.

INSPECTION OF IMPORTED ANIMALS.

The number of animals imported from Mexico and inspected at the ports of entry along the boundary line comprised 177,772 cattle, 64,207 sheep, 104 swine, and 3,053 goats.

There were imported from Canada for slaughter, milk production, grazing, feeding, etc., and not subject to quarantine detention, 79,907 cattle, 184,352 sheep, 374 swine, 2,998 horses, 2 goats, 8 mules, 1 deer, and 6 buffalo, of which 385 cattle, 6,867 sheep, and 217 swine were for breeding purposes.

Below is a statement of the animals imported and quarantined for the prescribed period at the different quarantine stations:

Animals imported and quarantined at different stations.

Stations.	Cattle.	Sheep.	Swine.
Littleton, Mass.	1		
Garfield, N. J.	282	303	10
St. Denis, Md.	10		
Houlton, Me.	43	52	1
Eastport, Me.	1		
Island Pond, Vt.	13	8	
Beecher Falls, Vt	89	50	
Newport, Vt	108		
Richford, Vt.	16		
St. Albans, Vt.	62	96	
Rouse Point, N. Y.	26		
Ogdensburg, N. Y.	144		
Cape Vincent, N. Y.	51		
Buffalo, N. Y.	85		
Port Huron, Mich.	44		
Total	973	509	11

There were 2 dogs, 2 deer, 14 goats, and 6 camels at the Garfield station, making a total of 1,519 animals quarantined.

TO PREVENT DISSEMINATION OF SHEEP SCAB.

In order to prevent the dissemination of scabies, it was required that sheep intended for feeding or breeding purposes should be dipped before being permitted to leave the stock yards, if they were affected with the disease or had been exposed to contagion. Accordingly, 535,501 sheep were dipped under the supervision of inspectors of this Bureau, various preparations being used for this purpose.

INSPECTION OF HORSES.

The appropriation for the coming fiscal year carries a provision "that live horses and the carcasses and products thereof be entitled to the same inspection as other animals, carcasses, and products thereof" named in the bill. In accordance therewith regulations are being formulated to govern the work of inspection of horses at abattoirs and of export horses.

WORK OF THE BIOCHEMIC DIVISION.

During the past year the routine work of the Biochemic Division, in the preparation and shipment of tuberculin and mallein and of ink for use in stamping meat, has continued steadily, and demanded much time from the divisional force. During the winter and spring

months tuberculin sufficient to inject about 5,000 animals is sent out
each month, while a slightly less quantity is used during the summer.
The ink used for stamping the meat continues to give satisfaction;
the work is more easily performed and at the same time considerable
money has been saved.

EXPERIMENTS WITH HOG CHOLERA.

The experiments conducted in the fall of 1897 upon hog cholera and
swine plague proved so encouraging that a special appropriation was
made by Congress for the purpose of continuing the work during the
present year. Owing to the late date of the passage of the bill making this appropriation available, the work has been somewhat delayed;
besides it was necessary first to erect barns at the Bureau station, and
also to make the necessary purchases of animals and other material,
in order to begin the experiments on a sufficiently practical scale.
Material to inject about 1,000 animals was sent to the agent of the
Bureau in Iowa, where the first test is being made, and his reports
already received indicate that about 80 per cent of the animals treated
are saved, while the loss in the check herds is about 85 per cent. A
full report of this test will find its proper place elsewhere in this report.
On account of the time required to secure a supply of this serum,
the quantity so far produced has not been sufficient to give the necessary data upon which to base definite conclusions, but the results from
the use of the comparatively small amount so far distributed have
been so gratifying that I deem it desirable to continue the work
another year. The production of serum is being steadily increased,
and in the course of two or three months a large and regular output
will be assured. It remains only to test the remedy upon a sufficient
scale and to perfect the method of procedure.

ADDITIONAL HELP AND ROOM NEEDED.

The proper conduct of these experiments has very materially
increased the work of this laboratory. While two assistants have
been added to the force, there is still need of additional help. The
increased duties of the laboratory employees make it absolutely necessary that more room be provided if good results are to be obtained.
The working space is so crowded that it not only interferes with the
rapid conduct of investigation of various kinds, but the excessive
weight of desks, tables, cases, etc., on the floor has reached the limit
of safety.

GERMAN TOYS AND COLORED GOODS POISONOUS.

In connection with an examination of those imports coming from
Germany which might be injurious to the health of our people, it was
shown that toys and colored goods of German origin were poisonous.
All of the highly painted German toys may be considered very dan-

gerous to the health of the children of this country if the paint is sucked or chipped off and swallowed through any inadvertence.

ESTIMATING NICOTINE IN SHEEP DIPS.

Some examinations of the tobacco dips used in connection with sheep scab indicate that the methods in common use for the determination of nicotine are very misleading. Several experiments have therefore been made to find an easy and satisfactory method for estimating nicotine, and one has been worked out which is both practical and of easy execution.

OBSERVATIONS RELATIVE TO TUBERCULOSIS.

The study of tuberculosis, with reference to both men and animals, has been continued, and the reports received from a tuberculosis sanitarium, where the serum supposed to have curative properties for tuberculosis has been used to some extent, indicate that in incipient stages of the disease this material is of considerable value. The results also indicate that further experiments in the line already begun should be continued, as there is a prospect of still more satisfactory results. An easy, convenient, and important method for staining and differentiating tubercle bacilli from other germs which might be confused with them has also been worked out in this laboratory.

A fact which should be emphasized and carefully considered in connection with investigations of this character is the salary paid to the individuals engaged in the study of bacterial products. These men are at all times exposed to the danger of contracting a dangerous disease which may destroy their usefulness throughout life. Under these circumstances, salaries commensurate with the high character of the work required and the dangers to which they are exposed should be paid.

WORK CONTEMPLATED.

It is contemplated by this division to undertake investigations relative to Texas fever, anthrax, and other diseases of animals.

WORK OF THE DIVISION OF PATHOLOGY.

DIPPING FOR TEXAS FEVER.

Experiments in the dipping of cattle with a view to destroying the ticks which spread the infection of Texas fever have been continued, and a substance has been found in which the cattle may be immersed without suffering any serious injury, and which will destroy all the ticks on an animal in a single dipping. This is great progress over last year's experiments, as it was then considered absolutely necessary that cattle should be dipped twice before it would be safe to send them into any territory where cattle are susceptible to Texas fever. The preparation in which the cattle are dipped is a light lubricating oil containing dissolved sulphur. During the summer experiments have been made with a view to ascertaining whether this method of treating cattle could be carried out on a large scale, and for this purpose several train loads of cattle have been dipped at Fort Worth, Tex., and shipped to various places north of the quarantine line.

Two train loads of cattle, consisting of about 500 head, were sent to the northern part of Illinois, where they were placed in pastures with susceptible cattle in order to ascertain whether the dipping had rendered them safe against transmitting the fever. The experiments have proved to be a success, in so far as all the ticks were destroyed on the dipped cattle and that no disease was transmitted by them. About 600 head have also been dipped with perfect success at Mammoth Spring, Ark. Preparations are now being made to adopt the dipping method generally, by means of which the cattle from the infected districts may be shipped north of the quarantine line during the entire year, while they are at present restricted by quarantine during ten months of the year. The importance of this measure can hardly be overestimated, and is considered by prominent stockmen and farmers to be worth millions of dollars, both to the cattle raisers below the quarantine line and to the cattle feeders and grain producers north of the line. Late in the season reports of some injuries to cattle by dipping have been received. These were due partly to the condition of the cattle and partly to the strength of the dipping mixture. Experiments are now in progress which it is believed will enable the Department to remove all difficulties.

Applications have been received to permit the establishment of a large number of dipping stations along the quarantine line, and owing to the great importance of giving a free market to cattle from the quarantined district, it is only proper that such permits should be granted at central points where the trade is sufficient to warrant such action. This new service will, however, require a considerable increase in the inspection force, as it will not be safe to allow cattle to be dipped otherwise than under expert supervision.

BLACKLEG INVESTIGATIONS.

The preparation and distribution of blackleg vaccine have been continued throughout the year, and the demand for the vaccine has increased very much. More than 355,000 doses have been distributed, and the reports sent in by the recipients of the vaccine show that the annual losses from blackleg have been reduced from an average of from 10 to 20 per cent to less than 1 per cent. This means a saving of at least $500,000 worth of cattle, and when all stock owners become familiar with the method and it is adopted throughout all the cattle-raising districts where blackleg prevails it will not alone save millions of dollars, but also tend to eradicate the disease completely.

RABIES.

In the course of the year a number of supposed cases of rabies in dogs have been brought to this laboratory for determination. In some cases the dogs had bitten one or more persons, and it was consequently of great importance to determine whether the animals were suffering from rabies or not. In two cases it was proven that the dogs had been suffering from rabies and the health officer of the District of Columbia was notified to that effect, and the five people which had been bitten by these dogs received the antirabic treatment of Pasteur.

MISCELLANEOUS WORK.

The usual routine work of examining pathological specimens sent to the Bureau from veterinary inspectors and private parties has been continued, and a number of outbreaks of infectious and contagious diseases among the domesticated animals in the vicinity of Washington City have been investigated and the owners advised as to the proper care and treatment of the animals.

WORK OF THE DAIRY DIVISION.

The general survey of the condition of the dairy industry of the country at large, which was begun upon the organization of the division, has been continued, together with inquiries as to special branches, such as the milk supply of cities and large towns. Some reports have been printed and others are in hand awaiting revision and publication.

The collection of dairy data in general continues, with a view to its proper arrangement and future use in the form of circulars of information, popular bulletins, and the like. So far as the clerical force of the office permits, the material collected has been indexed for ready reference.

The routine work of the office constantly increases, including general correspondence, calls for specific information, and the preparation of manuscript for publication.

During the year there have been published two bulletins and one circular prepared in the division, besides contributions to the Yearbook of the Department and to the Annual Report of the Bureau, in all comprising 284 printed pages.

The chief and assistant chief of the division have visited during the year centers of dairy interest in twenty-one States and collected information for future use. In order that the Department might be represented at as many as possible of the annual conventions of State dairy associations and similar organizations, Mr. John II. Monrad, of Illinois, was appointed temporarily as a special agent of the division, and assisted in attending public dairy meetings. In all, twenty-four States were visited and dairy meetings attended in nineteen of them.

In this way, officers and employees of the division have been enabled
to meet hundreds of the representative men connected with this
industry in various parts of the country, and to establish relations
which will be of material future benefit to the general work.

BUTTER SHIPMENTS TO GREAT BRITAIN.

The experimental exports of butter by this Bureau to Great Britain,
which were commenced in the spring of 1897, and partially reported
upon a year ago, were continued until the close of the active creamery
year of 1897 and resumed at the opening of the season of 1898 upon an
enlarged scale.   These exports have constituted the principal current
work of this division during the fiscal year now reported, and have
involved much detail, occupying the greater part of the time and
attention of the office force.   A complete report of the operations
during the commercial year of 1897 has been prepared and is ready
for publication in the Annual Report of the Bureau for 1898.

Without anticipating the results of the present (or second) season
of these trial exports, it can now be confidently stated that much additional information has been obtained in the line desired, and a decided
gain is evident in the favorable impression made by butter of the first
quality from creameries in the United States upon the best class of
the butter trade in London and Manchester.

An exhibit in the nature of an object lesson, illustrating the com-
ponent parts of the various products and by-products of the dairy,
has been recently prepared, and is included in the display of the
Bureau of Animal Industry at the Trans-Mississippi and International
Exposition now in progress at Omaha, Nebr.

PROPOSED LINES OF WORK FOR 1898-99.

It is proposed that the work of the dairy division for the fiscal year
1898-99 shall include continuation of the different lines of effort
reported as receiving attention during the years previous and still
incomplete.

As already indicated, a large part of the energies of the division
will be required for the experimental exports of butter, to which some
trials with cheese and eggs, and perhaps dressed poultry, may be
added.   Material extension of these trial exports, in frequency, quantity, and variety of new markets, is made possible by the provisions
incorporated in the current appropriation bill for this Department, in
accordance with last year's recommendations, and by which the net
proceeds of the sales of the products purchased for experimental
export are available for a continuation or repetition of such exports.

It seems expedient to continue the weekly experimental exports of
butter in progress during the summer of 1898 through the autumn
and the following winter, in order to complete the trial of a full year's
offerings in the market of Manchester, if not also in London.

Meanwhile it is proposed, by correspondence and the services of special agents, some voluntary, to investigate the prospects of trade in the dairy products of the United States, on the islands of the Pacific, Japan, and China, and also in the West Indies and South America. It is not unlikely that such inquiries will render it desirable to make experimental exports in those directions before the close of the present fiscal year and during the next one. An appropriation similar to the one now available is therefore to be desired for the new fiscal year.

It is expected to prepare, in part, during the current year, for the proper presentation of the dairy interests and products of the United States at the coming Paris Exposition.

RECOMMENDATIONS.

The following recommendations are respectfully made for the fiscal year ending June 30, 1900:

(1) A sufficient appropriation for extending and developing foreign markets for dairy products of the United States, under provisions similar to those applying to the funds now available for this purpose. The reasons for this have been already stated.

(2) That legislation be sought by which the existing system of Government inspection and certification of meats and meat products for export may be extended (with suitable modifications) to include butter, cheese, and condensed milk for export from the United States.

Reasons for such new legislation were given a year ago, as follows:

The combined efforts of the Government and commercial enterprise may succeed in the early establishment of a high reputation for American butter in desirable foreign markets; but as soon as accomplished, this becomes liable to be destroyed by the cupidity of those who, trading on this reputation, flood the same market with butter of low grade, yet still entitled to export and sale as "produce of the United States." This will disgust merchants and consumers alike and reverse the reputation of our butter, just as the fine market in Great Britain for our cheese was recently ruined by the quantity of low-grade and counterfeit cheese which was exported without being marked to show its true character. The remedy seems to lie in extending and adapting the provisions of law regarding the inspection of meats exported from this country so as to make them apply to butter and cheese. The brands of "pure butter" and "full-cream cheese" should then be affixed by United States inspectors to such products only as are of a fixed minimum standard of quality. Such precautions, duly legalized and properly executed, would place the good butter and cheese of this country in foreign markets under the identifying label and guaranty of the United States Government, leaving similar merchandise of lower grade to find a place for itself upon its own merits. It should be borne in mind that dairy products of Denmark and Canada, which are the chief competitors of the United States in the markets of Great Britain, bear the inspection certificate and guaranty of quality from their respective Governments and thereby maintain a great commercial advantage.

Such a system of inspection is much desired by the most reliable exporters, and the proposition has met with decided approval wherever considered by fair-minded, interested parties.

(3) That the estimates for the Bureau of Animal Industry be made to include $8,500 for "Salaries" and $20,000 under "Salaries and expenses," to be definitely set apart for this division, with the expectation that it will all be needed and used. (This besides any special provision for experimental exports of perishable products other than dairy products which may be ordered supervised by this division.)

ERADICATION OF SHEEP SCAB.

In the report for 1897 it was noted that experiments were being made by the Bureau with different sheep dips for the purpose of determining which is the most efficacious and at the same time least injurious to the animal. These experiments were concluded, and the results appear in an exhaustive article entitled, "Sheep scab: Its nature and treatment," in the Annual Report of the Bureau of Animal Industry for 1897, mentioned elsewhere in this report. In addition to the character of dips, this article gives a full history and description of the mite causing common sheep scab and also descriptions of the various kinds of apparatus used in dipping.

Inspectors of the Bureau have been zealous in enforcing Order No. 5, relative to the transportation of sheep having scab, which is as follows:

TRANSPORTATION OF SHEEP AFFECTED WITH SCABIES.

U. S. DEPARTMENT OF AGRICULTURE,
OFFICE OF THE SECRETARY,
Washington, D. C., June 18, 1897.
To the Managers and Agents of Railroads and Transportation Companies of the United States, Stockmen, and others:

In accordance with section 7 of the act of Congress approved May 29, 1884, entitled "An act for the establishment of a Bureau of Animal Industry, to prevent the exportation of diseased cattle, and to provide means for the suppression and extirpation of pleuro-pneumonia and other contagious diseases among domestic animals," and of the act of Congress approved April 23, 1897, making appropriation for the Department of Agriculture for the fiscal year ending June 30, 1898, you are hereby notified that the contagious disease known as sheep scab, or scabies of sheep, exists among sheep in the United States, and that it is a violation of the law to receive for transportation or transport any stock affected with said disease from one State or Territory to another, or from any State into the District of Columbia or from the District into any State. It is also a violation of the law for any person, company, or corporation to deliver for such transportation to any railroad company, or master or owner of any boat or vessel, any sheep, knowing them to be affected with said disease; and it is also unlawful for any person, company, or corporation to drive on foot or transport in private conveyance from one State or Territory to another, or from any State into the District of Columbia, or from the District into any State, any sheep, knowing them to be affected with said disease. All transportation companies and individuals shipping, driving, or transporting sheep are requested to cooperate with this Department in enforcing the law for preventing the spread of the said disease. Inspectors of the Bureau of Animal Industry are directed to report all violations of this act which come to their attention.

In order more effectually to accomplish the object of the above-mentioned laws, it is hereby ordered that any railroad cars, boats, or other vehicles, which have been used in the transportation of sheep affected with said disease, shall be immediately cleaned and disinfected by the owners or by the transportation companies in whose possession said cars or vehicles may be at the time the animals are unloaded, by first removing all litter and manure which they contain, and then saturating the woodwork with a 5 per cent solution of crude carbolic acid in water. Inspectors of the Bureau of Animal Industry are directed to see that this order is carried into effect.

JAMES WILSON, *Secretary.*

The information which is now available for the public is sufficient to enable anyone to cure this disease with a minimum of trouble and expense. There will hereafter be no excuse for those who claim that they are unacquainted with the nature of the disease or with the methods of treatment.

AGRICULTURAL ATTACHÉ AT BERLIN.

The tendency has been growing in Germany to assume that all diseased or unwholesome meat is of American origin. The Department of Agriculture having certified, through the inspection of the Bureau of Animal Industry, that all pork shipped to Germany is free from trichinæ, and produced from healthy animals, the time had arrived when it became necessary to learn the truth in the matter, in order, first, to correct the error, if it existed, in the system of microscopic inspection conducted by the Bureau, or, second, to deny authoritatively the charge. Accordingly, Dr. Ch. Wardell Stiles, zoologist of this Bureau, was commissioned as agriculutural attaché of the American embassy at Berlin in the latter part of March, with instructions to trace to a conclusion every such rumor or charge of German origin. The account of his work will necessarily appear in the report for the fiscal year 1899; and in that report he will be able to show that in many of the cases there is no trichinæ infection, and that in others where it has existed it was not of American origin or had not been certified as microscopically inspected.

It would be rash to assert that there could have been no oversight in the inspection of 120,271,659 pounds of pork, which was the amount inspected last year, but it is certain that such errors are reduced to the minimum; and the purpose of sending Dr. Stiles abroad on this mission is both to reassure the American people and to convince the German people so far as possible that the most painstaking efforts are made by the Bureau to inspect all pork exported to Germany, and that our microscopic inspection is as rigid and safe as that made by any country.

PUBLICATION WORK.

A list of the publications of the Bureau appears in the report of the chief of the Division of Publications. On March 1 a clerk was appointed to have special charge of the editorial work of the Bureau.

This character of assistance has been needed for some time, as the time of the chief of the Bureau and the divisional chiefs was wholly consumed in executive work or pressing investigations. One of the first duties of this assistant was the preparation of the Annual Report of the Bureau for the fiscal year 1897. For ten years previous to 1897 the reports of the Bureau were issued biennially, owing principally to lack of time to compile them, but it is proposed hereafter to issue one each year as the law authorizes. The report for 1897 was late in reaching the printer, but it will soon be issued. Its principal contents are the usual report of the Chief of the Bureau to the Secretary; a review of the contagious diseases of animals in Europe; an exhaustive article on the nature and treatment of sheep scab; the State and Territorial laws relative to contagious diseases of animals not published heretofore in the reports of the Bureau, and a complete collection of the dairy laws; also the orders issued by the Bureau since its organization.

An index is being made, which will embrace not only all of the publications of the Bureau, but all documents of the Department which relate in any way to animal industry. This is being prepared as time can be spared from editorial work, but it will probably be ready for publication before the end of the fiscal year 1899.

NEEDS OF THE BUREAU.

In the report for last year attention was directed to the importance of an experiment station, to be the property of the Department, and also of greater laboratory facilities. The conditions have not been changed for the better, while the demand becomes more imperative. If these matters could receive the favorable action of Congress the work of this Bureau would be greatly facilitated and the interests of public economy be subserved at the same time.

BLACKLEG IN THE UNITED STATES AND THE DISTRIBUTION OF VACCINE BY THE BUREAU OF ANIMAL INDUSTRY.

By VICTOR A. NÖRGAARD, V.S. (Copenhagen),
Chief of Pathological Division, Bureau of Animal Industry.

PRELIMINARY REMARKS.

In the beginning of 1895 the writer, who was then stationed in southern Texas, was directed by the chief of the Bureau of Animal Industry to ascertain so far as possible to what extent blackleg prevailed in Texas and what precautions were taken against the spread of this disease, which in certain parts of the State was said at times to decimate the annual calf crop. For this purpose a number of letters were addressed to prominent stockmen in various parts of Texas, making inquiries as to the occurrence of blackleg in their respective parts of the State, but only two or three of the answers received contained any information on the subject. These answers came from stockmen in the "Panhandle;" and, as verbal inquiries at various cattlemen's conventions also pointed to the fact that blackleg was a common disease in northern Texas, the writer was instructed to change his location to that place. Just then, however, the disease broke out in the vicinity of Alice, Tex., and shortly afterwards appeared on the ranch where the writer was located. This ranch is the property of Mrs. H. M. King, of Corpus Christi, Tex., and as the manager, Mr. R. J. Kleberg, is secretary of the live stock sanitary board of Texas and was anxious to obtain as much light on the subject as possible, there was here as good an opportunity to study the disease as could be found anywhere. Several typical cases were seen and careful observations made, which will be recorded in this article. As the herd in which the disease first appeared consisted of full-blood or high-grade Durham cattle, it was of importance to check the outbreak as soon as possible, and it was decided to try the effect of the French blackleg vaccine. This was done with very satisfactory results, only a small number of cattle dying between the first and second vaccination and one or two after the second. The method of double vaccination was, however, found to be very cumbersome, even though the original operation of injecting the vaccine in the tail was discontinued and injections made in front of the

27

shoulder on the lower part of the neck. Under date of July 24, 1896, the writer reported as follows in a letter to the chief of this Bureau:

The most objectionable feature of vaccination with Arloing's lymph is that the process requires two inoculations, with an interval of eight to ten days. On large ranches, with a yearly crop of several thousand calves, it would be questionable whether the annual loss from blackleg would ever exceed the additional expense of a double "round-up." If a single inoculation were sufficient it might be profitable to vaccinate the calves at the branding round-up, provided they have passed the age of 6 months. It is claimed that prior to this age vaccination does not produce immunity. But when, during an outbreak of blackleg, the disease attacks younger calves, it is advisable to vaccinate them. In an outbreak at Santa Gertrudes' Ranch during last spring several high-bred calves succumbed to the disease before having reached this age, wherefore all the calves past the age of 3 months, in the infected pastures, were vaccinated. Subsequently none of them became affected.

As a rule, however, the calves are branded before they are 6 months old, and the objection might be made that vaccination and castration should not take place simultaneously, and consequently vaccination alone will require that the calves be gathered twice for this special purpose. On large ranches this will be a considerable additional expense to the unreasonably high price of the vaccine, which amounts to from 15 to 25 cents per dose, according to the quantity purchased, and it is to be feared that vaccination against blackleg will never become popular so long as it requires two separate inoculations. It is therefore desirable that some vaccine which will produce immunity after one inoculation be introduced in this country.

INVESTIGATIONS IN TEXAS.

In the meantime investigations were continued with a view to ascertaining the prevalence of blackleg in Texas, but the information elicited was practically to the effect that most of the stockmen who were addressed on the subject very rarely lost cattle from blackleg. These unsatisfactory results were probably due to the fact that up to a short time ago the stock owners were extremely reticent when asked about the prevalence of any disease among their stock, as they were naturally afraid that publicity, through newspapers or otherwise, of such a statement might tend to reduce the value of their stock in the estimation of cattle buyers. Besides this, there was a vague dread of quarantine restrictions in case the disease should prove to be of a contagious or infectious nature. They consequently preferred to leave well enough alone, and, rather than ask the advice of the State or Government experts, they would let their cattle continue to die, looking upon such losses as an unavoidable evil, or else content themselves with old and well-tried remedies, such as those recommended for hollow-horn or wolf-in-the-tail.

But fortunately things have changed of late, and with the introduction of full-blood and high-grade stock, in connection with good prices and a scarcity of cattle throughout the country, the stock owners have come to realize that each calf saved means more than the immediate value of that one animal, and that it pays better to adopt modern scientific methods for the prevention of losses among the live stock than the crude and often cruel old-time remedies, which are frequently more harmful than beneficial.

The blackleg investigation was therefore discontinued until the fall of 1896, when the writer was placed in charge. of the Pathological Division of this Bureau, and when numerous inquiries indicated that the disease prevailed in many and widely separated districts of the United States. As the disease seemed to affect the graded stock in preference to the common or native stock, complaints were received principally from the progressive stockmen, who, through the introduction of blooded stock, had endeavored to improve their herds. The continued existence of this disease had a very detrimental effect on the cattle industry in the districts where it appeared regularly, and it became urgently necessary that the Bureau should devise some measure through which the steadily increasing losses might be arrested or reduced as much as possible.

In Europe the disease had prevailed for years, and the method of vaccination had been adopted wherever the annual losses were sufficient to justify the expense. Three French scientists, Arloing, Cornevin, and Thomas, were the first to recommend preventive vaccination against blackleg, and their method, which consists in injecting into each animal two doses of highly attenuated blackleg virus, is still used in a great many farming and dairy districts. But the process requires that each animal be treated twice, with an interval of ten days between the two inoculations. This, when we consider the labor and expense of vaccinating large herds, becomes very inconvenient and expensive. For this reason the double vaccination did not become popular with the ranch owners, either in Europe or America, and was subsequently modified by the German scientist Kitt, who reduced it to a single vaccination with less attenuated virus. Kitt's method was adopted in eastern Europe and northern Africa with very satisfactory results, and, as the conditions obtaining there were very similar in many respects to those of the cattle-raising districts in this country, his method was taken as the foundation for the work undertaken by this Bureau. While the blackleg vaccinations in Europe are almost exclusively made by veterinarians, it was obvious that if the same rule was to be followed in this country the majority of the stock owners would be excluded from the benefits of the method. It was therefore decided to prepare a single vaccine, somewhat similar to the one used in Europe, and to place it directly in the hands of the cattle owner, with such instructions as would enable him to apply it without the assistance of professional experts. This probably is the first time in the history of preventive vaccination that the hypodermic syringe and attenuated virus (an overdose of which may prove fatal to the animal) has been handled by laymen in great numbers; and, though it was not without misgivings that such heroic measures were adopted, still it was the only effectual way to reduce to a minimum the annual losses of thousands upon thousands of cattle. ·

The districts in which blackleg especially prevails are the vast plains and cattle ranges of the West and Southwest, where the nearest veterinarian is often a hundred miles away; stock owners in these regions would either have to vaccinate their own cattle or else do without it. However, they accepted the proposition, and the several hundred thousands of successful vaccinations performed by the ranch owners or their employees tend to prove that the preventive inoculation for blackleg may be carried out satisfactorily by any ordinarily intelligent person who will make himself thoroughly familiar with the printed directions before he attempts to administer the vaccine. In the more densely populated districts the farmers in many cases have engaged a veterinarian to prepare and inject the vaccine, but the general rule has been for the stock owners to do it themselves, and the testimonials received are all to the effect that the printed directions are plain and that no difficulties were experienced in following them.

DISTRIBUTION OF THE VACCINE, AND ITS RESULTS.

The effect of the vaccine prepared by this Bureau in preventing outbreaks of the disease and in immediately abating outbreaks already in progress has been highly satisfactory, and it is not to be doubted that thousands of young cattle have been saved to the stock owners during the eighteen months in which the vaccine has been distributed. More than 700,000 doses have been sent out during this period, and from reports received it is safe to conclude that at least 500,000 animals have actually been injected, whereby the percentage of loss from blackleg has been reduced to less than one-half of one per cent. When it is considered that in regions where blackleg prevails the losses from this disease alone exceed those from all other causes combined, and in certain badly infected regions amounts to more than 10 per cent of the annual calf crop, then it is plain that the general introduction of preventive vaccination must be of material benefit to the cattle raisers in the infected districts.

In order to obtain as full information as possible regarding the etiology of blackleg, as it appears in this country, it was agreed with every stock owner who received vaccine from this Bureau that he would make careful observations on all questions pertaining to the disease and its prevention and to report them when so requested.

For the sake of uniformity an inquiry blank containing eighteen questions was prepared and a copy sent to each stock owner in from eight to twelve months after vaccine was sent to him. This allowed sufficient time to observe the preventive effect of the vaccine through one or two blackleg seasons. In order that every stock owner may understand the nature of the information desired by the Bureau, a copy of these questions, as given below, is attached to the printed directions for the use of the vaccine:

QUESTIONS.

1. What time of the year does blackleg prevail in your section of the country, and how long does it generally last?

2. According to your observations what climatic or other conditions seem to favor an outbreak of blackleg, and what circumstances tend to allay or discontinue it?

3. Do you find that certain pastures or localities on your ranch or farm furnish a larger number of deaths from blackleg than others? If so, please describe the nature of such places or pastures as compared to the surrounding country, stating the kind of soil, whether it is high and dry or low or swampy.

4. Have you noticed any difference as to the sex, condition, and class of the cattle that become affected?

5. What is the lowest age at which you have seen calves affected with blackleg and how many cases of this disease have you seen in cattle over 2 years old? State as nearly as possible the exact age of each case under 6 months and over 2 years.

6. Have you ever seen an animal recover from a recognized case of blackleg? If so, please describe as fully as possible.

7. What precautions are taken in your neighborhood to prevent the spread of blackleg? Are the dead animals burned or buried or simply left where they died?

8. How many head of stock did you vaccinate and what ages were they? Below 6 months. Between 6 months and 1 year. More than 1 year old. Date of vaccinations.

9. Did blackleg prevail among your cattle before vaccination? And if so, how many had died the same season previous to vaccination?

10. How did you secure the animals during the operations? Was the injection made while standing or thrown down or secured in a chute? In the latter case please describe the chute.

11. Did any animals die from blackleg after vaccination? And if so, how many and how soon after the injection?

12. Referring to the above question, are you satisfied that the vaccine was prepared according to the printed directions sent to you, and that no mistake was made in either the preparation or injection of the vaccine?

13. If any animals became affected after vaccination, did you notice whether the symptoms and post-mortem lesions differed in any way from those observed in nonvaccinated cattle?

14. Were the vaccinated animals placed in a pasture where blackleg was known to have prevailed at any time?

15. Did any of your neighbors who had not vaccinated continue to lose cattle after yours had stopped dying?

16. Did you ever castrate and vaccinate, or brand, dehorn, and vaccinate at the same time? If so, did you observe any ill effect from the vaccination in either case?

17. Did you find any difficulty in preparing and injecting the vaccine according to the printed directions? If so, please state in full what directions did not seem plain to you, and what parts of the process you found difficult.

18. Have you used any kind of blackleg vaccine other than the one prepared by this Bureau? And if so, with what success?

The distribution of blackleg vaccine was begun in the summer of 1897, and from August 14 of that year until April 30 of the following year there were vaccinated, in eight different States and Territories, 127,369 cattle. The following table is compiled from the reports received from the 522 stock owners who vaccinated these cattle. Altogether there have been returned about 560 reports, but the table below does not include any but those from the States named.[1]

Table showing the number of cattle vaccinated and the percentage of loss before and after vaccination.

State or Territory.	Number of reports.	Number of cattle vaccinated.	Average annual loss from blackleg.	Died before vaccination.		Died after vaccination.	
			Per cent.	*Number.*	*Per cent.*	*Number.*	*Per cent.*
Texas	164	50,609	13	1,462	2.95	227	0.45
Nebraska	71	20,898	17.2	796	3.80	52	.25
Kansas....................	140	19,508	11	919	4.76	115	.58
Colorado..................	53	12,609	12.8	230	1.83	138	1.09
Oklahoma	37	7,915	17.5	471	5.96	37	.47
Indian Territory	20	7,418	17.5	504	7.81	95	1.28
North Dakota	22	6,118	12.75	133	2.18	25	.41
South Dakota.............	15	2,299	12.75	74	3.32	11	.48
Total.................	522	127,369	14	4,589	3.63	700	.54

From the above it will be seen that 522 stock owners in eight different States and Territories vaccinated 127,369 cattle, or an average of 244 each. Previous to using the vaccine they had lost during the same season 4,589 cattle from blackleg, or an average of nearly 9.

It must be borne in mind that these 4,589 deaths, which form 3.63 per cent of the total number vaccinated, do not represent the average annual loss from blackleg, but simply a fraction of it, as the death rate in all instances was either greatly diminished or ceased altogether immediately after using the vaccine. In computing the statements made by the stock owners in answer to question 3 on the regular application blank for blackleg vaccine (which reads: "To what extent does blackleg prevail in your part of the country, and how great is your annual loss from this disease?") it appears that the annual loss in these blackleg districts, which are no doubt highly infected, varies from 5 to 35 per cent, or an average of 14 per cent. These figures in the majority of cases undoubtedly refer to bad blackleg years, and would probably be greatly diminished if averaged for a number of consecutive years. At any rate we have before us an actual loss of 3.63 per cent at the beginning of the blackleg season; and, though it is impossible to estimate how large the loss would have been if the

[1] The remaining 40 reports are divided between many other States, and do not warrant any conclusions to be drawn from them. They will therefore be retained until a sufficient number have been received to form a basis for an estimate of the prevalence of blackleg in the remaining States.

animals had not been vaccinated, we are justified in believing that it would have been considerably greater, as the majority of stock owners state that those of their neighbors who did not vaccinate continued to lose cattle from blackleg long after the mortality had stopped among the vaccinated animals. The total loss after vaccination amounts to 700 head, which forms 0.54 per cent of the number vaccinated, or, in other words, a little more than one-half of 1 per cent. This does not seem to be very much, but when it is considered that the vaccinations here referred to in the majority of cases were first attempts by the operators in this kind of work, we are justified in believing that as the stock owners become more expert in preparing the vaccine and handling the instruments the loss after vaccination will be reduced to practically nothing. (See table on p. 76.)

LOSSES DUE TO CARELESS OPERATORS.

Many of these 700 deaths after vaccination are due either to mistakes or to carelessness on the part of the operator in preparing and injecting the vaccine. When the vaccine is made at the laboratory, a certain amount—as a rule, from 12,000 to 15,000 doses, or 4 to 5 ounces—of the powder is heated, tested, and packed as a batch by itself, which is given a number and kept entirely separate from other batches. It takes about two weeks to finish a batch, consequently a number are handled at the same time, which, however, does not necessitate that they come in contact with each other. When finally it is sent out a record is kept of the number of the vaccine sent to each applicant, together with the amount and the date when sent. If now, for instance, such a batch of 15,000 doses is distributed among 50 to 60 applicants and then a few weeks later one of these stock owners reports that, although he prepared and injected the vaccine according to the printed directions, he still lost a number of animals from blackleg, while none of the others make any complaints or report satisfactory results, then it is evident that the fault does not lie with the vaccine, but that some mistake has been made in this special case. There also seems to be, at least in some instances, a prejudice against the vaccine prepared by this Bureau, simply because it is distributed free of charge; and for the same reason there is sometimes an inclination to be negligent or careless in using it, an indulgence which no stock owner permits himself when he purchases one of the various blackleg vaccines on the market and pays from 15 to 25 cents per dose.

In Europe it is claimed that many of the failures to produce immunity through vaccination—that is, when several of the animals die from blackleg subsequent to vaccination—are due to negligence on the part of the operator either in preparing or administering the vaccine. It is especially charged that frequently the solution is filtered

10317——3

too much, leaving it perfectly clear and consequently less effective. This the Bureau has endeavored to remedy by substituting absorbent cotton for paper as a filtering medium, but nevertheless it is stated that some difficulty has been experienced in getting a solution of the right strength. This, however, will be overcome by experience if care is taken to follow the printed directions explicitly.

ATTITUDE OF THE BUREAU IN DISTRIBUTING VACCINE.

In this connection, it may be well to mention that the distribution of blackleg vaccine by this Bureau was undertaken simply for the purpose of aiding the stock owner to combat this fatal disease, and that there was no thought of entering the field for the sake of competing with the manufacturers or venders of blackleg vaccine, whatever may be the virtues or faults of their remedies; and if any stock owner thinks that he can get more satisfactory results, and save a greater number of animals by using any of these, there can be no objection to his doing so.

By introducing the single vaccine into this country and distributing it free of charge, the Bureau has succeeded in disseminating information on the subject of blackleg and its prevention to such an extent that during the eighteen months covered by this report there have been vaccinated in this country more cattle than had previously been vaccinated in all other countries since the first introduction of vaccination for blackleg fourteen years ago. And the results (if we may judge from the first 127,000 vaccinations) in reducing the mortality among the vaccinated stock to about one-half of 1 per cent compares favorably with the loss of 0.47 per cent as reported on 499,096 vaccinations in Europe and other countries for the period of 1884–1895. (See table on p. 63.) These latter figures include both single and double vaccinations and also the various methods of injecting the vaccine in either the shoulder region or in the tail. The latter method is in Europe considered the safest, and single vaccinations in the shoulder region are recorded with a subsequent mortality of 0.63 per cent, in comparison with which the results obtained in this country are highly gratifying.

It may be added, finally, that blackleg vaccine in the form it is now used in every country may be manufactured for less than 1 cent per dose; and, with the facilities at the disposition of this Bureau, the cost of production does not exceed 1 cent per ten doses. The price of 15 to 25 cents per dose, as is generally charged for the blackleg vaccine sold by the various companies in this country, has no doubt been one of the chief factors in preventing vaccination for blackleg from becoming more popular than was the case before the Bureau took the matter up.

Under these circumstances, it was clearly the duty of the Bureau of Animal Industry, under the law by which it is established, to take up the problem of preventing and ultimately eradicating the disease; and it has been a great satisfaction to all concerned to observe the alacrity with which thousands of stock owners have entered into the spirit of cooperation. No effort has been spared to make the vaccine as effective as possible without passing the danger line, and, if care is taken to follow the directions for its preparation and use, there is reason to hope that when employed wherever blackleg prevails the annual loss from this disease will, before many years shall have passed, be an unknown factor in the live-stock industry of this country.

HISTORICAL REVIEW OF BLACKLEG.

Although it is not until the last quarter of this century that black-leg, or symptomatic anthrax, has been definitely recognized as a distinct disease caused by a specific microorganism, still there can be little doubt that it has existed for many centuries, and that a large number of the epidemics among cattle which are referred to by early historians and clinical observers as anthrax, or *Ignis sacer*, were really blackleg and not anthrax. This supposition is based upon the fact that their description of the symptoms and post-mortem appearances in many cases correspond more exactly with our present knowledge of blackleg than it does with anthrax.

A French scientist, Chabert, one of the most brilliant observers of his time, attempted as early as 1782 to bring some system into the classification of the anthracoid diseases, and proposed to divide them into three classes, namely, anthrax fever, true anthrax, and symptomatic anthrax. When the disease manifested itself without the appearance of an external swelling he called it anthrax fever, and when swellings appeared it was either true anthrax or symptomatic anthrax. The first symptom observed in true anthrax was always the swelling, which at first was small, hard, and very painful, and in its further development was accompanied by fever and other general symptoms. When incised the tissues of the swelling appeared to be black and gangrenous. When, on the other hand, the appearance of the swelling was preceded by a febrile stage, with loss of appetite and general depression, he called it symptomatic anthrax. This classification was a great improvement over the former confusion, but, although it was not generally accepted by contemporary scientists, it remained in force for nearly a century.

In 1797 another French scientist, Boutrolle, mentioned a disease which he called *mal de cuisse* (quarter evil), because it affected the animal in the thigh and made it lame in one of the hind legs. He stated that the disease was of a gangrenous nature and nearly incurable. No doubt this author had reference to blackleg, although he did not recognize it as such.

In 1850 Rayer and Davaine discovered the anthrax bacillus in the blood of sheep which had died from anthrax, but, although a number of scientists verified this discovery, they did not recognize the bacillus as the cause of the disease, but considered its presence in the tissues and blood of affected animals as the result of the disease. Not until 1877 did Pasteur succeed in demonstrating that the bacillus was the one essential for the appearance of the disease, and in 1879 it was proved by Arloing, Cornevin, and Thomas that symptomatic anthrax. or blackleg, is caused by an entirely different microorganism and consequently is a distinct disease. The following year the same authors published a description of the blackleg bacillus and demonstrated that the disease could be produced in susceptible animals by inoculation, and that immunity might be produced by introducing the bacillus into the circulation of such animals under certain favorable circumstances. This discovery was the beginning of a series of experiments which finally led to the introduction of preventive vaccination by hypodermic injections of blackleg virus which had been attenuated by means of heat.

GEOGRAPHICAL DISTRIBUTION OF BLACKLEG.

There are but few countries in the world where blackleg does not prevail to some extent. The ravages of this disease are not confined to certain zones or altitudes, but occur as frequently in the extreme north as in the tropical regions, and as often on the highest mountain pastures as in the lowlands of the valleys. It is therefore evident that the contagion of blackleg possesses an unrivaled power of resistance against the destructive influence of varying climatic conditions. In Europe it occurs as far north in Norway as cattle are kept, and it is doubtful whether a disease which often causes great loss among the reindeer herds in Lapland, northern Russia, and Siberia is not identical with blackleg. Furthermore, in Denmark, Germany, France, Spain, Italy, Austria-Hungary, Netherlands, and England the disease is known and dreaded by cattle owners. On the summer pastures on the Alps, in Switzerland, where for five months of the year the ground is covered with snow and ice, the disease appears regularly every summer when the cattle are brought from the lowlands, and sometimes carries off as high as 25 per cent of the young stock.

In France blackleg is regarded as the most destructive disease among the cattle, and it is especially the dairy districts and the mountain pastures which suffer the greatest losses. In the latter places the disease is called *mal de montagne,* or mountain disease, but statistics show an equally great mortality among the cattle on the rich meadows and pastures along the great rivers. In the Bavarian Alps, in Tyrol and Vorarlberg, the disease is very severe on the young stock.

In Denmark the disease is well known, and has for more than a century been distinguished by laymen from other anthracoid diseases under the name of *raslesyge,* which means rattle disease. In 1821

Viborg described the disease as occurring regularly in certain districts where it still appears up to the present time.

In Africa blackleg occurs both in the northern and southern colonies, especially in the French possessions in Algeria, where it frequently decimates the herds of young stock. Also in the southern republics, especially that of Natal, it has been reported to be very prevalent. The same seems to be the case with the English colonies in Asia, although no definite statistics to that effect can be obtained. .

BLACKLEG IN THE UNITED STATES.

Up to the time when this Bureau undertook to investigate the prevalence of blackleg in the United States it was merely known that it occurred in certain districts in this country. Both Huidekoper and Liautard advised the above-mentioned French scientists to that effect, but were unable to furnish any statistics as to the extent of the disease in the various States. From the reports received during the present investigation it became apparent that the loss from blackleg in certain portions of several States exceeds that of all other causes combined. The States and Territories which principally suffer are Texas, Indian Territory, Oklahoma, Kansas, Nebraska, Colorado, North Dakota, and South Dakota; but it will be seen from the accompanying map that quite a number of the other Western States are badly affected. Every county marked with red, irrespective of the shading, is infested with blackleg, and the degree of shading indicates the approximate number of vaccinations which have been made in each county. (See explanation on the margin of the map.) It is, however, easy to judge from the shading as to the extent to which blackleg prevails in each county, as naturally the greatest number of vaccinations have been undertaken in those regions where blackleg occurs most frequently and where the direct loss from this disease has been greatest in relative proportion to the number and value of the cattle.

The following table shows the proportionate number of counties infected in each of the eight principal States and Territories:

Total number of counties in affected States and Territories and number of counties affected.

State.	Total number of counties in State.	Number of counties infected.	Percentage.
Texas	246	100	46
Kansas	106	84	79
Nebraska	90	55	61
South Dakota	78	33	49
Colorado	56	37	63
North Dakota	45	18	40
Oklahoma Territory	24	19	80
Indian Territory	5	4	80

As shown in the table on page 32, the stock owners in the infected communities enumerated above reported an average annual loss of 14 per cent from blackleg alone; but, as already stated, it must be borne in mind that most of these reports are probably based upon the losses during especially bad blackleg years.   It is nevertheless apparent that the disease prevails in the above-mentioned States and Territories to an extent far greater than is the case in Europe, where the Swiss scientist Strebel estimates the annual loss for a period of eleven years among unvaccinated stock in blackleg regions to average 1.67 per cent.   The actual loss from blackleg among 127,369 cattle which were vaccinated in the above-mentioned eight States and Territories amounted to 4,589 head during the same season, but previous to vaccination.   This constitutes 3.63 per cent of the total number, and would no doubt have been considerably greater if no preventive measures had been taken to arrest the mortality.

In the East a number of outbreaks have been reported from Virginia, West Virginia, and Pennsylvania, and scattering outbreaks have occurred in Vermont, New York, Ohio, Kentucky, Tennessee, and North Carolina.   In the Central States outbreaks have been reported from Michigan, Indiana, Illinois, Wisconsin, Minnesota, Iowa, and Missouri; but it is principally in the cattle-raising and cattle-feeding regions, which are bounded on the east by the Missouri River and Mississippi River and on the west by the Rocky Mountains, which suffer the most.   In the extreme west the disease seems to prevail to a considerable extent in the States of Washington, Montana, Oregon, Idaho, Utah, California, and Arizona.

With exception of the southern Atlantic and the eastern Gulf States there are but few districts in the United States where the disease has not been observed.

AGE, CLASS, SEX, AND CONDITION OF CATTLE MOST FREQUENTLY AFFECTED BY BLACKLEG.

Every stock owner who lives in a district where blackleg occurs knows that it is the young animals, especially those between the ages of 6 and 18 months, which are most liable to become affected.   Occasionally animals above and below this age may contract the disease, but the vast majority of cases occur in cattle between 6 and 18 months old.

In Europe exact statistics have been compiled regarding this question, and M. Hess, of Switzerland, tabulates his observations on 989 cases of blackleg as follows:

> 374 cases between 6 months and 1 year.
> 439 cases between 1 year and 2 years.
> 83 cases between 2 years and 3 years.
> 65 cases between 3 years and 4 years.
> 10 cases between 4 years and 5 years.
> 18 cases between 5 years and 6 years.

From this it appears that 82 per cent of all the cases occurred among cattle from 6 months to 2 years old, and that above the latter age the mortality decreases rapidly and becomes insignificant at the age of 4. It will be noticed that not a single case below 6 months is recorded in this list, and both M. Hess and the French authors Arloing, Cornevin, and Thomas are of the opinion that, although a few cases have been observed, the number is so insignificant that cattle below 6 months old may, for all practical purposes, be considered immune from blackleg.

In this country the case is somewhat different. From a number of blackleg districts it has been reported that the calves frequently begin to die at the age of 4 to 5 months, and cases of blackleg in even younger animals can not be considered exceedingly rare, although not numerous enough to be of any importance in the contemplation of preventive measures. It seems, on the other hand, to be very unusual for cattle in this country to contract the disease when past 2 years old. Only 59 cases have been reported by 550 stock owners to have been observed by them throughout their entire career in the cattle business. (See question 5 on the inquiry blank.) These cases are divided as follows:

> Between 2 and 3 years old, 40 cases.
> Between 3 and 4 years old, 7 cases.
> Above 4 years old, 12 cases.

It must, however, be taken into consideration that a large majority of the stock owners in the blackleg districts are cattle raisers who seldom retain their cattle, except the breeding stock, for any length of time after they have reached a marketable age, which is from 2 to 4 years; and according to the Swiss statistics (Hess) cows when past 3 years old are almost absolutely immune from blackleg.

Of cases below 6 months there have been reported to us 355. They may be classified as follows:

> Below 1 month old 6
> Between 1 and 2 months 30
> Between 2 and 3 months 47
> Between 3 and 4 months 113
> Between 4 and 5 months 120
> Between 5 and 6 months 39

The increase in number of cases with the increase in age is very characteristic, and suggests that natural or inherited immunity against blackleg, which is so pronounced in young animals, gradually wears off with the approach to the fateful half-year mark. The sudden drop from 120 cases between 4 and 5 months to 39 cases between 5 and 6 months is most probably due to the fact that calves past 5 months old are so close to the age when blackleg is expected to affect them that stock owners, as a rule, report such cases as being half a year old.

As to the class of cattle most frequently affected by blackleg the majority of reports agree that full-blood or high-grade stock are more subject to the disease than the common or low-grade range cattle. In a series of experiments conducted in southern Texas for the purpose of ascertaining the relative effectiveness of various kinds of blackleg vaccine, it was found to be very difficult to produce a characteristic case of blackleg in yearling calves of the ordinary longhorn breed, even when inoculated with 10 centigrams of highly virulent blackleg meat, which was known to kill guinea pigs in the course of eighteen to thirty-six hours after inoculation with only 0.2 milligram. It was therefore impossible to use this class of animals for experimental purposes, and graded Shorthorns were substituted. The only animal of this class inoculated died promptly from typical blackleg.

It has been claimed by Makoldi that the range cattle in Hungary are immune from blackleg, which statement is partially borne out by Hutyra, who states that this class of cattle seldom become affected, and that the course of the disease takes a much milder form than is the case in western Europe. Cornevin claims that the buffalo is immune from blackleg, but this statement is based upon the inoculation of only two buffalo calves, which remained unaffected except for a slight rise in temperature. M. Bremond states that the cattle of Algeria possess a much greater resistance to blackleg than European cattle and that when affected they frequently recover.

In this country it is a noticeable fact that blackleg has been on the increase ever since the stock owners began to improve their cattle. A large number of ranchmen state that up to a few years ago their losses from blackleg were insignificant, while others state that last year was the first time they ever heard of it; and when we consider the nature of the disease and the manner in which the infection takes place, we must admit that the more thin-skinned the animal is the more liable it is to become infected. It is generally conceded that the infection is almost always introduced into the system through abrasions of the skin in the form of minute punctures caused by thorns, spines, and grass-burs (not through open wounds), and that to take effect the virus must penetrate into the subcutaneous tissue. Consequently the thicker and tougher the skin of the animal the less liable it is to become infected.

On large ranges, where both ordinary and graded stock are kept, it is not difficult to observe that the majority of deaths from blackleg occur among the graded stock. The common-bred range cattle of Texas and the Western States are as hardy a race as ever existed, and there is no reason to doubt that in regions where blackleg has prevailed for a number of years the native stock, through the "survival of the fittest," have acquired or inherited a partial or complete immunity from the disease, in a similar manner as they have been enabled through constant exposure to resist a fatal attack of Texas fever.

Whether there exists any perceptible predisposition for either sex is very doubtful. A number of the reports received state that steer calves are more frequently affected by blackleg than heifers, but the greater majority of stock owners are of the opinion that both sexes are equally susceptible. That this is correct so far as calves and yearlings are concerned is highly probable, as the sexual characteristics are but slightly pronounced in the young animals.

In older animals there seems to be a predisposition to blackleg among the males. M. Hess, of Switzerland, has shown that among cattle over 3 years old the bulls and steers were much more frequently attacked than the cows. From two outbreaks in Canton Berne, in 1882 and 1883, he has gathered the following statistics:

Animal.	1882.	1883.	Average.
	Per cent.	Per cent.	Per cent.
Bulls	5.05	10.10	7.58
Steers	3.05	5.21	4.13
Cows	0.21	0.72	0.47

The limited number of cases of blackleg recorded in this country among cattle over 3 years old is not sufficient to warrant any conclusions to be drawn therefrom.

As to the condition of the animals, by far the greater majority of cattle owners hold that it is the best cattle in the herd which principally become affected. Nevertheless, it is not uncommon for cattle in very ordinary or rather poor condition to contract blackleg. There seems, however, to be a predisposition in young cattle which are rapidly improving in flesh, as is the case when they are turned on fresh grass in the spring. On the other hand, the change from grass to hay in the fall does in many localities have an equally fatal effect on the stock. A cattle raiser in Nebraska states that "young cattle rapidly improving or declining in flesh seem to be most susceptible." Another says that "poor cattle that pick up rapidly are more susceptible than those which remain in fairly good condition all the time." And still another says that "spring calves are mostly affected in the fall, when they are very fat and are changed from grass to hay, while yearling steers are affected in the spring when turned on grass." Other stock owners are inclined to attribute the appearance of blackleg to a lack of exercise, and claim that driving the herd for a considerable distance will temporarily check the disease. This theory, for several reasons, appears to be very plausible. In the spring, when the young stock suddenly find themselves in the midst of plenty, they do not have to feed over but a very limited area before they are filled up, when they lie down to ruminate. Under these circumstances, namely, plenty of food and little exercise, there is a tendency to an accumulation in the system of lactic acid, which, as will be discussed later in this article, has the property of greatly increasing the virulence of the blackleg bacillus. So great is the effect of lactic acid in this respect, that a few drops, added to a solution of blackleg vaccine, will in the course of five to six hours restore to the highly attenuated spores their original virulence, and vaccine treated in this way will, if injected into a susceptible animal, produce a fatal attack of blackleg. As the lactic acid in the system is found principally in the muscles, and is excreted by them through their activity, there is every reason to believe that lack of exercise while the grass is fresh and abundant is a predisposing factor in the appearance of blackleg.

As will be seen from the above, it is the spring and the fall which seem to be the seasons most favorable for the development of blackleg.   The disease is, however, not confined to these seasons, but appears at all times of the year with more or less frequency. In the North, for instance in the Dakotas, the real blackleg season lasts from April to September or October, but outbreaks are reported in every month of the year.   In Nebraska and Colorado the outbreaks are more evenly distributed over the whole year, with a slight increase during spring and fall, and the same may be said of Kansas, but with a slightly higher percentage of cases during fall and spring.   In Oklahoma, Indian Territory, and the Panhandle of Texas, it is difficult to single out any season as being more favorable to blackleg than others; but in central and west Texas the principal number of outbreaks occur during fall, winter, and spring, with but few cases during June, July, and August.

As to the meteorological and geological conditions, we have already seen that blackleg occurs at all seasons of the year and in almost every country in the world; so it is not surprising that the answers received to questions 2 and 3 on the inquiry blank sent out by this Bureau (which read: "According to your observations what climatic or other conditions seem to favor an outbreak of blackleg, and what circumstances tend to allay or discontinue it?" and "Do you find that certain pastures or localities on your ranch or farm furnish a larger number of deaths from blackleg than others? If so, please describe the nature of such places or pastures as compared to the surrounding country, stating the kind of soil, whether it is high and dry or low and swampy") have embraced every known climatic condition and every recognized geological formation, deposit, or strata as either favorable or unfavorable to the development of blackleg. But most stock owners agree that when the disease has broken out there is nothing short of a hypodermic syringe and vaccine or the immediate removal of the affected herd to another pasture that will have any effect in checking the disease, and one of the two is generally resorted to in preference to awaiting the interference of frost or rain. According to the writer's personal observations, there is no climatic condition, however extremely opposite to the one prevailing, which will in any way influence an outbreak of blackleg already in progress.

SYMPTOMS.

The symptoms of blackleg are so characteristic that the disease is easily recognized. The first symptoms may be either of a general or of a local nature, though more frequently of the latter. The general symptoms are high fever, loss of appetite, and suspension of rumination, followed by great depression. Respiration becomes accelerated; the animal moves around with difficulty, frequently lies down, and, when water is near at hand, drinks at short intervals and but a little at a time. The visible mucous membranes are at first dark red and congested, but they change in the course of twelve hours to a dirty leaden or purplish color.

The most important diagnostic feature is the development of a tumor or swelling under the skin. The swelling may appear on any part of the body and limbs, except below the knee or hock joint or on the tail. It is frequently seen on the thigh or shoulder, and, owing to the extensive discoloration of the swollen parts, as observed after the animal has been skinned, the disease has been popularly named "blackleg," or "black quarter." Tumors may also appear on the neck, the chest, the flank, or the rump. At first they are small and very painful. They increase rapidly in size and may in a few hours cover a large portion of the body. One or more of these tumors may form simultaneously, and when in close proximity to each other may become confluent. The neighboring lymph glands become considerably swollen.

As to the location of the tumors there seems to be a decided preference for the right side of the body. According to M. Hess, who has made observations along this line on 1,547 cases, the tumors appeared in 209 cases on the right hind quarter and in only 143 cases on the left; in 168 cases on the right front leg and in 98 on the left; in 59 cases on the right side of the neck and in 4 only on the left side. No explanation is offered for this peculiar preference for the right side, and as no observations have been made in this country and the question is of small economic importance, the writer will not venture to express an opinion.

If slight pressure is made on the tumor a crackling sound is heard and percussion gives a clear resonant tone due to the collection of gas in the affected tissue. The tumor is cool to the touch and painless in the center; the skin over it is dry and parchment-like. When the tumor is lanced a frothy dark-red fluid is discharged. If the incision is made while the animal is alive or immediately after death, there is no offensive odor to the discharge, but decomposition takes place very soon after death. No pain is manifested when the center of the tumor is lanced, but as soon as the knife reaches the warm inflamed part the animal will bellow loudly and flinch.

The swellings usually appear before the general symptoms [1] and they may even reach such an extent as to cause complete paralysis of the affected parts while the animal still looks bright and has a good appetite. This condition is, however, of short duration. As the swelling increases in size the general symptoms become more intense. The temperature may reach 107° F., while the respiration may exceed 140 per minute. The animal is unable to rise; the extremities become cold, and some time before death the temperature falls and may become subnormal. There is trembling of the muscles, which, as death approaches, may develop into violent convulsions.

With very few exceptions the disease terminates fatally, death generally occurring from twelve to thirty-six hours after the first appearance of the symptoms. A few cases linger from three to four days, and, as will be discussed later, the disease may sometimes terminate in recovery.

APPEARANCE AFTER DEATH.

The carcass of an animal which has died from blackleg soon becomes very distended by gas, partially through fermentation in the intestines and partially through the formation of gas in the subcutaneous tissue, due to the presence of the blackleg bacillus. This distention, which is especially pronounced in the region of the blackleg tumors, extends for a considerable distance from the tumors and in the directions where it meets the least resistance—that is, where there is plenty of loose areolar tissue. This is especially the case on the back and sides of the chest, on the shoulder and between the shoulder and chest, and on the external surface of the hind quarter. This tympanitic condition frequently causes the two legs on the upper side of the carcass to stand out straight without touching the ground.

A dark, blood-colored frothy discharge flows from the nostrils and the anus. Decomposition takes place soon after death, except in the affected muscles, which retain their sweetish-sour odor without developing any putrid odor, even when the rest of the carcass has decomposed.

On the surface of the body may be seen one or more of the characteristic emphysematous blackleg tumors. The skin covering these

---

[1] Arloing, Cornevin, and Thomas believe that the general symptoms always precede the tumor, but that they subside temporarily after the appearance of the latter. This I am not prepared to contradict, my opinion being based upon a number of observations where the animal was found with a well-developed swelling, but otherwise without showing any general symptoms.

swellings is affected with dry gangrene. The connective tissue beneath the skin is infiltrated with blood and bloody serum and is distended with gas. The affected muscles are dark brown or black, are easily torn, and the spaces surrounding them are filled with bloody liquid and gas. The muscle tissue is distended with numerous smaller or larger gas-filled cavities, often to such an extent as to produce a resemblance to lung tissue. Upon incision it does not collapse perceptibly, as the gas cavities are not connected with each other. The discoloration is deepest at the center, shading off toward the edges, and becomes brighter by contact with the air. On compression thick blood escapes, which is charged with gas and has a disagreeable sour odor. The blood in the remaining parts of the carcass is normal and coagulates easily after death, forming a solid clot. The gas of the tumor is combustible and burns with a blue flame, being, according to Bollinger, carbureted hydrogen. The abdominal cavity sometimes contains a considerable quantity of bloody effusion. The mucous membrane of the intestine may be congested or inflamed, and the contents of the bowels may be covered with blood. The liver is congested, but the spleen is always normal.

It is often desirable to determine whether an animal is affected with blackleg or with anthrax tumor or with a swelling caused by the bacillus of malignant edema. The anthrax tumor may be distinguished by its hardness and solidity and by the fact that it contains no gas. The spleen is enlarged in anthrax and is unaffected in blackleg. The blood in anthrax is very dark and of a tar-like consistence, while it is normal in blackleg. It is difficult to distinguish between the swellings of blackleg and malignant edema, since they resemble each other very closely and both are distended with gas. Malignant edema, however, generally starts from a wound of considerable size; it often follows surgical operations, and does not usually result from the small abrasions and pricks to which animals are subjected in pastures.

THE BLACKLEG BACILLUS.

A microscopic examination of a drop of fluid taken from a blackleg tumor shows the presence of a number of microorganisms, which vary considerably in shape. The young and actively growing blackleg bacillus is rod-shaped and cylindrical, the ends being more or less rounded. They are actively motile, moving in various directions and turning around their axes. Besides these, a number of spindle-shaped bodies may be seen, which form the first stage of sporulation. The tenacity to life of the blackleg virus is dependent upon the power of the bacillus to form spores. These constitute a dormant form of the microorganism, which possesses a very high degree of resistance to all destructive agents, but which under ordinary circumstances are unable to multiply.

The spindle-shaped bodies soon differentiate a small portion of their substance, which forms a bright oval spot in their interior, usually located at one end, producing very characteristic racket, or club-shaped, forms. The bright body, the spore, is soon liberated, and is surrounded by a hard, shell-like substance, which enables it to resist heat, cold, light, moisture, dryness, and other unfavorable conditions, and even decomposition in a dead body, which would more quickly result in the destruction of unprotected bacilli.

The blackleg bacillus is not able to multiply in the presence of oxygen. In technical language, they are anaerobic. This explains the fact that while they do not develop on parts of the body exposed to free air, such as the skin and mucous membranes, the germs find the conditions necessary to their growth in the parts underneath the skin, as the underlying connective tissue to which the air does not have access. With the spore stage to protect it the blackleg germ may exist for a long time outside of the body, and it is very difficult to eradicate the disease from a pasture which has once become infected. Experience shows that the spores may exist almost indefinitely in the ground, and that animals may become infected on the same pasture year after year. According to Arloing, Cornevin, and Thomas, the virulence of blackleg germs, after they have left the animal body, depends greatly on whether they are deposited immediately on swampy soil or in water, or on dry bodies (stone or wood), where they are dried quickly by the sun.

In the first case the virus becomes diluted, sinks to the bottom, or penetrates into the ground, where in the course of a few months it loses its virulence. In the other case it dries quickly, forming numerous spores, which are extremely resistant to all destructive agents which may afterwards be applied to them. Such dried virus may be exposed for many hours to temperatures, high or low, which are unknown in nature without losing its virulence. An exposure for twenty-four hours to $-120°$ C. does not in the least reduce the fatal effect of the virus, as shown by subsequent inoculations in guinea pigs. In order completely to destroy the virulence of dried blackleg material by heat it is necessary to expose it for six hours to a temperature of 110° C. Exposure to lower degrees (90°, 95°, or 100° C.) only produces an attenuation of the virulence, as will be discussed later. The fresh virus, on the other hand, may be destroyed completely by heating for two hours and twenty minutes at a temperature of 70° C., or for twenty minutes at 100° C.

The same is the case with the action of the various chemicals. The dried virus resists a stronger solution and a longer exposure than the fresh. A 2 per cent solution of carbolic acid destroys the latter in eight hours, while it requires fifteen to twenty hours for the former. For disinfecting purposes it is therefore necessary to use at least a 5 per cent solution of carbolic acid, or else corrosive sublimate, 1–2000.

MANNER OF INFECTION.

As already mentioned, the blackleg bacillus gains entrance to the body through abrasions of the skin, and perhaps in rare cases through the mucous membranes. In order to meet the requirements for the development of the spores—that is, an absolute absence of oxygen—it is necessary that the abrasion be minute in size and sufficiently deep to penetrate through the skin into the subcutaneous tissue; consequently incised or open wounds are not favorable to the development of blackleg, even if the infection is present in abundance. Punctured wounds, such as those received from barbed-wire fences or from stubbles and briers in the pasture, seem to be the most likely method of infection and correspond most closely to the only manner in which the disease may be produced artificially—that is, through hypodermic injection of the virus. It is doubtful whether the infection ever takes place through ingestion. In any case, it has proved exceedingly difficult to produce the disease, even by feeding enormous doses of highly virulent material to susceptible animals.

The fact that in 99 per cent of all cases the tumors develop on the surface of the body seems also to indicate that the infection takes place through the skin, and the few cases recorded where the deeper-seated muscles have been affected—for instance, the muscles of the diaphragm, or those popularly known as the tenderloin—without the presence of tumors on the surface may be due to the germs gaining direct entrance into the lymph stream, which carries them directly to muscle groups located in the interior of the body.

Blackleg may be produced in susceptible animals by inoculating with a small amount of virulent material taken from the swelling of an animal which has died from the disease. This material may be introduced by means of a hypodermic syringe under the skin or directly into the muscles. Certain places on the body, where the subcutaneous connective tissue is very dense and elastic—for instance, on the legs below the knee and hock joint or on the tail—offer greater resistance to the development of the germs than where there is plenty of loose areolar tissue.

When the virus is introduced directly into the blood stream the germs multiply rapidly, but owing to the presence of oxygen in the blood the disease does not develop, and animals treated in this way are subsequently immune to the disease. This fact was first noted by Arloing, Cornevin, and Thomas, who employed it for preventive vaccination; but the method required great skill in manipulation, as a minute amount of the virus, if it gained entrance into the subcutaneous tissue at the place of inoculation, would be sure to produce a fatal case of blackleg. Furthermore, if the animal at the time of inoculation was suffering from a severe contusion, the germs would gain entrance, through the extravasating blood, to the bruised muscle tissue and a blackleg tumor develop at this place. The same may occur when animals are castrated or dehorned or otherwise injured at the time of vaccination.

As already stated, it is exceedingly rare that an animal affected
with blackleg recovers. In Europe very few of the veterinarians and
scientists who have made investigations along this line have ever
been fortunate enough to observe a case of recovery. Arloing, Cornevin, and Thomas claim that they have seen a few cases of artificially produced blackleg, which in the course of three to four days
began to improve, and which after a long period of convalescence
finally recovered.

In Algeria M. Bremond thinks that blackleg among the native cattle
not infrequently terminates in recovery, but it is highly probable that
the stock owners in that country, upon whose statements his opinion
is based, are very often mistaken in their diagnosis. He states that
although he has never succeeded in rescuing an animal which was
affected, he has been assured by many reliable stock owners that what
they supposed to be characteristic blackleg sometimes terminated
spontaneously in recovery. An animal which showed a number of
scars from deep incisions and cauterization, and which was claimed
to have recovered from blackleg, was shown to M. Bremond, who, in
order to ascertain whether the diagnosis had been correct, obtained permission to inoculate the animal with blackleg. This was done, and in
the course of thirty hours the animal died from typical blackleg, which
demonstrated that it could not have previously been affected, as it
would then have been immune to the disease. He concludes, therefore, that the Algerian disease, which is characterized by extensive
local swellings, and which sometimes is cured through rational treatment, is not always true blackleg. It seems, nevertheless, that the
cattle of Algeria possess a greater resistance to blackleg and to other
infectious diseases than do the European animals, and no doubt the
chances of recovery among the native stock in that country are far
better than is the case in Europe.

In 1883 Bremond writes that out of a number of animals affected
with blackleg he chose a 4-year-old steer which presented an enormous crepitating tumor in the region of the shoulder. He made incisions into the tumor and cut out a piece of the affected muscular tissue,
with which he inoculated two guinea pigs, both of which died within
thirty-six hours with symptoms of typical blackleg. With material
from one of these guinea pigs he inoculated a 5-months-old calf and
a lamb, both of which died from blackleg at forty-nine and thirty
hours, respectively, after inoculation. The steer, however, which had
furnished the virulent material commenced to improve on the fourth
day and had completely recovered a week after the appearance of
the first symptoms. The author does not state how the enormous
crepitating tumor was resolved. The diagnosis can not be doubted,
but the complete recovery in the course of a week excludes the possibility of healing taking place through sequestration of the affected

SECTION OF MUSCLE FROM A BLACKLEG SWELLING.

tissues and the wound filling up with granulations, and leaves us to infer that the hemorrhagic exudation was resolved and that the affected tissues returned to their normal functions and appearance. This is of interest as bearing upon the same subject in this country, where several cases of supposedly typical blackleg are reported to have recovered in the course of a week or so, but where, for lack of professional knowledge on the part of the observers, it has been necessary to accept their reports with reservation. M. Bremond's case, however, indicates that a speedy recovery may take place even after extensive tissue changes have occurred.

Commenting on this case the three French scientists say that the curability of blackleg in Algeria is probably not alone due to a greater resistance on the part of the animals, but may, to some extent, at least, be due to a diminution of virulence through the influence of climate. They suggest that an attenuation similar to that which is produced artificially in the incubators or ovens in the laboratory may take place under the influence of the heat and radiation of the African sun, and many circumstances point to this theory being correct. We know that a large percentage of the hardy range cattle in Algeria, Hungary, and the southwestern part of the United States are immune to blackleg, but whether this is due to a natural or inherited power of resistance, or to what is called acquired immunity, is very difficult to decide. Arloing, Cornevin, and Thomas believe that there exists a mild form of the disease which only manifests itself through a slight fever and loss of appetite, and which leaves the animals immune (acquired immunity) to subsequent fatal attacks, but no actual observations of such cases are on record. When no external or local lesions appear, it is very difficult to diagnose blackleg; in fact, we do not see how it could be done except by laboratory methods, which rarely are convenient where such cases might present themselves. When the local lesions do appear, the result, as we know, is almost invariably death. But our experience with artificially attenuated virus—that is, vaccine—shows that a very mild form of the disease can be produced, so mild that clinical observations fail to notice it. The attenuation of the virus is accomplished by heating it in an oven at a temperature between 90° and 95° C. from six to seven hours. When virus is kept in the laboratory for several years, it undergoes a slight attenuation; that is, a larger dose of old virus is necessary to produce a fatal case of blackleg than is required when fresh virus is used. It is therefore natural to conclude that a similar attenuation takes place in nature, only to a greater extent, and that virus which has been left exposed to sun and rain for years may reach the same degree of attenuation as we produce in the laboratory by heating in a moist condition for a few hours.

Such naturally attenuated virus, when it gains access to the subcutaneous tissue of a susceptible animal, has the same effect as the hypodermic injection of vaccine; but owing to the minuteness of the

dose—that is, the few spores which may be attached to a spine or
thorn which penetrates the skin—it is obvious that a number of such
infections must take place before the animal acquires the same degree
of immunity as is produced through the injection of thousands of
artificially attenuated spores contained in a dose of vaccine.

If this theory of natural attenuation is correct, it would explain to
us at once why some animals are much more susceptible to blackleg
than others, and especially why cattle born and raised in a blackleg
district are more resistant to spontaneous blackleg and to artificial
inoculation than is otherwise the case. It might also explain why
cattle more than two to three years old are practically immune to
blackleg.   Arloing, Cornevin, and Thomas claim that aged cattle
which have been raised in districts where blackleg does not occur are
when placed in an infected pasture as susceptible as young animals,
and if this statement is correct it goes far to prove the theory of
naturally acquired immunity.   But, as already mentioned, there are
several other factors which may influence the degree of susceptibility
or power of resistance possessed by each individual.

In this country recoveries from blackleg do not seem to be extremely rare, if one may judge from the observations made and
reported by the stock owners.   Question 6 on the inquiry blank sent
out by this Bureau reads: "Have you ever seen an animal recover
from a recognized case of blackleg? If so, please describe it as fully
as possible." In reply thereto 120 stock owners out of 522 state that
they have seen animals recover from blackleg.   There is, however,
the same objection here as in the old country, namely, that the stockmen may be mistaken in their diagnosis; but as anthrax does not
prevail to any extent in most of the districts from which these recoveries have been reported, it is highly probable that a large percentage
of the cases referred to are really blackleg, and many of the stock
owners describe the cases which come under their observation in such
a manner as to leave very little doubt.

The number of recoveries reported may be classified as follows:

State.	Total number of reports.	Number of stock-men who reported cases.	Number of cases reported.	Number of stock-men reporting recoveries.[a]
Texas	164	37	50	8
Kansas	140	38	60	4
Colorado	53	8	22	3
Nebraska	71	14	20	2
Indian Territory	20	5	5	1
Oklahoma	37	9	15	1
North Dakota	22	4	3	1
South Dakota	15	5	10	0
Total	522	120	185	20

a Number of stockmen who reported that they have seen "a few" or "several" or "a number" of recoveries.

The above figures do not represent the number of cases observed in any given length of time, but refer to the entire experience which each stock owner has had while engaged in the cattle business, and, as already stated, it should be borne in mind that the vast majority of these cases are reported by men who are not in a position to distinguish between blackleg and other anthracoid diseases.

Nevertheless, it is fairly well established and understood by the stockmen that anthrax appears but very seldom among the range cattle, but is confined to certain districts, where it affects the horses and mules in preference to cattle, and aged cattle in preference to young stock. Furthermore, it is the low, swampy coast regions, especially along the Gulf and certain parts of California, and the swampy meadows on the bayous and backwaters of rivers which form the so-called anthrax regions in this country; and from none of these places has blackleg been reported to occur to any extent. It is therefore reasonably safe to conclude that a stockman who is located in a well-known blackleg district and who reports that he has seen one or more cases of recovery has reference to blackleg and to no other disease.

In reporting these cases of recovery, a number of the cattle men describe the various therapeutic and surgical efforts to which they attribute the recoveries. An examination of the reports shows that the treatment generally adopted when the cattle are on range consists in profuse bleeding and violent exercise in connection with deep incisions into the affected parts. In many cases an attempt is made to destroy the virus at the point of infection by pouring turpentine, various acids, concentrated lye, petroleum, vinegar, etc., into the incisions. The bleeding is done by opening the jugular vein, cutting off the tail, or "nerving" between the hoofs, which generally means to make an incision between the hoofs and severing the artery which is located there. The violent exercise consists in tying the affected animal to the saddle horn and dragging it for one or more miles. The following quotations are taken from the reports received and will illustrate some of the methods generally adopted:

I roped and dragged the animal through a pond of cold water and cut the end of its tail off, and it came out all right.

I saved three out of four by nerving or bleeding them in the foot and running them. One I cured by nerving and giving 20 drops of aconite every two hours. Tried the same on a number of others without effect.

One recovered. I started him on a run and kept it up for 3 miles. Then he seemed easier and recovered. But ninety-nine times out of a hundred they will not run, but just lie down and die.

One stock owner in Nebraska confines himself to the bleeding, but in a more comprehensive way. When an animal becomes affected, he bleeds, rowels, dehorns, and castrates it at the same time. This certainly is heroic treatment, but he claims to have saved five out of fifteen by it.

A stock owner in Colorado describes a case of recovery as follows:

The calf was about 9 months old. I had a man chase it around, so as to heat it up, and then an incision was made in the shoulder where it was swollen. A little dark blood ran out. Then a slit was made at the root of the tail and the end of the tail was cut off. These wounds bled more freely than the one in the shoulder. Then the animal was chased again, and two days later it was dehorned and vaccinated. One two-year-old heifer was treated the same way, except for dehorning and vaccinating, and died the following day.

A ranchman in Oklahoma writes:

Last year, about two days after vaccinating with double vaccine, a yearling heifer was lame with blackleg. I roped it, cut the tumor open and rubbed it with turpentine and salt until it bled freely, and then ran it for about 3 miles. The sore filled with screw worms, but the animal recovered and is a milch cow to-day.

That exercise alone can accomplish the same is seen from the following report from Nebraska:

A 2-year-old steer took lame in the morning with a large swelling of the hind leg. A man on horseback dragged the animal for half an hour, when it began scouring, and in the course of a few days it had recovered.

From these reports, which are fair samples of the average, will be seen that the majority of recoveries are placed to the credit of exercise and bleeding. The condition in which this treatment leaves the unfortunate sufferer is, however, in many cases, deplorable. When the disease has developed to a point where it is safe to conclude that an experienced stockman can not well mistake it—that is, when a crackling tumor has appeared and the animal is lame—the only way to recovery is either through resolution of the sero-sanguinolent exudation, before the affected muscles have been destroyed and the covering skin become gangrenous, or else the affected tissues must slough away and be replaced by cicatricial tissue. In all cases where the recovery is reported to have taken place in the course of a few days or a week, the first way is the only possible one in which it could occur. But here we must accept the owners' diagnosis with reservation, as no authentic cases are recorded in this country.

The following quotations, however, undoubtedly have reference to genuine cases of blackleg. A statement from Nebraska reads:

I have one steer on my ranch that had blackleg a year ago. It left his front leg crooked and his shoulder all sunk in like a "sweenied" horse.

Another ranchman of Yuma County, Colo., says:

I have a calf about 8 months old that lived more than six weeks after it became affected. All the flesh came off the shoulder and left the shoulder blade exposed. Nevertheless the animal would have recovered, but screw worms infested the sore and it became impossible to keep it free from maggots; consequently the animal was killed.

A stockman in Texas writes:

I have seen a few cases of recovery from blackleg, but the animals never amounted to anything after an attack.

And another in the same State writes:

I have seen one recovery, and the animal is still living. The affected part was slit open to let the bloody matter out. The muscles of the leg perished, but otherwise the animal made a good recovery.

Still another Texan writes:

A 2-year-old steer was affected with characteristic blackleg in the shoulder. The swelling was cut open and the affected parts sloughed out. It took four months for the wound to heal up.

A farmer in Kansas says:

I have seen a fine young yearling which had a very bad case of blackleg and recovered from it. I saved him by bleeding—almost to death—but he never amounted to anything afterwards.

Another Kansan writes:

A sucking calf was vaccinated when 1 month old, but developed blackleg a few months later. As soon as noticed, the affected part was lanced and rubbed with turpentine. The calf is still alive, but matter continues to run out of all the openings and it looks as if all the flesh is going to rot off the leg.

The following case reported from Kansas leaves no doubt as to the correctness of the diagnosis:

A 7-months-old steer had blackleg so bad that the blood under the skin crackled and the animal was very lame. Incisions made in the feet caused a slight flow of black clotted blood. The animal was then driven for two hours until exhausted, when it was physicked with linseed oil. It gradually improved; but although now more than 18 months old and completely recovered, it has never done well.

The following cases, all of Kansas, may be added:

A yearling heifer recovered from blackleg. Her right shoulder decayed and ran out and the shoulder blade could be seen. She always remained lame and worthless.

I have a heifer which was affected with blackleg while a sucking calf. Although now more than 2 years old, she is only the size of a 6-months-old calf—a knotted, knurly thing.

I have seen two cases of recovery, but they have never amounted to anything.

The above quotations are only a few out of many, and they tend to prove that after the local symptoms have appeared and the tumor begins to develop there is still a possibility of preventing a fatal issue; but it is a great question whether the cure is worth the treatment. If the animal survives the first five to seven days, it seems that the disease has exhausted itself, and if the depleted system has strength enough left it enters upon a long convalescense, constantly retarded by the extensive local tissue destruction, which must heal through granulation under a constant drain upon the system from suppuration, and which in most cases leaves the animal a cripple or a runt for life. And when it is remembered that the majority of the 120 stock owners who have recorded one or more cases of recovery as a result of certain treatment have applied the same treatment and remedies in dozens of cases without success, it seems to be in every respect wiser and more humane either to leave the affected animals alone or dispatch them as quickly as possible, for there can be no doubt that chasing an animal affected with blackleg over miles of ground, virulent blood oozing at every step from a number of incisions in the swollen parts, is to scatter the infection in a manner which could never occur under natural circumstances, and is bound to bring to grief many a succeeding generation of calves. For this reason it is strongly advocated never to use the knife on an animal suffering from blackleg unless it is kept confined in a place which can afterwards be disinfected thoroughly or from which healthy animals are constantly excluded; and it should be borne in mind that the spores of the blackleg bacillus retain their disease-producing properties for years after they have left the body of the affected animals, and that, although they do not multiply outside of the animal economy, they are merely awaiting an opportunity to regain an entrance thereto and continue their destructive work.

PREVENTIVE MEASURES.

From the preceding discussion it will be seen that treatment is of little avail, and consequently our principal resource against the disease is prevention.

The various measures employed for this purpose may be classified in two groups: (1) Those which aim at destroying or preventing the spread of infection in all places where cattle are kept, and which may be termed *hygienic* measures; and (2) those which operate to fortify the systems of susceptible animals against an effective invasion of the blackleg germ, and which may be called *prophylactic* measures.

HYGIENIC MEASURES.

When it is known that blackleg occurs with more or less regularity in a pasture, feed lot, or stable, it is due to the presence of the blackleg germ, either in the ground of these places or in materials (coarse feed, etc.) brought there regularly. Whenever an animal becomes affected, the germs multiply by the million in its system, and their liberation, through natural or artificial means, tends to preserve, increase, or spread the infection. In the large pastures of the West and Southwest an affected animal is rarely noticed until after death, when the swarms of buzzards or other birds of prey indicate that there is "something dead," and an investigation is made. It is then frequently too late to attempt to prevent the spread of infection, for wolves and other vermin usually attack the carcass in short order, without even waiting for the animal to die, and only the bones and pieces of the hide are found scattered over an acre or more of ground.

In more densely populated districts, where a sick animal is readily discovered, there is, as mentioned earlier in this article, often an inclination to "doctor" the animal, usually by means of a jackknife, and the result is the same as in the other case—the infection is scattered broadcast from incisions made in the affected part.

In some districts the cattle that die from blackleg are skinned in order at least to save the hide, and the remaining parts of the carcass are left to take care of themselves. This process naturally assists in scattering the infection. It is therefore of the utmost importance that cattle owners in the infected districts be made to realize that an animal affected with blackleg may be the cause of large subsequent losses from the same disease, maybe not immediately, but within a period of years to follow, and it can not be recommended too urgently that they make every effort to reduce the danger by taking adequate measures to destroy as completely as possible this source of renewed infection.

For this purpose the French scientists recommend various methods, some of which, however, are impracticable under the conditions which obtain in the infected districts of this country. They propose, for instance, to place the dead animals in a tank of sulphuric acid until completely dissolved. Where wood is plentiful the best method is to cremate the carcass. In order to insure its complete destruction, the dead animal should be placed on a couple of logs and plenty of dry wood heaped around it. A couple of quarts of kerosene oil should then be poured on and fire set to it. It is necessary that the carcass be entirely destroyed; if any part of it remains, another fire should be built over it.

In a pasture where wood is scarce, the carcass may be buried. This method is always more or less unsatisfactory, as the infection is not destroyed but merely removed to a few feet below the surface, whence it may return through various means of egress—for instance, as demonstrated by Pasteur, through the agency of the earthworms. It is therefore of importance that the hole in the ground be made at least 6 feet deep and the carcass well covered with lime before the earth is filled in. The lime has no special germicidal effect on the blackleg bacillus but may prevent the infection from being carried to the surface. The place where the animal was lying before being buried, as well as the top of the grave, should be freely sprinkled with a 2 per cent solution of creolin, or any of the carbolic sheep dips or disinfectants which are guaranteed to contain thymol or eucalyptol. The two latter substances are especially recommended by the French scientists because of their destructive action on the blackleg germs. Owing to the difficulty of destroying the infection, it may be well to repeat here that all attempts at treating an animal affected with blackleg through scarifications or incisions into the affected part should be abandoned as dangerous and unprofitable. It is far better to destroy the animal as soon as all doubt as to the diagnosis has been dispelled, and to burn the carcass immediately, without removing it from the place where found. As stated before, the fresh virus is much more easily destroyed than the dried, and by quick action a better result is always insured. If an animal dies from blackleg in a stable it becomes necessary to remove the carcass to a proper place for cremation or burial. Care should be taken to scatter straw or hay wherever there is a possibility of infecting the stable floor or the ground with the discharges or exudations from the carcass while it is being removed. All litter should be removed from the stable and burned, together with that used in removing the carcass. The woodwork and floors of the stable should be thoroughly and repeatedly soaked with one of the above-mentioned disinfectants or with corrosive sublimate (1–2000).

The question of how completely to eradicate the disease from a pasture has been much discussed, but no sure means have been found. The usual method of preventing the infection from renewing itself by keeping cattle away from the pasture until it had died out can not be employed in this case, as outbreaks have been recorded in this country in pastures where no case of blackleg had occurred for eleven years, and few people can afford to keep a pasture unstocked for that length of time or even longer. It has been claimed that complete drainage and cultivation of the soil for several years will prevent further outbreaks, but where the question is about large pastures which are unfit for anything but cattle raising this measure is, of course, out of consideration.

Several ranch owners, especially in Texas, have reported that blackleg never caused losses of any consequence until after it became impossible to burn the pastures off regularly every winter, and this statement, which in some cases is based upon actual observations, is no doubt correct. Whether this condition is due to overstocking or to an actual decrease in the annual rainfall needs not be discussed here, but the fact remains that in many of the Southwestern cattle-raising districts the winter grass, as a rule, is barely sufficient to keep the stock alive until spring, and not a straw remains to be burned off at the end of the winter. As stated before, no agent has a more destructive effect on the blackleg germs than heat, and no doubt it might be profitable for owners of badly infected pastures to allow grass in them to grow rank and burn it off during the winter. It is held by the French scientists that when the infection on the surface becomes attenuated through exposure to varying climatic conditions it may have its virulence reenforced through lactic acid formed during the natural fermentation in the soil. Such an acidity of the soil would, however, immediately be neutralized by burning off the pastures, thereby depositing on the surface a layer of alkalies in the form of ashes, and the attenuation of the germs which escaped destruction through the heat might continue without interruption.

When blackleg appears in a herd, a common remedy is immediately to move the animals to another pasture. From a number of reports received, this seems in certain regions to be considered the only sure means of stopping the disease, but in most cases the effect is but temporary. If the new pasture to which the animals are taken is free from infection, it is natural that no more cases should occur, if none of the animals were infected previous to leaving the old pasture. Such cases would develop in the course of a few days, and if no precautions are taken, infect the new pasture to a greater or less extent. But, as a rule, conditions are very much alike in all pastures on the same ranch or farm, and after a while, when the animals have become familiar with their new surroundings and begun to thrive again, the disease reappears. The results seem, however, to be better when the pasture to which the afflicted herd is taken is of decidedly poorer quality than the one where the disease first broke out. This, in connection with the fact that the change, which generally gives the cattle more or less exercise in rounding up and driving, produces a temporary lull in the outbreak, seems to indicate that the animals under certain conditions are less susceptible to the disease, and that the temporary increase in power of resistance must be due to certain chemical or metabolic processes in the animal economy which are dependent upon the relative proportion between the amount of exercise and the amount of nutrition of which the animal partakes. All cattle owners in the infected districts agree that a reduction in flesh, no matter in what condition the animals may be, tends to allay or stop an outbreak of blackleg. But, as it is contrary to the interests of stock raisers to interfere in any way with the growth and development of the young cattle, it is obvious that preventive measures along this line should be avoided or resorted to only as a temporary relief, while less injurious and more certain remedies are provided in the meantime.

PROPHYLACTIC MEASURES.

The same may be said of setoning, or roweling. Granting that a speedy reduction in flesh affords a certain amount of protection, there may be some excuse for roweling an affected herd, but the method (which consists in producing a large running sore in the dewlap or on the shoulder, and which, through profuse suppuration, drains the vitality of the animal) should only be resorted to as a temporary measure. When practiced regularly it simply prevents growth and stunts young animals, besides affording an opportunity for the introduction of other disease germs. In England, where public opinion is against vaccination, this method has been employed extensively and much has been written for and against it. The two principal authors on this question, Stewart Stockman and J. McFadyean, are both of the opinion that roweling is of no value as a preventive measure, the former even holding that it has the opposite effect. In support of this statement he quotes the following case:

At the request of a client, whose losses from black quarter are annually very high, a friend of mine setoned fifteen yearlings. For some reason a sixteenth animal was not setoned. The sixteen animals were all pastured on the same meadows. All the setoned animals died of black quarter, and were survived by the one that had not been setoned.

Such evidence speaks for itself. The fatal result in this case is no doubt due to a too prolonged action of the seton. The same author has proven experimentally that animals which have been setoned for one month succumb more readily to an inoculation of blackleg virus than animals which have not been setoned at all, and a number of stockmen in this country who have been in the habit of roweling their cattle declare that the protective effect of the seton soon wears off, although it seems effective for a while. In the writer's opinion, the seton, if used at all, should not be left in the sore for more than a week or ten days, or sufficiently long to allow the owner to obtain blackleg vaccine and use it on his cattle.

Preventive vaccination.—To Arloing, Cornevin, and Thomas belong the honor of first discovering that animals may be protected against blackleg by inoculation with more or less virulent material obtained from animals which have died from blackleg. They found that the hypodermic injection of minimal doses of fluid from a blackleg tumor did not necessarily result in death, but frequently produced a mild attack of the disease, unaccompanied by any swelling, and that animals treated in that way were afterwards possessed of a very high degree of resistance against the disease. There are, however, few diseases where the individual susceptibility varies to a greater extent than is the case in blackleg, and, as it was impossible to ascertain beforehand the degree of susceptibility or power of resistance possessed by each animal, the exact dose to employ in each case could not be determined and the method was abandoned as being too dangerous. Even when the inoculation was made at the extremity of the tail it frequently resulted in the development of a swelling which spread to the rump and killed the animal, or else the tail became gangrenous and dropped off.

When the virus, either fresh from a tumor or dried, is introduced into the blood stream or into the trachea, the animal shows great resistance to its effect and subsequently becomes immunized. It is, however, rather difficult to inject the virus either into the jugular vein or into the trachea without infecting the surrounding connective tissue, and the technique of the operation is too complicated to be of practical value when large numbers of cattle are to be vaccinated. Nevertheless, the French scientists practiced it on five hundred animals with one death only resulting from the operation.

Attenuated virus.—Prolonged exposure to a high temperature serves to attenuate the virulence of either fresh or dried virus. The fact was employed by the above-mentioned authors for the preparation of a vaccine which may be used in everyday practice with little danger of injuring the cattle. The material used for the vaccine is obtained from a fresh blackleg tumor, by pounding the muscle tissue in a mortar with the addition of a little water and squeezing the pulp through a piece of linen cloth. The juice is spread in layers on plates and dried quickly at a temperature of about 35° C. This temperature does not in the least affect the germs, and the dry virus obtained in this way retains a high degree of virulence for a couple of years or more.

When vaccine is to be prepared, the dried material is pulverized and mixed in a mortar with two parts water until it forms a semifluid homogeneous mass. This is spread in a thin layer on a saucer or glass dish, and placed in an oven, the temperature of which may be regulated with exactness. The reason for mixing the virus with water is to insure a quicker and more uniform attenuation. The temperature of the oven is previously brought up to 100° to 104° C., and the virus is allowed to remain in it for seven hours. When removed, it appears as a brownish scale, which is easily detached from the dish. This scale is pulverized and mixed with water, and when inoculated under the skin of calves in doses of 1 centigram per head it produces partial immunity. Subsequent inoculation with virus which has been heated for the same length of time, but at a temperature of 90° to 94° C., serves to reenforce the immunity. The inoculation is followed by insignificant symptoms. In a few cases there is a slight rise of temperature, and by close observation a minute swelling may sometimes be noted at the point of inoculation. Eight to ten days are allowed to pass between the first and the second inoculation. For reasons already explained, the vaccine is injected at a place where the subcutaneous connective tissue is dense and unelastic, generally at the extremity of the tail or the external surface of the ear, as far from the base of either organ as possible. The immunity conferred in this way lasts for at least eighteen months, but animals which are vaccinated before they are one year old should be revaccinated the following year.

This method of vaccination for blackleg, popularly known as "the French method," "Arloing's method," or the "Lyons method,"[1] was first introduced in 1883 and was generally adopted the following two years. Several thousand cattle were vaccinated in France, Switzerland, and Germany, and the results were highly satisfactory. The operation, however, is very cumbersome on account of the great density of the subcutaneous tissue of the tail, which makes it difficult

[1] The laboratories of Arloing, Cornevin, and Thomas are located at Lyons, France.

to insert the needle; in fact, it is necessary first to punch a hole with a strong trocar and loosen the skin sufficiently to form a sack or pocket large enough to receive the vaccine.   Afterwards a ligature is tied around the tail to prevent the vaccine from escaping through the hole, and this ligature must be removed a short time after, so as not to interfere with the circulation.   When the inoculation is made too close to one of the joints the needle is liable to wound the cartilaginous disks and cause the formation of an abscess, which may result in necrosis and the dropping off of the tail.   In any case, the operation has to be performed by an expert, besides requiring considerable time.   Consequently, when large numbers of cattle were to be vaccinated the method was both expensive and inconvenient, and when a modification was suggested it was eagerly accepted.   In 1888 Professor Kitt, of the veterinary college in Munich, Bavaria, took up the question, and, after experimenting with Arloing's vaccine on a number of animals, came to the conclusion that the second vaccine may be injected alone without any danger to the animal, and that such a single vaccination confers immunity against subsequent attacks of the disease.   He went even further and prepared a vaccine which was heated for six hours only at a temperature from 85° to 90° C., which, as compared to Arloing's second vaccine (90° to 94° C. for seven hours), was considerably stronger, but which he proved by experiments to be free from danger, even when injected in doses tenfold larger than those ordinarily used.   A single injection with this vaccine was found to produce complete immunity when treated by subsequent inoculations with fatal doses of blackleg virus.   He further modified Arloing's method by making the injections in the shoulder region, where the skin is loose and easily pierced by the needle.   For the preparation of the vaccine Kitt employed the affected muscles from a fresh blackleg tumor, which he cut in thin strips and dried at a temperature of 35° C. and then pulverized in a coffee mill.   This process in the manufacture of the vaccine was also an improvement on Arloing's method, which, as will be remembered, consists in pressing the juice from a blackleg tumor and drying it on plates.

In his publication on this matter Kitt recommends that experiments be made on large numbers of cattle with injections of Arloing's second vaccine—in the shoulder region—and that the results be published for the benefit of others who might wish to employ this much quicker and more convenient method.   He adds that before vaccinating a large number of animals the vaccine should be tested on guinea pigs or on a few head of young cattle to ascertain the quality of the material.

Acting on these suggestions, a number of veterinarians undertook vaccinations with second vaccine alone, and in most cases the results were equally satisfactory to those obtained through double vaccination. In Algeria, M. Bremond vaccinated 4,000 head of the half-wild range cattle with second vaccine alone, making the injections behind the shoulder. The subsequent loss from blackleg was even smaller than that reported in Europe as resulting after double vaccination, but it must be remembered that the range cattle of Algeria are very resistant to blackleg.

Subsequently a stronger vaccine, as recommended by Kitt, was prepared at various veterinary institutes—for instance, at Edinburgh, Scotland—but it proved to be too strong. The vaccine was heated for six hours at 90° C. and was proved experimentally to be harmless; but in one instance, when used on 15 head of cattle, it caused 5 to die in the course of three days, and 2 more died three to four weeks after vaccination, from typical blackleg. This highly unfavorable result can not well be explained. It is generally conceded that when the vaccine is strong enough to cause one or more cases of blackleg as a result of the inoculation, the surviving animals must be strongly fortified against subsequent infection. In this case, however, 2 of the vaccinated calves died of typical blackleg at a time when, for obvious reasons, the disease could not be attributed to the operation.

This experience caused considerable prejudice against protective vaccination for blackleg, which later experiments failed to dispel, and up to the present time the method has never become popular in Scotland and England. In the meantime double vaccination in the shoulder region had been very generally accepted as preferable to inoculations in the tail. M. Strebel stated in 1892 that 40 to 45 animals may be vaccinated in an hour by the former method, and also that of a total of 13,022 animals treated by this method only 5 head, or 0.038 per cent, died directly from the inoculation, while the immediate loss among cattle vaccinated on the tail amounts to twice as much. Out of a total of 158,579 vaccinated animals (both methods), 493 head, or 0.31 per cent, died from spontaneous blackleg; that is, the vaccination had in these cases failed to produce immunity. On the other hand, the loss among 106,787 unvaccinated animals amounted to 2,049 head, or 1.92 per cent—more than six times as great as among the vaccinated ones. These results were highly satisfactory, and proved that preventive inoculation with attenuated virus was a safe and effective remedy against the disease. It was furthermore observed that blackleg occurred with less frequency among the unvaccinated cattle in pastures where vaccination was practiced to some extent for a number of years. This is the natural result from a decrease in the infectious material which is ordinarily deposited in pastures where no vaccination is practiced. The fewer cases of blackleg, the less opportunity for reinfecting the ground.

About 1890 or 1891 Professor Kitt published the results of a series of experiments which he had undertaken for the purpose of producing a vaccine which would confer absolute immunity in a single inoculation and still be considered safe. Although the grand total of vaccinations up to that time was extremely satisfactory, there were several instances recorded where a high percentage of individual herds had died as a direct result of the vaccination. The statistics also indicated that a certain number of the vaccinated animals failed to become immunized, and died later from spontaneous blackleg (0.37 per cent). The new vaccine prepared by Kitt had been exposed to streaming steam of a temperature 98° to 102° C. for about six hours, at the end of which time the virulent pulverized meat was sufficiently attenuated to be inoculated in comparatively large doses into guinea pigs, sheep, and calves without fatal result, while producing a high degree of immunity. The preparation of this vaccine is very simple, but the product varies considerably in strength, and before being used in practice it is necessary thoroughly to test it on a number of sheep. Guinea pigs are very unreliable for this purpose and cattle are not easily obtained for such experiments in sufficiently large numbers.

This vaccine, known as Kitt's dry vaccine (to distinguish it from a fluid vaccine which he prepared later), was extensively used in many countries in Europe, and according to statistics published in 1893 the results obtained with it were better than those obtained by double vaccination on the tail and nearly as good as from double vaccination on the shoulder with Arloing's vaccine. The question remaining was, therefore, whether a single or a double vaccination was to be preferred. Although he was the originator of the single-vaccination method, Professor Kitt did not claim it to be superior to Arloing's method, as repeated inoculations necessarily must reenforce the power of resistance; but he thinks that the same degree of immunity can be obtained with a single inoculation with his dry vaccine as with a double vaccination with the French vaccine. More recently Professor Kitt has prepared a vaccine from pure cultures of the blackleg bacillus; but, as will be seen from the table below, its protective value was comparatively low, and consequently it was never used very extensively.

At the International Veterinary Congress in Berne, Switzerland, in 1895, Professor Strebel published the total results from vaccination for blackleg, compiling all the statistics which he had been able to obtain. They cover the period from 1884 to 1895, and embrace the various methods of inoculation already mentioned.

Methods of vaccination, total number vaccinated, and accidents after vaccination in Europe.

Method of vaccination.	Number of animals vaccinated.	Accidents.					
		Deaths from vaccination.	Deaths per thousand.	Deaths from natural blackleg after vaccination.	Deaths (per cent).	Combined losses.	Per cent.
Double vaccination on the tail	325,898	188	0.56	1,245	0.38	1,438	0.44
Total vaccinations in shoulder region	91,086	77	0.84	365	0.40	441	0.48
Double vaccination in shoulder region	37,410	8	0.22	157	0.42	165	0.44
Single vaccination with Kitt's dry vaccine	30,084	61	1.56	187	0.48	248	0.68
Single vaccination with Kitt's pure-culture vaccine	5,643	8	1.41	81	1.43	89	1.58
Total	490,096	341	0.68	2,035	0.40	2,376	0.47

The total shows that nearly half a million head of cattle were vaccinated, and that the loss resulting from the operation, together with the number of deaths from blackleg contracted naturally subsequent to inoculation, amounts to less than one-half of 1 per cent. In order fully to appreciate the protective value of the vaccine it is necessary to compare the mortality among vaccinated animals with that of unvaccinated ones under the same circumstances. To this end Strebel furnishes the following figures: Of the cattle treated with double vaccination on the tail, 129,705 were pastured together with 245,560 head of unvaccinated stock. Of the former 550 head, or 0.42 per cent, died from spontaneous blackleg, while 4,136 head, or 1.76 per cent, of the latter died from blackleg. The mortality among the unvaccinated animals was, consequently, four and one-half times greater than among those vaccinated.

Of the cattle vaccinated in the shoulder region 62,158 were pastured with 82,334 head of unvaccinated cattle. The respective losses from blackleg amounted to 282 head, or 0.45 per cent, in the former, and 1,350 head, or 1.64 per cent, in the latter. Mortality among unvaccinated was three and three-fifths times greater than among those vaccinated. Of the animals which received a double inoculation in the shoulder region 25,849 were pastured with 13,452 unvaccinated animals. Of the former 119 head, or 0.46 per cent, and of the latter 321 head, or 2.38 per cent, died from blackleg; difference in mortality five times greater among unvaccinated stock. Of the animals treated with Kitt's single vaccine 30,123 were pastured with 57,867 unvaccinated cattle. Eighty-five head, or 0.28 per cent, of the former died from blackleg, while the loss among the latter was 921 head, or 1.59 per cent, or nearly six times greater. The results from Kitt's pure-culture vaccine show a loss of 1.58 per cent among the vacci-nated animals, while the loss among 13,183 unvaccinated cattle in the same pasture amounted to only 1.45 per cent.

It appears from these statistics that vaccination in the shoulder region is not quite so safe as vaccination on the tail, especially when the inoculation accidents are included; while, on the other hand, the single vaccination on the shoulder with Kitt's dry vaccine confers the highest degree of immunity. His pure-culture vaccine, however, was very unsatisfactory.

In 1896 M. Strebel stated that the percentage of inoculation acci-dents had increased during the previous year from 0.028 per cent to 0.724 per cent, or twenty-two times higher than the record for eleven years. This he attributed to a less attenuated vaccine which, at his own request, had been prepared by Arloing and Cornevin. The unfortunate results caused the Swiss Government to order an investi-gation for the purpose of determining the best preparation for black-leg vaccine. A double vaccine was prepared at the veterinary college in Berne, while the laboratories at Lyons furnished an equal amount of their double vaccine for comparison. Of the 4,202 vaccinations not less than 123 animals died from inoculations for blackleg, by far the greatest percentage falling on the Berne vaccine, and espe-cially on animals which had been vaccinated in the shoulder region. As a result of these experiments the Swiss authorities, again aban-doned the latter method and returned to the slow and cumbersome inoculations on the tail.

The Bureau vaccine.—As already stated, experiments were begun in the Pathological Laboratory of the Bureau of Animal Industry in the fall of 1896 for the purpose of preparing a blackleg vaccine which by a single inoculation would produce practical immunity and still be sufficiently attenuated to cause only a minimum amount of loss at the time of inoculation. All the various methods already mentioned were tried, and it was finally decided to adopt Arloing's principle with Kitt's modifications. The finely ground and sifted blackleg meat was heated in moist condition for six hours at a temperature of 93° or 94° C. and the dried crust pulverized and divided in packets containing ten to twenty-five doses each. It was found that heating to 90° C. for six hours, as recommended by Kitt, did not attenuate sufficiently to make the vaccine safe in all instances. The same was the case with virus heated at 91° and 92° C.

To insure absolute uniformity of temperature, a special oven pro-vided with a 3-inch oil jacket was constructed, and the vaccine pro-duced gave, so far as could be ascertained by numerous inoculations, such uniformly good results that it was decided to place a limited number of doses in the hands of reliable stockmen in order to have them test it in practice on their cattle. For this purpose the following announcement was sent to about 100 stock owners in various localities where the disease was known to prevail:

PREVENTIVE VACCINATION AGAINST BLACKLEG.

For several years frequent reports have come to this Bureau concerning the great mortality from blackleg among young stock in many widely separated districts of the United States. In some of the Southern and Western States especially the annual losses from this fatal disease have been so great as to equal or exceed the losses of cattle from all other causes combined. These losses have been particularly felt by the progressive stock owners, as by far the largest percentage of the calves which became affected were either full-blood or high-graded animals, which seem to be more susceptible to this disease than the ordinary common-bred stock. As the continued existence of this disease has a very detrimental effect upon the cattle industry in general, and especially upon those stock owners who, through untiring efforts and great expense, have endeavored to improve their herds, an investigation has been made by this Bureau with a view to devising some measure through which the steadily increasing losses might be arrested, or reduced as much as possible.

In Europe, where this disease has long prevailed, the annual losses in certain badly infected districts became so disastrous that cattle raising had to be abandoned. About fifteen years ago three French scientists—Arloing, Cornevin, and Thomas—succeeded in producing a vaccine against blackleg, which is now extensively used in many countries where the disease prevails to a serious extent. The method consists in injecting into each calf two doses of highly attenuated blackleg virus, with an interval of ten days between the two inoculations. The first inoculation is made with a very mild vaccine, the so-called "first lymph," and the subsequent one with a stronger virus, the "second lymph," and in each case the vaccine is introduced by means of a hypodermic syringe under the skin of the lower part of the tail. This method, which is very inconvenient, especially where a large number of animals are to be treated, was later modified by a German scientist, Kitt, who reduced the process to a single injection with less attenuated virus, and who chose the loose skin on the side of the chest, just behind the shoulder, for the point of inoculation. Kitt's method has been adopted to a very large extent in eastern Europe and northern Africa with very satisfactory results, and it has, for that reason and on account of its simplicity, been taken as the foundation for the investigations made by this Bureau.

A "single vaccine" has been prepared in the pathological laboratory, and subsequently tested on a large number of calves in Texas, both common and high-grade stock, and the results warrant the conclusion that this vaccine is in every way satisfactory. It is desired, however, before distributing the vaccine to stock owners in general, to obtain a record of several thousand successful vaccinations. For this purpose a quantity of vaccine will be distributed to such parties as may desire to make preliminary vaccinations and report the results to this Bureau. Those stock owners will be preferred who already have experience in vaccinating stock for blackleg and are in possession of a vaccinating outfit. Explicit instructions will, however, be sent with the vaccine, to secure uniformity of operation and to assist those without previous experience in the vaccinations. Persons lacking the necessary outfit should procure one if they propose to test the vaccine. It consists of a graduated 5 c. c. syringe with detachable needles, a small porcelain mortar and pestle, a glass funnel, and some filters. This outfit can not be supplied by the Department, but must be purchased of some house which supplies such articles.

10317——5

Upon applying for vaccine please answer the following questions:

1. To what extent does blackleg prevail in your part of the country, and how great is your annual loss from this disease?

2. What experience have you had in vaccinating calves against blackleg?

3. How many head do you wish to vaccinate, and what class of cattle are they. common, graded, or full blood?

4. What is your express office?

Name, ———.

P. O. address, ———.

D. E. SALMON,
Chief of Bureau of Animal Industry.

Approved:

    JAMES WILSON,
        Secretary of Agriculture.

WASHINGTON, D. C., *June 22. 1897.*

With very few exceptions, all of the stockmen addressed responded and signified their willingness to cooperate with the Bureau.

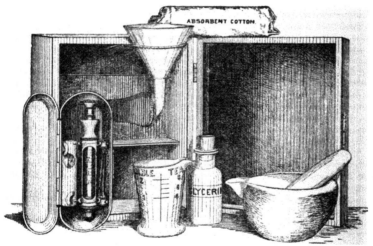

FIG. 1 —Vaccinating outfit.

Through them the information that blackleg vaccine was being distributed for experimental purposes spread quickly, and applications for vaccine became so numerous as to convince the officials in charge that they had entered upon a field of work of great importance. Every applicant testified to severe and repeated losses from blackleg and to a total inability to cope with the disease in spite of efforts made. Preparations were immediately made to meet this unexpected and steadily increasing demand for vaccine, and, though the supply at times has run short, the Bureau has succeeded in filling the thousands of applications within a reasonable time after receiving them.

In order to insure uniformity in preparing the vaccine powder for injection and to make the instructions as simple and explicit as possible, it became necessary to adopt a standard set of instruments (see fig. 1), which was recommended to those who wished to experiment with the vaccine and who had had no previous experience in this kind of work. The price of such an outfit, including a hypodermic syringe, and put up in a neat case, is $4.[1]

DIRECTIONS FOR USE OF BLACKLEG VACCINE.

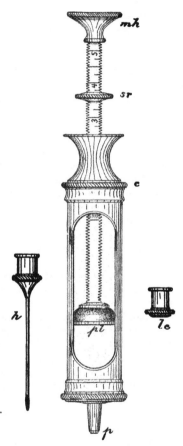

FIG. 2.—Hypodermic syringe.

The blackleg vaccine, as prepared by this Bureau, consists of a brownish powder, which is put up in packets containing either ten or twenty-five doses each. To prepare this powder in such a way that it may be injected hypodermically, it is necessary to obtain certain implements, which, together with the hypodermic syringe, are known as a vaccinating outfit. This consists of a porcelain mortar with pestle, a small glass funnel, and a measuring glass. For filtering the vaccine we have found absorbent cotton to be most suitable. All of the utensils, including the hypodermic syringe and a package of absorbent cotton, are fitted in a strong, polished oak box, which by means of an adjustable wire loop serves also as a support for the funnel when the vaccine is filtering. The syringe, two hypodermic needles, and an extra glass barrel are packed in a separate small metal box. The syringe, needles, and glass barrel are attached by means of clamps to a loose metal plate which fits snugly into the bottom of the box. This serves to keep the different parts together when the outfit is being sterilized.

The syringe (fig. 2) has a capacity of 5 cubic centimeters, and the piston is graduated from 1 to 5, each division being subdivided with half and quarter notches. The screw regulator (fig. 2, *sr*) may be

---

[1] Until such an outfit is for sale by other dealers the name and address of the manufacturer will be furnished upon application.

placed at any mark on the piston, and thus insure that the animal to be vaccinated receives only the exact dose intended for it. The plunger (fig. 2, *pl*) is made of rubber; it should fit air-tight in the glass barrel and still be susceptible of being moved up and down smoothly. By means of the milled head (fig. 2, *mh*) at the free end of the piston the rubber of the plunger may be expanded or contracted simply by screwing the head to the right or left. By this arrangement a close fit may always be obtained without taking the springs apart. If the plunger should become dry, or for other reasons not move smoothly up and down in the barrel, it is necessary to unscrew the milled cap *c* and pour a drop of glycerine into the barrel. For this purpose a small bottle of glycerine is furnished with each outfit; oil or grease should never be used, as these substances destroy the rubber. Extra washers to be placed inside of the cap at each end of the glass barrel are also to be found in the syringe box. It is of the greatest importance that the syringe be perfectly tight, in order that not a drop of vaccine may escape, except through the point of the needle. If a leak occurs, unscrew the cap of the syringe, withdraw the glass barrel, and replace the old washers with new ones. In order to prevent the plunger and washers from drying out, the small loose cap *lc* should always be tightly adjusted to the peg *p* when the syringe is not in use. The hypodermic needles should be kept very sharp at the point, in order to pass easily through the skin, and when not in use should have a fine brass wire passed through each to prevent rusting on the inside.

Whenever the point of the needle gets blunt it becomes very difficult to pass it through the skin, and the fingers of the operator become sore from attempting to force it through, and frequently the needle either bends or breaks. It is, therefore, of importance to have a small oilstone at hand on which to sharpen the point of the needle. Before using the syringe it should be tested thoroughly with pure water to ascertain that it is in perfect working order. To this end, fill the syringe slowly by withdrawing the piston. If the syringe is perfectly tight, it should fill completely; if it contains air bubbles, turn it with the point upward and press the piston until the water comes out of the point, then refill. The same precaution must be taken when filling the syringe with vaccine.

Sterilization of utensils.—Before preparing the vaccine all the utensils, together with the syringe, must be sterilized thoroughly. This is done by putting the mortar, pestle, measuring glass, and the metal plate, with the syringe and needles attached, in a pan of cold water, placing all over the fire. After boiling for ten minutes, the pan with the contents should be allowed to cool off slowly; then remove the utensils from the water and wipe them dry with a clean linen cloth which has been previously boiled. When the vaccine has been prepared the utensils should again be cleansed thoroughly and replaced in the box. After injection, the syringe and needles must be washed with a 5 per cent solution of carbolic acid, carefully wiped, and the brass wire adjusted in the needles.

Preparation of the vaccine.—Place the contents of one packet of the vaccine in a porcelain mortar and add a few drops of boiled water. (The water must have been previously boiled and allowed to cool.) Work the powder thoroughly with the pestle and then add, little by little, as many cubic centimeters of water as the packet contains doses. As the syringe contains exactly 5 cubic centimeters, it may be used for measuring the water. A packet containing 10 doses of the vaccine should be dissolved in two syringes full of water, and one containing 25 doses in five syringes full. Care should be taken that the syringe is full every time. To filter the vaccine, place the wooden box on end, as shown in the illustration, and adjust the wire loop in the two eyelets. Place in the funnel a small piece of absorbent cotton and press it lightly into the upper end of the neck, sufficient to keep it in place; moisten the cotton with a few drops of boiled water and let it drip off. Stir the mixture in the mortar thoroughly and, before it has had time to settle, pour it into the funnel under which the measuring glass has been placed. The solution should not be perfectly clear. If this is the case, the cotton has been pressed too closely into the neck of the funnel. The straining is done simply to prevent the coarser parts of the powder, which are suspended in the solution, from clogging up the needle when the vaccine is injected; and as the effectiveness of the vaccine depends upon the number of attenuated spores in the solution, it is obvious that a perfectly clear solution can not be as effective as one which is cloudy. It is therefore of the greatest importance that much time and care be spent in grinding the vaccine powder as fine as possible before the bulk of the water is added, as otherwise the greater part of the germ-carrying particles are left on the cotton instead of passing through it. If too much water is added at first it is almost impossible to grind the powder, and it becomes necessary to place the mortar with its contents in a warm and airy place in order to allow some of the water to evaporate. Only sufficient water should be added to the powder to make it form a paste, in which form it is easy to grind it extremely fine.

When a large number of animals are to be vaccinated at the same time, three or four packets of the vaccine may be dissolved at once, care being taken that the requisite amount of water is used, as otherwise the solution will be too strong or too weak. When the vaccine is prepared at home, a small sterilized medicine bottle may be substituted for the measuring glass under the funnel. The stopper of this bottle, if cork, must have been thoroughly soaked in boiled water. The vaccine is carried in the bottle to the place of operation, where it may be transferred, a little at a time, to the measuring glass; from this it may be conveniently drawn into the syringe. In doing this it is of importance to remember that, when standing for some time, a slight sediment will form at the bottom of the vessel or bottle, and the vaccine should therefore always be well shaken or stirred before the syringe is filled. When some time elapses between the vaccination of two animals, and the syringe still contains one or more doses of vaccine, the operator should turn the syringe up and down frequently to insure an even distribution of the germ-carrying particles throughout the vaccine.

No more vaccine should be prepared at one time than can be used the same day. While the vaccine powder will remain unchanged for more than a year, the solution deteriorates very quickly, and must be used within twenty-four hours after it is made.

ANIMALS TO BE VACCINATED.

Calves, as a rule, should not be vaccinated until they are 6 months old. Under this age they are practically immune against blackleg, and it has been claimed that when vaccinated before they are 6 months old they are liable to lose the artificial immunity induced by means of vaccination and become susceptible again. Animals more than 2 years old, as stated above, are seldom affected, and the mortality among them is so small that it makes vaccination unprofitable. It is the animals between 6 months and 2 years old which should be vaccinated.

Vaccination has no ill effect on calves under 6 months old, but it should be a rule that when very young animals are vaccinated they should be revaccinated the following year.

The time to vaccinate depends greatly upon circumstances. In nearly every part of the country where blackleg is known there is a distinct blackleg season, and the proper time to vaccinate is just before the arrival of this season. Every practical ranchman and farmer, as a rule, knows when to look for blackleg, and as the disease may appear a little sooner or later, according to climatic conditions, it is always better to vaccinate two or three weeks before the beginning of the blackleg season. In some parts of the country it is not unusual that the calves commence dying when only 4 months old, while in others they seldom become affected until they are 8 months old. It is, therefore, much a matter of judgment when to vaccinate and what should constitute the minimum age at which the calves should be treated.

Vaccination and castration should not be performed at the same time. Castration is always a severe operation, and in some cases decreases the vitality of the animals to such an extent as to make them unable to resist the effect of the vaccination. The same principle applies to all surgical operations (castration, spaying, dehorning, etc.) as well as to those cases where the constitution of the animal has been impaired from injuries external or internal.

Ten days to two weeks should be allowed to pass after vaccination before any surgical operation is undertaken, and, if performed before vaccination, ample time should be allowed for the part to heal and for the animal to regain its lost strength.

THE DOSE TO BE INJECTED.

Animals 1 year old or over are injected with a full dose of vaccine; that is, 1 cubic centimeter of the solution. Under this age the dose may be reduced to one-half or three-fourths of a full dose, according to the size and development of the animal. Less than a half dose should never be injected. In determining the dose for each animal more consideration should be given to the size and development of the animal than to its exact age.

HOW TO OPERATE.

When the animals to be vaccinated are gentle and accustomed to being handled, vaccination may be performed on the standing animal. Range cattle or other half-wild animals must be thrown or secured, as in a dehorning chute.

The most convenient place to inoculate is on the side of the neck, just in front of the shoulder, where the skin is loose and rather thin. If the animals are secured in a dehorning chute, it is easier to vaccinate them on the side of the chest just behind the shoulder.

All animals should be vaccinated on the same side and marked in such a way that they may be easily recognized. The best way to mark them is to use a small branding iron in the shape of a V, or to fasten a metal tag in the ear.

As calves which have been vaccinated for blackleg frequently command a higher price than the unvaccinated calves, it is of importance that they be plainly marked.

When the animal is secured, fill the syringe with vaccine and ascertain that it contains no air bubbles; then insert the needle by grasping a fold of the loose skin between the thumb and forefinger of the left hand and pushing the needle through the skin. The operator now adjusts the peg of the syringe tightly in the cap of the needle and injects the dose, which has been previously limited by the screw regulator on the piston. The needle is then withdrawn without detaching the syringe, and, to prevent any of the vaccine from escaping through the hole of injection, the skin is pressed tightly around the receding needle. The latter is then detached, the regulator screwed back to its proper place, according to the size and age of the animal to be next vaccinated.

When a large number of cattle are to be vaccinated, it is of importance to have a sufficient number of assistants, as otherwise the process becomes exceedingly tiresome and fatiguing both to the operator and to the assistants. The herd to be treated is confined in a pen, from which a small number, from five to ten, according to the number of assistants at hand, are driven into a smaller pen, where the assistants throw them and hold them down. Very wild range cattle must be lassoed, but graded or fine stock, being less unmanageable, should be seized by the head and thrown. The first method requires a larger pen, but when the assistants are skillful in handling the lasso it is by far the quickest way. The animals should all be thrown on the same side. One assistant sits across the side of the thrown animal, with his face toward its head and holding the upper foreleg pulled back and up. When secured in this way it is almost impossible for a well-grown yearling to free itself.

With older and stronger animals it is safer to have two men to hold each, as an animal which succeeds in getting up before all have been

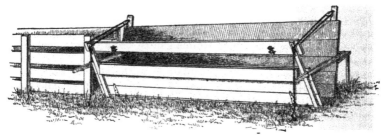

Fig. 3.—A vaccinating chute.

injected and marked will frequently make things very unpleasant for the operator and assistants, chasing them from the pen and necessitating a repetition of the whole process.

The operator should have an assistant insert the needle, while he himself adjusts the regulator. After inserting the needle, the assistant lifts the skin fold, presenting the cap of the needle so that the operator may easily grasp it and attach the syringe. In this way from 90 to 100 head of yearling calves may be vaccinated in one hour, with ten men to handle the animals and one assistant to insert the needle; but such a rate can only be maintained for a limited time without changing the men. With one set of men not more than 400 or 500 head should be vaccinated in one day, according to the age and size of the animals.

On many large ranches, where vaccination for blackleg is practiced as regularly as branding, special vaccinating chutes have been constructed which in principle resemble the ordinary squeezer, or branding chute.   One side of the chute is hinged to the base and may by means of a block and tackle be pulled over against the opposite side, thus squeezing the calves and preventing them from struggling while the needle is inserted and the vaccine injected.   One of the planks in the movable side, at a proper distance from the ground, is loose and hinged to the plank below it so that it may be opened and give the operator access to the side of the animals.   The chute may be built as long or as short as desired or may be made portable and carried to any pasture on the ranch and connected with the stationary chutes and pens.   Such a chute enables three or four men to vaccinate the same number of calves as ten to twelve men can vaccinate in the same length of time when every animal has to be lassoed or thrown.

SYNOPSIS OF VACCINATION PROCESS.

(1) Sterilize outfit by boiling.

(2) Place one powder in the mortar and add a few drops of water.

(3) Work the mixture well with the pestle.

(4) Add two to five syringefuls of water, according to the size of the packet, and stir well.

(5) Place cotton in glass funnel and moisten with water.

(6) Filter vaccine into the glass or bottle.

(7) Secure the animal to be injected.

(8) Insert the needle through the skin.

(9) Fill the syringe and adjust the screw regulator on the piston. If the first animal is a yearling or older, place regulator at No. 1.

(10) Fit the peg of the syringe into the cap of the needle and inject the dose.

(11) Withdraw syringe and needle together.   If the syringe is removed from the needle before this has been drawn out of the skin, some of the injected vaccine will flow back through the needle and be lost.   In this case the animal does not get its full dose and will consequently be insufficiently protected.

MEASURE OF SUCCESS SO FAR REACHED.

The distribution of vaccine was begun in July, 1897, and by April 30, 1898, there had been sent out about 200,000 doses.   Eight to twelve months later an inquiry blank with eighteen questions (see page 31) was sent to each stock owner who had received vaccine, in order that he might report the results.   By far the greater majority of the stock owners took pains to answer the questions and return the blanks promptly, and in the table below will be found the principal data obtained from all the reports which were received from the eight States and Territories enumerated in the column to the left.   About forty additional reports were received from other States, but not in sufficient numbers from any single one to warrant their tabulation. They will therefore be included in next year's report:

Table showing for eight States the number of cattle vaccinated and the percentage of loss before and after vaccination.

State.	Number of reports.	Number of cattle vaccinated.	Average annual loss from blackleg.	Deaths same season but previous to vaccination.		Died after vaccination.					
						Within 48 hours.	From 3 to 7 days after.	Within 1 year.	Number of cases admitted to be due to mistakes.	Total number.	Per cent.
			Per cent.	Number.	Per cent.						
Texas	164	50,609	13	1,462	2.95	20	7	141	59	227	0.45
Nebraska	71	20,893	17.2	796	3.80	7	1	39	5	52	0.25
Kansas	140	19,508	11	919	4.76	36	24	52	3	115	0.58
Colorado	53	12,609	12.8	230	1.83	6	8(?)	120(?)	4	138	1.09
Oklahoma	37	7,915	17.5	471	5.96	2	......	20	15	37	0.47
Indian Territory	20	7,418	17.5	504	7.81	......	......	51	44	95	1.28
North Dakota	22	6,118	12.75	133	2.18	......	......	25		25	0.41
South Dakota	15	2,299	12.75	74	3.32	1	1	7	2	11	0.48
Total	522	127,369	14	4,589	3.63	72	41	455	132	700	0.54

These figures, as will be seen, are based upon the reports received from 522 stock owners who vaccinated about 127,000 head of cattle. The average loss from blackleg in these eight States and Territories was estimated in the reports to be 14 per cent. This percentage, as already stated, is based upon the losses sustained in well-known blackleg districts and not upon the total number of cattle in each State, and refer, of course, to unvaccinated herds. At least 90 per cent of the 522 stock owners lost cattle from blackleg previous to vaccination and the actual number of deaths reported to have occurred during the same season before the cattle were vaccinated amounts to 4,589 head, or 3.60 per cent.

After vaccination 700 head died. These may be classified as follows: 72 head died within forty-eight hours after vaccination and can not justly be charged to the effect of the vaccine. In every one of these cases the owner reported that he was losing cattle every day before vaccination, and the period of incubation for blackleg being from two to five days, it is reasonable to assume that these animals were infected before being treated. Consequently they should be left out of consideration in judging the effect of the vaccine. Forty-one head died in from three to seven days after vaccination. It would doubtless be safe to consider these cases as being due to the immediate effect of the vaccine, and to term them cases of inoculation-blackleg.

During the year following vaccination 587 head died from blackleg. In 132 of these cases the owners admit to having made one or more mistakes, either in the preparation of the vaccine or in injecting it. A number also state that the animals which died were under 5 to 6 months old when vaccinated, some being only 2 to 4 months old. Mistakes are no doubt also responsible for some of the 455 deaths, but only in cases where the owners expressly state that such occurred have the deaths been classified in the column headed "mistakes." Take, for instance, the large number of deaths reported from Colorado—138 cases. Only 4 of them are acknowledged to be due to mistakes, while 6 died within two days after vaccination. Of the remaining 128 cases, 52 head or nearly half, were lost by one man who vaccinated 1,700 head. In reply to question 18 on the inquiry blank this man states that he used Pasteur vaccine the year previous with the same result. This is an equal loss of 3 per cent with either single or double vaccine, and indicates that either some abnormal conditions obtain in that neighborhood, or else the same mistake in using the vaccine was made in both cases.

Another stock owner in Colorado, who vaccinated 600 head, says that he lost 17 from blackleg three months after vaccination. Evidently the number of cattle failed to become immune from the vaccination. He states, however, that in withdrawing the syringe after making the injection a part of the fluid escaped. This can not occur when the directions are followed, and, as no complaints were received from any of the other stock owners who obtained vaccine from the same lot, the writer is inclined to believe that the unsatisfactory result can not be charged against the vaccine. A third stock owner vaccinated 2,350 head and lost 24 head during the following winter. In reply to question 18, he states that he has also used the Pasteur vaccine, and that the subsequent loss among the vaccinated ones was equally as great as among those which had not been vaccinated at all. These three cases account for 93 of the 128 deaths, leaving but 35 deaths among the remaining 7,959 vaccinated animals, or 0.44 per cent.

The Indian Territory also figures in the table with a very high percentage of deaths which occurred several weeks after vaccination. Of the 95 which died, 40 belonged to one man, who states that he lost a quantity of vaccine by working in "too much of a rush."

A Texas stockman made the signal mistake of injecting 400 doses into 200 animals, and subsequently suffered considerable loss. This was the only case of its kind. A number of deaths occurred, however, by vaccinating and castrating or dehorning at the same time. Two men lost heavily—about 20 head each. They stated that none of the heifers became affected, but a number of the castrated bull calves swelled very badly around the castration sores, down the hind legs, and along the belly. Although a large number died many more were similarly affected and recovered. On the other hand, a number of stock owners have continued to vaccinate and castrate at the same time, disregarding the warning contained in the blackleg circular sent out by this Bureau, and claim to have seen no ill effect from it. There is, in the mind of the writer, little doubt that sooner or later the practice will cause heavy losses to those who practice it. Dr. A. T. Peters, of the Nebraska Agricultural Experiment Station, claims to have seen blackleg tumors develop when animals were branded and vaccinated at the same time, the swellings appearing at the place where the hot iron had been applied. None of the stock owners, however, who have used our vaccine, and most of whom vaccinated and branded at the same time, report to have had any such experience.

The results obtained by a great majority of the stock owners have been uniformly good. Less than a dozen out of more than 500 report to the contrary. In some of these the losses were probably due to deviations from the printed directions, and it is justifiable to eliminate from the total of "deaths after vaccination" at least those losses which are admitted by the stock owners to be due to mistakes in preparing or administering the vaccine. But in order to estimate correctly the value of the vaccine as a preventive of blackleg, it is necessary to deduct the 72 deaths which occurred within forty-eight hours after vaccination, because they most likely were due to previous infection. It may be added that a number of cases occurring within this limit, and where no cases had been observed previous to vaccination the same season, were placed in the second column of accidents, as being due to blackleg.

The final results, consequently, appear as follows:

Table showing number of reports, number of cattle vaccinated, percentage of loss before and after vaccination, etc.

State.	Number of reports.	Number of cattle vaccinated.	Average annual loss from blackleg.	Deaths, same season, previous to vaccination.		Died after vaccination.				Mortality before vaccination.
						From 2 to 7 days after.	Within 1 year.	Total number.	Per cent.	
			Per cent.	*Number.*	*Per cent.*					
Texas	164	50,609	13	1,462	2.95	7	141	148	0.29	10 times greater than after.
Nebraska	71	20,893	17.2	796	3.80	1	39	40	0.19	20 times greater than after.
Kansas	140	19,508	11	919	4.76	24	52	76	0.39	12 times greater than after.
Colorado	53	12,609	12.8	230	1.83	8	120	128	1.01	1.8 times greater than after.
Oklahoma	37	7,915	17.5	471	5.96	....	20	20	0.26	23 times greater than after.
Indian Territory	20	7,418	17.5	504	6.81	....	51	51	0.69	10 times greater than after.
North Dakota	22	6,118	12.75	133	2.18	....	25	25	0.41	5 times greater than after.
South Dakota	15	2,299	12.75	74	3.22	1	7	8	0.35	9 times greater than after.
Total	522	127,269	14	4,589	3.63	41	455	496	0.39	9 times greater than after.

With these figures before us there is every reason to believe that, with the continued use of blackleg vaccine in all districts where the disease is known to occur and an earnest effort on the part of the stock owners to prevent the reinfection of their pastures by following the directions given by this Bureau, blackleg may be kept in check and gradually eradicated.

The danger of infection must naturally diminish in proportion to the decrease in the amount of virulent material deposited upon the pastures. With a mortality after vaccination of only one-ninth as great as that before vaccination (the estimated loss of 14 per cent is not considered, but only the actual loss of 3.60 per cent), it is obvious that this preventive measure serves a double purpose in combating the disease. It is therefore to the interest of every stock owner who vaccinates his cattle to induce his neighbors to take the same precaution, especially in districts where it is difficult to find the animals dead of the disease and dispose of them before they are attacked by vermin.

THE WORK TO BE CONTINUED.

The distribution of blackleg vaccine will be continued by this Bureau until further notice, and adequate measures have been taken to avoid all delay in sending the vaccine immediately on receipt of the application. It is advisable that all stock owners in infected districts should vaccinate their young stock regularly, without awaiting an outbreak of the disease, as heavy losses may be sustained in the course of a few days. The Bureau can not undertake to keep stockmen supplied with vaccine simply for the purpose of keeping it on hand for use in case of an outbreak.

As it has been reported to this Bureau that persons representing themselves as Government employees have offered for sale and sold the vaccine prepared here, or have offered to vaccinate and have vaccinated cattle for a stipulated compensation with the same vaccine, it may be well to call attention to the fact that the Bureau vaccine is never furnished to any person for distribution among others, excepting the State sanitary officials or State experiment station veterinarians, and any charges made for the same are fraudulent.

For the benefit of those who have not yet obtained vaccine from this Bureau the following is quoted from Circular No. 23 (revised) of this Bureau:

HOW TO APPLY FOR BLACKLEG VACCINE.

A regular application blank will be mailed to any stock owner who so requests, and in accepting the vaccine he pledges himself to report the results.

During the past year a number of stock owners have obtained vaccine in excess of what they actually needed, simply to have it on hand in case they should want to use it. This practice has caused unnecessary work for this Bureau, and, on the other hand, stock owners whose cattle were actually dying from blackleg had to wait on this account from two to three weeks or even longer before they could be supplied.

It has, therefore, become necessary to attach a certificate to each application blank, and make it obligatory for each stock owner who wishes to obtain vaccine from this Bureau to certify on his honor that the number of doses of blackleg vaccine applied for by him are actually needed at the time the application is made, and that they will be used within four weeks after receipt, on his own cattle, or on cattle in which he is actually interested, or of which he is actually in charge.

Attention is called to the rule that under no circumstances will blackleg vaccine be sent to any one person for distribution to others, except in the case of State officials or sanitary officers. Each stock owner must apply directly to this office for the amount of vaccine required for his own cattle, and this will in each case be sent to him direct.

EXTRACTS FROM REPORTS.

In order to encourage those stock owners who still are skeptical regarding the value of vaccination, it may be well to quote a few of the unsolicited recommendations received from the various States where the Bureau vaccine has been used: ·

TEXAS.

I did not lose any of the 110 head I vaccinated, but out of 6 head which were not vaccinated 2 died of blackleg.—C. M.

It is a dead shot. After I took the cattle out of the pasture in May I put in 65 heifers; they commenced dying. I lost 5 head before I could vaccinate and 1 after vaccination.—W. H. C.

We failed in finding about 40 head when vaccinating and lost 4 of them. We put an extra brand on all animals we vaccinated.—F. M. R. & Bros.

I did not lose any from blackleg, while my neighbors did. I have no hesitancy in saying that the vaccine prevented a loss.—J. F. S.

I consider the vaccine a perfect success as a preventive of blackleg, and recommend the use of it to every stock raiser.—A. S. S.

I vaccinated 50 head in September or October with your virus: turned them loose in pasture. In November I turned 150 in same pasture not vaccinated. Lost of the latter 6 head from blackleg, and none of the 50. I am a firm believer in vaccination.—G. C. A.

I sold to Mr. S. S. Springvale, Kansas, 330 head of vaccinated cattle. In the same train he had about an equal number of unvaccinated calves. During the winter he wrote me that he had lost 25 out of the unvaccinated calves, and that they were dying 4 or 5 every day, while he had lost none out of mine; stating at the same time that vaccination was the right thing, and that all cattle he bought in Texas in the future would have to be vaccinated.—L. H. & W. C. L.

I am well pleased with the success of the operation, and quite a number of my neighbors will vaccinate this fall.—R. N. D.

After losing 27 head I vaccinated 300 and lost none after vaccination. In April I vaccinated 40 high-grade heifer yearlings for a neighbor. One had died of blackleg the night before. The cattle were put back in the same pasture with a registered bull. Another neighbor put 2 fine yearlings in the same pasture to remain a few months; in the course of six months they both died of blackleg. The vaccinated ones are all living.—S. J. G.

Twenty head were put in my pasture that were not vaccinated, and 5 head of the 20 died of blackleg.—N. B. F.

I feel under grateful obligations to your honorable Department for its successful efforts to advance the live-stock interests along this and other lines; and my hope is that the periphery of your usefulness may be greatly enlarged in the future.—R. H. K.

Out of 360 animals vaccinated I lost but 1 calf, which was given one-half doses when only 3 months old. It died in May, 1898, after being vaccinated in October, 1897. All of my neighbors who did not vaccinate continued to lose cattle during the fall, winter, and spring of 1897-98.—J. W. M.

I think your vaccine is the best, and hope your Department will continue to prepare it and let stockmen have it at cost or at a low rate.—W. W.

I have never used any other vaccine, as I am satisfied from the experience I have had that the vaccine prepared by your Bureau can not be surpassed. It is a grand success and has saved me many dollars in cattle.—E. R.

I had 650 yearling steers, of which I vaccinated 500 and put a small "c" on left jaw to designate them from the 150 that were not vaccinated. Twenty-three head died, and only one of them had "c" on jaw.—H. H. H.

I vaccinated 600 calves, and I think 2 died afterwards. The year before I used vaccine I lost 120 head out of 600.—R. H. O.

KANSAS.

I was the first to vaccinate here. The results were so good men came to me for advice and instruction. I told them all how to get the vaccine, loaned them my instruments, and assisted in many ways. I think at least 1,000 head have been vaccinated in this neighborhood, and not one animal has died from blackleg after vaccination. One man lost 14 out of 40 head. I gave him part of my vaccine. He vaccinated his calves and never lost another animal, having them in same lots where others have died. I want to thank the Department for its assistance. I have every confidence in the vaccine.—E. C.

Last year I lost nearly all my calves and some yearlings; this year I have not lost one. I vaccinated this year; last year I did not. I think your vaccine has been worth a great deal to me.—H. M. K.

I am sure it is a very valuable remedy. It has saved me many dollars. It has made cattle raising profitable instead of a losing business.—R. J. M.

All of the people in this county are satisfied that the vaccine is all right, for we haven't had any losses since we used it.—G. B.

I vaccinated 100 head; lost 20 before and none afterwards. I have great faith in your vaccine.—G. H. G.

My loss is usually 10 per cent, and I believe if I had not used the vaccine it would have been fully that great this year. I consider it a very effective remedy for calves. I have had no experience with other cattle.—G. W.

I vaccinated 51 head, none of which became affected, although my neighbors continued to lose. I had 1 heifer about 11 months old which was heavy with calf, so did not want to catch and throw her. She was not vaccinated and died a month later from blackleg.—W. J.

INDIAN TERRITORY.

I was losing from 10 to 15 per day when I received the vaccine, but never lost a head after applying it.—N. B. R.

It is the only remedy we have found so far that prevents death from blackleg among cattle, and I think your Department is doing important work in assisting the farmers in preventing disease and losses among their cattle.—J. C. R.

My experience with your vaccine, and my observations on my neighbors' stock, leave me to think it a perfect preventive of blackleg. The vaccine is conceded to be a perfect success.—R. C. F.

OKLAHOMA.

I think the vaccine a sure preventive, and you are doing a noble work for the stockmen.—B. T. L.

I let my neighbor have about 75 doses; he vaccinated that many cattle and had about 100 that he did not vaccinate. He lost none of the calves that were vaccinated, but lost several that were not vaccinated.—H. C. C.

SOUTH DAKOTA.

None died after vaccination. The effect seemed to be marvelous. In all cases where Government vaccine was used in this locality the ravages stopped immediately.—C. F. R.

I lost 1 when I vaccinated, castrated, and branded at the same time, and 1 when I vaccinated and castrated at same time, but never any when vaccinating and branding at same time.—C. H. M.

Am fully convinced that this remedy can't be beat, and is all right if used right.—W. F. B.

COLORADO.

I am well pleased and heartily recommend the vaccine as a preventive for blackleg.—A. N. T.

NEBRASKA.

I have the utmost faith in this vaccine. This is the first summer that I haven't lost cattle with the blackleg.—H. C.

I believe your vaccine is all right, and I am satisfied that it saved me a big loss.—C. F. C.

We have vaccinated about 500 head at different dates, ages from 6 months to 18, and so far have not lost one after treating; but we have not treated them till some died. We know your remedy is a sure preventive.—W. & F.

We lost none of those we vaccinated, but 1 got away from us without being vaccinated and it was neglected. It alone became affected and died.—M. T.

Everybody vaccinated his cattle this year, and I believe it has saved the cattle industry in this part of the country.—M. N. P.

NEW MEXICO.

Inclosed you will find blank for recording the result of vaccination filled out, and I am very pleased with the result of same. I have only lost 2 head since I used the vaccine, and I have vaccinated 400 head. Last year I lost about 40 head of calves out of 150 from blackleg, and most of them had been weaned and were eating hay in the yard. I am sure they contracted the disease in the feed lot, for I heard afterwards that a man lost 8 or 10 feeding in the same pen. Just before I wrote to you for the vaccine I bought a bunch of cattle and they were in a pasture, watering at rain-water holes. It was hot weather, and the yearlings and calves began to die; 23 head died. I moved them away to another pasture and they had good lake water. I lost 3 head just after moving, but as soon as I got your vaccine I vaccinated all the yearlings and only lost 2 head after vaccinating. One of these had the horn broken off when thrown. A neighbor of mine got some vaccine from someone in Kansas. It was put up in capsules, and he inserted it in the necks of the calves by cutting the skin with a knife and putting the capsule under the hide. In a great many cases it formed a large sack of matter, and had to be opened and a quantity of pus came from it. He lost 27 head out of 175, and a great many of the others were very sick for some days. These calves would swell up and could hardly walk, and would die in from two to five days. I have not heard of anyone losing any calves who used your vaccine, and I have vaccinated a good many for persons in the neighborhood.

Thank you for the vaccine you sent me. I will always vaccinate all my calves from this on, as I have had heavy losses every year till this winter.—E. G. A.

IDAHO.

We lost none of the 480 head we vaccinated, but 7 head slipped past the operator and escaped from the chute before receiving the injection or the brand with which we marked those treated. All 7 of these died of blackleg, which is conclusive evidence to us that our total loss, had we not vaccinated, would have been very heavy.—S. & B.

CALIFORNIA.

The vaccine supplied by you has been of inestimable benefit in helping to stamp out the disease. We are comparatively free from it this year, many having used the free vaccine before suffering losses. We owe your Bureau many thanks.—J. S. A.

ARIZONA.

I vaccinated 100 bulls after losing 10 head, and not one of the vaccinated animals died. I am satisfied the vaccine prevented a loss, as a number of my unvaccinated cattle died from blackleg. Dr. J. C. N. prepared and injected the vaccine, as I think it best to employ a skilled veterinarian to do the work.—C. C.

10317——6

desire to extend the market for creamery butter, especially from the large producing districts of the West and Northwest, it was deemed expedient for this Department to ascertain the facts experimentally and make them known to all concerned.

It was decided to make the trial shipments of the season to London. There was good reason for making the first effort to promote an increased demand for fine American butter in the markets of England. That country is the greatest of all buyers of foreign-made butter. Great Britain imported butter during the year 1897 to the value of $77,000,000. This was 45 per cent in excess of like imports five years before, and the demand seems to be steadily increasing.[1]

Creamery butter of the grade known commercially as "extras" was selected as the standard for trial exports, because this represents the great bulk of the product for a part of which it seems desirable to obtain a foreign demand, and because of the purpose to demonstrate the high quality of butter obtainable in this country. The butter was produced from creameries in eleven different States, in order to further demonstrate that this production is not confined to any particular and limited portion of the United States.

The butter exported was made in accordance with special instructions from this office at creameries in Connecticut, Iowa, Kansas, Massachusetts, Minnesota, New Hampshire, New York, Ohio, South Dakota, Vermont, and Wisconsin. Creameries were selected for the purpose which were known to have won high honors at public butter exhibits and contests, or which were designated, at the request of the Department, by State dairy officials or State dairy associations. The instructions given were based upon the available knowledge regarding the particular requirements of the London market, and in the preparation of the later lots the makers had the benefit of experience derived from the earlier shipments. The Department paid for the butter used the regular market price for the product of the creamery concerned, at its own shipping station, at the time of shipment. Whatever extra labor and special care was necessary, in the use of unusual packages, modification of usual methods to conform to instructions, promptness in making and shipping and rendering reports, was cheerfully contributed, without charge, by the managers and butter makers of the respective creameries. A list of the creameries which cooperated with the Department in this public-spirited manner is appended at page 108, together with the places and times of manufacture. Acknowledgment is hereby made for the material assistance thus rendered.

The butter was made in all cases from the regular factory supplies of milk or cream and in substantially the same way as prepared for home markets, so that the shipments as a whole fairly represented the best product of the active creamery districts of the country.

---

[1] See table of British imports of butter, appended, p. 108.

Detailed reports were rendered in every case, and a full history was obtained of every lot of butter experimentally exported.[1] To complete the record, sample packages were carefully examined and scored by commercial experts and analyzed by competent chemists, as later described.

Several interesting experiments were made incidentally to determine facts along certain lines connected with the subject. Important among these were trials of the relative merits, upon reaching the London market, and the comparative keeping quality of butter as usually made and that from pasteurized cream; also experiments in sending to such a distant market "sweet," or wholly unsalted butter. Although these trials were insufficient to furnish conclusive results, they were satisfactory in the main and fully justify repetition, with the same ends in view. Special reports upon these subjects are included in the Appendix. (See pages 110 and 125.)

It is already evident that pasteurization of milk or cream, in connection with butter making, deserves careful study and persistent trial, especially in connection with the export trade. The prevailing creamery methods result in a product which has general characteristics and shows a vast improvement in almost every particular over the great diversity in butter consequent upon the practice of farm dairies. But there is still altogether too much variation in creamery butter for the good of the trade, not only among different factories but in the product of the same creamery at different times. Natural methods of ripening cream are uncertain, even under expert management; when inexperience and carelessness are involved, the opportunities become almost infinite for variety in flavor and other qualities. Pasteurization, necessarily accompanied by "starters" in cream-ripening, being preferably of known and special ferments, or "cultures," certainly tends to much greater uniformity in butter, even from widely separated sources, and produces a flavor slow in development and well adapted to foreign trade, besides apparently improving keeping quality, which is an important factor in the same connection. At least 95 per cent of the export butter of Denmark is now made from milk or cream which has been pasteurized, and there can be no doubt that to this fact is largely due that remarkable uniformity in flavor and general character which gives Danish butter such a strong hold in the best English markets.

The butter which brings the highest price of all in London is entirely without salt and called "fresh" and "sweet." The supply is mainly from the north of France, although some is made in England and some obtained from Ireland and from Italy. The favorite form is a 2-pound roll, packed twelve in a box. The rolls are not separately wrapped, but the box usually has linings of both cloth and paper. When the best salted butter is selling in London at 25 cents

---

[1] For an example of these reports, see Appendix V, p. 109.

per pound, these Normandy and Brittany rolls sell at 30 cents per pound. The supply is quite constant, and this butter is delivered so as to be consumed within a week or ten days from the time it is made. It usually contains a small quantity of borax or other preservative to assist in keeping it sound. During the early autumn the Department sent over two lots of unsalted butter, made at Eastern creameries. This was packed like the French rolls and also in other ways. Parts of this butter molded badly on the way, but this could be avoided in future. These trials, the first of their kind ever·made so far as known, met with several accidents and in several particulars gave unsatisfactory results, but enough was learned from them to show that it is entirely practicable to make butter of this class and place it in London just as fine in quality and condition as that which is above described as supplied from France.

The butter exported was sent in packages which varied much in size, form, material, and treatment. For general trade, a package holding from 50 to 60 pounds is wanted in Great Britain as well as in this country. Fifty-six pounds (or a half hundredweight) is an approved size in London, and "quarters" (of 28 pounds) are acceptable in limited quantity. Smaller or family-sized packages, to be sold unbroken, which are gaining in popularity in the best American markets, are not favored in London by either wholesale or retail merchants. Packages holding from 1 to 7 pounds were objected to as innovations; but, although retail merchants in London prefer to adhere to old methods and cut from a large lump for their customers, there were indications that consumers would soon learn to like the unbroken, convenient-sized packages, and by persistent offering these would come into demand, especially in connection with suburban trade.

There is great variety in form as well as size among the butter packages appearing in the London market. Firkins or small casks holding from 50 to 120 pounds are very common, and the cubical box, which originated in Australia and bears that name, is a prime favorite. This box holds just a cubic foot of butter, which usually weighs a little over 56 pounds. The cubical or other rectangular package unquestionably has intrinsic merits and decided commercial advantages. As an export package it is already generally advocated. But it would be highly objectionable to have one form of package demanded for export purposes and a different one for domestic use, and it will certainly be a long time before the "Welsh" tub, or more properly the American creamery tub, ceases to be the standard butter package of the United States. It is a great mistake to suppose that London or any British market yet demands its butter in Australian boxes. A small fraction of the butter sold in London is in this form. By far the greater portion is in "kiels" or casks in every respect inferior to the creamery tub. It has already been demonstrated that if the quality is satisfactory London will pay as much for its (salted) butter in one form as in another. It will be an easy matter to compromise by cutting the capacity of the creamery tub from 60 pounds to 56, and thus making a package acceptable both at home and abroad.

The chief objection to the creamery tub at present in British markets is that poor butter from the United States has been so largely exported in that form that this package is closely associated in the minds of English buyers with a low grade of goods. This prejudice is so strong that it is hard to get an English merchant who is seeking good butter to even take time to examine the contents of a package recognized by him as a "States tub."

The materials approved for tubs are white ash and spruce, without marked preference in London. For boxes, spruce and poplar are used, and the latter seems to be preferred by the foreign buyers. More important than the kind of wood is its thorough seasoning, in order to be absolutely odorless and tasteless.

The packages alone are an insufficient protection to their contents against the exposure of the voyage and the incidental transfer. Hence all packages need good parchment-paper linings well put in place. Double linings are desirable. These are used by foreign countries as a rule and are much heavier and better in quality than those used in this country. Besides linings, different methods were tried of coating the inside of the boxes with suitable material, to insure against unseasoned wood and to render the packages as nearly air-tight as possible. Paraffin was used for this purpose, applied hot, so as to thoroughly coat the inner surfaces, including the cover, and fill all cracks and joints. A patent application, a sort of enamel, was also tried. These extra precautions to guard the butter from exterior injury were found to be worthy of general adoption. The parchment linings may be regarded as essential; otherwise, the interior box coatings may depend upon the quality and tightness of the package.

A package with a clean exterior is attractive at the place of ultimate sale. Boxes and tubs are exposed to much rough handling and soiling between a Western creamery and a British market. It has been found that a coarse burlap sack or cover fitted to the box or tub and drawn tightly over it helps materially in keeping the package clean, prevents changes of temperature, and facilitates handling. In the trial shipments butter from different places was sent abroad with parts of the same lot sacked and partly without. Reports showed that while packages of butter thus protected did not actually sell for more than those of like contents sent without this covering, the sacked packages were first chosen because cleaner, and English merchants advised that the burlap covers be used in all cases. Early in the season of 1897 these sacks cost in quantity only about 4 cents each; later, changes in tariff caused a rise in price to 10 cents, and still later the price settled down to about 8 cents each.   At this rate it seems to be true economy to use them on all packages of fine buttter exported.

The Department trials included butter in prints (variously called blocks, tablets, lumps, rolls, and pats) of pound and half-pound weights, in separate paper wrappers, some packed in cases of different sizes and some with every print in a box of heavy paper.   Also, butter in small boxes of tin and paper board, hermetically sealed and suited for ocean voyages and use in hot climates.   With proper care, it will not be difficult to send print butter from this country to English markets in good condition and to make this form popular with retail merchants and their customers.   For butter in sealed packages there is always a demand from the shipping trade, but as the contents of these packages can not be examined, the sales must depend upon an established reputation as to quality, and this is a matter of time and business effort.   The whole question of exporting small packages and novelties in form and material, including print butter, requires much further attention.

With the exception of two lots, the butter selected for the export trials was carefully sampled and submitted to chemical analysis. These analyses were made in nearly all cases at the agricultural experiment stations in the States furnishing the butter, and acknowledgment is due to these stations for their prompt and gratuitous assistance.   Additional analyses were made by the Chemical Division of this Department, and in order to have a still further check upon the work the butter was sampled in a number of cases while on the London market and examined by a public analyst in that city.   The object of this chemical work was to determine as exactly as possible the important components of the butter in question, especially the proportions of fat, water, and salt.

In order that the butter exported might be closely compared with high-grade butter from other countries on sale at the same time in London, sample packages of the best butter to be found in that market, from various sources of supply, were purchased several times during the season and their contents were also analyzed.   In two instances packages of these foreign-made butters were sent over from London to this country, being subjected to exactly the same conditions as to time, distance, and transportation as the States butter exported, except that the movement was in the opposite direction. The butters thus obtained for comparison were as follows: Best English Dorset, in keg; Irish creamery, in pyramidal box; "Royal" Danish, in "kiels" or casks; Dutch creamery, in firkin; Finnish, in keg; Brittany rolls, unsalted, in boxes; Normandy, in basket; New South Wales, in cubical box; New Zealand, in oblong box; Australian, in cubical box.   Some of these were analyzed by a London chemist, but most of them at this Department and by the experiment stations in Connecticut and Iowa.

So far as practicable, the different lots of butter exported and those imported for examination were inspected by an expert and scored upon a scale of points. The butter inspector of the New York Mercantile Exchange was selected for this duty and performed it very acceptably. In this way a fair basis for comparison was established. For further information packages of butter from export lots were placed in cold storage in New York, held there and examined again about the time the same lots were on sale in London, and some of the export butter was sent back from London to be compared in New York, after its double journey, with packages of the same lot retained in New York. Several of the foreign butters were also scored in Chicago.

It was found impracticable to have the American butter included in the export trials scored in London and compared in that way with other butter on sale there, because this method of examination seems to be unknown in that market. Diligent inquiry failed to find anyone known to the trade in London who had ever scored butter upon a scale of points. Some attempts were made to use a score card sent over, but the inspectors were so unaccustomed to this method that, although doubtless good commercial judges of butter, the reports from them were of little value.

The records of the various analyses and scores referred to are appended in tabular form, with some explanatory notes. (See pages 128 to 134, inclusive.)

The distance and the danger of injury incident to the long journey by land and by sea being appreciated from the first, the matter of transportation received the closest attention throughout the trials made. Shipments were allowed to follow commercial lines and be subjected to commercial conditions as closely as possible, but they were watched at all points by agents of the Department, in order to ascertain the exact facts, as a basis for subsequent improvement in the existing conditions.

Railroad transportation facilities for perishable commodities are excellent in this country from all the principal producing regions to important points on the eastern seaboard. Similar facilities abroad are unusual and inferior. The various lines of refrigerator cars are well equipped and admirably managed here, so that little criticism of the present service is possible. The cleanliness of the cars, the temperature at which they are kept, the time schedules, and the freight tariffs, including these special facilities, were examined, tested, approved, and commended. All the large creamery districts of the West are well served by refrigerator lines, and butter is carried thence to markets 2,000 miles or more distant and delivered in as good condition as at the starting point.

Carload lots which can be moved unbroken from the creamery or creamery town to destination have great advantages, especially in hot weather. Small lots necessitate opening the cars, causing more or less fluctuation in the temperature of the butter, and involve transfers from car to car at interior points, sometimes including an open-air haul across a city or town. These transfers receive in many cases the attention of special agents, if they are duly notified by shippers, but still afford opportunity for improvement. It is practicable to lessen the exposure of butter at these transfers by reducing distances, avoiding midday hauls and handling, and protecting the packages while on wagons and drays.

Terminal facilities at the principal markets, including deliveries to consignees, have been greatly improved, but are yet far from perfect. Butter arriving unexpectedly, perhaps a day ahead of time, may remain at the terminal shed for several hours in a constantly rising temperature; it is not uncommon for notices of such arrivals in the early morning to reach consignees after 1 o'clock p. m. By efficient cooperation between railroads and merchants, it seems possible to materially lessen the average time which now elapses between the discharges of butter from refrigerator cars and its storing in cellars and cold rooms.

The Department trials included nineteen shipments over five refrigerator lines west of Chicago and four others reaching New York City. These shipments being all intended for export upon steamers with latest receiving hours named well in advance, estimates were made for as close connections as possible between railroad and vessel. Of the nineteen shipments mentioned, fifteen arrived at New York on time, and four were so late as to miss the sailing day desired. Three of these were from west of Chicago and one from central Ohio; they were delayed upon three different transportation lines. These delays were not due to railroad accidents or detentions of trains, but to avoidable circumstances in connection with transfers, showing points for improvement in the service.

It is not usually a matter of consequence to the merchant at an Eastern market if a consignment of butter arrives late by some hours, or even a day or two. But with butter intended for direct export, economy in handling and protection of quality render close connection between railroad and steamer quite important. Time, tide, and ocean steamers wait not for railroads. This kind of special service by the latter must be made as nearly perfect as possible. Some detentions by rail are unavoidable; and, to provide against these, the terminal facilities of the transportaion lines should include cold-storage accommodations, well located and ample in capacity, so that butter for export may arrive two or three days in advance of sailing time and (where the refrigerator car can not be held) be stored without charge until the proper hour for delivery to the vessel. There have been a few attempts to make such provisions in a small way, but nothing commensurate with the requirements of enlarged traffic.

Six trial shipments had to be brought to New York City by express from creameries in the States of New Hampshire, Massachusetts, Connecticut, and New York because refrigerator car service could not be obtained. Local traffic is still lacking such accommodations in the East. It cost more per pound in every instance to bring butter to the port of export from creameries 100 to 300 miles distant than to bring it from points ten times as far distant, and the butter coming 2,000 miles arrived in better order. Such conditions require no comment.

In accordance with special instructions from the Secretary of Agriculture, much attention was given to ascertaining the present and prospective facilities for the transportation of perishable farm products by sea, including ports from which few exports of this character have yet been made.

During a great part of the year accommodations for first-class ocean freight are good and sufficient. But there are several months in which butter for export is most abundant, when the quality of a high-grade article can only be safely preserved by cold storage during the voyage. The same provisions are needed for the preservation of other perishable products. A good many ocean steamers now have large commercial refrigerators fitted to be maintained at any desired temperature above the zero of Fahrenheit. Up to the present time, however, the demand for such accommodations has been so small and infrequent for commodities other than fresh meat that the expense of keeping these refrigerators ready for general purposes has not been justified. Nearly all of the commercial refrigerators upon vessels sailing regularly from ports of the United States consequently have been, and still are, contracted for by the large exporters of beef and other fresh meats and used by them exclusively throughout the season. During the summer of 1897 one commercial refrigerator was open to the general public on the steamers of the American Line from the port of New York weekly for three weeks out of every four. This was the extent of the accommodations of this kind which could be depended upon as available. Other lines from New York opened a refrigerator for general use occasionally. Inquiries at Portland, Me., Boston, Philadelphia, Baltimore, Charleston, New Orleans, Galveston, San Francisco, and Portland, Oreg., failed to find like facilities offered to shippers. From a few of these ports fresh meat was exported in refrigerators under exclusive contracts. Occasionally a vessel fitted with a refrigerator would clear from one of them, but these occasions were so rare and irregular as to be of no practical benefit to shippers. Earnest efforts to arrange for experimental exports of dairy products, fresh fruits, and other perishables over new lines, under the auspices of this Department, failed because suitable refrigerated ocean transportation could not be obtained. The same state of affairs seems probable for the season of 1898, although there are partial promises of a line of steamers with refrigerators available to the public from Boston to Bristol, and an occasional additional refrigerator on a Liverpool steamer from New York.

While this unfortunate lack of refrigerated space available to all exporters exists in this country, the butter makers and merchants of Canada, who are competing with those of the United States for position in the markets of Great Britain, have export facilities which can hardly be excelled. Under the fostering care of the Dominion government, which has borne a large part of the expense of initial equipment, seventeen steamers sailing from Montreal during the past season have been fitted with refrigerators, and the use of these has been secured to shippers in general at extremely low rates. There has thus been weekly refrigerated service from Montreal to London, Liverpool, and Bristol, and fortnightly service to Glasgow. There has also been fortnightly service from Halifax and St. Johns to London, and monthly service from Prince Edward Island. The system of refrigeration on all these vessels is mechanical, securing the best insulated compartments, and duplex machinery makes accidents next to impossible. Under the contracts between the Canadian government and the steamship lines these extra facilities are offered to shippers of butter made in the Dominion at a charge not exceeding 10 English shillings per ton, or about 1 mill per pound, above the prevailing rates for first-class freight. During the season of 1897 the rate on butter in refrigerators from Montreal to London averaged about 50 shillings per ton of 2,240 pounds, or half a cent a pound. Of course, these rates were secured only for Canadian produce, and, indeed, refrigerated accommodations could be obtained upon the steamers from Montreal for other produce only in case the Canadian offerings did not fill the compartments.

The combined railway and ocean rates from the Northwestern States to Great Britain were so much more favorable by way of Montreal than by way of New York that considerable States butter was sent by that route during the past season. The quantity of butter which crossed into Canada from the United States at Detroit, Mich., and Champlain, N. Y., during the year 1896–97 was three times as great as during the year next preceding.

The trial shipments for this Department were made from New York to London via Southampton. The commercial refrigerators were used as much as possible, and at other times, through the courtesy of the International Navigation Company, the butter was carried in the ships' own cold rooms at current rates. The temperature preferred during the voyage was 30° to 32°, and this was easily obtained and evenly held. There is no reason to believe that there was any deterioration of quality in the butter of the several lots exported consequent upon the voyage itself and the detention on shipboard for seven to nine days. Entirely satisfactory transportation facilities can be provided on vessels, as now on land, whenever the demand is such as to secure the supply.

Terminal facilities and the conditions pertaining to the necessary transfers at both ends of the voyage are far from what is needed. The steamers while loading are ready to receive certain classes of freight only at certain hours. These hours seldom agree with those of arrival by rail and delivery at the docks. Hence there is detention and exposure at the wharves, there being no provisions there for temporary cold storage or special protection until taken on board. Butter is subjected to similar exposure on arrival at Southampton and while awaiting the forward movement to London. There is one large refrigerator on the wharf at Southampton, owned by the steamship company, but this is without subdivisions, is used indiscriminately for all kinds of perishable products detained, meats especially, and is not a suitable place for holding butter. The Southwestern Railway Company have large masonry vaults under their tracks at Southampton, and these are kept clean and sweet and ventilated with electric fans. They would do for temporary storage of butter even without refrigeration, except in such extremely hot weather as rarely occurs at that place. Refrigerator cars on the line to London are furnished only for carload lots and shippers must provide their own ice. The railroad ordinarily offers no special accommodations, but the journey to London is short. The train carrying perishables makes the trip by night in about four hours, and the merchandise is very promptly delivered in the city during the early morning hours. The transfer from railway terminal to the warehouses of merchants is attended with less delay, and this service is better otherwise, than in New York. Early in the season there was complaint of much carelessness in the way butter was handled and exposed when taken from the steamer and while held at Southampton, and the packages arrived in London soiled and sometimes showing very hard usage. Department agents gave this matter attention, and before the season closed the conditions at Southampton were reported as greatly improved. Better cold storage at British ports and the more general use of refrigerator cars on British railways are improvements required for commerce of this kind.

If the transportation facilities were as good all the way from the American creamery to the European market as those afforded by the railroad lines in the United States and the trans-Atlantic steamers (when their refrigerators are available), the journey might be even longer and slower without injury to butter exported over this route. The chief danger of damage, as already stated, arises from the delays, exposure, and changes of temperature incident to the transfers on railways and those from land to water and water to land again. For perfecting this service attention should be directed to reducing the number of these transfers and improving the conditions pertaining to those which are unavoidable.

With the accommodations which were available during 1897, by the New York City route, and without material variation from usual commercial practice, this Department was able to transport butter from the creameries where made in the several States and deliver it to merchants in London in the number of days indicated as follows: Vermont, New Hampshire, Massachusetts, and Connecticut, ten or eleven days; New York, ten; Ohio, thirteen; Wisconsin, fourteen; Iowa, twelve to fifteen; Minnesota, sixteen to eighteen; Kansas and South Dakota, seventeen or eighteen. It is doubtful whether this time can be materially reduced, and fortunately a few days more or less seems to make no difference, if the butter is in a good refrigerator, on land or sea. The cost of the transportation service described, from the creameries to London, ranges from $1\frac{3}{4}$ cents to $3\frac{1}{4}$ cents per pound of butter, net weight. The least was from Ohio and the greatest from Vermont. The average from Iowa was rather less than $2\frac{1}{4}$ cents and from Kansas about $2\frac{3}{4}$ cents. These rates included transfer, cartage in New York, and the drayage on delivery in London, and were for single ton lots. The cost from the time the butter left the refrigerator car on arrival in New York until delivered to the London merchant averaged for the season almost 1 cent per pound. The extra expenses in cases of late arrival in New York and detention there in cold storage are not included. Butter shipped in carload lots secured much better rates, the difference being mainly in the tariff west of the Mississippi River. From different points in Kansas, rates of \$1.20 to \$1.40 per 100 pounds were obtained; allowing for packages this made about $1\frac{1}{2}$ cents per pound on the net weight of butter.

The butter sent to London by this Department was handled in that city in various ways. Some went to large wholesale houses and from them reached consumers through the regular course of trade, some was first taken by jobbers who placed it in varying quantities in the hands of others to sell again, and in a few cases shipments were delivered directly to retail dealers who sold the butter at once to consumers. One of the main objects of the trials was to have merchants of different classes make critical examinations of this States butter, compare it with the best butters in the market, and give opinions as to its merits. This was found to be a difficult matter, especially during the early part of the season. The wholesale merchants all had their favorite sources of supply and were unwilling to admit that any butter from this side of the Atlantic was at all equal to the English, Irish, Scandinavian, French, and colonial products. The prejudice shown against States butter was truly remarkable. All sorts of trivial faults were found with it, some of which were proved to be absolutely groundless, and the conclusion was forced that the object was to justify grading the American butter low and paying prices for it much below its actual comparative merit. These first buyers persistently refused to tell the prices at which they sold the butter, although several of them accepted it upon a definite promise to give this information. There is reason to believe that in several instances the butter was sold to retailers at prices much above the grade first assigned to it and at which the wholesalers made settlement. As the season advanced and the true quality of the butter bearing the Department brand became known in certain trade circles, it was accorded more justice and paid for at relatively better rates. The opinions of merchants were given in very general terms, yet, on the whole, they were favorable to the butter. And it was noticeable that the nearer the butter got to the consumers, the better satisfied the people were who handled it. Although paid for at second-grade rates, or lower, retailers generally placed it on sale as first-class goods and got the highest market prices for it from their customers. The opinions obtained from consumers were nearly all highly commendatory, although in most cases they believed it to be "Best Dorset" (English) or Danish butter—the favorite brands in the high-class retail trade for cured, or salted, butter in London. The prejudice against butter from the United States extends to the consumers, and hence the action of retailers in general in concealing the identity of American butter when they sold it. In a few instances, by special effort, dealers were induced to advertise and placard what was sent by the Department, as "Selected creamery butter from the United States." To sell it readily, as such, they were obliged to place the price rather lower than that of butter of greater reputation, but (by them) admitted to be no better, on sale at the same place. Twenty-four cents was a usual price for the former and 26 for the latter. In one case the States butter sold rather slowly at this comparative rate, so the merchant removed the sign and sold it unidentified at the higher price, apparently to the entire satisfaction of the consumers. One merchant who followed the wishes of the Department throughout the season closer than any other retailed the butter under its true name, and reported that he was constantly receiving inquiries from customers whom he had urged to try it for the first time, asking specifically for more of the United States butter.

Evidence was not lacking that, in contradiction of adverse opinions, some merchants really recognized the merits of the States butter. All exported by the Department had the same marking (quoted above), but no indication of the creamery or even the State from which it came. All was represented alike as "Produce of the United States." But several merchants who had received sample lots or packages from these experimental exports inquired privately of the Department agents for the addresses of the creameries at which the butter was made, with a view to corresponding with them in regard to future supplies. At least two creameries have since made direct shipments of butter to England upon orders thus received.

As already indicated, there were certain features of the trade nota-

ble throughout these London trials. The prejudice against anything
new or from a new source was such that merchants would buy the
new article, even after becoming convinced of its actual merits, only
when obtained at a price materially lower than that willingly paid
for one of established reputation and usually handled, yet no better in
quality. When the United States butter was sent to a wholesaler,
its identity was lost completely before reaching the consumer. The
dealers knew just what they were selling, but they took good care
that the consumers did not know. The custom of London retailers
in exposing their butter "stripped"—or turned out from casks, tubs,
and boxes and held in mass, with no package or marking in sight, to
be cut from in quantity to suit buyers—contributes to this conceal-
ment of the true origin of the butter. Dorsetshire has the reputation
in London of producing the best butter to be found. It occupies the
place there which "Goshen" and "Orange County" formerly held in
New York, and which "Elgin Creamery" now holds in this country—
although the latter term, as used, is actually very general, indefinite,
and deceptive. Therefore even the best Danish butter is largely
retailed in London as "Best Dorset." The retail merchant is evidently willing to deceive his customers so far as he can in this way if
his margin of profit is thereby increased. As an example, one London merchant who favored the representative of the Department by
showing his books was found to be purchasing during the same week
Danish butter at 118 shillings per hundredweight (25½ cents per
pound), Normandy butter at 106 shillings (23 cents), and United
States butter at 100 to 96 shillings (22 or 21 cents), and was retailing
all of them at the same rate of 1 shilling 2 pence (or about 28 cents)
per pound. And nearly all of it was sold as Dorset butter.

The usual commission for wholesaling butter in London is 4 per
cent besides the incidental expenses, and retailers depend upon
getting an average of 3 or 4 cents a pound for cutting out butter in
pounds and half pounds to serve to customers. Some make a better
profit, as above indicated, by using a well-selected, good article, from
a source lacking special reputation and hence bought at an advantage. Others sell butter incident to other business at little or no profit
to attract trade, as many grocers sell sugar. Although the London
wholesale butter market is subject to great fluctuations in the course
of the year, retailers endeavor to vary the price to consumers very
little. During 1897 the best salt butter sold in London at 24 to 28
cents per pound, seldom going outside these limits in the hands of
the largest retailers. There was a temporary drop to 22 cents in May
and June, but choice lots remained at this minimum only a few days.

The London wholesale market for the year presented features
familiar in this country, but less extreme, and the extremes reached
did not accord in time with those of New York. The highest London
prices realized for choicest Danish butter were 25 and 26 cents in Jan-

uary, September, November, and December, and the lowest was 20½ cents in May and June. The average for the year on this grade was between 23 and 24 cents. In New York creamery extras were highest in February and March, temporarily, and in October, November, and December, and lowest in May, the range being from 14 to 24 cents, and the average 19 cents per pound. For three months during the summer Danish butter stood from 5 to 6 cents higher in London than creamery extras in New York; this was the favorable time for export, although States butter was quoted for some weeks in London at about 18 cents. During certain weeks in the spring creamery extras brought nearly as much in New York as best Danish did in London, and in October the one actually sold at a higher price in New York than the other did in London. The export season was therefore short, and was delayed at the outset and checked at the close by home conditions. The rise began simultaneously in the two great markets early in August, with a mutual reaction in September, but after that the advance was steadier and longer continued in this country. The public quotations of States butter in London were 5 to 7 cents below those for Danish all through the earlier months of the year and until fresh arrivals from Australian and New Zealand creameries ceased in April. Then the gap began to close and in August and September it had been reduced more than one-half. Before the end of September, however, American creamery butter was worth as much in New York as it would bring in London, and exports ceased. These conditions were plainly detrimental to establishing a continuous foreign trade. Some of these facts and relations are shown graphically in the accompanying diagram of butter prices in London and New York during 1897. (See Appendix XII, p. 135.)

The question of profit was not regarded as of special importance in connection with these experimental exports. Information was the prime consideration. Yet the financial results were not disregarded. Commercial conditions were adhered to as closely as practicable and profit was sought so far as compatible with the more important object. But circumstances incident to the trials were unfavorable to gains from the purely business standpoint. The quantities of butter handled were so small as to be unattractive to buyers, and at the same time the incidental expense per pound was unduly large. The shipments were irregular and successive sales made through different channels, so that the advantages of a regular supply and demand were lost. In order to accomplish the main purpose of the work, expenses were incurred which would not occur in the usual course of trade.

The purchases for these exports were made during the seven months from April to October, inclusive, at prices ranging from 13 cents per pound, paid in Kansas in July, to 25 cents, paid in Connecticut in October. The sales in London ranged from 15¼ cents in May, to 21¾ cents in October. Butter sent in rather more than half of the several

10317——7

shipments was sold at more or less profit, and this was the result with almost half of the different lots of butter. Notwithstanding the unfavorable conditions mentioned, butter from Minnesota and Ohio sold at a net profit of 2¼ cents per pound, from Kansas at 2 cents profit, and from Wisconsin at about 1 cent. The average cost of these lots at the creameries where made, at current market rates, was 14¼ cents, and the average selling price of the same in London was 18¼ cents. (The fractions stated are not exact, but approximately correct.)

Every lot of butter obtained in New England, as well as one lot from New York, was sold in London at a decided loss. This was due partly to the disproportionate cost of transportation to New York, already noted, but more particularly to the higher prices which the creameries of this region are able to maintain because of the local markets for their product. It was plain enough, in advance, that butter which during the summer was in active demand at 20, 22, and 25 cents a pound at the creamery door could not be exported at a profit.

On the other hand, all the butter bought at creameries in Ohio or States farther west, at the current wholesale rates for "extras," was sold at a net profit in England, with the exception of a few lots at the two ends of the export season, when the market relations were known to be unfavorable to such transactions.

All considered, the operations of the year may be regarded as reasonably satisfactory in a business way, as well as otherwise, while at the same time a number of points were developed where greater economy could be practiced another season.

Following are a number of extracts from written and verbal statements made by merchants, retail dealers, consumers, and agents of the Department regarding the butter sent to London in the experiments of 1897, and these include some comparisons with other butters found in that market during the same season:

STATEMENTS FROM WHOLESALE MERCHANTS.

We have examined the packages of butter ex S. S. *St. Paul* and are favorably impressed with the quality of all. The boxes and tubs of 56 pounds net weight or more are the style of packing most likely to command the attention of buyers here, and we should recommend strict adherence thereto in fair proportions of each.

The American trade has been spoiled hitherto by inferior butter. United States butter must now make a good name by degrees; the quality must be high and uniform, the supply regular.

This last lot I think a perfect salt butter and very suitable for the English market. I have no doubt it would find a ready sale if it could be sold (wholesale) delivered to the tradesman during the spring and summer months at 88s. to 102s. per hundredweight [19 to 22 cents per pound] and in the autumn and winter months from 108s. to 124s. per hundredweight [23¼ to 27 cents per pound].

We have carefully inspected your American butter and find the quality and condition better than any of the kind we have yet seen, but it contains too much liquor, which runs when defrosted.

We have carefully and repeatedly examined the American butter, assisted by expert buyers, and all are of the opinion that the boxes and pails are suitable for the London trade. The butter is well packed, but contains too much water. This causes rapid deterioration directly the frost is gone, and in a normal temperature the water runs from the butter.

I have inspected samples of butter and consider the quality to be very fine. There is but one fault that I can find, and that is that the firkins contain too great a percentage of water. I am sure that this class of butter would be taken up very largely by the consumers in London and the suburbs if it could be shipped in large quantities regularly throughout the season and the quality kept equal to this lot. I should like to take up 2,000 to 3,000 packages per month for my customers.

My opinion of the States butter sent to me in June is in every way satisfactory for our London trade, both in quality and color. I do not hesitate in saying that if the manufacture of it can be kept to this standard it will make a very successful departure in the supply for this market. I shall be glad to receive further consignments.

I am very pleased with the general turnout of these American butters which I have had from you. With more attention to details heretofore referred to, there would be no difficulty in creating a good demand for butter of this description, and prices obtainable would be equal to finest Australian, New Zealand, and Canadian butter.

STATEMENTS FROM RETAIL DEALERS.

The package of American butter which I got from the lot you indicated to me was found in every way satisfactory. By this I mean that the butter was well made, carefully packed, and seemed possessed of the very best keeping quality. The flavor was most agreeable, and the amount of salt just about right to suit the general English taste. I truly believe that a standard of butter as good as this would bring the very highest prices on the London market.

There was a brightness of flavor, a certain bouquet, about that American butter which assured me that it had been churned—may I say the milk set and churned?—in an atmosphere pure and wholesome, and imparting to it a dewy freshness not always found in the very highest priced butters. Great credit is due to somebody for preparing such an excellent article, and it affords me great pleasure to say so.

The quality is only a good second. It does not compare favorably with the French, Danish, and colonial butter, the flavor being much poorer and the texture weaker. It also contains too much water and salt. Tested after being exposed out of the packages for two days, the quality has been found to have become impaired, and this shows that the quantity of liquor contained in the butter causes it to deteriorate rapidly upon exposure to the normal atmosphere.

For the London trade it savors too much of the Irish "twang," is a little too salt, and the color too high. The best standard of butter for you to imitate, if I may say so, is the finest Danish, which gives satisfaction nearly the whole year round.

The sample of butter I consider remarkably good, grass flavor, and equal to the "Best Dorset" in style and make, and if put on our market would undoubtedly meet with a ready sale.

This is, indeed, the best States butter I have tasted in England, but still there is room for improvement. A little less water and a trifle more salt would be in the right direction.

The lot of butter received from you I was very much pleased with, being just the class of butter which is appreciated by my customers. As you have asked my individual opinion, I beg to say that I consider the texture, coloring, and salting can not be improved upon and the flavor is A1; in fact, I regret not being certain of obtaining further supplies of this butter.

You promised me the first parcel of States butter you had in like the last; I should have some. I hope you have not forgotten, as my customers still continue to ask for it. If you have any now, please let me have three boxes tomorrow. If you have not same quality as before, do not send any. United States butter, as a rule, comes very inferior and all goes wrong after being exposed in the air a few hours.

Messrs. H. Brothers purchased box No. VI, Lot I, at 90s. per hundredweight [19½ cents per pound] and retailed the same at 1 shilling a pound (24 or 25 cents). They considered this butter to be fair in quality, though lacking in body. At the same time they purchased other United States butter at 88s. and Irish butter at 104s. The United States butter they regarded as rather better than the Irish. All three of these butters they retailed at the same price—1 shilling—being the highest price at which butter was then sold to their line of trade.

STATEMENTS FROM CONSUMERS.

The sample of United States butter was excellent. It came, saw, and conquered. It was such a decided success that if you can furnish me with the address of a place where it can be regularly procured, the dealer can be sure of one customer.

Referring to the small package of American butter lately procured on your suggestion, both Mrs. C. and I thought the butter very good, although a little more salt than we are accustomed to using. It arrived in splendid condition and was beautifully packed. As regards the packing, however, you are doubtless aware that in small households it is the custom to buy butter in small quantities, probably in pound pats, as by this means it can be obtained more frequently and consequently fresher. I should think this 5-pound package would be suitable for hotels, clubs, and large establishments.

In regard to the United States butter, of which you put me in the way of getting a small package lately, won't you please tell me where I can purchase more of it?

I purchased a small quantity of American butter from Messrs. H. Brothers. It is very good, similar to Irish creamery butter I have used, but I think the quality superior. It is rather light in color, otherwise, in my opinion, it is excellent.

STATEMENTS FROM REPRESENTATIVES OF THE DEPARTMENT OF AGRICULTURE.

Butter from the United States has not a good reputation at the present time in the London market. Consequently the same class of butter as the Danish, or even if better in quality, will not bring so high a price on account of the excellent reputation of the latter. Of course, this applies mainly to the wholesale trade, as the butter entirely loses its identity when sold to the retailer. Salt butter is, as a rule, retailed in London as "Best Dorset," irrespective of its actual place of manufacture.

So much inferior butter from the United States has been sent to England that some of the dealers laugh at us as soon as we mention United States butter to them. Consequently we have had much difficulty in getting some dealers to handle the butter at all. Had we been trying to sell the butter outright to them they would have had nothing to do with us.

Some dealers have objected to handling our butter, fearing, on the one hand, it might not suit their customers, and, on the other, thinking it might please them so well that they, the dealers, would be embarrassed by being unable to procure a further supply of the same, or other equally good.

These people dislike very much to acknowledge that the United States butter is better than that which has a good reputation, because, while not so admitted, they are able to buy it at a low rate wholesale and then get full price for it when sold to the consumer. Yet I have repeatedly compared the United States butter with the Danish and "Best Dorset" with friends who are in the butter trade and have invariably found the butter of the trial shipments superior in quality, flavor, and body.

The butter trade of London is a very queer one. Even the largest consumers have only a daily supply left at their doors. This is done to save the cost of private refrigerators and ice, and is one reason why large dealers object to the family-sized packages. Many people only purchase a half pound at a time. The hotels and restaurants have contracts with retail houses to supply them with a certain quantity of prints ready to put on the table every day. Still, I think the oblong and square boxes, holding from 3 to 7 pounds, would be very useful in a suburban trade where it was not convenient to have butter brought to the door every day.

The butter in the cases of carriers, in half-pound prints, was of a very good quality, the only objection being the fact of being in such prints. Retailers customarily buy the half firkin, or 56-pound box, and divide the butter up into pound or half-pound rolls, wrapping each roll with parchment paper bearing the dealer's name and address. I firmly believe, however, that with a little time and work spent upon the introduction of the print package, it could be made to sell largely in the London and suburban market, provided, of course, that the package is not too expensive.

The butter now coming in the trial shipments is undoubtedly better in quality than most of the Danish and Dorset—just as good in flavor and much better in body.

The fact of the —— stores, as well as —— & Son, selling this butter at 1s. and 1s. 1d. [about 26 cents] a pound, which are the very highest current retail prices, proves beyond doubt that the butter was of excellent quality when made, was well packed, and arrived in London in fine condition.

Messrs. —— and ——, as well as the two houses already named, told me that this United States butter compared favorably with the "Best Dorset." The latter is the best salt butter on the London market, some of it being made in Dorsetshire, but most of it coming from Denmark.

Wherever possible, we have ascertained from the retailers the prices obtained for the butter sold from our different lots, and find that they realized the full price for the best butter, 1s. and 1s. 1d. a pound, according to the locality of the store. This proves conclusively that if the creameries of the United States will put up the same grade of salt butter, and are able to guarantee the weight and quality, it will not be long before such butter will bring the highest price in the London wholesale market. But it must be sold squarely, in the right way, and the returns not eaten up by excessive charges.

In my opinion, if the United States butter is honestly made, properly packed, carefully transported, and then fairly handled in this country (Great Britain), it will soon be able to compete with the best Danish or any other first-class butter that is sent to British markets.

Many butter dealers in London are very anxious, owing to our efforts here this year, to handle United States butter; but in order to do so successfully and build up a remunerative trade they must be guaranteed a regular supply of butter of uniform good quality. Those who had handled butter from the States previous to these Government consignments complain that it has not been uniform, and that no reliability could be placed on the comparative merits of successive consignments. This has injured the trade much, and fear of this prevents building it up. These difficulties could be overcome by the Department supervising the butter and cheese export trade in a way similar to that done for live cattle, dressed beef, and packed meats. If all butter exported could be examined by an expert inspector and given a Government certificate of purity and quality, it would give such butter a standing in the markets of Great Britain and enhance its value to a great extent.

Box No. 7—E I retained for trial at my house. This box was opened November 13, 1897, and I supplied a family of six persons until February 16, 1898, or about three months. During this time it was kept in a larder without ice, and remained sweet, firm, and good throughout. If we had been using butter purchased at the retail stores, such butter being either Danish, Dorset, or Australian—the best salt butter on the London market—I know from my previous accounts that we would have consumed 67½ pounds. There was but 57½ pounds in the States box. I consider this another strong argument in favor of our United States butter, and also proof that such butter does not contain too much water, but is actually firmer, more solid, than most other salt butter sold in London.

Comments are necessary upon these expressions of opinion, else they might be misleading.

English dealers generally seemed to consider it necessary to find some fault with butter from the United States, and as most of them were already convinced that butter from this country was, as a rule, soft and briny, their criticism was very apt to include these points. Several of them referred to other butters as having the desirable "body" which ours lacked. But the facts, determined with an exactness far beyond the power of human judgment, did not sustain these complaints.

The following is a tabular comparison of the water and fat found in the butters embraced in the Department trial exports as the result of chemical analyses made in this country and in London, with the same facts as to the composition of selected lots of the best butter to be found in London from nine foreign sources. The highest and lowest results are given in each case, as well as the averages obtained:

Comparative composition of butter, United States and foreign.

Butter: Where made and where analyzed.	Water.			Butter fat.		
	Lowest.	Highest.	Average.	Lowest.	Highest.	Average.
United States:	*Per cent.*	*Per cent.*	*Per cent.*	*Per cent.*	*Per cent.*	*Per cent.*
American analyses	8.12	12.87	10.85	84.21	89.49	86.84
London analyses	8.08	11.73	10.13	86.71	90.09	88.06
Foreign, United States analyses	8.63	15.50	12.40	78.59	89.27	84.57

These figures show at a glance the much greater dryness of the butter from the United States, especially when determined by the London official analyst, and the superior richness of the States in pure butter fat. Only one lot of the export butter showed less than

85 per cent fat and none reached 13 per cent water by home analyses.
The English analyst reported only three cases above 11 per cent of
water, and made an average of over 88 per cent fat. Among the foreign butters, half were above 13 per cent water and only four reached
88 per cent of fat. The produce sent over by the Department, therefore, gave its buyers (according to English tests) three and a half
pounds more of actual butter in every hundredweight than was found
in the best foreign articles. The English Dorset, regarded as a standard, was found carrying almost 14 per cent water (which is not excessive) and only 84½ per cent fat. The Danish, constantly referred to
as a pattern, was found by the Department to average much better—
10.45 per cent water and 86.79 per cent fat; but this is better than
given by Danish authorities, who claim the water content of their
export butter ranges from 12 to 16 per cent and averages about 14½
per cent. There are other points for judging butter on a chemical
basis. The foreign matter in butter is represented by the casein, or
curd; of this, the less the better. The foreign samples examined
contained from 0.48 to 2.40 per cent of casein (with sugar, albumen,
etc.) and averaged 1.03 per cent. The States butter exported contained 0.33 to 1.30 per cent and averaged 0.81 per cent. Besides
this, none of the United States butter contained preservatives of any
kind, while all of the foreign butters, excepting the English, Danish,
Finnish, and New Zealand, were "borated" more or less, some quite
heavily. Yet some of the foreign butter was exceptionally well made;
and the Danish and French particularly, even although in some
cases testing pretty high in water, appeared to be dry and had a texture or body superior to most of that included in the experimental
exports.

As to the degree of color preferred for butter, the opinions of merchants and consumers in London differ materially. It is evident that
the London market does not want its winter butter colored much, but
in summer it accepts the "natural June color" of grass butter without complaint. On the whole, the conditions in this respect seem to
be about the same as in New York. It was noticeable that in the
lots of foreign butter brought from London as representative of the
preference of that market several were decidedly deeper in tint than
the average of the best in New York at the same time. The Danish
packages were included among those having the most color. Where
complaints are made in London of too much color in American butter, it may be generally attributed to sheer prejudice and not true
market judgment.

Opinions as to salt differ still more and naturally vary with individual taste. Three or four English merchants examining the same
lot of States butter separately gave as many different judgments as
to the salting. And the same critic declared one lot of butter too salt
and another too fresh, when the records of the making, sustained by

chemical analysis, proved the former actually to contain less salt than the latter. The facts as to the London market judgment in this particular seem to be that the very best butter should have no salt, and that the more salt butter contains the lower the grade to which it is assigned. Yet if butter is to have any salt, from one-fourth to two-thirds of an ounce per pound will be accepted, as tastes vary, and the average preference seems to be for half an ounce, or from 2½ to 3 per cent of salt remaining in the butter as placed in market.

Grading butter closely, or scoring it upon a scale of points, is a matter of individual judgment, but to secure figures which have any value for purposes of comparison, the work must be done by an expert. Such a comparison of the different lots sent to London by the Department, with the best from other countries found in that market, was much to be desired, made from the British standpoint of perfection. As already explained, the expert necessary for the purpose was not to be found in London. In place of such a comparison we only have the general expressions of merchants; those which have been quoted are in most cases very indefinite and contain no satisfactory comparisons. The few cases given and others in which comparisons were made, upon being merged in a "composite" form, seem to place the best States butter as second to the Danish, Swedish, and best French, and no more than equal to the best Irish, Australian, and Canadian. Yet a good many persons were entirely satisfied with our butter, and the evidence is conclusive that it was retailed to consumers in nearly all cases at the very highest prices for butter containing any salt.

The definite lessons from these transactions are not numerous, but the following conclusions and recommendations may be deduced, including some repetitions from the foregoing report upon the work:

The demand for butter of good quality in Great Britain and the steady increase in this demand offers a market for large quantities of the best creamery product of the United States.

The relative rates have been such for a number of years in the two countries that during the greater portion of every year it is probable that first-class butter can be profitably exported from America to England.

For a time, butter from the United States will be most acceptable in British markets to take the place of the large arrivals of fresh "Colonial" or Australian butter, which begin to fall off in April and do not recur until October. But this is a secondary position commercially and should not satisfy American ambition. There is no reason why butter from this country should not compete successfully with Canadian and Australian butter in the markets of the United Kingdom at all seasons of the year. Moreover, if the supply be made regular and the quality brought to a standard which may be easily attained and maintained, States butter is certain soon to take place, in British estimation, as the equal of Danish and other supplies now ranking first.

The disadvantage of distance and the difficulties of transportation can be overcome. At present the facilities are better for delivering butter in Great Britain from Canada than from the United States. Effort will be necessary to improve the conditions in this respect, as already explained.

The local requirements of markets in different parts of England and Scotland will have to be further studied and care taken to prepare butter especially to meet these varied tastes, in order to insure success. As a rule, the British demand a butter freer from brine, more waxy in texture, firmer, or "better in body" than the average "extras" of the American creamery. For export butter, more time and care in making and packing are essential; less attention to securing a "quick" high flavor and more attention to good body. The flavor may be mild, rather slow in development, but should be "clean" and uniform month after month.

It seems probable that pasteurizing cream and the use of pure cultures for ripening will be well adapted to making successful export butter, and probably necessary where special skill in cream-ripening is lacking. The color in British markets is permitted to vary somewhat with the season, but very little artificial coloring is desirable at any time, and natural grass yellow is generally regarded as too deep. Some English markets prefer butter very pale, or a light shade of straw color. In salt there is almost as much difference in taste as in our domestic markets, with a tendency there, as here, to use butter with less and less salt.

For packages, nothing is now so acceptable as the rectangular or block form, modified by a slight taper to the four sides. The top is thus a little larger and the contents can be easily turned out ("stripped") in good shape. This pyramidal form has been adopted by the best Irish creameries. Next in favor stands the cubical box, used for two or three years in Australia, Canada, and the United States. Then follows the oblong box from New Zealand. All these packages should contain, when sold, 56 pounds, or a full half hundredweight of butter, but should not run to 57 pounds or over. The Danish kiel, or cask, is in special favor in Great Britain, simply because it is recognized as meaning good Danish butter. The chief objection to the American creamery tub has been already stated; also the fact that British buyers will not quarrel over shape and style of package, or even its size, if once convinced that the butter in it suits them.

Packages for export should be strong enough to stand a long journey and some hard usage; lumber five-eighths of an inch thick is none too heavy for cubical 56-pound boxes, or others similar. All packages should be well finished, with tight joints and well-fitted covers. Merchants prefer covers fastened with screws, but these must not exceed six in number, as customs officers are impatient, and where covers can not be easily removed they break open the packages to be inspected. A better fitting cover for boxes than heretofore used, and some simple but efficient fastener, like the tub clip or fastener, are needed package improvements. Linings, sufficient and strong for protection, are essential. Burlap bags to cover packages, whether boxes or tubs, are advised, especially for exports made in hot weather.

Shrinkage must be provided for. The usual loss is about one-half of one per cent on the net weight; the range of loss one-fourth to three-fourths of one per cent. The Department investigations were not conclusive on this point, but if 57 pounds of weighed butter of suitable texture are packed into an export box, the net weight in any market of Great Britain, within a month's time, will be pretty certain to exceed 56 pounds and avoid allowance being claimed for short weight.

Success will doubtless reward the enterprise of anyone who will export fine butter in pound prints or convenient small packages for delivery unbroken to consumers, and press it persistently in London and other good English markets, but the desired end will be slow to reach. In such a venture it will be necessary to allow for shrinkage of weight on every small package, roll or print, as the market laws require full weight in all commodities at retail and are strictly enforced.   .

Export butter, if it is to have suitable transportation facilities and to be retailed when two to three weeks old, should be well chilled, but not frozen, before shipped from the creamery, and then carried to destination at a temperature held between 31° and 45° F. Care should be taken to avoid a rise above 50° at any time before exposure for retail.

For all lots less than a carload, special arrangements should be made in advance for proper attention by agents of transportation companies, to avoid delay and exposure of butter at transfer points; and unless the dispatch companies will perform like service efficiently at the place of export, and foreign consignees are of proved reliability, prudence demands the assistance of experienced export agents or brokers at the seaboard terminals. Experienced exporters must continue to conduct the bulk of our export trade for a long time to come.

It is evident that successfully to introduce fine creamery butter from the United States and establish a demand for it in British markets, with full recognition of its merits, there must be a considerable period of persistent effort, during which there will be some unsatisfactory results. English merchants of standing and in control of a reliable high-class trade must be interested in the effort and induced to act as agents for States butter. These agents must then be regularly supplied with butter uniform in quality and quantity and suited to the markets they represent for seven or eight months in the year. The desired end will be sooner attained if the supply is continued throughout the year, whether or not the returns are satisfactory for all the months. No regular demand can be built up unless retail merchants of a desirable class can be continuously supplied, so as to secure and hold customers for the new line of goods; and the conditions must be constantly insisted upon that the butter shall be always marked, known, and sold as produce of the United States. In short, States butter will have to be introduced to Great Britain by enterprising, persistent, long-continued effort, supplying only the best, and always as States butter, just as a place for American beef was made in those same markets.

The Department can not establish this foreign trade in high-class butter or even commence it; but it may do something toward ascertaining the conditions which control such trade, present and prospective, and assist in making them known to many interested parties.

The results of the trials made during the year 1897 appear to justify a repetition of the experimental shipments in 1898 upon an enlarged scale and in a broader field, to include, besides butter, other perishable farm products which this country has to sell.

APPENDIX I.

EXPORTS OF BUTTER FROM THE UNITED STATES.

[Selected and representative fiscal years, ending June 30.]

Years.	Pounds.	Years.	Pounds.	Years.	Pounds.
1790	470,440	1870	2,019,288	1888	10,455,651
1800	1,822,341	1873	4,518,844	1890	29,743,042
1810	1,620,538	1875	6,300,827	1891	15,187,114
1820	1,039,024	1877	21,527,242	1892	15,047,216
1830	1,728,212	1878	21,837,117	1893	8,920,107
1840	3,755,993	1879	38,248,016	1894	11,812,092
1850	3,876,175	1880	39,236,658	1895	5,596,812
1860	7,640,914	1882	14,794,305	1896	10,373,913
1865	21,559,892	1885	21,683,148	1897	31,345,224

Pounds.

For the twelve months ending December 31, 1896.. 27,220,218
For the twelve months ending December 31, 1897.. 30,914,783

APPENDIX II.

ANNUAL EXPORTS OF IMITATION BUTTER AND OLEO OIL FROM THE UNITED STATES.

Years.	Imitation butter.	Oleo oil.	Years.	Imitation butter.	Oleo oil.
	Pounds.	*Pounds.*		*Pounds.*	*Pounds.*
1884	1,537,682	37,785,159	1891	1,986,743	80,231,035
1885	761,938	37,120,217	1892	1,610,837	91,581,708
1886	928,053	27,729,885	1893	3,479,322	113,939,363
1887	834,574	45,712,965	1894	3,898,950	123,295,865
1888	1,729,327	30,146,595	1895	10,100,897	78,098,873
1889	2,192,047	28,102,534	1896	6,063,699	103,276,756
1890	2,535,926	68,218,098	1897	4,864,351	113,505,152

APPENDIX III.

IMPORTS OF BUTTER INTO THE UNITED KINGDOM.

[For the countries named and for the stated calendar year.]

Countries.	1886.	1890.	1894.	1895.	1896.	1897.
	Cwt.	*Cwt.*	*Cwt.*	*Cwt.*	*Cwt.*	*Cwt.*
United States	42,390	84,553	29,996	66,982	141,553	154,198
Canada	31,522	24,318	20,887	38,949	88,357	109,408
Denmark	400,556	824,740	1,102,493	1,162,770	1,228,784	1,334,723
Other countries	1,069,098	1,094,097	1,421,459	1,557,011	1,579,253	1,619,475
Total	1,543,566	2,027,717	2,574,835	2,825,662	3,037,947	3,217,801

APPENDIX IV.

LIST OF SHIPMENTS, WITH DATES OF EXPORT AND NAMES OF CREAMERIES AT WHICH BUTTER WAS MADE EXPRESSLY FOR THESE TRIALS.

Export.	Date.	Creameries.
I.	May 5	College Creamery, State Agricultural College, Ames, Iowa.
		Diamond Creameries, Monticello, Iowa.
		Hillside Creamery, Cornish, N. H.
II.	May 26	College Creamery, Ames, Iowa.
		Jersey Hill Creamery, Ryegate, Vt.
III.	June 16	Star Lake Creamery, Strout, Minn.
		Conway Creamery, Conway, Mass.
IV.	July 7	Hesston Creamery, Newton, Kans.
V.	July 28	Mount Pleasant Cooperative Creamery, Mount Pleasant, Ohio.
		Bentley & Son's Creamery, Circleville, Ohio.
		Jensen Creamery Company, Beloit, Kans.
VI.	Aug. 25	Sennett Creamery, Sennett, N. Y.
		Edmunds Creamery, Sherman, N. Y.
		Hilton & Nimmo's Creamery, Knapps, N. Y.
VII.	Sept. 15	Hoard's Creameries, Fort Atkinson, Wis.
VIII.	Oct. 6	College Creamery, Ames, Iowa.
		Vernon Creamery, Rockville, Conn.
IX.	Oct. 27	Big Stone Creamery, Big Stone City, S. Dak.
		Star Lake Creamery, Strout, Minn.

APPENDIX V.

EXAMPLE OF REPORT MADE UPON EVERY LOT OF BUTTER PREPARED FOR AND EXPORTED BY THE DEPARTMENT OF AGRICULTURE.

From College Creamery, Ames, Iowa.   Lot A, of Export VIII, October:

1. The cows supplying milk to creamery are mostly grades.   Shorthorn blood predominates.
2. During the time milk was produced from which this butter was made the cows were at pasture and without additional feed.
3. The whole milk is hauled daily to the creamery by the producers, the average distance hauled by the patrons being about five miles.
4. The cream is obtained by passing the milk through a De Laval separator immediately after reaching the creamery, at a temperature of 85° F.
5. The average per cent of fat in the milk received is 4, and in the cream, as separated, 23.
6. The cream is cooled to 75° F. and held from twelve to eighteen hours for ripening; the temperature meantime varies from 69° to 75°.
7. A portion of the cream was pasteurized, and to that, after cooling down, a homemade skim-milk "starter" was added.
8. Mann's test was applied to determine acidity of the cream, and the degrees noted as shown in churning record below.
9. No coloring matter was used.   One-half ounce of salt used per pound of butter.
10. Working: The butter was worked two minutes, incorporating the salt, then allowed to stand in cool room for eighteen hours, worked a second time four minutes, and packed at once.
11. The skim-milk from separator was tested and showed barely a trace of fat. The buttermilk was tested and showed one-tenth of 1 per cent of fat.
12. Very warm weather prevailed during the days this butter was made—about 70° F. in the morning, and from 85° to 90° during the midday hours.

Churning report on butter made for Export VIII.

Information required.	Number and date of churning.		
	First, Sept. 27.	Second, Sept. 29.	Third, Sept. 30.
Milk separated at degrees F	85	85	85
Per cent of fat in cream	25	20	23
Cream ripened at degrees F	75	75	73
Acidity of cream at churning	87	87.2	88
Cream churned at degrees F	52	52	52
Buttermilk, temperature when drawn, degrees F	54	55	54
Length of time in churning, minutes	85	25	70
Butter washed, number of times	1	1	1
Wash water, temperature, degrees F	46	46	47
Butter worked, times	2	2	2

Description of packages as filled:

First churning: Tubs, A 1, A 2; spruce boxes, A 7, A 8; poplar boxes, A 13, A 14.

Second churning: Tubs, A 3, A 4; spruce boxes, A 9, A 10; poplar boxes, A 15, A 16.

Third churning: Tubs, A 5, A 6; spruce boxes, A 11, A 12, poplar boxes, A 17, A 18.

All packages of third churning, butter made from pasteurized cream.
Packages parchment lined: A 1, A 2, A 9, A 10, A 17, and A 18.
Packages lined with paraffine coating: A 3, A 4, A 11, A 12, A 13, A 14.
Packages covered with burlap sacks: Tubs, 1, 3, 5; boxes, 7, 9, 11, 13, 15, 17.
Weights, gross and net, of several packages as per list attached.
Butter well chilled in packages until October 1.   Delivered to refrigerator car
on Chicago and Northwestern Railroad at Ames, 7 a. m.; waybill 15; Pennsylvania
Railroad car 41241; train No. 38; weather, cloudy; temperature, 69° F.

G. L. McKAY, *Superintendent Creamery.*

AMES, IOWA, *October 2, 1897.*

APPENDIX VI.

PASTEURIZING CREAM FOR BUTTER.

INTRODUCTION.

In connection with preparing butter especially suited to export, the question
arose as to the efficacy of pasteurizing cream for the purpose of improving the
keeping quality of the butter and also of producing an article more uniform in
texture and flavor.   Upon inquiry it was learned that, although several creameries
in different States had made some experiments in pasteurization both of the whole
milk and the cream, none had fully adopted the system or acquired experience
which gave definite results.

In the course of correspondence on the subject with different parties, the late
J. L. Hoffman, president of the Hesston Creamery Company, of Newton, Kans.
(also at that time president of the Kansas State Dairy Association), offered the
use of his creamery, with its supplies and working force, for any experiments in
pasteurizing which this Department might wish to conduct.   This location, in a
new creamery district, far distant from large markets either at home or abroad,
and subject to extremely hot weather during its active butter-producing season,
presented conditions particularly favorable for such experiments.

Accordingly, Mr. J. H. Monrad, of Winnetka, Ill., special field agent for the
Dairy Division, was detailed to proceed to Newton, Kans., and supervise during
the month of June a series of experiments in making butter for export from cream
pasteurized for the purpose.   Mr. Monrad approved the selection of the Hesston
Creamery because it seemed desirable to make the experiments under normal conditions at a creamery of average character.   If pasteurization proved desirable
under such circumstances, it would emphasize the usefulness of the practice more
than if much better results were obtained from experiments at a carefully managed dairy school or at some new and perfectly equipped creamery.

Considering season, place, and general conditions, it was not expected to make
butter of the highest quality, but a good article was sought, suitable for export,
and opportunity to make fair comparisons in the quality when fresh, and in the
keeping properties, of considerable quantities of butter made from the same lot of
cream, under good control, partly treated by usual factory methods and partly
pasteurized.

Recognizing the difficulty of obtaining cold water in Kansas for cooling cream
at separating stations and keeping it at a proper temperature during the haul to
the central factory, Mr. Monrad had made the original suggestion at the State
dairy convention at Abilene (1896) that it might be expedient to heat cream at
stations immediately after separating, or to separate at a high temperature and
haul the cream hot to the main factory, where pasteurization might be completed.
Mr. Monrad was authorized, in connection with the other work proposed, to make
a practical test of this suggestion.

The full report of this work follows. Although the bulk of butter made in these experiments passed at once out of his possession, was shipped to New York, and thence exported to London, the data regarding it was preserved and furnished to Mr. Monrad to embody in his report.

It is not felt that the results of these experiments in Kansas are at all conclusive, but they constitute an instructive contribution to experience in pasteurizing for making butter during the early stages of this practice in America.

H. E. A.

Record of Experiments in Pasteurization made at the Hesston Creamery, Newton, Kans., June, 1897.

By J. H. MONRAD,

Special Agent of Dairy Division, Bureau of Animal Industry.

Pasteurizing cream for butter-making can not in itself be properly called an experiment, as the practical benefit of this system was long ago proved in Denmark and elsewhere. But the work to be here reported was truly experimental under the conditions which existed and bore upon it.

My first duty was to select the apparatus needed and set it up at the creamery. From previous study of the subject, I at once discarded all tank heaters and sought "continuous" appliances as being the only ones practical for creamery use. Of these but two were found on the market, being made and sold by A. H. Barber & Co. and by the De Laval Separator Company. Each firm generously placed an outfit at my service, free of charge. These were forwarded to Newton, and I followed, reaching that place the 8th of June. Before reporting the experiment I give herewith a short description of the creamery and its regular system of butter-making.

THE NEWTON CREAMERY.

The milk is taken from an elevated driveway and dumped into the weigh can, which is on a small platform, high enough to run it into the milk vat. The latter is on a lower and larger platform in the separator room; on the same platform is also the cream vat for receiving the cream from the ten skimming stations connected with this factory.

From the receiving vat a 1¼-inch pipe 8 feet long conducts the milk to the milk heater and thence to the separators. There are two separators of the Alpha No. 1 pattern, which are on the same level as the cream room. The door to the latter is near the separators and the cream is carried in 10-gallon cans to the ripening vats in that room.

In the separator room is the wash tank, the 15-horsepower engine, and a No. 3 Barber refrigerator compressor. The boiler room, with a 20-horsepower boiler, is on a lower level, and still lower is the cellar. Here is the churn room with two combined churns and workers (a Disbrow and a Fargo) and also a Mason worker. Also in this basement and under the cream room is the printing room, 14 by 12 feet; an ante-storage room, 14 by 8 feet; and the refrigerator, 14 by 15 feet—all cooled with direct expansion coils.

In the churn room the floor is of fine flagstones, but not being laid in cement some of the smell in the room may have been caused by seepage into the sand on which the stones rest. In one corner is a sink hole from which the buttermilk, as well as washings, etc., are pumped into two large elevated tanks outside; from these the washings are hauled and scattered over a field, the city authorities having prohibited the use of an adjacent sluggish creek as means of drainage. This is not only a very unlucky situation, but an expensive arrangement, and the owners have a very difficult problem to solve. Indeed, the solution may lose the town of Newton the creamery, with its appendix of a large cash trade from the patrons, as it would be cheaper to build anew elsewhere than to provide a private sewer for a long distance.

Above the churn room and just opposite and on the same level as the separators is a storage room and in it the pump which raises the drainage to the outside tanks. This room was the only space available for the pasteurizing apparatus, and the smell from the pump was kept down by repeated rinsings with limewater. The creamery company kindly allowed me to pull down the partition between this and the separating room, giving better access and more fresh air.

The cream room, 15 by 35 feet, is newly built, well insulated, and has a brine tank, 6 by 11 feet and 30 inches deep, suspended close under the ceiling. The temperature of this room was from 52° to 55°[1] during the week, running up to 60° or 62° Sunday evening when the compressor had not run after 12 o'clock Saturday night. In this room are ten vats U-formed, made of tinned copper; they are 10½ feet long and 2 feet wide and hold about 1,500 pounds. There are no cooling jackets to the vats, and, cooling by air being too slow, ice is put directly into the cream. The vats are placed one a little higher than the other, so that enough slant may be given to the conductor which leads the cream to the churns below. A rotary pump circulates the brine (when desired) through a Bair copper cooler, and over this the cream flows between the receiving tank and the vats in the cream room.

In one test, the cream, flowing at the rate of about 1,200 pounds per hour, was cooled 10°, but the company has secured two more coolers of same size and will thus have better control of cream received from outlying stations.

The system of working is as follows: At 6 a. m. the day force arrives. W. S. Andis takes charge of the boiler, engine, compressor, and the separators. S. W. Hank receives the milk, which comes in slowly at first, and so much so, indeed, that it is often half past 8 before separating can begin. In the cellar the chief butter maker, D. S. Brandt, prepares for work in the printing room, while his son makes shipping boxes, and in the churn room J. R. Lewellen and N. P. Reed take turns at churning and helping in the printing room. As a rule, the churns are full of cream in the morning and often one has been already churned by the night man, C. S. Stouffer.

Let us first follow the work of Mr. Andis. He starts the deep-well pump, which gives an alkaline, salty water, and runs this over the Bair cream cooler, filling one of the cream vats with water at 52' or 54°, ready to be used for washing the butter by running it into the churns by the cream conductor. He starts the separators and carries the cream into the vat, where it is allowed to cool, ripening without a "starter." About 11 o'clock the separating is finished and then he cleans his separators. In the afternoon he helps Mr. Hank in cleaning the cream cans as they come in.

The first load of cream arrives at 1.30 or 2 p. m. and is dumped through a large fine wire strainer into the receiving vat and run over the cooler, being, as a rule, reduced to 66° or 70°. This is also allowed to ripen without a starter, and is indeed often half ripe before it arrives; acidity in one case was 21.5 cc. When there is any half-churned lumpy cream left on the strainer it is melted in a water bath and stirred into the cream.

The rest of the afternoon is occupied by the two men named in receiving cream, cleaning cans, and cleaning upstairs. Mr. Andis also has his boiler and engine, etc., to attend to.

The night man keeps the compressor running and receives cream, which comes in as late as midnight, washes the cans, and cools the cream by putting crushed ice in it and stirring. This cream, as a rule, stands at 55° or 56° in the morning,

---

Fahrenheit thermometer in all cases in this report.

at which temperature it is run into the churns. The acidity of the cream churned the first day of my visit was 20 to 23 cc. by the test. The buttermilk was 60° to 61°, showed an acidity of 31 to 33 cc., and was quite salt from the previous churning.

After drawing the buttermilk, the granules are washed with the water cooled as described above, salted with one ounce salt, and worked in the churn from two and a half to three minutes. It is then left thirty to sixty minutes and given a second working, this time six to eight revolutions on the Mason worker, and then either packed in tubs or boxes or taken to the other room to be made into prints or rolls. The refrigerator is kept at about 42°.

I at once set about ascertaining the acidity of the milk as delivered at the creamery and the general conditions there under which the work must be done. To my great regret both were found less satisfactory than expected. The acidity of the milk as determined by the Mann test (one-tenth normal to 50 cc.) varied from 9 cc. to 20 cc., the average of the last in the vat being 16 cc. But the cream as it came from the separator showed 8.5 cc. at 10 a. m., 9.6 cc. at 11.15 a. m., and 10.6 cc. at noon, when the separating was finished; consequently I had no fear of being unable to pasteurize it.

The creamery possesses an ice machine and has a very fine cream room, but part of the building is old and the churn room is located in the basement, where the air is musty. I saw no way of giving pasteurization a perfect test unless a complete annex was newly built and equipped, but undertook to improve existing conditions.

On the 14th we unpacked and commenced placing the apparatus, and I also tested the milk and cream for acidity. The temperature in the shade was 95° and the acidity of the first can of cream was 9 cc., the second 10 cc., the fourth 12 cc., and the last 14 cc. The smell in the churn room was somewhat improved by the use of lime and an improved ventilating fan in one window, but anyone conversant with pasteurization will acknowledge I had a right to be discouraged.

Indeed, I wrote to Jensen Bros., of Beloit, Kans., asking them to let me know the acidity of their cream, whether the conditions were right at their creamery, and whether I would be welcome if I decided to move there. This was done pending the effect of the following circular letter which I sent to the patrons of the Hesston Creamery Company:

NEWTON, KANS., *June 15, 1897.*

To the patrons of Hesston Creamery:

DEAR SIRS: The Agricultural Department at Washington is about making an experimental shipment of butter from this creamery.

In order to give it keeping quality the cream is to be pasteurized (heated to 160° and cooled).

I regret to say that I find nearly all the milk delivered too sour for this purpose, and hence I ask the favor of your help for two weeks by taking a little extra care.

First, in cleanliness in milk; next, in the care of the cans. They should be emptied at once and rinsed with cold or lukewarm water, then scrubbed with soda or lye water, rinsed again, and finally rinsed with boiling water and placed without wiping in a slanting position (bottom up) where the air is pure.

Same care should be taken in cleaning milk pails, strainers. etc.

When milking, place the shipping can in cold water and leave the cover off, stirring often, until the milk is as cold as the air, then cover.

The morning's milk should also be cooled, even if only for twenty minutes. If stirred or dipped, that will be a great help.

When hauling the milk cover the cans with a wet blanket and keep it wet until delivered.

By doing this you will serve your own interest and not compel me to give up the experiment and report that the Kansas farmers can not deliver milk sweet enough for this purpose.

Hoping you will help me all you can for a couple of weeks, I remain,

Yours, truly,

J. H. MONRAD,
Field Agent, Dairy Division, U. S. Department of Agriculture.

10317——8

Meanwhile I tried to pasteurize the cream as it was and made some preliminary churnings, the details of which will be given later.

From Jensen Bros. I received by wire a hearty invitation; but the following letter showed me that the average condition of the milk received at Beloit was no better than at Newton:

THE JENSEN CREAMERY COMPANY (ESTABLISHED 1894),
Beloit, Kans., June 17, 1897.

Mr. J. H. MONRAD, Newton, Kans.

DEAR SIR: Your letter of June 16 received, and note all you say. I wired you this morning: "Come here sure; will do everything to make the experiment a success; have a pasteurizer." Of course, we will have some difficulties, but we will arrange it all right. We don't take milk on Sundays generally, but should think we could for this purpose and have the whole creamery to our disposal during the experiment. We will have plenty of milk, as we receive 40,000 pounds per day here, and I could notify our best customers to fetch that day. I have Mann's acid test. I tested the cream from the separator this morning and it took 12 cc. to give it the red color. This sample cream was taken at about 10 a. m. Yesterday and last night we had thunder and cyclone weather, it being over 100° and a warm wind blowing. Under ordinary conditions we can get the cream all light. We are pasteurizing 50 gallons every day for a starter, and sterilizing all our skim milk. Ought to be able to pasteurize the cream. We have not got a small cream vat, but can get one. We have got a regular cream cooler. Will help you myself and supply whatever you need. Have got pipe-fitting tools and fittings. Hope that you will decide to come here, as I am very much interested.

Yours, very truly,

THE JENSEN CREAMERY COMPANY.
By W. F. JENSEN.

While we might have selected the best milk, it would not fill the demand for a practical test if we did so. Hence the only choice was to give up the experiment or try it under the existing conditions. Although it was evident that the best results could not be obtained under these circumstances, the condition of the cream (testing as high as 13 cc.) after being pasteurized, encouraged me in the belief that some practical value might be extracted for the benefit of the creamery men, even if the butter made under my direction did not score high enough to be creditable. I was also encouraged by having read the claims made by some experimenters in this country that improvement resulted from pasteurizing cream gathered twice a week, and completely sour.

As will be seen, the work done here under my direction is nothing more than can be easily done at any creamery having plenty of ice or a refrigerating machine; indeed, it was more difficult here than it would be if the creamery was pasteurizing regularly from day to day.

SETTING UP THE APPARATUS.

It was hoped to arrange the pasteurizers so as to catch the cream from the separators and run it directly over the coolers, but this could only be done by using a dark corner in the churn cellar, where the air was not good enough to expose the cream on the coolers, and where the heat from the heaters would be objectionable. I also suspected, what was proved later on, that both machines were of too great capacity for the heat to be kept down between 155° and 165°. Consequently the storage room was selected, just opposite the separators, and we removed the partition.

The Barber apparatus was placed as shown in fig. 4, the only difference being that there were four Bair coolers instead of three.

The heater, a cross section of which is shown in fig. 5, consists of a cast-iron base I, in which a turbine flyer (ff) is inserted and driven by steam from the pipe fs. It also has a pipe T for the exhaust, but this is, as a rule, closed by the damper K, when not less than 1,000 pounds of milk per hour is treated.

G is a galvanized cylinder riveted to the base and provided with an annular tin gutter *H*. *D* is a slightly conical tinned copper drum soldered to a tinned brass

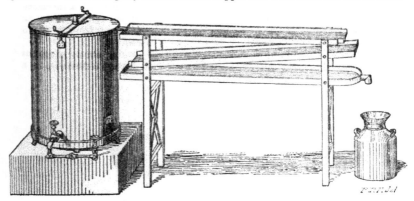

FIG. 4.—Barber pasteurizing and cooling apparatus.

bottom with a spindle which fits in the cup *C*, revolved by the turbine flyer *ff*, running on ball bearings. Drum *D* is strengthened by a hoop at the top, into which

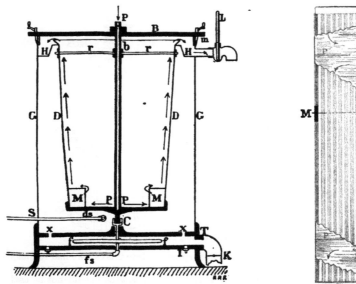

FIG. 5.—Cross section of heater for Barber apparatus.

is riveted a cross (*r*) of four rods, which again brace the 1-inch pipe *P* that acts as spindle for the drum. The cylinder *G* has a flat cover with a crossbar *B*, which is held in position by two thumbscrews *m*. In the center of this bar is the upper bearing. The cream enters at *P* (the hollow shaft) and is distributed from four holes at the bottom, but the chamber *M* (which was designed for hold-

Cross Section NM

FIG. 6.—Bair cooler.

ing back any possible dirt when heating new milk) is not used in the cream
heater.   The cream flows in a thin film all the way, as shown by the arrows, and
is thrown into the gutter *H*, leaving through the spout arranged with a thermometer at *l*.   The exhaust steam from the flyer *ff* passes up through six holes *xx*
into the cylinder and is the usual medium for heating the drum *D*.   The pipe *S*
supplies direct steam for this purpose, in addition, if needed.

I had no regulating cup, and simply placed a tin can holding about 16 gallons
on a shelf above the heater and ran the milk from that through a faucet with a

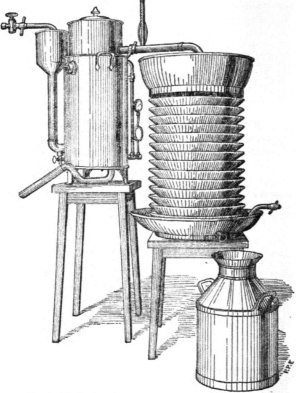

Fig. 7.—The De Laval pasteurizing and cooling apparatus.

pointed nozzle which fitted into the hollow spindle.   Into this can we had to dump
the cream, and the uneven pressure thus created made constant watching a necessity. in order to keep an even temperature.   The apparatus should not be used
without a regulating cup of some kind like those used for separators.

The Bair cooler (fig. 6) is in this case 8 feet long and 18 inches wide, like a wide,
shallow gutter with a corrugated bottom, shown in the cross section *NM*, and a
double bottom where the cooling water circulates in an alternating current,
caused by the partitions *PP*.   The water flows as shown by the arrows on the
sketch, entering at *W* and escaping at *A*.   The milk or cream flows over the top
and, of course, in the opposite direction.

These coolers were given a drop of only about 2 inches, having a total drop from heater spout to the cooler spout of 18 inches. The two upper coolers were made of tin and connected with the overflow from the condensing tank of the refrigerator, the water showing from 80° to 85°, and the two lower (made of copper) were connected with the Bair cooler in the cream room and the rotary pump, so that brine could be turned on at will. The brine was, as a rule, at a temperature between 30° and 32°.

The De Laval apparatus.—This neat and well-made apparatus, imported from Sweden, was placed next to the Barber in a similar manner, as shown in fig. 7. Soon after it became necessary to remove it to a skimming station.

The heater, a cross section of which is shown in fig. 8, is explained by the following key:

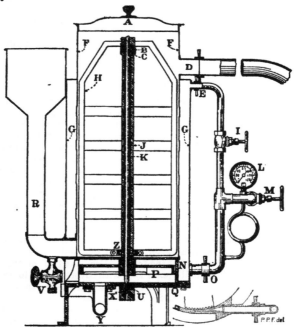

FIG. 8.—Cross section of heater for De Laval pasteurizing apparatus, with connecting pipes.

A—Cover.	I—Three-eighths-inch valve.	Q—Bottom plate.
B—Nut for balls.	J—Tubular shaft.	R—Feed pipe for milk.
C—Steel balls.	K—Shaft.	U—Footstep bearing.
D—Discharge pipe for milk.	L—Manometer (pressure gauge).	V—Milk-outlet faucet.
E—Pipe union.	M—Three-fourths-inch valve.	X—Steel ball for bearing.
F—Milk can.	N—Turbine housing.	Y—Outlet tube.
G—Mantle.	O—Pipe union.	Z—Center for stirrer.
H—Stirrer.	P—Turbine.	

In operating this apparatus the cream and the steam are turned on at the same time, and when a pressure of 45 pounds is maintained the right speed of the dasher (stirrer) *H* is obtained. When finished, the remaining cream (about 5 or 6 gallons) is drawn out by the faucet (outlet tube) *Y*. No oiling is required, as the bearing runs in water from the condensed steam, which is held back by a water lock. Direct steam may be applied by the valve *I*.

The disk cooler, which is shown in fig. 7 as accompanying the De Laval pasteurizer, has a distributing cup considerably smaller than the one shown in fig. 7, and it is at the same time to some extent a regulating cup, as it may be adjusted to distributing various quantities of cream. The cooler is really more like the one shown in fig. 9, and consists of a series of disks over which the cream flows in thin sheets, the cooling water (in this case brine) flowing inside the hollow disks from the bottom to the top.

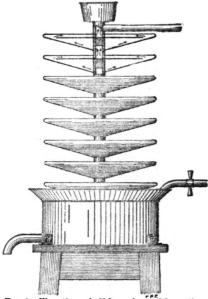

When the under vessel is placed fairly level, the cooling cylinder may be leveled perfectly by the three set screws in its supports.

This cooler was also connected with the brine tank and pump, and, small as it is (only 14¼ inches in diameter and 14 inches high, with eight disks and a total drop of 24 inches), its cooling capacity astonished all who saw its work.

PRELIMINARY CHURNINGS.

As it seemed unlikely, at the first attempt, to do justice to either the system or the apparatus used, under these conditions, novel and far from perfect, I arranged for a few preliminary churnings, and Messrs. A. H. Barber & Co. kindly consented to take the butter from these churnings and keep it for tests as to keeping quality, I agreeing to stand half of whatever loss might result.

FIG. 9.—Elevation of disk cooler, with section through the two upper disks.

First churning.—June 17 the first four 10-gallon cans of cream separated at the factory were pasteurized on the Barber outfit, the temperature being kept between 155° and 165° and cooled to 62°. The acidity of the first can was 9 cc. and of the fourth 14 cc. At 11 a. m. the pasteurized cream was dumped in a small cream vat (with cover) placed in the cream room and 10 per cent of a starter made (according to directions) from Hansen's lactic ferment. The acidity of this starter was 54 cc., and the flavor did not suit me perfectly (having been developed at too high a temperature), but I had to use it.

At 6 p. m. the pasteurized cream tested 17 cc. acid at 62°, and next morning 20 cc. Having cooled it to 55° with crushed ice in the cream, it was churned in 48 minutes, the buttermilk being 59°, with an acidity of 30 cc. It was washed once with the deep-well water, cooled at 54°, and salted and worked in the manner usual at the creamery. The only precaution taken was to rinse the churn and butter worker with iced limewater, of which I had two barrels prepared.

It may be in order here to put in a strong plea for a more common use of limewater. Get a barrel or hogshead and fill with clean water; stir into this unslaked lime enough to make an inch or two of sediment form after settling; stir up two or three times, then let it settle, and use when clear as crystal. Rinse everything used with this, after the usual cleaning and before using; and never mind what adheres to the churn after draining, as it will not hurt the butter.[1]

---

[1] The cleansing properties of lime and limewater can not be doubted. But this advice to add more or less limewater to cream in the churn ought to be further explained and qualified.—H. E. A.

This butter was salted with one ounce of salt per pound and packed in 60-pound tubs. It was scored by Messrs. Barber and Mittelstadt on the 28th of June on this scale: Flavor 50, grain 30, color 10, salt 10 = 100 points. Marked: Flavor 44, grain 29, color 10, salt 10 = 93 points.

Second churning.—June 18, the best milk I found for pasteurizing for starter tested 12 cc. This time I took every other can of cream from the separator, and my fourth can had 14 cc. acid; the pasteurized cream, before adding the starter, was 12 cc., and 63° in temperature. The starter used had an acidity of 49 cc. and showed a little better flavor than on the day previous.

At 5.30 p.m. the temperature of the cream was 62° with 17 cc. acidity, and the next morning (5 o'clock) the same temperature with an acidity of 26 cc. Cooled with ice in the cream to 48°, but the churn heated it up to 53° by the time gas was let out, and it churned in twenty-five minutes, buttermilk being 56° with acidity of only 29 cc. It was worked and salted the usual way, and scored, June 28, flavor 45, grain 29, color 9½, salt 10 = 93½ points.

I believe that the higher acidity produced a gain of one point in flavor.

A tub made from the unpasteurized cream of same day's separating (every other can) scored 44, 28½, 9, 10 = 91½ points.

July 1, Mr. Sleighton, of Manchester, and Mr. Barton, of Chicago, looked at these two tubs, and while Mr. Sleighton thought there was not much difference, Mr. Barton declared the pasteurized to be considerably better than the other.

July 2, Mr. W. D. Collyer, of Chicago, scored them 97 and 97½, giving one-half point in favor of the unpasteurized on flavor.

Third churning.—On the 19th there was a little improvement in the milk, some of the patrons having evidently taken notice of my circular letter. The milk used for starter tested only 10 cc. The cream from 9 to 13 cc., and this was heated to 160° in the De Laval heater and cooled to 68°, this being the lowest the cooler could bring it at the flow (1,200 pounds per hour) needed to keep the temperature down to 160°.

As no work is done at this factory on Sundays, I ran the cream over the cooler twice, getting it down to 51°. The pasteurized cream showed 11.5 cc. acidity at 2 p.m., and Sunday at 10 a.m. 12 cc., temperature 56°. At 5.30 p.m. the cream room was 59°, the pasteurized cream 56°, with 18.5 cc. acid, while the regular corresponding cream was 51°, with 26.5 acid.

Monday morning the acidity was 26 cc.; the cream was cooled but not churned till 2 p.m. (when the acidity was 27 cc.) at a temperature of 55°. It took one hour and seven minutes to churn, and the buttermilk was 58°, with 33 cc. acidity.

A tub was selected by the butter maker, Mr. Brandt, from his regular product of the day, to compete with this churning, and the comparative scoring of these two, June 28, was as follows:

Pasteurized—flavor 45½, grain 29, color 9½, salt 10 = 94 points; regular—flavor 42½, grain 28, color 9½, salt 10 = 90 points. On July 2 Mr. Collyer scored them with this result: Pasteurized—flavor 41, grain 30, color 9, salt 10 = 90 points; regular—flavor 40, grain 30, color 9, salt 10 = 89 points.

Fourth churning.—The milk delivered Monday, June 21, was somewhat improved, the last can of cream being 11.5 cc., the milk used for starter 11 cc., and the worst milk accepted 23 cc., whereas on a previous day 30 cc. had been taken in. The cream was taken alternately from the two separators, one to the regular vat and one set aside for pasteurizing. When four cans of each were secured the half for pasteurizing was heated to 160° and then cooled to 65°.

The starter was added, and at 6.30 p.m. the cream was 64°, with 13 cc. acidity. Next morning at 6.30 it had the same temperature and 23 cc. acidity. It was drawn into 8-gallon cans, set in ice water at 11.30 a.m., with an acidity of 26 cc. and cooled to 54°, but owing to one of the combined churns breaking down it was not churned till 5 p.m., being then at a temperature of 54° and acidity 27.5

cc.; time of churning, forty-five minutes; buttermilk being 61°, with 31 cc. acidity. The temperature in churn room was 79°. This churning was salted with only three-fourths of an ounce of Genesee salt and packed in export boxes.

A control tub of 20 pounds was scored by Messrs. Barber and Mittelstadt on July 1: Flavor 46½, grain 29, color 9¾, and salt 10 = 95¼ points. Mr. Collyer scored it on the 2d, flavor 44, grain 30, color 9½, salt 10 = 93½ points.

The unpasteurized cream had been treated the usual way, dumped in the cream vat as it came from the separator at 85°, and allowed to cool gradually to 62°, when plenty of ice was put in. On the morning of the 22d it had a temperature of 54° and acidity of 26 cc.; was churned at 53° in one hour and ten minutes, the finishing temperature being 57°. This was also salted with three-fourths of an ounce of Genesee salt. The scoring box of this "regular" churning was examined by Messrs. Barber and Mittlestadt and marked—flavor 42, grain 28¾, color 9¾, and salt 10 = 90½ points; and by W. D. Collyer—flavor 38, grain 30, color 9, and salt 10 = 87 points.

EXPORT CHURNINGS.

First churning, June 23.—Milk delivered on June 22 was decidedly better; the milk haulers nearly all had blankets over the cans, and milk used for starter showed 11 cc. acidity; the first can of cream 8.5 cc. and the last only 10.5 cc. Pasteurizing was done at 11.30 a. m., but the cream was not started till 2 p. m., as there was only one cream vat. At 6 p. m. it had 17 cc. acidity at 64°, and next morning at 6 o'clock 22 cc. at 63°, and at 11.30 a. m. 25 cc. at 62°. It was cooled in cans, as before described, and churned at 5 p. m. in fifty minutes at a temperature of 51°. The buttermilk was 59°, with an acidity of 31 cc.

The butter from this churning was packed in export boxes and was scored in New York by Mr. W. H. Healy, scale and results as follows: Scale: Flavor 40, grain 30, color 15, salt 10, package 5 = 100. Marked: Flavor 33, grain 30, color 14, salt 10, package 5 = 92.

NOTES.—Lacks flavor, but clean to taste; body good; color mottled.

The unpasteurized cream, handled the usual way, churned at 51°, buttermilk 61°, with 29 cc. acidity, made butter which was scored in New York by Mr. Healy, with the following comparative record: Marked: Flavor 31, grain 29, color 13, salt 10, package 4½ = 87½.

NOTES.—Flavor not clean, bitter. Body short; grain little salvy; color badly mottled; salt good; packing "slack."

Second churning, June 24.—Having found it impossible to get enough butter for three export boxes of each kind, apart from desired control boxes, I consulted with Messrs. Hoffman and Lewelling; and as they, as well as Mr. Brandt, declared that cream sent in early by express from a skimming station would be fully as good as the home cream, it was decided to have this done in order to eke out the unpasteurized cream and to pasteurize enough.

Milk received on the 23d was even better than that of the previous day, the first can showing only 7.5 cc. acidity and the third one 8 cc. The pasteurized cream was started in the usual manner, with about 8 per cent starter of an acidity of 49.5 cc., and next morning, at 5 o'clock, it was 63°, with 27 cc. acidity, increasing to 28 cc. at 9 a. m. Then it was set to cool, and churned at 3 p. m. at 49° in one hour and fifteen minutes, the buttermilk being 56°, with 34 cc. acidity. This butter was packed in boxes and scored in Chicago by three inspectors, and averaged—flavor 42⅔, grain 29, color 9¾, and salt 10 = 91 5/12 points.

The corresponding unpasteurized cream was churned at 52° in thirty-three minutes, buttermilk being 60°, with 26 cc. acidity. The boxes of butter made from this were scored—flavor, 40⅛, grain 28⅝, color 9⅞, and salt 10 = 88⅝ points.

Third churning, June 25.—Acidity of the cream pasteurized was: First can, 8.8 cc.; the fourth, 10 cc., and the last, 12 cc. The cream next morning (25th), 6 o'clock, was 63°, with 29 cc. acidity, increasing to 30 cc., when it was cooled and churned at 47° in fifty-seven minutes; buttermilk, 54°, with 38.5 cc. acidity. This butter scored—flavor 44¼, grain 29¼, color 9⅓, and salt 10 = 93¼. The unpasteurized butter, which was churned at 52° in fifty minutes, with buttermilk 57°, and acidity 24.1 cc., scored—flavor 40⅔, grain 28⅔, color 9¼, and salt 10 = 88⅔ points.

Fourth churning, June 26.—Friday, the 25th, I pasteurized the whole run of cream, dumping it into one of the regular vats and starting it with fully 10 per cent of starter. Mr. Brandt took charge of it, and it was cooled the next day by direct ice, acidity 28 cc., and churned at 49° in one hour, the buttermilk being 56° and 30 cc. acid. Of this a box was scored by three persons in Chicago, the average results being—flavor 44, grain 29¼, color 10, salt 10 = 93¼ points. For comparison, Mr. Brandt selected a tub from the regular make of the day, and this was similarly scored, its record being—flavor 42¼, grain 28⅝, color 9⅓, and salt 10 = 91 points.

SHIPPING HOT CREAM.

Fifth churning, June 28.—Having tried the De Laval heater once at the creamery, I then had it taken to the Halstead skimming station and prepared for heating cream there. On the 26th we drove over at 4 a. m. and set it in place. Knowing it would take care of more cream, I had requested Mr. Lewellen, in charge of the separators, to change them so as to give me more and thinner cream, and the heater was placed so as to catch the cream as it came from the two Alpha separators, there being just drop enough to place a cream-carrying can under the heater. We decided to divide the cream so that the first carrier was left unheated; the next three were heated and the last two not heated. This was fair enough, so far as the acidity was concerned, as the first can was 10 cc. and the last one only 11 cc.

It turned out that the temperature could not be kept below 170°, but I did not object to this, because it became a severer test as regards the "cooked" flavor, which I feared would result from not immediately cooling the cream after pasteurizing.

By 10.30 o'clock we had finished skimming and the cream hauler was ready to start. The three heated cans then showed 150°, 155°, and 158° temperature, the cans having cooled the cream that much. The unheated cream was 82°, also in three cans.

The cream arrived at Newton at 1.05 p. m. in good condition, the three heated cans at 138°, 140°, and 142°; this cream was immediately run over the Bair coolers and reduced to 64°.

The unheated cream was 85°, 84°, and 88°, the last being the carrier next to those containing the hot cream. This cream was somewhat churned and was treated the usual way, being run over the factory Bair cooler, reduced to 66°, and tested 21.5 cc. acidity at 3 p. m.; at this time the pasteurized cream tested only 8.5 cc. Starter was then added (8 per cent) to the latter, and next morning (Sunday), 7 o'clock, it had a temperature of 63° and 26 cc. acidity. At 11 a. m. it was 62° with 29 cc. acidity, and it was chilled to 52° in 8-gallon cans placed in ice water; but I also put in a couple of pounds of ice in each can. At 4 p. m. it was 46°, and Monday morning the acidity had only advanced to 31 cc. The churning was started at 50° and finished in one hour, with buttermilk at 59° and acidity 34.5 cc.

It must be observed that this cream hauled hot had, when cooled, considerably more "cooked" taste than the cream heated in Newton and cooled at once, but it is uncertain whether this was due to the higher heat or to keeping it hot for about three hours. As the ripening process went on the cooked flavor seemed to diminish, but both Mr. Lewellen and myself imagined we could detect it, even in the butter. Yet three days later, when asked about any peculiar flavor, none of the judges could find this cooked taste. This butter scored—flavor 43¼, grain 29¼, color 9¼, salt 10 = 91⅝ points. The unpasteurized cream was churned at 53° in thirty-five minutes, buttermilk being 59°, with acidity of 28.5 cc. The butter scored—flavor 43¼, grain 29¼, color 9¼, salt 9⅝ = 91⅝ points.

THE PACKAGES.

It was the plan to have the boxes prepared in sets of three—one with paraffin, one with Dowdell's enamel, and one unprepared. I had ordered spruce boxes, these being in my estimation the best looking, but through a misunderstanding I received poplar boxes, uncrated and unburlapped, dirty, and short count, and had to do as well as possible with these. In applying the paraffin it was found essential to have the boxes perfectly dry and warm; with these conditions it gave a satisfactory coating. The Dowdell enamel was contributed for trial by its inventor, Mrs. F. D. Shaw, through the agency of F. A. Tripp. It seems to give a very nice coating, but is too complicated in its application to be practical in a creamery. It is not unlikely, however, that this difficulty can be overcome later.

The first six boxes being thrown out, some spruce boxes from the home supply of the factory were substituted, and thus I to VI, IX, and XII were untreated spruce; VII, X, XIII, XVI, XIX, and XXII were untreated poplar; VIII, XI, XIV, XVII, XX, and XXIII were paraffined poplar; and XV, XVIII, XXI, and XXIV were treated with Dowdell enamel.

GENERAL REMARKS.

These experiments, made under many difficulties, are not claimed to have been exhaustive enough to have scientific value, but they at least indicate what may be done in this line, and may encourage creamery men to follow up the matter. The results of pasteurization in these trials is best shown by comparing the scoring records of the different lots of butter, pasteurized and not pasteurized, as given in the table following:

Table of comparative scorings of butter, pasteurized and unpasteurized, made as per report.

Dates of churning.	P.[a]	First scoring, June 28 and July 1.					Second scoring, July 23.				
		Scale and points.					Scale and points.				
		Flavor, 50.	Grain, 30.	Color, 10.	Salt, 10.	Total score, 100.	Flavor, 50.	Grain, 30.	Color, 10.	Salt, 10.	Total score, 100.
1897.											
June 18	P.	44	29	10	10	93	39½	29½	9⅚	10	88⅚
19		41	29	9	10	89	36	29⅙	9⅓	10	84½
19	P.	42⅙	29⅓	9⅓	10	90⅚	38⅙	29⅙	9⅙	10	87½
20		41⅚	28⅚	9⅙	10	89⅚	35⅙	29⅓	9⅙	10	83⅔
20	P.	44	29⅙	9⅙	10	92⅓	40	29⅙	9⅚	10	89
22		40⅔	29⅙	9⅓	10	89⅙	37⅚	29⅙	9⅙	10	86⅙
22	P.	45⅓	29⅙	9⅚	10	94⅓	41	29⅙	9⅚	10	90
24		40⅙	28⅔	9⅚	10	88⅔	35⅙	29	9⅙	10	83⅓
24	P.	42⅔	29	9⅔	10	91⅓	38⅚	29⅙	9⅙	10	87⅙
25		40⅚	28⅚	9⅙	10	88⅚	36	28⅚	9½	10	84⅓
25	P.	44⅙	29⅙	9⅔	10	93	38⅙	29⅓	9⅙	10	86⅔
26		42⅓	28⅚	9⅚	10	91	37⅙	29	9⅙	10	85⅓
26	P.	44	29⅙	10	10	93⅙	38	29⅙	9⅓	10	86½
28		43⅙	29⅙	9⅙	9⅚	91⅓	38⅙	29⅙	9⅙	10	86½
28	P.	43	29⅙	9⅙	10	91⅓	37⅚	29⅙	9⅙	10	86⅙
Average for pasteurized						92⅓					87⅝
Average for not pasteurized						90					85
Points in favor of pasteurized						2⅓					2⅝

[a] P equals "pasteurized."

NOTE.—All the figures are averages from marks of the three judges, acting separately.

The sample or control packages were taken from the several churnings. These were kept in the cold room of the Hesston creamery until all were ready and then sent together to Chicago. There the butter was kept by Mr. A. H. Barber in his sales room, which, although refrigerated, had a variable temperature of 42° to 45°. The judges had no knowledge whatever of the history or differences in the contents of the different packages while the scoring was being done.

As an additional contribution to the same subject, I procured sample packages of butter from Messrs. Jensen Bros., of Beloit, Kans., who were pasteurizing a part of the product of their creamery at the same time I was at Newton. The two packages were from the same lot of cream, the butter of one being pasteurized while the other was made up "raw." The packages were sent together to Chicago, scored on the 23d of July by the same judges, and their averages follow:

Score.	Flavor.	Grain.	Color.	Salt.	Total.
Scale	50	30	10	10	100
Pasteurized butter	45½	29½	10	10	94½½
Regular make	44½	29½	9½	10	93 7/12

The difference in favor of pasteurization, 1½ points.

A portion of the samples described were kept undisturbed at Chicago until August 13, when they were examined and scored by Mr. D. C. Wolverton, an excellent judge, with the following result. This gentleman was also in entire ignorance as to the butter in the various packages until his judgment had been recorded:

Place and date of making..	Scale.	Hesston creamery, Newton, Kans.								Jensen creamery, Beloit, Kans., July, 1897.	
		June 22.		June 24.		June 25.		June 26.			
		P.a	R.b	P.	R.	P.	R.	P.	R.	P.	R.
Flavor	50	44	40	38½	38	38	39	42	40	45	44
Grain	30	29	29	29½	29	29	28	29	29	29	29
Color	10	10	10	10	10	9½	9½	10	9½	10	10
Salt	10	10	10	10	10	10	10	10	10	10	10
Total	100	93	89	88	87	86½	86½	91	88½	94	93

a P = Pasteurized.   b R = Raw cream.

Averages: Flavor, P=41½; R=40½. Total: P=90½; R=88½.

The butter made at the Hesston creamery, as described, was duly exported to London and there subjected to criticism. An attempt was made to have it scored there upon the same scale of points as used in Chicago, and score cards were sent over for the purpose. This duty was assigned to the most competent person who could be found in London, but when the report was received (the middle of August) it was found to be useless for purposes of comparison. The examiner was evidently unaccustomed to the score card or to recording his judgment of butter by numerals, and the variations and inconsistencies in the report render it worthless. In general, this examiner reported that he failed to find any appreciable difference between butter made from cream which had been pasteurized and that from raw cream. As a matter of personal preference, he was rather inclined to favor the butter from raw cream at the time of his comparative examination in London.

Theoretically, the pasteurizing should have operated to preserve the flavor and increase keeping quality, and should have appeared in the later scorings. The tables above show that although all the American judges somewhat favored the butter which had been pasteurized, this butter did not appear to increase its advantage with age.

In the matter of flavor alone I find that the average of the pasteurized samples in June was 43½ against 41½ for the other, or a superiority of 2 points. In July the comparative averages on flavor were 39 and 36¾, difference 2½, or practically the same as in June. Mr. Wolverton gave the pasteurized lots an average in August of 1½ points in flavor over the others.

CONCLUSIONS.

As the result of this Kansas work, and some experience in confirmation of it, my conclusions are as follows:

(1) That even for the home market, pasteurization will make some improvement in the butter of at least 75 creameries in every 100.

(2) That fully as good "body" can be obtained in butter made from pasteurized cream as from raw cream.

(3) That heating cream even to 170° and hauling it 12 miles while hot is perfectly practicable, although the butter thus made did not show any higher scoring at the first trial as a result of this treatment.

(4) That with the proper arrangements the pasteurization of cream need not be much extra work aside from the cleaning of apparatus; but an extra man is needed if the preparing of starter and the care of the cream, as well as the extra cleaning, is to be given the proper attention.

(5) That a large supply of ice or a refrigerating machine is necessary in order to chill the cream sufficiently to get a good "body."

(6) That in ripening cream a lower acid seems better adapted to a very rich cream, and there are indications that a better flavor can be obtained from thin cream.

(Professor McKay, of Ames, Iowa, was the first to draw attention to the vagueness of the acid test unless the richness of the cream is known. This is an important subject and needs more investigation. The cream at Newton I calculated to have about 37 per cent of fat and the Halstead cream 29 per cent, but as the testing there is done by perambulating tester, the means were not available for verifying these estimates. The correlation of acidity in cream and in the buttermilk is also worth investigating.)

I can not conclude this report without expressing my appreciation of the kind treatment given me by Messrs. Hoffman and Lewellen, and the good-natured way in which all the employees humored my demands for cleaning, including the use of limewater, and performed all the extra labor caused by my work.

I must also thank Messrs. A. H. Barber and John Mittelstadt, of Chicago (who acted as judges at the Exposition of 1893), and Mr. W. D. Collyer (of C. F. Love & Co.) for the cheerfulness with which they scored the butter under conditions prescribed by me. There was greater difference in the scoring than usual, because each judge worked by himself, in my presence, and had no chance to consult the others or afterwards modify his decision. A different "key" was therefore very likely to be used. Consequently it has been thought best to give the average marks of these three judges instead of the figures reported by each. Creamery men can not too highly appreciate this volunteer work, taking up valuable time, a service which I did not find all butter experts willing to render.

THE FUTURE.

As a rather curious coincidence I will mention that upon my return home I received a letter from Mr. J. D. Frederiksen, dated Denmark, June 24, in which he wrote: "It has been interesting to observe the progress made, especially in the cooperative creameries and bacon factories, as well as in the sugar factories. It is the small farmers rather than the large 'estates' who have made this progress. Ninety-nine per cent of the creameries have pasteurizing outfits and 90 per cent pasteurize the cream, whether it is good or bad. There is no question but what the American creameries must follow suit. The Americans will adopt the English demand for mild-flavored butter, and ten years hence all cream in America, or at least the cream in all good creameries, will be pasteurized."

The introduction of this system will promote a higher standard of cleanliness in our creameries and compel the owners to give the needed extra help. If the Department desires to assist its introduction, it would be well to offer the aid of experts to creameries willing to pay their expenses while giving factory employees the necessary instruction in this new line of work.

I estimated the cost of an extra man, interest on apparatus, cost of cooling, and loss in yield of butter by the reduction in water content to meet export requirements to be about 1 cent per pound. It remains to be determined whether the above-mentioned advantages are worth this cost.

But it seems to me that uniformity, with a mild, clean flavor, is the only basis for building up an export trade, as well as for general improvement in the quality of the home market.

APPENDIX VII.

THE EXPORT OF FRESH (UNSALTED) BUTTER FROM THE UNITED STATES.

In the foregoing report the fact has been noted that butter without salt sells at a higher price in London than any other, and some description has been given of this butter as usually supplied from France for the London market. (See pp. 85 and 86.)

The custom of using unsalted butter has been slowly increasing in the United States for several years, and a considerable quantity of it, called "fresh" and "sweet" butter, now finds a market weekly in New York, as well as in other cities to a less extent.

It was therefore decided to try, in connection with the other experimental exports of the Department, the shipment of fresh butter from New York to London. So far as known, this form of butter had never before been exported from this country, at least upon a commercial basis.

Several hundred pounds of unsalted butter were engaged, to be made in August by two factories which have won a high reputation for this special product. They were the Sennett Creamery, of Sennett, Cayuga County, N. Y., and the Edmunds Creamery, of Sherman, Chautauqua County, N. Y. The officers of both these establishments did everything in their power to conform to the suggestions and instructions from this Department and to make this trial a success.

The butter was packed, at both factories, in bulk and in rolls. The former was put in cubical boxes, holding between 56 and 57 pounds net, to be sold as a half hundredweight. The boxes were coated inside with paraffin, besides being lined well with parchment paper. The rolls were made up (or intended to be) of 2 pounds weight each, in imitation of the Brittany fresh rolls, and a part of these were packed in a similar way, 1 dozen rolls in a box. The boxes were made exactly the size of those bought in the London market and imported (with the French butter they contained) as patterns. These were also paraffin coated inside and lined with parchment. Besides these extra precautions, each roll was wrapped in parchment paper, which is not the custom with the French rolls sold in London. From each factory a part of the rolls were wrapped in parchment, packed and shipped in a "portable refrigerator" or metallic chest with ice box.

The thorough making and density of the butter of this character as made in Brittany were developed in an interesting way in connection with these trials. The imported Brittany rolls were weighed on a standard scale and found to average 2 pounds each, "down weight." The rolls were then measured and molds made which would produce rolls of exactly the same size. The 12-roll packing boxes were also accurately duplicated, as already stated. But when the butter was made and molded, the rolls at one factory averaged 1 pound 14 ounces in weight and at the other factory only 1 pound 13 ounces. The sizes were right, and twelve of these rolls just filled the packing boxes made for them. When rolls of 2 pounds full weight and of the same shape were made up by hand, it was found impossible to get a dozen of them into one of the boxes provided. (This error in the rolls was discovered too late to have new molds and boxes made; so the short-weight rolls were shipped, and this defect had a very unfavorable bearing upon their sale in London.) Thus the pound of fresh butter as prepared in this country by very careful and skillful makers had a bulk materially greater than the similar butter made in Brittany, France. A natural conclusion was that the American butter was insufficiently worked and too porous. London critics said that it contained too much water. But the results of several analyses, by different analysts, shows that the American butter averaged 12.16 per cent water and 88.02 per cent fat, while the French butter averaged 13.10 per cent water and 85.93 fat. The other components averaged 0.82 of 1 per cent in the former and 0.97 of 1 per cent in the latter; this difference is accounted for, however, by the borax found in the Brittany butter, of which there was none in that from the United States. Chemically the American butter was the better, but the French butter excelled in its mechanical condition; it was uncommonly firm, fine grained, and dense, without being at all overworked. And while the French butter, as stated, carried a higher percentage of water, the latter was so thoroughly incorporated that this butter appeared to be very dry. These points are interesting and deserve attention from some of our experimenters in butter making.

Care was taken to have the butter made as late as possible to catch the export steamer, and transported with every precaution to avoid delay and exposure. The two lots of butter were made August 21 and 22, held in chilled rooms till evening of 23d, then sent by night express, reaching New York City at 6.30 a. m. of 24th. They were delivered at the vessel's side at 10.30 a. m., and an hour later were in its commercial refrigerator, at a temperature of 30° F. The atmospheric temperature at New York that day was 68° at 9 a. m. and 72° at noon. The steamer sailed from New York August 25, arrived at Southampton September 1, and the butter was delivered to merchants in London on the 2d of September, or the twelfth day after it was made.

Upon arrival in London some of the small boxes of rolls, made of light lumber, had been crushed and their contents spoiled. It was found also that the entire lot of butter, with the exception of some of the rolls in the two iron trunks, was damaged with mold. This trouble and the light weight of the rolls, already explained, caused the roll boxes to sell at a low rate. The bulk butter was slightly moldy on the outer portions of the cubes as removed from the packages. Upon cutting these parts away the greater portion of the butter was found in excellent condition. But as fresh butter is not sold in bulk in London this had to be worked up into rolls before being retailed, and this was a disadvantage. These several causes prevented realizing a satisfactory average on the sale of this butter in London, and it is fairer to the trial to name the prices of portions of the shipment, representative of the whole when starting, but which reached the foreign market free from accident and in the best of condition. These parts sold at a little less than 22 cents per pound wholesale and retailed at 24 to 27½ cents. The best fresh Brittany rolls were then selling at 28 to 30 cents per pound. The Normandy Pro.

duce Company took a good deal of the short-weight roll butter, including some
from the iron trunks, and retailed it all as "Normandy fresh butter" at a shilling a pound. The butter cost 20 cents per pound when placed on the export
steamer at New York and about 21 cents when delivered to merchants in London.
The two lots of butter constituting this shipment were examined and scored in
New York by the inspector of the Mercantile Exchange, with the following result:

Scoring of unsalted butter in New York City.

	Flavor.	Grain.	Color.	Salt. a	Style.	Total.
Scale for perfection	40	30	15	10	5	100
Sennett Creamery	33	30	15	10	5	93
Edmunds Creamery	35	30	15	10	5	95

a To follow scale, all marked perfect on salt, although having none.

In London all the packages, except those injured and rejected, were examined
and scored on the same scale, with the average result following. Comparisons
were made by the same examiner—a novice in scoring—with French fresh butter
and Danish salt butter judged at the same time:

*Scoring of United States and French unsalted butter and Danish salted butter in
London.*

	Flavor.	Grain.	Color.	Salt.	Style.	Total.
Sennett	33	28	12	10	3	86
Edmunds	35	28	12	10	3	88
Edmunds in trunk	37	28	15	10	a 1	91
French	38	29	14	10	5	06
Danish	37	28	14	9	4	92

a Package unsuitable because too heavy. But for this deduction on "style," or package, this
butter would have scored within one point of the French, which stood at the top of the market.

From various opinions given by the dealers and other critics who examined this
butter in London the following are culled: Graded as second to best Brittany
fresh rolls. The butter arrived bright, sweet, and in excellent condition except
for the moldy spots inside the wrappers already described; texture not sufficiently hard when thawed from hard state in which it arrived, showing too
many water globules; rather too much color [the butter was not colored]
to compare favorably with the standard French supply. Some of the boxes
had cloth at the bottom and top inside the parchment lining; the ends of the
rolls touched this cloth and all received a distinct odor and taste from it.
"Cotton cloth should never touch butter in packing for market." [Yet the boxes
from France as found in London market ordinarily have two pieces of cotton cloth
inside the paper lining, one at the bottom and the other at the top, in direct contact with both ends of all the rolls.] The butter which was not moldy sold
readily at a price next to the best of its general class in the market. The short-
weight rolls were objected to and had to be sold at a rather lower rate.
Special mention should be made of the patented carriers in which some of this
butter was sent. They were made of galvanized iron and had within them boxes
for holding ice free from contact with the butter. Each carrier or trunk was
intended for four dozen 2-pound rolls, but the short weight of the rolls reduced
the total contents from 96 to 90 pounds. Fifty pounds of ice was placed in each

carrier on leaving the creamery (August 23) and examined at New York the next day when put in steamer's refrigerator, when each was found to contain 15 to 20 pounds of ice. On reaching London there was still (September 2) a little ice in one trunk. In the other the ice had all melted and the water had reached the butter and injured its appearance. The butter in these trunks when opened in London was found to be hard, firm, and excellent in quality except for a few spots of mold. As the trunks were practically airtight, it is evident that the germs of this mold started with the butter from the creameries where made or at least from New York. The mold developed most in the 2-pound rolls in small boxes and least in the "portable refrigerators." While the latter carried the butter well, the weight of package and ice exceeded that of the butter contained, and it seems to be impracticable on that account alone, although efficient in its service.

Careful investigation satisfies the writer that the mold was preventable and not necessarily incident to the export of butter of this class. Salt butters sent before and after were exported free from mold, but some sent at the same time with these fresh lots was slightly affected. Fresh butter can undoubtedly be sent to London without being injured in this way. But for the mold and the short-weight rolls, the returns from the shipment would have been much better.

Although this trial can not be regarded as conclusive, its results justify repetition, and indicate that, with proper measures to secure the desired texture or "body" for the butter and further experience in packing and shipping, it will be possible for fresh roll butter made in the United States to be placed in the London market of such quality and in such condition as to equal the present favored product of the north of France. Whether the latter can be competed with commercially at a satisfactory profit will remain to be determined.

H. E. A.

APPENDIX VIII.

RECORD OF SCORING OF BUTTER EXPORTED.

No.	Mark.	Where made.	Where.	When.	Flavor, 40.	Body, 30.	Color, 10.	Salt, 10.	Package, 10.	Total, 100.	Notes.
1	P.	Connecticut	New York .	Oct. 5	37	30	10	10	10	97	
2	P.	......do	London	Oct. 16	36	28	8	8	10	90	Same as No. 1.
3	A.	Iowa	Chicago....	May 1	37	29	10	9.5	10	95.5	
4	A.	......do	....do	May 22	34	28	9.5	9.5	10	91	Same as No. 3.
5	A.	......do	....do	June 4	35	28	9	10	10	92	Do.
6	A.	......do	London	May 15	35	25	10	6	10	86	Do.
7	A.	......do	Chicago....	May 22	38.5	28.5	10	10	10	97	
8	A.	......do	....do	June 4	36.5	28.5	10	10	10	94.5	Same as No. 7.
9	A.	......do	New York .	Oct. 7	38	29	9.5	9.5	10	96	
10	A.	......do	....do	Nov. 12	36.5	28	10	10	10	94.5	Same as No. 9.
11	H.	Kansas............	Chicago....	July 2	33.5	29	9.5	10	10	92	Pasteurized.
12	H.	......do	....do	July 2	32.5	28	9.5	10	10	90	Raw cream.
13	H.	......do	New York .	July 7	33	30	9	10	10	92	Pasteurized same as No. 11.
14	H.	......do	....do	Aug. 26	32	30	9	10	10	91	Do.
15	H.	......do	....do	July 7	31	29	8	10	10	88	Same as No. 12.
16	H.	......do	....do	Aug. 26	30	29	8	10	10	87	Do.
17	H.	......do	London	July 19	38	27	10	9	9	93	Do.
18	J.	......do	Chicago....	July 27	36	29	10	10	10	95	Pasteurized.
19	J.	......do	....do	July 27	35.5	28.5	10	10	10	94	Raw cream.

Record of scoring of butter exported—Continued.

Sample.			Scored.		Points and scale.						Notes.
No.	Mark.	Where made.	Where.	When.	Flavor, 40.	Body, 30.	Color, 10.	Salt, 10.	Package, 10.	Total, 100.	
20	J.	Kansas	New York	July 29	36	29.5	10	10	10	95.5	Same as No. 18.
21	J.	do	do	Aug. 26	35	29.5	10	10	10	94.5	Do.
22	J.	do	do	Aug. 26	31	30	10	10	10	91	Pasteurized. Box sent to London and back to New York.
23	J.	do	do	July 29	35	30	10	10	10	95	
24	J.	do	do	Aug. 26	34	30	10	10	10	94	Same as No. 23.
25	J.	do	do	Aug. 26	31	30	10	10	10	91	Box exported to London and sent back to New York.
26	J.	do	London	Aug. 7	33	27	8	8	10	86	Pasteurized.
27	J.	do	do	Aug. 7	31	27	8	6	10	82	Raw cream.
28	F.	Massachusetts	Boston	June 18	35	30	10	10	10	95	
29	F.	do	New York	June 28	35	29	10	10	10	94	Same as No. 28.
30	F.	do	do	July 21	33	30	10	10	10	93	Do.
31	F.	do	London	July 25	36	30	10	9	10	95	Do.
32	E.	Minnesota	Minnesota	June 17	38	29	9.5	9.5	10	96	
33	E.	do	New York	June 28	36.5	30	10	10	10	96.5	Same as No. 32.
34	E.	do	London	July 14	35	30	10	9	10	94	Do.
35	E.	do	Minnesota	Oct. 25	39	30	9.5	10	10	98.5	
36	E.	do	New York	Nov. 1	36	30	10	10	10	96	Same as No. 35.
37	E.	do	do	Nov. 12	35	30	10	10	10	95	Do.
38	E.	do	London	Nov. 14	35	28	10	9	10	92	Do.
39	C.	New Hampshire	do	May 15	35	27	10	7	10	89	
40	K.	New York	New York	Aug. 26	33	30	10	10	10	93	
41	K.	do	London	Sept. 10	33	28	8	10	10	89	Same as No. 40.
42	L.	do	New York	Aug. 26	35	30	10	10	10	95	
43	L.	do	London	Sept. 10	37	28	10	10	10	95	Same as No. 42.
44	G.	Ohio	Ohio	Aug. 6	38	26	10	10	10	94	
45	G.	do	New York	July 29	34	29	10	10	10	93	Same as No. 44.
46	G.	do	do	Aug. 26	33	29	10	10	10	92	Do.
47	G.	do	do	Aug. 26	30	29	10	10	10	89	Same lot. Returned from London.
48	G.	do	London	Aug. 7	32	24	8	8	10	82	Same as No. 47.
49	I.	do	Ohio	Aug. 6	35	28	9	10	10	92	
50	I.	do	New York	Aug. 2	32	29.5	10	10	10	91.5	
51	I.	do	do	Aug. 26	28	29.5	10	10	10	87.5	Same as No. 50.
52	I.	do	do	Aug. 26	31	29.5	10	10	10	90.5	Same lot, back from London.
53	I.	do	London	Aug. 9	26	18	8	7	10	69	Same as No. 52.
54	O.	South Dakota	Madison	Nov. 1	39	30	9.5	8	10	96.5	
55	O.	do	New York	Nov. 8	36	30	10	10	10	96	Same as No. 54.
56	O.	do	London	Nov. 14	27	20	10	6	10	73	Do.
57	D.	Vermont	Boston	June 1	37	30	10	10	10	97	
58	N.	Wisconsin	Madison	Sept. 12	37	28	10	8	10	93	
59	N.	do	New York	Sept. 16	35	30	10	10	10	95	Same as No. 58.
60	N.	do	London	Sept. 25	35	27	9	6	10	87	Do.
		Average of all 60 records			34¼	28½	9½	9½	10	91½	
		Average of 45 records in United States			34¾	29	9¾	9¾	10	93½	London omitted.

NOTES UPON APPENDIX VIII.

The scoring in London was much lower than elsewhere, and upon omitting this, as may fairly be done, the general average is seen, to be much better. Chicago scoring averaged flavor a point higher than New York, and body a point lower. The packages appear to have been uniformly satisfactory. Salt and color were generally marked as perfect by American scorers, while in London both were "discounted" as being too high or strong. In body, the average of all is 28½ out of a possible 30, which shows generally well-made butter; yet in this particular local differences in opinion are shown in the averages, being 29½ in New York, 28½ in Chicago, and 26½ in London. In the right-hand column, "notes" indicates certain packages which are recorded as scored two or three times at different dates and places. For example, Nos. 3, 4, and 5 represent the same box of butter, held in Chicago, out of a lot of Iowa butter exported and scored May 1, then three weeks later, and two weeks later still; while No. 6, marked "same as No. 3," means a box of the same lot of butter, the same churning, scored after reaching London. A similar instance occurs with Nos. 28, 29, 30, and 31. No. 27 is the score of a package exported to London and brought back to New York; it was rated seven points better when it reached New York than when in London (No. 48) and but four points less than when it left New York (No. 45); and this deterioration is shown to be wholly in the flavor. Another instance is the score No. 52, as compared with No. 53 and No. 50; No. 58 shows the poor work done in London, and indicates the effect of such figures on the general average; it may be noted in this case that the butter lost but one point (on flavor) by its journey to and from London, while another box of the same lot which remained in New York dropped off four points in the same time, August 2 to 26.

In three cases—Nos. 11 and 12, 18 and 19, 26 and 27—there are opportunities for comparing butter from pasteurized cream and from raw cream, otherwise the same; in these cases the former scored higher than the latter. Nos. 11 and 13, the same butter, scored alike in Chicago and New York and lost but one point by being held from July 2 until August 26; Nos. 12 and 15, the same (raw cream) butter, which scored two points lower in New York than in Chicago, lost only one point by being held the same period. In all there are eight scores of pasteurized butter, and these give an average total of 93 points, which is just above the total average. The only butters which scored above 95 points when examined in New York prior to exportation were the following: No. 1, Connecticut, in October; No. 33, Minnesota, in June; No. 9, Iowa, in October; No. 36, Minnesota, in November; and No. 55, South Dakota, also November. In other respects these figures, which at first appear to have little significance, are susceptible of interesting comparisons.

APPENDIX IX.

RECORD OF SCORING OF FOREIGN-MADE BUTTERS.

No.	Where made.	Form.	Where.	When.	Flavor, 40.	Body, 30.	Color, 10.	Salt, 10.	Package, 10.	Total, 100.	Notes.
	Sample of butter.		Scored.		Points and scale.						
1	Brittany, France..	Fresh rolls; no salt.	New York	June 28	36.5	30	10	10	10	96.5	
2	....do............		.....do....	Nov. 3	35	30	10	10	10	95	
3	....do............		Chicago..	Nov. 10	26	30	10	10	10	86	Same as No. 2
4	....do............		London ..	Sept. 29	38	29	9	10	10	96	
5	Normandy,France	Firkin ...	New York	June 28	31	29	10	10	10	90	
6	....do............	.....do....	.....do....	Aug. 26	29	29	10	10	10	88	Same as No. 5
7	....do............	Basket ...	.....do....	Nov. 3	33	30	10	10	10	93	
8	....do............	.....do....	Chicago..	Nov. 10	27	30	9.5	10	10	86.5	Same as No. 7
9	Denmark	Cask	New York	June 28	35	30	10	10	10	95	
10	....do............	.....do....	.....do....	Nov. 3	35.5	30	9.5	10	10	95	
11	....do............	.....do....	Chicago..	Nov. 10	28	30	9.5	10	10	87.5	Same as No. 10
12	....do............	Sealed tin	New York	July 21	33	30	10	10	10	93	
13	....do............	Cask	London ..	July 25	37	30	10	10	10	97	
14	....do............	.....do....	.....do....	Sept. 29	37	28	9	9	10	93	
15	Dorset, England...	Keg	New York	June 28	30.5	29	10	9.5	10	89	
16	....do............	.....do....	.....do....	Aug. 26	28	29	10	9.5	10	86.5	Same as No. 15
17	Ireland (creamery)	Box	.....do....	June 28	26	28.5	9.5	10	10	84	
18	....do............	Sealed tin	....do....	July 21	27	29	10	10	10	86	
19	....do............	Box	.....do....	Nov. 3	34	29.5	10	10	10	93.5	
20	....do............	.....do....	Chicago..	Nov. 10	26	29	10	10	10	85	Same as No. 19
21	Holland...........	Keg	New York	Nov. 3	32.5	29.5	9.5	10	10	91.5	
22	....do............	.....do....	Chicago..	Nov. 10	24	30	8	10	10	82	Same as No. 21
23	Finland...........	.....do....	New York	Nov. 3	33	30	9.5	10	10	92.5	
24	....do............	.....do....	Chicago..	Nov. 10	24	28	8	10	10	80	Same as No. 23
25	New South Wales.	Cub'l box	New York	June 28	29	29	10	10	10	88	
26	New Zealand	.....do....	.....do....	Nov. 3	33	30	10	10	10	93	
27	....do............	.....do....	Chicago..	Nov. 10	24	30	10	10	10	84	Same as No. 26

NOTES UPON APPENDIX IX.

These are scores upon foreign butter, made in this country by American judges, upon an American basis. The general average of the 27 records is as follows: Flavor 30¼, body 29½, color 9¾, salt 10, package 10; total 90. This indicates that the imported butter was found in good condition upon examination in New York and Chicago, with the exception of flavor, which had deteriorated nearly 25 per cent. "Notes" indicate records of the same butter examined at different times and places. Seven lots of butter which averaged 93½ points in New York on November 3 averaged 84½ points in Chicago a week later; the main disparity was that the New York scores averaged 8 points higher on flavor. This was manifestly due to difference in judgment rather than actual change in the butter; the same judges varied but half a point (average) on the "body" of the same samples.

The only lots of these foreign butters which scored above 94 points in New York were the two Danish casks brought over in June and November and the fresh Brittany rolls imported at the same time.

APPENDIX X.

RECORD OF CHEMICAL ANALYSES OF BUTTER EXPORTED.

		The butter sampled.	Analyzed.		Report of analysis.					Notes.
No.	Mark.	Where made.	Where.	When.	Water.	Fat.	Curd.	Natural ash.	Salt.	
1	P	Connecticut	Connecticut	October	10.90	85.68	1.00	(a)	2.42	
2	P	....do	London	....do	9.80	87.30	1.00	(a)	2.40	Same as No. 1.
3	A	Iowa	Iowa	July	8.12	88.59	1.06	0.40	1.83	
4	A	....do	....do	....do	12.87	84.21	1.23	0.70	0.99	
5	A	....do	....do	October	11.52	85.95	1.10	0.30	1.13	
6	A	....do	London	November	8.08	90.09	0.59	(a)	1.24	Same as No. 5.
7	H	Kansas	Iowa	August	8.54	89.49	0.94	0.25	0.78	Raw cream.
8	H	....do	....do	....do	10.73	86.37	1.19	0.94	0.77	Pasteurized.
9	H	....do	London	July	10.12	88.08	1.10	(a)	0.70	Raw.
10	H	....do	....do	August	8.33	89.43	0.93	(a)	1.21	Same as No. 8.
11	J	....do	....do	....do	9.35	88.86	0.67	(a)	1.12	
12	F	*Massachusetts	Mass	June	9.78	87.71	0.85	(a)	1.66	
13	F	....do	U.S.D.A.b	August	9.41	87.84	0.89	0.04	1.82	Same as No. 12.
14	F	....do	....do	....do	9.63	87.24	1.04	0.03	2.06	Do.
15	F	....do	London	July	8.64	88.82	0.75	(a)	1.79	Do.
16	E	Minnesota	Minnesota	June	11.41	86.81	0.52	(a)	1.26	
17	E	....do	U.S.D.A	August	12.39	85.06	0.91	0.03	1.61	Same as No. 16.
18	E	....do	London	July	10.80	86.96	0.96	(a)	1.28	Do.
19	E	....do	Minnesota	November	10.83	86.86	0.65	(a)	1.68	
20	E	....do	London	....do	11.20	86.96	0.66	(a)	1.14	Same as No. 19.
21	K	New York	New York	September	12.54	86.28	0.83	0.48	0.00	
22	K	....do	London	....do	11.72	87.73	0.49	0.05	0.00	Same as No. 21.
23	L	....do	New York	....do	12.63	86.30	0.33	0.04	0.00	
24	L	....do	London	....do	11.73	87.79	0.43	0.05	0.00	Same as No. 23.
25	M	....do	New York	....do	10.50	87.53	0.33	(a)	1.25	
26	M	....do	London	....do	9.82	88.54	0.52	(a)	1.12	Same as No. 25.
27	G	Ohio	Ohio	August	10.64	87.16	0.80	0.53	0.87	
28	G	....do	London	....do	10.17	88.21	1.07	(a)	0.55	Same as No. 27.
29	I	....do	Ohio	....do	9.42	87.33	0.73	0.78	1.64	
30	I	....do	London	....do	11.10	86.71	0.82	(a)	1.37	Same as No. 29.
31	O	South Dakota	Wisconsin	November	9.38	87.96	1.30	(a)	1.36	
32	O	....do	London	....do	8.77	88.89	0.92	(a)	1.42	Same as No. 31.
33	D	Vermont	Vermont	June	11.37	86.25	0.53	(a)	1.85	
34	N	Wisconsin	Wisconsin	September	10.66	87.35	0.98	(a)	1.01	
35	N	....do	London	October	9.52	88.86	0.76	(a)	0.86	Same as No. 34.
		Average of the 35			10.30	87.20	0.81	0.33	1.36	

a The "natural ash" or mineral constituents included in the "salt" in these cases.
b U. S. D. A. = United States Department of Agriculture.

NOTES UPON APPENDIX X.

The average of these 35 analyses shows the lots of butter to which they apply to have been exceptionally well made. The average of 10.3 per cent of moisture and 87.2 per cent of fat is much above commercial standards, while less than 1 per cent of curdy contents is correspondingly low and creditable. The range is not near as great as usual in the same number of samples from creamery butter as ordinarily made. Excepting two unsalted lots (Nos. 21 and 23), the water content exceeds 12.5 per cent in only one case (No. 4, July butter), and the same lot is the only one in which the fat fell below 85 per cent. The latter was the minimum standard which it was intended to maintain. The figures for ash and salt show variation which indicates the difficulty of getting reliable results in these particulars from small butter samples as ordinarily taken. All of these butters were intentionally light salted, but the aim was to make them carry from 2 to 2¼ per cent, and the uniformity of judgment in scoring these same lots, as per Appendix VIII, showed that they satisfied the taste of experts in this regard better than appears from this chemical record.

The butter exported appears even better from the records of the London analyst than from those made in this country. Thirteen lots were analyzed on both sides of the sea, and the results are compared below:

Analysis of United States butter in United States and in London.

	Water.	Fat.	Curd.	Ash.	Salt.
	Per cent.	*Per cent.*	*Per cent.*	*Per cent.*	*Per cent.*
Averages:					
In United States	10.77	86.56	0.81	0.51	1.35
In London	9.87	88.02	.76	....	1.35

This comparison indicates that, despite all precautions, the butter dried out somewhat in transit, thus decreasing the water content and increasing the percentage of fat. The results on curd were very close, but, curiously, the London analyst, although he did not separate natural ash and salt, found less mineral matter in his drier butter than was found by American chemists. This is probably another example of the uneven distribution of salt in butter and the difficulty of getting duplicate samples in this respect.

APPENDIX XI.

RECORD OF ANALYSES OF FOREIGN-MADE BUTTERS.

[Representative selections imported by the Department of Agriculture.]

No.	Form.	Where made.	Where.	When.	Water.	Fat.	Curd.	Natural ash.	Salt.	
1	Cask	Dorset, England	London	July	15.00	83.39	0.50	(a)	1.11	
2	...do..	.....do	U. S. D. A. c.	.....do	13.89	84.33	.48	0.08	1.27	
3	...do..	.....do	Connecticut	.....do	12.51	85.65	.08	(a)	1.16	
4	Box	Ireland (creamery)	U. S. D. A	.....do	14.63	79.54	1.67	.62	3.54	(b)
5	...do..	.....do	Connecticut	.....do	15.02	79.21	1.53	(a)	4.24	(b)
6	...do..	.....do	U. S. D. A	November	15.31	82.17	1.13	.14	1.25	(b)
7	...do..	.....do	Iowa	.....do	13.28	84.93	.88	.06	.85	(b)
8	Tin	Ireland (Cork)	U. S. D. A	August	15.31	78.50	2.40	.44	3.85	(b)
9	Keg	Denmark	London	July	12.08	86.29	.71	(a)	.92	
10	...do..	.....do	U. S. D. A	.....do	9.71	88.11	1.06	.03	1.00	
11	...do..	.....do	Connecticut	.....do	8.93	89.05	1.03	(a)	.99	
12	.do..	.....do	U. S. D. A	November	13.02	84.46	1.15	.05	1.32	
13	...do..	.....do	Iowa	.....do	11.57	86.10	1.33	.15	.85	
14	Tin	.....do	U. S. D. A	August	8.62	87.80	1.29	.06	2.23	
15	Cask	France, Normandy	.....do	July	12.22	83.12	1.18	.26	3.22	(b)
16	...do..	.....do	Connecticut	.....do	10.17	85.95	1.09	(a)	2.79	(b)

a The "natural ash" or mineral con. tituents included in the "salt" in these cases.
b Samples were found to contain preservative, generally borax.
c U. S. D. A. = United States Department of Agriculture.

Record of analyses of foreign-made butters—Continued.

[Representative selections imported by the Department of Agriculture.]

	The butter sampled.		Analyzed.		Report of analysis.					
No.	Form.	Where made.	Where.	When.	Water.	Fat.	Curd.	Natural ash.	Salt.	
17	Basket.	France, Normandy	London	October...	10.63	85.50	1.06	(a)	2.81	(b)
18	...do..	.....do	U.S.D.A.c..	November	11.91	85.55	1.13	.11	1.20	
19	...do..	.....do	Iowa	.....do	8.88	89.23	.79	.20	.90	
20	Rolls.	France, Brittany ..	U.S.D.A....	July	15.36	83.70	.75	.19	......	(b)
21	...do..	.....do	Connecticut .	.....do	15.52	83.80	.57	.11	......	(b)
22	...do..	.....do	London ....,.	September	13.56	85.36	.78	.30	......	(b)
23	...do..	.....do	U.S.D.A....	November	14.59	84.10	1.03	.28	......	(b)
24	...do..	.....do	Iowa	.....do	10.37	88.72	.81	.08	......	(b)
25	Cask .	Finland	U.S.D.A....	.....do	12.57	83.71	1.30	.04	2.38	
26	...do..	.....do	Iowa	.....do	11.29	85.47	1.43	.35	1.46	
27	Keg..	Holland	U.S.D.A....	.....do	12.86	83.75	1.16	.24	1.99	(b)
28	...do..	.....do	Iowa	.....do	10.56	87.17	1.01	.13	1.13	(b)
29	Box ..	Australia	London	August ...	10.40	87.51	.77	(a)	1.32	(b)
30	...do..	New South Wales.	U.S.D.A....	July	15.50	81.17	.98	.05	2.29	(b)
31	...do..	.....do	Connecticut .	.....do	14.94	81.88	.96	(a)	2.22	(b)
32	...do..	New Zealand	U.S.D.A....	November	10.80	86.62	.60	.03	1.86	
33	...do..	.....do	Iowa	.....do	8.65	89.27	.70	.06	1.33	
		Average of 33...	....	....	12.40	84.57	1.03	.17	1.83	

a The "natural ash" or mineral constituents included in the "salt" in these cases.
b Samples were found to contain preservative, generally borax.
c U.S.D.A. = United States Department of Agriculture.

NOTES UPON APPENDIX XI.

The first comparison suggested by this table is the general average composition of this foreign-made butter, with the analyses of an almost equal number, in Appendix X. The water is seen to be 2.1 per cent more and the fat 2.6 per cent less. There is also more curdy matter in this butter and more salt. The chemical preservatives used are included in the "salt," and, although the quantities were not determined, these may account for the rise in the salt results. The range is also noted as much greater than in the American butters. The water rises above 12 per cent in 19 instances and to 15 per cent and over in 7. The fat falls below 85 per cent in 16 cases and below 82 per cent in 5 cases. The European butter without salt resembles that made similarly in this country in carrying a relatively high per cent of water and low per cent of fat, a greater difference in these respects than is accounted for simply by the absence of 2 per cent or less of salt. It is notable that all this foreign butter was "borated," or treated with preservatives other than common salt, excepting the lots from England, Denmark, Finland, and New Zealand.

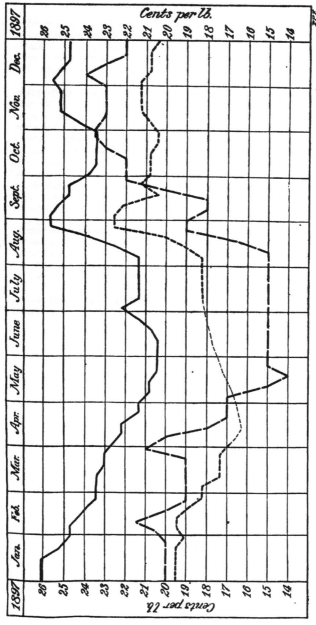

Diagram of butter price (wholesale) in London and New York for the year 1897

Best Danish in London ———   Extra Creamery in New York ———
"States" Creamery in London ———   (estimated) ———

FIG. 10.

NOTES UPON APPENDIX XII (DIAGRAM).

Upon the accompanying diagram the lines indicating the fluctuations in prices of butter in London and New York are based upon weekly quotations of the best grade of Danish and States, or "creamery extras," published by old and reliable merchants in the respective cities. The only exception is a period from early April to early July, when the London house failed to quote States butter. For this period the prices have been estimated from other data.

The most striking feature of the diagram is the difference between the prices of best butter in London and in New York during the greater part of the year. It is generally understood that American markets are so good in winter as to remove all inducement to export. The diagram does not support this view, except as to the last three months of 1897. The difference varies from nothing late in October to over 7 cents per pound less than two months earlier. With the exception of a few weeks near the close of the year, the difference was at all times greater than the cost of moving butter from New York to London. The explanation seems to be that during the winter months, when the margin in price might have encouraged export from New York, the supply of good "Colonial" (Australian and New Zealand) butter in England was such as to prevent any successful competition from this country.

The diagram also indicates the grade of butter exported. During seven months of the year States butter in London was quoted lower than "creamery extras" in New York. If the grade of exported butter had been "extras" it surely would have been kept at home and sold at the higher rate. In May, June, July, and August extras were very low in New York, and this appears to have started the shipment of that grade, which continued until New York prices rose again.

The notes upon the diagram are confirmed by the Treasury Department returns of the quantity and value of butter exported from the United States to the United Kingdom during the successive months of the year in question.

BREEDS OF DAIRY CATTLE.

By HENRY E. ALVORD, C. E.,

Chief of Dairy Division, Bureau of Animal Industry.

The domestic cattle of the world are probably descended from one parent stock, but variation began at a very early period. Through ancient sculptures and other records cattle can be traced back at least four thousand years, and the earliest evidence shows that animals of different types were then known. In various parts of the world there are now cattle so distinct in their characteristics as to justify their claim to be regarded as breeds, and these breeds exceed 100 in number. A subdivision of a family in the animal kingdom may be recognized as a breed when it has been subjected to and reproduced under the same conditions until it has acquired a distinctive character common to all the members and naturally reproduced with very slight variations. This definition, and the term breed, applies especially to domestic animals, and the differences which chiefly distinguish the breeds of the present day are the result of artificial treatment by man—the work of skillful breeders having definite objects in view.

The different breeds of cattle to be found in the United States all came from Great Britain and the western portions of Europe, and it is not at all unlikely that they have a common origin in the wild cattle which existed in the ancient forests of Europe. These were described by Julius' Cæsar, Pliny, and other Latin writers almost a thousand years ago, and by others who wrote of them a century or two later as abounding in the great forests around London. They were also mentioned frequently in chronicles of the middle ages.

In the early history of these cattle natural causes tended to divide them into two general classes; first, those adapted to the more mountainous and less fertile sections of country, and, second, those of the plains and richer regions. The former, owing to greater scarcity of food and more difficulty in obtaining it, were smaller, more rugged, and rougher in type than the better fed animals of the latter class. Later, breeding and artificial conditions, together with natural causes, resulted in additional variations among cattle, and led to the distinctions which became fixed in different breeds. The chief characteristics resulting from man's interference and control were first to be seen, on the one hand, in a tendency of the animals to mature at an early age and easily to lay on flesh and fat, and, on the other hand,

187

in prolonging the natural period of milk flow and increasing the milk product much beyond the needs of the calf.

At the present time each of the various recognized breeds of domestic cattle may be satisfactorily placed in one of two great classes designated, respectively, as beef cattle and dairy cattle. This article is intended to deal with the latter, giving something of the history and describing the characteristics of those breeds which are valued especially for their dairy qualities and of a few which belong primarily to the beef breeds, but also possess dairy merit. Some of the dairy breeds of Europe are not included; it seems enough to present those which are known in the United States—which have already made an impress upon the neat stock of this country, and which promise to be of value in promoting dairy interests.

Illustrations representative of the several breeds described accompany the text, being the likenesses of two mature animals, a bull and a cow, in each case.

The colored plate (frontispiece) is presented as an excellent example of a fine dairy cow. This animal is the Duchess of Smithfield 4256, American Ayrshire Record. She is descended in the seventh generation from stock imported from Scotland. The shape of head, horn, and udder are not typical of the Ayrshire, although she is a noted cow of that breed. She was dropped in Rhode Island in 1876, and always owned in New England. In 1885, when 8 years old, she won the first prize of the Ayrshire Breeders' Association, in an official test of seven days, by a record of 464 pounds of milk, which produced 19 pounds 6 ounces of butter. She calved in March and the test was made in June. Her udder measured 68 inches in circumference during this test. Her weight was 1,128 pounds, and she gave during one full year 10,748 pounds (or 1,242 gallons) of milk. Her color was a deep, rich red, with white in about equal parts. This cow belongs to what is known as the "Douglas family" of Ayrshires. She was a great winner of prizes herself at noted exhibitions, and her descendants of the first and second generations have been equally successful. They have also made records for milk and butter production which entitle them to the highest honors as dairy sires and dairy cows. Among those sired by sons of Duchess of Smithfield, was one which gave 12,172 pounds of milk in a year at the Vermont Agricultural Experiment Station, and several which have butter records ranging from 400 to 607 pounds in a year.

AYRSHIRES.

The county of Ayrshire, in the southwest part of Scotland, stretches for 80 miles along the lower portion of the river Clyde and the Irish Sea. The surface is undulating in large part, with moory hills, much woodland, and a climate moist and rather windy, although not severe. It is a region of moderate fertility, with natural pasturage so distributed that grazing animals must travel long distances in a day to satisfy their hunger.

In this county Ayrshire cattle were brought into their present fixed form. The breed is among the youngest of well-established type. Careful writers of a little more than a hundred years ago failed to even mention this breed, and the cattle of Ayrshire described in 1825 bear little resemblance to the present stock of the country and must have been only a foundation race, small, unshapely, and generally black; with white markings.

The Ayrshire breed has been built up within the nineteenth century by the liberal use of blood from the cattle of England, Holland, and the Channel Islands. The exact facts and methods are unknown, but the result testifies to the good judgment in selection and breeding of those who carried on the work. The Ayrshire of the present day— which is found best developed in Cunningham, the upper and most fertile of the three divisions of the county—bears strong resemblance to the Jersey in certain features; and in form, color, and horn it resembles the wild white cattle of Chillingham Park. Many people believe the cattle to be direct and but slightly varied descendants of the original wild cattle of Great Britain. There is a well-defined tendency in the improved Ayrshire to become lighter in color, many being almost white. This is additional evidence of a strong infusion of the blood last mentioned at some period in the history of the breed.

The first Ayrshires in America were brought to New York in 1822. They were imported into New England in 1830 and into Canada in 1837. In 1837 there was quite a large herd in Massachusetts, and several importations were made prior to 1845. From that time until 1875 there were more or less importations yearly, but there have since been less. This breed has been a special favorite for dairy purposes in Canada and highly esteemed in the New England States and parts of New York. Elsewhere in this country these cattle do not seem to be so well known as their established merits deserve.

Unless it be the little Irish Kerry, there is no cow which excels the Ayrshire in obtaining subsistence and doing well on a wide range of scanty pasture or in thriving and giving a dairy profit upon the coarsest of forage. "The natural hardihood of constitution renders these cattle admirably adapted to grazing on broken and rugged pastures and in sterner weather than would be conducive to the well-being of cows of some other breeds." The end sought in perfecting the breed has been a large yield of milk without extravagance of food. It is a characteristic of the Ayrshire that she carries her weight only, and lives only, to serve dairy interests with the utmost economy in the utilization of food. Yet, like all other good dairy cattle, the Ayrshire responds promptly and profitably to liberal feeding. The Scotch have a saying, taught by experience, that "the cow gives her milk by the mou."

Ayrshires are of medium size among dairy cattle. The bulls attain a weight of 1,400 to 1,800 pounds at maturity, sometimes being larger. The cows weigh 900 to 1,100 pounds, averaging probably 1,000 pounds in a well-maintained herd. They are short-legged, fine-boned, and very active. The general form is of the wedge shape, regarded as typical of cows of dairy excellence; and this shape is not from any weakness forward, but rather because of uncommon development and strength of body and hind quarters. Good specimens of the breed, when in milk, do not carry a pound of extra flesh. · The face is usually rather long and straight, but clean and fine, with a full growth of horn curving outward, then inward, and turning well up, with tips inclined backward. The general appearance of the horns is upright and bold, while usually symmetrical and often quite graceful. A black muzzle is the rule, although white seems to be allowable. The eye is peculiarly bright, with a quick movement indicating extreme watchfulness. The prevailing color of the body is red and white, variously proportioned; in spots, not mixed. Probably three-fourths of all the breed can be thus described as to color. A generation ago the dark markings predominated; but there is now a drift toward more white. Several prize winners at the Columbian Exposition might be called white cows. The red is sometimes bright, but often of a rich, shiny brown, like the shell of a horse chestnut, and the coat of a thrifty Ayrshire is equally bright and shining. Sometimes the color is a dull brown, and occasionally a brindle appears. Nearly all good animals of this breed have broad, flat, well-arched ribs, giving room for capacious digestive apparatus.

Dr. Sturtevant thus describes the milking parts of the Ayrshire cow: "The udder has been the point toward which the search after quality has been directed by the careful Scotchman for a long period of time. Although it differs in outward shape in individuals, it yet retains a certain uniformity which may be considered typical. This is in the gland and the teat. The glands are rather flattened than pointed or elongated, as in other breeds. These are well held up to the body, and in the types of the breed extend far forward and back, with a broad and level sole. The teats are small and of a cylindrical shape rather than cone-shaped, as seen in other cows. The udder is admirably fitted, by its elasticity, for the storage of milk, and when the glands are at rest occupies but little space. The eye accustomed to seeing the pendent fleshy udder so often met with in dairy animals is apt to underrate, in comparison, the capacity of the small bag of this breed, with its wrinkled and folded covering, so deceptive to the unskilled but so full of promise to the educated observer."

At the proper time these wrinkles smooth out, the folds expand, and the filled udder of the Ayrshire has come to be regarded as a model in shape for all dairy breeds. The teats are, however, often too small for comfortable milking; but careful breeders have remedied this defect, and whole herds can be found with superb udders and teats of good size, although rarely large.

The Ayrshire is of a highly nervous temperament. The cow has a superabundance of nerves and is willing to employ them, upon instant demand, in self-defense or self-support. The bulls, if properly handled, are not fractious, but the cows are rather inclined to be quarrelsome. They are always active and energetic, stop only for a purpose, move off with a brisk walk, and often trot without special provocation. Promptness is one of the characteristics of the breed.

Although these cattle can lay no claim to being specially adapted to beef production, the calves are thrifty and full fleshed, and steers and dry cows fatten readily on suitable feeding. Their carcasses are small, but they always give an unexpectedly large percentage of dressed meat, and its quality is excellent, fine grained, and well marbled.

The Ayrshire cow is a large and persistent milker. A yield of 5,500 pounds a year, as an average for a working herd in good hands, is depended upon and often realized. Records of 18 well-managed herds, collected from different sections and averaging 12 cows each, show an annual average product of 5,412 pounds. One noted herd, averaging 14 cows in milk, has an unbroken record for nineteen years with an average product of 6,407 pounds a year to the cow. In the last year recorded 19 cows averaged 6,956 pounds of milk. Four of the cows in this herd gave over 10,000 pounds in a year and one over 12,000 pounds. Butter records are not numerous, but in the herd last referred to the milk averaged 4¼ per cent of fat for the last year and the cows averaged 353 pounds of butter each, ranging from 244 to 512 pounds. In previous years single cows in this herd made butter records of 504, 546, 572, and 607 pounds within twelve months.

Another Vermont herd has a detailed record for eight consecutive years. The average yearly milk yield of the cows 3 years old and over has been, in different years, from 6,003 to 6,440 pounds; every year single cows exceed 7,000 pounds and sometimes 8,000. The milk of this herd averages over 4 per cent butter fat, and the yearly herd record ranges from 306 to 319 pounds of butter per cow; single cows have butter records of over 400 pounds per year. The most interesting fact connected with this herd is the economy of the rations upon which these records have been made: In summer, pasturage alone; in winter to each cow, daily, 1 bushel of ensilage of matured field corn, an average of 2 quarts each of corn meal and wheat bran, and plenty of good hay.

The milk of the Ayrshire is not exceptionally rich, but somewhat above the average. Herd records show 3½ to 4 per cent of butter fat in the mixed milk throughout the year. The milk of this breed is very uniform in its physical character, the fat globules being small, even in size, and not free to separate from the milk. Cream rises slowly and has comparatively little color. The Ayrshire is, therefore, not a first-class butter cow, but its milk is admirably suited for town and city supply, being safely above legal standards, uniform, and capable of long journeys and rough handling without injury.

A special reputation which this breed has enjoyed as superior cheese makers is not sustained by the facts. In the hands of capable makers Ayrshire milk will make little more cheese, if any more, from a given weight than from milk of other breeds. The uniform distribution of the fat is an advantage, and there is less liability to lose fat in converting this milk into cheese than in the case of richer milk with fat globules larger or irregular in size.

The breeders of Ayrshire cattle in America organized in the year 1863 and began the publication of a herdbook. The interests of the breed are now represented by the American Ayrshire Breeders' Association. The last volume of the Ayrshire Record is No. 12, issued in 1899. The total number of registered animals is about 22,000, and it is estimated that 6,000 of these are living and distributed among 500 or 600 owners, mainly in the New England and Middle States, Ohio, and Wisconsin.

The bull whose likeness has been selected as a good type of the Ayrshire is John Webb 5180. He was bred in this country, several generations removed from imported ancestry, was 6 years old when picture was made, and then weighed over 1,400 pounds. He was never shown, except at county fairs, where he always won first honors. His sire was a first-prize bull at New York State Fair, and the sire of noted dairy animals, among them a half sister to John Webb, which, at a fair-ground test, gave 50 pounds of milk in a day, from which 2¼ pounds of butter were made. The dam and granddam of this bull were also fine dairy cows, the latter having a record of 9,245 pounds of milk and 576 pounds of butter and two calves within eleven months. Young cows sired by him have given over 7,000 pounds milk a year, and one, 4 years old, about 10,000 pounds. Although well engraved from a faithful photograph, this likeness gives the bull rather too light and leggy an appearance, but shows his fine style and dairy quality. (See illustrations, p. 145.)

The cow selected to match is an imported animal, Red Rose 5566. This picture shows admirably the typical head, horn, and udder of the breed—the last in its best form; also the distinctly wedge shape which is believed to characterize fine dairy animals. She was brought from Scotland in 1875, and was the leading cow in the prize herd for her breed at the Philadelphia Centennial Exposition the next year. She was photographed at that time, being then 5 years old. Her milk product for one year was 8,578 pounds, or practically 1,000 gallons.

BROWN SWISS.

Switzerland has been famous as a dairying country for some centuries. It is especially noted for cheese, and it is said that seventeen different kinds are regularly exported to other countries. Two distinct races of cattle contribute to these products, and both are excellent dairy animals. In many respects they are unequaled by any of the other breeds of continental Europe.

The Brown Swiss is the breed better known in the United States.[1] It is called also Brown Switzer, but more properly Brown Schwyzer, from the Canton Schwyz, where the breed originated or, at least, has been bred longest and is still found of truest type. It is now common to the other cantons of eastern and central Switzerland and has a fine reputation throughout Europe. These cattle have been especially successful as prize winners at Paris, Hamburg, and other large exhibitions of live stock.

The first pure-bred animals of this breed brought to the United States comprised one bull and seven heifers, imported from the Canton Schwyz to Massachusetts in the autumn of 1869. It was not till 1881 or 1882 that other importations were made, but meanwhile this first little herd had been kept pure and had increased to nearly two hundred in number. During the years 1882 and 1883 several importations were made and there have been a number since. Where they have become known these cattle have made a favorable impression among dairymen, and herds of different sizes can now be found in States of all parts of the Union.

The Brown Swiss may be placed in the second class as to size among the distinctly dairy breeds. They are substantial, fleshy, and well proportioned, with very straight, broad back, heavy legs and neck, giving a general appearance of coarseness. But when examined they are found to be small-boned for their size and to possess a fine, silky coat, and rich, elastic skin, with other attractive dairy points. Although generally described as being brown in color, the brown runs through various shades and often into a mouse color and sometimes a brownish dun, especially for the saddle or body. Head, neck, legs, and quarters are usually darkest in color, often almost black. The nose, tongue, hoofs, and switch are quite black. Characteristic markings of the breed include a mealy band around the muzzle, with a light stripe across the lips and up the sides of the nostrils, a light-

---

[1] An account of the other Swiss breed, the Simmenthalers, appears at page 181.

colored tuft of hair between the horns, and a light-colored stripe extending all the way along the back to the tail. The eyes are full and mild, but bright, usually black. The horns rather small, white, waxy, curving forward and inward, with black tips. The ears are large, round, and lined with long silky hair, light in color. The barrel of the body is large and well rounded. The udder and teats are large, well formed, and white, with milk veins very prominent. The cows often carry remarkably well-shaped escutcheons. The animals of a herd are generally even in appearance, showing careful breeding extending through many generations. Bulls and cows are alike docile and easily managed. The cows are so plump and compact as to appear smaller than they really are. Mature animals weigh from 1,200 to 1,400 pounds, and often more; bulls run up to 1,800 pounds and over, yet are not so much heavier than the females as in most breeds. These cattle are extremely hardy and very active for their size, being necessarily good mountain climbers in their native country.

Developed as a dairy breed primarily, Brown Swiss cows yield a generous flow of milk and hold out well. Good specimens may be expected to give an average of 10 quarts for every day in the year. Six thousand pounds a year is an ordinary record, and single instances are known of 8,000 to 10,000 pounds. One Swiss cow owned in Massachusetts produced, by accurately recorded weights, 86,304 pounds of milk before 12 years old. The quality of milk is above the European average, $3\frac{1}{2}$ to 4 per cent of fat being usual. The cow mentioned above made a butter record ranging from 500 pounds to 610 pounds per year for four years, but this was exceptional. Ordinarily 22 pounds of the milk of this breed will make 1 pound of butter, and sometimes it does better.

The description given indicates that these cattle are good for beef as well as for the dairy. They are almost always full fleshed, easily kept so, and readily fattened when not in milk. The flesh is said to be fine grained, tender, and sweet. A barren heifer in Minnesota weighed 1,680 pounds; a mature cow in New York, fattened for butcher, weighed 1,925 pounds, and made 1,515 pounds of beef. A pair of Swiss steers at 13 months old weighed 2,200 pounds. The calves are large, often 100 pounds at birth, and make a vigorous growth. Weights 400 to 600 pounds at 4 to 6 months of age are not uncommon. Altogether, the Brown Swiss is able to present about as strong a claim as any breed to being a profitable "general purpose cow."

In their native country these cattle are ordinarily fed nothing but hay, grass, or other green forage, throughout the year, but they respond promptly to more various and generous feeding.

The Brown Swiss Breeders' Association in this country was organized in the year 1880 and has published three volumes of the Swiss Record. There have been 1,157 bulls and 1,714 cows registered (up to October, 1897), and it is estimated that 1,200 of these animals in all are now alive and owned by about 175 different persons, mainly in

FIG. 11.—Ayrshire bull John Webb 5180.

FIG. 12.—Ayrshire cow Red Rose 5566.

the States of Massachusetts, Connecticut, New York, Illinois, Wisconsin, Iowa, Minnesota, and Colorado.

Gilbo 720 was bred and owned in Illinois. This bull was placed first in his class at the State fair at Springfield in 1895, and was

10317——10

never exhibited afterwards. His likeness is from a photograph taken when 2¼ years old. He then weighed 2,150 pounds. The picture shows well the heavy frame, full flesh, strong muscles, and rugged appearance characteristic of this breed. The sire and dam of this bull were not show animals, but the dam gave 52 pounds (or 24 quarts) of milk a day with ordinary care, and the sire's dam when 10 years old gave an average of 65 pounds of milk, making 2¾ pounds of butter, for three days at the Fat Stock and Dairy Show, Chicago, in 1891.

Brienzi 168 was imported from Switzerland into Connecticut in 1882 and became the most noted cow of her breed in this country. More than this, she produced the largest quantity of butter fat in a day ever recorded in America at a public test. At the Chicago show mentioned above (1891) her average daily record for three days was 81.7 pounds of milk, containing 3.11 pounds of fat. This was equivalent to more than 3½ pounds of butter per day. The likeness of the cow was made at that time. She was then 11 years old and weighed 1,410 pounds. She was shown at numerous State fairs between 1886 and 1893, and always took first premium in her class; this was her award at the Columbian Exposition. . Calves of this cow of both sexes have also been first-prize winners at different ages at State fairs in Illinois, Iowa, and Missouri. (See illustrations, p. 147.)

DEVONS.

The peninsula which forms the southwestern portion of England is the home of a thrifty and attractive race of deep-red cattle, which take their name from the elevated region in the north of Devonshire, where they have been brought to the greatest evenness and fixity of type.

If solid color throughout and resistance to variation in all particulars be accepted as evidence of antiquity in a breed, the Devon must be regarded as among the oldest and purest. It certainly is one of the best defined of British breeds of cattle, although little is known of its origin. It was undoubtedly very gradually developed, but its greatest improvement since the record began has been at the hands of the brothers Quartley, Messrs. John T. and James Davy, and Mr. Coke, of Holkham, afterwards Earl of Leicester.

It is believed that Devons were among the very first cattle brought across the Atlantic, reaching New England on the ship *Charity* in the year 1623. Importations of some consequence were made in 1800, and to New York soon afterwards, but the first herd to be brought to this country and maintained pure, so that breeders can still trace to it, was a present of a bull and six heifers from Holkham, sent directly to Mr. Robert Patterson, of Maryland, and arriving at Baltimore

June 10, 1817. This Patterson herd has been kept up during the greater part of the century. Other importations occurred in 1818, 1820, 1835, 1855, and frequently in later years.

FIG. 13.—Brown Swiss bull Gibbo 720.

FIG. 14.—Brown Swiss cow Brienzi 168.

The characteristics of the Devon are compactness and general beauty, hardiness, activity, intelligence, docility, aptitude to fatten, and quality of milk. The prevailing red varies from a dark, rich

color to pale chestnut, but no black or white is admissible excepting a
little white patch on and in front of the udder, which sometimes
extends forward on the belly, and white hair in the switch of the tail.
The skin is yellow and unctuous, its richness being shown in an orange
ring around the eyes and more or less of the same encircling the muzzle. The hair is soft, fine, and often curls closely on the necks, shoulders, and faces. "The head is adorned, in the case of the female,
with particularly elegant, creamy-white, sharp-pointed, black-tipped
horns of medium length, having a good elevation at the junction with
the head and curving upward. In the bull the horns are shorter in
proportion to thickness, straighter, and less raised." Straight, broad,
level backs, roundness of form, fineness of bone, uncommon symmetry
of outline, make up an animal of great attractiveness.

Devons are of medium size, being about equal to the Ayrshires in
general average. Their docility, intelligence, and muscular activity,
already noted, combine to make steers of this breed especial favorites
as working cattle. Wherever working oxen are sought and appreciated, a common and justifiable ambition is to own a yoke of Devons.

These cattle thrive on meager pasturage and have shown remarkable adaptability to varied conditions of topography and climate.
They do well in the most hilly and rigorous parts of New England
and have proved well suited to the old field and pine lands of the
Gulf States.

As a rule, Devon cows do not yield large quantities of milk and are
not persistent milkers; yet some families, bred and selected for
dairy purposes, have made fair milk records, single animals producing 40 and even 50 pounds per day. The milk of this breed is rich
in quality, ranking next to the Channel Island cattle in percentage
of butter fat, total solids, and high color, being in these respects well
above the average of the dairy cows of the country.

While it is believed that the Devon is not commonly held in as high
esteem in the United States either as a dairy cow or a general-purpose animal as is really justified by its merits, the best friends of this
breed regard it as more particularly a beef producer. The calves
are always fat and lusty, showing a vigorous growth, while cows and
steers are easily kept in good order and fatten readily on demand.
At the famous Smithfield Fat Stock Show of London the Devons have
year after year won highest honors for butchers' meat. The beef is
fine-grained, usually tender, and well marbled, and the fat of a deep
yellow color, like the milk fat.

Capt. J. T. Davy began the publication of the Devon Herd Book in
1851, and animals bred and owned in America were for some years
entered in that book. Indeed, American pedigrees recorded run
back ten years further than the oldest published for English herds.
In 1859, herdbooks were published simultaneously in England and
America, and in March, 1863, the American Devon Herd Book, the

first volume of a new series, appeared. This publication has been continued by the American Devon Cattle Club. The last volume of the herdbook issued was No. VI, in 1899. This shows the animals registered to be 6,716 males and 11,627 females—a total of 18,343.

FIG. 15.—Devon bull Fine Boy of Pound 6185.

FIG. 16.—Devon cow Miss T 9605.

Of these, 10,000 are believed to be living, well distributed over the country, and in the hands of at least 900 different owners.

The preceding description relates to what may be regarded as the true Devon breed, although by some called the North Devon. This is to distinguish them from South Devons—a variation from the breed in its best form, giving a larger, coarser animal, not at all adapted to dairy uses.

Of the two animals selected to illustrate the Devon breed, the bull was imported and the cow was bred and owned in Pennsylvania.

Fine Boy of Pound 6185 began his public career soon after importation, in 1893, when 3 years old, and has won first prizes at all the principal fairs in the East and South. His sire took first honors and the Queen's cup once at royal shows in England. His progeny have furnished prize winners also, and his heifers are pronounced good milkers, although no special dairy records have been claimed for them. The picture shows this bull at the age of 4, when weighing 1,850 pounds.

Miss T 9605 has also been a first-prize winner for several seasons at Eastern fairs, and has a show-ring record equaled by few cows. Her calves have also won premiums at State and other fairs. Her dam, Matchless P 4065, was a fine dairy cow, her ordinary milk yield being 30 to 35 pounds per day, and 20 pounds of her milk always gave a pound of butter. The likeness of Miss T was taken when she was 7 years old, and her weight was then 1,450 pounds. Although faithful in outline, the picture does not do justice to this fine animal.

***

DUTCH BELTED.

The domestic cattle of Holland appear to have had a common origin, and the prevailing markings of all are black and white. The distribution of color differs, however, and one branch of this general stock has been so peculiarly marked for a century or two—some claim three—as to fix its name and secure recognition as a breed. What are known in Holland as "Lakenfeld" cattle are called Dutch Belted in this country.

The animals of this breed are all jet black, with a broad band or belt of pure white encircling the body. This belt or blanket differs in width, but rarely reaches so far forward as the shoulder blade or back to the hips. On cows the fore part of the udder is usually included. No white is admissible elsewhere on the body and no black within the white zone. In general conformation the cattle are of the dairy type, although not to such a degree as some others.

They are docile beasts and fairly hardy and vigorous in growth and action. In size they rank with the Ayrshire, although perhaps somewhat less blocky and with longer legs. Individuals are larger in frame, but not often heavier. This breed is not numerous either in Europe or America. A few specimens were brought to the United States in 1838, and for a long time there were more to be found in the famous dairying county of Orange, N. Y., than in all other parts of the country combined. They have become more scattered during recent years, and the interests of the breed are represented by the Dutch Belted Cattle Association of America. As milk producers these belted cows seem to give good satisfaction, although the milk is not above the

FIG. 17.—Dutch Belted bull Duke of Ralph 255.

FIG. 18.—Dutch Belted cow Lady Aldine 124.

average in quality. The claim of a leading breeder is that these cattle are "deep milkers, practical, profitable, thrifty, and picturesque in the extreme when seen as a herd at pasture."

The association mentioned publishes a herdbook, of which five volumes have been issued, the last in 1897. A total of 1,128 cattle have been registered, including 331 males and 797 females.   About 500 of these are believed to be still living, and they are mainly to be found in the States of Massachusetts, New York, New Jersey, Pennsylvania, Ohio, and Michigan, and the property of about 60 owners.

The two animals illustrating this strikingly marked breed are the bull Duke of Ralph 255 and the cow Lady Aldine 124.   Both are vouched for by prominent breeders as being good representatives of Dutch Belted stock.   The bull was 3 years old as shown in the picture and then weighed 1,200 pounds.   He came from a prize-winning family, although never himself shown in competition.   His dam, Belle of Crumwold 308, won the first prizes at the New England and other fairs.

Lady Aldine came from the old Orange County strain, her sire being Goshen 26, and her dam Elsie, who gave 32 quarts of milk a day for a week on grass alone.   The likeness shows the cow at 7 years old, when she weighed 1,200 pounds.   She was a first-prize winner at all the big fairs in Pennsylvania, New Jersey, and Delaware, and her progeny have won many honors at exhibitions.   She was a vigorous and productive cow until 18 years of age.

GUERNSEYS.

The island of Guernsey is the second in size of the Channel Islands, and lies farthest to the west in this group.   It is triangular in shape, being 9 miles long and about 4 in greatest width, with rough, rocky coasts, containing 16,000 acres, and has a population of 35,000, half of whom live in the principal town, St. Peters.   Market gardening is the chief occupation of the country people and dairy cattle form a secondary interest.   There are only about 5,000 cattle owned upon the island.   By a long-continued policy of excluding all live cattle from without its limits, the stock of this island has been built up into a distinct breed.   The origin and history of Guernsey and Jersey cattle are practically the same, but in the development of the former more of the characteristics of the parent stock of Normandy, France, have been retained.   At present, however, Guernseys can be better compared with Jerseys than with any other cattle.

It is difficult to say when Guernsey cattle began to come to the United States, but a few are known to have been owned near Philadelphia prior to 1850.   In America, as in England, all Channel Island cattle imported were long called "Alderneys," irrespective of the island from which they came.   Pure as they were at home, each within its own limits, the distinction was not properly preserved after they reached this country.   But between 1870 and 1875 the Guernsey became recognized here as a breed, and for twenty years importations have been made nearly every year. The breed has steadily increased in numbers and as steadily has gained in favor wherever introduced.

Guernseys are a size larger than Jerseys, stronger-boned, and a

FIG. 19.—Guernsey bull Sheet Anchor 3984.

FIG. 20.—Guernsey cow Fantine 2d 3730.

little coarser in appearance. They are claimed to be hardier and larger milkers, but both these points are stoutly disputed. They are generally very handsome and attractive cows.

The head of the Guernsey is rather long, the neck slender, the body large, deep, and rangy, the rump prominent, the flanks thin, thighs incurved, and twist open and roomy. Altogether the animal is at once recognized as businesslike and belonging to the pronounced dairy type. They are light in color, yellow and orange predominating, with considerable white, usually in large patches on the body and on the legs. Darker shades, approaching brown, are found upon some cows and are quite common on bulls. The muzzles are almost invariably buff or flesh-colored, surrounded by a fillet of light hair. Occasionally a black nose is found, showing the influence of some distant ancestor from Brittany. The horns are small, curved, fine, thin-shelled, and waxy in appearance, often showing a deep, rich yellow for a third of their length from the base. A characteristic of this breed is a very generous secretion of yellow coloring matter, which pertains to the whole skin, but is seen especially where the hair is white, in the ears, around the eyes, and about the udder. This gives a "richness" to the animal which is very noticeable and causes the butter produced to be of a higher color at all seasons of the year than that of any other breed. The udder and teats are large and admirably shaped and placed, in selected specimens, but these and other dairy markings do not, throughout the breed, appear to be as fixed as in the case of Jerseys, which have been subjected to a longer course of careful breeding.

The Guernsey possesses a nervous temperament, and yet the cows are extremely quiet and gentle when properly handled, and less trouble is reported in the management of aged bulls than with Jerseys of like age.

The cows of this breed produce liberal quantities of milk and it is of uncommon richness in butter fat and in natural color. They are to be especially recommended for butter cows, as well as for market milk where quality secures a relatively high price, and they are noted for rich production combined with especial economy in feeding. They possess great power of assimilating food and converting it into milk, yet are delicate feeders rather than gross, and will not generally bear much forcing. The grades, offspring of a Guernsey bull and well-selected cows of no particular breeding, usually make very satisfactory dairy stock. Guernsey cows average 1,000 pounds in weight, or a little more, and thus, being heavier than Jerseys, they are expected to give more milk. Records show, however, that the annual milk yield of good herds of these two breeds, of the same number, is just about the same. At the Columbian Exposition at Chicago, in 1893, 20 of the best Guernseys which could be found in the country were carefully tested and compared for five months with as many Jerseys and Shorthorns. The result so far as products are concerned is given on page 183. At home, the average Guernsey cow is expected to produce 5,000 pounds of milk and 300 pounds of butter in a year without high feeding. In this country these cows are fed higher and produce accordingly. Large herds have made records above the island standard just stated. One herd of 104 animals of all ages gave 5,317 pounds of milk and 318 pounds of butter per head in a year. Seventeen 3-year-old heifers in this herd, in the year 1896, averaged 6,035 pounds of milk and 355 pounds of butter. Another herd, of 15 cows, made ·a record (1895) of 6,626 pounds of milk and 418 pounds of butter. Still another, of 10 cows. averaged 6,347 pounds of milk in 1896 and 350 pounds of butter, Single cows have ranged up to 8,000, 10,000, 12,000, and almost 13,000 pounds of milk in a year, producing 500 to 700 pounds of butter. One cow gave 48 to 52 pounds of milk a day and 7,000 pounds in six months—a rate of over 25 pounds of butter per week and over 800 pounds per year. These records show what the best animals can do under the most favorable circumstances. The mixed milk of this breed is often found to average 14 to 15 per cent of total solids and 5 to 6½ per cent of fat. One herd record shows that for eight years it required 17 pounds of milk, on an average, to make a pound of butter. The fat globules in the milk are relatively large and the cream separates easily.

On the island of Guernsey, the beef of the native cattle is highly prized, and young animals are said to fatten easily at a profit. In the United States the friends of the Guernsey have laid no claim to its being a beef producer, and yet when an animal of this breed, if not too old, ceases for any reason to be profitable for the dairy, it is converted into beef without loss to the feeder.

The American Guernsey Cattle Club was organized in 1878. Volume IX is the current issue of the Guernsey Herd Register for 1899. This register includes the pedigrees of 5,600 bulls and 11,000 cows. Two-thirds of these are probably living and they are to be found scattered throughout almost every State of the Union.

Sheet Anchor 2934, chosen as the male representative of the Guernseys, is a noted animal. Few have such a prize-winning record; he has never been beaten in the show ring. Yet both parents were almost as successful, and his get are following in the same lines, the females supporting their show honors by records of dairy performance. This bull is American bred, dropped December, 1891, but both sire and dam were imported. The former, Lord Stranford 2187, won first prize on the island of Guernsey, in 1889, and first and sweepstakes at the Columbian Exposition in 1893. The dam, Bienfaitrice 4th 3657, was regarded as one of the best and most typical cows of her breed. After second calf she gave 41 pounds of milk a day. Sheet Anchor is a light yellowish red in color, with the white markings shown, and his skin is soft and pliable, with a wonderful golden hue, which shows through the silken hair on all parts of the body. The likeness shows him in his 4-year-old form, weighing

1,600 pounds, with long body, strong back and loins, ample constitution, dairy characteristics of the highest order, and fine style and finish. Heifers got by him have milk records ranging up to over 6,000 pounds per year, with $4\frac{1}{2}$ to over 6 per cent average fat tests; one made 329 pounds of butter before her second calf.

Fantine 2d 3730 stands in the very front rank among Guernsey cows, and is an excellent type of her breed. She and her dam were both bred in this country, while her sire and both parents of dam were imported. The likeness reproduced was made when she was 8 years old and within a few weeks of calving; her udder is shown not more than two-thirds filled. Her digestive capacity, good constitution, and strong dairy points are well shown in the engraving. At the age stated she made a record of 9,748 pounds of milk and 603 pounds of butter within eleven months. Her best day's yield was 47 pounds of milk, and her best month (the second—December) was 1,318 pounds of milk, containing 70 pounds of butter fat, equivalent to $81\frac{1}{4}$ pounds of butter. In four different months her milk yield was greater than her own live weight.

HOLSTEIN-FRIESIANS.

The strongly marked black-and-white cattle of North Holland and Friesland constitute one of the very oldest and most notable of the dairy breeds. The historians of this race claim that it can be traced back for two thousand years continuously occupying the territory named and always famous for dairy purposes. Tradition has it that two ancient tribes located upon the shores of the North Sea before the beginning of the Christian era; one possessed a race of cattle pure white and the other a kind all black. Men and cattle then became amalgamated, forming the people and herds which for centuries have occupied that region. Holland has been noted for dairy products for at least a thousand years, and the great bicolored beasts upon which this reputation has been gained have been slowly but surely developing their present form of dairy excellence.

These cattle have been known by several different names, in both Europe and America. "Holland cattle," "North Hollanders," "Dutch cattle," "Holsteins," "Dutch-Friesians," "Netherland cattle," and "Holstein-Friesians" are all the same. There was sharp contention in this country before the last name was agreed upon and generally accepted. It seems unfortunate that the simpler and sufficiently descriptive and accurate name of "Dutch cattle" was not adopted.

The large frame, strong bone, abundance of flesh, silken coat, extreme docility, and enormous milk yield of the Holstein-Friesians result from the rich and luxuriant herbage of the very fertile and moist reclaimed lands upon which the breed has been perfected, the uncommonly good care received from their owners and the close association of people and cattle. The Roman dominion brought improvements in draining and diking, in methods of cultivation and

FIG. 21.—Holstein-Friesian bull De Brave Hendrik 230, H.-F. H. B.

FIG. 22.—Holstein-Friesian cow Jamaica 1336, H. H. B., and calf.

of cattle breeding, but no mixture of blood occurred with the inhabitants or in their herds. "The preservation of the Friesian people and their continued adhesion to cattle breeding for more than two thousand years is one of the marvels of history. Always few in number, the conflicts of war and commerce have raged over and around them, yet they have remained in or near their original home, continuously following their original pursuits. Their farm houses are fashioned after the same general model; the one immense roof covers everything that requires protection. Here the cattle find shelter during the long and rigorous winter months. Here they are fed and groomed and watched for months without being turned from the door. Here the family is also sheltered, sometimes with only a single partition between the cattle stalls and the kitchen and living room. Everything is kept with a degree of neatness marvelous to those not accustomed to such system. The cattle become the pets of the household. At the opening of spring or when grass is sufficiently grown they are taken to the fields and cared for in the most quiet manner. Canvas covers protect their bodies from sun, and storm, and insects. The grasses upon which they feed are rich and luxurious, and the animals have to move about very little to gather sufficient food. On the first appearance of winter they are returned to the stable and the simple round of the year is completed. This round is repeated until the cattle are 6 or 7 years of age, when they are usually considered as past the period of dairy profit and are sent to the shambles. The object is always to produce as much milk and beef as possible from the same animal. With this twofold object in view, selection, breeding, and feeding have been continued for ages." (Houghton.)

This condensed description of the origin, development, and home treatment of this breed of cattle goes far toward explaining the characteristics of the breed as seen in this country.

The early Dutch settlers in America undoubtedly brought their favorite cattle with them during the seventeenth century, and there are definite records of three or four importations prior to 1850; but the credit of first introducing this breed to America and maintaining its purity here is due to Winthrop W. Chenery, of Massachusetts. He made three importations between 1857 and 1862. The Messrs. Gerrit S. and Dudley Miller, of New York, followed in 1867, and soon thereafter numerous others brought animals of this breed in considerable number to the United States. They have increased rapidly by importations and by breeding, and are now to be found in nearly all parts of this country.

The striking features in the appearance of this breed are the color markings of black and white and the large size of the animals of both sexes. The shining jet black contrasts vividly with the pure white, the fine, silky hair being upon a soft and mellow skin of medium thickness. In some animals the black predominates, and the white in others. Black has been rather preferred among American breeders, to the almost entire exclusion of white in some cases, yet a few very noted animals have been mainly white. The average animal

carries rather more black than white, and the distribution and out-
lines of the markings are extremely irregular. The black and white
are never mixed, the lines of demarcation being usually sharply
drawn. In Europe there are still some red cattle in this breed, and
occasionally a purely bred calf is dropped in this country with bright
red instead of black, showing the influence of some remote ancestor;
but none are admitted to the American Herd Book except those black
and white. In size the Holsteins are the largest of all the dairy
breeds. The big, bony frames are usually well filled out, and the
chest, abdomen, and pelvic region are fully developed. It is difficult
to prevent the males from becoming too fleshy for breeding animals,
and the females, when not in milk, take on flesh rapidly and soon
become full in form. The cows range in weight from 1,000 to 1,500
pounds, most of them being between 1,100 and 1,400, with an average
of about 1,250 pounds. The bulls at maturity are very large and
heavy, often above 2,500 pounds in weight. The head is long, rather
narrow and bony, with bright yet quiet eyes and large mouth and
nostrils. The horns are small and fine, often incurving, and frequently
white with black tips. The ears are large, thin, and quick in movement. The neck is long, slender, and tapered in the cows, its upper
line often quite concave. The back line is usually level, particularly
with the males, and the hips broad and prominent; some have well-
rounded buttocks, but a drooping rump is not uncommon. The legs
appear small for the weight carried and are quite long; the tail long
and fine and a white brush is required. The udder is often of extraordinary size, filling the space between legs set well apart, extending high behind and fairly well forward, with teats of large size and
well placed. Teats are sometimes cone-shaped and uncomfortably
large and puffy where attached to the udder. The milk veins are
usually prominent and sometimes remarkably developed. There is
a more marked inclination toward the beef form among the bulls
than among the cows; the latter are generally of the true dairy type.

In temperament these animals are quiet and docile, bulls as well as
cows, and the bulls exceptionally so. They have great constitutional
vigor. The calves are large at birth, almost always strong and thrifty,
and they grow fast and fatten easily. They mature early, heifers
reaching their full height at two and a half years and showing no
growth after four or five years except the addition of flesh and fat.
Animals of both sexes can be readily turned into very good beasts for
slaughter at almost any age, but they lack depth in the loin and ribs
and have not the finish and quality of the noted beef breeds. These
animals are very large feeders and at the same time dainty about their
eating. To do their best they must have an abundance of rich food
without the necessity of much exertion to get it.

These great black-and-white cows yield milk in proportion to their
size. The breed is famous for enormous milk producers. Records

are abundant of cows giving an average above their own live weight in milk monthly for ten or twelve consecutive months, and there are numerous authentic instances of daily yields of 100 pounds or more for several days in succession and 20,000 to 30,000 pounds of milk in one year. Cows giving 40 to 60 pounds (or 5 to 7 gallons) per day are regarded as average animals; 7,500 to 8,000 pounds per year is depended upon as a herd average. A known record of 11 cows from 3 to 8 years old is 11,286 pounds (or 5,250 quarts per cow), the average milking period being three hundred and forty-one days. Another herd of 12 cows averaged 8,805 pounds a year (or 4,064 quarts) for four years. The milk of these very large producers is generally pretty thin, low in percentage of total solids, and deficient in fat. The cows have been favorites for dairymen doing a milk supply business, but in numerous cases their product has been below the standards fixed by State and municipal laws. On the other hand, there are some families of Holsteins, and single animals are numerous, which give milk of more than average richness and show themselves to be profitable butter producers. Cows have frequently made from 15 to 25 pounds of butter a week, and 30 pounds in a few cases. Entire herds of good size have averaged over 17 pounds a week; a few cows have records of 90 pounds, and one almost 100 pounds, in a month. One of the herds already referred to averaged 308 pounds of butter per cow annually for four years, and there are several yearly herd records of over 400 pounds per head; also single records of 500 and 600 pounds, and one is claimed of 1,153 pounds of butter in three hundred and sixty-five consecutive days. A cow bred and raised in Texas made a remarkable record there, when five years old and weighing 1,350 pounds; she gave 707½ pounds of milk in seven days, which produced 22 pounds of butter, and in one month 2,958 pounds of milk containing fat equivalent to 86 pounds of butter. Holstein milk is characterized by fat globules of small and uniform size, separating slowly by the gravity method of creaming, and carrying very little color.

The breeders of "thoroughbred Holstein cattle" in America organized in 1872 and compiled the fi st herdbook. This was three years before any such published pedigrees appeared in Netherlands, the home of the breed. In 1877 another association of breeders formed and started the Dutch-Friesian herdbook. After a long and bitter contest these two organizations happily compromised and united their names and records as the Holstein-Friesian Association of America. The secretary of the association is editor of its register (a monthly journal) and of its herdbook. The sixteenth volume was published in 1899, and brought the recorded pedigrees up to 24,639 for bulls and 46,434 for cows. Previous issues of herdbooks upon this breed comprise nine volumes of the Holstein Herd Book, containing 15,364 bulls and 10,560 cows, and four volumes of the Dutch-Friesian Herd Book, containing 730 bulls and 1,937 cows. This makes a total registry of nearly 100,000, and it is estimated that half of these pure-bred animals are now alive in the United States. Although they are well distributed throughout the whole country, the animals of this breed are owned in greatest number in the States of Massachusetts, Connecticut, New York, Pennsylvania, Ohio, Indiana, Michigan, Wisconsin, Minnesota, Iowa, Missouri, Nebraska, Kansas, Texas, Colorado, and California.

It happens that both the selections for illustrating this breed represent imported animals and consequently comparatively little can be told about them and their immediate ancestors. It would be easy, however, to find many equally good types among American-bred Holsteins. Indeed, it is believed that in respect to size and dairy quality, the best animals of this breed in the United States are superior to those of their native country. De Brave Hendrik 230, H.-F. H. B., was dropped in North Holland in March, 1880, and during the years 1882, 1883, and 1884 won high prizes at Alkmaar, Gouda, and (first) at the great International Exhibition at Amsterdam. In March, 1883, he was designated by an official committee as the best bull in north Holland. He was imported in 1884 and owned in Pennsylvania. The likeness shows him as 4 years old, and he then weighed 2,300 pounds. This bull came from a great milking family, and the females sired by him proved uniformly excellent as dairy animals.

Jamaica 1336, H. H. B., was dropped in Friesland in 1880 and imported the same year to Orange County, N. Y. She had her first calf in December, 1882, and during a milking period of three hundred days gave 7,450 pounds of milk. Her second calf was dropped in December, 1883, and when one month in milk she had exceeded all known records for her age, and this upon the ordinary ration for milkers in the herd. Her feed was then carefully increased until she gave 73 pounds of milk a day, in January (1884), and a total amount of 2,026 pounds during that month. The milk yield continued to increase during February, notwithstanding unusually cold, rough weather, until she reached the maximum of 112 pounds 2 ounces of milk on the 2d of March, when she was 4 years old. She gave 535 pounds of milk in five days, 1,034 pounds in ten days, 2,102 pounds in twenty-one days, and almost attained an average of 100 pounds a day for a month.[1] In four months Jamaica gave almost 10,000 pounds of milk, and about 20,000 pounds during this her second milking period. From her milk for a week 23½ pounds of butter was made. The average of grain fed to the cow during her greatest yield was 28 pounds, costing 30 cents, with an abundance of cut beets and good hay, and she had access to spring water in the stable yard five or six times a day. She received no silage, slops, stimulating food, or drugs.

---

[1] The writer of this notice lived in the vicinity and verified the yield of this cow several days during the month; she was milked every eight hours, and there is no question about the accuracy of the record.—H. E. A.

Jamaica was of medium size for her race, handsomely marked, vigorous, and very stylish, as shown by her likeness. This was made about the time of her famous test; she then weighed 1,192 pounds. Her owner was offered $15,000 for this cow and her heifer calf, shown in the picture, before her milk yield reached 100 pounds a day. After her great performance this offer was increased to $25,000, and $10,000 was refused for the calf alone.

JERSEYS.

Lying in the English Channel, 30 to 50 miles from the southern extremity of Great Britain, is an interesting group of islands, the largest of which, but 13 miles from the coast of France, is the Island of Jersey. It is 11 miles long and less than 6 miles wide, being an irregular rectangle in shape, about the size of Staten Island, in New York Harbor. High rocky cliffs bound its coast on the north and west; thence the surface slopes gradually to the south, with valleys and plains of some extent. This is the home of one of the most important and widely distributed of the dairy breeds of cattle. The island was known by the Romans as Cesarea, and it is supposed that "Jersey" is a corruption of that name. Although one of the oldest and most loyal parts of the British Empire, this island, with its 60,000 inhabitants, is in appearance as much French as English, the curious dialect used by most of its people being old Norman. The foundation of the race of cattle developed here was probably the stock of Normandy and Brittany. But early in the eighteenth century steps were taken to prevent outside cattle coming to Jersey, and in 1779 a law was made, which has since been rigidly enforced, prohibiting under heavy penalties the landing upon the island of any live animal of the bovine race. Jerseys have therefore been purely bred with certainty for a longer time than any other breed of British origin.

The arable land of the island is in the hands of about 2,000 owners. The holdings vary from 3 to 30 acres, and herds exceeding a dozen cows are very rare. The soil is extremely fertile and its productiveness is enhanced by mildness of climate; the mean temperature of the year is 51° F. and the average rainfall is 30 inches. The ordinary yearly rental of land is $50 to $100 per acre. Extensive pastures, therefore, can not exist, and land and grass are so valuable that cattle are never permitted to roam at large. From time immemorial the custom has been to tether all animals, and they are moved several times a day. They are always led instead of being driven, and the handling is largely done by women. The cows remain out of doors the greater part of the year and are often milked in the fields. Very little grain is fed, but in addition to grass and hay the cattle are liberally supplied with roots, chiefly parsnips, which are abundantly grown for this purpose. Under these conditions a highly organized, delicate, and gentle race of cattle has been developed. It is at the

FIG. 23.—Jersey bull Pedro 3187.

FIG. 24.—Jersey cow Brown Bessie 74997.

same time a race of inherent constitutional vigor and peculiarly free in its island home from contagious, congenital, and other diseases.

A few Jersey cattle, then generally known as Alderneys, were brought to the United States prior to 1840, but importations did not become active until after the middle of the century. Connecticut,

Massachusetts, and New Jersey led in introducing this breed to America, and from 1860 to 1890 importations were very numerous. Year after year the little home island exported 2,000 animals or more, nearly all coming to this country. Jerseys have been so numerously imported, have increased so rapidly in America, have been so largely used for grading, and have proved so remarkably well adapted to a wide range of climate, that the characteristic markings of no other breed can be so frequently seen wherever dairy cows are kept, from the St. Lawrence to the Gulf, and from ocean to ocean.

Jerseys are the smallest in average size of the noted dairy breeds, cows ranging from 700 to 1,000 pounds and the bulls from 1,200 to 1,800 pounds. Yet the highest weights stated are often exceeded, and where effort has been made to build up a herd of larger size an average of over 1,000 pounds for mature cows has been easily attained. The average weight of Jerseys in America is considerably more than the average on their native island. In color this breed varies more than any other. For a time there was a craze for "solid-colored" animals in this country, and many persons have the idea that no pure Jersey has white upon it. This is entirely erroneous; all of the animals of the earliest importations were broken in color. There have always been such among the most noted cows, and at the present time few breeders object to white markings, if high dairy quality is maintained. At one time a careful examination of the foundation stock on the Island of Jersey showed that but one cow in ten was solid colored. The proportion is greater in the United States, but there are pure registered Jerseys of all shades of brown to deep black, and of various shades of yellow, fawn, and tan colors to a creamy white; also mouse color or squirrel gray, some light red and a few brindle. With all these colors and shades there may be more or less white, in large patches or small, and on any part of the animal. Bulls range much darker in color than cows. But there are always signs or markings about a pure Jersey or a high grade, or something in its appearance, hard to describe, by which the blood is unmistakably shown.

The head of the Jersey is small, short, broad, lean, and generally dished. The muzzle, including underlip, is black or a dark lead color, surrounded by a mealy fillet of light skin and hair. The eyes are wide apart, large, bright, and very prominent. The horns small, waxy, with thin shells, often black tipped and often much crumpled. Ears small and delicate. Neck small, clean, and fine; legs the same, and rather short. Body well rounded, with capacity for food and breeding. Tail long and fine, with a full brush often reaching to the ground. The skin is mellow and loose, with fine, silky hair. The udder of good size, more pendulent than in the Ayrshire, and with quarters more distinctly defined. Teats sometimes small and conically inclined. But udder and teats seem to be easily improved by judicious breeding. The square, close, "Ayrshire udder" is frequently well-nigh perfect. Milk veins highly developed, sometimes tortuous and knotty. This breed is second only to the Guernseys in the abundant secretion of coloring matter, which shows itself on the skin on various parts of the body, makes the fat of the body a deep orange, gives a rich tint to milk and cream, and a strong golden hue to the butter. Jerseys are irregular and sharp in outline, being picturesque rather than symmetrical, with the spare habit of flesh which is deemed favorable to dairy quality and enough muscular development for healthy activity and full digestive force. They are light, quick, and graceful in movement. Those of certain coloring are spoken of as "deer like" in appearance and action.

Jersey cattle are of the nervous order of temperament, highly developed. They are excitable for cause, but the females, when properly treated, are exceedingly placid and docile. The bulls have the reputation of being fractious and difficult to handle after attaining maturity. This is largely a matter of early training and judicious management. Although naturally active and disposed to self-assertiveness, good managers find no trouble in keeping Jersey bulls under perfect control throughout long lives. Owing to greater range, variation, and rigor of climate, and perhaps including rougher usage, the animals of this breed, reared for generations in America, have become larger, stronger boned, and more robust than on their native island. As dairy animals they are also decidedly superior to their island progenitors.

For scores of years Jerseys have been bred especially and almost exclusively for butter. There was no demand for milk on the home island, and the whole effort was to increase richness and add to the product of butter. In America breeders have striven with success to increase the milk yield, while maintaining its high quality. Two, three, and four gallons per day are common yields, and these cows are noted for persistence in milking, making a long season of profit, with great evenness of product until near its close. Herd records are numerous. Ten selected as having average dairy farm conditions include 140 cows and cover six years. The annual milk product per cow was 5,157 pounds, yielding 293 pounds of butter. Among these was one herd of 25 cows of all ages with a continuous record of seven years. The annual average per cow was 5,668 pounds milk and 342 pounds of butter. Several herd records for shorter periods show average yields of 6,000 and 7,000 pounds per cow. Single animals are on record producing 9,000, 10,000, 12,000, and, at least two, nearly 17,000 pounds of milk in a year. The characteristic of the milk of this breed is a high percentage of total solids, especially fat; 4 to 5 per cent of fat is a usual rate, in many instances higher. Jersey butter records are correspondingly large. Good herds are depended upon to produce 350 to 400 pounds of butter for every milking animal fed the full year. Individual cases are récorded by the hundred of cows making 15 to 20 pounds of butter in a week, and there are numerous weekly records of 25 to 30 pounds and more. Several tests for a full milking period have resulted from single animals, within twelve months of 600, 700, 800, and even 1,000 pounds. The butter fat in Jersey milk is in globules of uneven size, but mostly large, larger than with other breeds, and hence easily separated. The natural milk of cows of this breed is often too rich for their own calves, and it generally needs to be diluted when used for infants.

Jerseys are heavy feeders and have great capacity for assimilating and turning to profit all kinds of cattle forage. As a rule, they will bear rich feeding and forcing for long periods uncommonly well. In the good animals all the extra food is converted into milk. They do not fatten readily. The Jersey cow is essentially a machine for producing milk—butter-making milk—and may be considered worthless when she ceases to give milk. The owner should depend for profit solely upon the produce of the cow while she is alive. Yet Jersey steers and an occasional nonbreeding female have been found to take on flesh at a profit and make small butchers' beasts, with fine-grained, high-flavored flesh, very rich in color.

Breeders on the island of Jersey commenced the compilation of a herdbook in 1866, and a like association began similar work in this country the same year. The American Jersey Cattle Club was organized in 1868 and published the first volume of its Herd Register two years later. This is a strong organization, maintaining a business office in New York City. Volume 50 of its Register was published in 1898, bringing the recorded pedigrees up to 52,000 for males and 132,000 for females. It is estimated that there are 90,000 registered Jersey cattle alive in America, besides thousands pure although not registered, and hundreds of thousands of grades. The blood of this breed is more generally diffused and more highly prized than any other in the active butter-producing districts of the United States and among family cows in the country at large.

The illustrations of Jerseys represent two of the most famous animals of that breed.

Pedro 3187 was the second of several noted sons of the great cow Eurotas 2454,[1] having an authentic record of 778 pounds of butter produced in less than a year without forced feeding. Pedro was bred in New Jersey. His likeness is from a photograph by Schreiber. The bull was then 10 years old and weighed 1,760 pounds. His body color was gray, with very dark shadings, almost black, on head, neck, and quarters. He won numerous honors at important

---

[1] This cow furnishes an example of the impress which one animal may make upon a breed. Eurotas had 8 bull calves, which all reached maturity and became, collectively, the sires of 365 males and 449 females, registered.

fairs, individually and through his get, the climax being reached at the Columbian Exposition, when he was 16 years old. At this most remarkable contest in the history of the breed, Pedro won first prize in his class, led the first-prize herd, and took the sweepstakes for Jersey bulls. Several of his get won honors in the younger classes,

FIG. 25.—Normandy bull Americain 2.

FIG. 26.—Normandy cow Amie 8.

and the first-prize "young herd" were "all Pedros." This bull has 45 tested daughters, 33 of them having butter records averaging over 18 pounds in seven days, and 10 2-year-olds average 15½ pounds a week. When a young bull, Pedro was sold for $10,000 and proved to be a bargain at this price. The constitutional vigor of the animal is shown by his likeness and by the fact that he sired 138 registered sons and 120 daughters, besides others not recorded. He was in effective service until within two months of his death, which occurred in August, 1896, when almost 19 years old.

Brown Bessie 74997 became famous as the champion butter cow in the dairy tests, open to all breeds, at the Columbian Exposition (1893). She was in her prime at this time, 8 years old, and weighed 1,040 pounds. The likeness given is drawn from a photograph by Schreiber, taken while the cow was at Chicago. She was a Western animal, bred and raised in Iowa and Wisconsin, and later owned in Massachusetts. She was a rich brown in color, with a few white markings as shown. Her body was long and deep, with great storage capacity, and her milking parts and dairy points generally were of the best. During the public tests mentioned, under very unfavorable conditions, this cow averaged over 40 pounds of milk a day for five months, her total yield being exceeded (by 70 pounds) by only one of her seventy competitors. She made 3 pounds of butter a day several times, 20½ pounds a week, and 98 pounds more than any other cow in the entire test. Brown Bessie had a daughter and a full sister having butter records of over 20 pounds a week. Besides these, there are numerous other cows of record closely akin to her. She is one of a famous butter-making family; one grandsire was Combination 4389, and his grandsire was Sarpedon 930, also the grandsire of Pedro 3187. There are other noted dairy animals in this cow's pedigree, and the producing qualities of the get of her sons are adding to her reputation.

NORMANDIES.

As little is known of this breed as of any represented in the United States, and there are as few of them in this country. They are natives of the departments of Eure, Manche, Calvados, and Orne, in France, and are there esteemed for their dairy qualities. They appear, however, to lack a fixity of type, and are a coarse, rough race from which close selections must be made to get animals which are at all attractive.

A few were brought to America and taken to Illinois in 1885, others to New York in 1886, and to Massachusetts in 1887. Another importation was made in 1895, and these are owned in New York, New Jersey, and Vermont.

In size they may be classed with the large breeds, mature bulls ranging from 1,800 to 2,200 pounds in weight, and cows from 1,000 to 1,500 pounds. The animals are generally brindled and sometimes spotted, the coloring being red and reddish brown, shading dark and almost black. The head is coarse and rather long, with a large muzzle and mouth. The horns are long and extremely irregular, but with a

FIG. 27.—Polled Durham bull Young Hamilton 49.

FIG. 28.—Polled Durham cow Daisy 2.

tendency forward and downward, twisting in all directions on different specimens of the tribe. The body is long, deep, and irregular in outline, with narrow quarters, and covered with a thick, heavy skin. They have large, pendulent udders, prominent and tortuous milk veins, and long, widespread teats. They are believed to be particularly hardy and free from disease, and their generally rough appearance may be partly accounted for by the custom of the French farmers of never housing their cattle or giving more protection than is afforded by open sheds. These cattle are there almost entirely cared for by women and are very quiet and easily managed. They are hearty feeders and not dainty about their food.

The Normandies are claimed to belong to the "general purpose" class of cattle, being as good for beef as for the dairy. Large milk yields are reported from them, 7,000 to 8,000 pounds a year per cow, producing over 300 pounds of butter. Records made in this country show yearly yields of 4,000 to 7,000 pounds.

An organization has been perfected by the few persons interested in this breed in America, and a herdbook has been begun, but no publications have appeared up to 1899. (See illustrations, p. 167.)

The pictures furnished to represent this breed are those of the bull Americain 2, dropped in March, 1892, and imported three years later, and of the cow Amie 8, dropped in September, 1890, and imported February, 1895. "This cow calved April 20, 1895, and October 19, 1896, and to December 31, 1897, she had given 8,293 pounds of milk."

POLLED DURHAMS.

This is the only breed of cattle, if it may yet be called a breed, which has originated in America; but its foundation lies away back in the dawn of history regarding domestic cattle in England. At the time the earliest definite knowledge of improvement in the cattle of Great Britain begins, the middle counties formed the scene of activity, and "the district of Craven, a fertile corner of the West Riding of Yorkshire, bordering on Lancashire," seems to have been the place where the first decisive work was done which laid the foundation for a great race of cattle. The farmers of Yorkshire were well ahead of the rest of the country two or three centuries ago in their ideas of cattle improvement. The first group, or perhaps breed, to receive distinction and a name were the Longhorns. Their horns were as long as those of the typical Texan steer, but were drooping instead of erect.[1] The result of the next marked epoch in English cattle

---

[1] Mr. Pitt, writing two hundred years ago, mentioned the Longhorns of Yorkshire as giving milk that would produce more cheese and butter than any other cows known; and he told of 2 oxen fatted in 1794, and much alike, one of which dressed 1,988 pounds for the four quarters, besides 200 pounds of tallow and a hide of 177 pounds.

breeding was the Durham breed, which, by contrast with preceding favorites, were named Shorthorns. Another century has passed, and between "sports," selection, and artificial means, American breeders have been able to separate from the general Shorthorn stock a family

FIG. 29.—Red Polled bull Dobin 3462.

FIG. 30.—Red Polled cow Beauty 5th 2829.

retaining all the other features of that race, but with no horns at all. These are called Polled Durhams, and have become so fixed in type and in the potency of the hornless feature that they have been allowed a name and place as a distinct breed. It has taken shape within two or three decades, and one chary of new breeds is somewhat startled to find that animals registered as Polled Durhams are also admitted to the American Shorthorn Herd Book. Although thus largely of Shorthorn blood, the old familiar "muley" cow of the "native" stock of the country, often a brindle in color, was used to a considerable extent in the early work of building this breed and breeding out the horns. But, having served its purpose, this common blood is now rather despised, and one of the requirements for entry of animals in the American Polled Durham Herd Book is that after the year 1899 females shall carry at least 96$\frac{1}{2}$ per cent of Shorthorn blood, unless their parents are already registered. Besides this, they must have the "color and markings characteristic of the Shorthorn," but must be hornless. This branch or family of the Shorthorn breed—for that is what it is—was developed mainly in Ohio, and is best known in the valleys of the Ohio and Mississippi and in States to the westward.

As to size, color, and general appearance, the Polled Durhams answer perfectly to the description of the typical Shorthorn of the beef form (see later pages), without the horns. Red is the color preferred and prevailing. They should be, and usually are, classed as belonging to the beef breeds; yet so many animals of dairy excellence appear among them that they deserve this mention. One of their most careful breeders and earnest champions says of them: "They have the contour and general make-up of the grand old breed from which they have been mainly builded; besides, in their development the milking qualities have not been lost sight of, and among them are some excellent milkers."

In their dairy capacity they may also be said to practically duplicate "the milking Shorthorns," so that a separate description is unnecessary. The breed is not yet sufficiently strong in numbers and has not been handled enough for dairy purposes to furnish milk records of value for herds or single animals. In short, they have been from the first, and continue to be, bred primarily for the development of feeding quality for beef production as their dominant characteristic, and their service as milk producers must be regarded as a secondary consideration. It remains still to be determined to what extent this breed will affect the interests of dairymen. At the Columbian Exposition (1893) the Polled Durhams were entered as general-purpose cattle, and in the sweepstakes rings for that class they received the highest honor in competition with representatives of several other breeds of similar character.

Breeders of these animals organized in the year 1889 as the American Polled Durham Breeders' Association and at once began the compilation of a herdbook. The association has 116 members and has published one volume, containing the entries of 487 bulls and 834 cows. It is estimated that the breed comprises a total of 1,200 living animals, mainly owned in the States of Ohio, Indiana, Illinois, Iowa, and Kentucky.

Young Hamilton 49, a good type of the male Polled Durham, was bred in Ohio, and at the time his likeness was made he was 4 years old and weighed over 2,700 pounds. He was of a dark-red

FIG. 31.—Shorthorn bull Baron Cruickshank 106296.

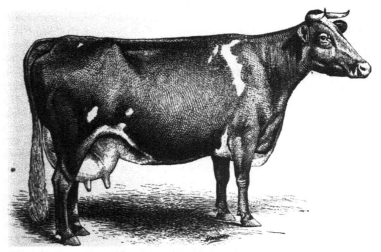

FIG. 32.—Shorthorn cow Kitty Clay 4th.

color with no white markings. His sire and dam are both recorded in the American Shorthorn Herd Book; whether either of them were without horns is not stated. This bull was the first-prize animal in his class at the Columbian Exposition, won the breed sweepstakes, and led the herd which won grand sweepstakes for general-purpose cattle. His get have been very successful show animals. "His daughters are a fine type of beef animals and regarded good milkers, but they have no dairy records."

Daisy 2 was bred and raised in Illinois and was one of the foundation animals of this breed. She was "strawberry roan" in color, old-fashioned Shorthorn marking, and was an uncommonly handsome and showy cow. She was also, as her picture indicates, an excellent milch cow, giving at times 24 quarts of milk a day. At her best she weighed 1,400 pounds and was a very easy keeper. One of her calves won first prize at the Columbian Exposition in 1893. (See illustration p. 169.)

RED POLLS.

This is another of the comparatively new breeds, as its independence has been recognized during the last half of the nineteenth century, and it is another without horns. Red Polled cattle resemble the Devons almost as closely as the Polled Durhams resemble the Shorthorns. Yet the two red races are probably not closely related; the Devons are natives of the Dartmoor region in the southwestern portion of England, and the Red Polls had their origin on the eastern plain, north of the river Thames, and particularly in the counties of Norfolk and Suffolk. The progenitors of this breed were "the little, old, red, horned cattle" of Norfolk and "the dun, or mouse, colored polled animals" of Suffolk. According to very early records, the latter were superior milch cattle. Arthur Young, in his Survey of Suffolk, published in 1794, mentions the hornless cattle of that country and says: "There is hardly a dairy of any consideration in the district that does not contain cows which give, in the height of the season, 8 gallons of milk a day, and 6 are common among many for a large part of the season. For two or three months a whole dairy will give 5 gallons a day on the average." And he adds: "Many of these beasts fatten remarkably well and have flesh of fine quality." Low, writing in 1845, after giving the breed, under the name of Polled Suffolks, a poor character in respect to almost everything except milking powers, suggested the probability of its immediate extinction. But since that time much enterprise has been shown among the cattle men of that part of England. The early stock of Norfolk and Suffolk has been merged (from about 1846), handled with skill, the horns eliminated on the one side, and all color but red upon the other. The traces of an infusion of Scotch Galloway and West Highland blood, doubtless once made, has been well covered, and the Red Polled cattle have now recognition as a breed and come well to the front.

They have not made much headway in Great Britain. however, outside of the two counties named.

Some of these hornless cattle, red and of other colors, were among those brought to the early English colonies in America, and the so-

FIG. 33.—Simmenthal bull Segg 1.

FIG. 34.—Simmenthal cow Jungferli 7.

called "muley" cows among our natives are probably descendants, more or less mixed with other strains, including the Scotch Galloways, of these early arrivals from Norfolk and Suffolk. But the first notable importation of the breed in its modern form was made in the year

1873 by Gilbert F. Taber, and this herd, to which he added in 1875 and 1882, was maintained for some years in Putnam County, N. Y. A number of importations to the United States have since been made and the State of Ohio has lately been the center of active interest in making these cattle known in this country.

The animals of this breed are about the same size as Devons, and, being of the same color and of the beef form, the resemblance is still greater. The absence of horns and the change thus caused in the shape of the head, which assumes a comparatively high and sharp crown, or poll, with a tuft of hair upon it, is the only noticeable distinction. The development of the milking parts has been better maintained in the Red Polls, so that at present their udders, teats, and milk veins show the better. In the matter of teats this may have been overdone, as with the Polls these are often unduly large, puffy, and conical. While red is the required color, it is permissible to have a white tip to the switch and some white upon the udder, although the latter is deemed undesirable. The Red Polled cattle are strong in constitution, hardy, good grazers, active in movement, and quiet in disposition.

In general appearance the animals of this breed are of the beef type—blocky, round, full, smooth, and fine boned. Their aptitude for making meat seems to be greater than for making milk. Their special friends claim them to be good at both, and press their merits strongly as the general farm cow. It is needless to present here the proofs of their excellence as butchers' beasts.

As dairy animals the Red Polls must be placed in the second class with the other breeds which aim to serve the dual purpose. They appear to give rather more milk than Devons on the average, but not quite so rich in quality. Being comparatively few in number in this country, dairy records of entire herds in the United States are lacking, and the available figures mainly pertain to records in Great Britain. Good herds there average 5,000 to 5,500 pounds of milk annually per cow, and when small and selected occasionally rising to 7,000 pounds. One record is claimed of 7,744 pounds each for 22 cows. In the year 1896 twelve herds reported 253 cows with an average yield of 5,786 pounds. Single selected cows give 30, 40, and sometimes 50 pounds of milk a day, and hold out well, making yearly totals of 6,000 to 8,000 pounds or more. One record is published of a 12-year-old cow giving 14,189 pounds of milk in a year. It must be admitted, however, that the tendency in this country among owners of these cattle is to add to the size and beauty of contour of their animals and improve the beef-producing capacity at the expense of dairy qualities.

The first herdbook for this breed was published in England in 1874, and in 1883 the Red Polled Cattle Club of America was organized, and issued its first volume in 1887. A few years later the English and American associations united their herdbooks, which have since been a joint issue, all animals of the breed in both countries being registered together. This is the only instance of its kind among the pure-bred cattle organizations of this country. Ten volumes of the joint herdbook have been published, the last in 1898, and the total records comprise 5,959 males and 13,109 females. The American data cannot be separately given, and no estimate is made of the number of Red Polls alive on this continent. The total is small, and they are held mainly in the Central and Western States.

Dobin 3462 was bred in Wisconsin, and both sire and dam were bred in this country. At the time the accompanying picture was made the bull was 6 years old and weighed 2,150 pounds. He is regarded as a typical bull of his breed and has been a winner at several of the important State fairs of the Northwest. No dairy records have been made by his dam or by his daughters.

Beauty 5th 2629 was bred in Vermont, both her parents being imported, and was afterwards owned in Ohio. The likeness shows her at 5 years old and weighing 1,250 pounds. She was a successful show animal in Ohio and Missouri and a good dairy cow, giving about 7,000 pounds of milk a year of more than average richness. She died of milk fever in 1890. (See illustrations, p. 171.)

SHORTHORNS.

The cattle which have been most famous as a breed in England and America, which have received the longest and closest attention of breeders and improvers, which have commanded prices, singly and in herds, far above all others, and which have made the most general impression upon the live stock of both countries during the nineteenth century, are the Shorthorns, or Durhams. Wallace says they are descended from the old Northeast of England breed, variously designated as "Durham," "Teeswater," "Yorkshire," and "Holderness," and adds: "The breed was probably originally formed, though perhaps several centuries ago, by crossing the aboriginal British cows with large-frame bulls imported from the Continent. Early Shorthorns were good milkers, and it may be presumed they in part inherited that quality along with the shortness of horn from their Continental ancestors. Little is known of the breed except from the uncertain authority of tradition down to the early part of the eighteenth century, though it is only right to infer that long before this time great care and even skill had been bestowed upon it. The earliest records show that purity of breed was fully appreciated, and this important fact could not have been universal without previous experience and attention."

The great county of York, extending along the east coast of England from the river Humber to the Tees, and westward almost to the

Irish Sea, has the honor of being the seat of the most noted examples of improvement in British cattle. It was this county which furnished the foundation stock upon which Gresley in Staffordshire, Webster in Warwickshire, and that greatest of all breeders, Robert Bakewell, in Leicestershire, labored to create the breed of Longhorns, which filled all the middle counties of England during the eighteenth century, and was then regarded as the most valuable in the Kingdom. And it was Yorkshire, helped somewhat by the smaller county of Durham, adjoining on the north, which brought the famous Shorthorns to the front, following closely upon the best days of the Longhorns. The former replaced and practically absorbed the latter, spreading over all middle England and northward across the island and well into the lowlands of Scotland.

Inseparably connected with the development of the Shorthorn breed are the names of Robert and Charles Colling, who brought their favorites into a new era of fame and popularity during the last decades of the eighteenth century and the first of the nineteenth. The Collings were shrewd advertisers as well as good breeders. In those days of slow communication and absence of fairs and shows they adopted the clever plan of sending specimen animals of their breeding on long tours about their own and adjoining counties. Two of these animals became especially famous. "The Durham Ox," which had a live weight above 1½ tons, and "The White Heifer that Traveled," weighing considerably over a ton, were driven about the country for several years and extensively exhibited. Almost equally valuable to this breed have been the later services of Bates and Booth and Cruikshank. Under these leaders, and in the hands of a host of able lieutenants and followers, this superb race of cattle has been raised to the highest rank in the United Kingdom, carried to the continent of Europe, and introduced into all British colonies. It was the first pure breed to make an impress upon the cattle of the United States.

The Revolutionary war was scarcely over before attention began to be given to improving the cattle in America. Virginia led in the work with several small importations between 1783 and 1800, and from these pioneer animals the first pure-bred Durhams were taken to Kentucky. In 1817 there was a special importation for Kentucky use, from which the descendants can be fully traced to the present time. This stock was popularly called the "milk breed," but they were improved Shorthorns, some of them from the Collings herd. Also in 1817 some of like breeding reached New York and Massachusetts. A few years later they obtained a foothold in Pennsylvania. Several importations followed prior to 1835, but up to this time the breed did not seem to do well east of the Alleghanies. In Kentucky and Ohio, on the contrary, great progress was made. Twenty years of special activity then followed in the development of American Shorthorns. During this time the famous herd of Thorndale, New York, was built up, and the Alexander herd at Woodburn, Kentucky. A quiet period of fifteen years was followed by another Shorthorn "boom," beginning after the civil war, and the climax came in September, 1873, when the celebrated New York Mills sale occurred. One hundred and nine head of Shorthorns were then sold at auction in three hours for $380,000. Eight cows averaged $14,000 each, and six others averaged $24,000; one sold for $35,000 and another for $40,600. British breeders acknowledged that the United States possessed better Shorthorns than could be found in England, and sent over agents to take back some of them at any price. During the last hundred years the Shorthorn blood has been more generally distributed through the United States than that of any other cattle, and it has proved most acceptable as the basis of improvement for the common, or native, stock, both for beef production and dairy purposes.

The aim of nearly all the improvers of Shorthorns has been to secure early maturity, size, form, and beef-producing qualities. "All is useless that is not beef" was the motto of an eminent breeder, and he has had many followers. Thomas Bates is the most noted of the few who have seemed anxious to retain good milking capacity. The Shorthorns are a beef breed and have been so for generations. They are classed among the beef breeds at all the great exhibitions, and, as a breed, do not even pretend to be general-purpose animals. But there have always been good dairy cows among them, and in England, especially, strains and families have been kept somewhat distinct and known as "milking Shorthorns." A few breeders in the United States have followed this example, and enough were found in 1893 to make up a herd which entered the famous dairy-cow test at the Columbian Exposition and there made a most creditable record, as shown in the Appendix. This alone entitles the Shorthorns to a place in these pages, although their best friends would hardly claim them to belong to the class of special dairy breeds.

In point of size the Shorthorns are probably the largest among pure breeds of cattle. In their modern form they are not so tall and have not so large a frame as some of their English ancestors, but the lower, blockier, fuller form maintains the maximum weight. Bulls ordinarily weigh a ton and more, sometimes running up to 3,000 pounds; mature cows range from 1,200 to 1,600 pounds, sometimes falling a little below and sometimes exceeding these limits. "The colors of the breed have always been red and white, with various blendings of these two. Many of the best among the early Shorthorns were pure white, but that color has lost caste, and red is especially fancied in this country. In England, however, the roan color is much more common than any other, and this peculiar blending of the red and white, popularly called 'roan,' is rarely, if ever, seen in any animal of the bovine race which does not possess some portion of the Shorthorn blood." (Sanders.) The head is comparatively short, broad, finely finished, and attractive; the nose, lips, and eyelids flesh-colored and free from dark markings; eyes clear, bright, yet mild; ears thin, delicate, and creamy yellow inside; horns short and blunt, more or less curved downward, of a waxy yellow throughout, free from black tips, laterally flattened, and wide apart at the base; the neck is short and fine in the cow, heavy and well crested in the bull. All the special masculine and feminine features should be strongly represented in both sexes. The lines of the body are straight, the rectangular form, with well-filled points, broad, level back, full loin, heavy, thick buttocks, wide apart, brisket wide and full, legs rather short, close, fine boned and well proportioned to size of body. Yet this describes the beef type. In the best milking strains the cows are rather more rangy and angular in outline, with large, hairy udders and good-sized straight teats, well placed. The skin over the whole body is flesh colored, soft, oily to the touch, and covered with fine short hair. The animals are quiet and kind in disposition. Nearly all show evidences of long-continued high breeding, and this has been carried to such an extent in many cases as to cause more or less delicacy of constitution and sometimes "shyness" in breeding.

It has been already noted that among the early Durhams and Teeswater cattle there was much dairy excellence, and that Shorthorns when first brought to America earned the name of "the milk breed." Among old records are those of cows giving 6, 8, and even 9 gallons of milk a day on grass alone. Although now latent in most lines, there seems to be a dairy quality inherent in the breed which some careful managers are able successfully to develop and propagate. Records of several dairy herds in the United States within a quarter century show a milking season of about two hundred and seventy-five days and an average product of 6,500 pounds of milk. One herd of 10 cows, from 3 to 12 years old, gave 7,750 pounds each in a year. Single cows have averaged much more, several instances being known of 10,000 to 12,000 pounds in a season. The Shorthorn milk is of good quality, rather above the average; the fat globules are of medium and fairly uniform size, so that cream separates easily; it is rather pale in color. In 1824 a cow near Philadelphia made over 20 pounds of butter in a week without special feeding. Herds of 40 cows have averaged 209 pounds of butter a year; the herd of 10 cows mentioned above averaged 325 pounds, and single cows have records of 400 pounds and over, one being of 513 pounds.

The first Shorthorn herdbook was published in England in the year 1822, but for nearly a century before pedigrees of some fine bulls had been kept with reasonable accuracy. The American Shorthorn Breeders' Association was organized in 1842 and publication of the herdbook of this country began in 1845, connecting with the Coates series in England.   Volume 43 was issued in 1899, bringing the number of bulls to 134,566 and of cows to 231,979.   At the time this volume was issued nearly 15,000 pedigrees were in the secretary's hands for record and publication, making the total number of animals to be registered prior to the year 1900 more than 381,000.   How many of these pure Shorthorns are now living in the United States it is impossible to determine, but a rough approximation places the number at 130,000 to 150,000.

Second Baron Tuberose 118023 was the bull selected to represent milking Shorthorns, because of his individual merits and the quality of his get, but it was found impossible to make a satisfactory engraving from the only available photograph of this animal.   A likeness of Baron Cruickshank 106296 has consequently been substituted. He is an imported bull and an excellent specimen of the breed in general, but not of the dairy type.   He was bred in Scotland, his sire being Collingwood (57074), and his dam, Maria 10th, a famous cow, was sired by Field Marshal (47870).   This bull was imported into Illinois in 1891, and weighed 2,100 pounds when 3 years old.

Kitty Clay Fourth (vol. 29, p. 553), a Pennsylvania animal, although bred in New York, was one of the cows chosen to represent the Shorthorns at the great dairy test at Chicago in 1893, and was the champion cow of her breed in the butter test.   In the thirty-day trial her yield of milk was 1,593 pounds, which made 62¼ pounds of butter. Two years later she gave almost 5,000 pounds of milk in three months, her best day being 65 pounds.   At a fair-ground trial, when only 2 years old, she gave over 28 pounds of milk in one day, which made 1¼ pounds of good butter.   She is a member of one of the best milking families of Shorthorns in America, and her "general purpose" has been shown in one of her sons, which, after satisfactory service as a dairy sire, was slaughtered when 5 years old; his live weight was 2,080 pounds and the dressed weight of his four quarters 1,456 pounds. The accompanying likeness of this fine cow by no means does her justice, although it was the best that could be obtained.   It shows her at the age of 10, when her weight was 1,348 pounds.   Her sire was Dick Turpin 50740, S.-H. H. B.   (See illustrations, p. 173.)

SIMMENTHALERS.

The spotted race (Fleckvieh) of Swiss cattle has its home in the Canton Berne, and is believed to have been best developed in the valley of the Simme.   Hence the names applied of "Bernese," "Berner spotted," "Simmenthal," and "Simmenthalers."   Remains of the prehistoric lake dwellers of Switzerland indicate that these cattle are the direct descendants of animals which occupied the same territory centuries ago. It may therefore be presumed that this breed, as a breed, originated in the region where it now exists in its best form. It is to be found, however, with slight variations, throughout western Switzerland and along the frontiers of France.

Few representatives of this breed have been brought to America. The first importation was in 1886, when a small herd was taken to Texas. A year later a few of these cattle were imported by an Illinois farmer. One small herd of choice animals is being kept pure in northern New Jersey. The chief use to which the blood of this herd is being put is an experiment in cross-breeding with Jerseys, the Simmenthal being used as the sire. No results can yet be reported.

The animals of this breed are large framed and heavy, the cows ranging from 1,200 to 1,700 or 1,800 pounds, and averaging 1,400 pounds or over, while the bulls, when mature, weigh 2,200 to 2,500 pounds, and frequently more. The color of these cattle is a creamy white, or a white ground with large, irregular spots of a light yellow or cream shade.

They have a rather small, well-shaped head, light-red or white nose, large nostrils and mouth, small horns turned forward and upward, yellowish white and waxy to the tips. Rather long, shapely ears, well fringed with hair. The neck is short, with a strong dewlap. The mature bull has a high, well-arched crest. Animals of both sexes, and especially the males, have loose, pendent skin under the throat, a peculiar characteristic of the breed. The back is straight and broad, body well rounded on the ribs, hind quarters broad, long, and prominent, legs round and well formed, rather short, muscular, and strong. The skin is in most cases smooth, soft, and very loose, with fine hair, quite thick. The udders are large and well formed, rather fleshy, with skin soft and yellow.

Simmenthal cattle of both sexes are generally gentle, tractable, and easily managed. The Swiss farmer uses his cows to plow his land, haul manure, harvest the hay crop, and do general farm draft service. They are not overfastidious as to food, and are noted for excellence at the pail when fed little else but hay or pasture grass, yet they require good care, comfortable stabling, and abundant food to do themselves justice in milk, labor, or flesh making.

This breed has a good reputation as dairy stock, although not quite equal to that of their Brown Swiss kindred. Cows yield 6,000 to 8,000 pounds of milk a year, superior animals producing 10,000 pounds or more. Among the few in this country, records made conform to these figures. Their milk will make about 4 pounds of butter per hundredweight.

This strain of Swiss cattle shows at a glance their natural hardiness, vigor, and strength of constitution; also their adaptability to labor and beef production. There are several offshoots of this Simmenthaler breed, but they have little more than local reputations in and near Switzerland. The best known of these is the so-called Freiburg breed, which is simply a variation from the parent stock, common to the canton of that name. Their chief distinction is in having spots of black instead of cream or yellow, or red, as is sometimes the markings of the Simmenthaler. The Freiburg cattle are still heavier and coarser, and decidedly inferior for dairy purposes.

The American Simmenthal Herd Book Association was organized in New York in June, 1896, but up to 1899 only 10 males and 15 females have been registered, and no volume published.

The two illustrations of this breed represent animals imported in May, 1895, and owned in New Jersey.

The bull is Segg 1, dropped in 1893, and 5 years old when this likeness was made. The cow is Jungferli 7, dropped in 1890, and shown as 8 years old. The spots upon the cow are in fact not so dark as they appear in the print. These two pictures are regarded as fairly representing the mature animals of this breed now in the United States. (See illustrations, p. 175.)

APPENDIX.

COMPARISON OF DAIRY BREEDS.

Summary of results of tests of dairy cows at the World's Columbian Exposition, Chicago, 1893. Open to all breeds. Entered for competition: Guernseys, Jerseys, and Shorthorns.

No. 1, cheese test, 15 days, May.

Cows in test.	Milk produced.	Fat in milk.	Cheese made.	Price of cheese per pound.	Cost of feed.	Net gain.
	Pounds.	Pounds.	Pounds.	Cents.	Dollars.	Dollars.
25 Jerseys	13,296.4	601.91	1,451.8	13.36	98.14	119.82
25 Guernseys	10,938.6	488.42	1,130.6	11.95	76.25	88.30
25 Shorthorns	12,186.9	436.60	1,077.6	13.00	99.36	81.36

No. 2, 90-day butter test, June, July, August.

Cows in test.	Milk produced.	Fat in milk.	Butter credited.	Proceeds of butter.	Cost of feed.	Net gain.
	Pounds.	Pounds.	Pounds.	Dollars.	Dollars.	Dollars.
25 Jerseys	73,486.8	3,516.08	4,274.01	1,747.37	587.50	1,323.81
25 Guernseys	61,781.7	2,784.56	3,360.43	1,355.44	484.14	997.64
24 Shorthorns	66,263.2	2,409.97	2,890.87	1,171.77	501.79	910.12

Summary of results of tests of dairy cows at the World's Columbian Exposition, Chicago, 1893, etc.—Continued.

Average per day and per cow (test No. 2).

Cows in test.	Milk produced.	Fat in milk.	Fat.	Cost of feed.
	Pounds.	*Pounds.*	*Per cent.*	*Cents.*
Jerseys..	32.7	1.56	4.78	26.1
Guernseys	27.5	1.24	4.51	21.5
Shorthorns.......................................	30.7	1.12	3.64	23.2

No. 3, 30-day butter test, September.

Cows in test.	Milk produced.	Fat in milk.	Butter credited.	Proceeds of butter.	Cost of feed.	Net gain.
	Pounds.	*Pounds.*	*Pounds.*	*Dollars.*	*Dollars.*	*Dollars.*
15 Jerseys	13,921.9	685.81	837.21	385.59	111.24	274.13
15 Guernseys	13,518.4	597.96	724.17	329.77	92.77	237.00
15 Shorthorns...............	15,618.3	555.43	662.67	303.69	104.55	198.99

Summary of results of comparative tests of cows of several dairy breeds of cattle, made at the Agricultural Experiment Stations of Maine, New York, and New Jersey. Averages for all breeds and lactation periods.

[From compilation by Prof. F. W. Woll. 1897.]

Breed.	Cows included.	Lactation periods.	Average yields per lactation period.		Average fat.	Average cost of—		
			Milk.	Butter fat.		Food eaten per day.	Producing 100 pounds of milk.	Producing 1 pound of fat.
	Number.	*Number.*	*Pounds.*	*Pounds.*	*Per cent.*	*Cents.*	*Cents.*	*Cents.*
Ayrshire	10	20	6,909	248.5	3.60	14.5	78.5	21.5
Devon	3	5	3,984	183.3	4.60	10.3	94.0	20.5
Guernsey	8	10	6,210	322.9	5.20	13.5	82.8	15.8
Holstein-Friesian .	9	10	8,215	282.0	3.43	17.2	74.7	21.5
Jersey	9	18	5,579	301.1	5.40	13.9	94.7	17.4
Shorthorn..........	4	5	8,696	345.4	3.97	14.3	78.7	19.4
Total	43	68	....	....	....	....	....	....

Average composition of milk of different breeds.

[From report of comparison of breeds at the New York Agricultural Experiment Station, 1891.]

Breed.	No. analyses.	Water.	Total solids.	Solids not fat.	Fat.	Casein.	Milk sugar.	Ash.	Nitrogen.	Daily milk yield.
		Per ct.	*Per ct.*	*Per ct.*	*Per ct.*	*Per ct.*	*Per ct.*	*Per ct.*	*Per ct.*	*Lbs.*
Ayrshire	252	86.95	13.06	9.35	3.57	3.43	5.33	0.698	0.543	18.40
Devon	72	86.26	13.77	9.60	4.15	3.76	5.07	.760	.595	12.65
Guernsey ...:........	112	85.39	14.60	9.47	5.12	3.61	5.11	.753	.570	16.00
Holstein-Friesian ...	132	87.62	12.39	9.07	3.46	3.39	4.84	.735	.540	22.65
Jersey	238	84.60	15.40	9.80	5.61	3.91	5.15	.743	.618	14.07

POINTS OBSERVED IN JUDGING DAIRY CATTLE.

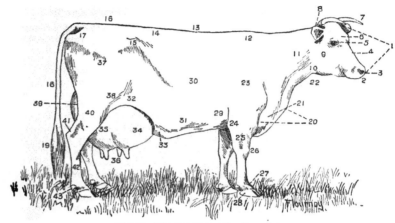

FIG. 35.—Diagram of cow showing points.

1. Head.	12. Withers.	23. Shoulder.	34. Fore udder.
2. Muzzle.	13. Back.	24. Elbow.	35. Hind udder.
3. Nostril.	14. Loins.	25. Forearm.	36. Teats.
4. Face.	15. Hip bone.	26. Knee.	37. Upper thigh.
5. Eye.	16. Pelvic arch.	27. Ankle.	38. Stifle.
6. Forehead.	17. Rump.	28. Hoof.	39. Twist.
7. Horn.	18. Tail.	29. Heart girth.	40. Leg or gaskin.
8. Ear.	19. Switch.	30. Side or barrel.	41. Hock.
9. Cheek.	20. Chest.	31. Belly.	42. Shank.
10. Throat.	21. Brisket.	32. Flank.	43. Dew claw.
11. Neck.	22. Dewlap.	33. Milk vein.	

REGISTERED, OR PEDIGREED, CATTLE OF SELECTED BREEDS.

Estimates of the number living in the United States, 1898.

Breeds.	Number registered.	Number living.
Ayrshires	22, 00	6,050
Brown Swiss	2,871	1,200
Devons	18,343	10,000
Dutch Belted	1,128	500
Guernseys	16,600	11,000
Holstein-Friesians	100,000	60,000
Jerseys	184,000	90,000
Normandies	25	25
Polled Durhams	1,321	1,200
Red Polls	a 19,068	(?)
Shorthorns	366,545	140,000
Simmenthalers	25	25
Total	731,926	320,000

a Includes all in Great Britain and United States.

AYRSHIRE BREEDERS' ASSOCIATION.

Scale of points for Ayrshire cow; adopted February 21, 1889.

The following scale of points for the Ayrshire cow were adopted, being similar to the scale adopted in Scotland in 1884, and changed in a few points to render them applicable to this country:

	Points.
1. Head short; forehead wide; nose fine between the muzzle and eyes; muzzle large; eyes full and lively; horns wide set on, inclining upward	10
2. Neck moderately long and straight from the head to the top of the shoulder, free from loose skin on the underside, fine at its junction with the head, and enlarging symmetrically towards the shoulders	5
3. Fore quarters: Shoulders sloping, withers fine, chest sufficiently broad and deep to insure constitution; brisket and whole fore quarters light, the cow gradually increasing in depth and width backwards	5
4. Back short and straight; spine well defined, especially at the shoulders; short ribs arched; the body deep at the flanks	10
5. Hind quarters long, broad, and straight; hook bones wide apart, and not overlaid with fat; thighs deep and broad; tail long, slender, and set on level with the back	v
6. Udder capacious and not fleshy, hind part broad and firmly attached to the body, the sole nearly level and extending well forward; milk veins about udder and abdomen well developed; the teats from 2½ to 3 inches in length, equal in thickness—the thickness being in proportion to the length—hanging perpendicularly, their distance apart at the sides should be equal to one-third of the length of the vessel, and across to about one-half of the breadth	20
7. Legs short in proportion to size, the bones fine, the joints firm	3
8. Skin yellow, soft, and elastic, and covered with soft, close, woolly hair	v
9. Color, red of any shade, brown or white, or a mixture of these, each color being distinctly defined	3
10. Average live weight, in full milk, about 10 hundredweight	3
11. General appearance, including style and movement	10
12. Escutcheon large and fine development	3
Perfection	100

Scale of points for Ayrshire bull; adopted February 21, 1889.

The points desirable in the female are generally so in the male, but must, of course, be attended with that masculine character which is inseparable from a strong and vigorous constitution. Even a certain degree of coarseness is admissible; but then it must be so exclusively of masculine description as never to be discovered in a female of his get.

1. The head of the bull may be shorter than that of the cow, but the frontal bone should be broad, the muzzle good size, throat nearly free from hanging folds, eyes full. The horns should have an upward turn, with sufficient size at the base to indicate strength of constitution	10
2. Neck of medium length, somewhat arched, and large in those muscles which indicate power and strength	10
3. Fore quarters: Shoulders close to the body, without any hollow space behind; chest broad, brisket deep and well developed, but not too large	

Points.

4. Back short and straight; spine sufficiently defined, but not in the same degree as in the cow; ribs well sprung, and body deep in the flanks.. 10
5. Hind quarters long, broad, and straight; hip bones wide apart; pelvis long, broad, and straight; tail set on a level with the back; thighs deep and broad 10
6. Scrotum large, with well-developed teats in front..................... 7
7. Legs short in proportion to size, joints firm. Hind legs well apart, and not to cross in walking 5
8. Skin yellow, soft, elastic, and of medium thickness 10
9. Color, red of any shade, brown or white, or a mixture of these, each color being distinctly defined 8
10. Average live weight at maturity, about 1,500 pounds.................. 10
11. General appearance, including style and movement.................... 15
12. Escutcheon large and fine development................................. 8

Perfection.. 100

BROWN SWISS BREEDERS' ASSOCIATION.

Scale of points adopted for Swiss cattle.

FOR COWS.

1. Head medium size and rather long...................................... 2
2. Face dished, broad between the eyes and narrow between the horns.... 2
3. Ears of a deep orange color within.................................... 1
4. Nose black, square, and with the mouth surrounded by a light, meal-colored band; tongue black 2
5. Eyes full and placid 1
6. Horns rather short, flattish, and regularly set, with black tips.......... 5
7. Neck straight, rather long, and not too heavy at shoulders............. 4
8. Chest broad and deep 4
9. Back level to the setting on of the tail and broad across the loin 6
10. Barrel hooped, broad and deep at the flank 8
11. Hips wide apart, rump long and broad 4
12. Thighs wide, with heavy quarters 4
13. Legs short and straight, with good hoofs 4
14. Tail slender, pliable, not too long, with good switch 4
15. Hide thin and movable.... 8
16. Color shades from dark brown to light brown, and at some seasons of the year gray; slight splashes of white near udder not objectionable; light stripe along the back 6
17. Hair between horns light, not reddish; hair on inside of ears light. (No points.)
18. Fore udder full in form and carried up, reaching far forward on the abdomen 10
19. Hind udder not too deeply hung, full in form and well up behind....... 10
20. Teats rather large, set well apart and hanging straight down 5
21. Milk veins prominent... 4
22. Escutcheon, high and broad and full in thighs.......................... 7
23. Disposition quiet and good natured.................................... 4

Perfection... 100

In judging bulls and heifers omit Nos. 14, 15, and 16, and for color they should be dark brown.

AMERICAN DEVON CATTLE CLUB.

Scale of points for Devon cattle; adopted at third annual meeting of club,
Chicago, November 11, 1886.

FOR COWS.

Points.

1. Head moderately long, with a broad, indented forehead, tapering considerably toward the nostrils; the nose of a flesh color, nostrils high and open, the jaws clean, the eye bright. lively, and prominent, and surrounded by a flesh-colored ring, throat clean, ears thin, the expression gentle and intelligent; horns matching, spreading, and gracefully turned up, of a waxy color. tipped with a darker shade.............. 6
2. Neck, upper line short, fine at head, widening and deep at withers, and strongly set to the shoulders 4
3. Shoulders fine, flat, and sloping, with strong arms and firm joints...... 4
4. Chest deep, broad, and somewhat circular in character 8
5. Ribs well sprung from the backbone, nicely arched, deep, with flanks fully developed 6
6. Back straight and level from the withers to the setting on of the tail, loin broad and full, hips and rump of medium width and on a level with the back.. 16
7. Hind quarters deep, thick, and square............................... 8
8. Udder not fleshy, coming well forward in line with the belly and well up behind; teats moderately large and squarely placed................. 20
9. Tail well set on at a right angle with the back, tapering with a switch of white or roan hair and reaching the hocks........................... 6
10. Legs straight, squarely placed when viewed from behind, not to cross or sweep in walking; hoof well formed 2
11. Skin moderately thick and mellow, covered with an abundant coat of rich hair of a red color; no white spot admissible, except the udder..... 8
12. Size, minimum weight at 3 years old, 1,000 pounds...................... 2
13. General appearance as indicated by stylish and quick movement, form, constitution, and vigor, and the under line as nearly as possible parallel with the line of the back................................... 8

Perfection... 100

FOR BULLS.

1. Head masculine, full and broad, tapering toward the nose, which should be flesh-colored: nostrils high and open; muzzle broad; eyes full and placid and surrounded with flesh-colored ring; ears of medium size and thickness; horns medium size, growing at right angles from the head, are slightly elevated, waxy at the base, tipped with a darker shade... 10
2. Cheek full and broad at root of tongue; throat clean.................. 2
3. Neck of medium length and muscular, widening from the head to the shoulders and strongly set on................................... 4
4. Shoulders fine, flat, sloping, and well fleshed; arms strong with firm joints... 6
5. Chest deep, broad, and somewhat circular....... 10
6. Ribs well sprung from the backbone, nicely arched, deep, with flanks fully developed 10
7. Back straight and level from the withers to the setting on of the tail; loin broad and full; hips and rump of medium width and on a level with the back 20
8. Hind quarters deep, thick, and square... 12

Points.

9. Tail well set on a right angle with the back, tapering, with a switch of white or roan hair and reaching the hocks.................................. 2
10. Legs short, straight, and squarely placed when viewed from behind, not to cross or sweep in walking; hoof well formed......................... ?
11. Skin moderately thick and mellow, covered with an abundant coat of rich hair of a red color; no white spot admissible unless around the purse. 8
12. Size, minimum weight at 8 years old, 1,400 pounds...................... 4
13. General appearance, as indicated by stylish and quick movement, form, constitution, and vigor, and the under line as nearly as possible parallel with the line of the back... 8

Perfection.. 100

DUTCH BELTED CATTLE ASSOCIATION.

Scale of points adopted for Dutch Belted cattle.

FOR COWS.

Points.

1. Body: Color, black, with clearly defined continuous white belt; the belt to be of medium width, beginning behind the shoulder and extending nearly to the hips.. o
2. Head: Comparatively long and somewhat dishing, broad between the eyes; poll prominent; muzzle fine; dark tongue.......................... 6
3. Eyes black, full, and mild; horns long compared with their diameter... 4
4. Neck fine and moderately thin, and should harmonize in symmetry with the head and shoulders... v
5. Shoulders fine at the top, becoming deep and broad as they extend backward and downward, with a low chest............................. ?
6. Barrel large and deep, with well-developed abdomen; ribs well rounded and free from fat... 10
7. Hips broad, and chine level, with full loin............................ 10
8. Rump high, long, and broad.. 6
9. Hind quarters long and deep, rear line incurving; tail long, slim, tapering to a full switch.. 8
10. Legs short, clean, standing well apart............................... 8
11. Udder large, well-developed front and rear; teats of convenient size and wide apart; mammary veins large, long, and crooked, entering large orifices... 20
12. Escutcheon... 2
13. Hair fine and soft; skin of moderate thickness, of a rich dark or yellow color... 8
14. Quiet disposition and free from excessive fat........................ 4
15. General condition and apparent constitution......................... 6

Perfection.. 100

FOR BULLS.

The scale of points for males shall be the same as those given for females, except that No. 11 shall be omitted and the bull credited 10 points for size and wide spread placing of rudimentary teats, 5 points additional for development of shoulder, and 5 points additional for perfection of belt.

AMERICAN GUERNSEY CATTLE CLUB.

Scale of points adopted for Guernsey cattle.

FOR COWS.

	Points.
Quality of milk, 30 points:	
Skin deep yellow in ear, on end of bone of tail, at base of horn, on udder, teats, and body generally................................	20
Skin loose, mellow, with fine, soft hair............................	10
Quantity and duration of flow, 40 points:	
Escutcheon wide on thighs, high and broad, with thigh ovals..........	10
Milk veins long and prominent	6
Udder full in front...	6
Udder full and well up behind...................................	8
Udder large, but not fleshy	4
Udder teats squarely placed	4
Udder teats of good size..	2
Size and substance, 16 points:	
Size for the breed	5
Not too light bone...	1
Barrel round and deep at flank	4
Hips and loins wide..	2
Rump long and broad	2
Thighs and withers thin	2
Symmetry, 14 points:	
Back level to setting on of tail.................................	3
Throat clean, with small dewlap................................	1
Legs not too long, with hocks well apart in walking..............	2
Tail long and thin...	1
Horns curved and not coarse	2
Head rather long and fine, with quiet and gentle expression	3
General appearance	2
Perfection..	100

For bulls, deduct 20 counts for udder; for heifers, deduct 20 counts for udder.

HOLSTEIN-FRIESIAN ASSOCIATION OF AMERICA.

Scale of points with a uniform system of discredits.

NOTE.—The items of description following each head of the scale should be passed upon separately and the amount of discredit marked down on the margin. The uniform discredits to be given are noted under each full description. V. s. means very slight deficiency; s., slight; m., marked; v. m., very marked; e., extreme. The difference between the sum of such discredits and 100 will be the standard of the animal by this scale.

FOR COWS.

	Points.
Discredits:	
Head—	
Decidedly feminine in appearance................................. }	2
Fine in contour... }	
Discredit, v. s. ¼, s. ½, m. ¾, v. m. ⅞, e. 1.	
Forehead—	
Broad between the eyes... }	°
Dishing .... }	
Discredit, v. s. ¼, s. ½, m. ¾, v. m. ⅞, e. 1.	

Discredits—Continued.

	Points.
Face—	
Of medium length	2
Clean and trim, especially under the eyes, showing facial veins	
The bridge of the nose straight	
The muzzle broad	
Discredit, s. 1/8, m. 1/4, e. 1/2.	
Ears—	
Of medium size	[illegible]
Of fine texture	
The hair plentiful and soft	
The secretions oil, and abundant	
Discredit, m. 1/8, e. 1/4.	
Eyes—	
Large	2
Full	
Mild	
Bright	
Discredit, s. 1/8, m. 1/4, e. 1/2.	
Horns—	
Small	2
Tapering finely toward the tips	
Set moderately narrow at base	
Oval	
Inclining forward	
Well bent inward	
Of fine texture	
In appearance, waxy	
Discredit, m. 1/8, e. 1/4.	
Neck—	
Long	[illegible]
Fine and clean at juncture with the head	
Free from dewlap	
Evenly and smoothly joined to shoulders	
Discredit, v. s. 1/8, s. 1/4, m. 1/2, v. m. 3/4, e. 1.	
Shoulders—	
Slightly lower than hips	3
Fine and even over tops	
Moderately broad and full at sides	
Discredit, v. s. 1/8, s. 1/4, m. 1/2, v. m. 3/4, e. 1.	
Chest—	
Of moderate depth and lowness	6
Smooth and moderately full in the brisket	
Full in the foreflanks (or through at the heart)	
Discredit, v. s. 1/4, s. 1/2, m. 1, v. m. 1 1/2, e. 2.	
Crops—	
Moderately full	2
Discredit, v. s. 1/4, s. 1/2, m. 3/4, v. m. 1 1/2, e. 2.	
Chine—	
Straight	3
Broadly developed	
Open	
Discredit, v. s. 1/8, s. 1/4, m. 1/2, v. m. 3/4, e. 1.	

Discredits—Continued.

Barrel—   Points.
  Of wedge shape .... ⎫
  Well rounded .... ⎪
  With a large abdomen .... ⎬   .
  Trimly held up (in judging the last item age must be considered) ⎭
       Discredit, v. s. ⅛, s. ¼, m. ½, v. m. ¾, e. 1.

Loin and hips—
  Broad .... ⎫
  Level or nearly level between hook bones .... ⎪
  Level and strong laterally .... ⎬   ·
  Spreading from chine broadly and nearly level............... ⎪
  Hook bones fairly prominent................................... ⎭
       Discredit, v. s. ⅛, s. ¼, m. ½, v. m. ¾, e. 1.

Rump—
  Long.. ⎫
  High.. ⎪
  Broad, with roomy pelvis.. ⎬   ·
  Nearly level laterally... ⎪
  Comparatively full above the thurl .... ⎭
       Discredit, v. s. ⅛, s. ¼, m. ½, v. m. ¾, e. 1.

Thurl—
  High .... ⎫   ₄
  Broad .... ⎭
       Discredit, v. s. ¼, s. ½, m. 1, v. m. 1¼, e. 2.

Quarters—
  Deep .... ⎫
  Straight behind .... ⎬   ₄
  Roomy in the twist.. ⎪
  Wide and moderately full at the sides........................... ⎭
       Discredit, v. s. ⅛, s. ¼, m. ½, v. m. ¾, e. 1.

Flanks—
  Deep.. ⎫   ₂
  Comparatively full .... ⎭
       Discredit, v. s. ⅛, s. ¼, m. ½, v. m. ¾, e. 1.

Legs—
  Comparatively short... ⎫
  Clean and nearly straight .... ⎪
  Wide apart... ⎬   ·
  Firmly and squarely set under the body.......................... ⎪
  Feet of medium size, round, solid and deep...................... ⎭
       Discredit, v. s. ⅛, s. ¼, m. ½, v. m. ¾, e. 1.

Tail—
  Large at base, setting well back .... ⎫
  Tapering finely to switch .... ⎬   ₂
  The end of the bone reaching to hocks or below .... ⎪
  The switch full.. ⎭
       Discredit, s. ¼, m. ½, e. ¾.

Discredits—Continued.

Hair and handling— Points.

Hair healthful in appearance ....

Fine, soft, and furry ....

The skin of medium thickness and loose........................

Mellow under the hand...................................... } 10

The secretions oily, abundant, and of a rich brown or yellow color ....

Discredit, v. s. ¼, s. ½, m. 1, v. m. 1½, e. 2.

Mammary veins—

Very large ....

Very crooked (age must be taken into consideration in judging of size and crookedness).................................... } 10

Entering very large or numerous orifices.....................

Double extension ....

With special developments, such as branches, connections, etc..

Discredit, v. s. ¼, s. ½, m. 1, v. m. 1½, e. 2.

Udder and teats—

Very capacious...

Very flexible ....

Quarters even...............................

Nearly filling the space in the rear below the twist and extend- } 12 ing well forward in front.................................

Broad and well held up.....................................

Teats well formed, wide apart, plumb, and of convenient size..

Discredit, v. s. ¼, s. ½, m. 1, v. m. 1½, e. 2.

Escutcheon—

Largest .... } 8

Finest ....

Discredit, v. s. ½, s. 1, m. 2, v. m. 3, e. 4.

Perfection... 100

General vigor—

For deficiency, inspectors shall discredit from the totals received not to exceed 8 points.

Discredit, v. s. 1, s. 2, m. 3, v. m. 5, e. 8.

General symmetry and fineness—

For deficiency, inspectors shall discredit from the total received not to exceed 8 points.

Discredit, v. s. 1, s. 2, m. 3, v. m. 5, e. 8.

General style and bearing—

For deficiency, inspectors shall discredit from the total received not to exceed 8 points.

Discredit, v. s. 1, s. 2, m. 3, v. m. 5, e. 8.

Credits for excess of requirement in production—

A cow shall be credited one point in excess of what she is otherwise entitled to for each and every 8 per cent that her milk or butter record exceeds the minimum requirement.

In scaling for the Advanced Register, defects caused solely by age or by accident, or by disease not hereditary, shall not be considered; but in scaling for the show ring such defects shall be considered and duly discredited.

A cow that in the judgment of the examiner will not reach, at full age, in milking condition and ordinary flesh, 1,000 pounds, live weight, shall be disqualified for entry in the Advanced Register.

No cow shall be received to the Advanced Register that, with all credits due her, will not scale, in the judgment of the examiner, at least 75 points.

10317——13

FOR BULLS.

Discredits: Points.

Head—
    Showing full vigor .... }   2
    Elegant in contour .... }
       Discredit, v. s. $\frac{1}{4}$, s. $\frac{1}{4}$, m. $\frac{1}{4}$, v. m. $\frac{3}{4}$, e. 1.

Forehead—
    Broad between the eyes....................................... }   .
    Dishing .... }
       Discredit, v. s. $\frac{1}{4}$, s. $\frac{1}{4}$, m. $\frac{1}{4}$, v. m. $\frac{3}{4}$, e. 1.

Face—
    Of medium length .... }
    Clean and trim, especially under eyes....................... }
    The bridge of the nose straight .... }   2
    The muzzle broad .... }
       Discredit, s. $\frac{1}{4}$, m. $\frac{1}{4}$, e. $\frac{1}{4}$.

Ears—
    Of medium size.. }
    Of fine texture .... }
    The hair plentiful and soft................................. }   .
    The secretions oily and abundant .... }
       Discredit, m. $\frac{1}{2}$, e. $\frac{1}{2}$.

Eyes—
    Large .... }
    Full.. }
    Mild .... }   2
    Bright .... }
       Discredit, s. $\frac{1}{4}$, m. $\frac{1}{4}$, e. $\frac{1}{4}$.

Horns—
    Short .... }
    Of medium size at base .... }
    Gradually diminishing toward tips .... }
    Oval .... }
    Inclining forward... }   2
    Moderately curved inward.................................... }
    Of fine texture .... }
    In appearance waxy .... }
       Discredit, m. $\frac{1}{2}$, e. $\frac{1}{2}$.

Neck—
    Long .... }
    Finely crested (if animal is mature) .... }
    Fine and clean at juncture with the head . ... }   5
    Nearly free from dewlap..................................... }
    Strongly and smoothly joined to shoulders .... }
       Discredit, v. s. $\frac{1}{4}$, s. $\frac{1}{4}$, m. $\frac{1}{4}$, v. m. $\frac{3}{4}$, e. 1.

Shoulders—
    Of medium height .... }
    Of medium thickness and smoothly rounded at tops .... }
    Bread and full at sides .... }   .
    Smooth over front... }
       Discredit, v. s. $\frac{1}{4}$. s. $\frac{1}{4}$, m. $\frac{1}{4}$, v. m. $\frac{3}{4}$, e. 1.

Discredits—Continued.

	Points.
Chest—	
Deep and low	
Well filled and smooth in the brisket	
Broad between the forearms	
Full in the foreflanks (or through at the heart)	
Discredit, v. s. ¼, s. ½, m. 1, v. m. 1½, e. 2.	
Crops—	
Comparatively full	
Nearly level with the shoulders	
Discredit, v. s. ¼, s. ½, m. 1, v. m. 1½, e. 2.	
Chine—	
Straight	
Broadly developed	3
Open	
Discredit, v. s. ⅛, s. ¼, m. ½, v. m. ¾, e. 1.	
Barrel—	
Well rounded	
With large abdomen	6
Strongly and trimly held up	
Discredit, v. s. ¼, s. ½, m. 1, v. m. 1½, e. 2.	
Loin and hips—	
Broad	
Level or nearly level between hook bones	
Level and strong laterally	5
Spreading from the chine broadly and nearly level	
The hook bones fairly prominent	
Discredit, v. s. ⅛, s. ¼, m. ½, v. m. ¾, e. 1.	
Rump—	
Long	
Broad	
High	5
Nearly level laterally	
Comparatively full above the thurl	
Discredit, v. s. ⅛, s. ¼, m. ½, v. m. ¾, e. 1.	
Thurl—	
High	
Broad	
Discredit, v. s. ¼, s. ½, m. 1, v. m. 1½, e. 2.	
Quarters—	
Deep	
Broad	
Straight behind	5
Wide and full at sides	
Open and well arched in the twist	
Discredit, v. s. ⅛, s. ¼, m. ½, v. m. ¾, e. 1.	
Flanks—	
Deep	2
Full	
Discredit, v. s. ⅛, s. ¼, m. ½, v. m. ¾, e. 1.	

Discredits—Continued.

Legs—   Points.

     Comparatively short ...

     Clean and nearly straight ...

     Wide apart ...   9

     Firmly and fairly set under the body ...

     Arms wide, strong, and tapering ...

     Feet of medium size, round, solid, and deep ...

         Discredit, v. s. $\frac{1}{4}$, s. $\frac{1}{2}$, m. $\frac{3}{4}$, v. m. $\frac{3}{4}$, e. 1.

Tail—

     Large at base, the setting well back ...

     Tapering finely to switch ...   2

     The end of the bone reaching to hocks or below ...

     The switch full ...

         Discredit, s. $\frac{1}{4}$, m. $\frac{1}{2}$, e. $\frac{3}{4}$.

Hair and handling—

     Hair healthful in appearance ...

     Fine, soft, and furry ...

     Skin of medium thickness and loose ...   10

     Mellow under the hand ...

     The secretions oily, abundant, and of a rich brown or yellow color ...

         Discredit, v. s. $\frac{1}{4}$, s. $\frac{1}{2}$, m. 1, v. m. $1\frac{1}{2}$, e. 2.

Mammary veins—

     Large ...

     Full ...

     Entering large or numerous orifices ...   10

     Double extension ...

     With special developments, such as forks, branches, connections, etc ...

         Discredit, v. s. $\frac{1}{4}$, s. $\frac{1}{2}$, m. 1, v. m. $1\frac{1}{2}$, e. 2.

Rudimentary teats—

     Large ...

     Well placed ...   2

         Discredit, v. s. $\frac{1}{4}$, s. $\frac{1}{2}$, m. $\frac{3}{4}$, v. m. $\frac{3}{4}$, e. 1.

Escutcheon—

     Largest ...

     Finest ...   2

         Discredit, v. s. $\frac{1}{2}$, s. 1, m. 2, v. m. 3, e. 4.

     Perfection ...   100

General vigor—

     For deficiency inspectors shall discredit from the total received not to exceed 8 points.

         Discredit, v. s. 1, s. 2, m. 3, v. m. 5, e. 8.

General symmetry and fineness—

     For deficiency inspectors shall discredit from the total received not to exceed 8 points.

         Discredit, v. s. 1, s. 2, m. 3, v. m. 5, e. 8.

General style and bearing—

     For deficiency inspectors shall discredit from the total received not to exceed 8 points.

         Discredit, v. s. 1, s. 2. m. 3, v. m. 5, e. 8.

Credits for offspring—

A bull shall be credited 1 point in excess of what he is otherwise entitled to for each and every animal of which he is sire actually entered in the Advanced Register, not to exceed 10 in number.

In scaling for the Advanced Register defects caused solely by age, or by accident, or by disease not hereditary shall not be considered. But in scaling for the show ring such defects shall be considered and duly discredited.

A bull that, in the judgment of the examiner, will not reach at full age, and in good flesh, 1,800 pounds, live weight, shall be disqualified for entry in the Advanced Register.

No bull shall be received to the Advanced Register that, with all credits due him, will not scale, in the judgment of the examiner, at least 80 points.

AMERICAN JERSEY CATTLE CLUB.

Scale of points adopted at the annual meeting held May 6, 1885.

FOR COWS.

	Points.
1. Head small and lean; face dished, broad between the eyes and narrow between the horns	2
2. Eyes full and placid; horns small, crumpled, and amber colored	1
3. Neck thin, rather long, with clean throat, and not heavy at the shoulders	8
4. Back level to the setting of the tail	1
5. Broad across the loin	6
6. Barrel long, hooped, broad and deep at the flank	10
7. Hips wide apart; rump long	10
8. Legs short	2
9. Tail fine, reaching the hocks, with good switch	1
10. Color and mellowness of hide; inside of ears yellow	5
11. Fore udder full in form and not fleshy	13
12. Hind udder full in form and well up behind	11
13. Teats rather large, wide apart, and squarely placed	10
14. Milk veins prominent	5
15. Disposition quiet	5
16. General appearance and apparent constitution	10
Perfection	100

In judging heifers omit Nos. 11, 12, and 14.

FOR BULLS.

The same scale of points shall be used in judging bulls, omitting Nos. 11, 12, and 14, and making due allowance for masculinity; but when bulls are exhibited with their progeny, in a separate class, add 30 points for progeny.

RED POLLS.

The "standard description" of Red Polled cattle.

[NOTE.—The Red Polled Cattle Club of America having adopted no scale of points for judging animals of the breed, the following "standard description" is published instead, being taken from the introduction to Volume I of the Red Polls Herd Book.]

ESSENTIALS.

Color, red. The tip of the tail and udder may be white. The extension of the white of the udder a few inches along the inside of the flank, or a small white spot, or mark, on the under part of the belly by the milk veins, shall not be held to disqualify an animal whose sire and dam form part of an established herd of the breed or answer all other essentials of this "standard description."

Form: There should be no horns, slugs, or abortive horns.

POINTS OF A SUPERIOR ANIMAL.

Color, a deep red, with udder of the same color, but the tip of the tail may be white; nose not dark or cloudy.

Form: A neat head and throat; a full eye; a tuft or crest of hair should hang over the forehead; the frontal bones should begin to contract a little above the eyes and should terminate in a comparatively narrow prominence at the summit of the head.

In all other particulars the commonly accepted points of a superior animal are to be taken as applying to the Red Polled cattle.

SHORTHORNS.

Scale of points for judging Shorthorn cattle.

[NOTE.—The American Shorthorn Breeders' Association has adopted no scale for judging cattle, but the following has been established by the Massachusetts State Board of Agriculture.]

STRUCTURAL POINTS FOR COWS.

	Points.
1. Head small, lean, and bony, tapering to the muzzle	3
2. Face somewhat long, the fleshy portion of the nose of a light, delicate color	″
3. Eye is of great significance, and should be prominent, bright, and clear, "prominent" from an accumulation of "adeps" in the back part of its socket, which indicates a tendency to lay on fat, "bright" as an evidence of a good disposition, "clear" as a guaranty of the animal's health; whereas a dull, sluggish eye belongs to a slow feeder, and a wild, restless eye betrays an unquiet, fitful temper	″
4. Horns light in substance and waxy in color, and symmetrically set on head; the ear large, thin, and with considerable action	″
5. Neck rather short than long, tapering to the head, clean in the throat, and full at its base, thus covering and filling out the points of the shoulders	″
6. Chest broad from point to point of the shoulders, deep from the anterior dorsal vertebra to the floor of the sternum, and both round and full just back of the elbows, sometimes designated by the phrase "thick through the heart." These are unquestionably the most important points in every animal, as constitution must depend on their perfect development, and the ample room thus afforded for the free action of the heart and lungs	14
7. Brisket, however deep or projecting, must not be confounded with capacity of chest, for though a very attractive and selling point, it in reality adds nothing to the space within, however it may increase the girth without. It is, in fact, nothing more nor less than a muscular adipose substance, attached to the anterior portion of the sternum, or breastbone, and thence extending itself back. This form, however, of the brisket indicates a disposition to lay on fat generally throughout the frame, and in this point of view is valuable	″
8. Shoulder, where weight, as in the Shorthorn, is the object, should be somewhat upright and of good width at the points, with the blade-bone just sufficiently curved to blend its upper portion smoothly with the crops	″
9. Crops must be full and level with the shoulders and back, and is, perhaps, one of the most difficult points to breed right in a Shorthorn	6

Points.

10. Back, loin, and hips should be broad and wide, forming a straight and even line from the neck to the setting on of the tail, the hips or hucks round and well covered 8
11. Rumps laid up high, with plenty of flesh on their extremities........... 5
12. Pelvis should be large, indicated by the width of the hips (as already mentioned) and the breadth of the twist 2
13. Twist should be so well filled out in its "seam" as to form nearly an even and wide plain between the thighs 3
14. Quarters long, straight, and well developed downwards 5
15. Carcass round, the ribs nearly circular and extending well back 4
16. Flanks deep, wide, and full in proportion to condition.................. 3
17. Legs short, straight, and standing square with the body 2
18. Plates of the belly strong, and thus preserving nearly a straight underline.. 3
19. Tail flat and broad at its root, but fine in its cord, and placed high up and on a level with the rumps.. 2
20. Carriage of an animal gives style and beauty; the walk should be square and the step quick, the head up 2
21. Quality. On this the thriftiness, the feeding properties, and the value of the animal depend; and upon the touch of this quality rests, in a good measure, the grazier's and the butcher's judgment. If the "touch" be good, some deficiency of form may be excused; but if it be hard and stiff nothing can compensate for so unpromising a feature. In raising the skin from the body, between the thumb and the finger, it should have a soft, flexible, and substantial feel, and when beneath the outspread hand it should move easily with it and under it, as though resting on a soft, elastic, cellular substance, which, however, becomes firmer as the animal ripens. A thin, papery skin is objectionable, more especially in a cold climate......................... 15
22. Coat should be thick, short, and mossy, with longer hair in winter; fine, soft, and glossy in summer.. 2
23. Udder pliable and thin in its texture, reaching well forward, roomy behind, and the teats standing wide apart and of convenient size..... 8

Perfection.. 100

STRUCTURAL POINTS FOR BULLS.

As regards the male animal, it is only necessary to remark that the points desirable in the female are generally so in the male, but must, of course, be attended by that masculine character which is inseparable from a strong, vigorous constitution. Even a certain degree of coarseness is admissible, but then it must be so exclusively of a masculine description as never to be discovered in the female of his get.

In contradistinction to the cow, the head of the bull may be shorter, the frontal bone broader, and the occipital flat and stronger, that it may receive and sustain the horn, and this latter may be excused if a little heavy at the base so its upward form, its quality and color be right. Neither is the looseness of the skin attached to and depending from the under jaw to be deemed other than a feature of the sex, provided it is not extended beyond the bone, but leaves the gullet and throat clean and free from dewlap.

The upper portion of the neck should be full and muscular, for it is an indication of strength, power, and constitution. The spine should be strong, the bones of the loin long and broad, and the whole muscular system wide and thoroughly developed over the entire frame.

ORGANIZATIONS OF BREEDERS OF PURE-BRED CATTLE AND AD-
DRESSES OF THEIR SECRETARIES FOR THE YEAR 1899.

Ayrshire Breeders' Association, C. M. Winslow, Brandon, Vt.
Brown Swiss Breeders' Association, N. S. Fish, Groton, Conn.
American Devon Cattle Club, L. P. Sisson, Wheeling, W. Va.
Dutch Belted Cattle Association of America, H. B. Richards, Easton, Pa.
American Guernsey Cattle Club, W. H. Caldwell, Peterboro, N. H.
Holstein-Friesian Association of America, F. L. Houghton, Brattleboro, Vt.
American Jersey Cattle Club, J. J. Hemingway, No. 8 West Seventeenth street,
New York, N. Y.
American Polled Durham Breeders' Association, J. H. Miller, Mexico, Ind.
Red Polled Cattle Club of America, J. McLain Smith, Dayton, Ohio.
American Short Horn Breeders' Association, J. H. Pickrell, Springfield, Ill.
American Simmenthal Herd Book Association, John Mayer, No. 120 Broadway,
New York, N. Y.

FIFTY DAIRY RULES.

Fifty short, practical dairy rules which should be observed in the production and handling of pure milk have been printed by the Department on large cardboards for posting in stables and dairy rooms and widely distributed to milk producers. These rules are based on matter in Farmers' Bulletin No. 63, "Care of Milk on the Farm," which was prepared in the dairy division and sent to a large number of creamery and cheese factory patrons and city milk producers. Some creamery and dairy associations have reprinted the rules for distribution in their neighborhoods, and the dairy commission of one State issued 30,000 copies for the dairymen of that State. The demand for these rules has been so great that it is deemed worth while to republish them in this report. They are as follows:

THE OWNER AND HIS HELPERS.

1. Read current dairy literature and keep posted on new ideas.
2. Observe and enforce the utmost cleanliness about the cattle, their attendants, the stable, the dairy, and all utensils.
3. A person suffering from any disease, or who has been exposed to a contagious disease, must remain away from the cows and the milk.

THE STABLE.

4. Keep dairy cattle in a room or building by themselves. It is preferable to have no cellar below and no storage loft above.
5. Stables should be well ventilated, lighted, and drained; should have tight floors and walls and be plainly constructed.
6. Never use musty or dirty litter.
7. Allow no strongly smelling material in the stable for any length of time. Store the manure under cover outside the cow stable and remove it to a distance as often as practicable.
8. Whitewash the stable once or twice a year. Use land plaster in the manure gutters daily.
9. Use no dry, dusty feed just previous to milking; if fodder is dusty, sprinkle it before it is fed.
10. Clean and thoroughly air the stable before milking. In hot weather sprinkle the floor.
11. Keep the stable and dairy room in good condition, and then insist that the dairy, factory, or place where the milk goes be kept equally well.

THE COWS.

12. Have the herd examined at least twice a year by a skilled veterinarian.

13. Promptly remove from the herd any animal suspected of being in bad health and reject her milk. Never add an animal to the herd until certain it is free from disease, especially tuberculosis.

14. Do not move cows faster than a comfortable walk while on the way to place of milking or feeding.

15. Never allow the cows to be excited by hard driving, abuse, loud talking, or unnecessary disturbance; do not expose them to cold or storm.

16. Do not change the feed suddenly.

17. Feed liberally, and use only fresh, palatable feed stuffs; in no case should decomposed or moldy material be used.

18. Provide water in abundance, easy of access, and always pure; fresh, but not too cold.

19. Salt should always be accessible.

20. Do not allow any strong-flavored food, like garlic, cabbage, and turnips, to be eaten, except immediately after milking.

21. Clean the entire body of the cow daily. If hair in the region of the udder is not easily kept clean it should be clipped.

22. Do not use the milk within twenty days before calving nor within three to five days afterwards.

MILKING.

23. The milker should be clean in all respects; he should not use tobacco; he should wash and dry his hands just before milking.

24. The milker should wear a clean outer garment, used only when milking, and kept in a clean place at other times.

25. Brush the udder and surrounding parts just before milking, and wipe them with a clean, damp cloth or sponge.

26. Milk quietly, quickly, cleanly, and thoroughly. Cows do not like unnecessary noise or delay. Commence milking at exactly the same hour every morning and evening, and milk the cows in the same order.

27. Throw away (but not on the floor, better in the gutter) the first few streams from each teat; this milk is very watery and of little value, but it may injure the rest.

28. If in any milking a part of the milk is bloody or stringy or unnatural in appearance, the whole mess should be rejected.

29. Milk with dry hands; never allow the hands to come in contact with the milk.

30. Do not allow dogs, cats, or loafers to be around at milking time.

31. If any accident occurs by which a pail full or partly full of milk becomes dirty, do not try to remedy this by straining, but reject all this milk and rinse the pail.

32. Weigh and record the milk given by each cow, and take a sample morning and night, at least once a week, for testing by the fat test.

CARE OF MILK.

33. Remove the milk of every cow at once from the stable to a clean, dry room, where the air is pure and sweet. Do not allow cans to remain in stables while they are being filled.

34. Strain the milk through a metal gauze and a flannel cloth or layer of cotton as soon as it is drawn.

35. Aerate and cool the milk as soon as strained. If an apparatus for airing and cooling at the same time is not at hand, the milk should be aired first. This must be done in pure air, and it should then be cooled to 45 degrees if the milk is for shipment, or to 60 degrees if for home use or delivery to a factory.

36. Never close a can containing warm milk which has not been aerated.

37. If cover is left off the can, a piece of cloth or mosquito netting should be used to keep out insects.

38. If milk is stored, it should be held in tanks of fresh, cold water (renewed daily), in a clean, dry, cold room. Unless it is desired to remove cream, it should be stirred with a tin stirrer often enough to prevent forming a thick cream layer.

39. Keep the night milk under shelter so rain can not get into the cans. In warm weather hold it in a tank of fresh cold water.

40. Never mix fresh warm milk with that which has been cooled.

41. Do not allow the milk to freeze.

42. Under no circumstances should anything be added to milk to prevent its souring. Cleanliness and cold are the only preventives needed.

43. All milk should be in good condition when delivered. This may make it necessary to deliver twice a day during the hottest weather.

44. When cans are hauled far they should be full, and carried in a spring wagon.

45. In hot weather cover the cans, when moved in a wagon, with a clean wet blanket or canvass.

THE UTENSILS.

46. Milk utensils for farm use should be made of metal and have all joints smoothly soldered. Never allow them to become rusty or rough inside.

47. Do not haul waste products back to the farm in the same cans used for delivering milk. When this is unavoidable, insist that the skim milk or whey tank be kept clean.

48. Cans used for the return of skim milk or whey should be emptied and cleaned as soon as they arrive at the farm.

49. Clean all dairy utensils by first thoroughly rinsing them in warm water; then clean inside and out with a brush and hot water in which a cleaning material is dissolved; then rinse and lastly sterilize by boiling water or steam. Use pure water only.

50. After cleaning, keep utensils, inverted, in pure air, and sun if possible, until wanted for use.

MEAT AND MILK INSPECTION IN SHANGHAI.

The following communication on the meat and milk inspection in Shanghai has kindly been furnished this Bureau by the Surgeon-General of the United States Navy:

U. S. S. MONOCACY,
Shanghai, China, October 1, 1897.

SIR: Through the courtesy of Drs. Edward Henderson and N. Macleod, of Shanghai, and the kindness of Mr. John Christie, inspector of markets, I was enabled during the months of August and September, 1897, to make a complete investigation of the abattoir, markets, and dairies of Shanghai, and beg to submit the following report compiled from health officers' reports and my own observations, in the hope that the information thus gained may be of service in protecting the health of the men and officers of the United States Navy, when visiting the harbor of Shanghai.

Very respectfully,

W. J. BLACKWOOD,
Passed Assistant Surgeon, U. S. N.

The SURGEON-GENERAL OF THE NAVY.

Anyone who has held a public office, in the discharge of the duties of which it has been necessary for him to attempt the introduction of reforms, be those of the most beneficial character for the public good or not, knows of the struggles through which he had to pass in order to sway public opinion his way, but his labors are but infantile in comparison with those of the foreigner who attempts to draw the Chinaman out of his rut of filth, superstition, and conservatism, and get him to adopt ideas of modern hygiene and sanitation.

Against a combination of these two powerful forces Dr. Edward Henderson fought for over twenty years before he could bring the people of Shanghai to such a position of mind that they were willing to take steps to protect themselves against the great dangers from the consumption of unhealthful foods, which are everywhere so prevalent in China.

To him are almost entirely due the present abattoir, market, and dairy systems, which, though still far from perfect, are yet the entering wedge to greater reforms, and confer upon the foreign community a blessing in the matter of healthful food supply which can best be appreciated by those who knew the old order of things. To well understand the difficulties and dangers to be overcome to gain healthful food supply, one must know something of the topographical divisions of the foreign and Chinese settlements that compose the "cities" of Shanghai. Following along the course of the Whang-poo

River from north to south, we first come to Hongkew, or the so-called "American concession;" crossing the Soo-Chow Creek we pass into the British concession, which is separated from the French concession on the south by the Yang-king-pang Creek. These concessions occupy the river front and have a breadth of about one mile, over which territory foreigners hold jurisdiction, and which is governed by the municipal council.

Surrounding this narrow strip are the Chinese settlements, and to the south the native city of Shanghai. To the west of Hongkew the native settlement is called Li Hongkew, while that to the west of the British concession is known as Pah-sien-jaoh, and it is with these two settlements that we will have to do, as they are the sources from which the largest part of the meat and milk supply for foreign consumption in Shanghai is drawn.

Practically all of the cattle which come to the markets of Shanghai come down by boat from the country, are landed at a small settlement called Jessfield, and from there are taken across country to Pah-sien-jaoh, where they are purchased by the various butchers and at their convenience sent to the isolation sheds in Hongkew, and thus they may remain some time in Pah-sien-jaoh. This part of the settlement is also the home of the grease shops and slaughterhouses that supply meat to the lowest class of Chinese, who consume it whether it is diseased or not. If any animal is sick, suspected of being so, or dies, this is the quarter to which it is sent.

Animals, from buffaloes to goats, ponies, or donkeys, are all utilized here. To give one an idea of this district would be next to impossible, for to get that one must visit the place on a warm summer day, when the air is reeking with the vilest stenches and the ground covered with the worst forms of decomposing matter. But let me quote the words of the health officer of Shanghai in a report on the subject, made twenty-four years ago, the conditions then described being practically the same as those existing to-day:

The land has been occupied as now for some ten or twelve years, and during all that time no single well-directed effort has been made, either by draining, scavenging, or building, to clean or to improve the place. The result is not difficult to imagine, but to be realized it must be actually seen.

The sheds, boiling-down houses, and slaughterhouses are, for convenience' sake, placed in close proximity to one another. These, with very few exceptions, are huts of the poorest possible description, the walls constructed of bamboo or loose boardings, the floors of earth, clay, or loosely laid bricks.

Drains exist in name only, being but shallow trenches dug in the earth and terminating either in the soil itself or in stagnant pools in the immediate neighborhood of the sheds. These channels are filled with the refuse and scourings of the slaughter and boiling-down houses.

The contents of the paunches of slaughtered cattle, mixed with dung from the stalls, is collected in heaps and suffered to remain drying in the sun until such time as it may be conveniently disposed of for manure.

The filthy surroundings of a native village, over which no foreign supervision has ever been exercised, contribute largely to the objectionable features of the place. Besides all this, rinderpest has prevailed extensively and with little abatement among the cattle stalled in this depot for nearly two years past, and without doubt the land and all connected with it is tainted beyond hope of remedy save through the lapse of time.

Seizures of diseased meat have been both frequent and extensive during the past year, and I have no hesitation in affirming that the protection which the public has enjoyed against the consumption of the flesh of animals affected with the plague has been mainly due to the activity and zeal displayed by the market inspector. I am fully aware that many have denied any risk to health from the use of such food, and, therefore, from a wish to avoid useless controversy, I have hitherto contented myself by stating that, while no one would knowingly eat such meat, the foreign community generally will require the governing body to use all possible diligence to prevent its introduction into the public market. * * *

It is practically impossible to distinguish beef taken from the carcasses of the diseased cattle from that which has been obtained from perfectly healthy animals, and it is obviously the duty of the governing body to insure that all cattle, the flesh of which is destined for foreign use, shall be inspected by foreign officers before being slaughtered.

Even after such reports as the one from which the foregoing is quoted, it took twenty-one years before public opinion and the municipality could be stirred up to the point of having a public slaughterhouse and thorough inspection of all cattle slaughtered, and it was not until 1893 that the present abattoir was completed and a beginning made to get a reliable supply for the meat markets of Shanghai.

The new slaughterhouses, which are situated in Hongkew, are in every way models of convenience and modern sanitation, and fully supply the wants of the community. These buildings consist of commodious high-studded rooms with cemented floors and walls, admirable systems of drains both for collecting the blood of the slaughtered animals and for carrying off the water used in washing and cleansing the place. There are separate rooms for the slaughter of different kinds of animals, and each room is complete as to contrivances for hanging and transporting carcasses and also as regards drains and water supply. In connection with the slaughterhouse proper is a system of cattle sheds, in which cattle are kept for a certain length of time to undergo the necessary inspection before being taken to the abattoir to be slaughtered, and in the construction of these sheds, which will accommodate hundreds of head of cattle, the same care and regard for cleanliness and convenience is displayed as in the other buildings of the system.

Following are the rules governing the cattle sheds and abattoir, which will explain themselves:

MUNICIPAL ABATTOIR.

1. Only licensed butchers shall be allowed to bring animals for slaughter to the municipal abattoir.

2. The hours of slaughter shall be: October 1 to May 31, from 8 a. m. to 6 p. m.; June 1 to September 30, from 6 a. m. to 9 p. m.

3. The following fees will be charged for slaughtering: Oxen, 10 cents each; calves, 5 cents each; sheep, 5 cents each; and pigs, 5 cents each.

4. No animal shall be allowed to be slaughtered before or after the hours mentioned in rule 2, unless the butcher has received a special permission signed by the inspector, and for which the following additional fees will be charged: Oxen, 10 cents each; calves, 5 cents each; sheep, 5 cents each; and pigs, 5 cents each. No hot water will be guaranteed for these special permits.

5. No carcass of any animal will be permitted to leave the abattoir until it has been inspected and stamped.

6. All ox tongues and tails shall have to be taken to the branding room to be branded, for which a charge of 1 cent for each tongue and tail will be made.

7. Half an hour after the time stated in rule 2 will be given the killers to clean up the killing booths, after which the lights will be extinguished.

8. Butchers or their coolies must cover all meats with a clean white cloth when taking any meats through the streets of the settlement; this rule to apply whether the meat is going from the abattoir to the shop or from the shop to the customer.

9. Coolies in charge of donkey carts or other vehicles conveying meats shall not sit on the meats while in transit.

10. All wheelbarrows, carts, or other modes of conveyance must be kept in a clean state. Any dirty conveyance will be stopped from going out of the abattoir until cleaned to the satisfaction of the inspector.

11. Butchers must send qualified men to kill their animals, for at no time will cruelty to animals be allowed to take place.

12. All animals must be killed within the places allotted for the purpose, and not in the open parts of the abattoir.

13. Any butcher, workman, or coolie who steals, disobeys orders, or otherwise breaks any of these rules will be bound to appear at the inspector's office, when the inspector shall have the power to withdraw his license, keep him outside of the cattle sheds and abattoir at all times, or otherwise dispose of the case as he may think best.

14. All complaints against the native staff, or against any other person within the abattoir, to be made at the inspector's office, when the complaint will be duly considered by the foreigner in charge at the time.

15. No nuisance to be committed within the slaughtering booths, but only in the places built for the purpose.

16. A fee of 2 cents per ox will be charged the grease shopmen and hide dealers for water used by them.

17. All offal, guts, or other decomposing parts of animals killed, to be removed the same day as slaughtering takes place. The inspector shall seize and dispose of any offal, etc., which he considers to be a nuisance.

18. Grease shopmen, when taking any offal, heads, guts, stomachs, etc., from the abattoir, must put them in large baskets properly covered over with cloths so that anything they are conveying through the streets may not seem unsightly to anyone passing.

CATTLE SHEDS.

1. All animals to be slaughtered for local supply must be housed at the municipal cattle sheds at least twenty-four hours before slaughter. As, however, animals are scarce at certain seasons, they may be passed for slaughter at discretion of inspector.

2. When passed for slaughter the following cattle-shed fees will be charged: Oxen, 75 cents each; sheep, 5 cents each; calves, 20 cents each.

3. All cattle brought to the cattle sheds must be properly fixed with ropes or

hooked to the chains provided for the purpose, so as to prevent them breaking away and doing injury to themselves or their surroundings.

4. All animals must be kept clean and provided daily with a sufficiency of food. Straw for bedding will be provided by the municipal council, and the sheds will be kept clean by the municipal staff of coolies.

5. The animals brought to the sheds will be inspected in the course of the morning, when any animal the inspector may consider unfit for the foreign market will be rejected, branded with the letter R, and sent off the premises.

6. The inspector will also in the course of the morning inspect any oxen, calves, or sheep intended for export, or going from this port on board any steamer, to see that they do not suffer from any contagious disease. The same fees will be charged as in rule 2.

7. All possible care and attention will be given to the animals housed at the municipal cattle sheds, but no responsibility will rest on the council or the municipal staff in case of loss or death.

After the cattle have passed the necessary inspection at the sheds while alive, they are taken to the abattoir and killed, after which the meat and internal organs are thoroughly inspected and if everything is found to be in perfect condition the meat is stamped with the official municipal "Chop" in such places that all cuts of the meat may possess the mark. If the meat is tough, the animal being old, a different mark is put on it called the "Stallman's chop," in which case it can be sold only in the open market and not in the butcher shops. If the animal is found, postmortem, to have been diseased, the carcass is condemned and removed to the grease shops. So that any meat bearing either of the official "chops" may be thoroughly relied on, though that with the "Stallman's chop" is inferior to the other.

To show the number of animals slaughtered during the year, and the extent to which the abattoir is used, I will quote the following figures for the year 1896: Oxen, 11,381; sheep, 20,626; calves, 1,967; pigs, 725, making a total of 34,699 animals, an increase of 4,119 over the year 1895. Of this number 41 oxen, 17 sheep, 2 calves, and 6 foreign-bred pigs were rejected as unfit for food.

The health of the animals in the sheds during 1896 was good, only 33 oxen and 21 sheep having been rejected.

After leaving the abattoir the meat is taken in carts to the various markets and shops for sale, but here again it is exposed to fresh sources of contamination. In 1891 the health officer, after an inspection of the butcher shops, reported as follows:

The point which chiefly attracted my attention was the dirty condition of the ice chests in which the meat is at present stored. In winter the joints, etc., are hung around the shop, the coolies employed by the proprietor sleeping, more or less crowded together. on boards projecting from the walls above the meat. The market inspector tells me that when these houses are opened in the morning the atmosphere with which they are filled is simply insupportable, and I can well believe it. Under existing circumstances the inspector is able to exercise but little control over the management of these shops; if, however, the butchers were licensed such matters as these just referred to could easily be put right. * * *

To prevent the sale of diseased meat in the shops from which foreigners derive

10317——14

their supplies the inspector has at present only one resource, the immediate destruction of the carcass found diseased. This he effects by cutting it up in such a manner as permanently to disfigure it, rendering it easily recognizable again if exposed for sale in the market, but of course not preventing it from being used as food by the natives, or by the Mohammedans, should they desire so to employ it. This proceeding is tolerably effective, but it is illegal, and fails to prevent the repetition of similar offenses by the same man. The only protection which the inspector has at present (1891) against suits instituted at the mixed court for the recovery of damages by the butcher whose meat he has destroyed, is the fear that the latter has of public exposure as a vender of bad meat.

These evils have now been remedied to a large extent, and all butcher shops and market stalls within the settlements are licensed by the municipal council, the following being the regulations governing them:

BUTCHER SHOPS AND STALLS.

1. All shops and stalls where butcher's meat is offered or exposed for sale shall be licensed by the municipal council. The license fee shall be $1 for one month, or for such part of a month as shall elapse until the license is withdrawn, payable in advance.

2. No butcher shall be allowed to offer or expose for sale any meat which has not been prepared for the market at the municipal abattoir. The inspector shall have power to seize and confiscate any such meat, and he shall also seize and confiscate any meats marked "Stallman" which he may find in any butcher's shop.

3. All butchers' shops and stalls must be kept perfectly clean and otherwise in order to the satisfaction of the inspector of markets, who shall have liberty to visit them at all times. No butcher shall occupy a shop which the inspector thinks unsuitable for the sale of meats.

4. No other business shall be carried on in the same shop, and no coolies' benches or sleeping places will be allowed to be in the same place that meats are either sold or kept.

5. All stallman butchers must after the closing of the market deposit their unsold meats in the abattoir. If the meat is found in their houses, it will be confiscated.

It may be thought by some that it is unnecessary to mention the condition of affairs before the now existing regulations were put in force, but in this they are mistaken, for the two conditions exist to-day side by side. Not, of course, within the limits of the municipality, but surrounding it on all sides, and in a country where people depend so much upon their Chinese servants, and especially so with messes on board United States men-of-war, it is absolutely necessary to know, not only what is right and correct, but what is wrong and to be guarded against.

The inspections and enforcement of the regulations within the limits of the municipality are most rigidly made and carried out, as I know from personal observation.

THE MILK SUPPLY.

The health of the cattle in the foreign and native dairies from which the settlement derives its milk supply suffered seriously during the year 1895; in the spring, autumn, and winter from cattle plague, and during the summer from a specific and apparently contagious fever, the exact nature of which has still to be determined. These constantly recurring epizootics made the business of the dairy farmer in Shanghai at all times a precarious one, and the question of the milk supply as affecting the health of the foreign community, of which infants and young children now form so large a proportion, is one of great and increasing importance. When in 1872 public attention was first drawn to an outbreak of rinderpest among foreign dairy stock it was pointed out that, although the disease was then for the first time recognized in Shanghai, it was well known and believed to be almost constantly present among the native cattle on the steppes of Russia and Great Plain of China. Since then recurrent epizootics here and elsewhere have justified the belief that the contagion of cattle plague is much more widely diffused throughout the Empire than was at first supposed; indeed, in the Shanghai district the dairy farmers of to-day have come with good reason to regard the disease as a constant menace to their cattle. It is one thing to recognize a danger, another and a very different thing to find means to avert it; and the council, possessing no authority beyond the limits of the settlement, being without either support or assistance from the Chinese Government, and encountering everywhere among the native farmers and cattle dealers the obstruction which arises from ignorance, is at present, it would seem, powerless either to prevent the introduction of the disease or to limit its extension.

Inspection of dairies.—I have lately, with the inspector, visited a number of native dairies and consider the present inspection is practically useless, the inspector having no power over the dairymen. The whole of the sanitary arrangements for dairy farming here are bad in the extreme. In fact, with few exceptions, the dairies are simply filthy and are certainly harboring disease for those who consume their products.

The water consumed by the cattle and used for washing bottles is in nine cases out of ten obtained from either native wells or dirty, stagnant creeks, into which in most cases whatever drainage there is empties itself. This probably is also the water that is used if the adulteration of milk goes on. For washing bottles, etc., this water may be boiled or partially so, but it is boiled simultaneously with and within a few inches of the boiler that contains the vegetables to be eaten by the Chinese. I do not think it is necessary to state what a source of danger this must be to the public health.

Drainage.—In many dairies there is no attempt at this, the water simply standing in a pool in one corner. In others, the slight attempt gives one the impression that it would not be made if it were not to prevent the shed from being a perpetual mud pond. And in the remainder that are drained the cesspools are immediately outside the building.

Ventilation.—This, one of the most important considerations for the well-being of the cattle, seems to be totally disregarded, consequently the atmosphere is heated and moist, which retards exhalation from the lungs and skin. The deleterious effete matters which should be thrown off by those organs must be removed in another way, and with a cow in milk there is no doubt a large quantity leaves the body with the milk, which is usually abundant, owing to suspension of functions of lungs and skin. Under this heading I do not think it out of place to also mention tuberculosis, the greatest scourge of cattle and perhaps human beings. The system of farming here is admirably suited for the propagation of this disease among cattle, which is admitted on all sides to be identical with that of the human subject. Upon recent investigations in England, 20 per cent of all milch cows are admitted to be tuberculous, and all foreign cows here originate from that stock. I do not know whether the disease is prevalent in Shanghai, but at any time through the milk source it may become so, and as the community is increasing, and especially the number of children, who are the largest consumers of milk, every precaution should be taken. With regard to infectious diseases being communicated to foreigners by means of the milk, it may be remembered that should disease of an infectious character break out among those attending to the cows the consumers of the milk would run a considerable risk.

As the result of the foregoing investigations I would most strongly urge, for the benefit of the health of all officers and men on United States men-of-war in the harbor of Shanghai, that no meats of any description be allowed aboard ship unless they bear upon them the official "chop" of the municipal abattoir, and that all stewards and compradores be cautioned to buy none other than these, and, if possible, to avoid purchasing even those which have passed through the abattoir, but are marked with the "Stallman chop;" and, lastly, that no milk be allowed on board ship, except it be condensed milk for ordinary use, except in cases of sickness where a milk diet is necessary, and that then the milk be most carefully boiled and sealed in properly cleansed bottles until it is to be used.

AGRICULTURE AND DAIRYING IN SCOTLAND.[1]

AGRICULTURAL DEPRESSION IN GREAT BRITAIN.

The agricultural difficulties caused by the drop in prices, which in Great Britain may be stated roughly as amounting to about 33 per cent within the last twenty years, have in the main been met by one of two methods—(a) reduction in expenses, (b) increase of production. Speaking broadly and subject to individual exceptions, it may be said that the first method has been chiefly resorted to in England and the second method in Scotland. The former has been effected chiefly by laying down land in grass, for the purpose of grazing with cattle or pasturing with sheep. A very large acreage of the country has been thus treated. In some instances the land has been simply left to cover itself, first with weeds, and by degrees with grasses indigenous to the locality. This process is, of course, the least costly of all, but it yields no return for a number of years, and only a small one at last. It has therefore been resorted to in exceptional and rare cases only. More generally the land has received more or less of cleaning and preparation and seeds of good permanent grasses have been sown, usually along with a grain crop. Great improvement has of late years been attained in getting such seeds pure and with a good percentage of germination. Most of the leading seedsmen now guarantee their seeds to be from within 1 to 5 per cent of absolute purity; and the percentage of germination is also guaranteed, though it varies to a greater extent, being generally about 90, though with a few species it is as low as 70 or 80. The expense of such seed, however, is considerable, varying from $5 to $10 per acre.

But even with the utmost care, and with no stint of expenditure, it generally takes from five to ten years to establish what (in England especially) is considered a good pasture; that is, one which will fatten cattle at the rate of about one beast per acre during the summer. In the majority of cases even this will not be attained without the addition of from 3 to 6 pounds of linseed or other oil cake per day. But subject to this outlay, and the expense of maintaining fences, the system of grazing on grass once established involves extremely little expense, and yields returns which may vary from $5 to $15 per acre, according to the character of the land.

---

[1] This paper was written by Hon. John C. Higgins, United States consul at Dundee, Scotland, and forwarded to the State Department under date of November 11, 1898, and thence referred to the Department of Agriculture. Mr. Higgins was for years a practical and successful dairy farmer in Delaware, where he owned a large and fine herd of Guernsey cattle.

METHODS OF MEETING LOW PRICES.

The economy, however, is obtained entirely from the cessation from employing labor. This means that laborers are displaced from the country districts and forced to migrate to the towns. The system is therefore one hostile to the interests of the nation at large. It has, in fact, always been viewed with disfavor by the English people, and statutes as far back as the Tudors were passed for the purpose of restraining the practice of converting arable land into grass.

The other method of meeting low prices has consisted in endeavoring to increase the production from cultivated crops, at the same time cultivating such only as give the best returns. This method necessarily tends rather to the employment of more than of less labor on the land, for it involves higher cultivation, the use of more manure, and the handling of larger bulk of crops. Nor, with the exception of mowing and reaping machines, has it been found possible to substitute, to any material extent, machinery for human (and horse) labor.

The chief alterations introduced in carrying out this system are the feeding of cattle in winter under cover and the increased use of commercial manures. Formerly cattle, though they had the option of a covered shed, were in winter generally kept in yards or courts, of which a great part was without roof. It was believed that they even throve better with this degree of exposure to the weather. But one consequence was that a large proportion of their manure was leached and rendered comparatively worthless. This system still survives in England, but it is nearly extinct in Scotland. In this country almost all farms now have their cattle yards entirely roofed over. The manure is thus doubled in value and the cattle fatten much more quickly and at less outlay for food.

FOODS AND FEEDING.

In addition to the foods produced on the farm it is also the universal practice to give all cattle which are at the fattening stage from 4 to 10 pounds a day of oilcake or meal of some sort of grain. This also greatly enhances the value of the manure. The cost of such foods has fallen considerably. Linseed cake, which cost at one time $60 or more per ton, is now only from $30 to $40. American maize and Asiatic barley cost only $20 to $25 per ton. The use of these more concentrated foods permits the straw grown on the farm to be used for feeding, and thus utilizes a part of the crop which was formerly considered merely as waste or at least only good for litter. By cutting the straw into "chaff," i. e., short pieces of one-half inch in length, and mixing it with the meal used for food, a value equal to $7.50 to $10 a ton is obtained from it in feeding. This is obviously an important addition to the profits of the farm. But in Scotland especially a great deal of the oat straw has always been, and still is, consumed without being cut, and it is reckoned as not greatly inferior to hay.

It should be kept in view that the feeding of cattle, and partly also of sheep, in winter is an essential element of husbandry in all parts of Great Britain. On the poorest land young stock, or "stores," are alone raised or kept, without any attempt to fatten. On medium lands, both classes, and on the richest lands cattle for fattening only are kept. The reasons are found, firstly, in the actual profits made in using hay, straw, or roots for growth or fattening, and, secondly, in the production of manure for subsequent crops. In connection with this system what are called "green crops"—that is, mangel-wurzel in the south and middle districts of England, replaced by turnips in the north and in Scotland—are a regular crop in the rotation. These have come in the place of the old fallow, when the land was allowed to lie without any crop during the whole summer, in order that by frequent cultivation weeds might be extirpated and fertility increased. These objects are now attained by the large amount of cultivation given to the green crops, which begins in spring and is carried on till they quite cover the ground in July, and by the heavy manuring always given to them. This, in the first place, produces a crop varying from 12 to 30 tons per acre, and at the same time the land is left clean and enriched, so that it yields a subsequent crop of oats or barley, followed generally by clover or grass, without further manure, or only with a dressing of commercial manure. These green crops, being consumed by cattle in the yards or by sheep penned upon them, furnish the manure for next year.

MANURES AND MANURING.

This manure is, however, in Scotland largely supplemented by commercial manures. That most in use is phosphate of lime, either in the form of superphosphate, basic slag, or bone meal, and this is principally applied to the turnips and potato crops, at the rate of about 3 hundredweights to the latter and 3 to 6 hundredweights to the former per acre. One or 2 hundredweights of nitrate of soda or sulphate of ammonia are generally added. A hundredweight of either of the two latter, with 2 hundredweights of superphosphate, is frequently used as a top-dressing to the grain crops in spring or upon grass intended to be cut for hay. Potassic manures, chiefly kainit, are used to the extent of 3 or 4 hundredweights per acre for potatoes, but rarely for other crops.

It must be remembered that the manure of the animals fed on the farm, which contains the manurial residue of much cake and meal and is wholly kept under cover till applied to the land, is of high value. It is carted and spread and plowed in either in autumn, in winter, or in spring, according as weather or work permit. No difference is perceived in results arising from the time of its application.

AGRICULTURAL PRACTICES IN FIFE COUNTY, SCOTLAND.

I have, while resident at Dundee, had an opportunity of observing the general application of the system above described in the highly cultivated adjacent counties of Forfar and Fife, more minutely in the latter.   Upon the North Sea, between the Firths of Tay and Forth for a distance of nearly 40 miles, lies Fife, one of the most fertile and not the least picturesque of the counties of Scotland.

With Edinburgh just south of it and Dundee just across the Tay, its northern boundary, it lies between two cities to which it offers sites of unsurpassed convenience and beauty for suburban villages, country residences, and landed estates.   I have had on several occasions the advantage of going closely over one of the latter under the guidance of its owner, and I can perhaps best illustrate the special characteristics of the best Scottish farming if I give in some detail an account of the practice which I there saw in operation.

The Lomonds are among the noted bits of Fife Highlands, nestled to the south of which lies Loch Leven; and to the north, just opposite, lies Ladybank, a station on the railway between Dundee and Edinburgh.   A branch road runs toward Perth, taking which 4 miles by train will place us at Collessie, a small village of quaint thatched roof houses and many evidences of a most respectable antiquity. One mile from Collessie brings us to the park entrance of Kinloch, the residence of J. Boyd Kinnear, esq., M. P., author, agriculturist, and country gentleman.   Kinloch house is by no means the largest of the stately homes of Scotland, but to say that there is not one more graceful or beautiful would probably not provoke an adverse opinion. The charming symmetry and delicate conceits of the softly shaded graystone that everywhere forms the prevailing building material of North Britain can only be well understood when we know that a brother of the present proprietor was a great architect, and that upon Kinloch he lavished his art with loving devotion.   Once the home of the historic Balfour, of Burleigh, it had many vicissitudes before it came (over a hundred years ago) to the Kinnear family, and for that reason gave a better opportunity for a full repair, that resulted in the Kinloch of to-day.   One hundred acres of park of stately trees, winding roads, and shaven turf, walled gardens, with the usual wealth of flowers, fruit, and vegetables, and parterres and turf immediately around the house, make Kinloch as charming a place as can be seen even in this land of homes.   The present proprietor devoted the earlier years of his life to the practice of the legal profession and to journalism in London.   But his health having given way under the pressure of these exacting pursuits, he was obliged under medical advice to abandon them entirely, and from 1870 to 1884 he lived almost entirely in the island of Guernsey.   This accident led him to an acquaintance with the breed of cows of that island, and being compelled, on succeeding his father in the Fife estate, to take a considerable part of it out of the hands of tenants who were unable to contend against the fall of agricultural prices, he resolved to have recourse to milk production from a herd of imported Guernsey cows, chiefly of his own selection, as the best means of meeting the difficulty. Through the kindness of Mr. Kinnear I am enabled to furnish the Department with the following particulars as to his methods and practice in handling this beautiful and profitable estate.

ESTABLISHING A GUERNSEY HERD AT KINLOCH.

Mr. Kinnear in farming adopts the system of cropping, already described as prevailing in Scotland, as a basis, but modifies or extends it to meet his special requirements. His live stock consists of a herd of (at present) about 120 pedigreed Guernsey cows, with some 60 or more of their produce in various stages of growth.

For the disposal of this milk without risk of adulteration by middlemen, he has two stores of his own, one in the small town of St. Andrews, containing a population of about 6,000, and the other in Edinburgh, the capital of Scotland. The former is distant by rail about 20 miles, the latter about 50 miles. In the former the milk is retailed at 8 cents and in the latter at 10 cents per quart. The whole expense of the stores, of distribution, and of carriage are of course to be deducted from these prices. They are, in each case, about 2 cents per quart higher than the rates current in the respective towns for ordinary milk. The demand for his milk is generally so large as to absorb nearly the whole supply; therefore butter is made only from such small surplus quantities as may not be required, and it is scarcely a regular product of the dairy. At certain seasons, however, when the demand falls off through the occurrence of vacations of schools or the departure of customers on visits or to country quarters, he makes a considerable quantity both of butter and of cheese, and the latter being made from the whole milk is very rich and sells readily at from 18 to 24 cents per pound. About 8 pounds of milk suffices to make 1 pound of cheese. So far as I know, this is the only instance in which cheese has been made from the milk of Guernsey cows, and it is of some interest to know that it can be successfully done.

FEED OF COWS DURING SUMMER AND WINTER.

The feeding of cows is, during summer—that is, from the middle or end of April (according to the season) to the middle or end of October—chiefly on pasture, which consists partly of fields that have lain for an unknown period in grass and partly of fields that have been laid down in grass within the last dozen years. About an acre per head suffices. The land is partly of good quality, lying on trap rock, partly very poor, being on drift gravel. Throughout the season the cows are brought into the sheds for the night, and they receive there a good feed of cut clover, or of tares or vetches. In addition, they have a few pounds of mixed meal, consisting of dried distillery grains, malt combs, and maize or rice flour. This costs on an average under 1 cent per pound. The quantity varies, because in the first flush of the grass the animals are scarcely inclined to eat it, and at all times it is proportioned to the quantity of milk each is giving. In the average, it is about 4 pounds a day during the summer season.

In winter the daily allowance of this mixed food is nearly doubled and 2 or 3 pounds of cotton-cake meal are added. In addition, the cows get as much hay and oat straw as they can eat, averaging about 12 pounds, and about half a hundredweight of turnips. The digestible nutriment in this diet may be represented as below, fat being reckoned as twice the value of carbohydrates and included in them.

Digestible nutrients in different kinds of foods.

Kind of feed.	Albuminoids.	Carbohydrates.
8 pounds mixed meal	1.2	5
2 pounds decorticated cotton meal	.7	1
12 pounds hay and straw	.5	5
56 pounds turnips	.3	3
	2.7	14

The above is, however, only to be taken as an approximation. Mr. Kinnear places great reliance on the German and American tables of digestible coefficients, viewed as averages, but modified according to the quality of each article. Where he thinks necessary he examines the digestible constituents of the actual foods available by analyzing them himself according to methods of his own, and sometimes by subjecting them successively to digestion in pepsin and pancreatic solutions.

METHODS IN THE STABLE AND THE DAIRY HOUSE.

In the stalls the cows are fastened by chains around the neck, the ring of which slides on a rod so as to rise and fall as required. The floor is of concrete, with a gutter by which the urine is at once conducted to a tank outside. The solid matter is removed as far as possible immediately it drops, and thus not a great deal of litter is required. The passages and gutters are washed every day till the water runs perfectly clear. The cows, when soiled, are first scraped, then the udder is washed, and the coats are brushed clean daily. The milkers, besides, use a basin of clean water to each cow to wash the teats before milking.

The milk when drawn is at once cooled by being run over a refrigerator. But it has been found that mere aeration, by being conducted in a very thin stream over wire gauze, is about as effective for preserving it fresh as refrigeration. When set for raising cream, shallow pans are used, without being surrounded by cold water, as it is found when milk is cooled, or even aerated, before it is set, the cream rises as rapidly as if continuously surrounded by cold water. But the making of butter being quite a secondary consideration, Mr. Kinnear is not careful to extract the last percentage from the milk. There is, in fact, always a sale for the skim milk at 8 cents a gallon.

THE YIELD OF MILK.

The yield of each cow is tested once a month by a day's milk being carefully weighed. Although there may be slight occasional varia-tions, Mr. Kinnear considers that this furnishes a practical basis of sufficient correctness on which to calculate the total production for the year, especially as he has not hitherto sold any cows, and only seeks information for his own judgment. He considers that the normal yield per head over the whole herd (including young and old) ought to be 6,000 pounds per annum. This has in some years been con-siderably exceeded, but during 1896 and 1897, owing to an epidemic of abortion, it fell to 5,850 and 5,350, respectively. The latter figure was brought down also by the introduction of an extra number of heifers to make up for loss of older cows. A few individual returns may be quoted, extending over the last three years.

Milk yield of individual cows in 1895, 1896, and 1897.

Name of cow.	1895.	1896.	1897.
	Pounds.	*Pounds.*	*Pounds.*
Violet XXII	7,110	5,770	11,020
Violet XXIV	6,200	7,720	8,580
Fleur de Lis III	7,750	7,530	7,530
Cowslip III	7,036	6,840	6,460
Lilac	8,360	8,920	9,040
Nerine III	7,710	6,970	7,950
Flora III	4,670	7,180	8,100

DISEASES AND REMEDIES.

To combat abortion most of the remedies (including Nocard's) rec-ommended have been tried, and it is believed it is now nearly extir-pated. The chief reliance is placed on injection of a weak solution of izal, one of the coal antiseptics. Milk fever, or more properly parturient apoplexy, is not now dreaded, since the discovery by a Scotch veterinary surgeon of the remarkable effect of chloral hydrate in this disease. It is given at first in a dose of 2 drams, followed by doses of 1 dram every second hour; but it is seldom, if taken promptly, that more than two doses are required.[1]

---

[1] The treatment now generally adopted for parturient apoplexy, and which con-sists of injections of iodide of potash solution into the mammary glands through the teats, was first recommended by the Danish veterinarian Kolding. Through its use the previous mortality of from 60 to 80 per cent has been reduced to about 20 per cent.

INFLUENCE OF FOOD ON MILK.

The large number of the herd and the keeping of a daily record of
the total milk yielded, over and above the monthly measurement of
the milk of each cow, has led Mr. Kinnear to form clear opinions as
to the influence of food on milk. A difference of even a quarter of
a. pint in each animal makes on the whole (supposing 100 cows to
be actually in milk) a difference of three gallons a day in the total
yield, and when the whole is required for the supply of customers,
such a sudden deficiency attracts attention and its correction becomes
urgent. Mr. Kinnear has thus been led to recognize that a very
slight diminution, either in the total amount or in the relative digestibility of the food consumed, produces a sensible effect at the very
next milking, while, similarly, an improvement in the diet will show
its influence a little more slowly, but quite distinctly, within the following twenty-four hours. In the same way the effect of stormy
weather, of cold, of annoyance by flies, or any other discomfort, is at
once apparent. The quality of the milk, however, is (over the whole
herd) not sensibly influenced by any such causes. The practical conclusion is, therefore, that, assuming sufficient food to be supplied, the
quantity of milk yielded may be materially affected by the ratio of
albuminoids to carbohydrates being made closer and closer up to
about one to five, but that quality depends wholly on breed and not
on feeding, within at least the ordinary practical limits.

At the same time his experience has led him to the conclusion that
exact adherence to a definite albuminoid ratio is not of material
importance, provided a full supply of food of good composition is
given and digested. The albuminoids will then in any case be sufficient to supply both the waste of the body and the demands of milk.
An extra allowance of albuminoids undoubtedly stimulates the processes both of digestion and metabolism, through which the milk is
formed, and thus is necessary in order to obtain the full supply which
the constitution of the animal enables it to furnish; but if this is
attained the essential point is to furnish digestible elements from
which the milk can be formed. As the fat can be derived, according
to the latest scientific researches, alike from the albuminoids, the
carbohydrates, and the fat of the food, it would seem not very important whether the one or the other is supplied in excess. This is supported by Mr. Kinnear's practical experience. He finds that within
reasonable limits the main point is to furnish the most digestible food
without too minute regard to its composition, and that such food will
generally approximate to a ratio of about one to five. On an average,
he has found that 1 pound of dry digestible matter in such food yields
1 pound of milk over the whole herd at one time; that is, including
cows dry, or nearly dry, as well as those in the full flush of milk.

There are, however, certain foods which appear to exercise a specific action on the milk glands and to cause an increased secretion. One of these is the carrot. This root is largely grown in Channel Islands, where a yield of 20 tons an acre is obtained. Given to cows in the quantity of 15 to 20 pounds a day, carrots will remarkably increase the yield of milk, to such a degree, indeed, that Mr. Kinnear has in Guernsey noticed that it is difficult to keep the cows which have this allowance from falling off in condition, no matter how much food of other descriptions is consumed. In a less degree turnips, which contain about 6 per cent of sugar, have a similar effect in increasing the milk flow. "Dreg," which is the liquor remaining in the stills after distillation of whisky, is in Scotland much used by town dairymen for a like purpose, but the milk produced by it is distinctly thin and watery.

BEST USE OF THE LAND.

In regard to the cultivation of the land, the first point kept in view is to obtain the largest quantity of cattle food, and the second is to obtain the largest amount of other salable produce. About 150 acres are employed for summer pasture for cows and young stock, 10 or 15 for the growth of the green food given at night in summer, 170 for hay, 160 are in grain crops, 40 in turnips, and 20 in potatoes. When there is a good crop of hay about half of it is sold, the price being from $12.50 to $16 per ton. The wheat and barley are all sold, and as much of the oats as are not required for the farm horses, of which 14 are kept, consuming about 2 bushels of oats each per week. The potatoes, also, are all sold, except when the price falls below $5 per ton, when they are given to the fattening stock, but not to the cows, as they tend to make the milk and butter white. On an average, the 120 cows consume during the whole year the produce of 180 acres of grass, 40 of turnips, and the straw of perhaps 30 acres of grain.

The grass cut for hay receives, as a rule, a top-dressing of 2 hundred-weights of sulphate of ammonia, 1 hundredweight of superphosphate of lime, and 1 hundredweight of kainit per acre. The grain crops receive half the above quantities. Potatoes receive 3 hundredweights of kainit and turnips 3 hundredweights of superphosphate, in addition to about 10 tons per acre of the farm manure. For the last few years Mr. Kinnear has given to the pasture grass the same top-dressing as to hay. He finds that it pays in bringing the grass at least a fort-night earlier, and in keeping it growing even in time of drouth, and in the enhancement of the nutritive quality of the grass. But what yields the largest amount of food is a mixture of Italian rye grass with red clover. This is sown with a grain crop. After the crop is removed it is lightly pastured, and in spring it receives a dressing of urine from the manure tank, put on by means of a barrel mounted on wheels and discharging into a trough pierced with holes. This treatment gives a growth of 2 feet or more in height by the beginning of May. As soon as this is cut a second dressing of the same description is given, which in six weeks yields a second cutting of the same bulk; a third and a fourth follow before the end of the summer. In this way from 30 to 40 tons of the most succulent and nutritious herbage are obtained per acre.

FARM ACCOUNTS.

All the accounts of the farm and herd are regularly kept by the system of double entry. There the herd is charged with the cost of the food grown on the farm, of purchased food, and of labor in attendance and milking, and expense of distribution; it is, on the other hand, credited with the amount received for milk, butter, etc., the value of the calves and of the manure produced. Each several crop is similarly charged with the cost of labor spent on it, seed, and manure, whether produced on the land or purchased, and it is credited with its price if sold or its value if given to the cows or other stock. Mr. Kinnear does not, however, take account of the residual value of manure after the first crop, this being of too uncertain an amount, and being fairly shared among all the crops by its addition to the general fertility of the land. He attributes the highest importance to the use of bookkeeping in this manner. It enables him to see the exact value of every crop and of every system of cultivation, and thus to abandon such as do not pay, while extending and improving those which are profitable.

COST OF LABOR.

It may be mentioned in conclusion that he adopts with the work people employed a modified system of what is known in Britain as "profit-sharing." When the accounts show a net profit after payment of expenses, interest on capital, and the normal rent of the land he divides it between himself and the work people in the proportion of their several interests, reckoning his own at the annual value of capital and land, and theirs at the annual rate of wages paid to them. In some years there has been no such profit; in others it has permitted of a bonus or dividend of from 2 to 7 per cent to each on their wages.

The laborers, both men and women, are, in conformity with the custom of the neighborhood, engaged by the year. They all occupy houses on the estate, which have gardens attached and are rent free. Men receive an average of $250 a year in wages, women and boys from $75 to $150. In addition the women employed in milking receive 12 cents a day. When there is a family thus working together the joint earnings may amount to from $500 to $900 a year. The total wages for labor employed on the farm are about $4,500 a year. From $2,500 to $3,000 a year is spent on purchased food and above $1,500 on commercial manures. The hours of labor are about nine in summer and eight in winter.

OTHER FARM OPERATIONS.

To an American the plowing is almost a revelation. The pair of heavy Clydesdale horses move slowly, time not being considered, but the land is left in furrows straight and practically alike in elevation and angles. The plowing matches are the great yearly events, forming gala days for the countryside. The teams are resplendent with plaits and ribbons.

The stacking is, however, no less a fine art. Fifty grain stacks about a single farm steading is not an unusual array—each ready to yield about 125 bushels of grain. Every stack is thatched and will withstand the heavy fall and winter rains, and as well the crows and rooks, which maintain the utmost freedom of intercourse with man and claim their full share of the products of his labor. They have not the shyness of their congener—the American crow. In Scottish farming the ultimate has been reached in tidiness, cleanliness of land, and thoroughness of cultivation. It is interesting to note that American implements are quite largely used in some of their operations.

This high farming speaks most emphatically in its results. This year affords instances where the yield per acre reached 81 bushels of barley, 64 of wheat, 80 of oats, and 350 of potatoes. Most of the grain crops are thrashing extremely well for quantity and quality. Weight per bushel of barley and oats has seldom been better. It is common to have ordinary Scotch barley up to 57 and even 58 pounds per bushel this year, and oats run from 43 to 44 pounds on almost every second farm on the low grounds. Wheat is also well up. Ordinary large crops might be said to be 40 bushels wheat, 48 barley, and 56 oats. A few crops of oats have run from 96 to 112 bushels per acre and the weight up to standard.

VITALITY AND RETENTION OF VIRULENCE BY CERTAIN PATHOGENIC BACTERIA IN MILK AND ITS PRODUCTS.

By CHARLES F. DAWSON, M. D., D. V. S.,
Veterinary Inspector, Bureau of Animal Industry.

That milk is a first-class medium for the development of many of the pathogenic bacteria needs no further proof than the fact that bacteriologists use it as one of the means to determine certain biological characters. Some species cause changes in the physical character and chemical composition of milk, these changes being peculiar to certain organisms and therefore diagnostic. Others cause no changes recognizable by the senses, yet have the power of infinite multiplication, and in this the danger mainly lies.

The bacillus of typhoid fever may be introduced into the milk supply of a family by ways too numerous to mention. The milk itself will give no evidence whatever to the consumer of the presence of typhoid bacilli, because no visible changes occur in the milk as a result of the multiplication of the typhoid bacilli in it. The same may be true of other diseases, the causes of which are yet undiscovered.

VIABILITY OF BACTERIA IN MILK.

That milk of itself has germicidal properties seems questionable, inasmuch as freshly drawn milk, taken under the most careful precautions in order to prevent the entrance from the air of bacteria, always contains them. It is believed that those found in carefully drawn milk come from the milk reservoirs in the udder, but opinion seems to be divided as to how far they penetrate the glandular structure of the udder. Their entrance into the teats from the atmosphere and external objects is admitted. Their presence in the udder itself is probably due to capillarity and growth by extension. It is possible, as the liquid portion of the milk and the dissolved salts come from the blood circulating through the mammary gland, that the milk may, like the blood, at some stage of its secretion possess slight germicidal property. If so, this property is speedily lost, as is indicated by the enormous numbers of bacteria usually found in freshly drawn milk. That some of the pathogenic bacteria continue to live in sour milk and also retain their original disease-producing qualities has been noted by numerous investigators. Hankin found infectious typhoid bacilli in an Indian milk product called "dahi." Heim says the bacillus of Asiatic cholera is viable for an indefinite period in sweet milk. It retains its virulence for some days in sour milk. Roland inoculated samples of certain cheeses with the bacilli of typhoid fever and of Asiatic cholera to determine the length of time they would survive on such soil. After a few days he tried to make subcultures

224

from the inoculated cheeses but failed. He kept up his observations for a period of nine months, but failed to get at any time growth upon ordinarily suitable media from the cheese cultures, showing that the bacilli of typhoid fever and Asiatic cholera are killed by a few days' contact with certain cheeses. Steyerthal writes: "A Hamburg family in 1892, during a cholera epidemic, went to Mecklenburgh and carried bread and butter with them. They ate it and two days after had Asiatic cholera, one of the children dying on the third day." Kossell writes: "Other fugitives from Hamburg to Mecklenburgh carried buttered bread, some of which was eaten by Mecklenburgh relatives. In three days one of them was sick with the cholera. Another had a suspicious diarrhea." Lafar found that tubercle bacilli lived and retained their virulence for one hundred and twenty days in butter. Fröhner states that foot-and-mouth disease (a contagious eczema of cattle) may be conveyed by the milk of the affected animals.

That not all pathogenic bacteria live and retain their virulence when they enter the milk and are carried over into the butter and buttermilk is proved by the following experiments made by the writer, in which it was considered of great importance to imitate as closely as possible the usual order of events in the ordinary manufacture of butter. The manner of procedure was as follows:

The virulence of a peptone beef-broth culture of the bacterium of swine plague was proven by the subcutaneous inoculation and subsequent death in eighteen hours of a healthy rabbit from swine plague. Ten cubic centimeters of the culture were added to one gallon of milk. The mixture was set aside for twenty-four hours at 70° F. At the end of this time the milk was acid, but not coagulated. A rabbit was inoculated subcutaneously with 1 cc. of the artificially infected milk and died in eighteen hours from swine plague. The bacterium of swine plague was demonstrated in the liver, spleen, and blood of the rabbit. The cream was removed by means of a clean spoon and placed inside the box for another twenty-four hours to "ripen." At end of this time another rabbit was inoculated subcutaneously with a small quantity of the "ripe" cream. The rabbit died within twenty-four hours, showing a decrease in the virulence of the swine plague organism after contact with sour cream. The cream was then placed in a clean jar and shaken until the butter had "come," which required about fifteen minutes. To this butter salt was added in the proportion of 1 to 16, and on the next day another rabbit was inoculated with a small quantity. This rabbit did not die or subsequently show any signs of being ill. In order to determine whether the addition of salt had anything to do with the absolute loss of virulence and possibly the death of the introduced swine plague bacteria, a small portion of the unsalted butter was used on another rabbit as a check. The check remained well, also, showing that the salt added was not the bactericide. We may therefore conclude from the result of these

10317——15

experiments that, in the case of the swine plague organism at least, something (acid) is formed in the milk during the manufacture of butter by the ordinary method which is in thirty-six hours present in sufficient quantity to lessen the virulence of the swine plague bacterium, and that in twenty-four hours it is present in sufficient quantity to render this bacterium nonvirulent or to kill it entirely.

As previously mentioned, similar observations have been made for some months upon the bacillus of hog cholera and the bacterium of tuberculosis.

EXPERIMENTS UPON THE BACTERIUM OF TUBERCULOSIS.

Method.—The guinea pig was chosen for the test on account of its susceptibility to tuberculosis and its being somewhat refractory to the septicæmias. A pea-size piece of butter was introduced beneath the skin. In order to get about the same quantity for each observation, a graduated glass tube was used as a sampler. This tube containing the butter was passed into an incision made through the skin of the abdominal wall and allowed to remain until the contained butter was melted by the heat of the animal's body, when the tube was withdrawn, leaving a pocket filled with the infected butter.

First observation.—June 28, 1895. Guinea pig No. 459, inoculated with a small piece of freshly infected butter made to-day. August 31, two months later, animal found dead; much emaciated. Local lesion large, and made up of creamy pus and pus-infiltrated tissue. Liver much enlarged, extensively diseased, and showed green and yellow necrotic areas. Spleen enlarged four times and extensively diseased. Mediastinal glands much enlarged, and those at bifurcation of trachea very large, and gritty on section. Lungs engorged and extensively invaded by yellow tubercles the size of a millet seed. Hydrothorax, the liquid being bloody. A cover-glass preparation from one of the least affected lymphatics showed, by differential stain, numbers of tubercle bacilli. The results of subsequent inoculation of butter infected with tubercle bacilli are here tabulated for the sake of brevity.

Table showing retention of virulence by the tubercle bacilli when placed in commercial butter, exhibited by its disease-producing property in guinea pigs.

Guinea pig.	Date of inoculation.	Date of death from tuberculosis.	Length of life after inoculation.	Age of infected butter.
No. 440	July 6, 1895	Aug. 16, 1895	1 month 11 days	8 days.
388	Aug. 5, 1895	Sept. 17, 1895	1 month 12 days	1 month 7 days.
9	Aug. 15, 1895	Nov. 12, 1895	2 months 27 days	1 month 17 days.
6	Sept. 10, 1895	Nov. 10, 1895	1 month 12 days	3 months 22 days.
63	Nov. 12, 1895	Feb. 20, 1896	3 months 8 days	4 months 14 days.
62	Jan. 29, 1896	May 12, 1896	3 months 15 days	7 months 1 day.
84	Feb. 28, 1896	(a)		8 months.

a Chloroformed and found affected June 28, 1896.

It may be seen from this table that the bacillus retains its virulence pretty uniformly for about three months, when it begins to attenuate. At the eighth month its virulence was considerably decreased, as may be seen from the fact that guinea pig No. 84 was inoculated four months previous to its death from chloroform. Although upon post-mortem examination it was found to be considerably diseased, it had appeared to be in fair health. These experiments also show that the bacillus of tuberculosis not only retains its life, but its virulence as well, in butter for eight months, and that butter may be considered a carrier of the germ of tuberculosis.

It would be of additional interest to determine if the tubercle bacillus, when placed in milk immediately after its having been drawn from the udder, would retain its virulence in the presence of the acids which are formed in the milk and cream previous to its being manufactured into butter by the usual methods. This was done in the case of the hog cholera and swine plague organisms, and it was found that the latter bacterium (swine plague) was either killed outright or rendered nonvirulent during the manufacture of butter. In the case of the hog cholera experiments the following table shows that it is an organism which retains its disease-producing property in conditions which were found to be adverse to the swine plague organism.

METHOD OF PREPARATION OF BUTTER TO TEST ITS BACTERICIDAL ACTION UPON THE HOG CHOLERA BACILLUS.

February 5, 1896, 10 cc. of a peptone beef-broth culture of virulent hog cholera bacilli was added to 1 gallon of milk. On February 6 the cream was removed and set aside to "ripen" until February 7, when it was shaken in a bottle until butter had "come." Salt was added in the proportion of 1 to 16.

Table showing retention of virulence by the bacillus of hog cholera in butter.

Rabbit	Date of inoculation.	Date of death from hog cholera.	Length of life after inoculation.	Age of infected butter.
No. 60	Feb. 5, 1896	Feb. 12, 1896	6 days	1 day.
63	Feb. 14, 1896	Feb. 21, 1896	7 days	9 days.
126	May 20, 1896	May 27, 1896	....do	3 months 15 days.
129	June 16, 1896	June 24, 1896	8 days	4 months 11 days.
133	July 5, 1896	July 12, 1896	6 days	5 months 1 day.
136	July 28, 1896	Aug. 8, 1896	11 days	5 months 23 days.
500	Sept. 5, 1896	Sept. 24, 1896	19 days	7 months.
156	Oct. 20, 1896	Nov. 1, 1896	12 days	8 months 15 days.
166	Nov. 19, 1896	Dec. 5, 1896	15 days	10 months.
169	Feb. 5, 1897	Feb. 15, 1897	10 days	12 months.

The foregoing observations show that the hog cholera bacillus is more resistant than the swine plague bacterium, and are a confirmation of the experiments made by Drs. Salmon and Smith upon these

organisms with various disinfectants, and also show that not until
the fifth month does the organism begin to lose its virulence.

They also show that hog cholera could be carried in sour milk and
in butter, and that the organism remains virulent for at least twelve
months in commercial butter.

BUTTER AND PORK AS CARRIERS OF INFECTION.

Owing to the similarity of the biology of this organism to the bacillus of typhoid fever and of the diseases they produce in man and in swine, respectively, might we not conclude that the typhoid bacillus, if it were in the milk, could retain its virulence in the butter made therefrom for at least a sufficient length of time to place butter in the list of edibles as a carrier of typhoid fever?

That tuberculosis can be spread by similar means is suggested by an outbreak of tuberculosis in swine[1] where all circumstances strongly pointed to the fact that the drove had become infected by feeding upon refuse from a creamery. It may be of interest to add that of the 9 hogs composing this drove 5 died of tuberculosis at the age of six months, and that in December, six months later, the remaining 4 were slaughtered for pork. They were, so far as external appearance went, in perfect health, weighing about 300 pounds each. Postmortem examination revealed calcified tubercles in the livers and spleens of three of them, and in the fourth the liver was liberally sprinkled with miliary tubercles. The spleen was the seat of large, caseous tumors, and the entire lymphatic glandular system was invaded by tuberculosis, some of the glands being infiltrated throughout their substance by small tubercles, and others, especially those of the mesentery, entirely broken down, indicating the primary focus of the disease. In all of the lobes of both lungs miliary tubercles were present, giving to the touch the impression of bird shot. This outbreak of tuberculosis also shows that swine, like cattle, may be badly affected with the disease and for a time give little or no evidence of its existence.

[1] Annual Report Bureau of Animal Industry, 1895 and 1896, p. 212.

COLORED SPOTS IN CHEESE.[1]

By R. A. PEARSON,

Assistant Chief of Dairy Division, Bureau of Animal Industry.

Numerous inquiries have been received by the Dairy Division of this Department concerning the "disease" of cheese sometimes called "cheese rust," which is more or less prevalent in certain sections of this country and has caused considerable annoyance and loss to some factories and dealers. Although this trouble has been in evidence for a number of years, it has received but little attention from our scientists and experiment stations; and cheese makers so unfortunate as to have it visit them have explained it in many different ways and dealt with it accordingly.

GENERAL DESCRIPTION.

From about fifty reports received at this office the following facts are gathered: The affection is noticed where white, or uncolored, cheese is made. It may not appear until after the cheese is sold, but is usually first discovered from one to three weeks after the curd is pressed, when there may be seen a number of red to reddish yellow spots on the outside and throughout the body of the cheese. The spots may be detected with the aid of a microscope some time before they are visible to the naked eye. These sometimes seem to be in irregular layers, and when a trier is inserted piercing the layers rings appear on the plug withdrawn. If a cheese affected in this way is cut across the layers it is found to be streaked. The spots increase in size from day to day and vary from mere specks to large patches; they are chiefly in the open spaces, or cells, or interstices, between the pieces of curd, and sometimes resemble a sprinkling of iron rust or red pepper. In some cases they are described as being the size of small shot and are scattered through the cheese as though they "had been dropped into the curd while putting to hoop." In other cases they are as large as silver quarters and occasionally, on the outside of the cheese, especially at the ends which come in contact with the shelves, there are colored patches as large as one's hand. This trouble occurs in hot weather and is at its worst in July and August. Sometimes it affects only a part of the output of a factory, but if it gains a good foothold it is liable to be found in the entire product.

---

[1] Published also as Circular No. 24 of the Bureau of Animal Industry.

EFFECT OF COLORED SPOTS.

So far as is known, these spots do not have any effect on the consumer. Professor Connell fed mice with cheese containing the reddish yellow spots and at the end of two weeks they were alive and well. Inoculation experiments with guinea pigs resulted in only slight local inflammation. But the unsightliness of the spots naturally has an unfavorable effect on sales, and reductions for this cause from one-fourth to one cent per pound are not uncommon. Such a shrinkage in returns, together with loss of reputation, can be ill afforded by any cheese factory and its patrons.

CAUSE OF COLORED SPOTS.

The cause of cheese rust is not generally known, and it is popularly attributed to numerous conditions, such as feed or water given to the cows, tainted milk, adulterated milk, rusty spots in milk utensils and vats, too quick ripening, poor rennet, uneven coloring (when color is used), uneven cooking, the curd mill, unclean benches in the curing room; in fact, almost everything which comes in contact with the milk or curd during manufacture and almost every step in the process has been suspected of being the cause of this disorder. It is sometimes confused with irregular coloring resulting from the use of a poor grade of color or improper mixing.

In recent years cheese rust and other affections of similar nature have been carefully studied by bacteriologists, and they have found that these troubles are usually caused by different kinds of bacteria. Some general characteristics of these tiny creatures are given in Farmers' Bulletin No. 63, "Care of milk on the farm," a publication of this Department.

USUAL REMEDY.

The remedy usually adopted is to color the cheese so the spots will be less visible or completely covered, but this is not entirely satisfactory, as it does not correct the cause, and frequently the market being supplied demands an uncolored cheese; sometimes the spots are so bad that color enough to cover them would spoil the cheese. Numerous other remedies are suggested, based on the supposed causes given above, but they are generally theories, and in most cases would fail in practice. As suggested later, hastening the ripening of the milk may have the favorable effect of retarding the growth of colored spots. The only perfect remedy is to do away with the cause, and the method of accomplishing this is shown below.

INVESTIGATION OF AN OUTBREAK.

Under the direction of the dairy commissioner of Canada a careful study and report of an outbreak of colored spots in a Canadian factory was made by Dr. W. T. Connell in the summer of 1896.

The factory was found to be well located but not well kept. As is too frequently the case with cheese factories, the utensils and vats in daily use were fairly well cleaned, but in general the factory had an untidy appearance; in particular, the drains were very defective and filthy. The drainage from the factory was intended to enter a drain under the floor, but a close connection between the floor and drain was not made and it had to fall about 18 inches to the trough; a considerable part of it splashed over onto the ground underneath, which was kept constantly saturated and in a slimy condition. The color of the slimy mass varied from reddish to reddish yellow or reddish gray. Bacteriological examination of this substance revealed many forms of low organic life, and bacilli were discovered which closely resembled a form found in the affected cheese. The salt, rennet, and samples of milk delivered by the different patrons were also examined, but without finding suspicious germs in any of them. There seemed little doubt but that the defective drain and its sur-roundings were the source of infection, and to prove that the chro-mogenic germ,[1] abundant about the drain, could cause the trouble, a lot of milk in a factory entirely free from the infection had a cul-ture of the bacilli introduced into it and was made into cheese; within a few days the spots appeared. Prof. F. C. Harrison reports that the same bacillus is found in dirty sinks, vats, etc.

In this instance it was easy to see how the germs could find their way from the infected soil to the vats. When the dried slime was stirred, dust arose and it was carried by the wind into the factory. Some particles settled directly in the vats and on the utensils; others fell in moist places and colonies were started, thus forming nearer sources of contamination. Moist slime and dried slime were tracked

---

[1] The organism found to cause the trouble is named by Professor Connell *Bacillus rudensis;* it is described as being in the form of short rods, sometimes curved, though usually straight, and measuring from one twenty-five thousandth to one fifteen-thousandth of an inch in length; they may be in pairs, but do not form long chains. It "stains well with ordinary aniline dyes in recent culture. It stains best with carbol-fuchsin or aniline water, gentian, violet. Older cultures often show rods with unstained beads, one or more. These are evidently not spores; no spores have been demonstrated."

As to its biological characters, it "is aerobic and facultative anaerobic, but grows more rapidly, and pigment is formed a little more freely, with plenty of oxygen. It does not liquefy gelatine. It is freely motile, but no flagella could be demonstrated by Van Ermengem's method."

"In gelatine stick cultures at 70° F. this organism is seen as a faint white growth along puncture line in twenty-four hours, showing as discrete small colonies under lens; in forty-eight hours the growth is clearly seen and has a faint yellowish tinge; growth is as free in depth as toward surface; in three or four days punc-ture line becomes of a faint reddish yellow. No liquefaction occurs, nor does growth extend over culture surface. In gelatine slope tubes growth occurs along the inoculating line as discrete, small, rounded colonies, with beveled edges, grad-ually acquiring a reddish yellow cast. If gelatine be faintly acid, pigment for-into the building by operators and visitors, and the germs were easily transferred from the floor to the milk by cloths, utensils, drafts of air, etc. No theory is given as to the original source of the germs, but it is plainly shown that after they became established a circuit was formed from the drain to the milk and whey and back to the drain again.

Experiments by Prof. J. A. Ruddick showed that when the germs were introduced into milk having considerable acid, less spots were found in the cheese than when they were added to comparatively sweet milk. This is evidently one reason why the makes are differently affected, the milk being riper when delivered on some days than others.

Just how a dairy originally becomes infected with objectionable bacteria which color the milk or cause it to be ropy, slimy, bitter, or soapy, or how a creamery or cheese factory which has had no previous trouble with bacteria is infected with troublesome forms, is not always known. Occasionally outbreaks occur which are as unexpected and inexplicable as are some outbreaks of infectious diseases in healthy communities. But it should be remembered that bacteria are extremely minute bodies and that many ways of moving about, even long distances, are possible to them. They can often successfully withstand what would seem to be very unfavorable conditions and thus for a long time hold their life as they are carried from place to place, or as conditions about them change, until they find themselves a favorable location for growth, and then immediately commence to multiply at a marvelous rate. They may first be introduced into a factory by impure water, milk from an infected dairy, cans which have been used for other than dairy purposes, and especially by dust or anything which carries dirt.

---

mation is not so great. On agar-agar colonies always remain small and white, not forming any pigment either at room temperature or at body heat."

"On milk growth readily occurs, causing clotting after two days at 70° F., and coagulum gradually acquires a faint yellow cast. Often, also, pigmentation occurs as faint, red, yellow dots on surface of coagulum."

"On neutral beef-peptone broth this bacillus grows slowly, causing a faint cloudiness, chiefly in lower half of tubes. On potato tubes its growth is, however, most typical. On potatoes kept at 70° F. there appear in twenty-four hours faint yellowish colonies which soon acquire a red tinge, gradually becoming in course of three or four days rust colored; these colonies are small, seldom becoming larger than a pinhead; the colonies are rounded and have raised centers and an irregularly sloping edge."

"Cultures in broth of these bacilli, forty-eight hours old, were heated to various temperatures to determine if spores formed. It was found that heating to 155° F. nearly always kills this bacillus, while a temperature of 148° F. for ten minutes was readily withstood. A temperature of boiling water for twenty to thirty seconds was found to kill the microorganism in all cases. If spore formation occurred, it is almost certain that higher temperature would be withstood for longer periods."

PREVENTIVE MEASURES.

After objectionable germs have once entered the factory three things are required for their growth or increase, namely, warmth, moisture, and food. It is impossible to keep the temperature from being favorable to them in the summer time, but by keeping the factory as dry as possible, the food supply scarce, and subjecting the germs to conditions which are fatal to them, such as high heat and disinfectants, it is possible to rid the factory of them.

Soon after a factory is infected with troublesome bacteria, colonies will become established in many places; they are hidden in cracks in the floors and walls, and any place which remains continually moist will contain large numbers of them. The entire building and all its contents must be scrupulously cleaned and the work must extend to the whey tank and drain leading to it. Every utensil should be thoroughly sterilized by exposure to live steam during at least ten minutes, and everything not so treated should be disinfected. The inside walls of the building and the outsides of the larger apparatus may be disinfected with boiling water or steam, but if this is not practicable a dilute solution of carbolic acid may be used, at the strength of 1 pound to 25 to 50 of water. This is an excellent disinfectant, but should not be applied to any surface which comes in contact with the milk. Sulphate of iron (copperas) is an efficient disinfectant for drains; they should be flushed daily with boiling water and have steam passed through them if possible, then have lumps of copperas placed in them.

At the same time or preceding the work of cleansing the factory its surroundings should be improved. Pools should be drained and the hollows filled with clean earth. If at any point the soil is saturated with milk or whey, the top part should be replaced with fresh earth, if practicable, and copperas sprinkled about. Treatment of this kind frequently repeated and accompanied by the replacement of decayed boards in the floor or elsewhere, and the repair of drains, waste pipes, etc., and followed by a good coat of whitewash, will usually remove all trouble. If, however, the conditions are not improved after these operations, it is probable the source of infection is external to the factory, and every effort should be made to quickly locate it. An affection once started readily travels from dairy to dairy, and unless it is promptly stamped out an entire district may suffer and great loss result. If it is found by handling the milk from the different dairies separately, or by the use of a fermentation or curd test, that the trouble belongs to a certain one, that dairy should be thoroughly cleaned and disinfected as described in Farmers' Bulletin No. 63. If the water is found to be to blame, a new supply should be obtained, or an arrangement provided to boil all the water used.

The infection of the factory above referred to was entirely overcome by remedying the faulty draining facilities and thoroughly cleaning and disinfecting the factory, its contents, and surroundings. In one factory which had been troubled for several years the difficulty disappeared with a change of operators; the new man gave everything a thorough cleaning and saw nothing of rust spots. In another case the renovation, and in fact the reconstruction, of a factory failed to remedy the trouble, which was finally located in the dairies of some of the patrons.

PHOTOMICROGRAPH OF HOG CHOLERA BACILLUS X 1000.

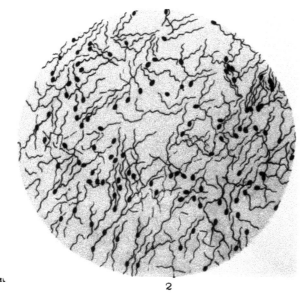

HAINES, DEL

2

HOG CHOLERA BACILLUS.
AGAR CULTURE, SHOWING FLAGELLA, LOEFFLER'S STAIN X 1000.

Fig. 1.
Agar Tube Culture of Swine-Plague Bacteria

Fig. 2.
Agar Tube Culture of Hog Cholera Bacilli, Four Days Old.

Fig. 3.
Swine Plague X 1000.

Haines, del.

A. Hoen & Co. Lith. Baltimore.

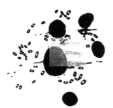

THE SERUM TREATMENT FOR SWINE PLAGUE AND HOG CHOLERA.[1]

By E. A. DE SCHWEINITZ, Ph. D., M. D.,

Chief of Biochemic Division, Bureau of Animal Industry.

The investigations of the Bureau of Animal Industry during the past years have demonstrated that the swine of the country are subject to two very serious diseases. The one of these called *swine plague* is produced by a short rod-shaped germ which is nonmotile. (Pl. V, fig. 3.) The other, *hog cholera*, is caused by a rod-shaped bacillus somewhat larger than the swine plague, which is motile (Pl. IV, fig. 1). These germs differ from each other in their manner of growth (Pl. V, figs. 1 and 2) on various media as well as in their shape, size, and pathogenic effects. In addition, the hog cholera germ is provided with flagella (Pl. IV, fig. 2), while these can not be demonstrated upon nonmotile bacilli, as the swine plague.

The cause of a disease having been found, the next problem is to find the means of destroying or controlling the baneful agent.

One of the most interesting and difficult problems which has engaged the attention of this Bureau for some years has been the discovery of a method or methods for the prevention or cure of the diseases known as hog cholera and swine plague among swine.

PRELIMINARY EXPERIMENTS.

In the year 1890 a study of the substances secreted by the hog cholera and swine plague germs was begun in the Biochemic Laboratory of the Bureau of Animal Industry by the writer of this article. From cultures of these bacteria he succeeded in isolating two substances albuminoid in character and others belonging to the group called amines, which produced, when injected into experimental animals, some of the characteristic symptoms of hog cholera or swine plague, respectively, and conferred upon these animals an immunity to subcutaneous inoculation with hog cholera and swine plague germs, respectively. The reports of this work were published in the Medical News, of Philadelphia, in September and October, 1890, and annual reports of this Department for 1890 and 1891.

---

[1] Most of the information in this article was published as Bulletin No. 23 of the Bureau of Animal Industry. It finds place here in order that both lines of investigations relative to hog cholera and swine plague in Page County, Iowa, may be recorded together. A report of the "stamping out" process immediately follows this.

A series of practical experiments were then carried on at the experiment station. The swine were injected with the products of the growth of the hog cholera and swine plague bacteria, including the contents of the cells themselves, as well as those products of excretion of the cells which were in solution in the culture liquid. In ten days after inoculation they were exposed to hog cholera and swine plague, respectively, by an intravenous inoculation with a virulent germ sufficient in quantity to kill the check animals in a week to ten days. In general these results were fairly satisfactory, in so far that, while the check animals died, about 50 per cent of the treated animals remained alive. The method of exposure, however, was unsatisfactory, as it was not always possible to be certain that the checks would die, and in a good many cases the exposure of the treated animals by this method of inoculation was very much more severe than that which they would in all probability have been subjected to in the field. In addition, the injection of these products of the bacilli produced disagreeable local leisons in the animals treated.

While the results of the work showed that considerable immunity to these diseases could be secured by this method of treatment, it did not appear practicable for field work, and consequently other laboratory investigations were begun.

A more through study of the substances produced by the hog cholera germ, the results of which were published in the Philadelphia Medical News of October, 1892, showed that if the cultures of this germ were made upon milk or other suitable media, it was possible to obtain from these cultures a small quantity of enzymes, or soluble ferments. These ferments secreted by the hog cholera bacillus were also tried for the purpose of producing immunity in experimental animals, with satisfactory results. The injection of quantities of these ferments below 0.01 of a gram was without ill effect. If the amount injected was increased beyond this point there was a rise of temperature in the animals for several days, and in several instances 0.05 of a gram was sufficient to kill the animals. A single injection of guinea pigs with 0.04 of a gram of the ferments served to make the animals immune from an inoculation with the hog cholera germ that was sufficient to cause the death of the checks in ten days. In the article referred to the opinion was expressed that the soluble ferments exert a very potent action in rendering animals insusceptible to disease, and that to the indirect action of the specific ferments secreted by the hog cholera and other germs the protective and curative influence of blood serum from immune animals may be traced, as well as the immunity produced by injecting animals with cell contents or the products of the cell growth. At about that time the writer published an article in the Philadelphia Medical News, September 24, 1892, upon the production of immunity in guinea pigs from hog cholera by the use of blood serum from other guinea pigs that had been previously immunized. The guinea pigs used as a source for the blood serum were immunized by means of the cell contents and products of the growth of hog cholera bacilli, and after they had withstood an inoculation of the germ of sufficient virulence to cause the death of the checks they served as a source of serum to be used for injecting other healthy guinea pigs or for treating guinea pigs infected with hog cholera. The results of these experiments were also satisfactory, but for various reasons they could not be pushed as rapidly as desired. The experiments were continued, however, in a quiet way, and the use of the products of other bacteria allied to the hog cholera germ, as the *Coli communis*, etc., were tried. The results were satisfactory for the purpose of securing immunity from hog cholera. As stated in one of the papers mentioned, it is probable that all gas-producing bacilli secrete a soluble ferment, and that this ferment is of considerable importance in connection with the production of immunity. While it is not probable that each germ gives rise to a distinctive ferment, it is probable that different germs secrete or cause the secretion of two or more ferments, and that the combined action of these ferments is necessary to secure satisfactory results in immunity.

RESULTS OF EXPERIMENTS WITH SERUM AS A CURATIVE AGENT.

During the years 1893, 1894, and 1895 it was possible to make some more experiments with the serum as a curative agent for hog cholera and swine plague upon a somewhat larger scale. These experiments were reported to the Society for the Promotion of Agricultural Science in Buffalo, N. Y., in August, 1896, and published in their proceedings, in the New York Medical Journal, September 5, 1896, and in Centralbl. f. bakt. u. Parasit., Vol. XX, No. 16–17, 1896.

The animals used for the production of the serum were treated for me by Dr. Schroeder, in charge of the experiment station of the Bureau.

After several months' injection of the cows with the virulent hog cholera culture, the serum was tested. The following is a record of one of the experiments:

Guinea pigs injected with serum from treated cows.

March 9, 1894, No. 219, weight 17 ozs., received 1.5 cc. of serum.
March 9, 1894, No. 220, weight 12 ozs., received 1.5 cc. of serum.
March 9, 1894, No. 221, weight 11 ozs., received 1.5 cc. of serum.
March 9, 1894, No. 222, weight 17 ozs., received 1.5 cc. of serum.
March 18, 1894, No. 219, weight 18 ozs., received 3 cc. of serum.
March 18, 1894, No. 220, weight 11 ozs., received 3 cc. of scrum.
March 18, 1894, No. 222, weight 19 ozs., received 3 cc. of serum.
March 18, 1894, No. 223, weight 14 ozs., received 3 cc. of serum.

No. 221 was found dead from pneumonia on March 16.
On March 20 No. 220 was found dead from pneumonia.

March 23, 1894, No. 219, weight 17 ozs., received 1.5 cc. of serum.
March 23, 1894, No. 222, weight 17 ozs., received 3 cc. of serum.
March 23, 1894, No. 242, weight 10¼ ozs., received 3 cc. of serum.
March 23, 1894, No. 243, weight 10¼ ozs., received 3 cc. of serum.
March 23, 1894, No. 246, weight 9¼ ozs., received 3 cc. of serum.
March 28, 1894, No. 219, weight 18 ozs., received 4.5 cc. of serum.
March 28, 1894, No. 222, weight 18 ozs., received 6 cc. of serum.
March 28, 1894, No. 223, weight 13 ozs., received 4 cc. of serum.
March 28, 1894, No. 242, weight 12 ozs., received 3 cc. of serum.
March 28, 1894, No. 243, weight 12 ozs., received 3 cc. of serum.
March 28, 1894, No. 246, weight 11 ozs., received 3 cc. of serum.

On April 9 the following guinea pigs were each inoculated with one-tenth cubic centimeter of peptonized beef-broth hog cholera culture:

No. 219, weight 28 ozs.   No. 261, weight 12 ozs.
No. 222, weight 18 ozs.   No. 262, weight 15 ozs.
No. 223, weight 12 ozs.   No. 263, weight 20 ozs.
No. 242, weight 13 ozs.   No. 264, weight 14 ozs.
No. 243, weight 13 ozs.   No. 241, weight 15 ozs. (check).
No. 246, weight 12 ozs.   No. 260, weight 12 ozs. (check).

Nos. 261, 262, 263, and 264 had not received previous injections with serum; Nos. 241 and 260 were checks; while the other animals had been treated with serum as above noted.

April 11, No. 261 received 3 cc. of serum.
April 11, No. 262 received 3 cc. of serum.
April 11, No. 263 received 5 cc. of serum.
April 11, No. 264 received 4.5 cc. of serum.
April 14, No. 261 received 3 cc. of serum.
April 14, No. 262 received 3 cc. of serum.
April 14, No. 263 received 4.5 cc. of serum.

The result: April 17, No. 260 (check) was found dead from hog cholera; April 19, No. 222 was found dead from hog cholera; April 20, No. 264 was found dead from hog cholera; April 25, No. 241 (check) was found dead from hog cholera; Nos. 219, 223, and 261 were also found dead from pneumonia. There had been quite an outbreak of pneumonia among the guinea pigs just at this time, accounting for the lesions which were not due to cholera.

Of the entire number of pigs treated, therefore, the checks died in from 8 to 16 days. Three of the pigs that had previously been vaccinated with 6 cc. of serum each recovered, and 2 of the pigs that had received 6 and 8 cc. of serum 2 days after the inoculation with the germ recovered from the disease. These experiments repeated later showed that while the blood contained a curative and protective substance the quantity present at the time would not cure disease by the injection of several small doses. Subsequently, by continued treatment of the animals, the curative material was increased in quantity, as will be seen from experiments reported later.

Already in 1894 some work had been done which served to emphasize the close relationship between the products in artificial media of the growth of the hog cholera germ and those produced by the growth of the bacillus *Coli communis* (the ordinary intestinal bacillus). A pig which had been immunized from hog cholera by long-continued injections of the *Coli communis* and subsequently inoculated with the hog cholera germs was used as a source for the serum for treating guinea pigs, as follows:

No. 425, weight 11 ozs., received 3 cc. of serum.
No. 426, weight 9 ozs., received 4.5 cc. of serum.
No. 422, weight 9 ozs., received 0.5 cc. of serum.
No. 423, weight 11 ozs., received 1.5 cc. of serum.
No. 424, weight 8 ozs., received 2 cc. of serum.

Fifteen days afterwards these pigs and 2 checks, Nos. 442 and 443, were inoculated with 0.1 cc. of a peptonized beef-broth hog cholera culture one day old. Seven and ten days, respectively, after this inoculation the checks were found dead from hog cholera while the other guinea pigs remained well. These experiments repeated upon another set of animals gave about the same results, which showed that an immunizing substance is produced in the blood of a hog that is protected against the cholera. Another set of experiments, the details of which need not be reported here, showed that while the hog itself might be immune from disease, its blood serum may have lost the power of conferring immunity upon other animals. This confirms the conclusion with reference to the use of blood serum in other diseases, namely, that the immunizing principle in the blood serum can best be obtained if the animals are inoculated from time to time with the culture, or toxins. So long as the animal receives continued injection of the cell contents or products of the germ the immunity of that particular animal continues, and in addition the antitoxic substance is found in the blood. After some time the antitoxic substance may no longer be noted in the blood, or only in small amounts, while the immunity of the individual animal from which this blood is obtained may still continue. The antitoxic substances are apparently the products of cell activity only.

These experiments with the serum of immune hogs and the serum of cattle and horses that had been made artificially immune warranted further investigation.

In practice, however, it is found that hogs are exposed not only to the disease of hog cholera but also to another disease called swine plague, both of which may occur together in the same animal, or there may be an outbreak of one or the other disease alone. As the experiments made in 1891 with the products of the swine plague germ as obtained from artificial media had shown that these could be used as immunizing agents, it was very reasonable to suppose, when the nature of the disease swine plague is considered, that an antitoxic[1] serum for this disease might also be obtained. A cow was used as the source of the serum after she had been repeatedly inoculated with cultures of the swine-plague germ. The preliminary tests of this serum were made upon rabbits. One-tenth cubic centimeter of a peptonized beef-broth culture of the swine plague, sufficient to kill a rabbit in fifteen to eighteen hours, was used. Several sets of experiments showed that while the check rabbits were killed within the specified time by the swine-plague cultures, others could be kept alive from six to ten days longer than the checks by the injection of 9 cc. of the serum per pound weight. As these results indicated that antitoxic, or curative, substances were present in the serum, its effect was tried upon guinea pigs. One-tenth cubic centimeter of swine plague culture was used, sufficient to kill the animals. The experiments gave the following:

No. 348 (check), weight 12 ozs., received 0.1 cc. swine plague culture.
No. 349, weight 8 ozs., received 0.1 cc. swine plague culture and 3 cc. serum.
No. 350 (check). weight 11 ozs., received 0.1 cc. swine plague culture.
No. 351, weight 9 ozs., received 0.1 cc. swine plague culture and 6 cc. serum.
No. 352, weight 8 ozs., received 0.1 cc. swine plague culture and 6 cc. serum.

While the check animals died the pigs which received the antitoxic serum recovered, about 6 cc. per pound weight being required to check the disease.

With the assistance of Dr. Dorset I next endeavored to isolate the antitoxic principle contained in the serum, according to a method prescribed by Brieger and Boer[2] for the isolation of diphtheria antitoxin, by the use of zinc sulphate, repeated solution in sodium hydrate and precipitation with CO_2. In this way from 90 cc. of serum about 0.152 gram of a practically ash-free white powder was obtained. The antitoxic properties of this substance when tested proved to be about the same as those of the serum. As we had therefore a serum which exhibited antitoxic or curative properties for hog cholera, and another which exhibited antitoxic or curative properties for swine plague, it was of interest to see if these serums would be of use interchangeably. The result showed, however, that the hog cholera serum protected guinea pigs from the cholera germ but not from the swine plague germ, and that the swine plague serum protected or cured guinea pigs from infection with the swine plague germ but not from the hog cholera germ. This demonstrated again the independent character of these two diseases, attention to which has often been drawn in previously published work.

As the preliminary experiments so far reported had shown that specific antitoxic serums for hog cholera and swine plague could be obtained, the work was carried forward on a somewhat larger scale,

---

[1] The word antitoxic is used in this article in the sense of curative.
[2] Zeit. für Hyg. u. Infectionskrank., Bd. XXI, Pt. 2.

and serums secured which were effective in much smaller doses upon experimental animals. The laboratory results seemed to warrant a trial of this method in the field, and experiments were made during the summer and fall of 1897 on this line in Page County, Iowa.

THE PREPARATION OF THE SERUM.

In preparing the serum for this work we have used cattle, horses, mules, donkeys, etc.; the animals received injections of the filtered, sterile, or live cultures of the hog cholera germ and swine plague germ, respectively, or the solutions of their products, including cell contents, extracts, and secretions. These injections were made either subcutaneously, intravenously, or intraabdominally, or a combination of two or more of these methods, depending upon the results obtained. The quantities given at first were small, but increased gradually until large amounts of the material used could be injected without bad results. This treatment of the animals must be carried out very carefully and requires six to eight months' time before the serum is sufficiently potent to be of any practical use. As the treatment continues the power of the serum to check the motility of the hog cholera germ increases with rapidity. The serum of animals treated with swine plague cultures also sometimes checks the motility of the hog cholera germ. The value of the serum was determined by the amount of serum necessary to protect or cure guinea pigs from an inoculation with the hog cholera germ or swine plague germ sufficiently virulent to kill the check animals in the usual time—a week to ten days.

The details of the method of treating these animals for preparing the serum, which were the results of numerous conferences between Dr. Schroeder, in charge of the experiment station, and the writer, will be given in another publication. Too much care can not be observed in selecting the animals and in observing proper precautions during the injections with the different products of the cultures that are used for producing in the animals a curative serum. The testing of the serum, as already noted, was usually made by treating animals that had been previously inoculated with a fatal dose of the culture. This method of testing is sometimes not altogether satisfactory so far as the cholera germ is concerned, although the results given with the swine plague are quite satisfactory. We have therefore used another method, namely, the injection of a quantity of the products of the hog cholera germ sufficient in quantity to kill the check guinea pigs, while the other guinea pigs so injected and treated with the serum will not succumb. This method promises more satisfactory results, and a better basis can thus be secured for estimating the amount of curative serum which should be used for injecting large animals.

In order to keep and utilize large quantities of serum, we have found it very convenient to concentrate it, and by making use of well-

10317——16

known principles we have accomplished this by freezing, so that a more concentrated material can be obtained and a less quantity of serum used for injecting animals. The preparation of a solid serum or an extract from the serum of the active products, secured by means of precipitation, has already been referred to, but for practical purposes it would appear that a concentrated serum is the best product to place in the hands of the individual veterinarian. If our experiments, continued on a still larger scale, give as satisfactory results as those obtained during the years 1897 and 1898 (and there is every reason to hope that such will be the case), it would appear that we have at hand a ·practical method which may be used for decreasing very materially one of the most serious losses to which the farmer is subjected.

THE PREPARATION OF A MIXED SERUM FOR THE TREATMENT OF HOG CHOLERA AND SWINE PLAGUE.

The experiments had shown that the serum prepared for the purpose of curing hog cholera was useful in protecting or curing small experimental animals from hog cholera only, and that serum prepared for the purposes of curing swine plague was useful in protecting from swine plague only. Other work had shown that if experimental animals infected with hog cholera were treated with a mixture of anti-hog cholera and anti-swine plague serum they responded generally a little bit more quickly to the treatment. Efforts were made therefore to prepare in one and the same animal a double serum, as it may be called. In order to do this, the animals which were to serve as a source for the serum were injected with hog cholera cultures and swine plague cultures, or their products, alternately or together, the doses being gradually increased until enough had been injected to impart to the serum the desired properties. The first tests upon experimental animals showed that a serum could be obtained in this way which exerted slight curative properties for both hog cholera and swine plague. The serum, however, was more active in checking swine plague than in checking hog cholera. The treated animals did not thrive under this treatment. The work, however, indicated the possibility of perhaps producing in the same animal a serum which may be specific for two distinct diseases. Experiments are being made now to ascertain to what extent this principle can be utilized in connection with other diseases of men and animals, especially tuberculosis.

CHARACTER OF IMMUNITY.

The length of immunity produced by the injection of serum is short, and more permanent immunity can apparently be secured by using in addition to serum the products of the germs. The serum has appeared most efficacious in treating herds where the disease had just begun.

DIFFICULTIES IN FIELD WORK.

A very important difficulty which is encountered in field work is that it is almost impossible to determine in the field whether animals are suffering from hog cholera or swine plague, or from a mixed infection, unless a careful autopsy has been made. And even when this is done, on account of the similarity of many of the lesions found in the two diseases, it is necessary to resort to a careful bacteriological examination of the cultures obtained from these animals in order to decide whether the disease dealt with is hog cholera or swine plague. This has already been pointed out in previous publications of this Bureau. On account of this practical difficulty the idea very naturally suggested itself that it would be well to treat animals in the field with a curative serum for hog cholera mixed with a curative serum for swine plague obtained from different animals, or with a mixed serum produced in the same animal, as has already been noted. The quantity of the serum used for treating pigs weighing from 40 to 60 pounds was 10 cc. When they were heavier, a larger quantity was used. In general, in the experimental as well as the practical work that has been done by the Bureau, a single injection of the serum was all that was given to each animal. Unless the serum to be used for this work is of such strength that one-half to 1 cc. of it will protect a 500-gram guinea pig from a fatal inoculation with hog cholera or swine plague it is not suitable for practical work.

WORK IN PAGE COUNTY, IOWA, IN 1897.

The Secretary of Agriculture requested the governor of Iowa to designate a county of the State of Iowa in which he would like to have experimental work carried on by the Bureau of Animal Industry. The governor selected Page County. The serum for treatment was prepared according to the methods that have been previously noted, conjointly under the direction of Dr. Schroeder, in charge of the experiment station of the Bureau of Animal Industry, at Washington, and the writer, in charge of the Biochemic Laboratory. The field work in Page County was in direct charge of Dr. Marion Dorset. The methods of treatment used were the following: Sick animals were inoculated with serum that had been found in the laboratory to be effective against either hog cholera or swine plague, or the swine were inoculated with mixed serums, or they were inoculated with the serums to which had been added the products of the hog cholera and swine plague bacteria and their cell contents, or cultures in which the germs had been killed without the application of heat, that might in any way have affected the secretions of the germ.

In order properly to note the efficiency of field work of this sort, it is very important that a large number of checks should be preserved. To accomplish this, in some instances a portion of the treated herd was reserved and not given serum. In other instances herds in which disease existed of about the same virulence as that in the treated herds were left as checks.

The conditions under which animals are placed in all diseases of course influence very greatly the results for the methods of treatment used. A child sick with diphtheria may be given an injection of anti-toxic serum, but if after this injection the child is otherwise neglected it will in all probability not recover, as while the antitoxin counteracts the specific poison of the diphtheria germ it does not give the further stimulation to the system which is also necessary for recovery. The case is similar in the diseases of animals. They should also be given proper care as to food, water, proper housing, and a moderate degree of cleanliness if any method of treatment whatsoever is to prove satis-factory. Very often the farmer has himself to blame quite as much as an outbreak of some particular disease for the loss which takes place in his herd. If he treats his animals as inanimate he must not be surprised if they finally become inanimate, nor can he hope that when they are almost dead the administration of some remedy will miraculously serve to revive them. In many instances where the animals used in this work were treated the farms were in a very good condition and the owner exhibited a sufficient amount of inter-est, care, and intelligence to warrant successful results. In other cases the farms were very poor and the farmers seemed indifferent as to whether their hogs had anything to eat or drink for two or three days. In order therefore to give the fairest test possible to the method of serum treatment, the better farms were the ones reserved for checks.

FIELD WORK IN 1897.

To give the general results with the work carried out under the direction of Dr. Dorset, it may be stated that out of 196 animals treated with the mixed serums 161 were saved, or about 82 per cent. The disease existed on all of the farms where treatment was carried out, a number of animals had already died, and about 50 per cent of the animals treated was ill at the time of injection with the serum. In the check herds there were originally 429 animals, and the disease had begun both in these check herds and in the treated herds about the same time. In the herds which were not treated only about 15 per cent of the animals recovered. Comparing these two sets it would appear that the serum had reduced the mortality about 67 per cent. It is understood, of course, that all of the ani-mals were under the same conditions after treatment as before. As a rule, the animals appeared to begin to improve very shortly after the injection of the serum. One herd was treated with a culture alone without any serum. Only 40 per cent of the herd so treated was saved. In another case a herd which was in a very poor condition at the time of inoculation was treated with a mixed swine plague serum and a dead culture. Eighty per cent of these animals was saved, while in a third similar case, where·the condition of the animals was very poor, only 30 per cent was saved. These results, obtained under rather adverse conditions, indicated that serum injection for swine diseases could be practiced with a fair degree of success when the animals are intelligently treated with a mixed hog cholera serum and swine plague serum and bacterial products, provided these serums are active. The material used in this way is perfectly harmless, so that a farmer need have no fear whatsoever in allowing his animals to be injected; if it should happen not to effect the desired cure it will not injure the animal in the slightest degree. In general, of course, the sooner the treatment of sick animals can be begun the better will be the results of the treatment, but unless the reliability of the serum has been carefully tested and established experimentally, it does not necessarily follow that a sick animal which has been injected with a serum that is said to be efficacious will be cured. If in the case of diphtheria the mortality has been reduced 50 per cent by the serum treatment after long years of careful trial with thousands of cases, it is fair to assume that this method of treatment of swine disease is worthy of a more extensive practical experiment..

The character of the disease in the animals treated, as well as in the check herds in the year 1897, was determined by careful autopsy or, so far as possible, by the identification of the cultures made from the diseased organs of some of the animals upon which autopsy had been performed. In most of the cases examined the hog cholera germ was found present, and specimens of blood which were examined for me by Dr. Dawson, Assistant in the Division of Animal Pathology of this Department, gave the characteristic reaction. The checking of the motility of the hog cholera bacilli, a reaction similar to that used for diagnosing typhoid fever, as has been suggested, might perhaps be useful in determining the character of diseases among swine in the field in a quicker way than would be possible if it was necessary always to work out the nature of the culture. While the majority of these blood examinations agreed with the culture tests, in a few instances the characteristic checking of the motility was observed in blood taken from animals which undoubtedly died from swine plague. These animals may have had in addition, however, a slight infection with hog cholera. At any rate, in chronic cases of disease in swine, when it is sometimes difficult to succeed in transferring to the laboratory a virulent culture from the diseased animals, it is possible that the blood test may be of service as a diagnostic agent.

So long as a serum is being used which has curative properties for both of the diseases to which the animals in the field are usually subjected, it is not of so much importance to be able to make a positive diagnosis or distinction between the two diseases. The acuteness of the attack is perhaps of more importance, as it serves to indicate the amount of serum which should be used in treating animals.

FIELD WORK IN 1898.

As the laboratory experiments and the field work of 1897 already reported had given such encouraging results, at the request of The Hon. James Wilson, Secretary of Agriculture, Congress made a larger appropriation which should be utilized during the year 1898 for making more thorough practical tests of this curative serum for swine. Unfortunately this appropriation was not made available as early as desirable. It was necessary after the needed funds were secured to erect additional stables to accommodate the large number of animals at the experiment station of the Bureau, to purchase the animals and other necessary facilities for carrying on the work. The experimental work in preparing the serum therefore could not be begun before the first of June, and consequently the amount of serum ready for use in the fall of 1898 was not so large as we had hoped, or as it might have been if the appropriation had been available three or four months earlier, when it was requested. Nevertheless, the field work was resumed again in Page County, Iowa. In July, Dr. McBirney, an inspector on the Bureau force, was put in charge of the work in that county, after being given instructions from the laboratory as to the quantity of serum to be used, the method of using it, the manner of treating herds, the method of keeping records, and so on. This work was carried out very faithfully by Dr. McBirney, according to the general directions furnished him, and the results reported up to date (December 1, 1898) have been exceedingly satisfactory and tend to confirm the results obtained in the year 1897. Between the 13th of July and the 11th of November, Dr. McBirney treated 35 herds containing 1,727 animals. Of these treated animals 403 died—a loss of 23.16 per cent in the treated herds. Cultures and specimens of blood were sent to the laboratory from most of these herds, and in 17 of the herds the presence of the hog cholera germ was demonstrated by tests upon experimental animals as well as by a careful study of the cultures. In 3 the presence of the swine plague germ was demonstrated. The examination of the blood and the motility test confirmed the presence of either hog cholera or swine plague, and indicated its presence in some of the herds the cultures from which had not given positive results. Autopsies were made upon one or more animals in each of these herds, and records carefully kept. They indicated in many instances the presence of acute or chronic hog cholera, in a few cases swine plague, or a combination of both diseases.

Thirty-three herds in whole or in part were reserved as checks upon those which were treated. In some of these herds the character of the disease was also demonstrated by cultures or blood reactions. In others the autopsy indicated the character of the disease and hog cholera was found predominant. The number of animals in these check herds was 3,197. Of these only 600 survived, or 81.24 per cent was lost. This shows about as large a percentage of animals saved in the treated herds as were lost in the nontreated herds, and leaves apparently but little doubt as to the efficacy of practical treatment of swine diseases in the field by the use of these mixed serums alone or with bacterial products, combined with simple methods of disinfection and slight care which every farmer should be willing to give to his animals. The serum is intended to cure disease simply, and should have such aids as clean, warm quarters and good food and water; it is no protection against freezing, smothering, or starvation.

The results of our work so far warrant the following conclusions: Animals treated with the hog cholera germs, their cell contents and secretions or those of allied germs, yield a serum which has curative properties for hog cholera. Similar results are obtained for swine plague by the treatment of animals with the germs or their cell contents and secretions.

The most satisfactory results in field work have been secured by treating the swine with a curative serum for swine plague mixed with a curative serum for hog cholera.

LOSSES FROM HOG CHOLERA AND SWINE PLAGUE.

It is estimated that the State of Iowa alone loses $15,000,000 per year in the number of hogs that die from disease. The work, which has been carried on as above reported, indicates that at least $11,000,000 of this loss might be avoided at a comparatively slight cost.

EXPENSE OF THE METHOD OF PREPARING AND USING SERUM.

The farmer should be able to have his hogs injected at a cost not to exceed 15 cents per head if the material for this purpose is prepared in a careful and legitimate way—for the benefit of the farmer rather than for the benefit of the manufacturer. If the latter simply desires to reap financial profits, irrespective of the fact that his material may or may not be useful, the results will undoubtedly be disastrous. Fifteen cents per head is but a trifle to the farmer if he is thereby enabled to save 60 to 80 per cent of his animals which would otherwise be lost.

SOURCES OF INFECTION AND NECESSITY OF DISINFECTION.

The fact that the cause of infection can be carried from one farm to another by animals, by birds, by water running through several farms, on some of which disease exists, by the farmers themselves visiting the pens and lots where their neighbors have sick hogs, can not be too strongly emphasized. Disinfection of the premises, of the farmer's boots, clothing, of the wagons, etc., are absolutely necessary. Hence in all cases pens and lots should be thoroughly disinfected with lime or 5 per cent carbolic acid, a pure water supply should be secured, and the hogs should from time to time have access to a mixture of salt, sulphur, and charcoal, or this should be put in their food. The animals should also have access to comfortable, well-protected sheds.

STATE SUPERVISION.

The results of the experiments conducted by the Bureau of Animal Industry indicate the advisability of certain State experiment stations carrying out this line of work in cooperation with the Bureau of Animal Industry.

Some expense is necessary for starting plants, building stables, and securing the animals, and a good deal of instruction for the men who undertake the work would be required. At the same time, as these experiment stations were inaugurated in order to advance the agricultural interests of the farmers, as they receive a very large amount of support from the National and State governments, it is presumed that they will gladly cooperate in every effort to promote the interests of the farmer. Undoubtedly commercial firms would be only too anxious to take up the manufacture of these serums, as the loss to farmers from these diseases of swine is so enormous. The moment that products of this sort, which can be so easily put up in a condition that they may be perfectly worthless and still appear satisfactory, are placed on the market for gain, the temptation is so great to sell an inefficient material that very often unsatisfactory results may be obtained and great discredit thrown upon the entire work. If private firms undertake the manufacture and sale of serum for treating swine, their products and prices should be subject to legal supervision. If the public is protected against the sale of utterly worthless fertilizers, as is the case in many of our States, most assuredly the sale of a material which may prove so essential to the farmer should also be subject to legislative control. No lot of serum should be sold unless it had been approved, and its value as a curative agent tested by careful official inspection and trial. As the Bureau of Animal Industry has now a plant for the manufacture of this material, has obtained a great deal of very valuable experience, and has worked out the theoretical and some of the practical principles of the use of serum, which promises such good results in treating swine, it is probable that for several years to come at least those who are working along these lines will prefer that the control of this material should remain either directly in its hands or under its supervision. The Bureau is endeavoring to push the work, and to supply larger and still larger quantities of serum for use, and will carefully note and report the results.

EXPERIMENTS IN "STAMPING OUT" HOG CHOLERA IN PAGE COUNTY, IOWA.

PREVALENCE AND EXTENT OF THE DISEASE.

There is no disease more disastrous to the live-stock interests of this country than hog cholera. No State is exempt from it, and in some communities it amounts to a calamity. It has been estimated that in Iowa alone the value of the animals lost by cholera was from $12,000,000 to $15,000,000 in one year, and some have placed the losses of the entire country at $100,000,000 per annum. These astounding figures, which are certainly not exaggerated, justify the General Government in adopting any methods or measures which have for their object the checking, the prevention, or the eradication of the disease.

OPPOSITION TO "STAMPING-OUT" MEASURE.

While it would appear that any effort in this direction would be welcomed by the farmers, considerable opposition is always manifested by individuals when it is proposed to slaughter their entire herds because they are infected with the disease or have been exposed to it. In attempting to eradicate any disease by the "stamping-out" process—one which may necessitate the slaughter of the diseased animals or the entire infected herd—it is not to be expected that stock owners will give that hearty and complete cooperation which is essential to success or to even a fair trial of any method.

GOVERNMENT EXPERIMENTS IN IOWA.

The State of Iowa suffered to such an extent from hog cholera that she was willing to accede to any proposition looking toward its eradication. Accordingly, when it was proposed that the Bureau of Animal Industry, acting for the General Government, should inaugurate a "stamping-out" method, the legislature of that State readily gave its consent and cooperation in the following law (Code of 1897), which took effect on May 4, 1897:

ERADICATION OF HOG CHOLERA.

AN ACT to cooperate with the United States in eradication of hog cholera or swine plague.

Rules and regulations.—SEC. 2350. The governor is hereby authorized to accept, on behalf of the State, any rules and regulations prepared by the Secretary of Agriculture of the United States for the eradication of hog cholera or swine plague in one or more counties of this State, and he, together with the State veterinary surgeon, may cooperate with the Government of the United States for the objects of this act.

Right of inspector.—SEC. 2351. The inspectors of the Bureau of Animal Industry of the United States Department of Agriculture shall have the right of inspection, quarantine, and condemnation of animals affected with hog cholera or swine plague, or suspected to be so affected, or that have been exposed to this disease, and for these purposes are hereby authorized and empowered to enter upon any ground or premises. It is hereby made the duty of sheriffs, constables, and peace officers to assist such inspectors when so requested; and said inspectors shall have the same powers and protection as peace officers while engaged in the discharge of their duties.

Compensation.—SEC. 2352. Whenever any swine in the district specified in the regulations are found to be affected with or to have been exposed to hog cholera or swine plague, said swine may be condemned and destroyed; and the owners of all swine destroyed under the provisions of this act shall be entitled to receive a reasonable compensation therefor, but not more than the actual value in the condition when condemned. In case of failure on the part of the inspector and the owner to agree as to the amount of compensation, the swine shall be appraised by a board of citizens of this State, one of whom may be appointed by the inspector, one by the owner of the swine, and the two thus appointed shall select a third, and these together shall proceed to appraise the amount to be paid to the owner for the animals destroyed. Such appraisal shall be made under oath, and shall be final when the value of the animals does not exceed one hundred dollars; but in all other cases either party shall have the right of appeal to the district court, but such appeal shall not delay the destruction of the diseased or exposed animals.

Expenses.—SEC. 2353. All expenses of quarantine, condemnation, and destruction of swine under the provisions of this act, and the expenses of any and all measures that may be used to eradicate hog cholera, shall be paid by the United States, and in no case shall this State be liable for any damages or expenses of any kind under the provisions of this act.

Penalty.—SEC. 2354. Any person violating any order of quarantine made under his act, or any regulations prescribed by the Secretary of Agriculture and accepted by the governor of this State for the eradication of hog cholera, shall be guilty of a misdemeanor, and upon conviction shall be punished by a fine of not less than twenty-five dollars nor more than one hundred dollars.

Under the authority conferred by the first section of this act, the governor designated Page County as the territory for the inauguration of the "stamping-out" experiments, to be conducted by the Bureau of Animal Industry. Dr. John McBirney, an inspector of this Bureau, was directed to proceed to Page County and take charge of the work, which covered the period from June 17 to December 31, 1897. Dr. McBirney's report forms the subject-matter of this article.

CENSUS OF HOGS OF PAGE COUNTY.

The first necessary piece of work performed was a census of the hogs of the county, which was taken by townships. This census furnished information as to the number of hogs on each premises, whether or not disease existed among them, and the date of infection, if any existed, number of deaths, and the losses for the two years preceding. The census, covering the 16 townships of the county,

was completed the first week in August, and gave the following statistics:

Number of hogs in county.. 97,192
Number that died from January 1, 1895, to January 1, 1897
  (two years) 48,695
Number of farms infected February to July, 1897 (six months)_   170
Number of farms infected August, 1896, to July, 1897 (twelve
  months)   503

SLAUGHTER OF DISEASED HOGS IN INFECTED HERDS.

Instructions from the Bureau, dated July 14, required the slaughter of all diseased hogs, the removal of healthy animals from affected herds to new ground or disinfected pens, and the administration of the cholera mixture[1] given in Farmers' Bulletin No. 24 of the Depart-

---

[1] Following are the formula and directions given in Farmers' Bulletin No. 24:

	Pounds.
Wood charcoal	1
Sulphur	1
Sodium chloride...	2
Sodium bicarbonate	2
Sodium hyposulphite	2
Sodium sulphate	1
Antimony sulphide (black antimony)	1

These ingredients should be completely pulverized and thoroughly mixed.

The dose of this mixture is a large tablespoonful for each 200 pounds weight of hogs to be treated, and it should be given only once a day. When hogs are affected with these diseases they should not be fed on corn alone, but they should have at least once a day soft feed, made by mixing bran and middlings, or middlings and corn meal, or ground oats and corn, or crushed wheat with hot water, and then stirring into this the proper quantity of the medicine. Hogs are fond of this mixture; it increases their appetite, and when they once taste of food with which it has been mixed they will eat it, though nothing else would tempt them.

Animals that are very sick and that will not come to the feed should be drenched with the medicine shaken up with water. Great care should be exercised in drenching hogs or they will be suffocated. Do not turn the hog on its back to drench it, but pull the cheek away from the teeth so as to form a pouch, into which the medicine may be slowly poured. It will flow from the cheek into the mouth, and when the hog finds out what it is, it will stop squealing and swallow. In our experiment hogs which were so sick that they would eat nothing have commenced to eat very soon after getting a dose of the remedy, and have steadily improved until they appeared perfectly well.

This medicine may also be used as a preventive of these diseases, and for this purpose should be put in the feed of the whole herd. Care should of course be observed to see that each animal receives its proper share. In cases where it has been given a fair trial, it has apparently cured most of the animals which were sick and has stopped the progress of the disease in the herds. It also appears to be an excellent appetizer and stimulant of the processes of digestion and assimilation, and when given to unthrifty hogs it increases the appetite, causes them to take on flesh, and assume a thrifty appearance.

ment of Agriculture. The slaughtered hogs were burned or were buried at least 4 feet below the surface of the ground.

The first diseased hogs were slaughtered on July 23. From that time to September 20 the sick animals in the 58 herds affected were slaughtered, the apparently healthy ones were removed to new or disinfected quarters, and the cholera·mixture mentioned above was used in all except the first herd. The owner of this herd desired to use a remedy of his own. The data given in Table No. 1 (appended hereto) show that 31 herds gave good results. In none of these did the subsequent deaths exceed 4. Of the 810 apparently healthy animals in the 31 herds, but 16 died—less than 2 per cent. Thirteen herds showed fair results and 12 poor, while in two instances no animals were left. When the work of slaughtering diseased animals was put into effect, there were 20 diseased or suspicious herds, and the small force in the field was unable to get them under control, for at that time new cases were of daily occurrence. For instance, 32 outbreaks were reported during the first two weeks in August.

Although, as is shown in Table No. 1, excellent results were obtained in 31 of the 58 herds treated and fair results in 13 others, it is true that beneficial results in the way of eradicating disease were not observed in more than one-third of the 16 townships. In order completely to control infection under this system and to enforce other restrictions which should be required of every owner, it would be necessary, as frequent visits would be required, that there should be at least an employee for each township and also the full cooperation of every owner. During August and the first half of September the disease spread rapidly in the western, southwestern, and southeastern parts of the county. At the latter date additional laborers were secured, but not until after the number of affected herds not having received official attention numbered 66.

WORK CONFINED TO EAST HALF OF COUNTY—SLAUGHTER OF ENTIRE INFECTED HERDS.

Amended instructions were sent to Dr. McBirney about the middle of September to the effect that the work be confined to the east half of the county, including the townships of Nodaway, Douglas, Valley, Nebraska, Buchanan, Amity, Harlan, and East River, and that all animals in affected herds be slaughtered. The west half of the county was reserved for serum experiments, which form the subject of a separate report. (See page 235.) The first entire herd was slaughtered on September 20, and from that date till November 24, 49 entire herds were destroyed and their pens disinfected. The data of the experiments which were conducted between September 20 and December 31 are given in Table No. 2 (appended hereto).

COMPARISON OF RESULTS BY TOWNSHIPS.

A comparison in results of the work in the townships of the eastern half of the county is made between the last six months of 1897 and

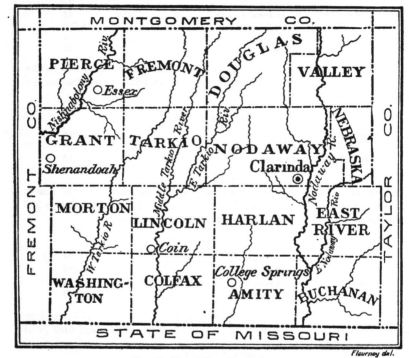

FIG. 36.—Map of Page County, Iowa.

Flournoy del.

the corresponding period for 1896.   The figures for the six months of 1896 are only approximated.

NODAWAY TOWNSHIP.

1896—Number of outbreaks	20
Number of head lost	3,594
1897—Number of outbreaks	12
Number of head lost	70

This is a showing favorable to 1897 of 17 outbreaks and net losses to the number of 3,524.   In this township 204 were condemned and paid for by the Government.

DOUGLAS TOWNSHIP.

1896—Number of outbreaks	23
Number of head lost	1,983
1897—Number of outbreaks	2
Number of head lost	106

This also is a favorable showing for 1897 of 21 outbreaks and net losses to the number of 1,877. In this township 48 head were condemned and paid for.

VALLEY TOWNSHIP.

1896—Number of outbreaks	49
Number of head lost	2,278
1897—Number of outbreaks	4
Number of head lost	88

An adverse showing for 1896 of 45 outbreaks and net losses to the number of 2,190. One hundred and thirty-six head were condemned and paid for in this township.

NEBRASKA TOWNSHIP.

1896—Number of outbreaks	12
Number of head lost	368
1897—Number of outbreaks	16
Number of head lost	191

These records show 4 more outbreaks than in 1896; but the losses in 1896 exceeded those of 1897 by 177 head. In this township 555 head were condemned and paid for.

BUCHANAN TOWNSHIP.

1896—Number of outbreaks	23
Number of head lost	1,015
1897—Number of outbreaks	20
Number of head lost	230

This statement shows 3 outbreaks and a net loss of 785 head in favor of 1897. In this township 785 head were condemned and paid for.

AMITY TOWNSHIP.

1896—Number of outbreaks	21
Number of head lost	65
1897—Number of outbreaks	11
Number of head lost	150

This shows 10 outbreaks in favor of 1897 and a net loss of 85 in favor of 1896. In this township 305 hogs were condemned and paid for.

HARLEM TOWNSHIP.

1896—Number of outbreaks	13
Number of head lost	1,233
1897—Number of outbreaks	2
Number of head lost	40

This is a remarkable showing in balances in favor of 1897 of 11 outbreaks and 1,229 deaths. Only 4 animals were here condemned and paid for.

EAST RIVER TOWNSHIP.

1896—Number of outbreaks... 48
Number of head lost.. 2,313
1897—Number of outbreaks... 13
Number of head lost.. 236

A statement showing balances favorable to 1897 of 35 outbreaks and 2,077 deaths. In this township 188 hogs were condemned and paid for.

RECAPITULATION.

Number of outbreaks in 1896 (six months) 218
Number of outbreaks in 1897 (six months) 80

Difference 138

Number of head lost in 1896 (six months) 12,849
Number of head lost in 1897 (six months) 1,111

Difference 11,738

THE SAVING AND THE EXPENSE.

This statement shows that 11,738 more hogs died of cholera in the last six months of 1896 than during the corresponding six months of 1897—the period covered by the operations of the Bureau—and there can be no question that this wonderfully favorable showing is due almost wholly to the method of procedure of the Bureau of Animal Industry. If, therefore, it is assumed that the average weight of the 11,738 hogs was 100 pounds, and their value 3 cents per pound, the saving to the 8 townships was $35,214. In Nodaway Township alone, where the effects of the work were especially obvious, the amount saved to the owners was $10,572.

The "stamping-out" method pursued against any disease is quite generally considered a very expensive one, and so it is; but when, as in this case, the resultant benefits are so apparent, the expense does not appear so extraordinary. It must not be forgotten that if the disease is really eradicated the benefits of the work extend over many years—until such time as it may be reintroduced by lack of vigilance. Now, the total expense of the Bureau's work in the eight townships was $10,157.12, and the estimated saving to the stock owners was $35,214, a net saving during the first year of $25,056.88.

DISINFECTION AND MEANS OF INFECTION.

During the time when only the diseased hogs of a herd were destroyed, the disinfection of pens was performed generally by the owner, and consequently was not so well done as when the entire herd was slaughtered, as in the latter case the work was done under the supervision of the employees of the Bureau. During the former period the lime and a portion of the carbolic acid used in disinfection were furnished by the owner, but when entire herds were slaughtered the owners were not so disposed to purchase disinfectants or to do much of the work of disinfection.

It will be observed from the tabulated statements that of the 110 herds that came under official action, all but 6 had been allowed to run in pastures, orchards, or yards too extensive for disinfection, except at large expense, so that the disinfected pens were only a small portion of the infected territory. The fact that so many herds were allowed to run in pastures was apparently the source of much of the infection that spread throughout Nebraska Township. There are many farms in this township and many of the herds have access to the line fences as well as the river. Thus a large number of herds were exposed at one time.

There are other sources of infection in this county. Carrion birds are very numerous, and along the Nodaway and East rivers many of the farmers keep hounds that are continually roaming from place to place. Dr. McBirney is of the opinion, however, that most of the infection was carried by the stock owners themselves. As many as three or four owners have been observed visiting infected premises, although they were aware that the disease existed there. During the fall months it is the custom in Page County for the farmers to "change work." The disease is in this way readily carried from one farm to many others. It was difficult to get owners to appreciate this source of danger and properly to guard against it. This method of dissemination was willfully undertaken in Buchanan Township, where a number of owners actively opposed the killing of entire herds. Because of such difficulties the eradication of hog cholera and swine plague has been a greater effort than it apparently should have been.

Of the 49 herds slaughtered, 12 were owned in the small villages where the pens were very closely situated. Four of the herds slaughtered were in Braddyville, Buchanan Township, and their infection was from a hog purchased from a herd recently infected. In the 49 herds there were 180 immune hogs, none of which died subsequently.

There was an outbreak in East River Township and one in Harlan Township which had not been officially disposed of on December 31, but the other six townships were practically free from the disease.

In order to expedite and facilitate the eradication of hog cholera and swine plague, it would be necessary rigidly to enforce regulations prohibiting owners from permitting their hogs from coming in contact with line or road fences, public roads, driveways, or have access to streams; nor should owners of infected premises be permitted to visit noninfected ones or the owners of noninfected ones to visit the infected ones.

THE METHOD OF ERADICATION PREFERRED.

Dr. McBirney adds, in concluding his report, that the first method employed—that of killing the diseased animals only of a herd, although it had some merit in controlling disease and proved to be of much benefit to owners—is a measure too slow in stamping out, unless a large force can be employed and very rigid quarantine regulations put in force. The killing of entire herds is evidently, from the results of the work, a quicker and safer method, although it does not generally meet with favor among the farmers. This method, too, should be accompanied by a rigid set of quarantine regulations, in order to produce the desired results within a reasonable time. If sufficient funds were available and the conditions present that existed in the county during August and September, a force should be employed consisting of one inspector or assistant inspector for each four townships and one employee of some experience for each township. This would insure the prompt disposal of diseased herds and prove a quicker method of arresting infection. One inspector can not visit the different premises with sufficient promptness when there are a number of diseased herds throughout the county, and consequently the owner last visited will have acquired some antagonism, as his herd will presumably be in a very poor condition or many of the animals will have died.

10317——17

TABULAR STATEMENT

Table No. 1.—*Report of diseased hogs slaughtered*

No.	Date.	Owner's name.	Township.	Section.	Number died previous to official action.	Number of sick hogs slaughtered.	Cost.
1	July 28	J. M. Campbell	Tarkio	25	29	11	$11.00
2	July 28	R. R. Montgomery	Lincoln	28	1	1	2.75
3	July 31	S. Hayner	Amity	24	4	23	15.00
4	Aug. 2	C. D. Johnson	Colfax	16	35	38	34.65
5	Aug. 2	F. J. Thrap	Lincoln	30	3	7	20.85
6	Aug. 4	R. T. Feltch	Amity	13	48	18	10.55
7	Aug. 5	Geo. H. Annan	Nodaway	31	....	17	25.70
8	Aug. 10	J. Knudsen	Lincoln	20	0	19	20.00
9	Aug. 16	Chas. Fulton	Nodaway	34	6	1	2.00
10	Aug. 18	F. J. Boreland	Tarkio	7	13	30	38.25
11	Aug. 18	J. F. Cozad	Grant	23	14	3	3.00
12	Aug. 19	Wm. T. Beckett	do	36	35	23	53.00
13	Aug. 19	A. O. Brewer	Tarkio	19	8	16	9.00
14	Aug. 20	P. J. Johnson	do	17	15	6	7.20
15	Aug. 21	Eliza McKee	Amity	24	20	22	12.10
16	Aug. 21	C. A. Hultine	Tarkio	8	10	4	5.75
17	Aug. 23	C. M. Conver	Lincoln	30	3	53	78.90
18	Sept. 1	Jacob Hamm	East River	34	62	1	1.50
19	Sept. 1	J. S. Crosby	do	3	0	2	2.00
20	Sept. 2	Jos. Burwell	Nodaway	22	1	6	7.70
21	Sept. 2	Isaac Mulkins	East River	22	5	1	.75
22	Sept. 3	L. W. Good	do	34	4	2	8.00
23	Sept. 4	T. E. Earhart	do	29	a 80	1	2.00
24	Sept. 4	F. W. Ammons	Nebraska	13	53	22	28.75
25	Sept. 4	C. H. Spaulding	do	13	18	19	15.20
26	Sept. 4	C. A. Gates	Buchanan	10	39	5	10.62
27	Sept. 6	C. H. B. Carlson	Nodaway	19	5	1	2.50
28	Sept. 6	S. R. Frank	Morton	36	8	33	23.74
29	Sept. 6	C. H. Varley	Tarkio	7	8	8	12.56
30	Sept. 7	J. F. Haley	Nodaway	31	35	5	8.26
31	Sept. 7	J. B. Damewood	Morton	26	0	20	20.00
32	Sept. 9	A. K. Christensen	Washington	1	30	50	32.90
33	Sept. 7	Fred. Boles	East River	34	30	6	10.20
34	Sept. 8	Jas. Whitmore	Washington	12	70	74	55.40
35	Sept. 8	Frank Morley	Nodaway	18	2	2	6.88
36	Sept. 8	A. C. Harland	Tarkio	22	30	3	3.75
37	Sept. 9	E. J. Caldwell	Lincoln	32	25	3	3.00
38	Sept. 9	Geo. T. Loy	Morton	36	25	28	34.95
39	Sept. 10	W. L. Gordon	Lincoln	29	12	6	2.40
40	Sept. 10	W. W. Montanye	Amity	17	4	4	3.20
41	Sept. 10	C. E. Worrell	East River	27	16	1	3.00

OF THE EXPERIMENTS.

in Page County, Iowa, July 23 to September 20, 1897.

Date of slaughter.	Number healthy hogs remaining.	Number of subsequent deaths.	Probable source of infection.	Results.	Where the hogs had been kept.	No.
July 23	16	0	Not known	Good	Pens and pasture	1
July 28	19	13	Montzingo, next farm	Poor	do	2
July 31	28	3	Not known	Good	Pens and yards	3
July 26 Aug. 2 }	28	1	Ikers, next section	do	Pens and pasture	4
July 28 Aug. 2 }	34	13	Dalby's, next farm	Poor	Pens, yards, and orchard.	5
Aug. 4	26	18	Not known	do	Pens and pasture	6
July 21 Aug. 5 }	2	0	Railroad yards, Yorktown	Fair	Pens and timber	7
Aug. 10	40	29	Disease in next section	Poor	Pens and cornfields	8
Aug. 16	200	0	Not known	Good	Pens	9
Aug. 13	12	0	Northwald's, next farm	do	Pens and pasture	10
Aug. 13	2	0	Rhodes's, next farm	do	do	11
Aug. 19	45	17	Not known	Fair	do	12
Aug. 19	13	0	Banner's, next farm	Good	do	13
Aug. 20	12	6	Northwald's, next farm	Fair	do	14
Aug. 21	21	4	Hayner's, next farm	Good	Pens and orchard	15
Aug. 21	29	10	Northwald's, next farm	Fair	Pens and pasture	16
Aug. 23	52	50	Wolf's, next farm	Poor	do	17
Sept. 1	31	0	Not known	Good	Pens and orchard	18
Sept. 1	3	0	Hamm's, next farm	Fair	Pens and cornfield	19
Sept. 2	121	0	Near asylum herd	Good	Pens and orchard	20
Sept. 2	23	1	Disease in next section	do	Pens and pasture	21
Sept. 3	5	0	Boles's, next farm	do	do	22
Sept. 4	18	1	Brought from Harlan Township	do	do	23
Sept. 4	11	0	Not known	do	do	24
Sept. 4	13	0	Ammon's	do	Pens and yards	25
Sept. 4	41	0	Not known	do	Pens, yards, and timber.	26
Sept. 6	50	0	do	do	Pens and pasture	27
Sept. 6	35	33	Disease in next section	Poor	do	28
Sept. 6	8	0	Not known	Good	Pens and timber	29
Sept. 7	6	0	Geo. Annan's, or railroad yards	do	Pens	30
Sept. 7	0	0	Disease in next section		Pens and pasture	31
Sept. 7 and 9.	23	18	Frank's, next farm	Poor	do	32
Sept. 7	13	0	Hamm's, next farm	Good	do	33
Sept. 8 and 13.	23	4	Disease in next section	Fair	do	34
Sept. 8	24	0	do	Good	do	35
Sept. 8	40	0	Not known	do	do	36
Sept. 9	9	3	Disease in next section	Fair	Pens	37
Sept. 9	13	3	Frank's, next farm	do	Pens and pasture	38
Sept. 10	10	3	Disease in next section	do	do	39
Sept. 10	40	0	Not known	Good	Pens	40
Sept. 10	9	0	Good's, next section	do	Pens and pasture	41

TABLE No. 1.—*Report of diseased hogs slaughtered in Page*

No.	Date.	Owner's name.	Township.	Section.	Number died previous to official action.	Number of sick hogs slaughtered.	Cost.
42	Sept. 10	Ruel Miller	Tarkio	29	40	8	$13.12
43	Sept. 10	Frank Johnson	....do	7	7	14	18.76
44	Sept. 11	C. G. Peterson	....do	8	11	5	5.00
45	Sept. 11	J. E. Davis	Lincoln	8	10	5	4.30
46	Sept. 11	F. M. Manifold	....do	19	12	7	6.00
47	Sept. 11	Amos Apple	Tarkio	23	19	4	3.25
48	Sept. 13	A. R. Clayton	Lincoln	32	2	11	21.00
49	Sept. 13	Clark Davison	East River	34	9	15	23.50
50	Sept. 13	L. E. Drodge	Lincoln	21	26	16	15.75
51	Sept. 13	W. W. Whitlow	Washington	14	225	26	19.50
52	Sept. 13	W. E. Newman	....do	14	1	7	7.00
53	....	Mary Friesz	Grant	14	28	3	4.95
54	....	J. D. Laughlin	Morton	29	3	25	19.68
55	....	Frank Brokaw	Nodaway	23	1	2	3.00
56	Sept. 15	H. E. Anderson	Amity	17	5	1	3.00
57	Sept. 25	John McCurdy	Buchanan	22	1	20	15.60
58	Sept. 20	P. D. Castle	Nodaway	19	2	7	12.60
					1,162	781	840.57

a This number died since April 1.

NOTE.—In all cases except No. 21 disinfection was performed in pens; No. 21 was disinfected in troughs. Many of the herds had access to public roads and driveways as well as to pens, pastures, and orchards.

County, Iowa, July 23 to September 20, 1897—Continued.

Date of slaughter.	Number healthy hogs remaining.	Number of subsequent deaths.	Probable source of infection.	Results.	Where the hogs had been kept.	No.
Sept. 10	15	0	Disease in next section	Good ...	Pens and pasture....	42
Sept. 10	9	4	.....do	Fair	.....do	43
Sept. 11	27	17	.....do	Poor ...	.....do	44
Sept. 11	65	4	Disease on farm all year	Good ...	Pens and yards......	45
Sept. 11	33	7	Disease in next section	Fair	Pens and pasture....	46
Sept. 11	50	0	.....do	Good ...	Pens and orchard ...	47
Sept. 9 and 13.	7	5	Caldwell's, same section	Poor ...	Pens and pasture....	48
Sept. 8 and 13.	17	1	Disease in next section	Good ...	.....do	49
Sept. 13	4	2	Bought hogs from infected farm..	Fair	Pens and yards......	50
Sept. 13	74	74	Disease in next section	Poor ...	Pens and pasture....	51
Sept. 13	145	73	Whitlow's, in same section	....do ...	.....do	52
....	7	2	Disease in next section	Fair	Pens, orchard, and road.	53
....	27	20	Disease in same section	Poor ...	Pens, orchard, and fields.	54
....	25	0	Burwell's, in section 22	Good ...	Pens and pasture....	55
Sept. 15	Sold..	0	Montanye's	....	Pens	56
Sept. 11, 15, 25.	63	1	F. McCurdy's, section 17	Good ...	.....do	57
Sept. 8 to 20.	16	0	Disease in next section	....do ...	Pens and pasture....	58
	1,732	439				

TABLE No. 2.—*Report of diseased and exposed hogs slaughtered*

No.	Date.	Owner's name.	Township.	Section.	Number died previous to official action.	Number sick hogs slaughtered.	Number exposed hogs slaughtered.	Cost.
1	Sept. 20	D. D. Stitt	Nodaway	30	0	31	25	$126.30
2	Sept. 20	H. D. Lucas	...do	31	1	1	3	7.00
3	Sept. 21	A. M. Collier	Nebraska	13	25	8	8	50.00
4	Sept. 20	E. N. Fowler	East River	12	0	10	15	72.50
5	Sept. 25	John Duncan	Amity	14	6	59	20	181.02
6	Sept. 27	R. T. Johnson	Buchanan	17	10	16	72	371.45
7	Sept. 27	F. McCurdy	...do	17	30	36	61	142.01
8	Sept. 27	O. B. Holton	...do	31	0	1	0	5.00
9	Sept. 28	J. D. Maxwell	...do	15	20	29	40	188.96
10	Sept. 28	J. A. Bloom	...do	20	9	9	30	88.20
11	Sept. 28	Caleb Hall	...do	31	0	1	1	5.60
12	Sept. 29	C. M. Collier	Nebraska	13	1	3	4	13.00
13	Sept. 29	J. S. Hayes	East River	1	·3	21	25	142.30
14	Sept. 30	J. S. McFarland	Nebraska	11	9	6	30	150.00
--	Sept. 30	J. D. Elliott	...do	13	2	4	37	170.91
16	Oct. 1	S. M. Elrick	Valley	4	54	3	50	166.80
	Oct. 1	Prichard Bros	Buchanan	15	34	33	180	510.00
	Oct. 2	Ambrose Beery	East River	33	5	20	10	88.00
	Oct. 4	Thos. Henry	Amity	24	18	1	0	2.25
	Oct. 6	N. W. Winter	Buchanan	31	1	2	4	19.76
	Sept. 21	B. F. Ennis	Amity	17	0	1	0	2.50
	Oct. 11	Edward Crosby	Buchanan	3	8	5	9	67.02
	Oct. 12	D. B. Holton	...do	31	3	1	1	5.50
17	Oct. 18	Ed. Hakes	Nebraska	24	25	30	158	360.00
25	Oct. 18	David Harris	...do	12	16	7	79	228.02
26	Oct. 19	Chas. Davison	Buchanan	5	5	8	60	250.00
27	Oct. 19	Phil. M. Crockett	Washington	12	6	2	0	1.50
28	Oct. 20	R. D. Farrens	Nodaway	22	16	24	66	158.50
29	Oct. 26	James Dunn	Buchanan	20	11	12	23	135.00
30	Oct. 26	A. C. Frisby	...do	20	2	2	19	50.00
31	Oct. 27	S. E. McAlpin	Nebraska	13	6	10	50	144.75
32	Oct. 27	J. S. Bently	...do	11	7	4	17	66.95
33	Oct. 28	A. C. Jackson	...do	13	0	5	0	10.00
34	Oct. 28	S. W. Kelley	East River	34	4	4	39	168.00
35	Oct. 29	Jno. W. Service	Amity	14	16	8	24	94.00
36	Oct. 29	L. L. Johnson	...do	28	0	6	44	155.02
37	Oct. 30	Edward Hollis	Nebraska	11	3	3	0	6.75
38	Oct. 30	Samuel Hollis	Valley	35	7	5	20	83.15
39	Nov. 4	W. T. Crain	Buchanan	14	23	27	109	375.01
40	Nov. 5	M. R. Ansbach	Nebraska	14	1	4	27	53.80
41	Nov. 6	C. P. Jackson	...do	13	3	4	0	10.00
42	Nov. 5	M. E. Miller	...do	11	20	4	6	15.00
43	Nov. 6	Geo. W. Dudley	...do	13	2	3	3	26.25
44	Nov. 15	A. A. Berry	Amity	4	4	33	46	161.00
45	Nov. 18	Rosena Carr	Buchanan	10	9	4	22	85.00
46	Nov. 20	Lewis Annan	Nodaway	30	1	3	10	21.60

in Page County, Iowa, September 20 to December 31, 1897.

Date of slaughter.	Number immune hogs remaining.	Number of subsequent deaths.	Probable source of infection.	Where the hogs had been kept.	No.
Sept. 13, 14, 20	0	0	Disease next section	Pens and yards	1
Sept. 20	0	0	Bought 2 exposed hogs	Pens (in Clarinda)	2
Sept. 21	0	0	From river	Pens and yards	3
Sept. 10, 20	0	0	Not known	Pens and pasture	4
Sept. 15, 20, 22, 25	0	0	Disease next section	....do	5
Sept. 16, 20, 22, 24, 27	2	0	McCurdy's, next farm	....do	6
Sept. 4, 13, 15, 20, 27	44	0	Not known	....do	7
Sept. 27	0	0	Bought from infected farm—Mrs. McKee.	Pen (in Braddyville)	8
Sept. 13, 15, 22, 28	0	0	Disease same section	Pens and timber	9
Sept. 17, 24, 28	0	0	Disease next section	Pens and pasture	10
Sept. 28	0	0	Exposed to Holton's	Pen (Braddyville)	11
Sept. 29	0	0	From East River	Pens	12
Sept. 14, 29	0	0	Disease next section	Pens and pasture	13
Sept. 30	0	0	....do	....do	14
Sept. 30	0	0	Disease same section	....do	15
Oct. 1	7	0	Not known	Pens and pasture; lives on county line.	16
Sept. 13, 15, Oct. 1	76	0	Disease next section	Pens and 200-acre pasture.	17
Oct. 2	0	0	....do	Pens and orchard	18
Oct. 4	8	0	Disease same section	Pens and pasture	19
Oct. 6	0	0	Exposed to Holton's	Pen (Braddyville)	20
Sept. 21	0	0	Exposed to Anderson's	Pen (College Springs)	21
Sept. 1, Oct. 11	0	0	Disease next section	Pen and fields	22
Oct. 12	0	0	Exposed to O. B. Holton's	Pen (Braddyville)	23
Oct. 18	a 105	0	Disease in next section and river.		24
Oct. 18	0	0	Disease next section	Pens and pasture	25
Oct. 19	0	0	Disease same section	....do	26
				Pens and yards	27
Oct. 20	40	0	Improper burials	Pens, yards, and timber	28
Oct. 26	3	0	Bloom's, next farm	Pens and pasture	29
Oct. 26	3	0	....do	....do	30
Oct. 27	13	0	Disease next section	....do	31
Oct. 27	2	0	Disease same section	....do	32
Oct. 28	0	0	....do	Pens (Hawleyville)	33
Oct. 28	5	0	Disease next section	Pens and pasture	34
Oct. 20	0	0	Duncan's, next farm	....do	35
Oct. 29	0	0	Not known	....do	36
Oct. 30	0	0	Disease same section	....do	37
Oct. 30	0	0	Disease next section	Pens	38
Nov. 4	5	0	....do	Pens and pasture	39
Nov. 5	1	0	....do	Pens and yards	40
Nov. 6	0	0	Disease same section	Pens (Hawleyville)	41
Nov. 5	2	0	....do	Pens and yards	42
Nov. 6	0	0	....do	Pens (Hawleyville)	43
Nov. 15	14	0	Carried from T. Buchanan's.	Pens, large yards, and driveways.	44
Nov. 18	3	0	Disease next section	....do	45
Nov. 20	20	0	Farren's, next farm	Pens and fields	46

TABLE No. 2.—*Report of diseased and exposed hogs slaughtered in*

No.	Date.	Owner's name.	Township.	Section.	Number died previous to official action.	Number sick hogs slaughtered.	Number exposed hogs slaughtered.	Cost.
47	Nov. 22	E. Beal	Buchanan	28	5	8	43	$100.75
48	Nov. 23	G. B. Hall	Valley	6	12	6	16	35.40
49	Nov. 24	O. A. Anderson	do	9	15	4	32	121.72
50 52	Dec. 7	G. H. Robinson	Douglas	17	72	48	0	64.32
	Dec. 8	J. C. Glasgow	Harlan	20	14	4	0	5.00
	Dec. 9	D. A. Farrens	Buchanan	22	18	2	0	3.00
					462	585	1,538	5,565.59

NOTE.—Disinfection in all cases was performed in the pens. Some of the herds had access to public roads and driveways, as well as to pens, pastures, and orchards. Nos. 50, 51, and 52 were disposed of under special instructions.

SUMMARY OF DATA.

Number of diseased herds	110
Number of diseased hogs died and not paid for	1,216
Number of diseased hogs slaughtered	1,306
Number of exposed hogs slaughtered	1,538
	2,904
Cost of 2,904 diseased and exposed hogs	$6,406.16
Cost of disinfectants and cholera mixture	183.23
Cost of incidentals, slaughtering, and disinfecting	21.28
Salaries of inspector and laborers (June to December)	2,276.29
Traveling expenses of inspector and laborers (June to December)	1,270.16
Total cost of work (June 17 to December 31)	10,157.12

Page County, Iowa, September 20 to December 31, 1897—Continued.

Date of slaughter.	Number immune hogs remaining.	Number of subsequent deaths.	Probable source of infection.	Where the hogs had been kept.	No.
Nov. 22	2	0	Not known	Pens and pasture	47
Nov. 23	3	0	.....do	.....do....................	48
Nov. 24	27	0	Thinks pigeon carried it from next farm.	Pens and large yards.....	49
Dec. 7	b 23	9	Not known	.....do....................	50
Dec. 8	c 6	....	.....do	Pens, orchard, and yards.	51
Dec. 9	Inoculated.		Next farm.................	Pens and pasture	52
	385	9			

a Had moved 20 pigs with 105 to another farm. Pigs all died.
b These were not immune.
c In addition there were 21 not immune, and 7 of the 21 died.

THE ENZYMES, OR SOLUBLE FERMENTS, OF THE HOG CHOLERA GERM.[1]

By E. A. DE SCHWEINITZ, Ph. D.,

Chief of Biochemic Division, Bureau of Animal Industry.

In the Archiv für Hygiene, 1890, vol. X, pt. 1, p. 1, Fermi describes the detection and isolation of soluble ferments from the cultures of a number of different germs. Some of these germs belong to the class that produce gas (principally CO_2 and H) when grown in media containing glucose or glucose-forming substances, and as a rule the gas-producing germs when cultivated upon proper media have been found to be ferment builders.

As has been shown by Smith and other investigators, the hog cholera germ produces large quantities of gas when grown in peptonized beef broth containing 2 per cent of glucose. About one-fourth of this volume is hydrogen and three-fourths carbon dioxide, the remaining liquid containing acetic and succinic acids, as I have found by analysis.

To detect and isolate the soluble ferments of the hog cholera germ, if any, several different culture-media have been tried, but the one that has given the most satisfactory results is sterilized milk. In plain peptonized beef broth media but very small amounts of these ferments were produced, sometimes none.

Upon agar-agar the growth of the germ is rapid, and from the watery extract of the surface growth a mixture of two ferments has been obtained that will convert starch into glucose and liquefy gelatine—in other words, ferments that act as diastase on the one hand and as trypsin on the other.

If now we take either skimmed or fresh milk, carefully sterilize it, and then inoculate it with the hog cholera germ, after about three weeks the milk will have become thin and watery in appearance, a curd-like coating will have formed on the surface, and the reaction, if the growth has been normal, will have become either neutral or alkaline. The germs may now be removed by filtering the milk through a carefully sterilized Pasteur tube, or they may be killed by heating the solution to 54°C. for several hours, or still better, by the addition of a saturated solution of thymol.

---

[1] Read before the Chemical Section of the American Association for the Advancement of Science, Rochester, August 17, 1892.

From the cultures sterilized in this way the addition of absolute alcohol throws down a voluminous precipitate consisting of albumose, a little peptone, and soluble enzymes.

A purification of this precipitate and partial separation of enzymes from the accompanying albuminoid matter is attained by a re-solution in water and precipitation with basic calcic phosphate. The enzymes are carried down mechanically by this, and can be dissolved out by water and reprecipitated with alcohol. After repeated treatment of this sort a small quantity of white powder is finally obtained, which will liquefy gelatine, digest fibrine and albumin, and convert starch into glucose.

To separate the diastase-like ferment from the liquefying ferment, the mixed ferments were rubbed up with glycerine and filtered. The solution in glycerine contained the hydrating ferment, while the undissolved portion taken up again in water and precipitated by alcohol does not act as a hydrating agent, but as a digestive agent.

The trypsin-like ferment can also be precipitated by means of saturated salt solution. This latter ferment seems to be formed in much smaller amount than the former.

The action of both of these ferments is destroyed by a temperature above 55° C. They contain nitrogen, but when pure do not give the general albuminoid reactions.

In order to try to obtain these ferments in a purer form, and possibly larger quantity, an artificial culture-medium proposed by Fermi, in the Archiv für Hygiene, vol. XIV, for use with other germs, was tried for the hog cholera bacillus. This contained 1 per cent ammonium phosphate, 0.1 per cent acid potassium phosphate, 0.02 per cent magnesium sulphate, and 4 to 5 per cent glycerine. The hog cholera germ grows vigorously in this liquid, and after from three to four weeks the cultures become alkaline in reaction. They also give the peculiar amine odor characteristic of the hog cholera cultures. From these artificial sterilized cultures I have so far been unable to separate the diastase-like ferment, but a small amount of the tryptic ferment has been obtained, showing that the ferment production is dependent upon the medium.

As for the physiologic effects of these ferments, Fermi holds that in general the soluble ferments are without great physiologic importance in the process of disease.

The initial experiments that I have made upon guinea pigs show that, so far at least as this particular disease is concerned, the ferments are of great importance in the production of immunity.

Guinea pigs about a pound in weight each have been injected with a sterile solution in water of these ferments, the amount taken varying from 0.003 gram up to from 0.02 to 0.05 gram. The injections below 0.01 gram were without ill effect; beyond that there was a rise of temperature for several days. The injection of 0.05 gram was in several instances sufficient to kill the animals. The autopsies showed some injection of the blood vessels of the intestines, but in other respects the animal was normal in condition.

A single injection of 0.04 gram of the ferments was sufficient to make the animals immune from an inoculation with the hog cholera germ that was sufficient to cause the checks to die in ten days.

It is probable, therefore, that the soluble ferments exert in their way, at least in some diseases, a potent action in rendering the animal insusceptible to disease.

It is possible, too, that to the indirect action of these specific ferments we may trace the protective and curative influence of the blood serum of immune animals.

THE PRODUCTION OF IMMUNITY IN GUINEA PIGS FROM HOG CHOLERA BY THE USE OF BLOOD SERUM FROM IMMUNIFIED ANIMALS.[1]

By E. A. de Schweinitz, Ph. D.,
Chief of Biochemic Division, Bureau of Animal Industry.

The important results obtained by Behring and Kitasato, Tizzoni and Cattani, Klemperer and Klemperer, and others, with diphtheria, tetanus, pneumonia, etc., led me to undertake a series of experiments upon guinea pigs for the purpose of studying the effect of the blood serum from animals immune from hog cholera. As a source for the blood serum, I used guinea pigs that had been immunified by means of the albumose extracted from artificial hog cholera cultures, and then exposed to the disease by inoculation with the virulent germ.[2] From this latter inoculation the animals had not suffered, and at the time of use had been well for several months. The blood was drawn from the carotid artery into a sterile test tube, and defibrinated by means of a sterilized glass rod, the overlying serum then being used for injection. Precautions were taken that the blood did not become contaminated while being drawn, and the absence of germs from the serum was carefully tested.

The experiments were as follows:

Experiment 1.—Two guinea pigs, weighing each about one pound, received 3 cc. of this blood serum by a single injection on the inner side of the thigh. This injection was followed by a slight rise in temperature, but no local lesion at the point of injection, though there was a slight inflammation of the skin for four or five days. After ten days these pigs, together with two checks, were inoculated in the thigh with 0.1 cc. of peptonized beef broth hog cholera culture one day old. The checks died in seven days. The autopsy showed characteristic hog cholera lesions; the hog cholera bacteria in the spleen were abundant. Both treated animals apparently recovered from the inoculation. Four weeks after the inoculation one of the pigs became paralyzed in the hind legs, and finally died five weeks after the inoculation. The autopsy showed the organs to be apparently normal, except for a few small dots on the surface of the liver. Culture showed an absence of hog cholera germs.

---

[1] Read before the American Association for the Advancement of Science, Rochester, August 15, 1892.

[2] The Medical News, October 4, 1890.

The second treated pig was found dead three months after the inoculation. The autopsy again showed the organs apparently normal, except for a slight congestion of the intestines.

There had been in these two cases, then, a considerable resistance to the disease from a single injection of the blood serum. As the germ could not be detected by cultures, and the organs, further, were apparently normal, it is probable that some other cause than hog cholera caused the death of the animals.

Experiment 2.—The experiment was repeated upon exactly the same number of animals, and in the same way, with the result that the pigs treated with the blood serum recovered entirely, while the checks died. The autopsies of the checks showed characteristic hog cholera lesions, and the germs were abundant in spleen and liver. The experiment repeated again gave the same results—a recovery of the treated animals and the death of the checks.

This work, taken in connection with my earlier results in immunifying guinea pigs,[1] made it apparent that the blood serum was a potent factor in the production of immunity.

While in the case of the use of the albumose extracted from the artificial sterilized cultures, or in the use of the simply sterilized cultures, from 10 to 15 cc., or the equivalent, were required for immunization, here only 3 cc. of the serum were necessary.

TREATMENT OF GUINEA PIGS INOCULATED WITH HOG CHOLERA WITH THE SERUM FROM IMMUNIFIED ANIMALS.

I next tried to cure guinea pigs with the blood serum.

Several pigs were taken, and all inoculated with 0.1 cc. hog cholera culture one day old. Two days afterward two of these animals received an injection of 1.5 cc. of the blood serum from an immunified animal. The other animals were reserved as checks. The injections with the same quantity of serum were repeated after two days. The result of the experiment was that while the checks died within ten days, the treated animals resisted from a week to ten days longer, finally, however, succumbing to hog cholera, as proved by the autopsies.

The experiment was repeated with the same quantity of material, and in the same way, and I succeeded in saving one of the animals, the recovery being entirely satisfactory. All of the checks died. This cure may have been accidental.

At present I am making a more extended series of experiments in this line, beginning the injections with the blood serum within twelve hours after the infection, and repeating them more frequently. In this way it may be possible to effect a cure in every instance.

Just at this point in my experiments the copy of Pasteur's journal[2]

---

[1] The Medical News, October 4, 1890.
[2] Annales de l'Institut Pasteur, May 25, 1892.

reached my hands, in which a series of experiments upon rabbits is described by Metschnikoff, with the germ which he considers to be identical with that of our hog cholera. His results were the same as those I had obtained, an easy immunization by means of the blood serum. Metschnikoff's injections of the blood serum were all intravenous and repeated several times. My injections were subcutaneous. The practical results, however, in both cases were the same.

A few tests were made in order to see if the action of the blood serum was due to its germicidal properties. These experiments showed that the serum outside of the body did not exert a germicidal action on the hog cholera bacillus, and on this point they also agree with Metschnikoff's work.

At the same time that the blood serum experiments were being carried on I had a number of guinea pigs that were being immunified with the albumose extracted from milk cultures, the products from purely artificial mineral salt and glycerine cultures, and with the soluble ferments that I have recently obtained from the hog cholera cultures.

In view of the observations of Roemer,[1] Neisser,[2] Canon,[3] Botkin,[4] and Tschistowitsch[5] I thought it would be of interest to learn if there was a noticeable increase in the number of white corpuscles in the blood of guinea pigs inoculated with the germ alone, and in the animals while being treated and after treatment, when inoculated.

The blood was taken daily from the ear of the animal, and the hemocytometer of Thoma-Zeiss employed for estimating the number of corpuscles. Toison's solution served for the staining fluid. Beginning twenty-four hours after each injection or inoculation the counts were conducted till the animals either died or recovered from the disease. To serve as a check upon the number of white blood corpuscles a healthy animal was also used. Comparing the figures thus obtained, allowing for natural daily variation and individual error in counting, we find an increase in the number of white blood corpuscles, both in the checks and in the treated animals. After the first injection for immunifying the animal the white blood corpuscles apparently increased and then returned to the normal as the animal became well. When these same animals were inoculated the increase of the white corpuscles and return to the normal were equally marked. In the checks those inoculated with the germ showed a decided increase and then decrease in the number of white blood corpuscles till the animal died. These results, though but preliminary as regards the disease of hog cholera, may be considered as throwing some light on Metschnikoff's theory of phagocytosis.

[1] Berl. klin. Woch., 1891, No. 36.
[2] Wiener med. Presse, 1892, Nos. 3, 4, and 5.
[3] Deutsche med. Woch., 1892, No. 10.
[4] Ibid., 1892, No. 15.
[5] Berl. klin. Woch., 1891, No. 34.

While writing this article Kanthack's[1] paper reached my hands. He reports observations upon the leucocytosis produced by the pyocyaneus cultures, and sterilized cultures of the vibrio Metschnikovi. As his injections were made intra-venously and with fairly large amounts of the material, the increase in the number of leucocytes was more rapid. He observed, upon repeated hourly examination, first a decrease and then an enormous increase in the number of white blood corpuscles. In my experiments this increase was not quite so marked nor was the decrease at first noticed, but as the

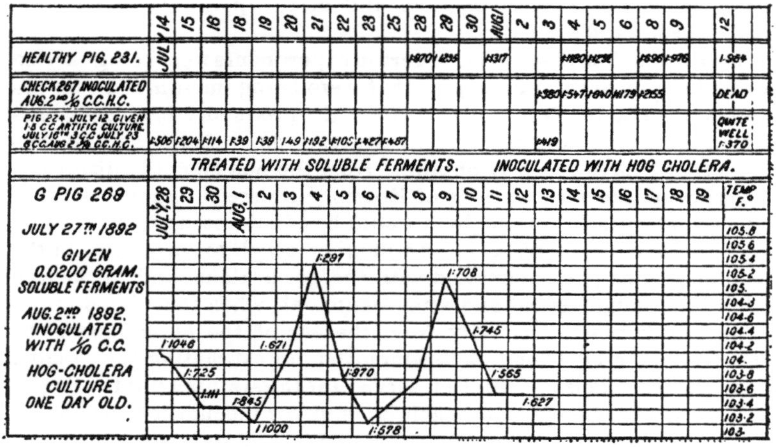

FIG. 37.—Ratio of white to red blood corpuscles.

counting of the corpuscles was not begun till twenty-four hours after the injections it would not have been observed.

In the accompanying chart is represented the relative number of white and red corpuscles as found in a healthy guinea pig, No. 231, in a check, No. 267, and in two treated and then inoculated pigs, Nos. 224 and 269. In the case of No. 269 the corresponding temperatures are also noted. I may take occasion here to acknowledge the help of my assistant, Mr. Emery, in the estimation of the leucocytes.

The results of my work show that there is an easy immunization of guinea pigs from hog cholera by means of the blood serum of immunified animals, and that there is a possible cure of infected animals by a similar treatment. Further, they point to an apparent education of the white blood corpuscles in the blood of guinea pigs by means of the bacterial products.

The work agrees practically with that of Metschnikoff upon rabbits.

[1] Brit. Med. Jour., June 18, 1892.

INOCULATION TO PRODUCE IMMUNITY FROM TEXAS FEVER IN NORTHERN CATTLE.

By E. C. SCHROEDER, M. D. V.,

In Charge of Experiment Station of Bureau of Animal Industry.

Dr. D. E. SALMON,

Chief of Bureau of Animal Industry.

DEAR SIR: I herewith respectfully beg to submit for your consideration a report on an experiment concerning the production of immunity in Northern cattle from the disease known as Texas fever.

The experiment was planned by Dr. V. A. Moore and myself, and was based on the results obtained from previous investigations made by the Bureau under your direction, and published in Bulletins Nos. 1 and 3. The work of immunizing the cattle, which with a proper number of checks were subsequently exposed to Texas fever in the permanently infected region, was done at the experiment station. During the exposure in the South the cattle were in charge of Dr. Cooper Curtice, and it is from his notes that all the facts in connection with the first year of the exposure are taken.

Much credit is due Mr. W. E. Cotton, first assistant at the experiment station, for making careful counts of blood corpuscles.

Very respectfully, yours,　　　　　　　　　　　　E. C. SCHROEDER.

OBJECT AND PLAN OF THE EXPERIMENT.

The object of this experiment is to demonstrate that it is possible, as has already been suggested in Bulletins Nos. 1 and 3 of the Bureau of Animal Industry, to produce a mild, nonfatal attack of Texas fever in Northern cattle, and that a very considerable amount of protection can be derived from such an attack by cattle which are subsequently exposed to the affection in the permanently infected Texas fever territory. For this purpose a number of young cattle were selected, because young animals suffer less severely from Texas fever than older ones. Each was given a hypodermic injection of blood drawn from the jugular vein of a Southern cow, this being the simplest and quickest method known to us by which the disease can be communicated to a susceptible animal. The injections were made during the fall and winter and the cattle exposed in the South during the following spring. The reasons for making the injection in the fall and winter are, on the one hand, that cattle probably suffer less severely from Texas fever during cool weather than during the warm months of summer; and, on the other hand, it seemed desirable to bring the time of recovery from the artificially produced disease and that of the exposure in the South as closely as possible together.

10317——18　　　　　　　　　　　　　　　　　　　　　　273

The severity of the affection resulting from the injection, and afterwards from the exposure, was ascertained in connection with each animal by measuring the degree and duration of the accompanying anæmia, which is probably the most constant determinable condition present in cattle suffering from Texas fever. This was done by estimating, at short intervals, the number of red corpuscles per cubic millimeter of blood. Attention was also given to the temperature, the absence or presence of parasites, and the changes in the character of the blood corpuscles. Beyond this the cattle received no treatment other than that given the healthy animals at the experiment station of the Bureau of Animal Industry.

The blood for injections was obtained from three Southern cows. Nos. 1 and 2 were received from North Carolina late in the spring of 1895, and No. 113 from North Carolina toward the end of the summer of 1889. No. 113 was not exposed to infection after her arrival at the experiment station.

The method of making the injections was as follows: A small incision was made through the previously shaved and disinfected skin over the jugular vein on the neck of the Southern cow which was to supply the blood. The vein was then caused to fill by compressing it below the cut, punctured with a large hypodermic needle, and an outward flow of blood established. A syringe was next connected with the needle by means of a short rubber tube, slowly filled, detached, and its contents immediately injected through a second hypodermic needle under the loose skin over the side of the neck of the Northern animal.

The total number of animals which received injections was 11. Of these, 9, together with 4 other cattle and 5 checks, were subsequently exposed to Texas fever at Manchester, Va. The 4, in addition to the injected and the check animals, will be sufficiently described in the following records of the cattle which were used in the experiment:

RECORD OF CATTLE.

Record of No. 8.

Black-and-white female about 5 months old. A little stunted from having been weaned too early.

October 3, 1895. Condition, fairly good. Number of red corpuscles per cubic millimeter, 7,800,000.

October 4, 1895. Injected with 10 cc. of blood from cow No. 2.

October 14, 1895. Texas fever parasites present in the blood. Number of red corpuscles per cubic millimeter of blood, 5,211,000. ·

October 21, 1895. Extreme variation in the size of the red corpuscles; number per cubic millimeter of blood, 4,166.000.

October 30, 1895. Parasite still present. Number of red corpuscles per cubic millimeter of blood, 4,766,000.

November 11, 1895. Some of the red corpuscles are very large. Number of corpuscles per cubic millimeter of blood, 8,100,000.

November 22, 1895. Number of red corpuscles per cubic millimeter of blood, 2,758,000.

December 3, 1895. Number of red corpuscles per cubic millimeter of blood, 3,390,000.

December 13, 1895. Number of red corpuscles per cubic millimeter of blood, 4,785,000.

January 6, 1896. Number of red corpuscles per cubic millimeter of blood, 5,896,000.

April 21, 1896. Number of red corpuscles per cubic millimeter of blood 6,800,000.

The normal temperature of No. 8 varied from 101° to 103° F. The first high temperature after the injection, 103.8°, occurred on October 12. The next day it rose to 106.5°; October 14 it was 106.3°, and on October 15 it fell to normal and remained so, with an occasional isolated elevation, lasting not more than twelve hours at a time, until November 23, when it rose to 104.8°. Remained at 104° during four days and then became permanently normal.

During the progress of the affection the heifer became quite thin, but was no time in danger of dying. About the middle of December she began to improve in condition, and by the end of April compared favorably with other cattle of about the same age.

May 11, 1896. Shipped to Manchester, Va., and exposed to Texas fever.

Her temperature was moderately high occasionally during July and August. The elevation never lasted more than twenty-four hours at a time. She became well sprinkled with ticks, and remained in fairly good condition. The number of red corpuscles per cubic millimeter of blood was estimated seventeen times during the summer. At its lowest it was 5,000,000 and averaged about 6,000,000. Beyond a slight reduction in the number of red corpuscles, no condition characteristic of Texas fever was observed.

The exposure was continued throughout the year 1897, at the end of which time she was sold in good condition.

Record of No. 10.

Female, black with white marks, about 15 months old.

October 4, 1895. Condition fair. Injected with 10 cc. of blood from cow No. 113.

October 5, 1895. Number of red corpuscles per cubic millimeter of blood, 8,297,000.

October 14, 1895. Number of red corpuscles per cubic millimeter of blood, 5,516,000. Texas fever parasites present in considerable number.

October 21, 1895. Some of the red corpuscles are very large. Number per cubic millimeter of blood, 3,640,000.

October 29, 1895. Number of red corpuscles per cubic millimeter, 4,690,000. A small number of parasites present.

November 11, 1895. Number of red corpuscles per cubic millimeter of blood, 4,941,000.

November 19, 1895. Number of red corpuscles per cubic millimeter, 6,126,000.

December 5, 1895. Number of red corpuscles per cubic millimeter of blood, 7,590,000.

January 4, 1896. Number of red corpuscles per cubic millimeter of blood, 9,191,000.

April 21, 1896. Number of red corpuscles per cubic millimeter of blood, 9,185,600.

The normal temperature of No. 10 varied from 100° to 102.5° F. The first elevation, 104.7°, occurred October 12. The day following the temperature was 105°; October 14, 106°; October 16, 103.6°. After the last-named date it fell to normal and remained so permanently, with the exception of an occasional moderate elevation, not above 104°, lasting not more than twelve hours at a time.

As a result of the affection the heifer became quite thin, but was at no time dangerously ill. About the middle of November she began to improve in condition, and by the end of December was as well and strong as before the injection.

May 11, 1896. Shipped to Manchester, Va., and exposed to Texas fever.

Her temperature was high from June 18 to June 21, from 104.5° to 106.4° F. The number of red corpuscles per cubic millimeter of blood at the end of June was 6,000,000, near which mark it remained until August 28, when it fell to 3,122,000.

September 10, 1896. Number of red corpuscles per cubic millimeter of blood, 3,931,000.

September 14, 1896. Number of red corpuscles per cubic millimeter of blood, 4,528,000.

September 21, 1896. Number of red corpuscles per cubic millimeter of blood, 5,070,000.

September 28, 1896. Number of red corpuscles per cubic millimeter of blood, 6,636,000.

Throughout the exposure the physical condition of the heifer was fairly good. Shortly after her arrival at Manchester she contracted a bad cold, which was accompanied by considerable discharge from her eyes, which were inflamed and swollen. Complete recovery from this trouble was not made until the middle of June, when she commenced to improve in condition.

The exposure was continued throughout the year 1897, at the end of which time she was sold in good condition.

Record of No. 14.

Female about 4 months old.

October 3, 1895. Condition fair; somewhat stunted from having been weaned too early. Number of red corpuscles per cubic millimeter of blood, 10,000,000.

October 4, 1895. Injected with 10 cc. of blood from cow No. 2.

October 14, 1895. A few large Texas fever parasites present. Number of red corpuscles per cubic millimeter of blood, 9,961,000.

October 15, 1895. Number of red corpuscles per cubic millimeter of blood, 6,600,000.

October 30, 1895. Number of red corpuscles per cubic millimeter of blood, 5,000,000. Parasites present in the blood. The corpuscles vary greatly in size.

November 11, 1895. Number of red corpuscles per cubic millimeter of blood, 4,550,000. Large parasites present.

November 21, 1895. Great variation in the size of the red corpuscles, which number 5,162,000 per cubic millimeter of blood.

December 3, 1895. Number of red corpuscles per cubic millimeter of blood, 9,160,000.

December 13, 1895. Number of red corpuscles per cubic millimeter of blood, 9,240,000.

January 6, 1896. Number of red corpuscles per cubic millimeter of blood, 9,415,000.

The temperature of this animal did not rise above 103.2° F. at any time. There was a slight loss in flesh, but restoration to the normal condition was very rapid. Retained at the experiment station for further observation.

Record of No. 16.

Red male about 8 months old.

September 12, 1895. Condition fair; probably a little stunted from having been weaned too early. Injected with 8 cc. of blood from cow No. 1. Number of red corpuscles per cubic millimeter of blood, 8,900,000.

September 23, 1895. Number of red corpuscles per cubic millimeter of blood, 9,764,000. Several large Texas fever parasites observed in the blood.

October 1, 1895. Number of red corpuscles per cubic millimeter of blood, 8,107,000.

October 14, 1895. Number of red corpuscles per cubic millimeter of blood, 2,814,000. A small number of large parasites present.

October 20, 1895. All the red corpuscles are larger than normal. The number per cubic millimeter of blood is 2,195,000.

October 29, 1895. Number of red corpuscles per cubic millimeter of blood, 2,649,000.

November 11, 1895. Number of red corpuscles per cubic millimeter of blood, 4,200,000.

November 22, 1895. Number of red corpuscles per cubic millimeter of blood, 8,925,000.

December 2, 1895. Number of red corpuscles per cubic millimeter of blood, 4,236,000.

December 11, 1895. Number of red corpuscles per cubic millimeter of blood, 5,186,000.

December 16, 1895. Number of red corpuscles per cubic millimeter of blood, 4,970,000.

January 6, 1896. Number of red corpuscles per cubic millimeter of blood, 6,712,000.

April 21, 1896. Number of red corpuscles per cubic millimeter of blood, 7,164,000.

The normal temperature of No. 16 varied from 101° to 104° F. A slight rise occurred September 20 and lasted until the 25th, the highest point reached was 104.8°. A second rise in temperature occurred October 12 and lasted until October 16; during this period the number of degrees varied from 104° to 106.8°. The temperature then fell to normal and remained so permanently.

The calf became very thin during the progress of the affection, and for a time his recovery was extremely doubtful. He began to improve toward the end of November. March 6, 1896, he was castrated. The operation was bloodless and was not attended by any evil conditions.

May 11, 1896. Shipped to Manchester, Va., and exposed to Texas fever. During the exposure, with the exception of a very slight reduction in the number of red corpuscles, the number of which per cubic millimeter was estimated twenty-eight times, and an elevation of temperature from July 11 to the 13th, and from the 27th to the 30th, no condition characteristic of Texas fever was observed. He lost a little in condition during the latter part of July, had an attack of diarrhea about the end of August, and was in better condition at the end of the year than at the time he left the experiment station.

Exposure continued throughout the year 1897, at the end of which time he was sold in good condition.

Record of No. 21.

Roan female about 15 months old.

October 4, 1895. Condition fairly good. Injected with 10 cc. of blood from cow No. 1.

October 5, 1895. Number of red corpuscles per cubic millimeter of blood, 5,470,000.

October 14, 1895. Number of red corpuscles per cubic millimeter of blood, 5,800,000. Texas fever parasites present in the blood.

October 20, 1895. Considerable variation in the size of red corpuscles; number per cubic milimeter of blood, 3,797,000:

October 29, 1895. Number of red corpuscles per cubic millimeter of blood, 4,050,000. All the red corpuscles appear larger than normal.

November 19, 1895. Corpuscles all appear larger than normal. Number of red corpuscles per cubic millimeter of blood, 1,502,000.

November 21, 1895. Number of red corpuscles per cubic millimeter of blood, 2,125,000.

December 5, 1895. Number of red corpuscles per cubic millimeter of blood, 3,252,000.

January 4, 1896. Number of red corpuscles per cubic millimeter of blood, 4,263,000.

April 21, 1896. Number of red corpuscles per cubic millimeter of blood, 6,154,000.

The normal temperature of No. 21 varied from 100° to 102.5° F. The first elevation after the injection occurred October 14 and lasted until October 22, during which time the variation ranged between 104° and 106.2°. A second rise in temperature, which reached its greatest height at 103.4°, lasted from November 18 to the 22d, after which the temperature fell to and remained normal.

During the course of the affection the heifer became very thin, and for a time it was very doubtful whether she would recover. She began to improve in condition about the end of November, but the improvement was very gradual and slow.

May 11, 1896. Shipped to Manchester, Va., and exposed to Texas fever. During the exposure she remained in good condition, and it was impossible to make a diagnosis of Texas fever. Her temperature did not rise above normal and there was no destruction of red blood corpuscles.

Exposure continued throughout the year 1897, at the end of which time she was sold in good condition.

Record of No. 23.

Black female about 3 months old.

October 3, 1895. Condition fairly good; probably a little stunted from having been weaned too early. Number of red corpuscles per cubic millimeter of blood, 9,750,000.

October 4, 1895. Injected with 10 cc. of blood from cow No. 1.

October 14, 1895. Number of red corpuscles per cubic millimeter of blood, 7,962,000.

October 20, 1895. Number of red corpuscles per cubic millimeter of blood, 5,880,000.

October 30, 1895. Number of red corpuscles per cubic millimeter of blood, 6,233,000.

November 11, 1895. Number of red corpuscles per cubic millimeter of blood, 4,566,000. One large Texas fever parasite observed in the blood.

November 22, 1895. All the corpuscles appear larger than normal. Number of red corpuscles per cubic millimeter, 4,692,000.

December 2, 1895. Number of red corpuscles per cubic millimeter of blood, 5,783,000.

December 13, 1895. Number of red corpuscles per cubic millimeter of blood, 7,480,000.

January 4, 1896. Number of red corpuscles per cubic millimeter of blood, 7,492,000.

April 21, 1896. Number of red corpuscles per cubic millimeter of blood, 9,700,000.

The normal temperature of No. 26 varied from 101° to 103.5' F. A rise occurred October 13 and was continuous until October 20; the highest mark reached was 104.6° and the average about 104°. Following this the temperature remained normal with the exception of one day, November 1, on which it was 105.6°. During the affection the calf showed only very little discomfort and remained in fairly good condition.

May 11, 1896. Shipped to Manchester, Va., and exposed to Texas fever. As a result of the exposure no Texas fever could be diagnosed. There was no elevation of temperature, no destruction of red corpuscles, and no reduction in physical condition.

Exposure continued during the year 1897, at the end of which time she was sold in good condition.

Record of No. 25.

Red-and-white male about 5 months old.

October 4, 1895. Condition fairly good. Injected with 10 cc. of blood from cow No. 113.

As the result of the injection he did not become noticeably affected with Texas fever. The temperature remained normal and there was practically no destruction of red blood corpuscles. The normal number of red corpuscles was about 10,000,000 per cubic millimeter of blood, and did not at any time fall below 7,500,000. Some variation in the size of the red corpuscles was observed. On March 5, 1896, he was castrated; bloodless operation.

May 11, 1896. Shipped to Manchester, Va., and exposed to Texas fever. He became well sprinkled with ticks, remained in good condition throughout the entire exposure, and with the exception of an elevated temperature from May 25 to May 27, and an occasional high temperature of short duration in July and August, showed no symptoms of Texas fever. The number of red blood corpuscles was estimated thirty times during the exposure and was found to vary from about 6,000,000 to 8,000,000 per cubic millimeter of blood.

Exposure continued through the year 1897, at the end of which time he was sold in good condition.

Record of No. 26.

Female about 5 months old.

October 4, 1895. Condition fairly good. Injected with 10 cc. of blood from cow No. 113.

As a result of the injection she suffered a slight attack of Texas fever, accompanied by a moderately elevated temperature. No parasites were observed in the blood. From October 14 till November 21 a gradual reduction in the number of red blood corpuscles occurred, which fell from 8,377,000 to 4,270,000 per cubic millimeter of blood. The diagnosis of Texas fever in No. 26 would have been impossible without careful estimates from time to time of the number of red blood corpuscles.

Retained at the experiment station for further observation.

Record of No. 29.

Dark-brown male about 5½ months old.

February 6, 1896. Condition poor. Number of red corpuscles, 6,550,000 per cubic millimeter of blood.

February 11, 1896. Injected with 10 cc. of blood from cow No. 1.

February 20, 1896. Number of red corpuscles per cubic millimeter of blood, 5,121,000.

February 27, 1896. Number of red corpuscles per cubic millimeter of blood, 4,402,000.

March 6, 1896. Castrated; bloodless operation.

March 11, 1896. Number of red corpuscles per cubic millimeter of blood, 4,032,000.

March 26, 1896. Number of red corpuscles per cubic millimeter of blood, 1,788,000. All the red corpuscles are much larger than normal.

April 22, 1896. Number of red corpuscles per cubic millimeter of blood, 5,364,000.

The temperature of No. 29 was very irregular both before and after the injection. It remained elevated at no time longer than two consecutive days. He was in poor condition when the injection was made, and afterwards became extremely emaciated, but at no time seemed in danger of dying.

May 11, 1896. Shipped to Manchester, Va., and exposed to Texas fever. During the exposure he became well sprinkled with ticks, gained rapidly in physical condition, and did not have an attack of Texas fever.

Exposure continued through the year 1897, at the end of which time he was sold in good condition.

Record of No. 30.

Black male about 5¼ months old.

February 8, 1896. Condition poor. Number of red corpuscles per cubic millimeter of blood, 8,726,000.

February 11, 1896. Injected with 10 cc. of blood from cow No. 1.

February 20, 1896. Number of red corpuscles per cubic millimeter of blood, 8,953,000.

February 27, 1896. Number of red corpuscles per cubic millimeter of blood, 5,906,000.

March 6, 1896. Castrated; operation followed by a considerable hemorrhage.

March 11, 1896. Large parasites present in the blood. Number of red corpuscles per cubic millimeter of blood, 2,538,000.

March 26, 1896. Great variation in the size of the red corpuscles. Number of red corpuscles per cubic millimeter of blood, 2,479,000.

April 22, 1896. Number of red corpuscles per cubic millimeter of blood, 4.643,000.

The temperature of No. 30 remained normal, with the exception of a moderate elevation, from February 21 to February 25· He was poor when injected and became very much reduced in condition, but at no time seemed in danger of dying.

May 11, 1896. Shipped to Manchester, Va., and exposed to Texas fever. He became well sprinkled with ticks, gained slowly in condition, and did not have an attack of Texas fever.

Exposure continued during the year 1897, at the end of which time he was sold in good condition.

Record of No. 32.

Black female about 3 months old.

February 8, 1896. Condition fair. Number of corpuscles per cubic millimeter of blood, 11,230,000.

February 11, 1896. Injected with 10 cc. of blood from cow No. 1.

February 20, 1896. Number of red corpuscles per cubic millimeter of blood, 11,000,000.

February 27, 1896. Number of red corpuscles per cubic millimeter of blood, 8,000,000.

March 11, 1896. Number of red corpuscles per cubic millimeter of blood, 6,046,000.

March 26, 1896. Number of red corpuscles per cubic millimeter of blood, 2,648,000.

April 22, 1896. Number of red corpuscles per cubic millimeter of blood, 5,376,000.

The temperature of No. 32 remained normal during the attack of Texas fever, with the exception of an occasional moderate elevation of not more than twenty-four hours' duration. She became very thin, but was at no time in danger of dying.

May 11, 1896. Shipped to Manchester, Va., and exposed to Texas fever. She became well sprinkled with ticks, gained rapidly in condition, and did not have an attack of Texas fever.

Exposure continued during the year 1897, at the end of which time she was sold in good condition.

Record of No. 12.

June 19, 1895. Born at the experiment station, daughter of cow No. 214. The mother was received from North Carolina in the summer of 1892, and a subsequent experiment proved that her blood still retained its infectious character, apparently in undiminished virulence.

June 29, 1895. Removed from her mother and turned into a field containing two Southern cows with ticks, Nos. 1 and 2, which had recently arrived at the station from the permanently infected region. One of the cows, No. 2, was made to adopt and raise the calf.

A number of adult cattle turned into the same field at different times during the summer became affected with Texas fever and died in consequence in from twelve to twenty days.

No. 12 remained in the field with her foster-mother throughout the entire summer and fall of 1895. Her temperature remained normal and her condition fairly good. About 5,000 ticks matured on her body. The number of red blood corpuscles, which was 8,666,666 when she was turned into the field, did not at any time fall below 6,288,000 per cubic millimeter of blood. Some variation in the size of the red corpuscles occurred, but no parasites were discovered in the blood. It can not be positively asserted that she suffered an attack of Texas fever.

May 11, 1896. Shipped to Manchester, Va., and exposed to Texas fever. As a result of the exposure No. 12 had a severe attack of Texas fever, accompanied by extreme anæmia. Her temperature was very irregular, high one day and low the next; never remaining either one or the other longer than a day or two at a time. The number of red blood corpuscles was 8,555,000 per cubic millimeter of blood shortly after her arrival in Manchester. On July 29 it had fallen to 5,340,000; August 3, to 2,368,000; August 4, to 2,114,000, and August 5 the lowest mark was reached, 1,448,000 per cubic millimeter. About August 10 the number of blood corpuscles commenced to increase, very slowly, however, and the normal number was not again reached until late in October. The animal became very thin and weak, and at times her recovery was very doubtful.

Exposure continued during the year 1897, at the end of which time she was sold in good condition.

Record of No. 17.

Red-and-white cow about 9 years old.

August 6, 1895. Condition good. Injected with 10 cc. of a suspension of recently hatched crushed ticks in sterile water. The suspension was opaque in a layer one-half an inch thick.

September 11, 1895. No result from the injection. Turned into a field containing North Carolina cows with ticks.

April 22, 1896. The exposure was followed by no symptoms of Texas fever, excepting a slight variation in the size of the red blood corpuscles, and a reduction of the same from 6,800,000 per cubic millimeter of blood to 4,900,000 per cubic millimeter.

May 11, 1896. Shipped to Manchester, Va., and exposed to Texas fever. During the first part of the exposure No. 17 improved greatly in condition and by the end of June was quite fat. July 3 her temperature commenced to rise; July 4 it was 106° F., at which mark it remained until July 8, when it began to fall slowly, reaching normal July 10. The number of red blood corpuscles at the end of June was 6,882,000; by July 8 it had fallen to 2,884,000 per cubic millimeter of blood. It then rose by the middle of August to about 5,000,000. A second destruction of red corpuscles commenced about August 20, and was continuous until September 7, at which time the anæmia was greatest. The number of red blood corpuscles per cubic millimeter of blood was only 1,200,000. September 28 she was six months pregnant, and aborted. During the progress of the affection she became very thin, and at times her recovery was very doubtful.

Exposure continued through the year 1897, at the end of which time she was sold in good condition.

Record of No. 18.

Jersey cow about 8 years old.

August 8, 1895. Condition poor. Injected with one-half cc. of blood from cow No. 113. The object of this injection was to find the minimum amount of blood from a Southern cow which would produce Texas fever.

September 11, 1895. No result from the injection. Exposed in field containing two North Carolina cows with ticks. She had a mild attack of Texas fever. No parasites were discovered in her blood. The number of red blood corpuscles was reduced from 5,208,000 per cubic millimeter of blood to 2,425,000 per cubic millimeter.

April 22, 1896. In fair condition and good health.

May 11, 1896. Shipped to Manchester, Va., and exposed to Texas fever. A severe attack of Texas fever resulted from the exposure. The temperature was high from June 14 to June 16, and again from July 28 to July 30. No reduction in the number of red corpuscles occurred until the end of August. From September 1 to September 7 the number of red corpuscles per cubic millimeter of blood dropped from 5,000,000 to 2,000,000. September 14 the anæmia was greatest—1,460,000 red corpuscles per cubic millimeter of blood. The cow remained in fairly good physical condition throughout the attack and made a slow but uninterrupted recovery.

Exposure continued during the year 1897, at the end of which time she was sold in good condition.

Record of No. 203.

Black cow about 10 years old.

September 10, 1894. Condition good. Infected with young ticks hatched in the laboratory of the Bureau of Animal Industry. The result was a very mild attack of Texas fever.

August 19, 1895. Turned into a field containing two North Carolina cows with ticks. In consequence she had a fairly severe attack of Texas fever. The normal number of red blood corpuscles was about 5,000,000, and this fell between August 30 and September 4 to 3,300,000 per cubic millimeter of blood, and remained at that mark until the end of September, when it commenced to rise, and regained normal by the middle of October.

November 15, 1895. Gave birth to a small but healthy calf.

May 11, 1896. Shipped to Manchester, Va., and exposed to Texas fever. As a result of the exposure she had a very mild attack of Texas fever, unaccompanied by a high temperature. The destruction of red corpuscles was only very small and her condition remained good.

Exposure continued during the year 1897, at the end of which time she was sold in good condition.

Record of No. 23.

Cow from 7 to 8 years old. Condition fairly good.

May 11, 1896. Shipped to Manchester, Va., and exposed to Texas fever as a check.

May 25, 1896. In good condition; well sprinkled with ticks.

June 16, 1896. The temperature was 105° F., at which mark it remained stationary until June 17, when it rose to 106.4°. On June 18 the temperature was 106.4°, and on June 19, 107.2°. Number of red blood corpuscles per cubic millimeter previous to the exposure, 5,071,000; on June 18, 5,100,000; June 19, 4,077,000; June 20, 2,050,000.

June 20, 1896. Cow died about 9 p. m.

June 21, 1896. Post-mortem examination made at 6 a. m.

Autopsy notes.—General condition fair. About 300 young ticks scattered over the body, principally on the abdomen. The spleen is from three to four times as large as normal; its substance is very soft and of a blue-black color. Liver is enlarged, friable, and stained a yellow color. The gall bladder contains about a quart of dark green bile. Kidneys are enlarged, softened, and congested. The urinary bladder contains about a gallon of dark, claret-colored urine. The pericardium is distended with blood-colored fluid. Ecchymoses are present under the epicardium and endocardium. Microscopic examination of tissues from the various organs shows the presence of Texas fever parasites in from 60 to 80 per cent of the visible blood corpuscles.

Record of No. 35.

Cow about 3 years old. Condition good.

May 11, 1896. Shipped to Manchester, Va., and exposed to Texas fever as a check.

June 30, 1896. Has been doing very well to this date, on which her temperature has risen to 105.6° F. Number of red blood corpuscles per cubic millimeter of blood, 6,000,000.

July 1, 1896. Temperature: Morning, 105°; evening, 105.6°. Number of red corpuscles per cubic millimeter of blood, 5,384,000.

July 2, 1896. Number of red corpuscles per cubic millimeter of blood, 5,000,000.

July 3, 1896. Number of red corpuscles per cubic millimeter of blood, 3,930,000. The cow is losing rapidly in physical condition. Temperature throughout the entire day, 106°.

July 4 and 5, 1896. Number of red corpuscles per cubic millimeter of blood, 3,000,000. Temperature from 107° to 107.4°. Urine clouded and of a pale red color.

July 6, 1896. Number of red corpuscles per cubic millimeter of blood, 2,507,000. Temperature, 107.4°.

July 7, 1896. Number of red corpuscles per cubic millimeter of blood, 1,225,000. Temperature, 107.2°. The cow is very thin and extremely weak.

July 8, 1896. Number of red corpuscles per cubic millimeter of blood, 1,540,000. The temperature has fallen to 102.2° in the evening; in the morning it was 104°.

July 9, 1896. Found dead in the morning; had died during the night.

Autopsy notes.—General condition very poor. Well sprinkled with ticks. The spleen is two to three times as large as normal; its substance is in the form of a dark, almost black, mush. The liver is firm, enlarged, and stained a yellow color. Gall bladder empty. The kidneys are softened and pale in color. The urinary bladder is filled with nearly 3 gallons of red wine-colored urine. Pericardium distended by 6 to 8 ounces of red fluid. Blood extravasation under the membranes of the heart and into its muscular tissue. Microscopic examination of cover-glass preparations from the various organs shows the presence of Texas fever parasites in 5 per cent of the visible blood corpuscles.

Record of No. 37.

Yearling steer. Condition fairly good.

May 11, 1896. Shipped to Manchester, Va., and exposed to Texas fever as a check.

June 20, 1896. In good condition and in good health up to this date, on which the temperature has risen to 104.8° F. Number of red blood corpuscles per cubic millimeter of blood, 7,569,000.

June 21, 1896. Temperature: Morning, 104.8°; evening, 106.2°.

June 22, 1896. Temperature 106.4°. Number of red corpuscles per cubic millimeter of blood, 6,800,000.

June 23, 1896. Temperature 106.4°. Number of red corpuscles per cubic millimeter of blood, 5,634,000.

June 24, 1896. Temperature 107.2°. Number of red corpuscles per cubic millimeter of blood, 3,670,000.

June 25, 1896. Temperature 106.8°. Number of red corpuscles per cubic millimeter of blood, 2,770,000.

June 26, 1896. Died this morning.

Autopsy notes.—General condition poor. Well sprinkled with ticks. The spleen is from four to five times as large as normal; its substance is dark red in color and very soft   Liver enlarged and stained a yellow color. The kidneys are pale and softened. The urinary bladder contains a few drops of clear urine. A few extravasations of blood under the epicardium. The blood generally is very thin and fluid. Microscopic examination of cover-glass preparations from the various organs shows the presence of Texas fever parasites in 5 per cent of the visible blood corpuscles.

Record of No. 38.

Yearling heifer. Condition fairly good.

May 11, 1896. Shipped to Manchester, Va., and exposed to Texas fever as a check.

From May 22 to 24 the temperature was slightly elevated, from 103.6° to 104.4° F. No destruction of red blood corpuscles has occurred; they number about 7,000,000 per cubic millimeter of blood. From June 30 till July 8 the temperature was constantly high, varying between 104.8° and 107.2°. The number of red blood corpuscles did not begin to fall until July 2, when it was 6,500,000 per cubic millimeter of blood.

July 3, 1896. Number of red corpuscles per cubic millimeter of blood, 5,185,000.

July 4, 1896. Number of red corpuscles per cubic millimeter of blood, 3,750,000.

July 6, 1896. Number of red corpuscles per cubic millimeter of blood, 2,800,000.

July 7, 1896. Number of red corpuscles per cubic millimeter of blood, 2,481,000.

July 8, 1896. Number of red corpuscles per cubic millimeter of blood, 1,800,000.

July 9, 1896. The heifer was killed at 6.30 p.m., in a dying condition, and was examined post-mortem.

Autopsy notes.—General condition poor. Well sprinkled with ticks. The spleen is four times as large as normal; its substance is dark red, almost black, in color and very soft. The liver is enlarged and stained a yellow color. Gall bladder nearly empty. The kidneys are pale and much softened. The urinary bladder contains a small amount of clear urine. Microscopic examination of cover-glass preparations from the various organs shows the presence of Texas fever parasites in 5 per cent of the visible blood corpuscles.

Record of No. 39.

Yearling steer.   Condition fairly good.

May 11, 1896.   Shipped to Manchester, Va., and exposed to Texas fever as a check.

Remained in good physical condition, with a normal temperature and no destruction of red blood corpuscles until the end of June. Normal number of red corpuscles per cubic millimeter of blood, 7,727,000. The temperature rose to 104.8° F. on June 30 and remained high without intermission until July 18. The highest temperature recorded is 107.8°; the average for the time specified is 106°. During the period of high temperature a rapid destruction of red blood corpuscles was in progress. July 2 the number per cubic millimeter of blood was 5,850.000 ; July 3, 6,353,000 ; July 4, 5,218,000 ; July 5, 3,577,000 ; July 6, 2,910,000, and July 7, 2,409,000. July 8 the number of red corpuscles reached the lowest point—2,173,000 per cubic millimeter of blood—at which it remained until July 18 and then commenced to rise, reaching 5,745,000 per cubic millimeter by the middle of August. A second destruction of red corpuscles then began, and by August 28 the number of red corpuscles had again fallen to 2,854,000 per cubic millimeter of blood. From the end of August the recovery was rapid and uninterrupted.

No. 39 is the only one of the five checks which survived the exposure. He suffered a severe attack of Texas fever, became extremely thin and weak, but by the end of October was restored to fairly good condition. He was exposed during the year 1897, at the end of which time he was sold in good condition.

During the second year of the exposure the cattle were carefully examined about the middle of March and again in the latter half of September. At the time of the first examination all, with the exception of No. 8, were in good health and condition, and had a normal temperature and a normal number of red blood corpuscles. No. 8 was very thin, covered with lice, and the number of red corpuscles per cubic millimeter of blood was only one-half what it should have been. When the last examination was made, all the cattle, with the exception of No. 293, were in excellent condition. No. 293 was a little thin. Her temperature and number of red corpuscles were normal. At the time the exposed cattle were examined in March, 1897, a number of native Southern cattle, which were to pass through the summer under similar conditions, were also examined. The Southern animals were again examined with the exposed herd in September. It was found that the condition of the exposed cattle was fully as good, in all respects, both in March and in September of 1897, as that of the native Southern animals.

It will be seen from the foregoing record that the disease produced in eleven susceptible cattle by the injection of blood from Southern cows, although severe in several individuals, was not followed by a single death. Only two animals, No. 16, injected September 12, and No. 21, a yearling, became so sick as to make their recovery appear doubtful. Among the injected cattle were four young males. Two were castrated after they had recovered from the injection and two during the active stage of the consequent affection. Excepting a considerable hemorrhage in one (No. 30) of the latter, the operation was unattended by complications. It is not to be inferred from this that castration is recommended at a time when cattle are suffering from an immunizing attack of Texas fever. On the contrary, the hemorrhage in No. 30 is largely to be attributed to the condition of his blood. It has been observed frequently that the blood of cattle, very anæmic as a result of Texas fever, flows with unusual freedom from very small injuries to the skin, and that it is often almost impossible to check this flow.

The injections were made on three different dates—September 12, October 4, and February 11. The first date is, for this climate, undoubtedly too early; the same is in some measure true of the second. February 11 may prove a little too late to allow time for a complete recovery before the exposure, which is a matter of much importance, because exposure means not only Texas fever but also changed climatic conditions. The best time probably is from the middle of December to the middle of January.

The blood for the injections was obtained from three Southern cows, Nos. 1 and 2, recent arrivals from the infected territory, and No. 113, a cow which had not been exposed to infection for six years. For some reason the disease produced by the blood from cow No. 1 was more severe than that caused by the blood from the two other cows. As this was not true of all the animals which received blood from No. 1, the circumstance may have no significance. Otherwise, investigations regarding the severity of the affection produced by the blood from different Southern cattle may lead to some interesting and practically useful conclusions.

The blood of No. 113, it will be seen, still retained its infectious character, a fact which was more perfectly illustrated earlier in the same year. July 19, 1895, an old cow received a hypodermic injection of 10 cc. of the blood of No. 113. The injection was followed by fever, a rapid destruction of red blood corpuscles, and death on the eleventh day after the injection. Blood preparations, examined the day before and immediately after death, showed the presence of large Texas fever parasites in from 50 to 75 per cent of the blood corpuscles.

Of the eleven injected cattle nine were exposed to Texas fever in the permanently infected territory. During the exposure they suffered to some degree from exceptionally warm weather. No. 10, one of the two older cattle which received an injection, suffered a mild but well-marked attack of Texas fever. Her companion in age, No. 21, remained perfectly well. The former had a mild, and the latter a very severe, affection previous to the exposure. This confirms the opinion previously advanced by the Bureau of Animal Industry that the amount of protection gained from one attack of Texas fever depends in a great measure more or less directly upon the severity of that attack. The remaining seven animals either escaped the disease entirely or suffered to so slight an extent that a diagnosis under ordinary circumstances would have been impossible.

Heifer No. 12 presents a remarkable condition. Her mother was a Southern cow carrying the infection in her blood, and her foster mother a cow recently removed from the infected territory. She was exposed almost from her birth to conditions similar to what she was expected to encounter in the South, and it was believed when she was sent South that she would be practically on a footing with native Southern cattle. In fact, she was regarded as the best protected animal in the herd. The result of the exposure was a very severe attack of Texas fever, accompanied by extreme anæmia. Standing alone, as a single case of the kind, it must be admitted that No. 12 does not furnish sufficient material for reasonable conclusions. The severe affection from which she suffered in the South, however, suggests that the offspring of Southern cattle inherit no immunity from Texas˙ fever, and that a simple exposure to Southern cattle and disease-carrying ticks during the early months of life north of the infected territory does not supply much power of resistance. The question also presents itself whether there is some source from which cattle born in the permanently infected territory acquire immunity from Southern cattle ticks other than by exposure from birth.

Cows Nos. 17 and 18 show that a very mild attack of Texas fever affords some protection. Whether No. 17 gained anything from the injection of crushed ticks, or No. 18 from the injection of one-half cc. of blood from cow No. 113, is not known, but appears very doubtful. A series of experiments to determine the effects of injecting crushed tick eggs and crushed ticks of various ages is very desirable, and may lead to means of protecting cattle with much less suffering than results from injections of infectious blood.

Cow No. 293 had suffered two attacks of Texas fever produced by exposure to ticks previous to her exposure in the South. She is principally interesting in connection with No. 12, as the conditions through which she gained a good practical immunity were similar to a part of the conditions to which No. 12 was subjected. No. 293 was an old animal, and hence it is surprising that she should have suffered so much less severely than No. 12.

Two of the cattle which were injected with infectious blood, Nos. 14 and 26, were not exposed in the South. They were carefully watched during the summers of 1896 and 1897, in a certain sense as checks. It was believed necessary to know whether any disease following the exposure of the injected cattle in the South was due to a new infection or to a recurrence of the affection resulting from the injection. Nos. 14 and 26 remained in perfect health.

The check cattle, five in number, were one cow, No. 22, younger than cattle Nos. 17, 18, and 293; one cow, No. 35, as nearly of the age of Nos. 10 and 21 as it was possible to obtain a suitable animal at the time the cattle were sent South; and three yearlings, Nos. 37, 38, and 39, the age of which corresponded with that of the younger protected cattle. Only one of the checks survived the exposure, a young male, No. 39, and he suffered a very severe attack of Texas fever, showing that the infection in the territory selected for the exposure possessed sufficient virulence to produce fatal disease in both old and young unprotected cattle.

Below a table is given showing in concise, practical form the character of the affection suffered by each animal before and during the exposure in the permanently infected Texas fever territory. The table is in three parts. The first embraces the cattle which received injections of infectious blood, the second the cattle which received other protective treatment, and the third the cattle used as checks:

Table showing the affection suffered by each animal before and during exposure in infected territory.

1.—RECEIVED INJECTIONS OF BLOOD.

Number of animal.	Affection before the exposure.	Affection during the exposure.
8	Severe	Very mild.
10	Severe	Well marked, but mild.
14	Mild	Not exposed.
16	Very severe	Very mild.
21	Very severe	No disease.
23	Mild	No disease.
25	Mild	Very mild.
26	Mild	Not exposed.
29	Severe	No disease.
30	Severe	No disease.
32	Severe	No disease.

2.—RECEIVED OTHER PROTECTIVE TREATMENT.

12	Practically no disease	Very severe.
17	Very mild	Very severe.
18	Mild	Very severe.
293	1 mild and 1 severe	Very mild.

3.—CHECKS.

22	No disease	Died June 20.
35	No disease	Died July 9.
37	No disease	Died June 26.
38	No disease	Died July 9.
39	No disease	Very severe disease.

INVESTIGATIONS CONCERNING TUBERCULOSIS AND GLANDERS.[1]

SOME RESULTS IN THE TREATMENT OF TUBERCULOSIS WITH ANTITUBERCULOSIS SERUM.

By E. A. DE SCHWEINITZ, Ph. D., M. D.,

Chief of Biochemic Division, Bureau of Animal Industry.

GENERAL REMARKS ON PRESENT STATE OF SERUM TREATMENT.

Although we occasionally find in the literature reports of cases treated with tuberculin as originally prepared by Koch, and in many instances improvement has been recorded, its use as a therapeutic agent has, except in special cases, been discarded. Its value, on the other hand, for the early diagnosis of tuberculosis in animals is generally recognized, and in some States, as in Pennsylvania, the law requires that all animals that are to be used for dairy purposes shall pass the tuberculin test. Following the careful methods proposed by Dr. Trudeau, tuberculin offers also a means of positive diagnosis in man, and of indicating whether the disease, after treatment, has been arrested or cured.

When tuberculin failed to give satisfactory results as a curative agent, attention was quickly directed to the preparation of a serum on the same principle as the diphtheria antitoxic serum. Maragliano, Babes, Behring, and others prepared such a material for the treatment of tuberculosis by injecting horses with tuberculin alone, or a combination of tuberculin and virulent tubercle cultures. After long-continued injections of the animals, the serum obtained was claimed to have antitoxic properties, and when this serum was injected subcutaneously into tuberculous animals, together with a dose of tuberculin, the fatal effects or characteristic rise of temperature from the latter were counteracted. The strength of the serum was based upon the quantity necessary to prevent a tuberculin reaction. This method, however, did not fulfill all the conditions. In the first place, as tuberculin is prepared from the cultures of the germ, it is submitted to such a temperature that some of the products of the germ life are

---

[1] Some of the articles appearing under this head have been published elsewhere, but they are brought together here in order to show the various stages of the progress of the work along these lines as pursued by the Bureau of Animal Industry.

changed or decomposed, and hence tuberculin as used does not represent the poisons of the tubercle germ as they are actually found in the animals suffering from this disease. Consequently a serum which counteracts the fever-producing properties of tuberculin does not necessarily exert a beneficial influence upon all the phases of the disease in man.

Assuming that while it may not be possible to establish a perfect artificial immunity in man, but that the disease may be checked by reenforcing the natural resistance which is always present, we have endeavored to secure, in a slightly different way from the one above described, a serum useful for treating tuberculosis. In the first place, as reported to the Medical Society some time ago, we had found that if an originally virulent tubercle bacillus was cultivated for many generations upon artificial media, while it did not lose the property of producing active poisons when so cultivated, it did lose the property of producing tuberculosis in animals when the latter were injected. Furthermore, the animals, as guinea pigs, after a time possessed a very marked resistance to tuberculosis when they were subjected to an inoculation with virulent tubercle bacilli that would cause disease and kill the checks in a month to six weeks.

This attenuated germ seemed to offer suitable means for treating animals for the production of a serum with active properties, and was used in large quantities upon both cows and horses. The entire culture medium, including the germs, was at first used for these injections. As the toxins of the tuberculosis germ are, however, found to a large extent within the cell wall, it seemed desirable to bring these into solution, so far as possible, and inject the animals with the extract. At the same time it should be advantageous to discard the excess of nitrogenous bases, glycerine, and pepton present in the culture media and unused by the germ. To accomplish this solution, I have used an ordinary milk-shake machine. The live germs in quantity are transferred to the sterilized tumblers and the liquid added which it is desired to use as a solvent. The whole is agitated as rapidly as possible until the cell contents have been pretty well extracted. The residual germs can then be separated and submitted to the same process. This germ extract, as it may be called, which contains the soluble products of the cells, is then used for injection. As the germs have not been submitted to a temperature above that at which they have been grown, this solution should contain the unchanged products of the cell life. This material is fairly well absorbed by the animals. The serum obtained from cows treated with a large amount of cultures had apparently little or no value in checking tuberculosis in experimental animals. The serum obtained from injected horses was at first without any apparent influence, but as their treatment progressed and more and more germ extract was injected, the serum gradually acquired properties of value. When given to tuberculous

guinea pigs, together with tuberculin, the serum would usually retard
or prevent the characteristic reaction, and, in addition, prolonged
their lives for a number of months.

USE OF ANTITUBERCULOSIS SERUM UPON MAN.

These results seemed to warrant the use of the serum upon man.
Through the courtesy of Dr. J. E. Stubbert, in charge of the Loomis
Sanitarium at Liberty, N. Y., I have been able to have a number of
patients treated with this serum. Dr. Trudeau, of Saranac Lake, has
treated a few cases from time to time, and also Dr. C. W. Richardson,
of Washington, D. C., has used it in small quantities. The effect upon
patients having night sweats and high temperature seemed to be in
general to reduce the temperature and cause the night sweats to cease.
There has also been noticed in some cases after using the serum a
tonic influence, with increase of the patient's weight, diminution of
expectoration, and, in some instances, apparent cure. To show the
effect upon lowering of temperature, if this was really due to the
action of the serum, the following cases may be noted:

A young man of about 20, in good condition, with consolidation at
the apices of both lungs, evening temperature about 100° F., was
given injections of the serum, beginning with 5 minims, increasing to
1.8 cc. every other day for twelve weeks. After the first week there
was a gradual fall in temperature until the morning temperature was
about 97.5° and the evening between 98.5° and 99° F. During this
time the patient improved greatly in physical condition, but was from
time to time affected with catarrhal gastritis. The number of tubercle
bacilli in the sputum decreased, and the consolidation partly disappeared. Another case, a young man of the same age, with consolidation of the left lung, moderate cough, numerous bacilli in the sputum,
high evening temperature (102° F.), and generally poor condition,
received injections of the serum for three months. Within three
weeks after the first injection the temperature had been reduced to
normal, he had gained materially in weight (11 pounds), the number
of bacilli in the sputum had decreased, and the physical signs greatly
improved. The cases I have referred to are from the sanitarium, and
the following table has been given to me by Dr. Stubbert:

PATIENTS TREATED WITH SERUM FROM BIOCHEMIC LABORATORY OF BUREAU OF
ANIMAL INDUSTRY, DEPARTMENT OF AGRICULTURE, IN CONNECTION WITH GEN-
ERAL HYGIENIC AND CLIMATIC TREATMENT ONLY.

Number of patients treated.

Incipient stage 16
Moderately advanced 15
Far advanced 3

Total 34

Physical signs. .

Improved 30
Unimproved 4
                                                               ___
    Total 34

Expectoration.

Decreased 28
Stationary 6
                                                               ___
    Total 34

Temperature.

Decreased 21
Unchanged 13
                                                               ___
    Total 34

Cough.

Decreased 26
Stationary 8
                                                               ___
    Total 34

Appetite.

Improved 27
Unchanged 7
                                                               ___
    Total 34

Tubercle bacilli.

Disappeared 4
Decreased 7
Stationary 20
Had none 3
                                                               ___
    Total 34

Weight.

Increased 25
Stationary 7
Lost 2
                                                               ___
    Total 34

These cases, compared with those treated in other ways or under climatic influences only, showed that the improvement with the use of serum was more marked.

In several other cases, where the disease was more advanced and almost beyond any treatment, the temperature was but slightly affected. The individuals, however, desired the use of the serum continued, as they claimed it had a bracing effect which they could not secure in any other way. In making a general review of 45 cases treated with this serum at Liberty, N. Y., we may say that 33 per cent were greatly benefited and improved by its use. The remainder showed neither good effects nor bad results. In general, the injection of the serum causes no local disturbances. Occasionally a slight rise of temperature may be noted, or a local irritation or abscess formation at the point of injection. These arise probably from some abnormal condition of the patients or infection during injection, and are not due directly to the serum.

The experimental work on guinea pigs and the results on man show that there is contained in the serum from horses treated as above indicated a substance possessing some value. That this particular substance has not been obtained in its strongest form is also apparent. Some attempts have been made to isolate this active principle, and by a long method of precipitation, solution, reprecipitation, etc., a small amount of a white powder, allied to the soluble ferments, as trypsin, etc., has been obtained. This substance appears to exert the same action as the serum from which it is derived.

CHARACTER OF THE ACTIVE PRINCIPLE IN ANTITOXIC SERUMS.

Granted that a curative substance can be produced in the serum of treated animals, so far obtained in very small amounts, however, the question naturally arises as to its character, as well as the character of the active principle present in all antitoxic serums.

A review of the work in general seems to warrant the theory that the value of so-called antitoxic serums lies in the fact that they contain in solution one or more soluble ferments which are able to digest and destroy in the animal body the toxic products that the germ forms. These ferments are probably secreted by the leucocytes or other cells acting under the stimulation of the toxins first elaborated by the germ of the disease. In the case of a germ like that of diphtheria, probably the secretion of only one ferment will be stimulated, while in the case of tuberculosis, where a larger number of toxic substances are produced, it is probable that several ferments are needed to counteract their effect.

These ideas seem to be supported by the properties of antivenomous serums described by Calmette and Fraser. They have found that the serum from an animal artificially immunized to the cobra venom will counteract the poison of venomous snakes in general. The poisons of snakes seem to belong to the class of true toxic proteids, differing principally in the quantity in the different species. I believe, therefore, that a soluble ferment which would destroy the venom of one snake would have the same effect on all. The isolation by Fraser of a principle which possesses antivenomous properties from the bile of serpents and in very much smaller amounts from the bile of the ox, is in accord with the theory of soluble ferments, although Fraser himself believes in a more direct chemical neutralization. I do not mean to imply that a distinct, separate ferment is produced by the toxins of each germ, but simply that certain ferments can be secreted by the leucocytes or other cells under certain conditions. Some germs require but one of these ferments for the digestion of their particular product. The toxins of another germ require a second ferment; the toxins of a third germ require both; while all these ferments are needed to destroy a large variety of toxins which a fourth germ produces. This probably accounts for the difficulty in treating tuberculosis. This bacillus produces at least three classes of poisons—a necrotic acid, a fever-producing substance, and one that acts as a direct poison. These are apparently more stable than the toxins produced by some other germs, and hence more difficultly and more slowly attacked by the soluble ferments. Just as different ferments digest the different classes of foods, so are two or more of these special ferments necessary for the destruction of the different germ poisons.

The application of Koch's tuberculin known as T. R., prepared by extracting finely ground virulent bacilli, has not in general, judging from the reports of many cases, given the hoped-for satisfaction. As noted by Trudeau and Baldwin and others, the material may contain live tubercle bacilli which are capable of producing disease, and, as I am informed that the firm at Höchst has discontinued the manufacture, there is good reason to believe that some unlooked-for difficulties have been encountered by the originator of this treatment.

Another method of treating tuberculosis has recently attracted attention, namely, the use of so-called oxytuberculin and oxytoxins in general. The first work in this direction was done by passing an electric current through the solutions of the toxins of the different germs. As this action always took place in the presence of salt, some hypochlorites were first formed, and these in turn partly destroyed the toxins. In reality, therefore, when this electrolyzed material was injected into animals a weak toxin was used, and it is well known that immunity can be produced by repeating small doses of toxins. The so-called oxytuberculin is said to be prepared by digesting tuberculin (which contains salt, 4 to 7 per cent glycerine, peptone-nitrogenous bases from the meat, and a small amount of the fever-producing principle which the germ forms) with hydrogen peroxide at 100° C. for several days. Sodium hydrate is then added to the solution, the precipitate formed filtered off, and the filtrate neutralized with boric acid. This mixture is the product called oxytuberculin. Submitted to an analysis it was found to contain 6 per cent solid matter, about 65 per cent of which, or 4 per cent of the whole, was mineral salts, chiefly sodium phosphate and borate. In addition some sodium glycerate was present. I am unable to speak as to its remedial properties, except that it has not, in my hands, appeared to cure tuberculosis in guinea pigs, and I fail to understand why a mixture of this sort, largely a solution of sodium salts, should be called a specific.

THE FUTURE OF SERUM TREATMENT.

Whether further application of the serum treatment in its present form will continue to prove beneficial and give better results; or whether this must be materially modified, can not be stated positively. The results obtained certainly show that the efforts are properly directed. Though many individuals hold that on account of the slight evidence that can be found in the clinical history of tuberculosis, there is little to lead us to believe that immunity ever occurs in the natural course of this disease, the experiments of Dr. Trudeau, and also of the writer, certainly show that artificial immunity is possible. In reporting the general results of some of his work Dr. Trudeau says: "One hundred and two pigs were used, 36 of which were checks and 66 were vaccinated with attenuated tubercle bacilli. All were then inoculated with a virulent germ. The average life of the controls was 50½ days, and of the vaccinated animals 154.3 days. The latter lived nearly three times as long as the controls." In some cases they lived eighteen months or longer. If the lives of experimental animals can be protected for six months to two years, and even longer, it is fair to assume that similar methods of treatment should give very much better results in man.

When the study of serum therapeutics and the treatment of diseases of bacterial origin are freed from a commercial aspect, still better results can be expected. It is just as necessary in this work that chemical principles should be considered as the fact that there is a specific germ that causes tuberculosis.

Perhaps it may be possible to prepare antitoxins by artificial means outside of the animal body, but it seems, from present results at least, that the active live cell and the intervention of the laboratory of the animal body are necessary adjuncts in the production of these curative substances.

THE COMPOSITION OF THE TUBERCULOSIS AND GLANDERS BACILLI.[1]

By E. A. DE SCHWEINITZ, Ph. D., AND MARION DORSET, M. D.,
Chief and Assistant, Biochemic Division, Bureau of Animal Industry.

While many examinations of the products of bacilli have been made during the past years, comparatively little attention has been paid to a comparison of the proximate and ultimate analyses of the germs themselves that are morphologically different and produce different pathological changes.

Cramer[2] gives the results and analyses of cholera germs from different sources, and concludes that upon easily assimilable media the

----

[1] Reprinted from the American Chemical Journal, August, 1895.
[2] Arch. f. Hygiene, 16.

composition of the bodies of the same germ from different sources, and which vary in virulence, is about the same. Where, however, the media supply a food that is not easily assimilable, the composition of the bodies of the germs will vary. The comparison which he makes between these and several other species shows a variation which indicates a distinct and characteristic composition for each germ.

We have had occasion to collect large quantities of the tuberculosis and glanders bacilli, and have submitted the germs grown upon the ordinary glycerol beef broth and on artificial media to proximate and ultimate analyses. The results are presented in tabulated form.

The germs were freed by filtration from the culture liquid and the last traces of the soluble products removed by washing either with water alone or with water with the addition of sodium carbonate. The germs were then dried over sulphuric acid, and just before analysis were further dried at 100° C. In drying the germs underwent but slight change of color if they had been thoroughly washed. The analyses were made with the germs obtained from one and the same original culture, but the growths of eight or ten different generations were mixed together to secure an average sample. The artificial media used for the cultivation of the tuberculosis bacillus had the following composition:

	Grams.
Water	1,000
Glycerol	70
Acid potassium phosphate	1
Ammonium phosphate	10
Sodium chloride	10
Asparagin	2
Magnesium sulphate	0.2

In Table 1 are given the determinations of the carbon, hydrogen, nitrogen, phosphorus, sulphur, ash—in column I calculated upon the weight of the sample dried at 100° C.; in column II, upon the ash-free substance. With the exception of the nitrogen, there seems to be but little variation in the composition of the germs grown on beef broth or on artificial culture media.

TABLE 1.—*Elementary analyses of bacillus tuberculosis.*

	Beef broth.		Beef broth.		Beef broth.		Artificial media.	
	I.	II.	I.	II.	I.	II.	I.	II.
	P. cent.	P. cent.	P. cent.	P. cent.	P. cent.	P. cent.	P. cent.	P. cent.
Carbon			60.12	62.61	62.98	64.06	62.16	63.85
Hydrogen	9.22	9.60	9.15	9.53	7.39	7.52	9.19	9.38
Nitrogen	7.34	7.64	7.27	7.40	8.04	8.18	8.94	9.14
Sulphur	.44	.45					.22	.23
Phosphorus soluble in dilute nitric acid	.66		.19					
Phosphorus, total (Carius)	.77		.83		.87		.06	
Ash	4.03		4.05		1.77		1.92	

Table 2 gives the elementary analyses of the bacillus of glanders. The germs for these analyses were filtered off, washed a number of times with water and cold absolute alcohol, and dried.

A comparison of these results with those of the bacillus of tuberculosis shows a great and distinctive variation.

TABLE 2.—*Elementary analyses of bacillus mallei.*

	Beef broth.	
	I.	II.
	Per cent.	Per cent.
Carbon	41.81	44.89
Hydrogen	5.89	6.20
Nitrogen	14.05	14.81
Phosphorus, total (Carius)	1.10	....
Ash	5.18	..........:

The variations in the composition of these two bacilli are still more apparent in a comparison of the amount of the proximate constituents as shown in Tables 3, 4, 5, and 6. The determinations were made according to the general methods prescribed for such analyses. The nitrogen determinations were made by the Kjeldahl method, and from these results the albuminoids were calculated. The figures reported in the table as cellulose were obtained by treating the residue from the alcohol extract with 1.25 per cent caustic soda for forty to sixty minutes, washing well, then digesting the residue with 1.25 per cent sulphuric acid for the same length of time, washing and drying. The loss by ignition of the dried residue should indicate cellulose.

The presence of cellulose in the organs of tuberculous individuals has been examined by Freund, Dreyfuss, Toyosaku, Nishimura, with somewhat discordant results. Freund[1] treated the organs and blood from twenty-five different cases, first by extracting with ether and alcohol, then with dilute sulphuric acid. In this way there were left behind hard round lumps about the size of tubercles, which, when insoluble in dilute sulphuric acid, were soluble in strong sulphuric acid. This solution diluted with water and heated gave the reduction test for sugar.

TABLE 3.—*Bacillus tuberculosis. Beef broth.—I.*

	1.		2		Average.	
	I.	II.	I.	II.	I.	II.
	Per cent.	Per cent.	Per cent.	Per cent.	Per cent.	Per cent.
Ether extract	39.04	41.29	38.95	40.82	39.20	40.80
Alcohol extract						
Albuminoids	45.81	47.31	45.87	47.85	45.84	47.53
Cellulose	6.95	7.24			6.95	7.24
Ash	4.12		3.94		4.03	

[1] Jahr. d. g. Wiener Aerzte, 28, 1886.

TABLE 4.—*Bacillus tuberculosis.   Beef broth.—II.*

	1.		2.		Average.	
	I.	II.	I.	II.	I.	II.
	Per cent.	Per cent.	Per cent.	Per cent.	Per cent.	Per cent.
Ether extract						
Alcohol extract	3.04	3.10			3.04	3.10
Albuminoids	50.25	51.12	45.43	46.25	47.84	48.68
Cellulose	7.87	7.68			7.37	7.68
Ash	1.67		1.87		1.77	

TABLE 5.—*Bacillus tuberculosis.   Artificial media.*

	1.		2.		Average.	
	I.	II.	I.	II.	I.	II.
	Per cent.	Per cent.	Per cent.	Per cent.	Per cent.	Per cent.
Ether extract	37.76	37.86	37.96	38.71	37.57	38.34
Alcohol extract	4.69	4.79	4.19	4.28	4.44	4.53
Albuminoids	55.87	57.12			55.87	57.12
Cellulose	3.82	3.89	5.69	5.80	4.75	4.84
Ash	1.98				1.98	

TABLE 6.—*Bacillus mallei.   Beef broth.*

	1.		2.		Average.	
	I.	II.	I.	II.	I.	II.
	Per cent.	Per cent.	Per cent.	Per cent.	Per cent.	Per cent.
Ether extract	7.91	8.26	7.67	8.09	7.78	8.17
Alcohol extract						
Albuminoids	89.81	94.68	85.71	90.43	87.76	92.55
Cellulose	5.87	6.19			5.87	6.19
Ash	5.18				5.18	

Schulze's method was also used. Lungs, spleen, peritoneum, and dried blood were cut up finely and subjected to the action of nitric acid and potassium chlorate. White round nodules or a flocculent substance were left behind, which, when submitted to analysis after solution in cupric ammonia and reprecipitation, gave results corresponding to cellulose.

Nishimura[1] used for experiment the lungs and blood of tuberculous cows and also of men. The organs, after being finely divided, were extracted with ether and alcohol and then with 2 per cent sulphuric acid.

The residue, when treated with strong sulphuric acid, gave a solution that yielded the Trommer sugar test only twice out of six experiments.

Nishimura then tried the alkali method. The material was fused

[1] Arch. f. Hygiene, 21 (1), 52.

with potassium hydrate in the oil bath at 180° C., the fusion acidified with sulphuric acid, then made slightly alkaline and allowed to stand until clear. The residue was filtered off and tested for cellulose. By this method, from the lungs of a grown person a slight reaction for cellulose resulted with Trommer's test. The spleen and liver treated in the same way also indicated cellulose. In two cases from children, lungs, liver, and spleen gave the cellulose test.

How should this cellulose content be present in the organs? The most plausible explanation is the assumption that this comes from the presence of the bacilli themselves, and that the bodies of the latter are rich in cellulose. Under this assumption Dreyfuss[2] examined several varieties of bacilli, *Bacillus subtilis*, pus bacillus, *Aspergillus glaucus*, and by the fusion method with caustic potash succeeded in obtaining the reduction and phenylhydrazine tests.

Nishimura found, however, that other bacilli, e. g., the water bacillus No. 28, did not show the presence of cellulose. He extended his researches to the tubercle bacilli themselves. He made four tests upon the tubercle bacilli from glycerol bouillon cultures, using the alkali method, but obtained no reduction. From this he concludes that cellulose is not present in the tubercle bacilli.

In our examinations of the tubercle bacilli, as indicated above, the digestion of the residue, after extraction with 10 per cent sulphuric acid, gave distinct reduction tests with Fehling's solution. In two experiments Hoppe-Seyler's method, by fusing with caustic potash at 180° C., was used. In the one a good reduction test was obtained; in the other the reduction test failed.

From these tests we would conclude that cellulose is present in the tubercle bacilli, but in very minute amount, which may in some instances escape detection by the methods generally adopted. Nishimura thinks that possibly the tubercle bacilli form cellulose when they grow in the body, but not on artificial culture media. The fact, however, that the analyses indicated cellulose, both when grown upon glycerol beef broth and upon the mineral salt cultures, would make it probable that the cellulose is a normal constituent and can be produced by the germ from whatever material it feeds upon.

The proximate analyses of the glanders bacilli show results which are markedly different from those obtained with the tubercle bacilli. While the determination of cellulose by the method of difference would indicate its presence, the fusion with caustic potash, according to the same method adopted for the tubercle germs and subsequent treatment with sulphuric acid, indicates the absence of cellulose. Care was taken in filtering the tuberculosis and glanders germs that they were not contaminated with cellulose from filter paper. The most of them were filtered through porcelain and then scraped off.

---

[2] Ztschr. f. Physiol. Chem., 18 (3, 4), 367.

In order to show more clearly the variation in the body composition of different germs, the table is given herewith which gives results obtained by Cramer and others with different germs upon varying media. The change in the nitrogen content is very marked, and while the difference of medium influences this to some extent, there is still sufficient variation in the different germs to permit of a possible distinction of species. While the products of germs are invaluable as an aid to identification, it would appear that the chemical study of the bodies of the germs and the differences in their proximate constituents, especially albuminoids and fat, and a more distinctive study of the albuminoids might be very useful in aiding classification.

In order to form some idea of the composition of the fat extracted from the tuberculosis and glanders bacilli, the fats were saponified with caustic soda and the fatty acid separated. The quantity of acids obtained, however, was small and it was only possible to make melting-point determinations. From these the acids of the glanders seemed to be oleic and palmitic; those from the tubercle bacilli palmitic and arachidic.

The difference in the fatty acids apparent in these two, and which would probably vary as much in other germs, could doubtless be made use of in classification. The study is being continued further and extended to the hog cholera, swine plague, and allied germs.

Table showing results obtained with different germs upon varying media.

Media	Albuminoids.			Ether and alcohol extract.		Ash.	
	1 per cent peptonized agar.	1 per cent peptonized agar.	1 per cent soda.	5 per cent peptonized agar.	1 per cent soda.	5 per cent peptonized agar.	1 per cent peptonized agar.
	Per cent.	Per cent.	Per cent.	Per cent.	Per cent.	Per cent.	Per cent.
Bacilli:							
Pfeiffer's capsule bacillus	66.6	70.0	....	14.06	....	9.10	....
Pneumonia bacillus	71.7	79.8	....	11.3	....	10.36	....
Bacillus of Rhinoscleroma	68.42	76.2	....	9.1	....	9.33	....
Spirillum of cholera	....	64.96	....	....	....	....	30.78
No. 28	73.1	79.6	....	17.08	....	7.79	....

	Nitrogen.						
	7 per cent glycerol beef broth.	7 per cent artificial media.	5 per cent glycerol beef broth.	1 per cent peptonized beef broth.	Carbon.	Hydrogen.	Ash.
	Per cent.	Per cent.	Per cent.	Per cent.	Per cent.	Per cent.	Per cent.
Tuberculosis	7.34	8.94	....	....	62.98	7.34	1.77
Glanders	....	....	14.05	....	41.89	5.89	5.18

NOTES UPON THE FATS CONTAINED IN THE TUBERCULOSIS BACILLI.[1]

By E. A. DE SCHWEINITZ, PH. D., AND MARION DORSET, M. D.,

Chief and Assistant, Biochemic Division, Bureau of Animal Industry.

In the Journal of the American Chemical Society for August, 1895, we published an article[2] upon the composition of the tuberculosis and glanders bacilli, and noted the probable composition of the fats which are present in these germs in considerable proportion. The amount of crude fat in the tuberculosis bacilli is very large, having been found by us to be in round numbers 37 per cent of the weight of the dried germs. In the article referred to the amount of fat at our disposal was very small, and we could at that time determine only palmitic acid, and a high melting acid, which we stated appeared to be arachidic so far as the quantity at hand could be utilized. Recently we have made some further study upon these fats, and the results so far obtained seem to be of sufficient interest to warrant publication as a continuation of our previous work.

The quantity of crude fat available, which had been extracted from the germs was about 3.5 grams, and this was examined in the following way: It was first saponified in a closed flask with sodium hydroxide, in accordance with the method prescribed for the determination of fats by the American Association of Official Agricultural Chemists, as this method seemed to give the most satisfactory results. The saponification yielded a hard soap which was difficultly soluble in water. The dissolved soap was acidified with sulphuric acid and submitted to distillation until 100 cc. of the distillate had been obtained, again in accordance with the usually prescribed method. The distillate had a pungent odor, something like that of sweet almonds, and when titrated with tenth normal hydroxide solution, required for neutralization 2.4 cc. of the latter. The total amount of volatile fatty acid was therefore exceedingly small. As the total amount of sodium hydroxide required to neutralize the volatile acid from 3.5 grams fat was only 0.0096 gram, the total quantity of volatile acid could probably not have been 0.05 gram, an amount too small to permit of a determination of its character.

The nonvolatile fatty acids which formed a hard layer in the distilling flask were filtered off and well washed with water to remove all sulphuric acid and salts. The mixture was partially soluble in cold 95 per cent alcohol, but readily soluble in hot absolute alcohol. The only method that appeared practical for the separation of the fatty acids in this mixture was a fractional crystallization. Even this was extremely troublesome, but finally by repeated efforts the

---

[1] Reprinted from the Journal of the American Chemical Society for May, 1896.
[2] See p. 295.

larger portion of the acid was found to have a melting point of 62° C., which remained constant upon recrystallization. The principal fatty acid was therefore palmitic. After the palmitic acid had been removed a residue remained which was partially soluble in cold 85 per cent alcohol, and partially in hot 85 per cent alcohol. The acid soluble in hot 85 per cent alcohol after the first crystallization melted at 85° C., while two subsequent crystallizations raised the melting point to 102° C. Unfortunately again the quantity of this high melting acid was too small for further crystallization or identification. It was evidently the same acid that in our first article we noted as probably arachidic acid.

The acid soluble in cold 85 per cent alcohol was further purified and gave white crystals that melted at 42°–43° C., which would correspond to lauric acid. The amount was too small to permit of a positive identification.

This examination of the tuberculosis fats has shown that it is principally a glyceride of palmitic acid. In addition there is a minute amount of the glyceride of a volatile fatty acid to which the tuberculosis cultures owe their characteristic odor, and very small amounts of probably lauric acid and an unusally high melting acid, an acid apparently with a larger carbon content, so far as we can find, than any before noted in plants.

We propose still to identify the volatile and nonvolatile acids found in such small quantities, but as it will require probably several years to collect the material for this work, it has seemed best to give the results so far obtained at the present time.

THE MINERAL CONSTITUENTS OF THE TUBERCLE BACILLI.[1]

By E. A. DE SCHWEINITZ, PH. D., AND MARION DORSET, M. D.,
Chief and Assistant, Biochemic Division, Bureau of Animal Industry.

In August, 1895,[2] the writers published the results of some analyses showing the composition of the tubercle bacilli when grown upon different media. Depending upon the character of the media used, the amount of ash varied from 2 to 4 per cent. It seemed desirable to make a careful analysis of the ash in order to see which of the mineral constituents of the animal body would be most largely utilized by the germ and consequently necessary for its satisfactory development. The bacilli used for this work had been grown upon neutral beef broth containing 1 per cent of peptone, ½ per cent salt, and 7 per cent glycerol. The cultures, after heating in order to kill the germs,

---

[1] Reprinted from the Journal of the American Chemical Society, August, 1896.
[2] Journal of American Chemical Society.

were filtered and washed well with boiling water. The washed bacilli were then dried over sulphuric acid, finely powdered, and thoroughly extracted with pure ether and 98 per cent alcohol. After the last extraction the bacilli were again dried and ignited at a low red heat until practically all the carbon had been burned. The ash, which was almost pure white in color, was dried to a constant weight at 100° C. The total ash available for analysis was 1.453 grams. Examination showed that sulphates, chlorides, and carbonates were not present in the ash. The method used for the determination of the constituents of the ash were those prescribed for the analyses of the ash of plants. The results calculated upon the dry ash were as follows:

	Per cent.
Na_2O	13.63
K_2O	6.85
CaO	12.64
MgO	11.55
C and Si	0.57
P_2O_5	55.23

The high percentage of phosphorus pentoxide and the absence of other acid radicals in this ash are very noticeable. While it is probable that some of the chlorides and sulphates may have been washed out of the germ in the process of preparing it for analysis, no chlorides were present in the germs after washing; the fact that the amount of phosphoric acid obtained in the ash is slightly lower than the total amount of phosphoric acid obtained from the whole germ, would indicate that chlorides and sulphates are practically of no importance in the composition of the germ, while their presence in the culture media in minute quantity appears to be necessary for the satisfactory development of the germ. Chlorides and sulphates if dissolved out would have been present probably as cell contents rather than as part of the germ.

Ash analyses of comparatively few germs have been made, and the only ones which give data that may be reported here are the analyses made by Cramer,[1] who found that the composition of the ash of the cholora germs varied greatly, depending upon the quantity of sodium chloride and sodium phosphate that were used in the preparation of the media. In normal media the results were as follows:

	Per cent.
Cl	17.02
P_2O_5	20.48
SO_4	8.55
K	6.32
Na	32.06
Ca	.98
Mg	trace

[1] Archiv. für Hygiene, 28, No. 1.

If the amount of sodium chloride in the media was increased, the percentage of chlorine in the ash was more than doubled, while the percentage of SO_4 found was reduced to 1 per cent, and the percentage of P_2O_8 was largely diminished, being reduced to 9.64 per cent. When sodium phosphate was added to the media the percentage of chlorine was found to be 9.99 per cent, the percentage of P_2O_8 34.30 per cent; SO_4 2.24 per cent, of potassium 4.97 per cent, of sodium 31.83 per cent, of calcium 1.29 per cent, of magnesium 0.12 per cent. These results differ greatly from those found in the examination of the ash of the tubercle bacilli. As noted above, the media used for the growth of these latter germs was a normal material containing one-half of 1 per cent of salt, but without the addition of any phosphates or other salts. Consequently the high percentage of phosphorus pentoxide can be attributed only to the fact that phosphorus as well as the calcium and magnesium are absolutely necessary for the development of the tubercle bacilli, and were derived by it from these elements as normally present in the media.

In arrested cases of tuberculosis in animals, we often find hard, gritty, calcareous nodules. These nodules in healed tuberculosis contain tubercle bacilli. In other cases of healed tuberculosis where calcareous nodules are not present no bacilli, as a rule, are found. It is easy to trace a very close connection between these nodules, in healed tuberculosis, and the composition of the ash of the germ.

The high percentage of fat contained in the body of the tubercle bacilli, which we have noticed in previous papers, in conjunction with this high percentage of calcium and magnesium phosphate in the ash, give grounds for some interesting speculation. Phosphates and cod-liver oil are two materials always strongly recommended in cases of tuberculosis. As the germs of this disease seem to demand a large quantity of food containing phosphorus and also rich in fat, it is but a fair supposition that in giving the drugs above mentioned, we are supplying to the animal body those constituents which are very important for its proper nourishment, the supply of which is constantly being levied upon by the germs of the disease. The question might be asked whether in this method of treatment we are not really feeding the bacilli rather than the individual. But just as an exhausted soil can be made valuable by the addition of constituents which are deficient, so we may assume that the administration of specific materials containing the elements that the germ has utilized, should act in a similar way in increasing the vitality in the animal body. These of course are speculations, based, however, on certain known data. We trust that a still further study which is in progress, including the albuminoid constituents of the tubercle bacilli, may throw some light upon their development and chemical action in the animal body.

A. Hoen & Co. Lith. Baltimore.

CRYSTALLINE SUBSTANCE ISOLATED FROM ARTIFICIAL LIQUID CULTURES.

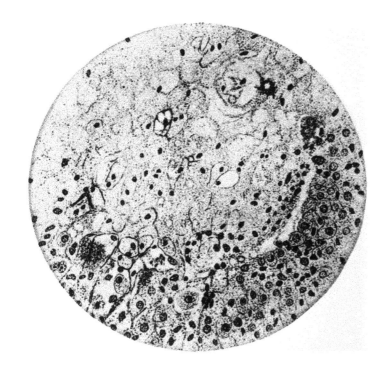

SECTION OF LIVER SHOWING NECROSIS PRODUCED BY CRYSTALLINE SUB-
STANCE ISOLATED FROM ARTIFICAL CULTURES

SOME PRODUCTS OF THE TUBERCULOSIS BACILLUS AND THE TREATMENT OF EXPERIMENTAL TUBERCULOSIS WITH ANTI-TOXIC SERUM.[1]

By E. A. DE SCHWEINITZ, Ph. D., M. D.

Chief of Biochemic Division, Bureau of Animal Industry.

So much has been written in regard to the poisons of the tuberculosis bacillus that a review on this occasion would demand too much time, and we desire to refer only briefly to the work which is of importance in connection with those substances which we will describe.

Tuberculin, as is well known, is the extract of the tuberculosis bacilli, including the media upon which they are grown. From specially prepared artificial cultures of the tuberculosis germ Kühne[2] and the writer[3] have obtained a substance corresponding to a nucleoalbumin which appeared to be the fever-producing principle of the germ. However, many conditions in tuberculosis were not accounted for by this substance, and as Mafucci,[4] Prudden and Hodenpyl,[5] Vissman,[6] and others had succeeded in producing tubercular nodules without necrosis by the intravenous injection of dead bacilli, it seemed as though it should be possible to isolate either from cultures or from bodies of the germs themselves some substance which might be considered accountable for the coagulation-necrosis of tissue which takes place—a necrosis which it appears is necessary for the progress of the disease. This problem was undertaken with the cooperation of my assistant, Dr. Dorset, more than two years ago. After many fruitless attempts we succeeded in isolating from artificial liquid cultures a crystalline substance having a melting point of 161° to 164° C., readily soluble in ether, alcohol, and water, which separated from these solutions in needlelike or prismatic crystals showing a slight yellow tint (Plate VI). They did not give the biuret reaction. The solution of this substance has an acid reaction to litmus, is acid in taste, and is optically inactive. The crystals give no precipitate with silver nitrate ($AgNO_3$), platinum chloride ($PtCl_4$), or barium hydrate ($Ba(OH)_2$). The analysis showed C = 50.88 per cent, H = 6.70 per cent, O = 42.42 per cent, giving a formula corresponding closely to $C_7H_{10}O_4$. This is the formula of teraconic acid, an unsaturated acid of the fatty series.

The culture media upon which the germs were grown and from which these crystals were obtained contained potassium acid phosphate, ammonium phosphate, asparagin, and glycerine, the media used

[1] Reprinted from the Transactions of the Association of American Physicians, 1897.

[2] Zeit. f. Biologie, Bd. xxx, 1894, p. 221.

[3] Bulletin No. 7, Bureau of Animal Industry, 1394.

[4] Centralb. für allg. Path., Dec. 15, 1893.

[5] New York Med. Journal, June 6 and 20, 1891.

[6] Archiv für path. Anat. u. Phys. und für klin. Méd., 1892, cxxix, p. 163.

306 BUREAU OF ANIMAL INDUSTRY.

and described by us[1] some years ago for studying their products. After the germ has been growing on this media for some weeks the liquid becomes light yellow in color, having the appearance of a pale urine, a change which does not take place in the uninoculated media kept under the same conditions. Efforts to obtain this same acid from the ordinary beef-broth cultures containing peptone and glycerine resulted in securing minute amounts of the crystals only, which it was never possible to purify. After noting some of the other properties of this acid substance we came to the conclusion that the presence of peptone and the nitrogenous bases of the meat resulted in their combination with the crystals, forming compounds from which the acid could not again be easily extracted, even after the addition of acid. Finally, a small quantity of the crystalline substance obtained from the artificial cultures was added to the glycerine peptonized beef-broth media, but it was impossible to recover it again by the methods used for the first extraction—namely, repeated precipitation with alcohol and extraction with water and ether. The ready solubility of this substance in water as well as ether probably accounts for the difficulty of obtaining it. The uninoculated media did not yield these crystals. When dissolved in water and injected into guinea pigs the following effects were noted. The injections were made subcutaneously in the thigh:

I. Healthy guinea pigs.

Guinea pig No. 314 received 0.015 gram of crystals.
    Temperature at time of injection, 102.6° F.
    Temperature at 11.50 a. m. (one hour after), 100.6° F.
    Temperature at 1.30 p. m., 100.2° F.
    Temperature at 3 p. m., 102.4° F.
    Temperature at 4 p. m., 102.2° F.
During the above period breathing was rapid, with an occasional rigor.
Guinea pig No. 422 (weight, 284 grams) received 0.0095 gram of crystals at 12.05 p. m.
    Temperature at time of injection, 99.8° F.
    Temperature at 2.30 p. m., 97.4° F.
On the next day there was quite perceptible swelling where the injection was made. Pig was chloroformed at end of twenty-four hours and showed considerable inflammation at seat of injection. Tissues were hemorrhagic and bathed in a serous exudate. The muscular tissue was much disintegrated, resembling the appearance from the action of a caustic.
▸ Guinea pig No. 511 (weight, 183 grams) received 0.0048 gram in 0.5 cc. water at 11.25 a. m., subcutaneously in thigh.
    Temperature at time of injection, 103° F.
    Temperature at 12.25 p. m. (one hour after), 101.8° F.
    Temperature at 1.15 p. m., 102° F.
    Temperature at 3.25 p. m., 100.8° F.
Chloroformed next day. Considerable inflammation, with serous exudate at seat of injection.

---

[1] New York Med. Journal, March 11, 1892.

Guinea pig No. 10 received 0.0274 gram at 10.10 a. m.
  Temperature at time of injection, 99.2° F.
  Temperature at 10.40 a. m., 100.2° F.
  Temperature at 11.15 a. m., 100.6° F.
  Temperature at 11.50 a. m., 100.6° F.
  Temperature at 2 p. m., 100.2° F.
During above period this pig showed signs of restlessness, breathed rapidly, and shivered.

II. Tuberculous guinea pigs.

Guinea pig No. 181 received 0.017 gram at 10.25 a. m.
  Temperature at 11.40 a. m., 101.4° F.
  Temperature at 1.50 p. m., 102.8° F.
  Temperature at 2.50 p. m., 103.4° F.
  Temperature at 3.50 p. m., 103° F.
Pig sat drawn up in cage and shivered.

Guinea pig No. 259 had received virulent tuberculosis two weeks previous to injection of crystals. Received 0.0172 gram at 10.45 a. m.
  Temperature at time of injection, 102.4° F.
  Temperature at 11.45 a. m., 101.6° F.
  Temperature at 3.20 p. m., 101.6° F.
Distinct rigors and rapid breathing.

Guinea pig No. 377 inoculated with sputum from tuberculous patient some time before injection of crystals. Received 0.023 gram at 11.35 a. m.
  Temperature at time of injection, 101.2° F.
  Temperature at 12.35, 100.6° F.
Trembling very noticeable.

Guinea pig No. 11 had been inoculated with attenuated and virulent tuberculosis culture (weight 448 grams). Received 0.0096 gram of crystals at 11.25 a. m.
  Temperature at time of injection, 103° F.
  Temperature at 12.25 p. m., 100.8° F.
  Temperature at 1.15 p. m., 101° F.
  Temperature at 3.25 p. m., 100.8° F.

The idea was suggested from these experiments that this acid, evidently a secretion of the bacillus, was one of its most powerful weapons; that by its action upon the tissue the cells were first destroyed, so that they could subsequently be utilized by the germ as food, and in this way the germ protected itself from surrounding leucocytes. To test this, crystals dissolved in sterile water were injected by means of a hypodermic syringe directly into the liver. At the same time an equal quantity of water was injected into a check in the same way. After forty-eight hours check and experimental animals were killed. The check failed to show any effect, while the other exhibited a liver with several light spots. A repetition of this experiment gave the same results.

No effort was made to recover these crystals from the liver, as the amount used was too small. We did not test the effect upon the liver by an intravenous injection, as would otherwise have been done, because we had found that there was a combination of this acid substance with the albuminoids or bases, and any intravenous injection would have resulted in its immediate conversion into a modification by uniting with the albuminoids in the blood. Further, the growth of the germ in the body is localized, and where localized the necrotic areas are apparent, so that the fairest test was to bring the substance as soon as possible in contact with the tissue. The experiments in injections of the animals and appearance of sections follow:

Injection of crystals from artificial cultures of Bacillus tuberculosis into the liver of guinea pigs.

Guinea pig No. 409 received 0.00178 gram in liver on left side at 11.45 a. m. Pig weighed 338 grams.

 Temperature at time of injection, 101.6° F.
 Temperature at 8 p. m., 102° F.

Chloroformed October 24, 1896, at 12 m. Liver dark, with one or two small white spots in it, and apparently a small inflamed spot at about the position where injection was made. Gall bladder injected and seemingly inflamed.

Guinea pig No. 412 received 0.0037 gram in liver at 1.45 p. m. Pig weighed 242 grams.

 Temperature at 1.45 p. m., 103° F.
 Temperature at 3.30 p. m., 100.4° F.

Chloroformed at end of forty-eight hours. Gall bladder was congested (not so much as in No. 409). Liver showed pale spots and one or two small white areas of apparent necrosis. Hardened in HgCl, on microscopic examination one area rather well defined where the liver cells do not take hematoxylon well, though stained nuclei could be seen.

Checks on injection of crystals into liver.

Guinea pig No. 510 received 0.25 cc. sterile distilled water in liver.

Chloroformed after forty-eight hours. Post-mortem: All organs, liver, lungs, spleen, etc., normal.

Guinea pig No. 387 received 0.50 cc. sterile distilled water in liver. Chloroformed after forty-eight hours. Post-mortem: All organs normal excepting one or two very small pale spots in liver ; no necrosis.

Injection of crystals. Guinea pig " C " received 0.0043 gram in liver. Chloroformed after six days. Pig weighed 600 grams.

Lungs very slightly congested. In large left lobe of liver there were two or three comparatively large areas of necrosis. These spots were on the side in which injection was made, and the liver appeared to show the track of needle. The guinea pig was otherwise healthy.

Guinea pig " E " received 0.0023 gram of crystals in liver. Chloroformed after two days. Pig weighed 345 grams.

All organs appeared normal, except stomach and liver. The stomach showed a slight inflammation in its wall on the side which lay next to a necrosed spot in the liver.

Besides this spot there were several others of considerable size in the liver on the side on which the injection was made. The section of pig "C," the one allowed to live six days after injection, showed on microscopic examination the following:

Stained with hæmatoxylon and eosin ; distinct areas of necrosis were noted, the most marked ones near the surface of the liver. Polynuclear leucocytes were present, though not in large numbers, in and around the necrotic areas, and there was also an increase in connnective tissue cells of the liver around these same areas. Plate VII is a drawing of the liver section, showing healthy and necrosed areas.

Prudden,[1] 1892, suggests that caseation, so constantly present in tuberculosis, is probably due to a specific metabolic product of the bacillus.

It seems very reasonable to conclude from our experiments that we have here the substance formed by the bacillus which is responsible for this necrosis.

The formula which can be deduced from the analysis makes this acid correspond closely to teraconic, which has properties very similar to those noted by us in connection with this new acid. Its identity we have not yet proved or disproved, as the preparation of teraconic acid is not completed. The amount of this acid obtained is very small, so that we have used only a very small portion of it for testing its immunizing property. A single injection of 0.0020 gram was sufficient to keep the animals alive some weeks longer than the checks, and its solution appeared to exert some slight bactericidal influence.

As this substance seemed to be a temperature-reducing principle in healthy and diseased animals, we endeavored to separate the fever-producing principle independently. The crystals were always found in the culture liquid, and only minute amounts could be obtained from the bacilli themselves that had been grown on liquid media. Accordingly, these bacilli, carefully filtered without heat, were washed in cold water, and next extracted with hot water. This hot water extract contained an albuminoid which caused the tuberculin reaction in tuberculous guinea pigs and calves upon repeated injections.

Roux and Nocard[2] state that they have a tuberculin which will give reactions almost indefinitely, but do not describe its method of preparation. Whether this is the same substance that we have obtained we are unable to say, but certain it is that the tuberculin prepared in the way we have indicated will give reactions four or five times in succession, where the reaction with tuberculin as prepared in the ordinary way fails after the second time. The conclusion is a fair one. We think that the fever-reducing principle having been removed, to an extent, if not entirely, the immunity from the fever-producing principle is much more slowly acquired. Our tests upon guinea pigs and tuberculous calves were made with only one day intervening between the injections. (See Table 1.)

In the Deutsche medicinische Wochenschrift for April 1, 1897, Dr. R. Koch[3] describes some new tuberculin preparations. The dried tuberculosis bacilli were taken (the culture medium used is not mentioned), finely powdered and centrifugalized with distilled water. The opalescent solution obtained, tested upon animals, gave the tuberculin reaction. The residual germs were submitted to this treatment a number of times, until finally all were practically dissolved.

---

[1] New York Med. Journal, September 10, 1893.
[2] Receuil de méd., 1897.
[3] Deut. med. Woch., April 1, 1897.

The latter solutions in large doses caused a reaction, but in small quantities did not produce this result, and seemed to exert both an immunizing and curative action in experimental tuberculosis. Koch used for this work virulent germs, and claims that attenuated germs do not give an active product. My own work was done with germs purposely attenuated by cultivation, and the results show that very active fever-producing, fever-reducing, and probably curative principles can be obtained from them. It hardly seemed justifiable to myself or others to powder dried virulent germs and have the dust floating in the air. Koch further refers to two fatty acids which, in conjunction with Proskauer,[1] had been found in the bodies of the germs. The writer[2] of this paper published in the American Chemical Journal for August, 1895, a preliminary study of the fats of the tuberculosis bacilli, showing the high content of fat in the bodies of these germs, which accounts for the difficulty in staining them with certain colors, as well as their difficult absorption.

In a later paper, 1896,[3] we described briefly the different acids obtained from the body of the germ, both high-melting and low-melting acids, but whether or not these are identical with those observed by Koch and Proskauer we can not tell from the brief mention made of them.

From our result it seems very reasonable to think that the necrotic acid is the fever-reducing principle, the albuminoid the fever-producing principle, and the reason the tuberculin ordinarily does not react continuously is on account of their presence at the same time. At any rate, tuberculous guinea pigs tested successively with tuberculin showed no reaction, while with this albuminoid, which we will call cell extract, a reaction was obtained.

The preliminary experiments published by the writer in 1894[4] upon the production of an immunity or resistance to tuberculosis by attenuated cultures have been continued and are confirmatory of the first results, showing the production of great resistance and in some cases complete immunity. A detail of two sets of these experiments may be given as an instance of their general results (Table 2).

The first effect of the injection of the attenuated germ was in some instances to cause a slight decrease in weight; sometimes a local swelling was noted at the point of injection, and occasionally an enlargement of the inguinal glands. This disappeared after some weeks. This local swelling is probably due to the mechanical action of the bodies of the germs, on account of their high fat content and possible presence of a minute amount of the acid, causing necrosis.

[1] Deut. med. Woch., April 1, 1897.
[2] Journal of the Amer. Chem. Society, August, 1895; Bulletin No. 13, 1896, Bureau of Animal Industry.
[3] Centralb. f. Bak. u. Parasit., vol. XIX, 18, 19, 1896.
[4] Med. News, December 8, 1894.

It does not always result from a subcutaneous inoculation, and an apparent immunity from this action is acquired by repeated injections. This is well shown in horses and cows submitted to treatment with the attenuated germ.

From six to eight weeks after the date of the injection of the germ guinea pigs seem to be entirely well, and are then inoculated with the virulent germ. As can be seen from the chart, the checks died within six weeks from date of inoculation, while the ones vaccinated remained well four months afterward. It has appeared from many experiments that if the inoculation with the virulent bacillus is made before complete recovery from the treatment with the attenuated bacillus the resistance is considerably less. The inoculation of the animals with the virulent bacillus, and subsequently with a single injection of the attenuated bacillus, showed that the latter produced a slight resistance, but no very material retardation of the disease.

The production of this partial immunity or artificial resistance by means of the attenuated cultures suggested already, in 1894, the availability of this same material for the purpose of treating animals for the production of a serum which would have some effect in curing tuberculosis. It suggested the idea further that possibly cattle could be vaccinated with this attenuated germ and made immune from tuberculosis.

Two cows and one heifer were selected for the work, which was conducted for us by Dr. Schroeder, in charge of the Experiment Station of the Bureau of Animal Industry. One of these animals was originally tuberculous, the other two healthy. The tuberculous animal received large doses of tuberculin until it had received altogether 19,407 cc. (19½ liters), and as much as 1,500 cc. of tuberculin at a single dose, from November, 1894, to April 20, 1897. The other animals received injections of the attenuated culture, the amount injected in fifteen months being 11,425 cc. and 18,100 cc., respectively; and by this is meant the liquid culture media in toto, including the germs, just as taken from the incubator, without any further treatment. At first the injections produced a slight reaction and occasionally a local edema and abscess. After they had been continued for some time this effect diminished or disappeared. The serum of all of these animals was tested a number of times. Guinea pigs were injected with the serum in quantities varying from 1½ to 6 cc., and subsequently inoculated, together with the checks, with a culture sufficiently virulent to kill the checks within four or five weeks, or the pigs were inoculated with the virulent bacilli and treated by subsequent injections of the serum. Without giving the detail of the experiments, we may say that the serum from the cow treated with tuberculin would cause in the pigs a slight resistance to the disease; the serum of those treated with the attenuated bacilli produced more resistance on the part of the animals or prolonged their life to some extent, but not sufficiently, as compared with the quantity of material injected, to make the use of cow serum appear practicable. The cow serum, although sterile, frequently produced abscesses in guinea pigs. This serum we expect to test again shortly, when it should be more potent.

While these experiments were in progress two horses had been pressed into service. They were treated by injecting the attenuated cultures, culture fluid, and bacilli. The first injection of 5 cc. caused a decided temperature reaction, local edema, stiffness, slight loss of appetite, recovering after a few days. At first local abscesses were formed, which healed fairly readily. After a time the abscess formation ceased or occurred occasionally. After eight months' treatment, the doses of the culture being gradually increased up to 300 to 400 cc.—the total amount injected in fifteen months = 4,459 cc.—the serum was used for testing. It separated out clear and well. Two sets of illustrations may be given to show its action on tuberculous animals. (Table 3.) In one set the checks and two treated pigs died; the other two treated pigs are alive and in perfect health, apparently, after a number of months. In another set the checks, four in number, died within four to five weeks, while the treated ones lived two or three weeks longer, showing, on autopsy, much less disease in the lungs than the checks. We endeavored further to isolate from the serum antitoxic substances by a slight modification of the Brieger-Boer method. We finally succeeded in obtaining a small quantity of a grayish powder giving the biuret reaction, soluble in water with difficulty, which was used for treating guinea pigs in the same way as the serum. The result was as in the first instance. The pigs, one-half pound in weight, were inoculated with a virulent germ and treated by a single injection of 0.008 gram of this solid substance. They lived three or four weeks longer than the checks, again showing considerably less disease in the lungs and less necrosis was noted in the liver.

The effect of the serum was also tried in preventing the rise of temperature in tuberculous guinea pigs, and in saving them from a fatal dose of tuberculin. As can be seen from the temperature reactions in Table 1, the injections of one-fourth cubic centimeter of diluted tuberculin, and at the same time of one-half cubic centimeter of the serum, either caused a decided reduction of the temperature or prevented a characteristic tuberculin reaction in animals weighing about 400 grams. This is one way of gauging the serum.

The result of all this work leads us to the conclusion that the injection of the live culture produces substances antitoxic to tuberculosis; that the quantity of this substance can be increased gradually; that the treatment of tuberculosis is and will be for some time still in the experimental stage. One point, however, must be remembered, namely, that while it may be difficult to cure the disease in a guinea pig, where its course is very rapid—a virulent bacillus requiring only from four to five weeks to kill—it might be much easier to check the disease when more prolonged in action, as in the majority of cases in man. Again, in addition to some form of specific treatment for the disease, man usually has the advantage of being placed under the best possible surroundings as to diet, climate, etc., and every effort is made to aid the improvement of the patient, while with experimental animals the conditions are different.

The experimental results obtained lead undoubtedly to the conclusion that while the treatment with antitoxic serum is still in the experimental stage, and should as yet be used only in sanitariums and under the best conditions, we are on the road to success in the treatment of this disease and nearer our goal than ever before.

In an experimental way, the antitoxic serum as prepared in my laboratory has been used by Dr. Stubbert at the Loomis Sanitarium, and some by Dr. Trudeau at Saranac Lake, as well as by Dr. Charles W. Richardson in Washington.

The serum used for these cases was of the same lot that cured the guinea pigs reported in Table 3. The treatment has not been continued long enough for positive conclusions to be drawn. One of the cases reported by Dr. Stubbert has been apparently cured, and the others much improved. Dr. Charles W. Richardson reports decided improvement in the cases upon which this serum has been used. Dr. Trudeau has not used the material long enough to come to any definite conclusions. He noted reduction of high temperatures under its influence in one of the cases tried.

Maragliano, Babes, and Behring are the other principal workers in the preparation of an antitoxic serum for tuberculosis. Paquin also has an antitoxic serum on the market.

Maragliano[1] gives the method he has used for the production of antitoxic serum, and notes that there is present in the cold-filtered cultures of the tuberculosis bacilli a substance which causes the reduction of temperature, and another, not destroyed by heat, which causes the rise of temperature. In all probability, without isolating the principle, Maragliano was using solutions of the crystalline substance we have described in the beginning of this paper. While this is not destroyed by heat, as he seems to think, it does undergo some change by combining probably with the albuminoid matter in the media, and thus losing its distinct property as a temperature-reducing substance; or, more probably, its temperature-reducing property is disguised by the presence of the temperature-producing principle extracted by hot water. The serum which he obtains from treatment of the animals with the different products of the bacilli is claimed to have some effect in reducing the temperature and apparently improving the disease.

In the Zeitschrift für Hygiene, Babes,[2] reviewing a portion of the

---

[1] Revue de la tuberculose, juillet, 1896, p. 131.
[2] Zeit. f. Hygiene, Bd. xxiii, Hft. 3.

work upon the treatment of tuberculosis with serum, comes to the conclusion that he is the first individual to have discovered any antitoxic properties in this serum; that there is an antitoxic substance present in treated animals, but that it has not yet been brought to a sufficient development to warrant general use.

Our experiments lead us to conclude that while the injection with tuberculin in healthy animals produces a serum containing antitoxic material, the amount of this is small, and that the injection of the live culture is the proper treatment. We can not agree with the statement made that horses are unsuitable for the work. Mules and donkeys may perhaps give quicker results, but horses seem to be eminently satisfactory. At no time have we found that the horse serum produces toxic effects, although this has been noted in the cow serum.

If the antitoxic serum treatment for tuberculosis could be freed for the present from its commercial aspect, and careful, systematic experiments continuously conducted in numerous hospitals and sanitariums, this or a similar modified method of treatment could be looked to for good results. When tuberculosis can be uniformly cured in guinea pigs as certainly as diphtheria, then does the commercial aspect become a fair and legitimate one.

TABLE 1.—*Test of cell extract, tuberculin, and serum.*

Date.	No. of animal.	Condition.	Weight in grams.	Substance injected.	Temperature. 11.20 a. m.	1.40 p. m.	3.05 p. m.
Mar. 26	XI	Tuberculous guinea pig.	423	½ cc. tuberculin + ½ cc. serum.	102.2	96.6	96.2
	492	.....do...........	255	½ cc. tuberculin...............	102.8	105.0	104.4
	VIII	Attenuated, tuberculous.	443	½ cc. tuberculin + ½ cc. serum.	101.0	102.4	103.8
	XIX	.....do...........	356	2 cc. cell extract = 0.0040 gram.	102.2	105.6	103.4
	513	Healthy (check)	210	1 cc. cell extract = 0.0020 gram.	104.4	101.6	101.0
					10.50 a. m.	12.25 p. m.	1.50 p. m.
Mar. 27	XI	Tuberculous guinea pig.	....	½ cc. tuberculin...............	101.2	102.4	102.4
	492	.....do...........	....	2 cc. cell extract = ½ cc. tuberculin.	103.0	103.8	105.0
	VIII	Attenuated, tuberculous.	....	½ cc. tuberculin...............	103.0	103.2	103.8
	XIX	.....do...........	....	.....do	102.8	103.8	103.0
	XX	.....do...........	....	½ cc. tuberculin + ½ cc. serum.	102.4	95.0	95.6
					10.25 a. m.	12.10 p. m.	1.45 p. m.
Mar. 29	VIII	Attenuated, tuberculous.	....	2 cc. cell extract = ½ cc. tuberculin.	101.8	103.8	103.6
	492	Tuberculous guinea pig.	....	.....do	102.8	104.4	104.6
	XIX	Attenuated, tuberculous.	....	.....do	102.2	105.6	103.6
					10.45 a. m.	12.15 p. m.	2.10 p. m.
Mar. 30	492	Tuberculous guinea pig.	....	2 cc. cell extract = ½ cc. tuberculin.	102.2	104.2	104.2
	XIX	Attenuated, tuberculous.	....	½ cc. tuberculin...............	102.2	103.2	103.6

TABLE 2.—*Two sets of experiments showing the average results in experiments in which the guinea pigs were vaccinated with attenuated bacilli and then inoculated with virulent bacilli.*

No.	October 24. Inoculation and amount of attenuated germ.	Weight. Oct. 24.	Weight. Nov. 2.	Condition.	December 9. Inoculation and amount of virulent germ.	Weight. Dec. 16.	Weight. Jan. 7.	Weight. Jan. 19.	Weight. Feb. 2.	Weight. Feb. 8.	Weight. Apr. 8.	Weight. Apr. 19.
		Ounces.	*Ounces.*			*Ounces.*	*Ounces.*	*Ounces.*	*Ounces.*	*Ounces.*	*Ounces.*	*Ounces.*
373	1½ cc. fiftieth generation	12	14	O. K.	Dead from pneumonia.							
374	do	10	11	O. K.	½ cc. of vir. tuberculosis; fourth generation from rabbit.	14	16	16	15½	16	16	14
375	do	16	15	O. K.	Dead from pneumonia.							
376	do	16	14½	O. K.	½ cc. of vir. tuberculosis; fourth generation from rabbit.	12	15	15	15	15	17½	18
377	Check	13	13¾	O. K.	Fourth generation from rabbit	12	13	12½	Dead.			
378	1½ cc. attenuated germ	14	14	Thin.	Dead from pneumonia.							

No.	Dec. 21.	Dec. 28.	Dec. 21.	Feb. 2.	Feb. 12.	Mar. 6.	March 8.	Mar. 16.	Apr. 6.	Apr. 19.	Apr. 21.
			Ounces.	*Ounces.*	*Ounces.*	*Ounces.*		*Ounces.*	*Ounces.*	*Ounces.*	
II	½ cc. of sixty-first generation.	1½ cc. of sixty-first generation.	13	14	16		½ cc. virulent germ	16	Chloroformed.		
III	do	do	12	15½	14		do	17	17	19	
IV	do	do	15	16	17		do	20	21	20	
V	do	do	13	15	16		do	17½	19	19	
VII	do	do	14	13	14		do	16	16½	18	
VIII	do	do	15	15	16		do	17	16	18	
IX	do	do	12	13	11		do	14	15	16	
X	(Check)	(Check)		16	16	18	do	17½	14	12	Dead.
XI	(Check)	(Check)		15	16	17	do	17½	Dead.		
XII	½ cc. of sixty-first generation.	1½ cc. of sixty-first generation.	16	16	16		do	18	19	19	
XIII	do	do	14	15	16		do	18	17½	16½	
XV	do	do	15	16	18		do	18	14		
XVI	do	do	15	15	17		do	18	18½	20	
XVII	do	do	12	12	13		do	15	15	14½	
XVIII	do	do	15	15	14		do	16	17½	17½	
XIX	do	do	14	13	18		do	13	13	12½	
XX	do	do	15	18	14		do	20	19	19	

TABLE 3.—*Effect of serum from horse injected with attenuated culture on tuberculous guinea pigs.*

No.	Weight (ounces).	October 24. Amount of virulent culture and serum injected.		Dates and amount of serum injected.					
				November 16.	November 17.	November 25.	Dec. 3.	Dec. 8.	April 19.
								Ounces.	*Ounces.*
434 (check)	10	¼ cc. of virulent tuberculosis culture		10 oz.	8¼ oz.	8 oz.	Dead		
435	9	do	1¼ cc. of serum	9 oz. +1¼ cc.	8 oz. +1¼ cc.	8 oz. +1¼ cc.		9	20
436	11	do	do	10 oz. +1¼ cc.	9 oz. +1¼ cc.	7 oz. +1¼ cc.	Dead		
437	14	do	do	13 oz. +1¼ cc.	11 oz. +1¼ cc.	10 oz. +1¼ cc.		10	20
438	9	do	do	8 oz. +1¼ cc.	8 oz. +1¼ cc.	6 oz. +1¼ cc.	Dead		
439	8	do	do	8 oz. +1¼ cc.	7 oz. +1¼ cc.	5 oz. +1¼ cc.			

TABLE 4.—*Test of dry antitoxic material from serum from vaccinated horse.*

Number of animal.	Weight (ounces).	Date.	Material for inoculation.	Date.	Weight (ounces).	March 8.	Date.	Weight (ounces).	Date.
464	Check 11	Feb. 4	¼ cc. tuberculosis virulent	Feb. 20	11		Mar. 6	10	Mar. 8. Dead.
476	12	Feb. 4	¼ cc. tuberculosis virulent +0.208 gram antitoxin.	Feb. 20	12		Mar. 6	10	Mar. 16. Dead; less disease than others.
478	Check 8¼	Feb. 4	¼ cc. tuberculosis virulent	Feb. 20	8	Dead; tuberculosis.			
479	Check 8	Feb. 20	do				Mar. 6	7	Mar. 8. Dead; generalized tuberculosis.
481	Check 10	Feb. 20	do				Mar. 6	9	Mar. 12. Dead.
482	13	Feb. 20	¼ cc. tuberculosis virulent +0.008 gram antitoxin.				Mar. 6	12	Apr. 7. Dead; less disease than others.
484	12	Feb. 20	do				Mar. 6	12	Apr. 12. Dead; less disease than others.

THE ATTENUATED BACILLUS TUBERCULOSIS: ITS USE IN PRODUCING IMMUNITY FROM TUBERCULOSIS IN GUINEA PIGS.[1]

By E. A. DE SCHWEINITZ, Ph. D.,

Chief of Biochemic Division, Bureau of Animal Industry.

It is well known that a number of the pathogenic bacteria decrease very greatly in virulence when cultivated for a long time outside of the animal body. This fact has also been noticed in the case of the *Bacillus tuberculosis,* and the literature is full of references to the decrease in virulence of the tubercle bacillus and the way of securing this, but some facts have been developed in this connection in my work on tuberculin, in a new direction, which should be recorded.

Cultures with which I started several years ago were obtained through the kindness of Dr. Trudeau, of Saranac Lake, N. Y., and were the second generation on blood serum from a rabbit. After growing for several generations upon glycerine agar, about two months to each generation, the culture was transferred to glycerine beef broth, which was to be used as a source for tuberculin. After the fourteenth generation I noticed that the guinea pigs that were always kept inoculated with tuberculosis, to test the tuberculin, did not succumb nearly as readily, and in the case of the fourteenth generation it required six months before the disease developed. I consequently inoculated a number of guinea pigs with the seventeenth, eighteenth, nineteenth, and twentieth generations of this germ, which was alive and would grow very readily on the liquid media. Some of these pigs inoculated had previously been treated by an injection of tuberculin; the others had never been used. After some months those that had been inoculated with the attenuated germ remained quite well, and one was chloroformed, and the autopsy showed that it was free from disease.

In order to see if this might be accidental, I then had nine pigs inoculated—four checks, four pigs previously inoculated with the attenuated germ, and one pig that had received tuberculin by feeding. These were all inoculated in the side with the material from the gland of a tuberculous cow that had just been killed. After seven weeks the checks were all found dead from tuberculosis. The other animals appeared perfectly well. One was accordingly chloroformed, and, although very careful examinations were made, no disease could be detected. Even the local lesion that was produced where the material had been injected had entirely healed. The animals were apparently immune.

Some experiments that had been made earlier with tuberculin prepared from a younger growth did not show that this material had a positive value in preventing disease, although it retarded it. As the

[1] Reprinted from The Medical News, December 8, 1894.

preparation of tuberculin continued, however, I noticed that the tuberculin was much more constant in reaction and that a larger amount of the active principle was yielded by cultures of the older germ.

At this time I had at the Experiment Station of the Bureau the calf of a tuberculous cow, which, however, although the mother was badly diseased, did not respond to an injection with the tuberculin. The calf was then drenched with 100 cc. of a growing active liquid culture of this attenuated germ, the twentieth generation. After three months the calf was again injected with tuberculin, and, failing to respond, was killed. The autopsy showed the animal to be perfectly healthy.

Another healthy Southern cow received into a vein an injection of the same generation from this liquid culture in July. On November 20 this animal, which was rather thin and had an initial temperature of 103° F., was injected with tuberculin, but did not show any reaction. Another animal known to be tuberculous, injected at the same time, with the same sized dose of tuberculin, showed a good reaction. The cow which had received the injection of attenuated culture had a small lump, the size of an egg, on the side of the neck, where inoculated. The diagnosis of no tuberculosis, as based upon failure of reaction to tuberculin, will be confirmed or disproved by an autopsy later. These experiments were kindly made for me by Dr. Schroeder.

So far as I have been able to find, the first note of successful cultivation of the tubercle bacillus upon liquids free from albuminoid matter was made by myself in the New York Medical Journal of March, 1893. Since then Uchinsky, Proskauer, and others have used similar media. None has, however, reported a better growth than that obtained by a slightly modified form of the original culture medium. It required some time until I could persuade the germ to grow in this liquid, but after considerable coaxing it will now multiply as well here as on glycerine-peptonized beef broth, the fourth generation having become accustomed to the change of food.

The formula that I have found eminently adapted to the growth of the tuberculosis bacillus and have used may be repeated here:

	Grams.
Water	1,000
Glycerine	70
Acid potassium phosphate	1
Ammonium phosphate	10
Sodium chloride	10
Asparagin	3
Magnesium sulphate	0.2

After a certain amount of growth has appeared in a definite volume of media the growth will entirely cease. The germ has exhausted the supply of nutritive material or eliminated enough poison to check its own development, and, although the germs may still float on the surface of the liquid, after from three to four months there is practically no growth in the liquid. Further, there is a distinct and peculiar odor generated in the culture media. This is due to a fatty acid which is difficultly volatile with steam. The reaction of the media when inoculated is slightly alkaline. As the growth increases it becomes less so, and finally it is acid in reaction.

In order to see if the apparent loss of virulence of the germ might be due to some of its products contained in the body of the germ, two guinea pigs were inoculated with the twenty-third generation of the germ, after the germs had been carefully and thoroughly washed with sterile water to remove all products. These pigs, after two months, are still well. The bacillus grown on purely artificial media might naturally be supposed to be still more attenuated than that grown on the ordinary culture liquid. To test this, some of these germs were used to inoculate guinea pigs, with the same results as those already noted.

In the case of a disease like tuberculosis, in which the incubation period is often an exceedingly long one, there is a possibility that what now appear to be immune animals may in time succumb. In view of the fact, however, that all of the checks died so promptly, so long a time has elapsed since, and that all the other animals remained well, it is fair to presume that we have here a true immunity secured by an attenuated germ.

The following notes give the experiments in detail, and in the table they can be noted in a comprehensive form. The autopsies are not given in full, as they appeared superfluous.

January 18, 1894. Guinea pigs Nos. 27, 28, 29, and 30, about three-quarters pound weight each, were inoculated with an emulsion of an agar-culture of tuberculosis, receiving 0.25 cc. each in the thigh. This was the eighteenth generation of the particular germ. On February 13, 1894, No. 27 was used to test some tuberculin and gave a good reaction, although apparently in good health. February 15, 1894, No. 28 was found dead, but the autopsy did not reveal any signs of tuberculosis. No. 27 was found dead on March 19, two days after it had been fed a large amount of tuberculin. The autopsy did not reveal the presence of any tuberculous lesions. Nos. 29 and 30 were subsequently, within six months, chloroformed and examined, but no signs of tuberculosis were apparent.

February 16, 1894. Healthy guinea pigs, Nos. 115, 113, 128, and 127, were fed varying doses of tuberculin, from 3 to 12 cc. Nos. 127 and 128 succumbed to the feeding, but this proved to be due to the glycerine with which the tuberculin had been mixed.

On March 30, 1894, Nos. 114, 115, 113, 109, and 112 were inoculated with 0.1 cc. of tuberculosis emulsion from the seventeenth generation of a liquid culture. June 5, 1894, No. 115 was chloroformed, but the autopsy did not reveal any signs of the disease. October 1, 1894, No. 114 was found dead outside of the cage; it had been killed by the rats and the head was badly eaten. The animal was in good condition and fat, and the autopsy did not reveal any signs of tuberculosis. There was a little thickening of the skin and a small non-tuberculous lump at the point of inoculation.

During April and May Nos. 113 and 112 were fed on three different dates with small doses of tuberculin, but did not show any reaction. Both of these pigs are apparently in good health and entirely well at the present writing, eight months after inoculation. During this time guinea pig No. 109 had been chloroformed, September 29, 1894, and examined, without any signs of disease being apparent. The seventeenth generation of this germ was evidently too attenuated to cause death.

April 4, 1894. Guinea pig No. 110 was fed with 9 cc. tuberculin, diluted with sterile water, without ill effect.

February 19, 1894. Pig No. 122 was inoculated with 0.25 cc. of tuberculosis culture, the seventeenth generation, and on April 4, 1894, was fed with 25 cc. tuberculin. The pig was rather thin; there was a lesion the size of a pea at the point of inoculation, but the temperature was normal. April 9, 1894, this pig, No. 122, was found dead. The organs were apparently normal, except that the blood vessels of the stomach and intestines were much congested. The pig had evidently been poisoned with the tuberculin; the contents of the intestines were thick and mucus-like.

February 19, 1894. Guinea pig No. 121, weight 13 ounces, was inoculated with 0.25 cc. tubercle culture. May 16 it was well, and was reinoculated with 0.25 cc. tubercle culture.

February 19, 1894. Guinea pig No. 118 was inoculated with 0.25 cc. of tubercle culture, the seventeenth generation. March 19 this pig was found dead, but the autopsy did not reveal any signs of tuberculosis.

February 19, 1894. Guinea pig No. 119, weight 14 ounces, received an injection of 0.2 cc. tubercle culture, and on March 24, 1894, an injection of 0.5 cc. tuberculin. The temperature reaction was very slight.

February 19, 1894. Guinea pig No. 120, weight 14 ounces, was inoculated with 0.2 cc. tubercle culture. On April 4, 1894, it was fed 3 cc. of tuberculin. At this time it appeared to be ill, but did not show any reaction to the tuberculin, and the next day was quite well.

February 19, 1894. Guinea pig No. 125 was inoculated with 0.25 cc. tubercle culture. March 24 it received an injection of a small quantity of tuberculin, which caused a characteristic reaction.

March 8, 1894. Guinea pig No. 141, three-quarters of a pound in weight, was given 18 cc. of dilute tuberculin.

March 8, 1894. Guinea pig No. 142, healthy, was fed 27 cc. of tuberculin, but did not show any reaction. April 11, 1894, this pig was dead; the lungs were hemorrhagic, and the blood vessels of the stomach and intestines much congested from tuberculin poisoning.

March 12, 1894. Guinea pig No. 136, healthy, was fed 12 cc. of tuberculin.

May 16, 1894. Guinea pig No. 135, weight 1 pound; guinea pig No. 141, weight 1 pound, and guinea pig No. 136, weight 1 pound, all received 0.25 cc. tubercle culture, the twentieth generation. Guinea pig No. 137, weight 1 pound, received 0.5 cc. of the twentieth generation of tubercle culture. Nos. 141 and 136 had both been fed tuberculin once; the others had never been used.

July 27, 1894. Guinea pigs Nos. 210 and 211, weight 1 pound each, received 0.5 cc. of attenuated culture of tuberculosis, the twenty-second generation. At the present writing neither of these animals shows the least signs of tuberculosis.

July 29, 1894. Pigs Nos. 135, 136, 120, 110, 141, 125, and checks, healthy pigs, Nos. 213, 214, 215, and 133, were all inoculated for me at my request by Dr. V. A. Moore, with the material from the tuberculous gland of a badly diseased cow, No. 286. The inoculations were made beneath the skin of the side. On September 11, checks Nos. 214 and 215 were both found dead, and the autopsy revealed extensive tuberculosis in lungs, liver, and spleen. September 21, check No. 213 was found dead, the autopsy showing advanced tuberculosis. September 17, guinea pig No. 133 was chloroformed for examination, which revealed extensive tuberculosis.

October 13, 1894. Guinea pig No. 136, one that had been inoculated in May with the attenuated culture, and subsequently inoculated with a tuberculous gland, was chloroformed for examination. Not a sign of disease could be detected and the local lesion from the inoculation had almost healed.

October 29, 1894. Guinea pig No. 110 was found dead. This was a pig that had been fed upon tuberculin on April 4, 1894, and inoculated with the gland July 29, 1894. The autopsy showed advanced tuberculosis. The other pigs that had been inoculated with the attenuated culture and then the active virus, Nos. 135, 120, 141, and 125, are, at the present writing, quite well, and show no signs of disease. I may find that some of the animals that are now considered immune will eventually succumb to the disease. This, however, does not appear probable, as pig No. 136, examined after the death of all the checks, did not show any signs of disease.

Further, animals No. 137, inoculated with the twentieth generation May 16, and No. 112, inoculated March 30; Nos. 120 and 119, inoculated February 19; No. 113, March 30; and No. 121 on February 19, and again on May 16, are, at this writing, to all appearances, perfectly well, having lived from six to nine months after the inoculation.

February 23, rabbit No. 141 was inoculated with 0.25 cc. of tubercle culture of the seventeenth generation. July 27, this same rabbit was reinoculated with the twentieth generation of a tubercle culture, 0.25 cc. being used. The animal remains apparently well.

These experiments, which, of course, in connection with so important and troublesome a disease, can be regarded as preliminary only, and must be confirmed by a large number of similar ones, serve to show that by the use of attenuated tubercle bacilli and their products we may be able to control pulmonary tuberculosis. If the twenty-second generation has shown such attenuation and produced so much resistance, then the thirtieth generation, or later, should give still more satisfactory results.

An examination of the table and accompanying notes will also show that tuberculin, when fed in very large doses to supposedly diseased or to healthy pigs, may cause the death of these animals by poisoning. The amount necessary varies from twelve to twenty times the quantity that would give a reaction in a tuberculous cow.

The digestion experiments referred to in my report, in Bulletin No. 7, Bureau of Animal Industry, have shown that the action of tuberculin upon diseased animals is not affected after twenty-four hours in a hydrochloric-acid pepsin solution, nor by warming with acetic acid. On the other hand, in two cases noted, feeding the tuberculin in small doses, while it did not prevent the disease, apparently retarded it. Possibly a combined feeding of tuberculin and the inoculation with the attenuated germ may be found more useful than either alone.

The fact must not be lost sight of that the number of bacilli injected into an animal may cause great differences in the length of time of the development of the disease. There could be no error of this sort, however, in the experiments recorded, as the emulsion of virulent and attenuated cultures used for inoculation were prepared in the same way, and a larger quantity of the attenuated culture was used than is necessary in case of a more virulent one to produce death, in five to six weeks.

What conclusions may be drawn from these experiments? We have guinea pigs made apparently distinctly immune to an active tuberculous virus by the use of an attenuated germ. We have guinea pigs in which a single injection of a small quantity of tuberculin increased, perhaps, the subsequent immunity secured by injection with the attenuated culture. We have other pigs the immunity of which has not been tested, it is true, by an active virus, but which were inoculated with the attenuated culture many months ago, and are still well, and in which an autopsy of other animals treated in exactly the same way and at the same time showed no signs of disease.

Recently Viquerat claims to have been able by means of subcutaneous injections of the serum of the ass, an animal naturally immune from tuberculosis, to effect cures and improvement in the disease in man. Our attenuated germ may possibly prove very valuable in checking or controlling tuberculosis in animals, especially cattle.

Table showing effect of attenuated tubercle cultures and

No. of animal.	Fed tuberculin.		Injected tuberculin.		Inoculated with artificial-culture attenuated tubercle bacilli.		Fed tuberculin.	
	Date.	Amount.	Date.	Amount.	Date.	Amount and generation.	Date.	Amount.
Guinea pigs. 27	1894.		1894.		1894. Jan. 18	¼ cc., eighteenth generation.	1894. Mar. 17	24 cc....
28					Jan. 18	.....do......		
29					Jan. 18	.....do......		
30					Jan. 18	.....do......		
115	Feb. 16	6 cc....			Mar. 30	¼ cc., seventeenth generation.		
113	Feb. 15	4 cc....			Mar. 30	.....do......		
110	Apr. 5	9 cc....						
141	Mar. 8	18 cc....			May 16	¼ cc., twentieth generation.		
142	Mar. 8	26 cc....						
136		12 cc....			May 16	Twentieth generation.		
135					May 16	.....do......		
137					May 16	¼ cc., twentieth generation.		
213	Checks.							
214								
215								
133			Mar. 24	½ cc.....				
210					July 27	¼ cc., twenty-second generation.		
211					July 27	.....do......		
125					Feb. 19	¼ cc., nineteenth generation.		
122					Feb. 19	.....do......	Apr. 4	25 cc....
121					Feb. 19	¼ cc., seventeenth generation.		
120					Feb. 19	0.2 cc., seventeenth generation.	Apr. 4	3 cc.....
119					Feb. 19	.....do......		
118					Feb. 19	¼ cc., seventeenth generation.		
114					Mar. 30	.....do......		
109					Mar. 30	.....do......		
112					Mar. 30	.....do......		
Rabbit.....141					Feb. 28	Seventeenth generation.		
Cow 217					July —	Twentieth generation in the vein.		

feeding tuberculin in guinea pigs, rabbit, and cow.

Injected tuberculin.		Inoculation with tubercular gland.	Reinoculated with attenuated culture.	Dead.	Chloroformed.	Autopsy.		Present condition. (Nov. 28, 1894.)
Date.	Amount.					Date.	Condition.	
1894. Feb.13	¼ cc	1894.	1894.	1894. Mar. 19	1894.	1894. Mar. 19	Poisoned with tuberculin; no tuberculosis.	
					Mar. 19	Feb. 15	Organs normal.	
							.....do.....	
					June 5	June 5	.....do.....	
						June 5		Well, fat, in good condition.
		July 29		Oct. 29		Oct. 29	Badly tuberculous.	Do.
		July 29						
				Apr. 11		Apr. 11	Tuberculin poisoning.	
		July 29			Oct. 1	Oct. 1	Organs normal.	
		July 29						Do.
		July 29						Do.
		July 29		Sept. 11		Sept. 10	Badly tuberculous.	
		July 29		Sept.11		Sept. 11	.....do.....	
		July 29		Sept. 21		Sept. 21	.....do.....	
		July 29			Sept. 17	Sept. 17	.....do.....	Do.
								Do.
Mar.24	¼ cc							Do.
				Apr. 9		Apr. 9	Tuberculin poisoning.	
			May 16, ¼ cc.					Do.
								Do.
Mar.24	¼ cc			Mar. 19		Mar. 19	Organs normal.	Do.
				Oct. 19. Killed by rats.		Oct. 19	No tuberculosis.	
					Sept. 29	Sept. 29	.....do.....	Do.
			July 27, ¼ cc. twentieth generation.					Well.
								Tested with tuberculin; no reaction Nov. 20, 1894.

A NEW STAIN FOR BACILLUS TUBERCULOSIS.

By Marion Dorset, M. D.,

Biochemic Division, Bureau of Animal Industry.

The large percentage of fat present in the bodies of the tubercle bacilli was first noted by Hammerschlag. Subsequently Dr. de Schweinitz and the writer, in the course of a general chemical study of the tubercle bacillus which is being carried out in this laboratory under the direction of Dr. de Schweinitz, found that the dried bacilli often contained as much as 40 per cent of ether soluble material. Reports upon some of the results so far obtained in the work mentioned above have already been published by de Schweinitz or de Schweinitz and Dorset in the Journal of the American Chemical Society, 1895, 1896, and 1898; the Centralblatt für Bakteriologie und Parasitenkunde, and in bulletins of this Department.

In pursuance of a suggestion made in one of these earlier publications, that the large amount of fatty material in the tubercle bacilli probably accounted for the difficulty experienced in staining the bacillus with the ordinary dyes, an effort was made by the writer more than a year ago to stain them with some of the ordinary dyes after the preparations had been extracted with ether and alcohol for varying lengths of time. The results obtained, however, were not satisfactory. Shortly afterwards my attention was called to the statement that Sudan III[1] was a useful stain for fat in histological and pathological work, and it was immediately tried upon preparations of the tubercle bacilli. This dye is insoluble in water, soluble, however, in alcohol with a red color, also in the various essential oils, in chloroform and xylol. Fat once stained with this material can be decolorized with difficulty. Daddi,[2] who first suggested the use of Sudan III in histological and pathological work, recommends that Müller's fluid and glycerine be used in hardening and fixing the tissues, and that absolute alcohol should not be used as a dehydrating agent, nor should the specimen be cleared in the essential oils or xylol nor mounted in Canada balsam. After trying various strengths of solutions of Sudan III in alcohol, it has been found that the following methods give the most satisfactory results:

I. STAINING OF TUBERCLE BACILLI IN PURE CULTURES.

Cover-glass preparations were made and fixed in the ordinary way and then immersed for five minutes in a saturated solution of Sudan III 80 per cent alcohol. The excess of stain was then

---

[1] Since the preparation of this paper it has been found that several different substances are on the market under the name of Sudan III.

[2] Arch. ital. di biol., Vol. XXVI, p. 143, 1896.   Orig. paper in Giornale d. R. Acc. di medicina di Torino, No. 2, 1896.

removed by washing for five minutes in several changes of 70 per cent alcohol. The results obtained were very satisfactory, and the characteristic appearance of the tubercle bacilli could be very readily noted. The bacilli are stained somewhat better if left in the Sudan III ten minutes and then washed in the 70 per cent alcohol. The germs are found stained a bright red and the beaded appearance is very distinct. Cultures of the bovine tubercle bacillus, and also of the tubercle bacillus obtained from swine, treated with this dye were not apparently so well stained as in the case of the bacillus of human origin. These results should be verified, however, and further work with these and tubercle bacilli from various sources is in progress. The human tubercle bacilli stained with Sudan III are not decolorized by washing for two minutes with dilute 1-25 sulphuric, hydrochloric, or nitric acid, or ammonia.

II. STAINING OF PREPARATIONS FROM A GLAND OF A TUBERCULOUS GUINEA PIG, AND FROM SPUTUM WHICH HAD BEEN PROVED TO CONTAIN TUBERCLE BACILLI.

The preparations were fixed as usual and immersed for ten minutes in a saturated solution of Sudan III in 80 per cent alcohol. They were then washed from five to ten minutes in 70 per cent alcohol. Upon examination the tubercle bacilli were found to be stained a distinct red and presented the characteristic appearance. No other bacilli present in the sputum had been stained by the Sudan III, though they were evident in quantity when the preparation was counterstained with methylene blue. The tubercle bacilli still retained their characteristic red color and appearance.

III. SECTIONS OF A TUBERCULOUS LUNG.

Sections from the lung of a man who died of bronchial tuberculosis[1] were stained from five to ten minutes in a concentrated 80 per cent alcoholic solution of Sudan III washed from five to ten minutes in several changes of 70 per cent alcohol, counterstained with methylene blue, dehydrated with absolute alcohol, cleared with clove oil, and mounted in Canada balsam. In this preparation the tubercle bacilli were stained red and could be distinctly seen lying in the tissue. The material from which the sections were made was prepared in the following way: Pieces of the lung were placed in absolute alcohol and allowed to remain for a week, then placed in a fresh lot of alcohol, and from that passed through alcohol and ether into celloidin in the usual way. The sections after staining were also dehydrated with alcohol, but in spite of this fact the tubercle bacilli were well stained by Sudan III. It is thus evident that their staining properties are

---

[1] The material was kindly furnished by Dr. Carroll, of the Army Medical Museum.

not influenced by the dehydrating action of the alcohol.   This differs
from the method prescribed by Daddi in staining sections for fat, as
he recommends that care should be taken not to dehydrate with alcohol or clear, with clove oil.   Possibly the fatty material in the bodies
of the tubercle bacilli is not as soluble as that deposited in the tissues.
It should be noted, however, that preparations stained with Sudan III
and mounted in Canada balsam did not retain a bright color after a
month's time.

To demonstrate further that Sudan III is apparently a selective
stain for tubercle bacilli, I endeavored to stain the numerous varieties
of bacteria found in decomposing sputa, pure cultures of hog cholera,
glanders, typhoid, anthrax, symptomatic anthrax, diphtheria, and
prodigiosus bacilli, the spirilla of Asiatic cholera, and the *Staphylo-
coccus pyogenes aurus*, with negative results.   Preparations of the
smegma bacilli were also made, but did not stain with Sudan III,
although they were stained with carbol-fuchsin according to the
ordinary method.   In a mixed preparation of tubercle and smegma
bacilli stained with Sudan III and well washed with 70 per cent
alcohol, the tubercle bacilli appeared characteristic, while the smegma
bacilli remained unstained, although this same preparation, when
subsequently stained with carbol-fuchsin, showed smegma bacilli
present in abundance.   It would appear from the results so far
obtained that Sudan III may be considered as a selective stain for the
tubercle bacillus, and that this selective action is due to the large
amount of fatty material present in the body of the germ.   When
stained with Sudan III the characteristic beaded appearance of the
tubercle bacilli is very distinct, and, as has been suggested, this beaded
appearance in the staining is probably due to the droplets of fatty
substance present in the body of the germ.   Although smegma bacilli
stain very readily with carbol-fuchsin, similarly to the tubercle bacilli,
the fact that the smegma bacilli do not stain with Sudan III would
indicate that their cell substance is very different from that of the
tubercle bacilli.

The practical value of Sudan III as a stain for tubercle bacilli will
be recognized where a rapid method is desired for staining the organism
in tissues, and for the purpose of differentiating without trouble
between smegma and tubercle bacilli in cases, as in urinary sediments,
where the smegma bacilli might be present, and throw some doubt
upon a positive identification of the tubercle bacilli by the ordinary
method of staining.   The method takes about the same length of time
as the carbol-fuchsin method for cover-glass preparations, but as the
stain is apparently a selective one for tubercle bacilli it appears to be
well adapted for routine work.

ASTHENIA (GOING LIGHT) IN FOWLS.[1]

By CHARLES F. DAWSON, M. D., D. V. S.,

Veterinary Inspector, Bureau of Animal Industry.

In January, 1898, two fowls were brought to the laboratory of the Bureau by Mr. Smith, of Hyattsville, Md., who requested an investigation of the disease from which they were suffering.

CLINICAL HISTORY.

The most noticeable departure from the normal condition in the fowls was their extreme emaciation. Their appetite was voracious. There was no evidence of an existing diarrhea; indeed, a slight constipation seemed to exist. There was no increase of temperature, and the comb and wattles were slightly paler than is usually found. Mr. Smith had 350 fowls, 30 of which had died and 100 of which were sick. The disease was a chronic one, lasting about three months before a fatal issue. The fowls were well cared for, the house in which they were kept at night being so built as to be free from drafts. Their diet consisted of a morning meal of bran mash made of six parts bran and four of middlings and two of Bradley's meat meal, with Sheridan's C. P. and a little charcoal. They had plenty of small gravel and crushed oyster shells. At night corn, wheat, and oats were fed. None of Mr. Smith's neighbors had the disease in their flocks, although they were only 75 yards away. The adult male Brahma variety seemed most susceptible to the disease, Mr. Smith having lost 15 roosters. He had never noticed any diarrhea. The disease made itself known only through loss of flesh, and some of Mr. Smith's neighbors called it "going light"; others said it was a new disease to them. Damp weather seemed to increase the symptoms. Although the sick fowls had mingled with swine and the dead ones had been eaten by them, no disease resulted in swine or other animals. Mr. Smith tried careful nursing in six cases, and they all seemed to recover.

POSTMORTEM APPEARANCES.

Postmortem examination revealed an extreme emaciation of the muscular system and viscera, with almost complete absence of fat. The crop and gizzard appeared normal and well filled with food material. The duodenum was the only organ noticeably affected. Here there was a reddening of the walls and the contents were mucoid in appearance.

---

[1] Since this manuscript was prepared another outbreak of disease in fowls has been investigated by Miss Louise Tayler, assistant in the Pathological Laboratory. The disease was proved by animal inoculations and other bacteriological experimentation to be identical with the one described in this article.—C. F. D.

ETIOLOGY.

As the duodenal catarrh was the only noticeable departure from normal, it was supposed the fowls were suffering from a bacterial intestinal affection. Inoculations into various culture media from the various organs gave no development. A culture carefully made from the duodenal contents, however, developed a single species of bacterium. A portion of the duodenal contents was mixed with sterile normal salt solution and injected subcutaneously into a guinea pig, with the result that the animal died in the course of twenty-four hours. Post-mortem examination on this guinea pig showed an extremely edematous and necrotic condition of the subcutaneous and muscular tissues of the ventral aspect of the body, simulating malignant edema. The germ was demonstrated in the liver, local lesion, spleen, abdominal exudate, heart blood, and lungs; none were found in the kidneys. Bacteriological comparison of the bacterium found in the edematous fluid and muscular tissue with the culture made from the duodenal contents of the fowl showed the two germs to be identical. Rabbits were inoculated subcutaneously and fed with cultures of the organism without fatal result or the production of any illness. If, however, a ½ cc. of bouillon culture of the germ be injected into rabbits intra-abdominally, the animals will die inside of twenty-four hours. As lesions a severe duodenitis and an inflammation of the omentum will be noticed. 'From the wall of the duodenum and its contents and from the liver the germ may be found in large numbers. Experiments upon chickens in which cultures of the germ, both in artificial media and in the organs of animals dead from disease, have failed to produce any other symptoms than a slight transient indisposition. Chickens have been inoculated intra-abdominally, subcutaneously, and intravenously without result. In one case 15 cc. of a liquid culture was introduced by catheter directly into the gizzard. Pigeons, mice, and rats were also refractory.

Although the required postulates have not been fulfilled, I am inclined to believe that the bacterium described below is the cause of this disease in chickens. I am also inclined to regard the organism as a heretofore undescribed variety of the colon species. It differs materially from the organisms found in similar situations by Klein and by Lucet.

BACTERIOLOGY OF THE DISEASE.

BACTERIUM ASTHENIÆ.

Morphology.—A bacterium with blunt ends, varying in size according to the medium on which it is grown, from 1 micron to 1¼ microns long and nearly ½ micron wide, and often occurring in pairs. It does not stain in acid or alkaline methylene blue, carbol fuchsin, or in any alcoholic solutions of the various stains. It stains well in aqueous solutions of fuchsin, methylene blue, Bismarck brown, night blue, and Gram's stain.

Biology.—An aerobic and facultative anaerobic bacterium.

Acid bouillon.—In this medium (peptonized beef broth not alkalinized) the organism flourishes well, causing a dense turbidity with a floating pellicle and a ring of deposit around the tube at the level of the liquid. The fluid has a putrefactive odor and is of a yellowish green color. On the third day considerable white deposit occurs.

Alkaline bouillon.—The culture is densely turbid the first day and a ring of deposit which is easily broken is noted at the surface of the liquid. The odor is putrefactive, resembling that in cultures of the swine plague organism. The reaction is slightly acid.

Glucose bouillon.—In 1 per cent solutions of this medium fermentation begins the first day and is completed in three days. The reaction becomes highly acid. Growth takes place throughout the fermentation tube. The odor is slightly sour. There is a slight surface deposit and the neck of the tube contains a whitish material. Total quantity of gas produced is 50 cm. By the addition of sodic hydrate to absorb the carbon dioxide, the gas formula reads—hydrogen, three parts; carbon dioxide, two parts, or $\dfrac{H}{CO_2} = 3/2$.

Saccharose bouillon.—Reaction becomes quite acid and other appearances similar to the glucose tubes, except in the amount of gas produced. Total amount of gas produced was 6 cm.; the gas formula was $\dfrac{H}{CO_2} = 2/1$.

Lactose bouillon.—In this medium there were no remarkable differences from the other two sugar solutions, except that 35 cm. was the total amount of gas produced. Of this two parts were hydrogen and one part was carbon dioxide, making the gas formula $\dfrac{H}{CO_2} = 2/1$.

Milk.—This is firmly coagulated inside of twenty-four hours. The whey is perfectly clear, highly acid, and odorless.

Gelatine stick cultures.—At 75° to 80° F. growth occurs both on the surface and along the track of the needle. Around the place of entrance is a spreading, brownish, deeply dentated growth, the whole surrounded by a delicate, peripheral, concentric growth seen only with magnifying glass. Growth appears like an anthrax colony, but is not so luxuriant. There were no annular markings. Along the track of the needle growth appears as small, yellowish, discrete, closely packed colonies.

Gelatine plate cultures.—In twenty-four hours at 78° to 80° F. colonies 1½ millimeters in diameter, with no annular markings or "overflow" border, appear. The border of colony is indicated by bright edge, showing it to be raised on a level with the rest of the colony, or is precipitous. There is a papillated center surrounded by a yellowish material. The rest of the colony contained clouded areas of irregular shape. The submerged colonies are yellowish and have irregularly lobulated margins with well-defined edges.

Agar slants.—A luxuriant white opaque growth, with slightly wavy margins, occurs along the line of stroke, attaining its maximum in twenty-four hours.

Potato.—On this medium in three days there occurs a yellowish, creamy growth, spreading around the base of the potato cylinder. Along the line of inoculation gas-containing blisters indicate its property of fermenting starch. Some of these have burst, causing crater-like depressions in the growth. The odor is pungent and disagreeable.

Effect of disinfectants.—Carbolic acid in solutions of ½ per cent does not kill the germ when immersed in it for five minutes. A 1 per cent carbolic acid solution kills it in five minutes. Aqua calcis does not kill it in forty-eight hours. Formaldehyde gas, generated by volatilization of 1 gram of paraform inside an inverted gallon bell jar, kills the organism when the culture tube, containing 10 cc. and not plugged, is placed inside the bell jar.

Maximum temperature at which the organism will vegetate.—Bouillon tubes inoculated with the organism and placed in an incubator at 55° C. showed no growth. Subsequent inoculations from these tubes into tubes kept at 37° C. showed the germ still viable. When similar tubes were kept overnight in an incubator at 49° C., growth took place.

Minimum temperature.—Inoculated tubes kept in an ice chest at 50° F. showed a slight clouding in three days. No growth occurred at 40° F.

Temperature at which the organism is killed.—Exposures of cultures of the germ in thin-walled narrow tubes deeply immersed in water showed the germ to be killed at between 57° and 60° C.

Freezing.—Inoculations from bouillon cultures kept frozen in freezing mixture for twenty-four hours into fresh tubes of bouillon showed that the germ retained its vitality.

Desiccation.—Sterilized tubes were smeared on the inside with a loop of a bouillon culture and placed in incubator at 37° C. overnight to dry. They were then placed in a window under the influence of drying and diffuse sunlight. After twelve days of such treatment development took place upon the addition of sterilized broth.

REMARKS.

Among the peculiarities of this organism are the wide temperature limits in which it will vegetate—from 50° to 120° F. Freezing for twenty-four hours does not kill it. Limewater does not kill it in forty-eight hours. Two weeks' drying in diffuse sunlight does not kill it. It ferments at least three of the sugars, and potato starch. It takes Gram's stain, but not alcoholic solutions of the various stains.

It was found in pure culture in the duodenal contents of chickens in an asthenic condition. It is pathogenic for guinea pigs and rabbits. The material obtained did not contain the germ with sufficient virulence to cause the disease in fowls.

Tests made for the presence of indol and phenol were negative in results. The distillate of liquid cultures has a strong odor of marsh gas.

TREATMENT.

This disease is one in which the vitality is being sapped by the multiplication of a parasitic bacterium in that part of the alimentary canal where the digestive process is most active and important. The food constituents elaborated and intended for absorption here are probably appropriated or decomposed by the parasite, and the starvation of the fowl, shown by the extreme emaciation, is thus slowly accomplished. In addition an inflammatory process is set up by the bacterium, which also interferes with the absorption process. Therefore the indications for the treatment are, first, the removal of the causative element—the bacterium—and the renewal of the lost vitality by medicinal tonics, easily digested foods, and careful housing.

As medicinal agents for the removal of the cause by purgation, castor oil in two-teaspoonful doses, or calomel in oft-repeated $\frac{1}{2}$-grain doses may be tried. Purgation should be followed by a stimulating tonic. Dr. Salmon recommends the following tonic in similar affections: Powdered fennel, anise, coriander seed, cinchona, each 30 grains; powdered gentian and ginger, of each 1 dram; powdered sulphate of iron, 15 grains. Mix. Add from 2 to 4 grains of this mixture for each fowl to the food twice a day.

Fig. 1. From a 24-hour-old growth on potato.
        × 3,000 diameters.
     2. From a 24-hour-old growth in bouillon.
        × 3,000 diameters.
     3. From a 24-hour-old growth on agar-agar.
        × 3,000 diameters.
     4. From a 24-hour-old growth on gelatine.
        × 3,000 diameters.
     5. From local lesion in guinea pig.
        × 3,000 diameters.

   334

Fig. 1.

Fig. 2.

Fig. 3.

Fig. 4.

Fig. 5.

Haines, del.

A.Hoen & Co. Lith. Baltimore.

BACTERIUM ASTHENIÆ.

LABORATORY METHODS FOR THE DIAGNOSIS OF CERTAIN MICROORGANISMAL DISEASES.

By CHARLES F. DAWSON, M. D., D. V. S.,

Veterinary Inspector, Bureau of Animal Industry.

The diseases here described have been placed according to the range of their occurrence in the lower animals; for instance, anthrax, malignant edema, and rabies may be found in most of the lower animals. Actinomycosis, Texas fever, tuberculosis, and blackleg are oftenest found in cattle—Texas fever and blackleg being two diseases peculiar to cattle. Tetanus and glanders, while they occur in other animals, are found oftenest in the horse. Hog cholera and swine plague, as their names indicate, are peculiar to swine. Entero-hepatitis, infectious leukæmia, chicken cholera, and roup are fowl diseases. The nodular diseases in fowls and sheep are included because of their resemblance to tuberculosis.

ANTHRAX.

Anthrax is probably the best known bacterial disease, because it was one of the first to be recognized as such. It received a great deal of attention in the early days of bacteriological research. It is one of the few bacterial diseases where a diagnosis can be made with tolerable certainty with the aid of a microscope alone. In an outbreak of this disease there will, in all probability, be a history of very sudden deaths, and its existence in more than one kind of animal. To make a diagnosis, take a bit of the spleen, blood, or liver of an animal recently dead, and smear it on a cover-glass. Allow it to dry, and pass the cover-glass with the smeared side up through the flame of a Bunsen burner three times, occupying one second each time. Now add, with a medicine dropper, a small quantity of Loeffler's alkaline methyline blue as a stain. The formula for this solution is as follows: To 30 parts of a saturated alcoholic solution of methylene blue, add 100 parts of a solution of potassium hydrate (1–10,000). Allow the stain to remain on the cover-glass for a minute. Wash off carefully in clear water. Lay the cover-glass, stained side up, between two pieces of filter paper and press to absorb the water. When perfectly dry, mount in balsam. If anthrax bacteria are present they can readily be seen, stained blue, under a microscope magnifying five hundred diameters. The bacteria will appear as rods with square ends, *never* blunt or round. They will also be seen in chains, containing a dozen or less cells with square ends in apposition. Spores are not found in the germ in fresh tissue. These appear very early in liquid cultures, occur about the middle of the cell, and do not cause any bulging.

With lenses of good definition, the ends of the stained rods frequently appear slightly concave. When the bacterium is sown in bouillon a profuse growth consisting of flocculi occurs in twenty-four hours slightly below the surface. If shaken the flocculi break up and fall to the bottom. A cover-glass preparation from the culture will show the germs arranged in bundles of long chains. The germ of anthrax measures from 1 to 1.25 microns in breadth, and from 5 to 20 microns in length. In gelatine stab cultures a fir-tree growth occurs along the line of puncture in a day or two, with saucer-shaped liquefaction of the surface. The organism is nonmotile.

An organism appearing in the blood of animals that have died suddenly, and answering the description above given, may with tolerable certainty be called the bacterium of anthrax. The bacillus of malignant edema may be mistaken for it; but here it must be remembered that while this bacillus may be found in chains with opposing ends square, the terminal cell will be found to be *round* on the free end. This germ is, moreover, anaerobic and is not found in the blood for sometime after death, while the anthrax bacterium is aerobic and thrives best where it can obtain a good supply of oxygen. This it can do in the circulating blood.

Another method of diagnosing the affection is by animal inoculation. Anthrax material will produce the disease in mice, guinea pigs, and rabbits; the degree of susceptibility in these animals being in the order in which the animals are named. The younger the animal, the greater is the degree of susceptibility. If such an organism is found in the blood or other organs of these animals after inoculation with a suspected tissue, it may safely be called anthrax, as there is no known pathogenic bacterium having a similar morphology. Dogs are immune from the disease. To test a suspected tissue by means of animal inoculation, grind up in a sterile mortar with salt solution of 0.6 per cent strength, or in neutral bouillon, a piece of the suspected tissue. Allow the undissolved tissue to subside, and inject a young guinea pig, mouse, or rabbit subcutaneously with $\frac{1}{4}$ cc. of the extract thus made. If the material is fresh and from an animal recently dead, the inoculated animal should die in a day or two. The bacterium may be found in abundance in the blood, spleen, or liver; or, cultures may be made in bouillon from the original material, incubated at 37° C. to 38° C., and from 0.3 to 0.5 cc. injected subcutaneously into animals. The germ can then be identified in the same manner as given above. (Pl. IX, fig. 1.)

MALIGNANT EDEMA.

Although this organism may affect several species, cases of the disease are comparatively rare, and it occurs only when large surfaces are exposed to infection.

The germ is an anaerobic organism 3 microns long and 1 broad, exists in all climates, and will withstand almost any ordinary physical condition. Its home is in the soil, and it perpetuates its species by reverting to the spore stage when conditions for its multiplication become adverse. It can be differentiated from anthrax by the fact that it causes a local disease, and is not found in the blood during life or just after death. Nor will the spleen or other internal organs be noticeably affected. It is said to be a motile organism, but the writer has never observed motility in artificial cultures. The spore may be seen in the center or slightly to one end of the rod, where it causes a slight enlargement. It may be observed in chains, and the opposing ends will be square, resembling the bacterium of anthrax. The terminal cell of the chain, however, will *always* be found rounded on the free end, *never* square. This at once differentiates it from the bacterium of anthrax. It greatly resembles the bacillus of blackleg, but it can be easily differentiated from the latter by animal inoculation. Guinea pigs are susceptible to malignant edema as well as to blackleg. Rabbits, however, do not die when inoculated with the blackleg organism, while they are very susceptible to malignant edema. In testing a tissue for the presence of this bacillus by means of animal inoculation, proceed in the same manner as described in the paragraph on anthrax, with the following changes. As the organism will not grow in the presence of oxygen, it is better to inject the material, or culture, deeply into the muscles of the gluteal region of a rabbit or guinea pig. If an attempt is made to use cultures for inoculation, they must be made in an anaerobic apparatus. For this purpose a fermentation tube having one end filled with neutral bouillon, and completely freed from oxygen by three consecutive boilings, is recommended. From 0.2 to 0.3 cc. drawn from the bottom of such a culture should kill a rabbit or guinea pig inside of twenty-four hours. The bacillus can be obtained in pure cultures from the liver or spleen a few hours after death. In cover-glass preparations made from the edematous fluid of the local lesion of an animal recently dead, the organism is rarely found spore-bearing, as is the case with the blackleg organism. In cultures, however, this organism soon reverts to the spore-bearing stage.

In the inoculated animal there will be found, as lesions of the disease, extensive edema of the subcutaneous tissues. The affected muscles will be found gangrenous and very friable. The liquid poured out into the tissues will be of a sero-sanguinous nature, and has a disagreeable odor. The internal organs will not be noticeably affected. (Pl. IX, figs. 2 and 3.)

RABIES (HYDROPHOBIA).

This disease is possibly more widely spread than we acknowledge at present. Like anthrax and malignant edema, but to a greater extent, it affects many species. Man and the farm animals usually become infected from dog bites.

10317——22

Although no bacterium has yet been isolated and proven to be the cause of the disease, it is assumed that it is of bacterial origin. That it is an inoculable disease is shown by the method of diagnosis, which is as follows: A pea-sized piece of the base of the brain or medulla-oblongata of the suspected animal is obtained under the strictest aseptic precautions. This is ground up in a sterile mortar with sterile water. A few drops of this emulsion is injected by means of an ordinary hypodermatic syringe beneath the dura-mater of a rabbit which has been carefully trephined. Usually two or three rabbits are used. The wounds are carefully closed and the rabbits are kept under observation. If the case was one of rabies, it will be noticed on the twelfth day or thereabouts that the rabbits become unusually excitable. This may last one, two, or three days, during which time convulsions generally occur. They then pass into a stage of paralysis, in which the posterior extremities are first affected, and die in a day or two. In rare cases the disease may not show in rabbits for a month. Recently, guinea pigs, which are said to be more susceptible to the rabies virus, have been used. In these animals the disease is said to develop in about a week. Attention is called to the fact that rabbits develop the paralytic, while guinea pigs develop the furious, form of the disease. When it is impracticable to perform the operation of trephining, the virus may be injected into the anterior chamber of the eye of the rabbit or guinea pig, care being taken to wound the iris to promote absorption. Of the several different methods of inoculation for this disease the subdural in rabbits has, in the experience of the writer, been found the only reliable one.

ACTINOMYCOSIS.

The disease is primarily a local one in cattle, but may occur in man and other animals. It occurs extensively in the cattle-raising States, as is indicated by the number of cases noticed in the large stock yards. It is due to a fungus, the actinomyces, or ray fungus. Infection takes place through an abrasion of the mucous membrane of the mouth or through a carious tooth. The fungus then grows, penetrates any tissue with which it may come in contact, and forms large tumors, usually in the upper jaw, which finally suppurate. The disease may affect any organ.

The diagnosis can be made with a microscope, magnifying two or three hundred diameters by taking one of the little yellowish granular bodies of about one-fifth inch diameter, found very plentifully in the tumor mass, and slightly compressing it under a cover-class, with or without glycerine as a mounting medium. If the fungus is present it will be seen as a mass of little rays projecting from a center, or of a rosette shape. The rays will appear clubbed at the peripheral ends. In some preparations, owing to the presence of detritus, the fungus may be ill defined. Washing in caustic potash solution or acetic acid previous to mounting will usually clear it away. The fungus may also be stained, if it is not visible without it, by Gram's stain. The formula for this stain and its mode of application is as follows: (1) Flatten out one of the small granules upon a cover-glass sufficiently to render it transparent, after having washed away all detritus. Fix by heat, immerse in a hot filtered solution of aniline water gentian violet from two to three minutes. (The aniline water gentian violet is made by dissolving a few drops of aniline oil in water, filtering off the excess of oil, and adding a few drops of a concentrated solution of gentian violet.) (2) Carry directly into Gram's solution of iodide of potassium, and allow it to remain from one to three minutes. (This solution consists of 1 part iodide, 1 part potassium iodide, 2 parts in 300 parts of distilled water.) (3) Wash in alcohol, 60 per cent, until a light-brown shade remains. (4) Remove the alcohol by washing in water. (5) Place in eosin, picro-carmine or Bismarck brown for contrast stain. The fungus will appear stained blue, and all else red or brown, according to the contrast stain employed.

Attempts to inoculate animals or make cultures as a means of diagnosis often result in failures, and is a superfluous procedure for the purpose of diagnosis. Upon glycerine-agar a yellowish growth is obtained in successful cultures, consisting of mycelia—the club-shaped or conical rays which are supposed to be the spore-bearing organs, not forming. (Pl. X, fig. 5.)

TEXAS FEVER.

This is a blood disease and exists only in cattle, so far as is known. The cause of it remained in doubt for a long time, owing to the many contradictory conditions surrounding the outbreaks. Dr. Theobald Smith, on October 23, 1889, read a paper before the American Public Health Association, describing an intra-corpuscular body, a parasitic protozoan, which he had discovered, shown to be the cause of the disease, and named *Pyrosoma bigeminum*.

In cases of the disease, the animal will have continuous high fever of 106°F. or more from four to fifteen days; afterwards a general weakness sets in, and this is followed in a few days by death. In the later stage of the disease the urine becomes highly colored with hæmoglobin, indicating a frightful loss of red blood cells. This amounts to a decline, in some cases, to one million to the cubic millimeter of blood; whereas the normal number is about five millions. The spleen will be found much enlarged and to contain a dark tarry substance instead of the normal pulp. A condition of this kind in cattle may be looked upon with great suspicion. In addition, when the animals are infested with the cattle tick the suspicion may almost be confirmed. The ticks may be so small as to escape notice at first, but a careful search will reveal them. The tick is regarded as the host of the parasitic protozoan, and in fastening itself to the skin of the animals it inoculates them with the parasite. The parasite multiplies rapidly, enters and destroys the red corpuscles, producing a train of symptoms pathognomonic of the disease.

The parasite may be demonstrated in the red cells during life in some cases. Make smear preparations of the blood drawn from an incision into the skin of the hip. These films are dried and fixed by passing them through the flame three times, film side up; or it is safer to heat the films in a hot-air oven for one hour at 110° to 120° C. Add a few drops of Loeffler's alkaline methylene blue (formula given above) to the smeared surface. After an interval of two or three minutes the specimen is washed free of the stain in clear water and mounted either in water or balsam as desired. If overstained, immerse for a moment in 0.3 of 1 per cent of acetic acid, and then wash in water.

If the case is one of Texas fever, in which the parasite can be demonstrated antemortem, blue dots, sometimes very small, sometimes in pairs, will be found inside of the red cells. The organism also frequently appears pyriform. Sometimes the parasite will be found outside of the corpuscle, or free. In many cases they are not found at all antemortem. They may always be found, however, postmortem, in the spleen, liver, or heart muscle. As no satisfactory method has yet been devised for the cultivation of protozoa on artificial media, the clinical history, the determination of the intraglobular parasite by means of the microscope, and the presence of the ticks will have to suffice in diagnosing Texas fever. There can hardly be any mistake, however, as these means are amply sufficient. (Pl. IX, figs. 4, 5, and 6.)

TUBERCULOSIS.

This disease may be found in any mammal, and cases have been reported in fish and frogs. It is, however, most common in cattle. In cattle affected with the disease there may be no manifestation for some time which is sufficient to arrest the attention. Finally, however, an animal will begin to cough, become feverish, slightly emaciated, and will eventually die. The symptoms will point plainly to trouble in the respiratory tract. In this disease we have an excellent method of detecting even those cases which are in their incipiency. It consists in the subcutaneous injection of a certain amount of toxin produced by the growth in bouillon of the tubercle bacterium. From injecting this tubercle toxin, known as tuberculin, an exacerbation of the disease occurs. There is a sudden rise of the temperature within a certain time after injection, with a corresponding increase in all other symptoms. This method is so accurate that it is safe to condemn all those which give a considerable rise of temperature after the injection of the tuberculin. Tuberculin is prepared by growing the tubercle bacterium in bouillon to which 5 per cent glycerine has been added. After the growth has gone on for two or three weeks the culture is freed of the live germs by filtration through unglazed porcelain tubes, or by boiling the culture for a short while to kill the bacterium, and subsequent filtration to clear the solution of the dead growth. Carbolic acid sufficient to prevent decomposition is added, and the material, a light-brown liquid, is packed in hermetically sealed, sterilized bottles. It is now a commercial article, and can be obtained from the large manufacturing-chemists.

To detect the presence of the tubercle bacterium in tissue by means of the microscope, smear preparations are made as in the case of the foregoing diseases. After fixing by heat, pour on some Ziehl-Neelsen carbol-fuchsin. (This is made by dissolving 1 part of fuchsin in 10 parts of alcohol, and 100 parts of a 5 per cent solution of carbolic acid.) Pass the cover-glass through the flame of a Bunsen burner thirty times, replacing the solution as it evaporates; or, better, heat the stain in a closed vessel. Allow to cool, remove the cover-glass, and wash off in clear water. Then add, as a contrast stain, a few drops of Gabbett's acid methylene blue. (This is made by dissolving 2 parts of methylene blue in 100 parts of a 25 per cent solution of sulphuric acid.) Allow this stain to act about one minute. Wash off, and dry between two pieces of filter paper. Mount in balsam or water, and examine with an oil-immersion lens. If the bacterium be present, it will appear stained red. All else will have been decolorized by the acid in the methylene blue solution, and have taken up the blue stain. Two other methods remain by which a diagnosis may be made. One of them is the histological study of the sections of the diseased glands, lungs, or other affected tissues. In these the characteristic tubercle structure may be made out, and in many cases also the bacterium, in preparations stained by Gabbett's method. Another method, probably the most certain, but which requires about three weeks, is the inoculation of some of the ground-up affected tissues into guinea pigs subcutaneously or intra-abdominally. This animal is quite susceptible to the tubercle organism. A tissue might contain too few of the bacteria for their recognition by the microscope, and yet they might be present in sufficient numbers to start up the disease in guinea pigs. As evidences of the inoculation disease in guinea pigs will be noticed extensive alterations in the lymphatic glands, lungs, liver, and spleen. The lungs will contain numerous round yellowish tubercular masses. There may be considerable hydrothorax. The liver will be somewhat enlarged and contain large yellowish necrosed areas, the result of the coalescence of numerous small tubercles. The spleen will be found much enlarged, engorged with blood, and to present upon its surface numerous grayish tubercular areas. The lymphatic glands will be found much enlarged and to vary from a cheesy to a crumby consistence. In some, deposits of salts will have taken place, and these will impart a grating sensation upon section. The bacterium may be demonstrated in properly prepared preparations. Should the inoculated guinea pig show no emaciation within three weeks, or die, it should be chloroformed and examined, as they frequently remain apparently healthy and yet upon postmortem may be found extensively diseased. (Pl. X, fig. 1.)

BLACKLEG.

Blackleg, otherwise known as black quarter, quarter ill, or symptomatic anthrax, is a disease found in calves ranging from 6 months to 2½ years old. The losses from this disease in the cattle-raising States make it one of the most important diseases of our animals. As its geographical distribution does not depend on climatic conditions, it may be found wherever a previous case has existed. At present, however, it exists mainly in the cattle-raising States.

The germ which causes blackleg much resembles the malignant edema bacillus, but is more slender, is often found in pairs, and never in chains like the latter. It frequently forms filaments. It may be differentiated from anthrax by the fact that in animals dead from blackleg the spleen and other organs are not noticeably affected. There may be some reddening of the intestine, but the disease is usually located in the muscles and subcutaneous connective tissue of the thigh and inguinal regions. If the infection takes place in the mouth or throat the disease will be localized in the anterior portion of the body. The animal becomes suddenly lame, usually in one leg. There is a rapid rise of temperature and in the respiratory rate. The animal gets down finally and dies in a day or two. The affected leg is much swollen. The abdomen contains much gas, and the tissues have a strong butyric acid odor. The best and fattest calves are the ones which usually become affected. If the animal is skinned it will have the appearance of having been beaten with a club.

In a typical case, the affected muscles are emphysematous, causing them to be very light and spongy. They exhibit, in addition to the highly inflamed appearance, spots here and there of free blood which has escaped from the vessels.

A differential diagnosis between this and three other diseases for which it may be mistaken—anthrax, malignant edema, and Texas fever—may be made with certainty. In anthrax we have the enlarged spleen; this is never present in blackleg. Anthrax may be found in several species in the same outbreak. Blackleg is not found in horses, adult cattle, or swine. Swine, have, however, been reported susceptible. The anthrax bacterium lives and multiplies in the blood. The blackleg bacillus is not found in the circulating blood. Cultures may be obtained from the blood, but this is because the spores are present, they having been absorbed from the local lesion. If the bacillus is present in the blood it is there by accident, and will not multiply so long as the blood contains oxygen, because it is a strict anaerobe. The anthrax bacterium is square on the ends, and grows in chains of several cells each, while the blackleg bacillus is blunt on the ends, and does not grow in chains, and is often a long oval in shape, or, if containing a spore, may be spindle-shaped. The anthrax bacterium does not form spores while it is in the bodies of live animals; the blackleg bacillus does. The anthrax bacterium may be grown on the surface of culture media, while the blackleg bacillus will not grow in the presence of atmospheric air.

The blackleg bacillus may be differentiated from the bacillus of malignant edema, an organism which it greatly resembles, by a study of their respective biological characters, as well as by their range of pathogenesis. The bacillus of malignant edema measures about 3 microns long and about 1 micron broad. The bacillus of blackleg is about the same length and half as broad. The bacillus of malignant edema kills rabbits and guinea pigs, while the bacillus of blackleg is not known to be fatal to rabbits. In malignant edema the fluid poured into the subcutaneous tissues from the blood vessels does not contain a large amount of coloring matter, and is therefore comparatively pale, while in blackleg the edematous fluid is very red, from the escaped corpuscles and coloring matter of the blood. Malignant edema rarely becomes epidemic, while blackleg does; blackleg appears throughout the year, and is most plentiful when the spore-containing soil is stirred up by worms, sprouting grass, or from other causes.

Blackleg may be distinguished from Texas fever without difficulty. In Texas fever the spleen is greatly enlarged; there is no lameness or swelling; the urine is wine-colored; ticks are usually present, and, above all, the intraglobular parasites may be demonstrated in the blood. The ages of the animals affected would also be a valuable guide in diagnosis. Cattle of all ages are susceptible to Texas fever, while blackleg is generally found in those ranging from 6 to 30 months of age. (Pl. X, fig. 2.)

TETANUS.

Tetanus is found mainly in horses. Like the germs of malignant edema, blackleg, and anthrax, the germ of tetanus lives as a spore in the soil. The spore enters a wound by being carried in on a nail, splinter, or similar wounding body. Being a strict anaerobe, the spore can not change to the bacillar stage until the wound has healed and shut off the air. When this occurs the spore develops into a bacillus. Each divides into two, and finally when they have become sufficiently numerous they produce by their physiological activity sufficient tetanus toxin to cause the well-known symptoms of the disease. The germ is very difficult to locate, and it is almost useless to look for it in animals when the point of inoculation is unknown.

Diagnosis must here depend upon the clinical history. Death may occur in four to five days. Difficulty in mastication and deglutition will be noticed as early symptoms in the horse, owing to the muscles partaking of the general tetanization. The nictitating membrane will also be noticed extending over the front of the eye from a recession of the eyeball caused by a contraction of its extrinsic muscles. Endeavors to force open the jaws will cause great nervousness and increased contraction of the jaw and neck muscles. The spine and legs become rigid and are moved with difficulty, the tail being elevated and motionless. The muscular system finally becomes tetanic, indicated by a constant tremor. There is cold perspiration, locked jaws, retracted eyeballs, drawn lips, and dilated nostrils, the whole constituting a perfect picture of misery, which is ended by death. In many cases the symptoms never reach an acute stage, but are all present in a mild form and are amenable to treatment. In others the symptoms are confined to head and neck muscles, while in others the head and neck may be exempt and the symptoms appear in the body and limbs.

The disease is most prevalent in warm climates, and can be produced in mice, rabbits, and guinea pigs by inoculation with earth from infected localities. The disease is inoculable into all the animals. The toxin produced by the tetanus bacillus is an extremely potent one, a one hundred-thousandth of a cubic centimeter of a filtered bouillon culture being sufficient to kill a guinea pig. (Pl. X, figs. 3 and 4.)

GLANDERS.

Glanders is a disease which is oftenest found in horses and mules. Cattle are immune. In this disease the primary lesions are usually in the nasal passages. Here the mucous membrane becomes reddened, infiltrated with tubercles, and finally ulcerated. The ulcers have the appearance of having been gnawed. When a capillary has been ruptured by the ulcerative process, the usual yellow discharge from the nostril becomes streaked with blood. The disease also manifests itself in the skin, causing the lymphatic glands to ulcerate. These ulcers and swellings are known as farcy buds, the names farcy and glanders being regarded as synonymous. The former is an external manifestation. The disease may invade the lungs, liver, and spleen, and does so frequently. In some animals glanders remains latent, and in these cases great difficulty is experienced in making a diagnosis. This difficulty can be readily overcome, however, by using the glanders toxin as a diagnostic agent. This toxin is prepared similarly to tuberculin and is known as mallein. Its mode of action is similar to tuberculin in that it causes an exacerbation of the disease. This is indicated by a rise of temperature and the formation within a certain period of a tumor at the point of injection. Another method of diagnosis is the inoculation of male guinea pigs with some of the nasal discharge or other infected material emulsified in normal salt solution or bouillon. Several guinea pigs should be used, and different-sized doses should be given—say 0.1, 0.2, 0.4, and 0.5 cc. should be injected intraabdominally into four guinea pigs. Those receiving the larger dose may die of septicemia. If the glanders bacterium is present in the injected material, and has not been killed or rendered inert by desiccation or other influences, the guinea pigs should be attacked in forty-eight to seventy-two hours by a violent orchitis. If the animals live six to eight weeks, the scrotum will ulcerate. The lips and feet, also, will show a tendency to ulceration. The presence of the germ can also be demonstrated by means of plate cultures and cultivation on the various media. The organism is a short rod with rounded, slightly pointed ends, a little shorter and much thicker than the tubercle organism. It takes the aniline colors in aqueous solutions rather feebly in parts of the cells, while in others the cellular protoplasm is deeply stained. It grows best upon glycerine-agar as a pale-white transparent streak along the track of the inoculating needle. (Pl. X, fig. 6.) Upon potato it gives a characteristic dirty-brown color in about a week. If, however, mallein injections and guinea pig inoculations fail of results, it may be doubted that the case is glanders.

HOG CHOLERA AND SWINE PLAGUE.

As these two diseases often coexist, it is deemed better to mention them together. Although in some of the text-books their identity is seemingly much mixed, they are regarded in this country as two distinct diseases. The former—hog cholera—is primarily a disease of the intestine, but may secondarily attack the lungs. Swine plague, on the other hand, has its primary seat in the lungs and may attack the intestine.

The germs of both diseases have been carefully studied and described by Drs. Salmon and Smith[1] as belonging to two distinct groups of bacteria. The hog cholera germ may be classed with the colon group of bacteria, while the swine plague germ may be classed with the hemorrhagic septicemia group. So much alike, indeed, are the members of the latter group of bacteria that it is almost impossible to distinguish one from the other. Their variations are mainly found in the degree of their virulence and range of pathogenesis, and not in their behavior when leading a saprophytic existence. For instance, it would be a difficult matter to differentiate between cultures of the germs of swine plague, chicken cholera, spontaneous rabbit septicemia, and a few plagues found in other animals. This group is widely distributed, is very vulnerable, and is sometimes found in the respiratory tract of animals in a state of

---

[1] Hog Cholera, B. A. I., 1889, and Swine Plague, B. A. I., 1891.

perfect health.   There are many varieties of the germ, each of which may differ in virulence from the type.   The hog cholera germ is fatal to rabbits, guinea pigs, and mice, requiring from four to seven days to produce death.   Virulent varieties of the swine plague germ will also produce death in these animals, but in a much shorter time—in some instances inside of twenty-four hours.

Hog cholera and swine plague are by far the two most important bacterial diseases in swine.   In fact, in any outbreak of disease in swine, if parasitism can be excluded (by this is meant the larger animal parasites), one or the other or both of them may be assumed to exist.   The postmortem appearances are at times quite puzzling. In the *acute* form of hog cholera the animals die suddenly, showing on examination a hemorrhagic condition in the heart muscle, the meso-colic, bronchial, and thoracic lymphatic glands, and infarcts in the kidneys.   Hemorrhages beneath the thoracic and abdominal serous membrane are of frequent occurrence.   The subcutaneous tissue also partakes of this general hemorrhagic condition.   Here it is indicated by bluish blotches on the ventral aspect of the body.   In some cases blood tumors form in the superficial muscular tissue. The mucous membrane of the stomach is usually deeply reddened. Sometimes there may be direct hemorrhages into the stomach.   In some cases the mucous membrane of the small intestine is dark red in color.   No ulcers will be found in these acute cases.   The *chronic* form is more common, and in this the disease is most manifest in the large' intestine.   The other organs become affected secondarily by degenerative processes through the absorption of poisons and the invasion of the bacteria from the intestine.

The disease in the intestine consists of the production of ulcers, or buttons.   These may be circular and projecting or depressed and ragged in outline.   They appear most frequently in the cecum and upper half of the colon.   The stomach is sometimes ulcerated.   The spleen, unlike in the *acute* form, is not always enlarged.

In swine plague the primary seat of the disease is to be looked for in the lungs.   Here there is inflammation and small and large necrotic cheesy areas.   The serous membranes also partake of the inflammatory process, and by the formation of fibrinous material become adherent.   When the disease invades the intestinal tract, which it frequently does, there will be congestion or inflammation of the mucous membrane, followed by fibrinous deposits.   The lymphatic glands often become involved secondarily.   In these two diseases a bacteriological examination and a histological study of the tissues from typical bases are often the means upon which we may absolutely rely.

The swine plague organism may be obtained with ease and with certainty from all the organs, including the blood, of a rabbit inoculated with swine plague material.   At the point of inoculation there will appear more or less necrosed tissue with zones of active inflammation surrounding it. If a drop of the blood be placed upon a cover glass and is scraped off with the ground edge of a slide, a thin film of blood will remain on the cover glass. This is to be dried and fixed by heat in the usual way. A drop of alkaline methylene blue spread out upon the film will stain the bacteria immediately. The surplus stain is washed off in water and the specimen is examined with an oil-immersion lens. An oval bacterium will be seen. Similar preparations should be made from the spleen, liver, and abdominal exudate, if any. The organism has a peculiar property of staining deeply at the ends. This may be plainly brought out by dipping the stained preparation made from the spleen or abdominal exudate for a second into three-tenths per cent acetic acid, care being taken to remove the acid by subsequent washing in water. The center is completely decolorized, while the ends retain the stain. So transparent does the central portion become that the stained ends may be mistaken for cocci in pairs. Careful focusing will, however, reveal the unstained central portion. This occurs only in preparations made from animal tissues. In cultures the organism takes the stain uniformly.

In a case where hog cholera and swine plague coexist the experimental animal, if a rabbit, will die of swine plague and the hog cholera germ will have no relation to the fatal issue. In these cases it is manifest that the hog cholera germ could not be so isolated by the inoculation of rabbits, because of the rapidity with which a fatal issue ensues. The hog cholera germ requires from four to seven days to kill a rabbit or guinea pig. We may resort to making cultures from samples of tissue at hand. This is done by thoroughly grinding the tissues obtained under aseptic precautions in sterile water and making plate cultures from the extract. The different colonies may then be studied and the two organisms isolated. Assuming that there are only two species present, if we find two different colonies and upon examination preparations from one colony show a rapidly motile bacillus, we may provisionally call it the hog cholera bacillus, while, on the other hand, if it is nonmotile it could be assumed to be the swine plague bacterium. Experiments upon rabbits would clinch the matter. The inoculation of a rabbit with two-tenths cubic centimeter of a bouillon culture made from the suspected hog cholera colony ought to require from four to eight days to kill, according to its virulence. The disease in rabbits is characterized by pin-head sized necroses in the liver and a dark swollen spleen in which the germ is plentiful.

The culture made from the suspected swine plague colony into bouillon ought to kill a rabbit in twenty-four hours in one-half cubic centimeter dose injected subcutaneously. In some cases, where the germ at hand is a weak one, a much longer time may be required, even seven days in extreme cases. On postmortem examination of these cases the experimental rabbit will not show the usual acute septicemia, but an extensive peritonitis. The cecum, liver, and spleen will be covered by a thin false membrane which contains large numbers of swine plague bacteria, while the liver and blood will contain very few. The swine plague germ will not grow in a temperature as low as 70° F., while the hog cholera germ will do so. Making plate cultures and keeping them at this temperature would be another way of isolating with some degree of certainty the hog cholera from the swine plague germ.

About a year ago the writer[1] published a method for diagnosing hog cholera in live animals, basing the method upon the Widal serum reaction, now so extensively used in diagnosing typhoid fever in man. Since then, ample opportunity has shown the method to be of value. The mode of procedure is as follows: A drop of blood is obtained from the cleansed ear of a hog or experimental rabbit and is smeared upon a cover glass in the usual way. As few corpuscles as possible should be present, as they interfere mechanically with the reaction. About ten times as much sterile water is added to the film of serum on the cover glass. To this diluted serum is added the smallest possible quantity of the hog cholera germs from a culture on agar twenty-four hours old, or a loop of a culture in bouillon twenty-four hours old. (The test culture should always be first examined for the presence of motility and the absence of clumps of the organism.) The cover glass so prepared is now inverted on a concave slide and observed with an oil-immersion lens. If the case is hog cholera, the hog cholera germs which were noticed to be actively motile and swimming independently of each other in the test preparation are now losing their motility and massing themselves in clumps. The reaction sometimes occurs immediately, or it may require from one-half hour to one hour. No such reaction has been observed in swine plague, nor does it occur under these conditions with other organisms. The method is therefore a ready one for the diagnosis of hog cholera. The reaction indicates the presence of hog cholera, but neither the absence nor presence of swine plague. This method could be made use of in differentiating the germ itself by making blood preparations from a known case of hog cholera and proceeding as described above for the diagnosis of the disease. The culture which gave the clumping and agglutination of bacteria could be called hog cholera. (Plate XI.)

Starting with the two germs obtained from an outbreak where there is a double infection of hog cholera and swine plague, they could be studied and identified as follows: Obtain cultures from dissimilar colonies on the plates as indicated above. Inoculate from each of them several tubes of media as follows: Two or three fermentation tubes of glucose bouillon, two or three gelatine and agar plates, and

---

[1] New York Medical Journal, February 20, 1897.

several tubes of potatoes and incubate them at 38° C. for several days. Allow the gelatine plates to remain at a temperature of 65° to 70° F. If the fermentation tubes show the development of gas in the next day or two and it contains a single species of a rapidly motile organism, the probability is that the culture is one of hog cholera; it is certainly *not* one of swine plague. One or more of the fermentation tubes may not show gas formation. If these cultures which have not formed gas show, in a hanging-drop preparation, a nonmotile organism, it is not hog cholera, and is probably swine plague. If a brownish growth is visible on the potato tubes, it is not swine plague, and may be hog cholera. If the surface of the potato is moist and glistening, the almost invisible growth is probably swine plague. No growth ought to take place on the gelatine plates inoculated with the suspected swine plague organism at low temperature. If growth has taken place, and it consists of a motile bacillus, the culture is possibly one of hog cholera. In ordinary tubes of bouillon and upon the incubated agar plates, the odor would also be a diagnostic point. If the culture be a pure one of the swine plague germ, the odor will be that of putrefaction, while the cultures, if of hog cholera, would be odorless. Bringing together of these points, testing the pathogenesis in the smaller animals, excluding the possibility of having obtained mixed cultures at the start, or subsequent contaminations, would furnish a correct diagnosis. (Pl. X, figs. 7, 8, and 9.)

There are four important microorganismal diseases in poultry in which the causes are well known. They are chicken cholera, infectious leukæmia, tuberculosis, and entero-hepatitis, or black head.

CHICKEN CHOLERA.

Chicken cholera is a disease characterized by the sudden onset of high fever, profuse diarrhea of a greenish tinge, darkened mucosa from congestion, and the presence of a bacterium in the blood resembling in all its biological characters the germ of swine plague, and of rabbit septicemia. The fowls become comatose and die suddenly in large numbers. The writer has never observed an outbreak of genuine chicken cholera, but a bacteriological study of the disease would be all that is sufficient for its recognition.

There could be no difficulty in diagnosing the disease, with laboratory facilities. The presence of the peculiar germ in the blood during life in large numbers and the clinical symptoms could leave no doubt as to its identity in the mind of anyone who had ever studied the hemorrhagic septicemia group of organisms to which the germ of chicken cholera belongs. The biological characters would correspond very closely to those of swine plague.

INFECTIOUS LEUKÆMIA.

Infectious leukæmia is a very important fowl disease. The clinical history is so pronouncedly like that of chicken cholera that there can be little doubt of its being often mistaken for that disease. It is possible that most of the reported outbreaks of chicken cholera are in reality outbreaks of infectious leukæmia. This disease was first described by Dr. V. A. Moore in the Twelfth and Thirteenth Annual Reports of the Bureau of Animal Industry, and is probably the most important one which occurs in poultry at the present time in this country. The fowl becomes suddenly dumpish; the feathers are ruffled; the eyes are closed, and there is a condition of drowsiness in which the head falls back; the comb and wattles early become congested; this is followed in a short time by extreme paleness; in fact, the comb becomes almost empty of blood during the last days of illness. The temperature reaches from 110° to 112° F. The blood becomes very thin, losing a large number of corpuscles daily. There is a profuse diarrhea. These discharges contain an enormous number of the *Bacterium sanguinarium*, which causes the disease. In cases of the disease artificially produced by feeding the animals upon grain infected with the germ, they live about eight days. After death, no particular lesions, other than the engorgement of the hepatic capillaries and the extreme thinness of the blood are noticed. If lesions occur elsewhere, as in the liver, they are probably due to the mechanical plugging of the capillaries by the bacterium. The germ may be readily isolated from the blood or liver. Smear preparations from these organs indicate the relative scarcity of the organisms. They are found most plentifully in the intestinal contents. The diseased fowls sometimes recover. The causative organism is a short bacterium, in pairs, devoid of movement, measuring 1 micron in width from 1.2 to 1.8 microns long. It grows well in all the ordinary media at the room temperatures. It coagulates milk in one day. In hanging-drop preparations the cellular protoplasm is seen thickened at the ends. In stained preparations the center is either transparent or very lightly stained. The periphery of the cell is densely stained. The organism does not form gas in the presence of sugars. It will grow fairly well at 13° C. It is killed in thirteen minutes by exposure to 58° C. Freezing has no apparent deleterious effect upon it. It will resist drying in diffuse sunlight for three weeks. A 1 per cent solution of carbolic acid is fatal to it in three minutes. It will kill rabbits when inoculated into them intravenously in three or four days. Guinea pigs die in from five to eight days when inoculated subcutaneously. Pigeons inoculated intramuscularly die in about three days. Healthy fowls placed in cages which retain the droppings of the sick ones contract the disease in some cases. The disease can also be produced by feeding fowls grain infected with cultures of the organism.

TUBERCULOSIS IN FOWLS.

Tuberculosis in fowls is a comparatively rare disease, but the possibility of an outbreak should be borne in mind. The disease is not considered identical with that of man. There are important differences between the germs of the disease in man and in fowls, probably due to environment. These differences occur not only in their biology, but in their pathogenesis as well. In fowls affected with the disease tubercles appear as hard, horny, or soft, cheesy swellings on the skin and joints. There is great emaciation, and they die after having shrunken to a mere mass of skin, bone, and feathers. A postmortem examination will show little yellow cheesy tubercles in the liver and spleen.

In 50 per cent of the cases the intestinal form will be observed. Here tubercles appear as dense round masses in the intestinal wall. The lungs and serous membranes, as in other animals, may be attacked and become infiltrated with the disease.

A histological study of the tissues could be carried out by means of. the same methods as indicated for the affection in mammals. In avian tuberculosis one of the important characters of the mammalian variety is said to be absent—that is, the giant cells.

ENTERO-HEPATITIS, OR BLACKHEAD.

Entero-hepatitis is a disease which exists to a considerable extent among turkeys. It occurs mainly in Rhode Island, where large numbers of turkeys are raised. The disease was first described by Dr. Theobald Smith, who claimed that it is caused by a parasitic protozoan, named by him *Amœba meleagridis*.[1] The parasites enter the digestive tract along with the food. They become lodged in the ceca, where they set up an inflammatory process, which results in partial closure of those parts of the intestine from great thickening and ulceration of their walls. The ceca sometimes becomes distended and very large from accumulations due to the disease process. From the ceca the parasites reach the liver, where they start up a violent inflammation, which results in the formation of yellow and green areas of necrosed tissue. The liver is generally much enlarged and engorged with blood. The disease seems to attack turkeys when they are quite young, as the progress made by it corresponds, as a rule, with the age of the turkeys.

In addition to the study of the clinical history and autopsies upon the bodies of the dead turkeys, which reveal the peculiar disease in the liver and great thickening of the walls of the ceca, the microparasite can be demonstrated in the stained sections of the liver and intestinal wall when prepared by the usual embedding and staining

---

[1] Bulletin No. 8, United States Department of Agriculture, Bureau of Animal Industry.

processes. Dr. Smith found that Delafield's hematoxylin and eosin gave the best general results as stains. The parasite appears as a nucleated body, measuring from 6 to 10 microns in diameter, having in sections stained with hematoxylin and eosin a bluish red tint more feebly stained than the surrounding tissue nuclei. It has not been observed as an intracellular body, but appears in the interstices and lymph spaces of the tissue. (Pl. XII, and Pl. XIII, fig. 3.)

ROUP (DIPHTHERIA).

Roup is very prevalent in poultry, more particularly among chickens. It is sometimes called diphtheria, from the fact that it is characterized by the formation of diphtheritic membranes in the air passages, notably in the nose, upon the pharynx and larynx, and also upon the tongue and eyes. As a first symptom of the disease will be noticed a watery secretion from the eyes and nose, followed by loss of appetite, coughing, sneezing, and obstructed breathing. At this time an examination of the larynx will reveal a thin grayish yellow membrane of recent formation upon the red and swollen parts. The discharge is characterized by a grayish yellow fibrinous exudate, which forms thick layers on the parts named. Attempts to remove it entirely will cause bleeding, showing its intimate connection with the tissues upon which it rests. In many cases the exudate is very profuse, becomes desiccated, and interferes with respiration from laryngeal obstruction, or with prehension of food by causing immobility of the tongue. In other cases the exudate accumulates upon the cornea, causing agglutination of the eyelids and consequent destruction of the eye from pressure. In these cases the fowl presents a sorry picture. The whole eyeball sometimes disappears, and in its stead is found a globular mass of cheesy material pushing the closed lids out to the utmost. When the discharge becomes infected with the organisms of decomposition a peculiar nauseating odor is noticed. There is rapid loss of strength, roughened feathers, and drooping wings.

In some cases the disease attacks the intestine, causing bloody discharges and rapidly fatal results. In other cases the disease may assume a chronic form in which the symptoms are more obscure, and in which a local disease may not be present. The disease varies in duration from a few days to a few weeks, according to its being acute or chronic in character. The acute form is very destructive, causing the death of a large number in a few days. In the chronic form few deaths occur, but on account of the depression caused the fowls are of little use for food purposes. There seems to be little or no basis for the claim made by some that this disease is the same as diphtheria in man. Were they identical, the same methods of isolation of the germ could be employed as in diphtheria in man. Loeffler has described a bacterium which he calls *Bacillus diphtheriæ columbrarum* as being the cause of a disease in pigeons having the general characters of roup. In this country Moore, in studying roup, described several species of bacteria, one of which is probably identical with the one described by Lœffler. It is a member of the hemorrhagic septicemia group of organisms, and was similar biologically to the bacterium of swine plague. In pathogenesis, also, it was similar to a somewhat attenuated swine plague organism.

In studying an outbreak of this disease bacteriologically, the exudate from the mouth, throat, nose, and eye of the affected fowl is ground up in salt solution, and varying quantities (from 0.5 cc. up) are injected subcutaneously into the small experimental animals—rabbits, guinea pigs, mice, fowls, or pigeons. If injected intravenously, the extract should be freed of solid particles by filtration. Scarification of the mouth parts and cornea and rubbing pieces of the exudate upon the abraded surfaces would also be logical. Little could be hoped from experiments in feeding, but they would be necessary in order to make the investigation more complete.

In case a microscopic examination of the exudate showed few bacteria, cultures should be made from them, and used as suggested above for the exudate.

Common colds and infectious catarrh are often mistaken for roup. The existence of these may be suspected when there is absence of the characteristic membranes in the air passages.

NODULAR TÆNIASIS.

Although this is not a microorganismal disease, its gross pathology is so strikingly like that of intestinal tuberculosis that it is included in this series.

The disease was first described as occurring in fowls in this country by Dr. V. A. Moore,[1] who determined the cause to be a tapeworm which embeds itself in the intestinal mucous membrane and causes the formation of the nodules. The parasite is quite small and might easily be overlooked in a macroscopic examination. In case of doubt, careful washing of the mucous membrane by a gentle stream of water will reveal the small worms attached.

Unlike tuberculosis, there will be no lesions in the liver or other organs in this disease. This fact and the presence of the small tapeworms embedded in the intestinal tumors would exclude tuberculosis.

NODULAR DISEASE IN SHEEP.

A nodular disease of the intestine occurs very frequently in sheep. It has been mistaken for tuberculosis. It is caused by a nematode (*Œsophagostoma columbianum*), first described by Cooper Curtice.[2]

The disease can only be diagnosed postmortem. The sheep will be

---

[1] Circular No. 3, Bureau of Animal Industry.
[2] Animal Parasites of Sheep, Bureau of Animal Industry.

generally debilitated—the eyes and lips bloodless, the sides and flanks thin, and the wool dry. There may be an excessive diarrhea, followed by death in severe cases. It is an insidious disease, and is characterized by the formation of nodules in the mucous membrane of the intestine. When these tumors become numerous they interfere with the digestive functions of the cecum, and cause the asthenic condition commonly noticed in outbreaks of the disease.

If some of the larger soft characteristic tumors from the intestine be slit open and their greenish cheesy contents be broken up in water, a small round worm, measuring 3 to 4 mm. in length, will be found. This is the embryonic stage, and it has been shown by Curtice that it is during this stage in the life history of the parasite that it enters the mucous membrane of the intestine and causes, by its activity, sufficient irritation to produce the nodules. The adult may be found free in the contents of the large intestine and measures from 12 to 18 mm. long.

As it is not the intention of this paper to discuss other than microorganismal diseases, the writer will refer those interested in the life history of this parasite to Curtice's work. Sufficient has been said to direct attention to these nodular diseases in fowls and sheep to prevent their being confounded with intestinal tuberculosis, and to give very brief methods of determining their presence. (Pl. XIV.) ·

PLATE IX.

Fig. 1. Cover-glass preparation from a 2-day-old bouillon culture of the anthrax bacterium. Some of the cells have already begun to form spores. Stained with Lœffler's alkaline methylene blue. (× 1000 diameters.) (Original.)

MALIGANT EDEMA.

Fig. 2. Cover-glass preparation of the bacillus of maligant edema from the edematous fluid from the side of inoculation in guinea pig. Note the formation of long threads and the absence of spores. (From Abbott.)

Fig. 3. Cover-glass preparation of the same organism from a culture. Note the absence of threads and the presence of spore-bearing cells. Some of the spores are lying free. (From Abbott.)

TEXAS FEVER.

Fig. 4. Cover-glass preparation from the spleen pulp. The parasite is seen as small dots inside the yellowish red blood corpuscles stained. blue. (× 900.) (After T. Smith.)

Fig. 5. Cover-glass preparation of the same organism from kidney of cow. Method of preparation same as above. The large blue body in the center of the group is one of the cellular elements of the kidney. The parasite appears as dots in pairs stained blue. This form is generally noted in stained preparations made after death. (× 1,000.) (After T. Smith.)

Fig. 6. Cover-glass preparation of the same organism made from the heart muscle. A preparation made in this way shows corpuscles from the capillaries which contain pyriform parasites in pairs. The large blue body represents a leucocyte. (× 1,000.) (After T. Smith.)

356

Fig. I.

Fig. 2.

Fig. 3.

Fig. 4.

Fig 6.

Fig. 5.

Organisms Causing Anthrax, Malignant Edema, Blackleg, and Texas Fever.

PLATE X.

TUBERCULOSIS.

Fig. 1. The bacterium of tuberculosis. A cover-glass preparation from human expectoration stained by Gabbett's method. The tubercle organism appears stained red; all else is blue. Slide prepared by Miss Louise Tayler. (× 1,000.) (Original.)

BLACKLEG.

Fig. 2. The bacillus of blackleg. Preparation made from the local lesion in a guinea pig and stained with gentian violet. This preparation shows great variation in morphology, and spore formation in the tissues. (× 1,000.) (Original.)

TETANUS.

Figs. 3 and 4. Fig. 3 represents the tetanus bacillus as it appears in gelatine cultures. Fig. 4 shows the same bacillus in the spore-bearing stages in agar cultures. (× 1,000.) (From Sternberg.)

ACTINOMYCOSIS.

Fig. 5. The actinomyces fungus as it appears in fresh preparations made from the little grains found in the affected tissues. (× 300.) (From Flügge.)

GLANDERS.

Fig. 6. The bacterium of glanders. Note the irregular way in which the cells take up the stain, giving the appearance of spores. (From Abbott.)

HOG CHOLERA.

Fig. 7. Cover-glass preparation of the bacillus of hog cholera from a 2-day-old bouillon culture. (× 1,000.) (Original.)

SWINE PLAGUE.

Fig. 8. Cover-glass preparation of the bacterium of swine plague from a 2-day-old bouillon culture. (× 1,000.) (Original.)

Fig. 9. Smear preparation from the spleen of an animal dead from swine plague. Note the manner in which the organism takes the stain. The light spaces do not occur in preparations made from cultures. (× 1,000.) (From T. Smith.)

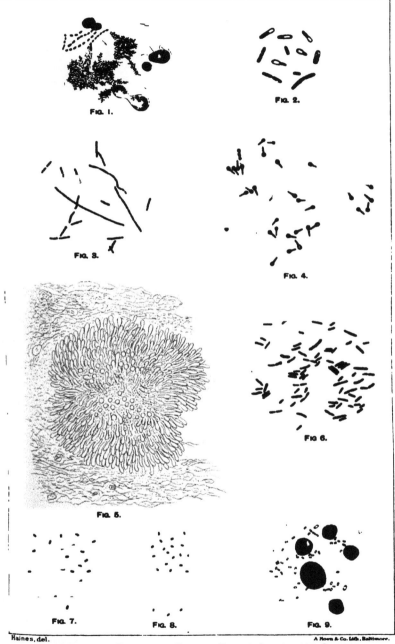

ORGANISMS CAUSING TUBERCULOSIS, BLACKLEG, TETANUS, ACTINOMYCOSIS, GLANDERS
AND SWINE PLAGUE.

PLATE XI.

THE SERUM DIAGNOSIS OF HOG CHOLERA.

Showing the peculiar way in which the bacillus of hog cholera groups itself
when brought in contact with the blood of an animal affected with hog cholera.
360

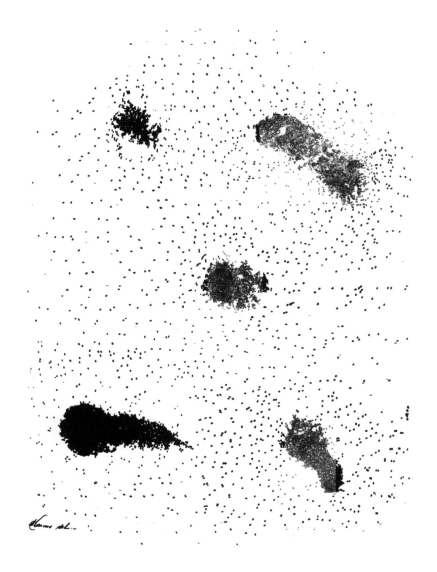

BACILLI OF HOG CHOLERA SHOWING CLUMPING

THE HELIOTYPE PRINTING CO., BOSTON.

PLATE XII.

ENTERO-HEPATITIS IN TURKEYS.

Fig. 1. One cecum of turkey, cut open longitudinally. The middle portion of the tube is greatly distended and occluded with an exudate which is firm in consistency. The upper portion contains small stones which have passed down from the gizzard. The irregular thickening of the wall of the tube is shown by a faint line bordering the exudate. (After T. Smith.)

Fig. 2. Left lobe of liver of turkey (convex surface). The large yellow area in the upper portion of the figure represents a mass of dead tissue penetrating nearly through the entire thickness of the liver. On the right the pale grayish spot represents diseased liver tissue which is undergoing repair. Similarly, the spots in the lower portion of the figure correspond to diseased regions partly healed. Several other spots readily detected in the specimen could not be clearly brought out in the figure. The diffuse change, probably reparative, is shown along the lower margin. (After T. Smith.)

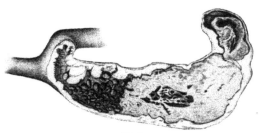

Fig. 1.

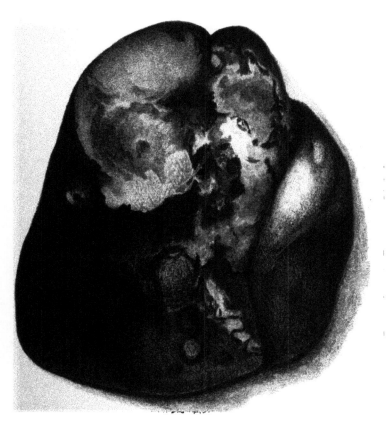

Fig. 2.

Hanes, del.

Cecum and Liver of Turkey Affected with Entero-Hepatitis.

PLATE XIII.

The morphology of Bacterium sanguinarium.

Fig. 1. Cover-glass preparation made from a bouillon culture 24 hours old. (× 1000.) (After V. A. Moore.)

Fig. 2. Cover-glass preparation of the spleen of a rabbit showing the deeply stained periphery and light center of *Bacterium sanguinarium.* Also its appearance in pairs. (After V. A. Moore.)

ENTERO-HEPATITIS IN TURKEYS.

Fig. 3. Section of the liver of turkey. A large collection of protozoa (*a*) occupying the space formerly occupied by the liver cells. They are probably somewhat forced apart by artificial pressure, for in other sections of the same liver compact masses of protozoa of equal size were not infrequently seen. The parasites are surrounded by capillaries (*b*) dilated and filled with red corpuscles; (*c*) round cells, or leucocytes. (After T. Smith.)

364

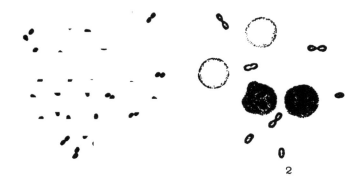

2

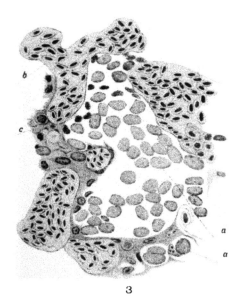

3

BACTERIUM SANGUINARIUM.—ENTERO-HEPATITIS IN TURKEYS.

THE HELIOTYPE PRINTING CO.. BOSTON.

PLATE XIV.

NODULAR TÆNIASIS IN FOWLS.

Fig. 1. (*a*) Piece of the intestine of a fowl showing the nodules (reduced one-third). (*b*) The mucosa of the intestine showing ulcerated areas; also several small and one larger tapeworm attached to the intestine (reduced one-third). (*c*) A cross-section of the intestine illustrating the thickening of the wall due to a large number of the nodules; also a portion of a tapeworm which has penetrated the mucous membrane, magnified. (After V. A. Moore.)

ROUP (DIPHTHERIA).

Figs. 2 and 3. Showing the formation of false membranes upon the tongue, the roof of the mouth, and around the glottis, in this disease. (After V. A. Moore.)

366

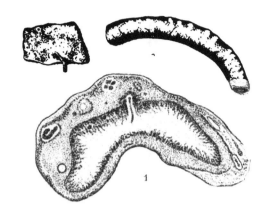

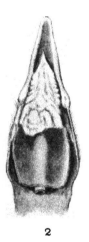

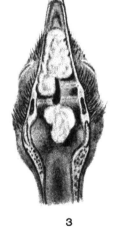

1

2

3

NODULAR TÆNIASIS IN FOWLS. DIPHTHERIA (ROUP)

THE HELIOTYPE PRINTING CO., BOSTON.

PLATE XV.

Fig. 1. Piece of the cecum exhibiting tumors caused by the embryos of *Œsophagostoma columbianum*, natural size. The various stages of growth are represented in the different sized tumors. (After Cooper Curtice.)

Fig. 2. Section through a worm tumor in its young stages. The worm is seen in the center of the mass surrounded by a thick capsule at *f*. (After Cooper Curtice.)

368

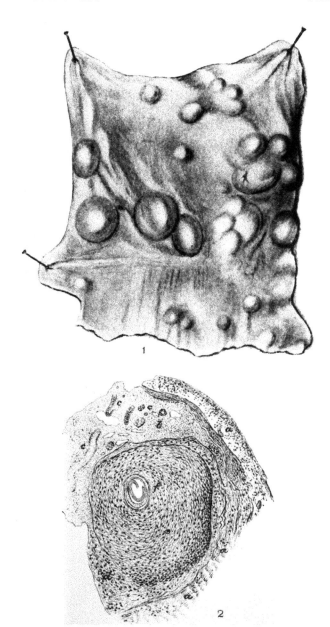

HAINES, DEL.

NODULAR DISEASE IN SHEEP

THE HELIOTYPE PRINTING CO., BOSTON

Plate XVI.

Zebroid Lordello, out of the Mare Stael by the Zebra Canon.

(one year old when photographed.)

Zebroid Lordello, out of the Mare Stael by the Zebra Canon.

One year old when photographed

ZEBRO.⊃ MÉNÉLICK, OUT OF THE MARE ELLA BY THE ZEBRA CANON.

Three months old when photographed

BREEDING ZEBROIDS.

The Brazilian minister has kindly forwarded to the Bureau of Animal Industry some interesting data regarding the crossing of the zebra with the common mare. Two photographs of the hybrids produced by this crossing accompanied the data and are reproduced for this report. This experiment was conducted by Baron de Paraná, of the Plantation Lordella, municipality of Sapucaia, State of Rio Janeiro, Brazil.

Hybrids of this sort have not been unknown, but they are exceedingly rare. Hybrids of the ass as the male parent and the horse as the female parent, which produce the common mule, are well known everywhere. Less common, but still well known, is the hybrid known as the "hinny" (sometimes called the "jennet"), which is the offspring of the horse as the male parent and the ass as the female parent.

The breed of zebra generally considered the best for crossing with any of the domestic species of Equus is Burchell's zebra (*Equus burchellii*), which is the best known zebra at this time. Messrs. Tegetmeir and Sutherland[1] give the following description and comparison with the mountain zebra: "The species is still common in some parts of South Africa, and is now being utilized in the coach teams in the Transvaal. The Burchell differs from the mountain zebra (*E. zebra*) in several essential parts. It is a larger and stronger animal, with shorter ears, which are rarely more than $6\frac{1}{4}$ inches in length, and have a much larger proportion of white, a longer mane, and a fuller and more horse-like tail. The general color is pale yellowish brown, the stripes being dark brown or nearly black."

Mr. Harold Stephens, who wrote of this zebra in 1892, speaks of their use in the harness in the Transvaal in a most encouraging way, and says they will largely be substituted for mules. They are said to be entirely free from that South African scourge called "horse sickness." He says: "The zebras, when inspanned (harnessed to the coach), stand quite still and wait for the word to go. They pull up when required and are perfectly amenable to the bridle, and are softer mouthed than the mule. They never kick, and the only thing in the shape of vice which they manifest is that when first handled they have an inclination to bite, but as soon as they get to understand that there is no intention to hurt them they give this up."

Mr. Stephens says that attempts are to be made to cross this zebra with the horse, with the object of getting a larger and handsomer mule than the ordinary cross with the ass, and probably superior in

---

[1] Horses, Asses, Zebras, Mules, and Mule Breeding, p. 51, 1895.

every way. He says further: "It will be interesting to watch the progress of these experiments, which may bring about a new and important industry, for if the cross between the zebra and the horse can be brought about without difficulty it will not be long before these animals will be preferred to ordinary mules."

When we consider these possibilities, one is reminded of the remarks of Thomas Bewick in 1824. While the records show that there were still earlier in the century zebras that had been broken to the harness, it was generally believed that they were among the most untamable of wild animals. Mr. Bewick said: "Such is the beauty of this creature that it seems by nature fitted to gratify the pride and formed for the service of man, and it is most probable that time and assiduity alone are wanting to bring it under subjection. As it resembles the horse in regard to its form as well as manner of living, there can be but little doubt but it possesses a similitude of nature and only requires the efforts of an industrious and skillful nation to be added to the number of our useful dependents."

The Burchell zebra is much better adapted by its structure and form to the uses of man than any of the wild asses, and there can be liltle doubt that its hybrids, especially where crossed with the horse, would be exceedingly valuable to man if the mating is done carefully.

In the case of the hybrids produced in the plantation of Baron de Paraná, to which he has given the generic name of zebroids, he was able to make some interesting and important observations. He produced five zebroids, as follows:

Lordello. Male; foaled December 5, 1896; out of the mare Stael, by the zebra Canon; is a brown bay striped with black.

Ménélick. Male; foaled January 15, 1898; out of the mare Ella, by Canon; gray, striped with black.

Saba. Female; foaled June 22, 1898; out of the mare Denise, by Canon; light bay, striped with black.

Salomon. Male; foaled July 2, 1898; out of the mare Ingleza, by Canon; a bright bay, striped with black.

Erythréa. Female; foaled December 30, 1898; out of the mare Ella, by Canon.; bay, the zebra stripes being dark brown.

The Baron states that these zebroids are very sprightly, but at the same time are gentle, becoming very docile in the hands of those who care for them. They feed as well from the manger as in the pasture, and are possessed of extraordinary muscular strength. Their size, slenderness of form, pace, and disposition depend upon the dam. Therefore they may be bred at will for the saddle or for heavy or light draft. It is only necessary to select the mare possessing the qualities desired. Thus the crossing with mares of the heavy Percherons, Suffolks, or Clydesdales gives zebroids that are large and very strong, but not so heavy and thickset as their dams. Crossing with mares of lighter races, such as the Arabs, Normans, etc., produces zebroids that are tall and slender, fully as strong as the former, but more tractable and suitable for work which requires quickness rather than strength alone.

A peculiarity of the breeding of zebroids, as pointed out by Baron de Paraná, is that copulation will not take place unless both the mare and the zebra are "in heat" at the same time; "that the domestication of the zebra is of very recent date, and consequently it preserves the characteristics of the wild animals, which never copulate except when male and female are in heat at the same time." The zebra, he says, is in heat in autumn and spring, especially in very warm countries, seldom covering in very warm weather and never in very cold weather.

It will be observed that the five zebroids named above are out of four different mares, but that the zebra Canon was the sire of all of them. This fact, taken in connection with the statement that Professor Ewart, at Penicuick, near Edinburgh, bred about twenty mares to a zebra with only one foal as a result, indicates that Canon was an unusually good getter or that there was mismanagement in the other instance.

Baron de Paraná is convinced that the zebroid will prove of great economic importance, especially in the warmer countries, and advises all who are engaged in breeding to take the new product into consideration. He believes that when the zebroid is better known there will be no further use for the common mule—"that the zebroid will be the mule of the twentieth century."

THE MILITARY ADMINISTRATION OF GERMANY IN ITS RELATIONS TO NATIONAL HORSE BREEDING.[1]

The war department takes the liveliest interest in the legalized efforts being made toward national horse breeding. The military administration recognizes in this matter, with the greatest thanks, the care being taken on the part of the Royal Saxon civil authorities, which have been called upon to devote special attention to the direction of horse breeding, to bring the material up to the demands of the military service; and the same is to be further undertaken, even though it can only indirectly operate, as is well understood, to promote this advancement. There is no doubt whatever that this looks toward an important move in political economy which must be advantageous to the country if it is made successful. At least an important part of the annual supply of horses for the cavalry of the Saxon army at home will be met, and thereby the large sums which go to the other countries for this purpose will more and more be saved to Saxony. The idea is, however, constantly recurring that the interests of agriculture and the wishes of the military authorities do not harmonize in the matter of horse breeding, but this opinion is not correct. When it is seen, without further comment, that horse breeding is dependent upon local conditions—as, for instance, that in mountainous and manufacturing regions this enterprise will never reach a prominent importance, such as is attained in the plains and especially in strips of land devoted to agriculture—then it may be asserted that under existing circumstances in the kingdom of Saxony horse breeding will never prosper as in the case possibly in eastern Prussia. Still it must be granted, on the other hand, that in Saxony, with its numerically not insignificant production of horses, it may be possible to breed a horse that will be useful as well for agriculture and the industries as for military service.

On the part of the Government there have been the greatest variety of efforts made to promote national horse breeding, the securing of good stallions, instructions for the breeders by word and writings upon breeding, arrangement of colt-raising stations, the inauguration of colt and mare inspection, etc. The war department on its part has responded to the wishes made known by the breeding circles, arranged market places for the sale of cavalry horses where the

---

[1] This is a free translation of a pamphlet recently issued by the war department of Germany. The careful descriptions of the kinds of horses required in Germany should be of no less importance to American breeders than to those of Saxony.

breeders might dispose of their product, and has shown that the foundation of a rational breeding is the selection of good animals for the mothers. Therefore the attention must be drawn to the continuance of good material in this respect, and to this end breeders, under certain conditions, may procure from the cavalry supply depot at Kalkreuth breeding mares at net cost price. It is, however, the duty of the breeder to grasp the proffered hand and by his own exertions aid in reaching the high point in breeding at which the country aims. The breeder must be clear as to what breed of horses he should raise for use in his own work. The nature of his soil will show him what he needs, and he must have regard to the use to which a horse may be applied in case it can not be sold in such a way as to yield him profitable returns. The lighter soils will require the breeding of lighter classes of work horses, while the heavier soils will need strong-boned horses. Horses with hereditary blemishes (such defects as misshapen legs, outward or inward turning forelegs, bandy legs, long weak backs with bad connecting lines, etc.) should naturally not be employed for breeding purposes. It is true without any doubt that in Saxony a high-bred horse, either heavy or light weight, can be utilized, if having fine figure, strong back, good legs, and plenty of energy with firm step, as well in the agricultural and industrial service or for luxury as for the military service. The breeder who operates after these rational methods will receive a better price and make easier sale for his product.

The army with its demand for strong, medium, and light horses will, when good cavalry material is bred in this country, always be a regular purchaser thereof. In order to sell his horse to the army he must take advantage of the important point that it must be three years old; otherwise a sale will be almost impossible.

In consideration of the fact that the greater part of our land is heavy soil, the breeding of strong-boned horses (artillery horses) will very naturally come first in line, then cavalry horses of heavy weight, and finally, in districts having a lighter soil, medium and lighter horses. There exists, however, much confusion as to what demands will be made by the military authorities in the supply of horses, and to the ignorance as to the demands of the army are traceable the greater part of the complaints which have been heard in breeding circles that the commission for the purchase of cavalry supplies make too high exactions and are too particular in their choice of horses, refusing good Saxon-bred horses, and preferring foreign-bred animals, etc.

In order to make this subject clearer the war department gives the following general statement as to what the army requires in the horses to be purchased for war purposes, and, to illustrate the same, have furnished some photographs taken at the time from horses in the troops, which show the requirements most to be desired in the cavalry service. These copies are added to this report. The demands of the army are in general as follows:

1. Thoroughbred, small head, good neck poise.
2. Strong, well-placed legs with broad joints.
3. Arched ribs, with good sloping shoulders.
4. A well-built, not too long, strong back with good connections and high-lying kidneys.
5. Healthy strong hocks.
6. Round good hoofs and healthy frogs.
7. Healthy constitution and good digestion.
8. A broad energetic step.

REQUIREMENTS FOR SPECIAL SERVICE.

1. *Artillery draft horse.*—Height at 3 years, 153 to 157 centimeters (61 to 62½ inches); full grown, 160 to 168 centimeters (62.73 to 65.73 inches).

An artillery horse can only meet the wants of the service when it has the above-named qualities and at the same time has strong bones, broad breast, especially strong hind quarters, and good collar shoulder. An artillery horse must at the present time be able to work under the weight of the rider and the free motion of the heavy wagons, with five other horses, and draw a load of 42 hundredweight on a heavy march, under the strain and endurance of an alternating trot and gallop in deep soil up an elevated point of land. That such a horse is impossible from inferior stock, which often has very long, weak backs and bad connections, with awkward, heavy upper parts of the body, badly set legs, weak hind quarters, and heavy deep-set neck, is easy to be seen. Such horses break down early and set the troops out of position in the attempt to perform what is to-day required of the war horse. Such horses still appear in the military supply market. Frequently these horses have lacked the necessary exercise in their youth, and have no development of muscle, and, again, through too early work, perhaps in too heavy draft, have been ruined, have thickened foot frogs, ruined fetlocks, crooked fore legs, hock protuberance, convulsive motion in the hocks, etc. Then the breeder is surprised and undeceived when such product is rejected by the military authorities.

2. *Heavy riding horse.*—Height at 3 years, 153 to 157 centimeters; full grown, 160 to 168 centimeters high.

The general build must fulfill the above-described requirements, and in addition the demands are activity, speed, broadness of gait, and endurance to compare with the artillery horse. The breast need not be so broad. The fetlock should not be too short; while, on the other hand, if too long, it bends too low and causes the heavy weight carried to produce fatigue on a long march. A good saddle place is as necessary in the cavalry horse as a good collar shoulder in the artillery horse.

3. *The medium and light riding horse.*—Height at 3 years, 146 to 155 centimeters; full grown, 152 to 162 centimeters high.

The medium and light riding horse differs only through the size, breadth, and strength of all bones from the heavy riding horse— differences which concern the size and weight of the rider and the kind of arms which are to be taken into account.

To raise military horses it is naturally requisite to have a good understanding of the breeding material, and the principal attention must be given to the selection of the sire and dam as to form, gait, and other external appearances in the offspring. Of just as great importance is the way of raising the young horse itself; that is, as to its food, its hardening, exercise, and muscle development, etc. It will still be a long time before the breeding material in Saxony will reach the desired height, and before the needful conditions therefor, as well as for the rational handling of the young horses, will be universally obtained. The department of war is therefore not at all in doubt that it must overlook certain faults for the time being when otherwise the national breeding can be made serviceable, and the producers will exercise more taste, in so far as this accords with their responsibility for the preparations for war in the army. Such faults are, for the artillery service, heavier head, somewhat steeper shoulders, short forearm, and leg from knee downward, somewhat longer back with absolutely good connections and high-lying reins, longer and more sloping fetlocks, heavy belly, smaller knees, slight variations from the normal setting of the limbs, and the normal gait. Absolutely to be rejected are, however, as war horses (for draft as well as for riding horses) those having any bone ailment, such as spavin, hareheels, deer's legs, bony excrescence on the sinews, heavy or badly twisted legs, bad hoofs, long backs and poor attachments, and horses having the so-called admitted, or guaranteed, faults.

In one case the described faults lie in the build or structure of the horse; in the other, in the faulty raising and training and in the premature use of the horse. This last fault, frequently occurring, is all the more incomprehensible, as the horse not only suffers in its ability to be of service in work, but also loses extremely in its market value.

CONDITIONS OF TAKING BROOD MARES FROM THE ROYAL CAVALRY SUPPLY DEPOT AT KALKREUTH FOR USE IN BREEDING.

1. For the removal of horses from the supply station for breeding purposes, there must be provided, outside the purchase money, also the transportation and cost of feed.

2. The selected dams are to be annually exhibited for six years by the military supply commission at the nearest supply depot or that at

Kalkreuth, and these shall be accompanied by their foals of the last year. Should the mare be barren or the foal be dead, then the colt of the previous year should be brought. It is also to be understood by the purchaser that the master of the government stables shall occasionally inspect the stations where the brood mares are kept.

3. The resale of the mares can only take place through the special permission of the military economic division of the war department.

4. The purchaser further obligates himself to provide for the annual covering of the brood mare and that by good half-blood stallions from the royal government stud. Private stallions can only be employed when the military authorities or the government master of the stables shall decide it to be suitable to make such a change.

5. The purchaser is further bound to so handle and feed these dams that they may serve as such for a number of years, and to this end the special conditions are fixed that the dams, with their offspring, shall be kept the summer through in the horse gardens and pastures.

6. The colts from these dams shall, at the age of 3 years, be offered to the supply purchasing commission for sale, in so far as the owner does not utilize them for further purposes of breeding.

7. When these dams die or become no longer serviceable for colt breeding, the military supply purchasing commission shall give notice of the same.

Plate XVIII.

ARTILLERY SHAFT HORSE FREGATTE.

Seven years old; dark-brown mare; 164 centimeters high.   East Prussia.

ARTILLERY FORE HORSE GERTRUDE.

Five years old: brown mare; 160 centimeters high.   Holstein.

Plate XX.

Heavy Riding Horse Strolch.

Six years old; brown Wallach; 169 centimeters high.   East Prussia.

Lancers Horse Nelson.

Plate XXII.

Hussars Horse Schnucke.

Seven years old; dark-brown mare; 156 centimeters high.   East Prussia.

THE CATTLE INDUSTRY OF COLORADO, WYOMING, AND NEVADA, AND THE SHEEP INDUSTRY OF COLORADO IN 1897.

By JOHN T. McNEELY,

Live Stock Agent, Bureau of Animal Industry.

CATTLE INDUSTRY OF COLORADO, WYOMING, AND NEVADA.

Many important changes have taken place in the cattle and sheep industry of the States of Colorado, Wyoming, and Nevada during the past few years. About seven years ago the price of cattle—then all grades, and comparatively at a high figure—began to decline. The reason was obvious. Up to that time most, if not all, of the herds roaming over the vast plains and uplands of the range States in the Far West had been kept as "breeding herds," and the result was that they accumulated in such numbers that there was an overproduction—the supply became greater than the demand. The slump in prices came, and for a season the cattle men hoped and believed the decline would be but temporary. But as prices went down and remained down, owners became panic-stricken, and in almost every locality they began reducing their herds by spaying heifers and shipping more cows and calves to market. This system was adhered to until 1893, when suddenly it dawned upon the minds of many of the largest owners that there was danger of a cattle famine in the near future unless the reduction was checked. The checking process really commenced in 1894, but was confined principally to a gradual cessation of spaying heifers.

The shipping of calves was kept up until 1896, during which year a smaller number was shipped, and during the present year but few calves have been shipped as compared with previous years. There was a perceptible falling off in the shipment of cows in 1896, but the present year, owing to the high prices of cattle, the shipments of cows have been heavier than usual. Last year but few heifers were spayed in the range States, and during 1897 not a single one was spayed in Colorado, Wyoming, or Nevada, so far as I can learn.

In the State of Colorado a few years ago (until the heavy decline in prices) every herd was a "producing herd," but after the decline they all merged into "steer herds." Such was the case in Wyoming and Nevada, and presumably so in most of the range States. Early in the present year the upward tendency in the prices of cattle, with a

377

widespread belief prevailing all over the Western range States and Territories that prices will remain high for years to come, has prompted the " cattle barons," as well as the small owners, to convert their steer herds into producing herds, as is evidenced by the non-spaying of heifers and the unprecedented small shipment of calves.

The universal opinion seems to be that after the present year there will be a tremendous falling off in the shipping of cows to market, as they will be held for breeding purposes. So it would seem that the fear of a cattle famine, indulged in a year or so ago, may be considered as dispelled. It is true there is still a shortage, and there will be in all probability for some time to come; but it will steadily grow less as the process of converting the herds into producing herds go on, and when the conversion becomes absolute—say, in three or four years—the shortage, if any, will hardly be perceptible. Then the question naturally arises, when that time comes, when every available cow is held for breeding, and the great bulk of calves held for beef or breeding, will there not soon again be an overproduction, followed by another decline in prices?

I have given this question a great deal of attention, discussing it personally and by correspondence with cattle men far and wide, and there seems to be but one sentiment expressed. Many of the old cattle ranges are things of the past. Lands over which immense herds of cattle roamed ten years ago have been taken up by home-steaders, preemptioners, and desert-land claimants. As an example, but a few years ago more than a dozen individuals in the State of Colorado, and perhaps three times as many in Wyoming, counted their herds in numbers from 5,000 upward, while in the State of Colorado to-day there is hardly more than one herd of more than 5,000, and in Wyoming not more than ten herds of more than 5,000 each. As the settlers have taken up and fenced large tracts of Government land the cattle ranges have been lessened, and in many instances but a few ranches fenced on each side of a mountain stream has rendered thousands of acres of vacant land worthless as a cattle range on account of the absence of water. Before these lands were taken up and fenced by settlers the great herds had unlimited Government range to feed upon and unlimited territory over which to drift with the storms. But these conditions have changed, especially in Colorado and Wyoming; and as the progress of immigration continues to march westward the same conditions will prevail in the territory lying to the west and northwest of these States, where the largest herds are now concentrated. So, for the lack of room, it will be impossible for herds to accumulate in numbers as they did in the years gone by; and as a natural consequence it can hardly be anticipated that with the constant increase in consumption making the demand greater each succeeding year, there can be a decline in prices, but, rather, higher prices will follow, which will stimulate the farmers in the range and feeding States to increase their male herds in numbers to suit the exigencies of the times, thereby guarding against future shortage.

There are more cattle being fed in Kansas and Nebraska this year than ever before in the history of those two States, the feeders having gathered them from wherever they could be found, taking everything they could get, of every grade and every mixture, and at higher prices than at any time for seven years last past—the direct result of the present boom. In Colorado, Wyoming, and Nevada they are feeding every animal they can get, feeders paying from 25 to 30 per cent more per head than last year. When these cattle now being fed in the above-mentioned and other localities are cleaned up and marketed, the Western ranges will be called upon for the next supply of feeders, which they can hardly furnish; but the shortage can be made up by the farmers of the country, who have been increasing their small herds, prompted so to do by continued high prices.

THE SHEEP INDUSTRY OF COLORADO.

The sheep industry of Colorado, which during the past three years has been very unsatisfactory and generally unprofitable to owners, began to revive in the early spring of the present year, and since that time a gradual, steady increase in the prices of wool and the value of different animals of the flocks have been going on, until now the industry is upon a good, healthly, paying basis, and the sentiment expressed by all sheep raisers with whom I have conversed is to the effect that so long as the present tariff exists, unless some unforeseen calamity occurs, the sheep industry of Colorado and other range States will be one of the best-paying branches of the live-stock business, in proportion to the amount of capital invested. There has been, and is now, a shortage of sheep, but this shortage will not last so long as the shortage of cattle, for the reason that the sheep can be renewed in number on the ranges in far less time than cattle. All over the sheep-growing districts of the State ranchmen, who for the last few years had become discouraged and neglected their flocks and in many instances went out of the business entirely, are now increasing their herds and going back into the business on a larger scale than ever before.

The sheep scab, through good attention and a thorough system of dipping, was almost eliminated from the State a few years ago, when the sheep industry was profitable. At least it was gotten under control to such an extent that it was considered of little consequence; but under the late depression in the industry it had been allowed to become quite prevalent in some portions of the State, especially in the southern counties, where a great portion of the animals are of the Mexican breed. In some of the southern counties, up to the latter part of September last, there was scarcely a sheep ranch that was not infected with the scab, while in the northern counties there was but one ranch at that time where the disease prevailed. At this writing (December, 1897) the disease has been entirely eliminated from the northern part of the State, and in the south the only counties where the disease exists to an extent worth mentioning are Las Animas, Huerfano, Costillo, Archuleta, and Saguache; and in these counties the disease is fast disappearing, owing to the determined efforts of county inspectors appointed by the State veterinary board, as provided by statute. The inspectors and owners of flocks are working in harmony, and the dipping process is being carried on with so much vigor that within ninety days, possibly by the 1st of March, 1898, the disease will scarcely be known to any flock of sheep in the State. Of course, we are liable to fresh infection from sheep admitted from other States, either for feeding or grazing. But with the disease once thoroughly under control in the State, a vigorous execution of the regulations adopted by our State veterinary board, together with the measures adopted by the Federal Government to arrest the progress of the disease by forbidding the interstate traffic in scab-infected sheep, will, it is believed, almost entirely prevent any movement of infected herds by trail into or through the State.

There is no contagious disease known to stock which is more easily controlled or cured than the sheep scab. Two dippings in a solution of lime and sulphur will work an absolute cure. The proportion used is 1 pound of lime, 2 pounds of sulphur, and 6 gallons of water.[1] The custom is to make the dippings two weeks apart. Sheep once cured of this disease will never have it again unless brought in contact with others that are infected.

The sheep industry of Colorado for the past two years (1895 and 1896) is estimated to represent a gross annual product in wool, mutton, and lamb of over $1,000,000. The estimate for this year, conservatively made, will reach over $1,500,000.

During the year 1896, according to the report of the veterinary board of Colorado, there were shipped into Colorado from New Mexico, Texas, Wyoming, Utah, Oklahoma, Oregon, and Idaho, for feeding and grazing, 233,136 head of sheep, distributed principally in the counties of Arapahoe, Larimer, Las Animas, Weld, Boulder, Eagle, Logan, Otero, Pueblo, and La Plata.

This year the following number of sheep from other States and Ter-

---

[1] For formulas for various dips, see Annual Report of Bureau of Animal Industry for 1897, p. 116.

ritories (**New Mexico, Utah, Wyoming, and Oregon**) were shipped into Colorado for feeding and grazing:

For feeding (principally lambs).

To Larimer County	161,034
To Weld County	72,429
To Otero County	45,351
To Bent County	18,727
To Logan County	10,889
To Morgan County	8,889
To Boulder County	2,500
To other counties	1,465
Total	316,184

For grazing (principally stock sheep).

To Arapahoe County	26,465
To Routt County	24,950
To Las Animas County	14,435
To Pueblo County	4,495
To El Paso County	2,231
To Montrose County	2,000
To Gunnison County	450
Total	75,026

This makes a total of 391,210 for the year 1897, as against 233,136 for the year 1896. The above figures for 1897 do not include lambs brought from southern Colorado counties for feeding in Larimer and other northern counties.

A CATTLE DISEASE IN MARSHALL COUNTY, KANSAS.

On February 15, 1898, Mr. Rice P. Steddom, assistant inspector for this Bureau, was given instructions to proceed to Blue Rapids, Kans., to investigate a disease of cattle in that vicinity which was alleged to be extremely contagious. Below is Mr. Steddom's report:

On February 17, accompanied by Commissioners Frank Weinshank and J. W. Johnson, of the Kansas Live Stock Sanitary Commission, and Dr. Paul Fischer, professor of veterinary science, State Agricultural College, Manhattan, Kans., I visited the farm of G. C. Rodkey, located 3 miles east of Blue Rapids, in Marshall County, Kans.

The herd of cattle in which the disease exists on the Rodkey farm consists of 25 animals, ranging in age from 10 to 14 months, grade Herefords and Galloways; in general condition good, some of them fat; most of them recently dehorned. Seventeen are steer cattle and 8 are heifers; of the latter, 6 are "Whitefaces" and 2 are Galloway grades.

The steer cattle appear to be in perfect health, while all the heifers are affected with a disease of the vulvæ. The ones exhibiting the severest forms of the disease presented the following symptoms: The lips of the vulvæ were infiltrated and swollen to twice their normal thickness. The mucous membranes of the vulvæ and vagina were dry and slightly congested. The vulvar integument was slightly congested, on which were a few pustules from 1 to $1\frac{1}{2}$ centimeters in diameter. These ulcers were covered with brown leathery scabs, which adhered tenaciously, and, on being removed, brought away a scanty amount of yellow pus, leaving an angry, granular, elevated ulcer, with pitted surface. These ulcers have been treated with caustic, which undoubtedly changed the character of the covering.

About December 15, 1897, these calves were placed in a feed lot with hogs, where they have since been continuously confined. The lot is small, poorly drained, and has been very muddy during the greater portion of the period. During said confinement these calves have received one-half ration, consisting of whole shelled corn six parts, rye one part, oats one part, and an abundance of fodder, consisting of about equal parts of prairie hay and millet. The water supply is from a well 16 feet deep, situated on the lower portion of the lot. Until recently these cattle and hogs drank from the same troughs. The milch cows on this farm (none of which have manifested any symptoms of the disease) have received the same kind of food, but are supplied with water from the Blue River. All these young cattle were bred and raised on Mr. Rodkey's farm, and no foreign cattle have been in contact with them.

The first appearance of this disease in the calves was noticed by Mr. Rodkey three weeks ago, and a week later treatment with medicine procured from Mr. C. F. Rice (nitrate of silver as a caustic and creolin—5 per cent solution—as a wash) was commenced. But one application of caustic and creolin has been given each animal. Mr. Rodkey states that they are all rapidly recovering, and that the muddy yard and common watering troughs are the causes of the disease.

On the same date, February 17, 1898, Mr. J. H. Duncan, of Blue Rapids, whose farm is 1 mile west of G. C. Rodkey's, was interviewed, and made following statement: "On February 10, 1898, I noticed some of my heifers presenting symptoms similar to those of the disease affecting the Rodkey stock. I at once procured medicine from C. F. Rice and treated them. They are at this time practically well."

On February 18, 1898, I visited the farm of C. F. Rice, 8 miles north of Blue Rapids, and, upon investigation of Mr. Rice's cattle herd, consisting of 2 milch cows and 60 head of yearling grade heifers, found that 59 of the latter were affected with a disease of the vulvæ, a majority of which presented symptoms similar to those affected in the outbreak on the Rodkey farm. One other was but slightly affected, and one presented a very aggravated form of the disease and exhibited the following symptoms: Loss of appetite; bowels constipated; temperature elevated; respiration accelerated; a tucked-up and general dejected appearance; vulvæ greatly inflamed, swollen, and covered with brown, leathery scab, resulting from confluent pustules; extreme tenderness in these parts, as manifested by stiff, straddling movement. These heifers have been confined in feed. lot with hogs and given full feed of shelled corn, Kafir corn, and cane. Water supply is from shallow well adjacent to feed lot. The early history, as given by Mr. Rice, is as follows: The 60 head of heifers were brought from Kansas City (Mo.) stock yards December 18, 1897, and placed in the feed lot, where they have since remained. At the end of the first week 5 animals were affected; second week, 20; third week, 40; fourth week, 60. The two cows which were with the herd were slightly affected. The vulvar lips thickened and continued to enlarge for four or five days. In the meantime certain pustular enlargements, varying in size from 0.1 to 2.5 centimeters, appeared. About the fifth day these pustules ruptured and discharged yellowish pus. In some of the more severe cases the skin of one entire side of the vulva and adjacent parts of the escutcheon had sloughed, leaving an angry, ulcerous surface 10 or 15 centimeters in diameter. The pus discharged from these surfaces accumulated in the hair, but produced no erosion. During the early stages of the disease there was loss of appetite, and wheat bran was substituted for corn. The latter is now given, full feed.

Mr. Rice contends that the herd was affected when brought to his farm, in evidence of which he called attention to a certain animal larger than the others which presents a marked depression on one side of the vulva, indicating that at some time there has been a waste of tissue of the part, which, as he claims, was caused by this same disease prior to their arrival at his farm.   There was no other indication of disease in this individual animal at the time of purchase, nor .has there been since.

On February 19, 1898, Mr. Hunt, whose farm joins the farm occupied by Mr. Rice, was interviewed, and stated in substance as follows: The 18 cattle (cows and heifers) on his farm were affected with a disease presenting symptoms similar to those of the Rice stock.   He is treating them with medicine obtained from Mr. Rice, and they are rapidly recovering.

A comparison of the herds of Messrs. Rice, Rodkey, Duncan, and Hunt, which have been similarly affected and have been treated by the application of caustic (silver nitrate) and a wash (5 per cent solution of creolin), as prescribed by Dr. Paul Fischer, of Manhattan, Kans., makes it evident that the care of the animals has much to do with the source of the disease, as all animals affected are rapidly recovering except those of one man, who has not given his cattle proper attention in protection and medical care.   In none of the animals affected have I seen the disease in its earlier stages, all presenting similar symptoms, differing only in degree of severity.

From the information gained from this investigation, I am led to conclude that the cause of the vulvar disease is of local origin, and although apparently contagious as regards a particular herd, there is no evidence of communication between the farm of Mr. Rice and the farms of Mr. Rodkey and Mr. Duncan prior to the existence of the disease on the latter farms, and there certainly has been no transfer of cattle between the farms above mentioned.

A CATTLE DISEASE IN URUGUAY.

The following letter from Hon. Albert W. Swalm, United States consul at Montevideo, addressed to the Assistant Secretary of State, is self-explanatory:

CONSULATE OF THE UNITED STATES,
Montevideo, May 16, 1898.

SIR: Having noticed the fact stated that the herds of cattle of Uruguay were largely affected by the disease known as the Texas fever, I addressed an official communication to the secretary of the agricultural and stock department, Señor Joaquin Suarez. In a letter of transmittal the chief of the bureau reported that the disease which had at first created much alarm, from its newness to the country, had almost entirely abated, and that it never had existed in any epidemic form in any of the departments. It was true that there had been a few deaths, but it was always among imported breeding stock, and never among the native cattle.

When the disease was at first reported the honorable minister of fomento at once put on foot an official investigation by telegraph. This was on April 4, the agricultural department calling to its aid all the civil officers for the investigation. In addition several veterinary experts were sent out into remote sections, or wherever an unfavorable report had been made and dissections were possible. All the departments reported themselves practically clear, save that of San Jose, where the sixth district reported that a disease had appeared among the imported and high-grade stock, and that the symptoms were: Head bent down to the ground, no appetite, hair roughed up, body contracted, eyes red and inflamed, in some cases abdomen swollen to very marked degree, and in all of these cases death followed in twenty-four hours, with the urine very red and excrement black and very foul. The veterinary surgeons did not make any dissections of the cases, as the disease had abated when they arrived and decomposition had destroyed those which had died. In another section of the same department the report was that the cattle showed these symptoms: Mouth and tongue dark, eyes unaltered, passed no urine, excrement dark, did not swell much. It is stated that the meat of some of these cattle was eaten by the peons, and they reported it normal both in color and taste. It has been the custom to report all cattle deaths as the result of Texas fever, as is usual in all countries, our own not excepted, where every hog that dies goes out because of cholera. It is surmised that the same weed or grass may be at the bottom of the trouble, and as the imported strains of cattle are the ones wholly affected by it, just about when pasturage is at its best, the supposition has much to support it. In no district has there been such a thing as an epidemic, and it is a pleasure to note that the department in charge here is keenly on the alert to bring about very decided repressive action, should anything of the kind occur.

The interest of our country in this matter lies in the fact that we import a very great number of hides from Uruguay annually, and there might be danger from infection, even after the thorough "poisoning" that is adopted in all the hides so imported.

I am, sir, your obedient servant,

ALBERT W. SWALM,
United States Consul.

Hon. WILLIAM R. DAY,
Assistant Secretary of State, Washington, D. C.

10317——25

THE CATTLE TICK AND TUBERCULOSIS IN NEW SOUTH WALES.

The following communication having reference to the ravages of Texas fever and the free use of tuberculous cattle for meat in New South Wales was received by the Chief of the Bureau of Animal Industry under date of September 10, 1897: ·

I had a very pleasant call, a few days ago, from a Mr. Gee, a packer of New South Wales, Australia. He told me that the cattle tick had practically ruined the cattle industry of his colony; that the Government had, at great expense, tried dipping the cattle, with only temporary benefit, as, while the oil used killed the ticks on the cattle at the time of dipping, it only prevented the accession of a new lot of ticks as long as the animal was on his feet; for the first time the animal lay down the oil rubbed off and the ticks swarmed over him. He stated that the Government had tried crude petroleum and several other oils, but found cotton-seed oil the best for the purpose, both on account of its nonirritating character and its cheapness. Owing to its never freezing there, the ticks are equally virulent at all times of the year, and in the early morning, before the sun got high enough to make it warm, the tops of the grass fairly swarmed with them. Lately the Government had begun some inoculation experiments, but they had not been carried far enough to warrant forming any conclusion as to their efficacy.

Asked as to whether they had a system of inspection, he said that they had, but as yet it was very crude. He said he had a call from the Government inspector a short time before he left, and the inspector pointed out a tuberculous steer being killed at the time. Asking how many they got like that, Mr. Gee replied, "Oh, quite a few." The inspector then asked him to keep a record of such cases as a basis for some statistics. The inspector did not ask him what he did with the cases. Mr. Gee stated in answer to a question of mine that they got a very large percentage of tuberculous animals. This appears more remarkable in view of the fact that they killed no cows whatever. He also said he was at that time filling a large contract for canned beef for both the French and Belgian governments, and doing it absolutely without inspection, except so far as related to the terms of the contracts.

Thinking that this condition of affairs, in a country that is a very strong competitor of ours in the meat markets of the world, might interest you, I take the liberty of submitting these facts.

Very respectfully,

GEO. S. BAKER, *Inspector,*
Bureau of Animal Industry.

PRELIMINARY CATALOGUE OF PLANTS POISONOUS TO STOCK.

By V. K. CHESNUT, B. S.,

Assistant, Division of Botany, Department of Agriculture.

In Bulletin No. 20 of the Division of Botany of this Department and in Farmers' Bulletin No. 86, also of this Department, an attempt was made to describe the plants native to the United States which are best known to be poisonous either to man or to domestic animals, and also to give a satisfactory account of their geographical distribution and poisonous qualities. No systematic attempt has as yet been made to study the poisonous plants of our new possessions. In the present catalogue there has been gathered together a few brief notes concerning a very much larger number of plants, mostly introduced or native, than was given in the bulletins named above, all of which have been reported to be more or less poisonous to stock.

Some of the species treated of in the bulletins have been omitted in this catalogue, either because stock are not poisoned by eating them, or because they are not known to have been eaten by stock. The leaves of the various species of poisonous Rhus, for example, are eaten by several, if not all, kinds of stock with impunity, and even with considerable relish. On the other hand, stock have not been known to eat the false jessamine. The plants which are well known to cause death in a purely mechanical way are excluded from this account beeause they are not poisonous. Bacteria and all living plants parasitic on animal organisms have also been excluded.

Those plants which are injurious or fatal in a mechanical way have been called "stock-killers" by Prof. J. II. Maiden, the well-known economic botanist of Australia. These contain no poisonous substances, but operate chiefly by clogging up the intestines, by perforating and inflaming the tissues of the eyes, the nose, or the mouth and intestinal tract, and perhaps by evolving gases which distend the stomach and intestines to such a degree that it is impossible for the lungs and heart to perform their function in aerating and circulating the blood. Instances of bloating are very frequent in stock, as is evidenced by the information contained in Bulletin No. 52 of the State Agricultural Experiment Station at Fort Collins, Colo. Prof. W. W. Cooke cites numerous cases of death in sheep, especially ewes, from bloat caused by eating green alfalfa. He estimates that over 5 per cent are killed by eating it and concludes that it is not a safe food for stock unless certain precautions are observed. The precautions enumerated are well worthy of careful consideration. While this action in several cases is mechanical, it seems probable that, under certain conditions, poisonous substances may also be formed in the stomach at the same time, and that these may also be a cause of death. Prussic acid may thus be easily formed from amygdaline, a nonpoisonous substance which exists in the leaves of several groups of plants belonging to the rose family.

The annoying or serious and sometimes fatal effect of the sharp barbed awns of certain grasses is especially well known to Western farmers, who experience much trouble from the fox-tail and squirrel-tail grasses (*Hordeum* sp.), which are so abundant in Western meadows. These grasses make excellent fodder when young, but when nearly mature the awns easily separate, and frequently work their way into the mouth and throat, or the eyes and ears, and cause such intense suffering that the animal must be killed. The hairs from the crimson clover (*Trifolium incarnatum*) act in a very different manner. In Circular No. 8 of the Division of Botany of this Department Mr. Coville has shown that if the overripe dried plants are eaten by stock the hairs become easily detached from the flower stalks and heads, and, by virtue of their barbed structure, accumulate in the intestines in the form of felt-like balls which gradually increase in size until the intestines become completely clogged. Several instances of death from this cause have been recorded. This is also true of some species of cacti which in Mexico and the southwest serve as food for stock. In the issue of the Transactions of the Academy of Science of St. Louis for November 30, 1897 (Vol. 7, No. 18), Prof. Trelease gave an account of an unusual accumulation of fine cactus bristles which caused the death of a bull at San Luis Potosi in Mexico. The animal being untamable, had been allowed to run wild, its chief food in winter having consisted of five species of Opuntia, which grew plentifully in the vicinity. Since the minute bristles had not been scorched or burnt off the plant in any way, they were swallowed with the fleshy part and gradually accumulated in the form of sixteen spherical masses which averaged about 4 inches in diameter and about 7 ounces in weight. A microscopical investigation of these balls showed that they were composed almost wholly of the minute barbed bristles characteristic of the Opuntias. Anyone who has attempted to gather the gorgeous blossoms of these species can not fail to remember the ease with which the bristles pierce the flesh and the pertinacity with which they cling to it. When the plants are properly singed, however, they may be used for fodder without danger. When the larger spines only are cut off and the remainder feed to stock, these concretions are to be expected.

At least one representative of the lower orders of fungi, the corn smut (*Ustilago maydis*), appears to be deleterious, and sometimes even fatal to stock in a mechanical way by virtue of the large quantity of the dry powdery spores which it contains when mature. These probably act by expanding, and thus obstructing the stomach.

In the case of some molds, such as the white mold (*Aspergillus glaucus*), found on corn and oats, it has been proved that the spores will germinate and grow within the tissues of the body. They cause death apparently from a poisonous compound which is produced simultaneously with the mold. Other plants are undoubtedly deleterious to stock on account of their dry, tough, fibrous, or indigestible character. Cases of blind staggers with marked cerebral symptoms have been cited to me by Dr. Albert Hassall, of the Bureau of Animal Industry, which were caused simply by the continued feeding of a large quantity of dry fodder for several days or weeks. The intestines were completely stopped, but when the impacting material was removed the symptoms speedily vanished.

The list as given is provisional for some species, as the reports upon which their reputation is founded are very meager, and sometimes even contradictory. A very interesting and instructive illustration of this was published in the Bulletin of Pharmacy for May, 1899. The chief portion of Mr. Theod. A. Melter's article entitled "When to Gather Plants" [for drugs] is devoted to a consideration of the time in various places in the Southern States, at which to gather the passion flower vine (*Passiflora incarnata*), which is very extensively used by pharmaceutical manufacturers. It is a well-recognized fact that, in order to get a drug of maximum and uniform strength, the plant should be cut off just above the roots when it is beginning to flower. The very interesting observation was made that, while the plant blossomed in March at West Palm Beach in Florida, the blossoms did not appear until April at Jacksonville, Fla., 300 miles northward; nor until May at Montgomery, Ala., and June at Nashville, Tenn., both of which latter places are, respectively, 300 and 600 miles north of Jacksonville. The drug collected at the flowering time at all of these places proved to be of equal potency. The most interesting fact, however, comes in right here. In July, 500 pounds of the drug was collected and offered for sale at Jacksonville. As the plant blossoms here in April, the drug was refused for medical use, but was purchased at a cent a pound to be used for hay. The horse to which it was fed ate it with relish so long as the supply lasted, and even preferred it to hay. No ill results were observed, and in fact the horse became not only very fat, but more high spirited. Eight months later, in March, the author of the article received 50 pounds of the fully potent drug from West Palm Beach, and, by accident or carelessness, his horse got access to it at night and ate over half of the quantity. The animal was found in a very stupid state the next morning, and it remained in this condition, but with loss of flesh, for six weeks when it died. When it is remembered that the other horse ate 500 pounds and became high spirited, the effect of the varying season on the drug is at once apparent.

Several doubtful plants are here enumerated, not necessarily because it is believed that they are poisonous, but with the view to eliciting more positive evidence either for or against them. Although comprehensive, the list is incomplete, for experience is slowly but constantly adding to the number already known or suspected to be poisonous.

A few plants not poisonous to stock are nevertheless objectionable to stockmen and should be mentioned in this connection. This class includes all of those which, when eaten, taint the milk or impart a disagreeable or more rarely poisonous quality to the animal's flesh. Wild garlic (*Allium vineale*) is a familiar example of a plant which taints milk. It is intended, however, to speak here only of those species which thus indirectly cause poisoning. Mention has been made of a few such plants in the catalogue, the most prominent being the bitterweed (*Helenium tenuifolium*) of the Gulf States, and the may apple (*Podophyllum peltatum*) of the Eastern States. More facts and further investigation are needed in this line of work.

In considering the circumstances under which stock eat this obnoxious vegetation the most stress should be laid upon unfamiliarity. The odor and the taste of the plants which are ordinarily eaten by stock are so varied that it is little wonder that any animal, when placed among plants with which it is unfamiliar, will eat one that is deleterious. Especially when hungry or thirsty such animals are apt to eat anything of the kind placed within their reach. The custom so prevalent in the West of driving large herds of cattle and sheep from one pasture ground over wide areas of barren country to another is especially conducive to severe losses from plant poisoning.

Another very important class of cases is due to a purely artificial cause, and may therefore be remedied by the exercise of due intelligence and care. This cause consists in the use of impure or unclean hay. The seed sown is sometimes contaminated with poisonous weed seeds or with the spores of ergot. Grass or meadow hay is still more apt to contain poisonous plants. These are, of course, generally rejected by all but the most hungry animals, but when the texture happens to be nearly the same as that of the hay itself it is very apt to be eaten by the animal. Bulletin No. 35 of the North Dakota Experiment Station contains an interesting account by Prof. E. F. Ladd of the poisoning of a bull by eating slough hay which was described as being badly contaminated with the water hemlock (*Cicuta maculata*). In the case investigated, evidence of the water hemlock poison was plainly detected in the stomach.

The practice of tempting stock to eat material which is more or less deleterious by cutting it up finely and mixing it with food of superior quality is also open to criticism. There is some question in regard to the merits of the seeds of the velvet bean as a food plant for stock. The plant is now largely cultivated in the South, but does not mature its seed well except in Florida and the adjacent parts of Georgia and Alabama. The nitrogen content of the seed is very high, but, according to Mr. J. F. Duggar, of the Alabama Station, the verdict of three out of four correspondents is against the use of the seed as a food for man. The fourth man, quoting from Professor Duggar's bulletin on the subject, says: "For human food they are by all odds the richest and best vegetable I have ever tasted. If eaten in large quantities they will nauseate the stomach, not from poison, but from richness." This recommendation is of rather doubtful value, especially when we consider there is one authentic case on record in which nearly fifty people were very badly poisoned by eating the seeds. Stock often refuse to eat the seeds, but as the hull is readily eaten alone, both the hull and seed are often ground up together in order to make the animals eat the seeds, which are considered very nutritious. It is possible, however, that, as in the case of the jack bean (*Canavalia ensiformis*), much of the nitrogen which they contain is in the form of amides, and is, therefore, not available for nutrition. If not absolutely poisonous, it may possibly be deleterious in the assimilation of other food.

Some plants useful for fodder in small quantities are deleterious when fed continuously as hay. In Bulletin No. 35 of the North Dakota Station Professor Ladd has shown that millet hay exercises a very marked action on the kidneys of stock to which it has been fed continuously, and he has succeeded in isolating a poisonous glucocide. Lupines (*L. plattensis* and *L. leucophyllus*) are esteemed as good fodder in Montana, but the enormous fatality which has occasionally attended its use show that it is poisonous under some conditions, probably when the ripe seeds are present in considerable quantity.

The most serious losses of stock due to poisonous weeds have been reported from the western half of the United States. In three cases that occurred in October and November, 1898, over 2,000 sheep are reported to have perished. Smaller fatalities have been reported from all parts of the United States, including Alaska. The money value of this loss can not well be estimated, but it must be a very considerable sum. The loss to one correspondent from loco in one year is estimated at $2,200, and, as is mentioned in the catalogue, the State of Colorado paid out $200,000 in bounties to rid itself of this pest. The loss from lupine poisoning in Montana during the fiscal year ending June 30, 1899, is estimated at about $10,000. The number of eastern cases of animal poisoning investigated by the Division of Botany during the fiscal year ending June 30, 1899, is only six, all of which were of minor importance only. Twenty cases from west of the Mississippi were investigated during the same period.

The information incorporated in the accompanying catalogue has been procured from the most diverse sources. Special treatises, including the works of Kobert, Blythe, Cornevin, Fröhner, Dammann, Millspaugh, White, Van Hasselt, and Rochebrune, have been constantly at hand, and free recourse has been had to the numerous articles found in the various botanical and chemical journals and agricultural bulletins; also the literature indexed in the Catalogue and Index Medicus of the Surgeon-General's library at Washington. Besides some actual experiments made in this Department, an important and most valuable source of information has been the correspondents of the Division of Botany. The letters from farmers and large stock raisers have done much to further our knowledge in these lines. The letters from botanists, chemists, and medical men have been especially esteemed for the more explicit information which they conveyed.

The problem of establishing the identity of a plant which has, or is supposed to have, caused poisoning in the field is not always easy, and it is frequently only by a combined knowledge of the sciences and of a variety of diseases that it can be solved. For the general facts as to the occurrence of losses, the number of animals affected, and the amount of the money loss we must look to those whose interests are immediately affected. The same class can also afford us general data, assisting in the identification of the plant which has inflicted the damage. For the final determination of the injurious plant, however, technical assistance is required, and here the veterinarian, the chemist, and the botanist can be of great service.

When, however, the plant has been identified we still need information concerning the nature of the poison, and need to know of a rational antidote. For this knowledge we must depend upon the chemist and medical man.

The cooperation of chemists and medical men is therefore especially solicited; but at the same time it is still necessary to impress upon others the desirability of their assistance in obtaining the fullest and most accurate information in regard to all the phases of plant poisoning which come under their observation.

CATALOGUE OF PLANTS POISONOUS TO STOCK.

PERISPORACEÆ (Rot-mold Family).

Aspergillus glaucus (L.) Link.—This is the common flocculent WOOLLY MOLD which sometimes develops to a dangerous extent on corn, oats, and other food grains which have either been harvested before full maturity or been stored in a damp place. The moldy growth is pure white at first, but changes with the ripening of the spores to gray and then green. The spores are apparently the cause of the so-called enzootic cerebritis, or "staggers," of horses, which, during the winter of 1898–99, has been reported as having caused very heavy losses throughout the Missouri Valley, in Illinois, Indiana, Tennessee, and Maryland. Experiments made in 1891 by Dr. N. S. Mayo, at Manhattan, Kans., confirm the results of European investigators, who have shown that the spores of this mold will grow inside of a living animal if they are introduced into the blood in any way. Death is probably caused by some poison which is simultaneously produced with the mold in the body of the animal.

HYPOCREACEÆ (Ergot Family).

Claviceps purpurea (Fr.) Tul.—This, the most common species of ERGOT, infests various species of native and cultivated grasses. It causes great loss of stock, especially in the West, where it is much more common than in the Eastern States.

USTILAGINACEÆ (Smut Family).

Ustilago maydis (DC.) Corda.—The black powdery fungus known as CORN SMUT is common throughout the corn-producing districts of the middle West and is occasionally reported as being fatal to stock. Experiments made in Wisconsin and elsewhere show that it is not a very active poison when eaten in moderate quantity. When fed in gradually increasing amounts up to 2 pounds, no effect was noted, but 4 pounds fed on each of two successive days caused the sudden death of one cow. Since corn smut has been shown to be less fatal when wet, it seems probable that its physical and not its chemical character may be responsible for the death of cattle which have eaten it in considerable quantity.

UREDINACEÆ (Rust Family).

Coleosporium solidaginis (Schw.) Theum.—This is a parasitic growth that is found on some species of golden rod and is possibly responsible for the cause of the so-called golden-rod poisoning in horses. (See Solidago sp.)

AGARICACEÆ (Mushroom Family).

Amanita muscaria (L.) Fr.—The well-known FLY AMANITA (FLY FUNGUS; DEADLY AMANITA) may be found from spring to early winter in pine forests throughout the United States. Cows are supposed to be killed by eating it, and almost every year the daily papers chronicle the death of several human beings who were led to eat the fungus through mistake for some edible species. The fresh cap is frequently rubbed up with milk and used to poison flies.

PHALLACEÆ (Stink-horn Family).

Clathrus columnatus Bosc.—In an article published in the Botanical Gazette (vol. 15, p. 45), Dr. Farlow, of Harvard University, gives an account of an investigation of a case of poisoning in hogs which was caused by eating this peculiar fungus. It grows in patches in oak woods and openings, and is quite common throughout the Southern States.

Fig. 38.—Fly amanita (*Amanita muscaria*): *a*, mature plant; *b*, top view of cap showing corky patches—both one half natural size.

POLYPODIACEÆ (Fern Family).

Pteris aquilina L.—In July, 1895, nineteen cattle died in Maryland, which were supposed to have been poisoned by eating the common BRACKEN FERN. Very few similar cases are on record, but one European authority cites one in which five horses were killed by eating hay contaminated with this fern, and another states that cases are quite frequent among cattle in England.

EQUISETACEÆ (Horsetail Family).

Equisetum arvense L.—The FIELD HORSETAIL was reported from Connecticut in 1871 as being poisonous to horses. Cases are very rare, and it is probable that this plant is deleterious only when eaten in considerable quantity and then perhaps only on account of its physical character. Experiments made in Europe show that a similar species (*E. palustre*) is fatal to horses when fed in considerable quantity with hay.

TAXACEÆ (Yew Family).

Taxus minor (Michx.) Britton.—The COMMON YEW, or GROUND HEM- LOCK of the northeastern United States, is called POISON HEM- LOCK in some places. The leaves of this shrub are probably poisonous to stock, as are those of the European yew. This species is more accessible to stock than the western yew (*Taxus brevifolia*), which grows only in deep canyons.

POACEÆ (Grass Family).

Lolium temulentum L.—The seed of the DARNEL, or POISON RYE GRASS, an introduced annual especially abundant on the Pacific Slope, is considered poisonous to both man and animals.

Stipa robusta (Vasey) Nash.—This is a perennial plant which is known in Arizona and New Mexico as SLEEPY GRASS. It pro- duces a narcotic effect on horses and cattle that feed upon it, but stock bred in that region rarely touch it.

Zea mays L.—The numerous deaths that are frequently attributed to INDIAN CORN are mostly due, not to any poison inherent in the plant, but rather to parasitic or saprophytic fungus growths, as noted under *Aspergillus* and *Ustilago*. The green fodder is very apt to cause severe and even fatal bloating if the animal's diet is not properly regulated. Death has also been attributed to the presence of niter (potassium nitrate) in the growing stalks. It is supposed that in very rich soil this substance will sometimes accumulate in the stalks in considerable quantity during a pro- longed drought.

MELANTHACEÆ (Bunch-flower Family).

Chrosperma muscætoxicum (Walt.) Kuntze.—The bulbous portion of the FLY POISON, or CROW POISON, an Eastern plant, is some- times eaten by cattle with fatal results. The bulbs, when mashed up with molasses, are used to stupefy flies.

Veratrum viride Ait.—The leaves of the COMMON SWAMP HELLE- BORE (AMERICAN WHITE HELLEBORE; FALSE HELLEBORE; INDIAN POKE) of the eastern and northern portions of the United States have proved fatal to man and to horses. Sheep eat the young leaves and shoots with apparent relish. The seed is poisonous to chickens.

Veratrum californicum Durand.—The root and young shoots of the CALIFORNIA FALSE HELLEBORE have been reported as being fatal to horses.

Zygadenus venenosus Wats.—The name DEATH CAMAS has been applied to this plant in the Northwest to distinguish it from the true camas (*Quamasia quamash*), which is highly esteemed for food by the Indians. In Oregon it is erroneously called

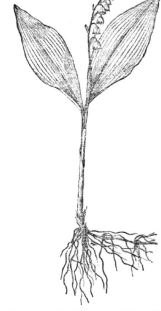

FIG. 39.—False hellebore (*Veratrum viride*), one-third natural size.

FIG. 40.—Lily of the valley (*Convallaria majalis*), one-third natural size.

"lobelia" by most stockmen and farmers. Horses, cattle, and sheep, as well as man, are poisoned by eating the bulb.

Zygadenus elegans Pursh.—The bulbs, and perhaps the leaves of the *Glaucous zygadenus*, or ALKALI GRASS, are poisonous to cattle.

LILIACEÆ (Lily Family).

Leucocrinum montanum Nutt.—This beautiful little plant is known throughout the Northwest as LEUCOCRINUM. It is supposed in Montana to be very fatal to sheep, especially after the fruit is developed.

Nothoscordum bivalve (L.) Britton.—The bulbs of a plant called CROW POISON were sent to the Department from Texas in March, 1898, with the information that they were suspected of being very fatal to cattle at that time of the year. The mature plants grown from these bulbs proved to be of the above species. Another common name for the plant is YELLOW FALSE GARLIC.

CONVALLARIACEÆ (Lily of the Valley Family).

Convallaria majalis L.—All parts of the LILY OF THE VALLEY are powerfully poisonous, and are liable to cause damage to cattle and horses.

HÆMODORACEÆ (Bloodwort Family).

Gyrotheca capitata (Walt.) Morong.—This is the RED ROOT, or PAINT ROOT, of the Atlantic Coast and Cuba, so called on account of the red color of its sap. White hogs are supposed, throughout the South, to be particularly subject to the poison contained in the plant.

AMARYLLIDACEÆ (Amaryllis Family).

Atamosco atamasco (L.) Greene. — The ATAMASCO LILY of the southeastern United States is supposed by some persons to cause the disease known as "staggers" in horses.

FAGACEÆ (Beech Family).

Quercus sp.—In Europe the acorns of various species of oaks cause sickness and death in hogs and cattle. This effect may possibly be due to bloating, but may also be due in some way to the tannin or the bitter principle which they contain.

URTICACEÆ (Nettle Family).

Urtica gracilis Ait.—The SLEN-ER NETTLE covers thou-

FIG. 41.—Slender nettle (*Urtica gracilis*).

sands of acres of reclaimed swamp land in Michigan and Wisconsin, which is made nearly worthless by its dense growth, horses refusing to pass through it to cultivate the soil.

CHENOPODIACEÆ (Goosefoot Family).

Sarcobatus vermiculatus (Hook.) Torr.—BLACK GREASEWOOD, or CHICO, is a scraggy shrub which grows in strongly alkaline soil in the southwestern and western portions of the United States. A correspondent in New Mexico states that on one occasion he counted as many as 1,000 sheep that had been killed by eating the leaves of this plant. It is claimed that cows are not affected by eating it at any time and that sheep can eat it quite freely in winter. Death is perhaps due more to the bloating effect rather than to any poisonous substance which the plant contains.

Fig. 42.—Pokeweed (*Phytolacca decandra*), one-half natural size.

PHYTOLACCACEÆ (Pokeweed Family).

Phytolacca decandra L.—The leaves of the common POKEWEED (POKE; GARGET; AMERICAN NIGHTSHADE) of the eastern half of the United States is occasionally eaten by cattle with fatal results.

ALSINACEÆ (Pink Family).

Agrostemma githago L.—The common CORN COCKLE (COCKLE; MULLEIN PINK) is an introduced weed from Europe. Poultry and household animals are occasionally poisoned by eating the seeds or the bread made from wheat contaminated with the seeds.

Silene antirrhina L.—The SLEEPY CATCHFLY, which is found throughout the United States, was stated to have poisoned sheep in southern Michigan a few years ago, but there is reason to believe that the poisoning was due to another source.

MAGNOLIACEÆ (Magnolia Family).

Illicium floridanum Ellis.—The leaves of this species of ANISETREE are supposed to be poisonous to stock.

RANUNCULACEÆ (Crowfoot Family).

Aconitum napellus L.—The EUROPEAN ACONITE (MONKSHOOD; WOLFSBANE) is very commonly cultivated in gardens and is therefore capable of doing great damage to stock. Horses and cattle have fre-

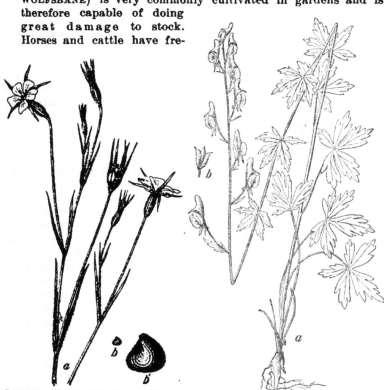

FIG. 43.—Corn cockle (*Agrostemma githago*): *a*, sprays showing flowers and seed capsule, one-third natural size; *b*, seed, natural size; *b'*, seed, four times natural size.

FIG. 44.—Aconite (*Aconitum columbianum*): *a*, flowering plant; *b*, seed capsule—both one-third natural size.

quently been poisoned by eating the leaves and flowering tops.

Aconitum columbianum Nutt.—The WESTERN ACONITE, or MONKS-HOOD, is native in the northwestern portion of the continent, where it sometimes poisons sheep.

Actæa alba (L.) Mill., WHITE BANEBERRY.—Actæa rubra (Ait.) Willd., RED BANEBERRY.—Very little damage is done to stock by these plants, because animals generally refuse to eat them.

Sheep are occasionally poisoned by eating the leaves of a closely related European species (*A. spicata*).

·Anemone quinquefolia L.—The COMMON WIND FLOWER which grows throughout most of the United States is extremely acrid and poisonous. Cattle seldom touch it: The plant loses most of its poison in drying.

Delphinium tricorne Michx.—The DWARF LARKSPUR, or STAGGER WEED, of the northeastern quarter of the United States has been especially reported from Ohio as fatal to cattle in April, when the fresh leaves appear.

Delphinium consolida L.—The seeds of the commonly introduced FIELD LARKSPUR are well known to be poisonous; the leaves are known in Europe to be fatal to cattle.

Delphinium menziesii DC.—The PURPLE LARKSPUR of the northwestern quarter of the United States is very common throughout Montana. In one case of poisoning reported by Dr. E. V. Wilcox of the Montana Experiment Station, over 600 sheep were affected, 250 of which were claimed to have been killed by the weed. An experiment made by Dr. S. B. Nelson, professor of veterinary sciences in the Washington State Agricultural College, shows that it is possible to feed as much as $24\frac{3}{4}$ pounds of the fresh leaves to a sheep within a period of five days without

FIG. 45.—Dwarf larkspur (*Delphinium tricorne*), one-third natural size.

any apparent ill effect taking place. An experiment made by Dr. Wilcox shows that the extract from less than an ounce of the dried leaves killed a yearling lamb in two hours, the dose having been given by way of the mouth.

Delphinium geyeri Greene.—The WYOMING LARKSPUR is well known throughout Wyoming, Colorado, and Nebraska under the name of POISON WEED. It is reported to be the most troublesome plant to stock in Wyoming, the dark-green tufts of foliage being especially tempting in spring when the prairies are otherwise dry and barren.

Delphinium recurvatum Greene.—This species of LARKSPUR grows in wet subsaline soil in the southern half of California. It has been reported from San Luis Obispo County as fatal to animals.

Delphinium scopulorum Gray.—The TALL MOUNTAIN LARKSPUR of the Rocky Mountains has been reported to the Canadian Department of Agriculture as poisonous to cattle in the high western prairies of Canada.

Delphinium trolliifolium Gray.—This plant is common throughout the coast region of northern California, Oregon, and Washington. In Humboldt County, Cal., it is known as COW POISON on account of its fatal effect on cattle. Its toxic character has been questioned. Perhaps it is not equally poisonous throughout all stages of its growth.

Helleborus viridis L.—The GREEN HELLEBORE is a European plant sometimes found as an escape from our gardens. All of the parts are poisonous. Cattle have been killed by eating the leaves.

Ranunculus sceleratus L.—The CURSED CROWFOOT, or CELERY-LEAFED CROWFOOT, is found throughout the eastern half of the United States and also in Europe. Cattle generally avoid all of the buttercups, but fatal cases of poisoning from this plant are recorded in European literature. When dried in hay, the plant appears to be non-poisonous. The BULBOUS

FIG. 46.—Cursed crowfoot (*Ranunculus sceleratus.*)

CROWFOOT (*R. bulbosus*) and the TALL CROWFOOT (*R. acris*) are well known to be very acrid in taste, and it is probable that all of the species which grow in water or in very marshy land are poisonous.

BERBERIDACEÆ (Barberry Family).

Podophyllum peltatum L.—The leaves of the COMMON MANDRAKE, or MAY APPLE, of the eastern half of the United States, are sparingly eaten by some cattle. Cases of poisoning are very rare, but the experience of one correspondent shows that the milk from a cow that had been feeding on the plant off and on for about three weeks was so extremely laxative as to be positively poisonous. The incident occurred during babyhood, when cow's milk was the sole source of food. The physiological effect of the milk was precisely like that of mandrake. It was shown that the cow ate the plant, which was abundant in one pasture, and when the animal was removed to a pasture free from the plant the illness stopped at once.

FIG. 47.—Mandrake (*Podophyllum peltatum*).

BUTNERIACEÆ (Strawberry-shrub Family).

Butneria fertilis (Walt.) Kearney.—The large oily seeds of the CALYCANTHUS, or SWEET-SCENTED SHRUB, contain a poisonous alkaloid, and are strongly reputed to be poisonous to cattle in Tennessee.

PAPAVERACEÆ (Poppy Family).

Argemone mexicana L.—The MEXICAN POPPY is reputed to be poisonous to stock both in the United States and in New South Wales. The seeds are narcotic, like opium.

Chelidonium majus L.—The yellow milky sap of the CELANDINE, an introduced weed common in the East, contains both an acrid and a narcotic poison. Both are powerfully active, but cases of poisoning are very rare, as stock refuse to touch the plant.

Papaver somniferum L., OPIUM POPPY, or GARDEN POPPY.— P. rhœas L., FIELD POPPY, RED POPPY, or CORN POPPY.—These plants are sometimes found as escapes from our gardens. Both contain acrid and narcotic poisons, and European literature records the death of various animals from eating their leaves and seed pods.

PRUNACEÆ (Plum Family).

Prunus caroliniana (Mill.) Ait.—The LAUREL CHERRY, or MOCK ORANGE, is native in the southeastern quarter of the United

States, and is there often cultivated for hedges. The half-wilted leaves and the seeds yield prussic acid and are poisonous when eaten by animals.

Prunus serotina Ehrh.—The WILD BLACK CHERRY is a valuable forest tree which ranges throughout the eastern half of the United States. Cattle are killed by eating the partially wilted leaves from branches thrown carelessly within their reach or

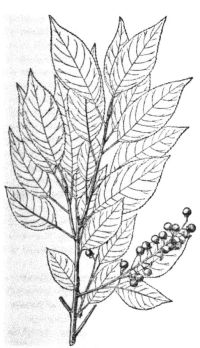

FIG. 40.—Stemless loco weed (*Aragallus lambertii*): *a*, flowering plant; *b*, seed pods; *c*, cross section of seed pod—all one-third natural size.

FIG. 48.—Black cherry (*Prunus serotina*), one-third natural size.

ignorantly offered as food. The leaves of various other wild and cultivated cherries are probably poisonous to cattle in the same way.

VICIACEÆ (Pea Family).

Aragallus lambertii (Pursh.) Greene.—The LAMBERT, or STEMLESS LOCO WEED is, next to the following species, the best-known representative of a large group of closely related plants which are native to the western half of the United States, and are known as loco weeds on account of the peculiar crazy condition which they induce in animals that eat of their leaves. Horses and cattle are both affected, but the chief damage is done to horses. After being permitted to graze on any of these plants the animal acquires an unnatural appetite for them and soon refuses all other kinds of food. It rapidly becomes unmanageable and crazy, and finally dies from the lack of proper nourishment.

Astragalus mollissimus Torr.—This, the WOOLLY LOCO WEED, is perhaps the best known of all the loco weeds. It is the species most abundant in Colorado, where from 1881 to 1885 nearly $200,000 was paid out in bounties in an attempt to exterminate it. The plant is still abundant in that State, and reports of the damage done by it continue frequent. Specimens of the three following species of *Astragalus* have been forwarded to the Division of Botany with the information that they were causing great financial loss in the districts noted. It is quite probable that other species are dangerous also.

Fig. 50.—Woolly loco weed (*Astragalus mollissimus*): *a*, whole plant; *b*, section of pod—both one-third natural size.

Astragalus bigelovii A. Gray.— Especially reported from Plainview, Tex.

Astragalus hornii A. Gray.— Stock are affected by this loco weed in the southern part of California.

Astragalus pattersoni A. Gray.— This was especially reported from Flagstaff, Ariz., as poisonous to horses and to sheep.

Crotalaria sagittalis L.—The RATTLEBOX (RATTLE WEED; WILD PEA) is an annual weed which grows on sandy soil throughout most of the eastern half of the United States. In some years it is especially abundant in the bottom lands of the Missouri Valley. Horses and sometimes cattle are killed in this region by eating grass or meadow hay which is contaminated with the plant.

Lupinus leucophyllus Dougl.—This herbaceous shrub is a representative of a very large genus of plants, many of which are widely and abundantly distributed throughout the West, and are generally known as LUPINES. The above species is very abundant in Montana, where it is said to have caused the death of a very large number of sheep. There is some question whether the animals are killed by a poisonous constituent of the plant or merely by bloat. The seeds of all the lupines are probably deleterious in the raw state. In Europe, however, the seeds of *Lupinus albus*, after the bitter taste has been removed by steeping and boiling, are eaten by human beings as well as by cattle.

Robinia pseudacacia L.—The common LOCUST TREE is native in the central and eastern parts of the United States, and is extensively cultivated for ornamental purposes throughout the Union. The bark and the leaves contain a powerful poison, and persons have been killed by eating these parts.

Sesbania vesicaria Ell.—The curious membranous-sacked seed pods of this annual vine were sent to the Department from South Carolina in November, 1897, with the information that similar seeds were found in the stomachs of cows that had died from eating some poisonous plant. This species was most strongly suspected.

Sophora secundiflora (Cav.) DC.—The beautiful bright-red beans of the FRIJOLILLO, or CORAL BEAN, of southern and western Texas contain a powerfully poisonous alkaloid. The plant is said to have poisoned stock in Texas and in northern Mexico.

Sophora sericea Nutt.—T h e SILKY SOPHORA of the southern Great Plains region has

FIG. 51.—Rattle box (*Crotalaria sagittalis*): *a*, whole plant; *b*, cross section of seed pod—both one-third natural size.

been somewhat vaguely reported as one of the plants that "loco" horses in that region. The seeds contain a very poisonous alkaloid.

Thermopsis rhombifolia (Nutt.) Richards.—This plant is known as the PRAIRIE THERMOPSIS throughout the northern part of the Great Plains region. The seeds have been reported to the Canadian Department of Agriculture as being poisonous to children. Since the plant grows abundantly in pasture lands, it is here mentioned as a plant to be suspected in cases of stock poisoning.

LINACEÆ (Flax Family).

Linum rigidum Pursh.—The LARGE-FLOWERED YELLOW FLAX is reported from Pecos Valley, Tex., as poisonous to sheep. An investigation made at this Department showed that the plant is poisonous.

MELIACEÆ (Umbrella-tree Family).

Melia azedarach L.—The CHINESE UMBRELLA TREE is much culti- vated for ornament, and sparingly escaped from cultivation in

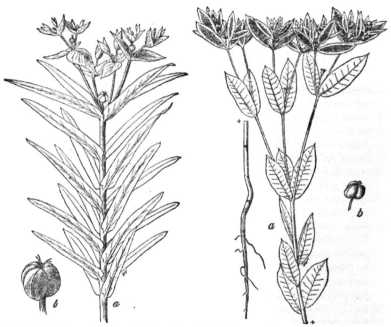

FIG. 52.—Caper spurge (*Euphorbia lathyris*): *a*, upper half of plant, one-third natural size; *b*, seed capsule, natural size.

FIG. 53.—Snow on the mountain(*Euphorbia mar- ginata*): *a*, whole plant, one-third natural size; *b*, seed capsule, natural size.

the South. A correspondent from Arizona states that three of his hogs were poisoned by eating the seeds, which were ignorantly offered to them for food.

EUPHORBIACEÆ (Spurge Family).

Euphorbia sp.—There are many species of SPURGE native to the United States, nearly all of which contain an acrid milky juice. Stock generally avoid them, but cattle have been poisoned by drinking water into which the plants have been thrown. The

juice of *E. marginata* and *E. bicolor* is used to some extent in
Texas to brand cattle, it being held to be superior to a red-hot
iron for that purpose, because screw worms will not infect the
fresh scar and the spot heals more readily.

Jatropha stimulosa Michx.—The seeds of the SPURGE NETTLE of the
Southern States are extremely poisonous. Stock avoid the plant
· on account of its stinging hairs.

Ricinus communis L.—The CASTOR OIL PLANT is quite commonly
cultivated in the warmer portions of the United States and has

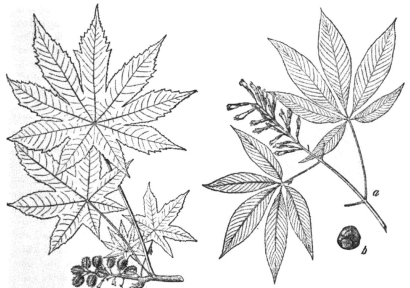

FIG. 54.—Castor oil plant (*Ricinus communis*).

FIG. 55.—Red buckeye (*Æsculus pavia*): *a*, flowering branch; *b*, seed—both two-ninths natural size.

escaped from cultivation in the South. The seeds have been
accidently eaten by horses with fatal effect, and they have been
strewn on pasture lands in the Northwest for the purpose of killing sheep that were trespassing thereon. A Frenchman has
discovered a method of making cattle immune to the effects of
the toxalbumin contained in the seeds, so that they may be fed to
stock without causing any apparent ill effect.

BUXACEÆ (Box Family).

Buxus sempervirens L.—The leaves of the COMMON BOX, which is
cultivated in the Eastern States for hedges, are poisonous to all
kinds of stock.

CELASTRACEÆ (Staff-tree Family).

Celastrus scandens L.—The CLIMBING BITTERSWEET, or STAFF-VINE, `s native in the northeastern quarter of the United States and in New Mexico. One case on record shows that a horse was badly, though not fatally, poisoned by eating the leaves.

ÆSCULACÆ (Buckeye Family).

Æsculus californica (Spach) Nutt. CALIFORNIA BUCKEYE.—*Æ.* **glabra Willd.** OHIO BUCKEYE, FETID BUCKEYE.—*Æ.* **hippocastanum L.** HORSE CHESTNUT.—*Æ.* **pavia L.** RED BUCKEYE.—

The leaves and fruit of these species are generally regarded as poisonous to stock. The fruit may be easily converted into food by washing and boiling. It is believed that a small quantity of the unprepared fruit of the California buckeye will cause cows to slip their young.

HYPERICACEÆ (St. John's-wort Family).

Hypericum perforatum L.—The common ST. JOHN'S-WORT is commonly believed to cause disagreeable eruptions on cow's udders and on the feet of white-haired animals. This species and the spotted St. John's-wort (*H. maculatum* Walt.) were brought into the Department by Dr. G. W. Bready, from Norwood, Md., who stated that five horses were poisoned in May, 1898, by eating

FIG. 56.—Water hemlock (*Cicuta maculata*), showing section of spindle-shaped roots and lower stem, the leaves, flowers, and fruit, one-half natural size; also fruit and cross section of seed, enlarged five times.

meadow hay which contained nearly 50 per cent of these plants. One horse died from the effects of the poison, and two were killed to prevent their further suffering.

APIACEÆ (Carrot Family).

Cicuta maculata L.—This is the WATER HEMLOCK (SPOTTED HEMLOCK; BEAVER POISON; COWBANE) which grows most abundantly throughout the United States. It is one of our best known poisonous plants. Stock are not infrequently killed by eating the fleshy roots or hay with which the plants are mixed.

Cicuta vagans Greene.—Cattle are frequently killed in Oregon and
Washington by eating the large fleshy rootstocks which have
been washed, frozen, or dug out of the soil, or by drinking water
in marshes where the roots have been trampled upon. The roots
of the other species of *Cicuta* are undoubtedly poisonous, but
cases have been reported against one other species only, namely,
C. bolanderi. It grows in marshy land in California.

Conium maculatum L.—The
well-known POISON HEMLOCK,
or SPOTTED HEMLOCK of Eu-
rope, is an introduced weed

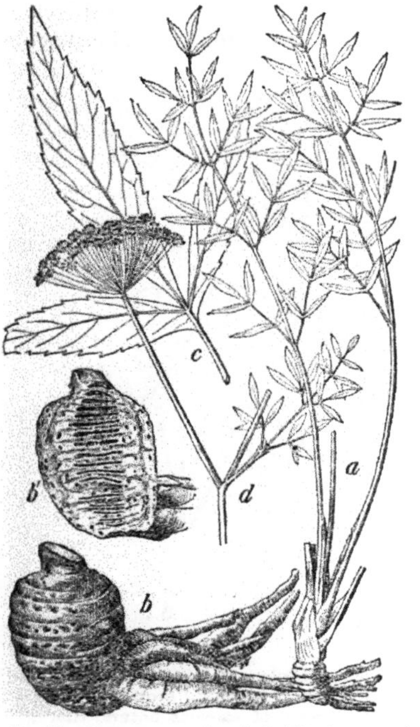

FIG. 57.—Oregon water hemlock (*Cicuta vagans*);
a, plant with leaves, one-sixth natural size; *b*
and *b'*, rootstock and horizontal roots, showing
section, half size; *c*, terminal leaflets, one-sixth
natural size; *d*, flowering spray, full size.

FIG. 58.—Poison hemlock (*Conium maculatum*), showing upper portion of plant with
flowers and seed, one-third natural size.

not uncommon in the northeastern section of the United States
and in California. The plant is generally avoided by stock on
account of its bad odor, but animals have been killed by eating
it in the fresh state. Since the poisonous constituent is volatile
the dry plants are not so dangerous.

Oxypolis rigidus (L.) Britton.—The COWBANE is natural in swamps
throughout the eastern half of the United States. The leaves
and roots are reputed to be poisonous to cattle.

Sium cicutæfolium Gmel.—The leaves of the HEMLOCK WATER PARSNIP, which is more or less common throughout the United States, are said to be poisonous to stock.

ERICAEÆ (Heath Family).

Andromeda polifolia L.—The WILD ROSEMARY, or MOORWORT, is a plant native to the northern regions of Europe, Asia, and America, entering the United States only in the extreme northeast. The leaves, which have been eaten by sheep with fatal effect, contain a narcotic poison known as andromedotoxin. The plant

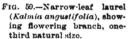

FIG. 59.—Narrow-leaf laurel (Kalmia angustifolia), showing flowering branch, one-third natural size.

FIG. 60.—Broad-leaf laurel (Kalmia latifolia); a, flowering spray, one-third natural size; b, vertical section of flower showing peculiar attachment of stamens, natural size; c, fruiting capsules, natural size.

is not very dangerous in its native habitat, because it grows in bogs which are inaccessible to stock.

Azalea occidentalis Torr. & Gray.—The CALIFORNIA AZALEA is very much dreaded by sheep men who drive their flocks into the southern Sierras for pasture. Investigation has shown that the leaves contain a poisonous substance.

Epigæa repens L.—The leaves of the pretty little TRAILING ARBUTUS (MAYFLOWER; GROUND LAUREL), so commonly known as one of the early spring flowers, are reputed to be poisonous to stock. A cow was reported to have been poisoned by the plant in Maryland in the winter of 1897. It contains no andromedotoxin.

Kalmia angustifolia L.—The NARROW-LEAF LAUREL is abundant in the northeastern section of the United States, where it is also well known as SHEEP LAUREL and LAMBKILL. The leaves contain andromedotoxin, and sheep and calves are quite frequently poisoned by eating them.

Kalmia latifolia L.—The BROAD-LEAF LAUREL is native throughout the greater part of the eastern half of the United States, and is known by a great variety of common names, the most important of which are LAUREL and IVY. The latter name is most commonly used south of Maryland. Scores of cattle and sheep are poisoned annually by eating the plant. It is probably the most dangerous of all the shrubs belonging to the heath family.

Ledum glandulosum Nutt.—The CALIFORNIAN LABRADOR TEA grows at medium elevations in the Sierra Nevada range in California and in the Coast Range northward from Mendocino County. In selecting pasture land and in driving sheep through the mountains sheep men are careful to avoid the plant so far as possible.

Ledum grœnlandicum Œder.— The LABRADOR TEA is an Arctic plant which may be found in bogs and swamps in the

Fig. 61.—Branch ivy (*Leucothoë catesbœi*): a, flowering branch; b, fruiting capsules.

colder regions of the northeastern States. It has a slight reputation as a stock poison.

Leucothoë catesbæi (Walt.) A. Gray.—This is the BRANCH IVY, HEMLOCK, or CALFKILL, of the Allegheny Mountains. It is well known in that region to be fatal to all kinds of stock.

Leucothoë racemosa (L.) A. Gray.—The SWAMP LEUCOTHOË of the Atlantic and Gulf States has been reported from New Jersey as especially fatal to calves.

Pieris floribunda (Pursh.) Benth. & Hook.—The MOUNTAIN FETTER BUSH is native in the mountains from Virginia to Georgia and is sometimes cultivated as an ornamental shrub. Sheep have been poisoned by eating the leaves.

Pieris mariana (L.) Benth. & Hook.—The STAGGER BUSH of the
Atlantic Coast region, Tennessee, and Arkansas is quite commonly known to be poisonous to calves and to sheep. The name
STAGGER BUSH was applied to the shrub on account of the peculiar
intoxicating effect of the leaves.

Rhododendron californicum Hook.—The CALIFORNIA RHODODEN-
DRON is native on the Pacific Slope from San Francisco to British
Columbia. The plant is re-
ported from Oregon as poison-

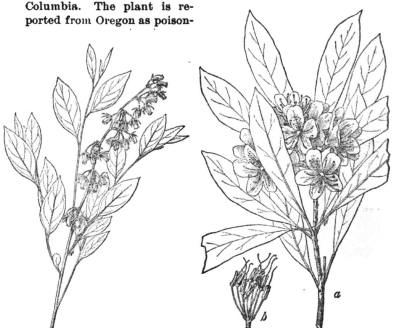

FIG. 62.—Stagger bush (*Pieris mariana*),
showing flowering branch, one-third natural size.

FIG. 63.—Great laurel (*Rhododendron maximum*): *a*, flowering branch; *b*, fruiting capsules—both one-third natural size.

ous to sheep. It is quite probable that the leaves contain andromedotoxin, but they have not been tested.

Rhododendron maximum L.—The GREAT LAUREL (ROSEBAY; MOUN-
TAIN LAUREL; RHODODENDRON) is a large evergreen bush or
small tree which is quite commonly cultivated for ornament, and
is found native in the Allegheny Mountains. The leaves contain
andromedotoxin, and they are occasionally eaten by stock with
fatal effect.

PRIMULACEÆ (Primrose Family).

Anagallis arvensis L.—The PIMPERNEL is a European plant which
has obtained a specially strong foothold in California, where it

grows luxuriantly and is sometimes known as POISON WEED. It is suspected of having caused the death of a horse at Santa Ana. Chemists have isolated a powerfully poisonous oil and a strongly active ferment from the plant.

OLEACEÆ (Olive Family).

Ligustrum vulgare L.—The PRIVET, or PRIM, is a garden shrub, introduced from Europe and Asia, which is much used for hedges in this country, and has escaped from cultivation in western New York and southward to North Carolina. Accidents have been occasioned in children both by the fruit and the leaves. The plant is to be suspected in cases of poisoning in animals.

APOCYNACEÆ (Dogbane Family).

Apocynum androsæmifolium L., SPREADING DOGBANE.—**A. cannabinum** L., INDIAN HEMP.—These plants are quite generally distributed throughout the United States. Stock generally avoid them in pasture fields on account of their acrid milky juice. When dry they are not so poisonous as when in the fresh state.

Nerium oleander L.—The OLEANDER is a common house plant throughout a large portion of the United States. It grows thriftily out of doors in the Southern and Western States, and has probably escaped from cultivation in some places. It grows wild in northern Mexico. The leaves are well known to be most powerfully poisonous, and stock are occasionally killed by eating them.

ASCLEPIADACEÆ (Milkweed Family).

FIG. 64.—Milkweed (*Asclepias eriocarpa*), one-sixth natural size.

Asclepias eriocarpa Benth.—This is the plant with broad mullein-like leaves which is known as MILKWEED in California. Several authentic accounts of the poisoning of sheep have been secured against the plant in Mendocino County. It is especially feared on very warm days by sheep men when they are compelled to drive their flocks through dry, barren valleys. It sometimes grows on cultivated land and is cut with hay.

Asclepias mexicana Cav.—This smooth NARROW-LEAF MILKWEED is native in dry ground in California, Oregon, and Nevada. Specimens of the plant were sent to this Department from Hanford, Cal., with the information that sheep and calves were not infrequently poisoned by eating the growing plant, and that cows were poisoned by eating hay which was contaminated with it.

Asclepias syriaca L.—This is the common MILKWEED, or SILKWEED, of the northeastern quarter of the United States. Experiments show that the milky juice so abundant in all parts of the plant is very acrid and poisonous. It is listed among the poisonous plants of Europe.

FIG. 65.—Jimson weed (*Datura stramonium*): *a*, flowering spray; *b*, fruiting capsule—both one-third natural size.

Asclepias tuberosa L.—The leaves of the BUTTERFLY WEED, or PLEURISY ROOT, of the eastern half of the United States are somewhat suspected of being poisonous to stock.

SOLANACEÆ (Potato Family).

Datura stramonium L.—D. **tatula** L.—These two species very closely resemble each other, and are most commonly known by the name of JIMSON WEED. They are European plants which have become vile weeds in waste grounds and about dwellings throughout the greater portion of the country. One or two instances are recorded in which cattle have been poisoned by eating hay containing the young leaves.

Hyoscyamus niger L.—The BLACK HENBANE is a vile, ill-smelling plant, a native of Europe, now naturalized in Michigan, and from New York northward. One or two cases are recorded in foreign literature in which stock have been poisoned by eating the plant of their own accord, but there is very little danger from it, on account of its ill odor and harsh texture.

Nicotiana tabacum L.—This is the TOBACCO most commonly cultivated in the United States. It is native to South America and has escaped from cultivation to some extent in the Southern States. According to some authorities stock are not always disposed to shun this plant on account of its characteristic ill odor and taste, but, on the contrary, will eat a small amount of the leaves with apparent relish, especially when they are somewhat fresh. Stock have, however, been poisoned by eating leaves which were placed within their reach to dry, and also by eating food contaminated with the juice of the leaves. Considerable precaution should be used in applying tobacco juice to fresh cuts or bruises in stock, as the poison is easily absorbed into the sys-

FIG. 66.—Bittersweet (*Solanum dulcamara*): *a*, flowering spray; *b*, fruit—both one-third natural size.

FIG. 67.—Black nightshade (*Solanum nigrum*), one-third natural size.

tem and may prove fatal. There are several native species of tobacco in the western half of the United States, all of which are undoubtedly poisonous if eaten even in moderate quantity.

Solanum dulcamara L.—The BITTERSWEET, or CLIMBING NIGHT-SHADE, is a European weed, now introduced in the northeastern quarter of the United States. The leaves are suspected of being poisonous to stock.

Solanum nigrum L.—The BLACK NIGHTSHADE (COMMON NIGHT-SHADE; GARDEN NIGHTSHADE) is a common weed in cultivated fields throughout the greater portion of the United States. Cattle seldom eat the plant, but a few cases of poisoning are recorded for calves, sheep, goats, and swine.

Solanum triflorum Nutt.—The SPREADING NIGHTSHADE is a native of the Great Plains, and also a common garden weed from Arizona and Texas to British America. Complaints of the poisoning of cattle by this plant have been sent to this Department from Nebraska. Experiments show that the berries are poisonous.

Solanum tuberosum L.—The small, immature tubers of the common cultivated potato and those that have turned green from exposure to the sun are slightly poisonous. The green fruit and the white sprouts from mature potatoes are likewise poisonous. In all of these cases the deleterious substance may be removed or destroyed by thorough boiling.

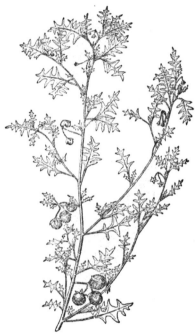

FIG. 63.—Spreading nightshade (*Solanum triflorum*), one-third natural size.

SCROPHULARIACEÆ (Figwort Family).

Digitalis purpurea L.—The PURPLE FOXGLOVE is a common garden plant which has sparingly escaped from cultivation and is naturalized to some extent on Cape Breton Island. Horses are occasionally poisoned in Europe by nipping the plants from gardens or by eating hay contaminated with it.

Gerardia tenuifolia Vahl.—The SLENDER GERARDIA is native to the eastern half of the United States, and has been specially reported as poisonous to sheep and to calves in the Southern States.

Gratiola officinalis L.—The HEDGE HYSSOP of the Southern States contains an acrid poison. The same plant grows in Europe and is there regarded as poisonous to stock.

Pedicularis sp.—The plants of this genus are commonly called LOUSEWORT. In Europe several species are suspected of being slightly poisonous to stock. One of these, *P. palustris*, occurs in Labrador, and there are over thirty species native to the United States, largely Western. They should all be suspected of being poisonous.

CAMPANULACEÆ (Bell-flower Family).

Bolelia sp.—One or more species of this genus are suspected of being poisonous to sheep in California.

Lobelia inflata L., INDIAN TOBACCO.—**L. kalmii** L., BROOK BOLE-LIA.—**L. spicata** Lam., PALE-SPIKED LOBELIA.—**L. syphilitica** L., GREAT LOBELIA.—All of the species in this genus contain an acrid and usually milky juice and are poisonous. None has been specially reported as poisonous to stock, but the above-named species are to be suspected because they frequently occur in grass and are sometimes found in meadow hay.

AMBROSIACEÆ (Ragweed Family).

Xanthium canadense Mill.—The young seedlings of the American COCKLEBUR are reported from Texas as being rapidly fatal to hogs.

Xanthium spinosum L.—The SPINY CLOTBUR is suspected of being poisonous, but few cases have been definitely recorded against it. The seeds apparently contain a toxic compound.

Xanthium strumarium L.—The young seedlings of the BROAD COCKLEBUR are reported from Georgia as being fatal to hogs. Experiments seem to show that the seed is poisonous.

CARDUACEÆ (Thistle Family).

FIG. 69.—Sneezeweed (*Helenium autumnale*), one-third natural size.

Helenium autumnale L.—SNEEZEWEED. (SNEEZEWORT; AUTUMN SNEEZEWEED; STAGGER WEED; FALSE SUNFLOWER) is found throughout the greater portion of the United States, being most abundant in the Southern and Eastern States. Sheep, cattle, and horses that are unfamiliar with the plant are often poisoned by it when driven to localities where it is abundant. Stock avoid it, as a rule, but it is claimed that they sometimes develop a taste for the plant and are killed quickly by eating it in large quantity.

10317——27

Helenium tenuifolium Nutt.—The FINE-LEAFED SNEEZEWEED has been reported from several of the Gulf States, where it is a troublesome weed, fatal to horses and mules. It is not known to what extent cattle may feed on the plant with impunity, but the bitter principle in milk and meat sometimes met with in the Southern States is quite generally supposed to be due to these plants.

Senecio jacobæa L.—The TANSY RAGWORT, or STAGGERWORT, is a European plant which grows as a weed in ballast about New York and Philadelphia. Farther north, in Nova Scotia, it has become extensively naturalized, and it is there regarded by stock men as poisonous. It is interesting to note that *S. guadalensis* of Mexico is also considered fatal to stock.

Solidago sp.—A species of GOLDEN-ROD growing in Wisconsin is suspected of being very poisonous to horses. The damage is perhaps due to a parasitic growth on this plant. (See *Coleosporium solidaginis*.)

LIST OF PLANTS KNOWN TO BE POISONOUS TO STOCK.

Ergot, *Claviceps purpurea* (Fr.) Tul.

Clathrus, *Clathrus columnatus* Bosc.

Fly poison, *Chrosperma muscætoxicum* (Walt.) Kuntze.

American white hellebore, *Veratrum viride* Ait.

Slender nettle, *Urtica gracilis* Ait.

Pokeweed, *Phytolacca decandra* L.

Corn cockle, *Agrostemma githago* L.

Aconite, *Aconitum napellus* L.

Western aconite, *Aconitum columbianum* Nutt.

Dwarf larkspur, *Delphinium tricorne* Michx.

Field larkspur, *Delphinium consolida* L.

Purple larkspur, *Delphinium menziesii* DC.

Wyoming larkspur, *Delphinium geyeri* Greene.

Green hellebore, *Helleborus viridis* L.

Cursed crowfoot, *Ranunculus sceleratus* L.

Celandine, *Chelidonium majus* L.

Opium poppy, *Papaver somniferum* L.

Field poppy, *Papaver rhœas* L.

Laurel cherry, *Prunus caroliniana* (Mill.) Ait.

Wild black cherry, *Prunus serotina* Ehrh.

Rattlebox, *Crotalaria sagittalis* L.

Locust tree, *Robinia pseudacacia* L.

Coral bean, *Sophora secundiflora* (Cav.) DC.

Chinese umbrella tree, *Melia azedarach* L.

Spurge nettle, *Jatropha stimulosa* Michx.

Castor oil plant, *Ricinus communis* L.

Box, *Buxus sempervirens* L.

Staff vine, *Celastrus scandens* L.

Common St. John's-wort, *Hypericum perforatum* L.

Water hemlock, *Cicuta maculata* L.

Oregon water hemlock, *Cicuta vagans* Greene.

Poison hemlock, *Conium maculatum* L.

California azalea, *Azalea occidentalis* Torr. and Gray.

Narrow-leaf laurel, *Kalmia angustifolia* L.

Broad-leaf laurel, *Kalmia latifolia* L.

Branch ivy, *Leucothoë catesbœi* (Walt.) A. Gray.

Swamp leucothoë, *Leucothoë racemosa* (L.) A. Gray.

Mountain fetter bush, *Pieris floribunda* (Pursh.) Benth and Hook.

Stagger bush, *Pieris mariana* (L.) Benth and Hook.

California rhododendron, *Rhododendron californicum* Hook.

Great laurel, *Rhododendron maximum* L.

Oleander, *Nerium oleander* L.

Milkweed, *Asclepias eriocarpa* Benth.

Milkweed, *Asclepias syriaca* L.

Jimson weed, *Datura stramonium* L.

Jimson weed, *Datura tatula* L.

Black henbane, *Hyoscyamus niger* L.

Tobacco, *Nicotiana tabacum* L.

Black nightshade, *Solanum nigrum* L.

Spreading nightshade, *Solanum triflorum* Nutt.

Purple foxglove, *Digitalis purpurea* L.

Sneezeweed, *Helenium autumnale* L.

LIST OF PLANTS PROBABLY POISONOUS TO STOCK.[1]

Mold, *Aspergillus glaucous* (L.) Link.

Fly amanita, *Amanita muscaria* (L.)Fr.

Bracken fern, *Pteris aquilina* L.

Yew, *Taxus minor* (Michx.) Britton.

Darnel, *Lolium temulentum* L.

California false hellebore, *Veratrum californicum* Durand.

Death camas, *Zygadenus venenosus* Wats.

Alkali grass, *Zygadenus elegans* Pursh.

Lily-of-the-valley, *Convallaria majalis* L.

Red-root, *Gyrotheca capitata* (Walt.) Morong.

White baneberry, *Actœa alba* (L.) Mill.

Red baneberry, *Actœa rubra* (Ait.) Willd.

Wind flower, *Anemone quinquefolia* L.

Larkspur, *Delphinium recurvatum* Greene.

Mountain larkspur, *Delphinium scopulorum* Gray.

Cow poison, *Delphinium trolliifolium* Gray.

Bulbous crowfoot. *Ranunculus bulbosus* L.

Tall crowfoot, *Ranunculus acris* L.

Calycanthus, *Butneria fertilis* (Walt.) Kearney.

Mexican poppy, *Argemone mexicana* L.

Lupine, *Lupinus leucophyllus* Dougl.

Silky sophora, *Sophora sericea* Nutt.

Large-flowered yellow flax, *Linum rigidum* Pursh.

Spurge, *Euphorbia* sp.

California buckeye, *Æsculus californica* (Spach) Nutt.

Ohio buckeye, *Æsculus glabra* Willd.

Horse chestnut, *Æsculus hippocastanum* L.

Red buckeye, *Æsculus pavia* L.

Spotted St. John's-wort, *Hypericum maculatum* Walt.

Cowbane, *Oxypolis rigidis* (L.) Britton.

Hemlock water parsnip, *Sium cicutœfolium* Gmel.

Wild rosemary, *Andromeda polifolia* L.

Pimpernel, *Anagallis arvensis* L.

Milkweed, *Asclepias mexicana* Cav.

Potato, *Solanum tuberosum* L.

Fine-leaf sneezeweed, *Helenium tenuifolium* Nutt.

Tansy ragwort, *Senecio jacobœa* L.

Spring clotbur, *Xanthium spinosum* L.

Broad cocklebur, *Xanthium strumarium* L.

LIST OF PLANTS SUSPECTED OF BEING POISONOUS TO STOCK.[1]

Cornsmut, *Ustilago maydis* Corda.

Golden rod rust, *Coleosporium solidaginis* (Schw.) Theum.

Field horsetail, *Equisetum arvense* L.

Sleepy grass, *Stipa robusta* (Vasey) Nash.

Leucocrinum, *Leucocrinum montanum* Nutt.

Crow poison, *Nothoscordum bivalve* (L.) Britton.

Atamasco lily, *Atamosco atamasco* (L.) Greene.

---

[1] The following explanation appears on page 388: "The list as given is provisional for some species, as the reports upon which their reputation is founded are very meager and sometimes even contradictory. * * They are here enumerated, not necessarily because it is believed that they are poisonous, but with the view to eliciting more positive evidence either for or against them. Although comprehensive, the list is incomplete, for experience is constantly adding to the number already known or suspected to be poisonous."

Oak, *Quercus* sp.

Black greasewood, *Sarcobatus vermiculatus* (Hook.) Torr.

Sleepy catchfly, *Silene antirrhina* L.

Anise tree, *Illicium floridanum* Ellis.

Mandrake, *Podophyllum peltatum* L.

Lambert locó weed, *Aragallus lambertii* (Pursh.) Greene.

Woolly loco weed, *Astragalus mollissimus* Torr.

Loco weed, *Astragalus bigelovii* A. Gray.

Loco weed, *Astragalus hornii* A. Gray.

Loco weed, *Astragalus pattersoni* A. Gray.

Sesban, *Sesbania vesicaria* Ell.

Prairie thermopsis, *Thermopsis rhombifolia* (Nutt.) Richards.

Trailing arbutus, *Epigœa repens* L.

Californian Labrador tea, *Ledum glandulosum* Nutt.

Labrador tea, *Ledum grœnlandicum* Oeder.

Privet, *Ligustrum vulgare* L.

Spreading dogbane, *Apocynum androsœmifolium* L.

Indian hemp, *Apocynum cannabinum* L.

Butterfly weed, *Asclepias tuberosa* L.

Bittersweet, *Solanum dulcamara* L.

Slender gerardia, *Gerardia tenuifolia* Vahl.

Hedge hyssop, *Gratiola officinalis* L.

Lousewort, *Pedicularis* sp.

Downingia, *Bolelia* sp.

Indian tobacco, *Lobelia inflata* L.

Brook lobelia, *Lobelia kalmii* L.

Pale-spiked lobelia, *Lobelia spicata* Lam.

Great lobelia, *Lobelia syphilitica* L.

Golden-rod, *Solidago* sp.

American cocklebur, *Xanthium canadense* Mill.

FEEDING WILD PLANTS TO SHEEP.

[Paper by S. B. Nelson, D. V. M., Professor of Veterinary Sciences, in Washington Agricultural College and School of Science, before the second annual meeting of the Association of Experiment Station Veterinarians, at Omaha, Nebr., September 8, 1898.]

For many years past there have occurred in the State of Washington, when sheep were being moved from winter quarters to summer pastures, serious losses in the flocks. According to the statements of the various sheep owners these losses have occurred in certain definite localities in the spring, but not in the autumn, when the sheep were returned to their winter feeding quarters. These fatalities happening under apparently the same conditions—at the same time and place each year—led the sheep owners to believe that the deaths were due to eating some grass or weed which acted as a poison to the sheep. This condition was brought to the attention of the experiment station and certain members commenced the work of investigating the cause of the great mortality in the flocks. As these experiments are not completed, it is not the intention of this paper to discuss the cause of the death of the sheep, but to record the results of feeding to sheep different plants, many of which have been and are considered poisonous to sheep and other domesticated animals.

The station botanist went into these various localities and ascertained what plants were there. About thirty-five different plants were observed, and as many as possible of these were fed and the results noted. The plants found were grouped into two classes: First, those from which might be expected a positive result; second, those from which a negative result might be looked for—judgment on both classes being based on public opinion about many of the plants; and also consideration being given to the abundance with which the plants were distributed. Following is the list of plants collected:

Class 1.—Delphinium menziesii, Castilleja pallescens, Crepis barbigera, Astragalus dorycnioides, Astragalus spaldingii, Astragalus palousensis, Zygadenus venenosus, Frasera albicaulis, Antenaria luzuloides, Sisyrinchium grandiflorum, Arnica fulgens.

Class 2.—Saxifraga integufolia, Lupinus ornatus, Leptotænia multifida, Peucedanum grayii, Synthyris rubra, Clematis douglassii, Heuchera glabella, Lithospermum pilosum, Geranium, Potentilla, Eriogonum heracleoides, Geum triflorum, Grindelia nana, Chænactis douglasii.

DELPHINIUM MENZIESII.

The first, and which was thought the most important, was *Delphinium menziesii*. Three sheep were used in this experiment. Prior to the experiment they had been kept in a lot where there was running water and were fed timothy hay.

421

Experiment No. 1.—May 17: At 4.30 p. m., sheep No. 1, a ewe, was tethered in a patch where Delphinum was very plentiful. She was returned to the stable at 8.30 p. m. There was evidence that she had eaten the blossoms of a few Delphinium. The next day she was placed in the patch at 5 a. m. and returned to the stable at 8 p. m. Besides the plants that she had cropped, there was given to her about 1 pound of gathered Delphinium plants, which she ate. On May 19 she was again tethered in the patch and given, in addition to the amount she obtained there, 1 pound of Delphinium. This was repeated on May 20; but she had only one-half pound of the gathered plant. She had, however, eaten everything within her reach except some scattered plants of *Brodiæ douglasii.* The following day she was staked out in a fresh place. She once in a while bit off the heads of the Delphinium, but did not seem to prefer it; however, by the evening she had eaten all the green material within the reach of her tether except the *Brodiæ douglasii.* May 22: She was tethered in a fresh place at 5.30 a. m., and by 9 a. m. she had eaten all the grass and Delphinium within her reach. On the 23d and 24th she was all right. Here we have an experiment in which a sheep is kept tethered in a patch of Delphinium for six days, and she ate all of the plant that she could obtain and was fed 2½ pounds besides, with a negative result.

Experiment No. 2.—This sheep was placed in a small pen, and on May 18 was given 5 pounds of Delphinium, consisting of stems, leaves, flowers, and unripe pods. May 19: He had eaten all that was given him yesterday. May 20: At noon he was given 2½ pounds of Delphinium that was gathered on the 18th. Probably considerable of the plant's water had evaporated; how much I do not know. In two and one-half hours he had eaten nearly all of it, and at this time was fed 5 pounds that had just been picked. The next day he had eaten all that had been given him the day before. He was given 3 pounds that was partially dried. It had been picked twenty-four hours. Four hours later he had eaten the 3 pounds and was then given 7 pounds just gathered. May 22: Removed 1¼ pounds that he had not eaten. He was given 3¼ pounds twenty-four hours old. The next day it was all eaten. May 24 and 25: He was well and the experiment was ended. This sheep was fed, in five days, 24¾ pounds of Delphinium, of which 15¾ pounds were freshly gathered, 6¼ pounds twenty-four hours old, and 2¼ pounds forty-eight hours old. All this with a negative result. Certainly this was more of the plant than a sheep would possibly gather on the range in the same length of time. During these five days he had nothing else to eat, subsisting wholly on Delphinium.

Experiment No. 3.—This was intended as a check on experiment No. 2; but this sheep did not eat the plant so readily. It consumed during the five days only 6¼ pounds. The result, however, was also negative.

These experiments certainly are strong evidence that *Delphinium menziesii*, at least when eaten fresh at this time of the year, is not poisonous to sheep.

CASTILLEJA PALLESCENS.

This plant was looked upon with distrust as being poisonous, for the reason that it occurs only in a few places in the State in abundance, and these places were where the sheep often died. Two sheep were used in this experiment, which began May 26. Fed to the first 1¾ pounds of Castilleja. The next day it was observed that he had eaten only a little, but he was given, in addition, the same amount as before. May 26: Only a little eaten. May 29: Nearly all eaten. May 30: All was consumed. In four days he ate 1½ pounds of the plant. On May 30, the second sheep was fed 2 ounces of Castilleja, which he ate immediately.

The results of both of these experiments were negative.

CREPIS BARBIGERA.

We were informed by a person very much interested in this matter that years ago he had seen *Crepis barbigera* fed to sheep with fatal results. I therefore looked for positive results from these trials. Two sheep were used.

May 26: There were fed to the first one 2 ounces of Crepis. The next day he had not eaten all of it. May 28: It was all eaten and he was given one-half pound, which was eaten by the following day. June 23: The second sheep was fed 1¾ pounds of *Crepis barbigera*, which he ate as if he relished it.

Nothing detrimental to the sheep resulted from either experiment.

THE ASTRAGALI.

These plants have at various times been suspicioned of causing trouble in our domestic animals. We used the three following species: *Astraglus spaldingii, A. palousensis, A. dorycnioides.* Of *Astragalus dorycnioides*, 5½ ounces were fed May 26. Of *A. spaldingii*, 12 ounces were fed June 3, and again to the same sheep were given 1¼ pounds on June 8, five days later. June 9: 2½ pounds of *A. palousensis* were fed to the third sheep. These sheep ate the various amounts given them during the night following without any ill effects resulting. Could these experiments have been continued for a longer period of time, it may be that pathological changes would have followed the continuous feeding.

ZYGADENUS VENENOSUS.

This plant is called "poison camas" by the Indians, and it is reported that the eating of the bulb has caused death in the human family. On May 31, June 1 and 2, a sheep was fed 1½ ounces daily. He would eat them from the hand with apparent relish. However, his appetite was kept sharpened so that he would eat almost anything. June 4: Fed to this sheep 1 pound of the plant, both in blossom and in fruit. This amount was all eaten during the night. The sheep remained well.

FRASERA ALBICAULIS.

This beautiful plant was next tried on one sheep. June 3: He was fed 1½ pounds, which he ate before next morning. June 5: Fed to him 5 pounds, of which he ate about one-half during the night. By the 8th he had eaten nearly all. On this day he was fed three-fourths pound more, which was four days old. He ate this last amount during the night. In all he received 7¼ pounds without any apparent injury.

SISYRINCHIUM GRANDIFLORUM.

The plants of this species that were fed were 4 years old and about 20 of these stalks were fed. The sheep ate them out of the hand. Result, negative.

ANTENARIA LUZULOIDES.

Three pounds were gathered and fed to one sheep. It was all eaten in less than twenty-four hours without any visible bad results.

ARNICA FULGENS.

This was the last plant in this class to be used. Fed to a sheep 2 pounds of the plant that had been gathered eighteen hours. The material was all eaten during the day. Results, entirely negative.

This closed the experiments with those plants from which we had some reason to obtain some clearly visible physiological effects. There was fed of the different plants from one-eighth to 7 pounds in one day.

In the second class the following were fed and eaten in about six hours' time: *Saxifraga integufolia*, 7 ounces; *Leptotænia multifida*, 1¾ pounds; *Grindelia nana*, 2 pounds; *Chœnactis douglassi*, 1¼ pounds. No poisonous symptoms followed.

LUPINUS.

On May 30 there was fed to a sheep 1¼ pounds at 11 a. m.; at 6 p. m. it was all consumed. The next day he was given 2¼ pounds more, which he ate greedily. June 1: That amount was doubled, giving him 5 pounds; this he consumed by the next day. This sheep was fed 8¼ pounds in a few hours less than three days. No untoward effects resulted.

PEUCEDANUM GRAYII.

On May 31 I fed 1⅛ pounds of this stinking plant, having much doubt that the sheep would eat it. The following morning it had, however, all disappeared. Two days later he was fed at one time 4 pounds, which he ate by the following morning. The sheep showed no ill effects from it.

The following five plants were fed to five different sheep: *Clematis douglasii*, 4 pounds; *Lithospermum pilosum*, 4 pounds; Geranium, 3½ pounds; Potentilla, 4 pounds; and *Eriogonum heracleoides*, 3½ pounds. Each sheep ate his allowance in less time than one day and showed no ill effects whatever from it.

Of the next three plants a smaller amount was given: *Synthyris rubra*, 1 pound; *Heuchera glabella*, 1½ pounds; and *Geum triflorum*, three-fourths pound. The sheep took nearly twenty-four hours to eat this, and the result again was negative.

In these experiments from three-fourths to 4 pounds of the various plants were fed in one day without appreciable effect on the sheep.

In conclusion, I wish to acknowledge the valuable advice and assistance of the station botanist, C. V. Piper, in carrying on these experiments.

COOPERATION BETWEEN THE EXPERIMENT STATION VETERINARIAN AND THE LOCAL VETERINARIAN.

[Paper by A. W. Bitting, D. V. M., Veterinarian of the Indiana Experiment Station, read before the Second Annual Meeting of the Association of Experiment Station Veterinarians, at Omaha, Nebr., on September 8, 1898.]

It may be possible to imagine an experiment station so well equipped and so liberally provided with funds that the veterinarian at the head of his department can use his discretion in the selection of the disease or the special problem for investigation; that he may go wherever the disease is present, stay as long as may be necessary to make a complete series of observations, or repeat his visitations until he has learned all that he can. In such a position he could be independent of public demands, and could utilize all his energy in prosecuting his work.

A veterinarian occupying a position in a State experiment station is confronted with a difficult set of conditions. The funds for maintaining this department are limited. He is usually compelled to make his studies upon outbreaks of disease and such sporadic cases as occur in the immediate vicinity of the station. If he visits localities at some distance from the station he is rarely permitted to have all the time that is necessary to complete the work or repeat his visitations because of exhaustion of the funds. Under the conditions existing at most of the stations the veterinarian can have at best only a small number of cases of any disease upon which to make observations or experiments. The public demands that he should be informed concerning the occurrence and distribution of contagious diseases, and in many instances that he shall give assistance in their suppression. Of all the members of the station staff he is the least independent. He can not order an outbreak of disease for his special study; he can not control the location or duration of the disease when one does occur; and he can obtain information upon the occurrence and distribution of contagious diseases in the State only through correspondence.

I believe the veterinary department of the experiment station and the veterinarians in the State should be on such friendly terms that cooperative work may be conducted to the advantage of both. The station can act as a medium to give the latest information upon the results of its own researches and announce the work that is being accomplished at other places. The station may also give assistance in diagnosis in certain cases where the microscope or other special equipment is necessary. The veterinarian, in turn, may be of great assistance to the station by reporting outbreaks of disease and the results of any experiments which he may undertake.

426

In 1896 and 1897 I made an attempt to determine whether cooperation was practicable and whether the station would gain information
to compensate for the work required. There were ninety-six qualified
veterinarians in the State. A circular letter setting forth the plans
and blanks for reporting the number of cases occurring in their practice each month were sent to each veterinarian. The list of diseases
upon which reports were desired were those most common in the
State. It included abortion (infectious) among mares and cows,
actinomycosis, anthrax, cholera, glanders, influenza, rabies, specific
ophthalmia among cattle, sporadic aphthæ, tetanus, tuberculosis,
azoturia, colic, other intestinal diseases, parturient apoplexy, periodic
ophthalmia, pneumonia, cerebro-spinal meningitis, bursatte, fistulæ,
lameness, etc. At first I received about thirty-five replies, but the
number gradually became smaller until only eight remained after
the month of August. In 1897 I tried a different plan and made my
blank upon a postal card and distributed them at the end of each
month. I sent the postal cards to about twenty-five addresses and
had fifteen reports for each month of the year. At the close of the
year there was much greater interest than at the beginning, and I
feel certain that I could have doubled the number of correspondents.
The work was abandoned, as I contemplated withdrawing from station work.

The time covered by this work is admittedly too short to draw conclusions from the reports, but they seem to indicate that certain
diseases, such as tetanus and parturient apoplexy, are of far more
common occurrence than is generally suspected; that certain diseases, such as fistulæ and bursatte, are common in some localities
and rare in others; and that seasonal influences are less marked than
is often asserted. The station received fifty-one species of parasites
for identification, and also a number of pathological specimens. At
the suggestion of the writer several new preparations were used and
reports received. The station supplied its own publications and gave
notice of all bulletins upon veterinary science as they appeared at
other stations and the Bureau of Animal Industry. Upon the whole
the station was well repaid for its part of the work, and the veterinarians expressed the desire to have it continued.

One of the good effects that was wholly foreign to the original
object was the increased interest which it developed in the State
Veterinary Medical Society. At the first three meetings of the society
which I attended only seven or eight members were present. The
three meetings held after the correspondence was established were
attended by from twenty to thirty members.

CONTAGIOUS DISEASES OF ANIMALS IN EUROPEAN COUNTRIES.

GREAT BRITAIN.

CONTAGIOUS PLEUROPNEUMONIA.

This disease, which at one time played such havoc among the cattle of Great Britain, has all but been stamped out. The official report for 1897 of Alex. C. Cope, chief veterinary officer for Great Britain, reviews the efforts which had previously been made to eradicate the disease, and also embodied a historical sketch of the disease in Great Britain. This sketch is given below:

HISTORY OF THE DISEASE IN GREAT BRITAIN.

There is a tradition, but I am unable to find its origin, that pleuropneumonia was introduced into the United Kingdom by some calves which were imported into Cork from the Netherlands about the year 1840, and that in the ordinary course of the cattle traffic it was conveyed to England and found its way into the London cowsheds, where it is known to have been rife in the year 1842. This may or may not have been the origin of the disease in Great Britain, but when we take into consideration the fact that fifty years ago the veterinary profession as a whole were unacquainted with the diseases of animals other than the horse, it may not be regarded as ungenerous or unfair to state that it is probable that the disease had existed here for some years prior to 1842.

Unfortunately, for many years after the disease had become prevalent. there were many in the veterinary profession in this country, including some of its leading men, who regarded pleuropneumonia as being due to climatic influences.

The fact, however, that of late years the disease has been nearly, if not quite, eradicated under the stamping-out system, not only here but in other countries, conclusively demonstrates the error of the views then entertained. It may be accepted that after its first introduction it was frequently imported by foreign cattle at the time when they were permitted to be moved into the interior of the country after an inspection and detention of only twelve hours at the port of landing. In connection with this I find in one of the veterinary journals for the year 1848 a letter from a veterinary surgeon who appears to have recognized the disease in 1837 among some cattle at Putney belonging to Lord de Grey. He refers to the disease as being identical with the lungenseucht, which he had seen among the cattle in India and in Germany, in which latter country he stated they then slaughtered and paid compensation for the diseased animal, and in his letter he animadverts upon the defective system of examination at the ports where foreign cattle were landed in this country. He gives no description of the clinical symptoms of the postmortem appearances of the cases which he saw, but from the fact that he regarded the diseases as identical with that for which the Germans legislated and paid compensation, it may reasonably be assumed that he believed the disease to be contagious pleuropneumonia. Assuming that he was correct in his view as to the nature of the disease, it would appear that it existed in this country prior to 1840.

428

The following table gives statistics of pleuropneumonia in Great Britain since 1870, at which date returns were first collected by this Department, and shows how rapidly the disease declined after the application of the stamping-out system in September, 1890:

Statistics relative to pleuropneumonia in Great Britain from 1870 to 1897.

Year.	Number of infected counties.	Number of fresh outbreaks.	Number of cattle attacked.	Diseased cattle.		Healthy cattle in contact slaughtered.
				Killed.	Died.	
1870	68	1,508	4,602	1,755	1,276	2,085
1871	68	1,669	5,869	2,207	1,339	1,836
1872	71	2,474	7,983	3,871	1,979	3,245
1873	72	2,711	6,787	5,061	1,028	2,030
1874	71	3,262	7,740	7,434	289	1,485
1875	71	2,492	5,806	5,584	190	1,417
1876	66	2,178	5,253	5,131	114	1,288
1877	70	2,007	5,330	5,223	107	1,353
1878	67	1,721	4,593	4,488	114	1,857
1879	63	1,549	4,414	4,296	119	2,042
1880	51	1,052	2,765	2,681	88	1,389
1881	45	729	1,875	1,797	78	914
1882	46	494	1,200	1,161	39	962
1883	40	349	931	897	35	981
1884	33	312	1,096	1,074	20	751
1885	41	404	1,511	1,469	42	1,167
1886	48	553	2,471	2,409	63	2,446
1887	47	618	2,437	2,384	52	3,817
1888	39	513	1,843	1,786	59	8,722
1889	41	474	1,646	1,603	42	7,297
1890 a	36	465	2,057	2,004	55	11,301
1891	27	192	778	778	....	9,491
1892	10	35	134	134	....	8,477
1893	4	9	30	30	....	1,157
1894	2	2	15	15	....	891
1895	1	1	1	1	....	43
1896	1	2	9	7	2	183
1897	3	7	46	46	....	741

a The contagious diseases (animals) (pleuropneumonia) act, 1890, came into force on September 1, 1890.

During the last two years pleuropneumonia has been confined to a comparatively small district in and around the east end of London. In 1896 only two outbreaks were discovered—one in the county of Essex and the other on the premises of a butcher in the east end of London. In 1897 seven outbreaks were confirmed. Of these five were in the London cowsheds, one in the county of Essex, and the other in that part of the county of Middlesex which borders on the northern boundary of the county of London.

In consequence of the persistence of the disease in the cowsheds of London, and it being impossible to trace the origin of the diseased animals, the board, in order to prevent the movement of infected or diseased cattle into the interior of the country, issued an order which came into force on the 23d August, 1897, prohibiting the movement of cows out of any licensed cowsheds in an extensive district in the east end of London, except for slaughter with a license to a registered slaughterhouse within that district.

At the time when the order was issued a general impression existed that there still remained in these sheds some cows in which the disease existed in a form unrecognizable during life, and the board therefore appointed three veterinary surgeons to grant these licenses and to attend the autopsy of each cow slaughtered under the provisions of this special order. The order had only been in force a few weeks when one of these veterinary surgeons discovered in the lungs of a cow, which during life appeared to be perfectly healthy and was fat and in very good condition, extensive lesions of pleuropneumonia of long standing. Sixteen other cows in the same shed were slaughtered and two more cases were detected. In one, the greater part of one large lobe was affected and portions of the lung structure had become necrosed and were in a friable condition. In the other, a small portion of encapuled necrosed lung was found, and from the thickness and density of the enveloping tissue there is no doubt that the animal had been infected months prior to its slaughter.

This center of disease would probably never have been detected but for the steps adopted by the board in requiring a postmortem examination at the time of the slaughter of these shed cows. The action taken has proved conclusively that the views of the Department as to the existence of unrecognizable cases in the living animal among the cattle in the London sheds were correct.

FOOT-AND-MOUTH DISEASE.

During 1897 several reports of foot-and-mouth disease were received at the office of the chief veterinarian and the services of experts were engaged to make a thorough investigation. The disease was reported among sheep in North Lincolnshire, and a veterinarian was sent to investigate the matter. On careful inquiries and examination he ascertained that the injuries to the feet of the 36 head of sheep affected were due to the improper use of an arsenical dip which had caused sloughing of the hoofs of the animals. The other cases reported were equally unreliable.

SWINE FEVER.

Every effort is being made to eradicate swine fever, good progress resulting. During 1897 the disease decreased more than one-half, being 2,155, as against 5,166 for 1896. The number of sets of viscera sent to the chief veterinarian for examination was 5,386.

RABIES.

It is stated that rabies has existed in England from time immemorial, but the hope is now expressed that the disease will soon be entirely eradicated. Mr. J. T. Tennant, assistant secretary of the board of agriculture, says this is the most important duty, so far as the general public is concerned, which engaged the attention of the board during the year. Much stress is placed upon the necessity of muzzling dogs which have been bitten or are suspected. Careful investigations are made of all deaths of dogs attributed to rabies, in order to ascertain the truthfulness of the statement frequently made that the disease is not so prevalent as reported, and a record of all such investigations is carefully kept. In 1897 there were 151 dogs and 16 other animals affected with rabies. The previous year had 438 cases in dogs and 22 in other animals.

GLANDERS AND FARCY.

During the year there has been an increase over the previous year of 235 cases of glanders. The greatest increase was in Scotland, where the number of cases rose from 98 in 1896 to 297 in 1897. Mr. Cope's remarks concerning this disease are given below:

For many years glanders has been prevalent among the horses of Glasgow, while the rest of Scotland has been comparatively free, and the local authorities of that city, with a view to eradicating the disease within their own district, invited the horse owners of the city to allow their animals to be tested with mallein, on the understanding that if those which reacted proved to be affected with glanders on postmortem examination one-fourth of the value of the animals would be paid, and full value if found free from disease. Under this arrangement the veterinary inspector of the Glasgow local authorities tested 320 horses; of these 147 reacted and were subsequently slaughtered. On a postmortem examination being made of the 147 horses which had reacted no glanders nodules could be detected in the lungs of 14 of the horses; in the remaining 133, however, the lesions of the disease were found to be present.

At the present time mallein is accepted by all veterinarians as a thoroughly reliable aid to diagnosis in occult cases of glanders, but until the horse owners generally become equally convinced of its value it is hardly to be expected that they will consent to have their horses slaughtered so long as they can perform their regular work with apparent ease and present no external evidence of disease, simply because their animals have reacted to mallein, unless they receive their full value.

At the present time there are still many points in connection with the pathology of glanders about which a great divergence of opinion exists among the members of the veterinary profession both here and abroad. By some it is asserted that the ordinary mode of infection is by the alimentary canal; others, who only recognize glanders by the presence of lesions in the lungs, hold that the infection, like that of contagious pleuropneumonia of cattle, is more probably contracted by inhalation; at the same time all admit that it may be produced by inoculation through the abraded surface of the skin or of the lining membrane of the nostril. That the disease can be produced by the introduction into the digestive system of fresh glanderous material is a fact with which the veterinary profession have long since been acquainted. This was repeatedly experimentally proved years ago.

It has lately been suggested that there is a much greater tendency on the part of some horses to recover from glanders than has generally been known, and the repeated injections of mallein have a curative effect, but whether horses which react to mallein and after repeated injections with that material having ceased to react can be properly regarded as recovered and incapable of infecting others is a very moot point.

With a view so far as possible to set at rest many points of a doubtful nature in connection with glanders, a series of experiments are being conducted by the veterinary officers of the board, and it is hoped that in the course of time a special report on this most important subject will be produced.

The following statement is from a recent issue of the London Times:

The appointment by the board of agriculture of a departmental committee, under the chairmanship of Lord Stanley, M. P., to inquire into and report upon the working of the diseases of animals acts in so far as they relate to glanders, and to consider whether any more effective measures can with advantage be taken to prevent the spread of that disease, will impart a special interest to the subjoined table. It shows for Great Britain the number of outbreaks of glanders in each year since 1877, inclusive, the number of counties over which these were distributed, and the number of horses attacked.

Number of outbreaks of glanders in Great Britain in each year, 1877 to 1898.

Year.	Counties	Out breaks	Horses attacked.	Year.	Counties.	Out-breaks.	Horses attacked.
1877	40	518	758	1888	30	1,007	1,581
1878	45	585	888	1889	25	1,262	2,246
1879	52	936	1,367	1890	24	959	1,808
1880	37	1,459	2,110	1891	28	1,351	2,435
1881	35	1,012	1,720	1892	34	1,657	3,001
1882	33	850	1,369	1893	40	1,381	2,133
1883	35	753	1,244	1894	33	965	1,437
1884	34	713	1,123	1895	36	964	1,594
1885	25	637	946	1896	31	817	1,294
1886	27	776	1,114	1897	31	900	1,629
1887	25	1,003	1,482	1898		751	1,380

The number of counties involved—this figure has not yet been officially announced for 1898—is seen to range between 52 in 1879 and 24 in 1890, so that in some years they have been more than twice as numerous as in others. The number of distinct outbreaks, which is far more significant than the number of horses attacked, was greatest, at 1,657, in 1892, and least, at 518, in 1877. The inspection by local authorities may, however, have been less stringent in the earlier years. The number of outbreaks last year, amounting to 751, was greater than in 1877, 1878, 1884, or 1885. Excepting in 1897 there has been a continuous decrease year by year since 1892, but something similar happened between 1880 and 1885, after which an increase again began to manifest itself. The introduction of the use of mallein as a diagnostic agent within the last two or three years may have had the effect of bringing under notice more cases than would otherwise have been detected. With regard to the number of counties, it is necessary to remember that the majority of outbreaks are restricted to three or four. The two black spots in Great Britain in connection with glanders center around London and Glasgow (Lanarkshire). Thus, in 1897, out of 839 outbreaks in England, 619 occurred in London, 48 in Middlesex, 35 in Essex, and 16 in Surrey. In other words, 718 of the outbreaks happened in what may be roughly described as the metropolitan area, leaving only 121 for the rest of England, of which 26 belonged to Lancaster, 13 to Warwick, 12 to Kent, 10 to Norfolk, and lesser numbers to 17 other counties. In the same year, out of 58 outbreaks distributed over 5 other counties of Scotland, 53 occurred in Lanark alone. Only three outbreaks were reported from Wales, all from Glamorganshire.

BELGIUM.

The record of contagious animal diseases in Belgium, as compiled below from official documents of that country, is not quite complete. A part of November, 1898, is missing. It will be observed that the status of diseases was about the same for the two years, with the exception of foot-and-mouth disease. This scourge appears to have prevailed there, as it did in adjoining countries.

Cases of contagious diseases among domestic animals in Belgium during the years 1897 and 1898.

Name of disease.	January.	February.	March.	April.	May.	June.	July.	August.	September.	October.	November.	December.	Total.
1897.													
Glanders and farcy	19	27	34	23	26	27	21	45	39	20	12	8	301
Foot-and-mouth disease	249	191	104	85	64	86	387	433	356	234	78	186	2,453
Rabies	8	8	6	3	1	2	2	9	28	5	7	6	85
Anthrax	22	24	35	21	25	32	43	40	30	45	32	29	378
Foot rot	3	20	36	30	1	30	102	15	225	....	....	....	462
Sheep scab	1	....	2	....	....	....	....	1	....	....	....	....	4
1898.													
Glanders and farcy	1	13	10	12	4	9	21	20	18	19	4	7	138
Foot-and-mouth disease	168	159	54	21	4	32	87	736	3,014	6,540	2,294	2,444	15,553
Rabies	12	8	18	14	13	7	11	17	15	14	7	15	151
Anthrax	37	26	27	40	29	21	30	49	36	47	29	31	413
Foot rot	52	10	20	....	13	....	....	6	31	125	....	270	427
Sheep scab	....	200	6	1	....	....	....	....	....	....	....	140	347

FRANCE.

Contagious diseases among domestic animals in France during the years 1897 and 1898.

Name of disease.	January.	February.	March.	April.	May.	June.	July.	August.	September.	October.	November.	December.	Total.
1897.													
Contagious pleuropneumonia:													
Number of outbreaks	14	11	20	16	15	15	12	16	15	13	17	17	181
Number slaughtered	38	19	39	30	40	34	14	45	39	20	48	38	404
Number inoculated	59	63	184	30	45	115	44	112	85	159	92	113	1,101
Aphthous fever (outbreaks)	459	388	255	97	106	117	87	36	15	64	52	25	1,601
Sheep scab (outbreaks)	69	41	134	39	88	77	21	12	4	37	30	58	619
Sheep pox (outbreaks)	17	9	8	10	28	23	14	32	35	40	43	27	286
Anthrax (outbreaks)	41	32	38	30	18	36	28	27	31	56	55	27	429
Blackleg (outbreaks)	77	61	63	57	102	64	58	159	95	138	209	151	1,234
Glanders and farcy (outbreaks)	87	62	84	88	83	92	80	67	72	60	68	57	900
Rabies (cases)	131	151	180	202	225	172	192	154	130	131	150	140	2,073
Rouget (outbreaks)	38	25	52	47	62	54	197	281	195	40	18	30	1,029
Hog cholera (outbreaks)	5	5	14	16	20	24	13	18	24	14	10	7	170
1898.													
Contagious pleuropneumonia:													
Number of outbreaks	18	11	....	5	6	7	11	9	10	....	14	19	110
Number slaughtered	41	18	....	25	16	15	31	19	30	....	42	53	290
Number inoculated	87	42	....	70	83	61	150	34	72	....	116	121	786
Aphthous fever (outbreaks)	115	604	....	507	182	488	750	471	1,902	....	2,032	2,317	9,458
Sheep scab (outbreaks)	16	18	....	66	47	61	7	8	3	....	20	32	278
Sheep pox (outbreaks)	36	15	....	8	11	43	16	28	61	....	80	96	474
Anthrax (outbreaks)	34	28	....	45	27	20	40	54	45	....	50	30	382
Blackleg (outbreaks)	103	79	....	56	81	57	69	70	78	....	96	127	825
Glanders and farcy (outbreaks)	67	72	....	69	60	48	54	80	61	....	77	69	657
Rabies (cases)	139	148	....	181	216	278	185	177	150	....	153	154	1,781
Rouget (outbreaks)	11	14	....	9	17	31	30	13	9	....	36	28	196
Hog cholera (outbreaks)	6	11	....	18	15	10	13	10	12	....	17	4	116

NETHERLANDS.

The table of animal diseases given herewith is not complete, but it shows in a general way the character and extent of the diseases affecting the animals of that country. As will be observed, an extensive outbreak of foot-and-mouth disease occurred during the past two years in this country, which has always been in the front rank in regard to veterinary sanitary service. Mr. Alex. C. Cope, the chief veterinary officer of England, points out the fact that "with a cattle population of great value on account of its milking qualities, and a total animal population beyond the requirement of the country for the supply of food for her inhabitants, Holland has always been an exporting country, and therefore in a position to exclude foreign animals, and has maintained a strict supervision and control over the movement of animals across her German and Belgian frontiers. Under these favorable conditions Holland has for a number of years been comparatively free from foot-and-mouth disease; but in the early part of 1896, when the disease was most prevalent in Germany, these safeguards broke down." The disease was apparently allowed to run its course, and it has been estimated that more than half of the total number of animals suffered from it.

Cases of animal diseases in Netherlands for the years 1897 and 1898.

Name of disease.	January.	February.	March.	April.	May.	June.	July.	August.	September.	October.	November.	December.	Total.
1897.													
Foot-and-mouth disease	11,096	21,396	25,397	41,119	69,647		208,349	94,013	40,000	48,212	21,414	2,980	699,623
Farcy or mange	15	10	8	9	5		1	11		16	35	5	115
Sheep scab	20	1	59	16	1,363		3,736	3,036	87	2,346	4,452	983	16,129
Rouget	3	5	13	5	28		311	1,649	306	375	123	16	2,126
Anthrax	29		31	18	25		17	24	7	16	20	31	218
Foot rot of sheep	9	1	44	45			326	11	6	6	99	5	553
1898.													
Foot-and-mouth disease	755	513	208	475	63		6	42	3,208	1,787	2,667		
Farcy or mange	1	5	6	3	6	5	3	3	2	16	4		
Sheep scab	196	376	508	219	62	112	188	311	225	577	1,385		
Rouget	16	8	5	4	25	76	150	296	214	104	64		
Anthrax	24	36	35	23	24	18	15	31	27	25	30		
Foot rot of sheep	8	6	3		1	45	45	348	156	98	129		

DENMARK.

A comparison between the diseases existing in Denmark in 1897 and 1898 may be made from the table which follows. The report for November, 1898, was not received. The totals do not materially differ from those for 1896.

Cases of contagious diseases in Denmark for the years 1897 and 1898.

Name of disease.	January.	February.	March.	April.	May.	June.	July.	August.	September.	October.	November.	December.	Total.
1897.													
Anthrax	7	10	21	17	11	7	6	11	7	12	12	16	140
Foot-and-mouth disease		3	1							1			5
Cerebro-spinal meningitis	4	1	4	1	1	2	4	1	1	2	3	1	25
Glanders	4	11	9				1	1	1	1			28
Malignant catarrhal fever	1	7	2	9	12	10	10	11	8	3	6	5	84
Swine plague or hog cholera		1		1	2	2				1			7
Rouget:													
Acute	40	36	45	24	34	38	65	80	69	63	69	49	925
Chronic	12	8	9	8	2	5	7	20	12	20	25	19	147
Nodular erythema	30	36	44	34	46	153	253	433	396	322	220	100	2,067
1898.													
Anthrax	13	12	17	18	16	7	7	0	2	7		18	131
Foot-and-mouth disease													
Cerebro-spinal meningitis	2	1	2	9	2		3		5	5		1	30
Glanders									9	8			17
Malignant catarrhal fever	3	5	7	8	4	6	9	9	8	4		2	65
Swine plague or hog cholera	3	3	1	2	2	1	2	4	5	2		1	26
Rouget:													
Acute	46	51	35	47	37	32	78	79	85	80		47	617
Chronic	18	16	11	9	3		6	14	16	22		13	123
Nodular erythema	62	53	43	46	64	81	266	324	535	448		118	2,040

NORWAY.

Cases of contagious diseases reported in Norway for certain months of 1897 and 1898.

Name of disease.	January.	February.	March.	April.	May.	June.	July.	August.	September.	October.	November.	December.	Total.
1897.													
Anthrax	17	37	35	51	39	42		19	20	28	25	23	396
Blackleg	1		2					1	1			2	7
Braxy	6	3	1		1	3				4	18	1	37
Malignant catarrhal fever of cattle.	14	26	35	24	20	34		21	19	15	13	61	239
Rouget	18	11	19	31	36	63		129	161	103	60	41	672
Hog cholera								25	50	6			81
1898.													
Anthrax	28			53	45	32		15					
Blackleg	1			2	4	2		2					
Braxy	12			7	5	16							
Malignant catarrhal fever of cattle.	31			44	28	30		9					
Rouget	21			47	39	34		94					

HUNGARY.

The following statements for the year 1897 are compiled from official documents of the Hungarian Government:

ANTHRAX.

The existence of anthrax was officially established on 1,426 farm premises, and affected 209 horses, 1,889 cattle, and 968 sheep. This is

88 more farm premises, 18 more horses, 109 more cattle, and 106 fewer sheep than suffered from the disease in 1896. The following number of animals died from the disease in 1897: Horses, 197; cattle, 1,739, and sheep, 968, this being 7 horses, 36 cattle, and 168 sheep more than in 1896.

The proportion of animals lost to the entire number of animals is stated below in percentages. The approximate value of the animals lost is also given:

Kind of animal.	1897.		1896.	
	Percent-age lost.	Value.	Percent-age lost.	Value.
Horses	0.010	$6,818	0.009	$6,298
Cattle	.080	55,243	.029	53,329
Sheep	.013	2,751	.010	2,117
Total		64,812		61,734

RABIES.

In 1897 rabies was reported as affecting 1,282 dogs, 22 horses, 120 cattle, 40 sheep, and 53 hogs. The number of animals affected has been greater than in 1896 by 8 dogs, 8 horses, 46 cattle, and 32 sheep, while 10 fewer hogs were affected. Seventy-five dogs died, 1,057 were killed, and 150 escaped. Suspected dogs, having been bitten, were killed to the number of 3,196; also 6 cattle, 3 sheep, 2 goats, 11 hogs, 208 cats, 9 fowls, and 19 animals not definitely named.

GLANDERS.

Glanders was reported from 496 farm premises, and 776 horses were affected. This showing exceeds that for 1896 by 143 farm premises and 148 horses. Of the horses affected, 755 were killed and 21 died. Besides, 155 suspected horses were killed, making a total loss on account of this disease of 931 horses. This was 0.039 per cent of the total number of horses in Hungary, valued at about $31,080.

FOOT-AND-MOUTH DISEASE.

This disease has not been so prevalent as in 1896. The following comparison shows a gratifying reduction in the number of cases:

	1896.	1897.
Counties where reported	63	50
Cattle affected	572,809	70,491
Sheep affected	178,612	25,450
Hogs affected	82,931	3,758

The table shows that reductions amount to 502,318 cattle, 153,262 sheep, and 79,173 hogs. Of the animals affected, there died 235 cattle, 48 sheep, and 13 hogs.

PLEUROPNEUMONIA.

This disease was identified on 109 farm premises, the number of cases being 262. In 1896 there were 313 cases. All affected animals were slaughtered by the authorities. Besides the 262 sick cattle, there were 735 killed at once because of suspicion, and 4,580 were sent to the slaughterhouse on account of exposure to the contagion.

SHEEP POX.

The number of sheep affected with sheep pox was 9,536, reported from 292 farm premises. This is an increase over 1896 of 273 farm premises and 8,598 cases. Of the sheep affected 8,010 recovered, the remaining 1,526 having died of the disease or were killed. The death rate of the affected animals was 16 per cent.

FOOTHALT.

Foothalt was reported from one county (Hajdu) where both stallions and mares were affected, but statistics are not given.

BLISTER UPON THE GENITALS.

This disease appeared on 143 farm premises in 16 counties. Eighty-one horses and 134 cattle were affected. Compared with 1896, this shows 95 fewer farm premises, 1 more county, 37 fewer horses, and 83 fewer cattle.

SCAB.

This disease existed upon 604 farm premises in 44 counties. Below is a comparison of its extent with 1896:

	1896.	1897.
Horses affected	1,713	970
Cattle affected	119	4
Sheep affected	4,156	3,222

RED MURRAIN OF SWINE.

This disease was reported from 2,764 farm premises in 49 counties. The number of swine attacked was 11,068. A comparison with 1896 shows 3,089 fewer farm premises for 1897, 3 fewer counties, and 17,738 fewer animals affected.

HOG CHOLERA.

Hog cholera appeared on 84,828 farm premises in 60 counties. A comparison of data with 1896 is given in the following table:

	1896.	1897.
Hogs attacked	868,777	514,291
Hogs died of the disease	639,765	360,838
Hogs killed	13,093	5,021

This statement shows a decrease of 354,466 in the number of cases, of 278,927 in the number of dead of the disease, and of 8,072 killed.

BUFFALO CHOLERA.

There were 99 cases of this disease reported from 69 farm premises. In 1896 there were 350 cases reported from 153 farm premises. Of the 99 cases, 94 died.

ITALY.

The tabular statement presented of the contagious diseases of domestic animals in Italy for 1897 and 1898 is not nearly complete, but enough is given to show what diseases prevailed in that Kingdom. Foot-and-mouth disease, which was so prominent in other European countries during 1897, appears to have been very prevalent in Italy.

Cases of contagious diseases among domestic animals in Italy during the years 1897 and 1898.

Name of disease.	January.	February.	March.	April.	May.	June.	July.	August.	September.	October.	November.	December.	Total.
1897.													
Maladie du coît				2	3								5
Foot-and-mouth disease				7				23	112	265	361	2,444	3,214
Rabies			1		19			38	8	4	11	4	96
Variolæ				10	25			9		1			45
Tuberculosis				1	8	4		5	2		5	2	31
Infectious agalactia				296				468	212	337	170	55	1,538
Hog cholera and swine plague				33	458	245	528	94	115	411	197	138	2,219
Epizootics of uncertain nature				33					75			32	140
Anthrax and blackleg *a*				22	100	229	399	129		397	108	117	1,471
Glanders and farcy			45		33	70	17	22	37	34		19	277
Tetanus					2								2
Sheep scab					10,758								10,758
Strangles					2								2
Purpurea hæmorrhagica					3	7							10
Barbone of the buffalo (buffalo disease)								59		25	16		100
Influenza among horses (pinkeye)						8				250	374	31	663
1898.													
Foot-and-mouth disease	4,299	2,023	4,352	6,605	5,545	9,739	5,801	1,918	1,248	1,572	2,456		45,497
Rabies	15	16	7	14	3	26	12	8	3	6	7		117
Tuberculosis	1	5	9	5	3	3	5			1	7		39
Infectious agalactia				10				141					151
Hog cholera and swine plague	91	61	347	229	245	518	667	155	68	61	197		2,634
Anthrax and blackleg *a*	92	48	69	136	161	166	243	236	63	60	159		1,433
Glanders and farcy	17	14	8	22	26	21	28	15	7	17	12		277
Sheep scab		472			1								473
Barbone of the buffalo (buffalo disease)	3							20	16	6			45
Influenza among horses (pinkeye)	241							216					457
Mange (psoroptic) of cattle			177	987	810	821				98			2,396

a These diseases are not separated in the documents from which these figures are tabulated.

SWITZERLAND.

The figures on contagious diseases of animals in Switzerland for 1897 and 1898 varied but little in most particulars·from the figures for 1896. The scourge of foot-and-mouth disease was larger in 1897, the number of animals affected being 10,342, while in 1898 the diseased increased to an alarming extent, the number of cases being 106,884. Of this large number 34,491 occurred in July and 32,431 in June. From that time till the end of the year, as will be observed by reference to the tabular statement, the disease decreased.

Cases of contagious diseases among domestic animals in Swizterland for the years 1897 and 1898.

Name of disease	January.	·February.	March.	April.	May.	June.	July.	August.	September.	October.	November.	December.	Total.
1897.													
Blackleg (dead and slaughtered)	10	10	16	27	52	81	149	124	98	72	21	12	672
Anthrax (dead and slaughtered)	30	24	36	24	28	32	33	27	37	28	13	14	324
Foot-and-mouth disease:													
Large cattle (dead and infected)	268	50	647	116	2	360	2,206	790	431	231	829	1,871	7,801
Small cattle (dead and infected)	65	41	310	72	....	84	545	316	49	4	148	907	2,541
Rabies (dead and slaughtered)	11	30	6	2	9	5	3	2	8	7	72	24	179
Glanders (dead and slaughtered)	.....	3	3	4	14	10	6	5	2	2	4	5	58
Rouget (dead and slaughtered)	271	200	177	190	208	465	422	443	350	278	135	108	3,247
Sheep scab (dead and infected)	.....	15	29	4	3	.....	1	......	30	232	.....	......	314
1898.													
Blackleg (dead and slaughtered)	9	5	12	16	39	108	162	127	95	42	15	15	645
Anthrax (dead and slaughtered)	29	18	28	29	28	25	24	25	22	20	21	37	306
Foot-and-mouth disease:													
Large cattle (dead and infected)	1,290	617	1,011	789	797	3,279	13,714	15,726	6,880	3,346	5,186	2,578	55,213
Small cattle (dead and infected)	312	200	85	79	223	3,506	20,777	16,705	3,590	2,972	2,120	1,002	51.671
Rabies (dead and slaughtered)	19	3	7	51	9	1	14	8	6	.....	1	......	119
Glanders (dead and slaughtered)	1	2	3	4	2	5	3	1	5	2	3	11	42
Rouget (dead and slaughtered)	78	85	42	54	194	142	226	307	221	199	119	111	1,778
Sheep scab (dead and infected)	158	65	....	....	2	351	.....	224	183	....	....		983

AMERICAN ANIMALS AND ANIMAL PRODUCTIONS IN GREAT BRITAIN.

By W. H. WRAY,

Inspector in England for Bureau of Animal Industry.

A comparison of the figures for 1896 with those for 1897 shows an increase in the importation into England of live cattle for 1897. The good quality of the live cattle entering Great Britain from the United States is still maintained. The losses at sea continue to be very small, averaging between 2 and 3 head per 1,000. This low rate of loss at sea is without doubt due to the system of vessel inspection conducted by the Bureau of Animal Industry and to the steamers which carry them to foreign countries.

DELAY IN TRANSSHIPPING CATTLE.

Of late it has been the custom of some transatlantic steamers when arriving at the port of London to delay entering the docks until the very last minute, just before the tide falls. This delay prevents the transshipping steamers from getting the cattle while the steamer is in the river and causes the cattle to remain on board the steamers from one to two hours longer than is necessary. All the facts possible with reference to this matter are being gathered with a view to placing them before the steamship owners or their agents, when a request will be made that the captains and pilots be notified to bring their steamers to the docks as soon as possible after arriving at the port, and that everything possible be done to have the cattle transshipped before the steamers enter the docks. The difference in time in getting the cattle to Deptford on the transshipping steamer, when the cattle are taken on board before the transatlantic steamer enters the dock and when they are transshipped inside the dock, is, at the lowest estimate, over two hours. This delay has often caused a cargo to arrive at Deptford too late for the market, causing the cattle to be held by the consignee for two or three days, until the next market day. This entails considerable expense and sometimes a loss in price.

INCREASE OF FOREIGN-ANIMALS WHARVES.

In June I held an interview with the chairman of the Southwestern Railroad Company in reference to a foreign cattle market at Southampton, with the result that plans are now being drawn for the landing place, abattoirs, etc., the construction of which will begin as soon as possible. Every new foreign-animals wharf that is opened in

440

England makes a new outlet for the live cattle of the United States. It is also another step toward preventing a certain few of the foreign cattle markets from holding a monopoly of the foreign cattle trade. With foreign cattle wharves at Southampton, Bristol, and Cardiff, the south coast of England will be pretty well supplied, and if a regular line of steamers, thoroughly fitted for the carrying of live cattle, would establish regular sailings to these points, I am quite sure the venture would prove remunerative.

CATTLE FROM THE ARGENTINE REPUBLIC.

During 1897 there were received from the Argentine Republic 7,836 more cattle than during 1896.

The South American cattle are still very rough and are not yet up to the standard of first-rate beef, but they are improving year by year. The voyage is a long one, and during certain seasons the cattle show the effects of the journey very much on their arrival in Great Britain. During 1897 the loss of South American cattle bound for Great Britain averaged more than 80 head per 1,000. The English board of agriculture are doing all they can to have the steamers engaged in this trade better fitted. It is almost an impossibility to compel the steamship owners to have permanent fittings on the boats which transport South American cattle. This condition obtains because the steamers are unable to get full cargoes often enough to warrant their owners in making regular trips. It is quite a common sight, however, to see a steamer from Buenos Ayres with no other cargo than live cattle and sheep.

Even should the breeders of South America succeed in improving their cattle up to the standard of those bred in the United States, there is not much danger, owing to the long distance and cost of transportation, of their cattle competing in the English markets with the United States cattle.

RECEIPTS OF CANADIAN CATTLE.

During 1897 there were shipped from Canada to England 24,893 more live cattle than in the preceding year. The Canadian cattle arrive in very good condition, but are not so well finished as those from the United States, but are a good second. Recently Minister Long made a visit to the foreign cattle market at Deptford, and, after inspecting the market and the cattle that were for sale, expressed surprise to see such excellent cattle from the United States and stated that they were in every way equal to British bred and were much more uniform than would be seen in the British market.

SHEEP AND LAMBS.

There were received in England from the United States 80,005 fewer sheep in 1897 than during 1896. This decrease is largely due to the large shipments of live sheep and frozen mutton from the Argentine Republic and New Zealand. The United States sheep that have reached Deptford did not all compare favorably with the sheep arriving from the Argentine Republic; but those shipped from the United States to Liverpool have been, as a rule, of very good quality and have brought as good prices as the Argentine Republic sheep.

During 1896 there were shipped to the British markets from the Argentine Republic 339,381 sheep, as against 345,217 in 1897. These sheep are well bred and arrive at the ports of Great Britain in very good condition. The loss at sea averages about 40 per 1,000. The Argentine Republic sheep are sold in the English retail shops as best "Welsh" and "English" mutton and bring good prices—from 9 cents per pound for the poorest cut to 24 cents for the best.

From Canada there were received 20,000 fewer sheep in 1897 than in 1896. This decrease is due to the same causes which influenced the shipments from the United States, namely, large shipments of live animals and frozen mutton from the Argentine Republic and New Zealand. There is much room for improvement in the breeds of Canadian sheep in order to make them a good mutton-producing animal. They do not bring as good prices as the sheep from the Argentine Republic, the average price being 9¼ or 9¾ cents per pound.

There can hardly be a doubt that it would pay the breeders of the United States to breed a good mutton sheep for export or one suitable for the English market. There is no reason why refrigerated mutton should not be shipped from the United States to Great Britain. The chilled or refrigerated mutton of the right quality would be much more preferable and bring higher prices than the frozen mutton from New Zealand or the Argentine Republic.

HORSES.

The trade with Great Britain in United States horses greatly increased during 1898. The horses are giving general satisfaction to purchasers. Many may be seen at work in the streets of London, and at Liverpool scores may be counted in a walk of a few minutes. If the breeders of the United States will produce a horse suitable for the English market, they will, as a rule, find here a good market at remunerative prices.

It is a pleasure to state that no contagious disease has been discovered in the American horses on their arrival in this country; in fact, they are found to be so healthy that the Glasgow corporation has decided to abolish the system of inspection of horses imported from the United States.

The trade in old, worn-out horses from London to Antwerp, Amsterdam, Rotterdam, and Ghent still continues, notwithstanding the fact that many cases of glanders have been discovered upon arrival. The Royal Society for the Prevention of Cruelty to Animals have been doing their utmost to stop this trade on account of the alleged cruelty practiced toward these horses. This trade is dangerous to the export horse trade of the United States, as many steamers bring the horses to Gravesend and London, whence they are transshipped on smaller steamers to the Continent. It may easily happen that these same small steamers also transport the worn-out glandered horses to the Continent; hence, if the steamers are not thoroughly cleaned and disinfected before the American horses are taken on board, there is great danger of infection. A thorough investigation will be made of this matter at the first opportunity. It is quite certain that the British law providing for the cleaning and disinfecting of boats and cars which carry cattle do not apply to steamers which carry horses.

BACON.

The shipments of bacon from the United States in 1897 exceeded the shipments of 1896 by 841,131 hundredweights of 112 pounds.[1] This was a very healthy increase; in fact, the shipments of bacon from the United States have generally been on the increase since 1893.[2] The receipts from Russia increased 8,712 hundredweights during 1897 over 1896, while the receipts from all other countries, except the United States, have decreased. This is notably true of Germany, from which 512 hundredweights were received in 1896 and 45 in 1897.

United States bacon loses its identity when it reaches the retail dealer in England. It is impossible to purchase a piece of United States bacon under that name in any of the retail stores of London.

RULES FOR THE LONDON PROVISION TRADE.

The following are the official rules, conditions of sale, and trade customs in the London provision trade as established by the Home Foreign Produce Exchange, Limited:

SECTION 1.—*Terms of credit and payment.*

RULE 1. Landed sales: The terms are payment by acceptance at two months to approved buyers, or by cash within seven days, less two months' discount, at the rate of 5 per cent per annum; if after seven days, discount at the same rate to be allowed upon the unexpired term of credit. (Excepting rules 11 and 25.)

The customary three days' grace is not allowable on country checks forwarded three days before the goods become due.

RULE 2. F. o. b. sales: Irish provisions by acceptance at sixty days. and Dutch at two months' date; or if paid in cash, 5 per cent per annum to be allowed upon the unexpired term of credit.

---

[1] The increase given by the Bureau of Statistics of the Treasury Department was 100,066,894 pounds, or 893,454 hundredweights of 112 pounds.—EDITOR.

[2] The exports of bacon, in pounds, from the United States to the United Kingdom, for the last six years, according to the Bureau of Statistics of the Treasury Department, were as follows: 1892, 425,050,161; 1893, 296,943,650; 1894, 342,606,950; 1895, 364,437,873; 1896, 334,042,167; 1897, 434,109,061.—EDITOR.

American and Canadian provisions by acceptance at sixty days' sight; or if paid in cash, a discount to be allowed at bankers' rate upon the unexpired term of credit. Buyers risk commences from date of bill of lading.

RULE 3. C. i. f. sales: By acceptance with bill of lading attached at sixty days' sight. Bill of lading to be given up in payment of acceptance; if before maturity, a discount to be allowed at bankers' rate from date of sighting upon the unexpired term.

RULE 4. Landed-to-arrive sales: Invoice to be dated from day of tender of goods, terms as in Rule 1. If name of vessel be specified at time of contract, sellers are not bound to replace in case of accident by sea.

SECTION II.—*American and Canadian bacon; English and Irish hams; pickled and mess pork, and beef.*

RULE 5. Irish and Continental bacon: If weighed at railway depot, to be weighed gross for average, 5 pounds to be deducted for every four-sided bale and 6 pounds for every five and six sided bale for wrapper and cord, which shall not exceed on an average 4½ and 5½ pounds, respectively; should, however, the wrapper and cord exceed these limits, an average of not less than five wrappers (unless the parcel in question be less) shall be taken, and the excess over and above 4 pounds and 5 pounds, respectively, be allowed. If weighed at wharf, buyers' warehouse, or bacon dryers' premises, the net weight to be taken for average.

RULE 6. Any claim except for taint to be made within three days from date of sale, or of landing if sold to arrive. Claims for taint must be made within ten days as above.

RULE 7. English and Irish hams: Sold on inspection, to be weighed within three days, and claims for defects to be made also within three days. Sold to arrive, to be weighed within three days, and claims for defects to be made within six days after delivery.

RULE 8. American and Canadian bacon, landed: After being swept to be weighed a box at a time, net; 2 pounds in 3 hundredweight to be allowed as beamage when packed in salt. Box bacon: Any box taken in average proving exceptionally overweight, the overweight will be charged; the same box not being included in the average. Any exceptional loss to be treated in a similar way.

RULE 9. Three days to be allowed for averaging and 10 per cent of bulk may be taken.

RULE 10. Pork and heads in barrels and tierces, seven days to be allowed for averaging.

RULE 11. Mess pork in barrels of 200 pounds and beef in tierces of 304 pounds each: Ten per cent may be turned out for averaging, and short weight allowed, if any. Overweight not chargeable. Terms: Payment by acceptance at two months to approved buyers, or by cash in seven days, less 1½ per cent discount.

SECTION III.—*Butter.*

RULE 12. Dutch f. o. b. sales: Shippers' weights and tares to be accepted. Landed: Six clear days allowed for weighing off, from date of purchase; after that rehoused at buyers' risk and cost. Tare, 16 pounds for each quarter and 8 pounds for each eighth cask. Factory average to be taken on net weight. Return of all goods sold with a guaranty to be made within three days from date of landing and (or) purchase.

RULE 13. Danish, Kiel, Swedish, Finnish, etc., f. o. b. sales: Shippers' weights and tares to be accepted. Landed: Six clear days to be allowed for weighing off from date of purchase, after which rehoused at buyers' risk and cost. Tares marked on each package, or according to specification of invoice. Two out of every ten casks may be turned for average.

Rule 14. Irish: Average to be taken upon net weight. French: 28-pound packages to be weighed to ¼ pound and 56-pound packages to ½ pound. Packages above 56 pounds to be weighed to 1 pound.

Rule 15. American: Weighed gross and average for super tare, or weighed net for average loss. Australian: Packages of about 56 pounds to be weighed net to ½ pound. Overweight on marked weights can not be included in average or charged for.

Rule 16. Average to be taken within three days, but in fresh and mild goods at the earliest possible time.

Rule 17. Ten per cent of the bulk to be weighed if required by the buyer or seller, but in case of hot weather not more than 5 per cent to be taken.

Rule 18. Packages of 56 pounds and under to be weighed to ½ pound. Above that, to be weighed to 1 pound. Box butters: Overweight on boxes of uniform marked weights can not be included in average nor charged for.

Section IV.—*Cheese.*

Rule 19. American and Canadian, landed: Cheddar shape to be weighed gross in drafts of 5, Flat cheese in drafts of 3, hundredweights, or box weights may be taken with an allowance for average loss taken on the basis of 10 per cent of total quantity sold or bought. Beamage, 1 pound on 3 hundredweights, to cover cloths and scale boards, but shall not be allowed when it is equaled or excelled by the overweight.

Rule 20. New Zealand and Australian: To be averaged, and allowance to be made for cloths, crate, and shrinkage. Ten per cent may be taken for averaging.

Rule 21. Weights to be taken within three days on buyer's application. If seller does not attend, wharfinger, storekeeper, or his agent to represent him.

Rule 22. Dutch landed sales: To be weighed not within seven days, with draft of 1 pound on 3 hundredweights, f. o. b. sales at shipper's weights.

Rule 23. English landed sales: To be weighed net within three days. No draft and no beamage. Terms same as American, i. e., two months' credit, less interest at 5 per cent per annum on the unexpired term, or cash within seven days.

Section V.—*Lard.*

Rule 24. Bladders, landed, to be weighed net, taking 1 in 5 for average. Kegs weighed to ½ pound; scale balance to be taken as weight alternately.

Rule 25. American tierces: Reweights, market tares, and super tares. Terms, fourteen days, less 2½ per cent discount. Beamage to be allowed ½ pound per hundredweight. Ten per cent may be taken for average. (This action does not apply to "refined" lard.)

Rule 26. Lard in 28-pound packages to be weighed two at a draft to ½ pound; 56-pound packages to be weighed to ½ pound, and hundredweight packages to 1 pound.

Section VI.—*Tinned meats.*

[In accordance with the rules of the chamber of commerce.]

Rule 27. Sold at described weights, but any short weight to be allowed if exceeding ¼ pound per case of 12 by 6 pounds, 18 by 4 pounds, or in proportion for other-sized cases.

Rule 28. Buyers to be at liberty to refuse any cases the short weight on which exceeds 2 pounds per case.

Rule 29. Unless otherwise expressed, boiled beef to be taken as meaning "boneless beef, without salt;" boiled mutton as "boneless mutton, without salt."

Rule 30. Examination to take place where the goods are lying, or if "to arrive," where stored after landing; buyer to have notice of time of examination, and to have the right of being present and examining personally or by his representative. Perfect tins only to be delivered to buyer. Wharfingers' charges in connection with the examination to be paid by the seller.

RULE 31. No claims to be made on account of goods after examination, except in respect of defective preservation or defective soldering, for which the packer shall be held responsible at any time within one year from time of sale by his agent; but intermediate agents or dealers shall not be held responsible or liable.

SECTION VII.—*General rules.*

RULE 32. The terms "about" or "more or less," when applied to quantity, shall mean a variation of not more than 5 per cent either way, and when applied to average sizes the extreme range allowable shall be 10 per cent. "Merchantable," as applied to lard, means sound, sweet, steam rendered.

RULE 33. In case of excessive loss on shipments, say, c. i. f. and f. o. b. sales, the seller may be called on for proof of his original weights.

RULE 34. The seller is liable for any distinct variation from the description of any goods bought or ordered on his representation.

RULE 35. In case of nonfulfillment of contract, either party shall have the right of repurchase or resale, as the case may be, either publicly or privately, during seven business days next ensuing, or within the like time may assess his own damages on giving notice and particulars thereof to the party in default; and should he dispute such assessment, he shall, by 12 o'clock on the second business day after receipt of such notice, demand an arbitration under rule 42, and in default of doing so, the assessment shall be deemed good. When the amount of damages has been ascertained by such repurchase, resale, assessment, award, or otherwise, the amount shall, on demand, be paid by the party in default, and be recoverable as a liquidated demand.

RULE 36. Weights to be considered as final between buyer and seller of all goods weighed or averaged at any public wharf or quay.

RULE 37. Invoices of goods sold "ex quay" shall date from the average date of landing, but such date shall not precede the day of sale or tender.

RULE 38. Where country of production, etc., is not stated, the foregoing rules are applicable.

RULE 39. Time for making claim limited to three days, unless the contrary is specified under any previous section.

RULE 40. Agents or merchants advancing on goods, either by cash or by acceptance, reserve to themselves the power of sale.

RULE 41. Should any dispute arise for which provision has not been made in the foregoing rules, such dispute to be settled by arbitration.

Charges for reweighing on goods sold f. o. b. : If the goods prove to be "weight," the cost shall fall on the buyer; but if "short weight," the cost shall fall on the seller.

SECTION VIII.—*Arbitration.*

RULE 42. In case any dispute shall arise out of the contracts made subject to these rules, the matter shall be referred to two arbitrators, one to be chosen by each party in difference, the said arbitrators having power, either before or after they shall enter upon the reference, to call in a third, if they shall deem it necessary.

RULE 43. In the event of one of the disputing parties appointing an arbitrator and the other refusing, or by 12 o'clock of the second business day following notice in writing of the appointment neglecting to do so (such notice to be delivered personally or left at the usual place of business of such other party), or in case the arbitrators appointed by the parties shall not within seven days after the appointment agree to an award; or in case of death, refusal to act, or incapacity within the like time of any such three arbitrators, then upon application of either disputing parties the question in dispute shall stand referred to two arbitrators, to be nominated by the chairman, for the time being, of the exchange; or in case of his absence, illness, or interest in the matter in dispute, then by the deputy chairman, if not interested; and in case of his absence, illness, or interest in the matter in dispute, then by the committee—the arbitrators so chosen having power, either before or after they shall enter upon the reference, to appoint a third arbitrator—and in case the two arbitrators so appointed, whether by the chairman, deputy chairman, or the committee, shall not within seven days agree to an award or appoint a third arbitrator, and shall in case of death, refusal to act, or incapacity of any such three arbitrators, from time to time substitute a new arbitrator in the place of the arbitrator so dying, refusing to act, or incapacitated.

The arbitrators appointed shall in all cases be members of the exchange, and no member having any interest in the matter in dispute shall be competent to act on any arbitration.

The award of any two arbitrators, in writing, signed by them (subject only to right of appeal hereafter mentioned), shall be conclusive and binding upon all disputing parties, both with respect to the matter in dispute and all expenses of the reference and award; and this agreement to refer shall not be revokable by either party.

No arbitrator shall be entitled to demand a higher fee than 21s. for every requisite sitting.

In case either party shall be dissatisfied with the award, a right of appeal shall lie to the committee of the exchange, provided it be claimed not later than 12 o'clock on the second business day after that on which the objecting party shall have notice of the award (Sundays and holidays not to be counted); provided also the appellant do pay to the exchange the sum of £10 [$48.66] as a fee for the investigation; and an award signed by the chairman of the meeting which shall hear such appeal, and countersigned by the secretary or his substitute, shall be deemed to be the award of the committee, and shall in all cases be final. The committee shall have power to direct by whom or in what proportion the expenses of the reference, appeal, and awards (including the amount of the said fee) shall be borne and paid.

No member of the committee having any interest in the matter in dispute shall vote on the question of the appointment of arbitrators, or in case of an appeal sit or vote on the committee; nor shall the arbitrator whose decision is appealed against sit or vote on the committee.

For the purpose of enforcing any award by attachment or otherwise this rule, and any contract referring thereto, may be made a rule of any court of record.

LIVERPOOL TERMS AND CONDITIONS.

I. (a) A buyer of provisions shall approve of bulk as soon as possible after day of sale or tender. Should no written notice be sent to the seller by 6 o'clock (Saturdays, 3.30 p. m.) on the third business day, inclusive of day of sale or tender if from warehouse, or 6 o'clock (Saturdays, 3.30 p. m.) on the second business day, inclusive of the day of sale or tender if from quay, rejecting the bulk and stating the cause, the bulk shall be deemed to have been accepted (subject to right of rejection in detail provided by rule 5).

(b) The seller shall be deemed to have accepted such rejection of bulk unless he shall have demanded arbitration upon the rejection before 6 p. m. (Saturdays, 3.30 p. m.) on the second business day (or, if on the quay, on the first business day) following that on which he received such notice of rejection.

II. (a) A tender on any business day except Saturday shall be made before 4 o'clock in the afternoon, and, if on a Saturday, before 1 o'clock in the afternoon;

but if a tender is made on any business day except Saturday after 2 o'clock, or on a Saturday after 12 o'clock, the same shall, for the purpose of calculating interest, but not otherwise, be deemed to have been made on the business day next following.

(b) A tender made on the last day of the period allowed for delivery shall stand good to any subpurchaser of the whole or part of the goods who shall receive his tender before 4 p. m. on the business day next ensuing, provided that no intermediary, availing himself of this by-law, retain the tender in his possession for more than one hour, except between the hours of 5 p. m. and 10 a. m. of any two consecutive week days, or between 4 p. m. of Saturday and 10 a. m. of the following Monday.

(c) Except to complete a contract, no tender shall be made of less than 25 packages of lard or meats or 50 boxes of cheese of any one mark or brand. The seller shall permit the buyer to sample as often as he pleases, provided the buyer indemnifies him from all loss and expense incurred after the first sampling; and the seller shall accept and act on the buyer's part orders for delivery where such part orders are for not less than 100 packages of lard or 50 boxes of meats or 100 boxes of cheese.

(d) Except where otherwise stipulated, goods sold for forward delivery may be tendered at such times within the period limited by the contract for delivery of the whole as the seller thinks fit, but each delivery shall be considered a separate contract, and the failure of any delivery or any delivery not in accordance with the contract shall not vitiate or affect the contract.

(e) Where the rejection of any tender is by consent or by final award held to be good, the seller shall have the right of making other tenders within the time for delivery stipulated by the contract; and if the rejection of a tender is not sustained the seller shall forthwith deliver and the buyer accept the goods tendered, but subject to the terms of payment provided for by the contract.

(f) In all cases where no valid tender is made a sum of 1s. per hundredweight, as assessed damages, shall be paid by the party in default, in addition to the difference, if any, between the contract price and the market price of the day on which default shall be made.

(g) If goods tendered shall have been rejected and any such rejection shall not have been upheld by a final award within the period of delivery stipulated in the contract, the goods so rejected shall be accepted by the buyer; but if it be afterwards awarded that the tendered goods did not fulfill the contract they shall then be invoiced back to the seller at the market price of the last business day of the said period, together with such sum, if any (not exceeding 1s. per hundredweight), as may be awarded, and all intermediate parties shall settle their differences as if a valid tender had been made.

(h) Should the seller be prevented from delivering during the period stipulated in the contract or the buyer from taking delivery as provided by the rules by reason of riots, strikes, or combinations of workmen, or lockouts at the place named for delivery, the time allowed for delivery shall be extended until the operation of the causes preventing delivery has ceased, but the seller shall not be entitled to claim the benefits of this clause unless he shall have declared before the expiration of the period stipulated the special parcel which he intends to deliver.

This provision shall apply also to delivery under contracts for shipment and delivery against which a declaration has been made before the ship's name appears in the bill of entry. The time for declaration to be extended to twenty-four hours after such appearance in cases where the ship brings her own advices.

(i) The following days shall be deemed holidays and not business days: Sundays, Good Friday, Saturday after Good Friday, Christmas Day, New Year's

Day, bank holidays, or any holiday appointed by the Liverpool Provision Trade Association at an extraordinary general meeting.

III. (a) The weight of cheese and boxed meats shall be ascertained by averaging from the American weights, and the loss, if any, allowed. For the purpose of this rule cheeses shall be weighed five at a time.

(b) Lard in tierces shall be delivered at the marked landing weights, and the tare ascertained by averaging from the American marked tares.

(c) Butter packages shall be reweighed singly, and the super tare, if any, ascertained by averaging shall be allowed.

(d) A buyer may, before goods are delivered or turned over to him, whichever shall happen first, demand that the whole be reweighed by the seller; but in such case the buyer shall pay to the seller the extra expense incurred, or the seller may reweigh the whole at his own expense. In the case of prime steam lard in tierces, a buyer may demand that the whole be reweighed at the seller's expense; but in that case he shall forego the customary draft, or the seller may reweigh the whole at his own expense, but in such case he must allow the draft.

(e) The customary allowance for draft on lard shall be 4 pounds per tierce. There is no draft in the case of cheese, butter, boxed meats, or meats in pickle.

(f) Each barrel of pork shall be considered as weighing 200 pounds net, and each tierce of beef 304 pounds net. All deficiency from this weight shall be allowed for on average.

(g) Except where otherwise agreed upon, the standard average weight of packages sold for forward delivery shall be 320 pounds net per tierce of lard and 500 pounds net per box for meats, and the difference in weights shall be settled for at the market price of the day. This clause shall not apply when brands are specified on the contract, in which case the weight of packages usual to the brand shall be the standard average weight.

(h) All boxed meats, cheese, and butter sold subject to these rules shall be cash in one month (or before delivery, if required); if paid within seven days, less full two months' discount; after that date, less equal to two months' discount from date of invoice. Discount to be at the rate of 5 per cent per annum.

IV. Where goods are sold ex quay, the buyer shall take delivery at the quay in carts or other conveyances provided by him, and in case he shall fail to do so before 5 o'clock of the following afternoon (in the afternoon of the day following) that on which the seller has given notice that he is ready to show samples within half a mile of the produce exchange and to deliver, the buyer shall pay all fines, demurrage, watching, and all other expenses which may be thereafter incurred, and after a further period of twenty-four hours the seller shall be at liberty to weigh over and warehouse the goods at the buyer's expense and risk. Buyers of lard having to draw their own samples shall be allowed forty-eight hours after tender for removal from quay, and such tender shall not be valid unless made after the discharge of the goods has commenced.

V. Deliveries of goods from or weighing over in warehouse must be commenced within ten running days from the day of sale. The risk of condition incident to the article from the day of sale or tender to be upon the buyer.

Subject to Rule I as to acceptance of bulk, the buyer shall be allowed with respect to goods in warehouse fourteen running days from the day of sale or tender or until weighed over, whichever event shall first happen, and with respect to goods on quay before taking same away to reject in detail anything not in accordance to contract.

VI. (a) In case of nonfulfillment of contract, either party shall have the right of repurchase or resale, as the case may be, either publicly or privately, during seven business days next ensuing, or within the like time may assess his own damages on giving notice and particulars thereof to the party in default, and

10317——29

should he dispute such assessment he shall, by 12 o'clock on the next business day after receipt of such notice, demand an arbitration (under Rule XII), and in default of doing so the assessment shall be deemed good. When the amount of damages has been ascertained by such repurchase, resale, assessment, award, or otherwise, the amount shall on demand be paid by the party in default and recoverable as a liquidated demand.

(b) Should either party to a contract for forward delivery at any time declare his inability to meet his engagements or become bankrupt or insolvent, all his outstanding contracts shall, within three business days next ensuing, be closed at the market price then current for the several periods for which they may be open, and the difference thus ascertained shall be a claim on or an asset of his estate.

VII. Rent on all goods in warehouse shall be borne by the seller for one month from the day of sale or tender unless delivery shall have previously taken place. The seller shall be entitled to charge the buyer with rent after one month until delivery, and shall have a lien on the produce for the amount of such rent.

VIII. Risk of fire shall be upon the seller until the goods shall have been delivered. Where delivery of part shall have been made, risk of fire as to the part delivered shall be upon the buyer and as to the undelivered part on the seller. Goods shall not be considered as delivered so long as they remain in the seller's own warehouse unless he shall, by memorandum in writing, have agreed to hold them as warehouse keeper (or so long as they remain in the name of the seller in the books of the warehouse keeper), or as to goods on the quay so long as they shall be in charge of a master porter. The seller shall be entitled to charge the buyer with premium of fire insurance after one month until delivery and shall have a lien on the produce for the amount of such premium.

Goods shall, for the purpose of this rule only, be considered as delivered and at the buyer's risk as regards fire: (a) When they shall have been transferred in the books of a warehouse keeper under a transfer order directing the warehouse keeper to transfer them into the name of the buyer; or (b) at 12 o'clock noon of the day next following that on which such a transfer order shall have been handed to the buyer.

IX. The mere act of weighing over shall not constitute a delivery, nor shall a delivery of part constitute or be considered as a delivery of the whole.

Invoices of goods sold ex quay shall date from the average date of landing, but such date shall not precede the date of sale or tender.

The seller's responsibility shall cease on delivery from the ship, quay, or from or in warehouse.

X. (a) The words "about" or "remainder" when used in contracts with reference to the weight of the parcel or the quantity shall mean within 5 per cent over or under that stated.

(b) The words "prompt shipment" shall mean shipment within ten days; "immediate" shall mean shipment within five days, both inclusive of day of sale.

XI. Unless otherwise stipulated, when goods are sold c. i. f. or f. o. b., the quality, condition, and weight contracted for shall be the quality, condition, and weight at the place of shipment, and the terms of sale shall be those of the market from which the goods are shipped.

XII. *Arbitrations.* (a) All disputes arising out of contracts made subject to these rules shall, on demand by any party, be referred to the arbitration committee of the association.

(b) When disputes arise of a similar nature on a series of contracts made subject to these rules, and which deal with the whole or part of the same goods, it shall be incumbent on the seller under the first of such contracts and the buyer under the last of such contracts to refer such disputes to the arbitration committee, and every buyer and seller to the intermediate contracts shall be bound by such reference and all awards made therein, so far as the same are applicable to their respective contracts.

(c) Every demand for arbitration shall be made in writing, accompanied by a deposit of £3 3s. ($15.32), to the secretary of the association, who shall convene a meeting of the arbitration committee to be held within two days from the receipt of the demand, and shall at the same time give written notice thereof to every party.

(d) No demand shall be entertained unless one party is a shareholder of, and an annual subscriber to the association, and if the party demanding arbitration is not, he shall with his demand pay to the association the said £3 3s. ($15.32) hereinbefore provided for and also the further sum of £1 1s. ($5.10).

(e) Any person dissatisfied with the board of the arbitration committee shall have a right of appeal to the appeal committee of the association, provided notice in writing, claiming such appeal, be given to the secretary not later than 12 o'clock on the second business day after that on which such party shall have received notice of the award (Sundays and holidays not to be counted), and provided he shall also pay to the secretary the sum of £10 ($48.66) as a fee for the hearing of the appeal.

(f) The secretary shall, upon receipt of notice claiming an appeal and payment of the said £10 ($48.66,) convene a meeting of the appeal committee to be held within three days from receipt of such notice and payment, and shall at the same time give written notice thereof to every party.

(g) In the event of any party refusing or neglecting to attend before the arbitration committee or appeal committee, after due notice thereof in writing, then the arbitration committee or appeal committee, as the case may be, may proceed ex parte, and the absence of any such party shall not bar the inquiry or prevent an award being made.

(h) The fees to be paid for every reference to the arbitration committee shall be £3 3s. ($15.32) for each requisite sitting.

(i) The arbitration committee and the appeal committee shall, respectively, have power to award by and to whom and in what manner, part, or proportion the expenses of any reference appeals and awards and all moneys paid under these arbitration rules are to be borne and paid.

(j) Every award of the arbitration committee shall be in writing and signed by such of the members as shall have heard the reference, or a majority of them.

(k) Every award of the appeal committee shall be signed by the chairman thereof and countersigned by the secretary or his substitute.

(l) Every award of the arbitration committee or of the appeal committee shall (subject as to an award by the arbitration committee to the right of appeal hereinbefore mentioned) be final and binding upon every party, both with respect to the matters in dispute and all expenses of the reference appeal and awards, and all fees and moneys paid pursuant to these arbitration rules.

(m) No complaint or objection shall be made as to the constitution or powers of the arbitration committee or appeal committee, respectively.

(n) Any notice required to be given by these rules may be given personally or left at the last known place of business of the party to whom it is addressed.

(o) In these rules, under the head of "arbitrations," unless the context otherwise requires, the word "party" means a buyer or a seller or a broker on a contract made subject to these rules and those claiming under them, respectively, and includes persons, firms, and bodies corporate and incorporate.

AVERAGE WEIGHTS OF PROVISION PACKAGES IN LONDON.

Subjoined are the range of weights of different kinds of provisions as nearly as can be ascertained:

BUTTER.

	Pounds net.
Irish: firkins	66–76
small firkins and kegs	50–56
kits	50–64
pyramids	28–56
boxes	14
Normandy: baskets	28–56
firkins	56–60
crocks	28–56
Saumur: crocks, "blues"	40–42
crocks, "greens"	42–44
crocks, "reds"	50–52
baskets, finest	28
other sorts	36
Paris, baskets	28–56
Danish and Swedish: casks	100–112
half casks	56–60
firkins and kegs	60–75
boxes	28–30
Finnish: casks	90–112
Russian: in Danish cwt. casks	112
Dutch: casks	90–100
firkins	50–60
Australian and New Zealand: boxes	56–60
Canadian and American: pails and tubs	30–70
boxes	56
Argentine: boxes	56

Margarin, tubs, firkins, boxes, and casks, all sizes, from 14 pounds upward.

Mixtures, in various sized packages, from 14 pounds up to 112 pounds as desired.

BACON.

	Cwts.	Qrs.		Cwts.	Qrs.
Irish, Hambro', Danish, Dutch, and Swedish, in bales, sizable from (net)	1	3			1
Sizes (net)	2	1			3
Stout sizable (net)	2	0	to		1
Heavy (net)	2	2	to	3	0

The various cures of bacon, branded and unbranded, are classed in the following order: Irish: Waterford, Limerick; sizable; stout; stout sizable; good; sizes; English lean; English stout. Continental: Sizable, No. 1 (lean); No. 2 (ordinary); No. 3 (medium). Sixes, No. 1 (lean); No. 2 (medium). Stout, No. 1 (lean); No. 2 (ordinary); No. 3 (outsize). Canadian "pea fed:" No. 1 selection, averaging 40 to 42; 46 to 48; 52 to 56; 58 to 62 pounds. No. 2 selection, averaging 46 to 50; 54 to 56; 58 to 60 pounds.

"Lean heavy" and "heavy" are, of course, over the above averages.

The different cuts of English "smoked" (including West of England) bacon may be classified as under "sides," "gammonless," "three-quarters," and "middles," all and each consist of "lean sizable," "sizable," "medium," and "heavy." "Unbranded" bacon is divided into "sides," "three-quarter sides," "gammonless," and "middles." "Fores" and "gammons" are classed as "sizable" and "medium;" and "chaps" are "smoked" and "green." "Green" bacon, branded, contains the same sizes as the leading ones for "smoked."

New Zealand bacon is imported in wooden cases containing six sides each and weighing 3½ to 4 hundredweight gross.

Canadian (pea fed) and American sides, middles, shoulders, and legs, in boxes about 4 to 6 hundredweight net.

Fine light American hogs weigh about 1 hundredweight each, and heavier ones run from 1 to 1½ hundredweight, or 180 pounds each. These are live weights, and differ from dressed weights, when the hogs are treated as dead meat, and sold with or without the heads, feet, etc. Sometimes in ascertaining the dead weight of pigs, the inside portions are reckoned in or thrown out, according to the mode of treatment adopted in certain localities; but technical knowledge of this sort can only be gained by serving for a time in a properly conducted curing establishment.

Pig's heads: Irish are the largest and Danish the smallest. There are usually 33 to 35 heads to one tierce, equal to 5 hundredweight each, or four tierces to a ton. They are seldom sold in lines of less than 50 tierces, which contain between 1,600 and 1,700 heads in all, and are consumed chiefly in Ireland.

HAMS.

American sugar-cured hams, in tierces, about 300 pounds net; in crates, about 400 to 540 pounds net. Irish and American dried hams, in casks, from 5 to 10 hundredweight. Casks and packages of Cumberland hams average from 3 to 10 and 12 hundredweight each.

BEEF.

American canned, from 2 pounds up to 14 pounds net. Mess beef, in tierces, about 304 pounds net.

PORK.

American mess pork, in barrels, about 200 pounds net. Bellies in pickle, from 300 to 320 pounds net.

LARD.

English: Tins of 25 and 28 pounds each net; in half-hundredweight boxes containing 1 and 2 pound packets, with parchment covers; in crates of 14-pound parchment-lined boxes; in barrels of 1¼ hundredweight, which contain a certain number of bladders, according to size, namely, barrels of 50 to 75 bladders, of 40 to 50, of 30 to 40, of 20 to 30, of 10 to 20, and of 10 bladders and under in each barrel.

Irish: Bladders, in barrels, 1 hundredweight net; kegs, from 50 to 56 pounds net. Hambro' and Danish: Bladdered, in barrels, 1 hundredweight net; kegs, from 40 to 56 pounds net. American: Tierces, 280 to 336 pounds net; barrels, 2 hundredweight net; half barrels, 1 hundredweight net; bladdered, in barrels, 1 hundredweight, 1 quarter, net; tins and pails, 14 to 28 pounds net. Canadian: Barrels, 1 hundredweight, 1 quarter, net.

In cabling the quotations of lard the term "point" is intended to mean 1 cent, a hundred of which go to the American dollar, and a single cent is equivalent to 1 halfpenny in English money. Thus 24 points are equal to 1 shilling, and with the dollar at 4s. 2d., $4.87 would be the exchange for 20 shillings.

CHEESE.

English: Cheshire, each average from 56 to 112 pounds; Cheddar, from 60 to 100 pounds; Derbys, from 28 to 30 pounds; double Gloucesters,[1] from 28 to — pounds; Wiltshire loaf, from 8 to 9 pounds; Stiltons, from 10 to 14 pounds; Canadian and American (in boxes), from 40 to 80 pounds; Cheddar shapes (in boxes), from 90 to 100 · pounds; Colonial (single cheeses), from 40 to 70 pounds.

New Zealand cheeses are usually packed in crates containing two to four each, the whole weighing from 120 to 180 pounds.

Dutch cheese is nearly always imported loose. One thousand Dutch round (or Edam) cheeses are equal in weight to about 2 tons, and the same number of "Flat" (or Gouda) cheeses weigh, as nearly as possible, 5 tons.

EGGS.

All foreign eggs are packed to the number of 1,440 eggs, equal to twelve long (or great) hundreds[2] in a single case, with the exception of extra and best Italians, of which 1,380 (or 11½ great hundreds) go to each case; or small eggs that take 1,620 (or 13½ great hundreds) and 1,680 (14 great hundreds) to fill a case.

There is an allowance to the merchants from the importers of 60 eggs (or one-half hundred) to compensate for any broken or bad eggs there may be in each case, and 30 eggs (one-fourth hundred) on each half case. This allowance, however, is not recognized as being due from egg merchants to retailers, as the egg merchants have often to repack the goods, on account of damage or other causes, and the half hundred is taken into account. All claims must be made within . three clear days from date of delivery order.

---

[1] Four double Gloucesters weigh 112 pounds, and eight singles the same.
[2] A great hundred equals 120.

The terms of payment of the London wholesale egg market are that on all accounts paid within seven days from date of invoice there shall be a discount of 2d. on every pound sterling.

The following rules of the London egg market (limited) came into operation on January 1, 1897:

RULE 1. The market shall be held every Monday, except when such Monday falls on Christmas Day or on a bank holiday, in which case it shall be held on the day following, or such other day as may be appointed by the committee. The committee shall also have the power to close the market at any time or times that they may think fit, by affixing a notice to that effect in the market, on or before the previous market day.

RULE 2. Sundays, Good Friday, Christmas Day, and bank holidays shall not count as business days.

RULE 3. All goods are to be paid for and the price of the same is payable at seven days from date of invoice (or before delivery if required at the time of sale), and on all goods which shall be so paid there shall be allowed a discount of 2d. on the pound.

RULE 4. A sale note given to and accepted by a buyer shall be equally binding on seller and buyer, and shall thereby constitute a valid contract, and the seller is in all cases the authorized agent of the buyer to sign the sale note on the buyer's behalf.

RULE 5. No person shall be at liberty to buy in the above market, unless he either buys personally or through some authorized agent, whose name and address is to be left in writing by such buyer at the office of the company; and such agent shall have authority to buy in the above market and to bind his principal by any purchase made by him therein; and the sale note accepted by such agent shall in all respects bind and be enforceable against such principal, as if he had signed such sale note n his own proper handwriting. The authority of the agent herein referred to shall continue until written revocation of such authority shall be left by the principal at the said registered office.

RULE 6. The market prices ruling on Monday shall remain in force until the following Thursday at noon. All goods sold or arriving after that time shall be subject to the following Monday's prices, unless distinctly stipulated to the contrary; but this provision is not to affect goods sold previous to noon on Thursday, should prices advance on the following Monday.

RULE 7. For all purposes the term "one hundred" shall mean 120 eggs.

RULE 8. An allowance of half a hundred shall be made on every case, and a quarter on every half case of fowl's eggs, to compensate for broken and bad eggs. Example: Should one hundred eggs be found broken or bad in a case, the extra allowance shall be limited to half a hundred.

RULE 9. Rule 8 is not to apply to sales made at so much per case, but all eggs sold at so much per case shall be considered to be sold with all faults (unless otherwise stipulated), and no claim whatever shall be made in respect thereof.

RULE 10. All claims of every description shall be made within three business days of the date of sale, or should the goods bought not have arrived on the date of sale, then within three business days from the date of arrival on railway, wharf, or docks, as provided by Rule 13 hereof; and unless this is done no claim will be entertained, allowed, or enforceable; and in no case shall any claim be allowed unless, simultaneously with the making of the same, sellers are invited to inspect the goods and have full opportunity of verifying claim.

RULE 11. When any claims in respect of the bulk on any parcel of eggs are made within the recognized time, an average of the waste shall be made by unpacking at the rate of three cases out of the first ten cases, and then by unpacking one case out of every additional ten cases, such cases to be selected by lot. Damaged cases to be unpacked apart, and not included in the average.

RULE 12. All eggs short-packed to be allowed for in full, the usual allowance of half a hundred per case not affecting this rule.

RULE 13. Unless otherwise stipulated, all goods are sold at the railway station, wharf, or docks in London, and will be at the risk of purchaser two business days after sale. If the same have not arrived at date of sale, then they will be at the risk of the purchaser two business days after arrival. Nothing herein is to affect the seller's lien for the price.

RULE 14. Delivery orders given to carriers at the request of buyers are to be considered as having been given to the buyers.

RULE 15. No buyer shall be at liberty to refuse delivery or acceptance, as the case may be, of goods after two business days after delivery of order has been received by the buyer or his carrier ; or, in case the goods have not yet arrived, then two business days after their arrival.

RULE 16. Factors, agents, or merchants making advances on goods shall have full power of immediate sale without any notice whatever.

RULE 17. In case of nonfulfillment of contract, either party shall have the right of repurchase or resale, as the case may be, either publicly or privately, during seven business days next ensuing. When the amount of damages has been ascertained by such repurchase or resale, the amount shall on demand be paid by the party in default, and be recoverable as a liquidated demand or debt. This rule does not apply to cases of default of payment by the buyer, which are dealt with and provided for in the next succeeding rule.

RULE 18. Sellers shall be at liberty to sell any goods sold by them and not paid for in accordance with the sale note, at such time and in such manner as they think fit, and to apply the proceeds of said sale toward the satisfaction of the price due to them, and to recover any balance due as and by way of liquidated demand or debt ; and such sellers shall not be accountable to the buyers in respect of such sales, unless in case of dispute it shall be found that the sellers willfully sold the said goods at less price than could have been reasonably obtained.

RULE 19. *Arbitration.*—In case any dispute shall arise out of the contracts made subject to these rules, the matter can, by arrangement between the parties, be referred to arbitration, provided that all disputes as to what were ruling market values on a particular day shall be settled under the arbitration clauses hereinafter set forth. When the parties agree to submit any dispute or disputes to arbitration, or a dispute arises as to market values on a particular day or days, the following arbitration clauses shall apply : (a) The matter shall be referred to two arbitrators, one to be chosen by each party in difference, the said arbitrators having power, either before or after they shall enter upon the reference, to call in a third arbitrator, if they shall deem it necessary. (b) In the event of any one of the disputing parties appointing an arbitrator and the other refusing, or by noon of the second business day following notice of the appointment neglecting to do so (such notice to be delivered personally or left at the usual place of business of such other party), or in case the arbitrators appointed by the parties shall not within seven days after the appointment agree to an award or appoint a third arbitrator, or, after the appointment of such arbitrator, they or any two of them shall not within seven days agree to an award, or in case of the death, refusal to act, or incapacity within the like time of any of such three arbitrators, then on application of either of the disputing parties the question in dispute shall stand referred to two arbitrators, to be nominated by the chairman (for the time being) of the market ; or in case of his absence, illness, or interest in the matter in dispute, then the vice-chairman, if not interested ; and in case of his absence, illness, or interest in the matter in dispute, then by the committee, the arbitrators so chosen to have power, either before or after they shall enter upon the reference, to appoint a third arbitrator; and in case the two arbitrators so appointed, whether by the chairman, vice chairman, or the committee, shall not within seven days agree to an award or appoint a third arbitrator, then the committee shall appoint a third arbitrator, and shall, in case of the death, refusal to act, or incapacity of any such three arbitrators, from time to time substitute a new arbitrator in the place of the arbitrator so dying, refusing to act, or incapacitated. (c) The arbitrators shall in all cases be members of the London egg market (limited), and such other persons as the committee may appoint, and no person having an interest in the dispute shall be competent to act on any arbitration. (d) The award of any two arbitrators in writing, signed by them (subject only to right of appeal hereinafter mentioned), shall be conclusive and binding on all disputing parties, both with respect to the matters in dispute and all expenses of the reference and award; and this agreement to refer shall not be revocable by either party. (e) No arbitrator shall be entitled to demand a higher fee than 21s. for every requisite sitting. (f) In case either party shall be dissatisfied with the award a right of appeal shall lie to the committee of the market, provided it be claimed not later than noon on the second business day after that on which the objecting party shall have notice of the award, and provided also the appellant do pay to the market the sum of £10 as a fee for the investigation; and an award signed by the chairman of the meeting which shall hear such appeal, and countersigned by the secretary or his substitute, shall be deemed to be the award of the committee and shall in all cases be final. (g) The committee shall have power to direct by whom or in what proportion the expenses of the reference, appeal, and awards (including amount of the said fee) shall be borne and paid. (h) In all cases of disputes of any kind between the sellers and buyers, and for all cases whatsoever, the arbitrators herein referred to shall have power to determine what were the ruling market values on any particular day. (i) No member of the committee having any interest in the matter in dispute shall vote on the question of the appointment of arbitrators, or, in case of an appeal, sit or vote on the committee; nor shall the arbitrator whose decision is appealed against sit or vote on the committee. (j) For the purpose of enforcing any award by attachment or otherwise this rule and any contract referring thereto may be made a rule of any court of record. (k) The fee shall be deposited with the secretary of the market before the arbitration is entered upon by each party in dispute. (l) After the award the secretary shall refund the fee paid by the party in whose favor the award shall have been given.

RULE 20. In any action of proceeding and for all purposes the production of a copy of these rules, certified by the secretary (for the time being) of the company, shall be admissible in evidence as being a true copy of, and as, and for the original signed rules, and it shall not be necessary for either party to produce in evidence such original rules.

Suggested conditions of sale note: "Sold to ———— ————, subject to and on the conditions of the London egg market (limited), passed by the committee and adopted by a general meeting of subscribers on the 12th day of November, 1896, a copy of which has been signed by the said -——— ————."

PRICES OF ANIMAL PRODUCTS IN LONDON.

The following are the prevailing prices in the London market, per hundredweight, f. o. b., for the fiscal year of 1898 as compared with 1897:

BACON.

Description.	1898.	1897.
	Shillings.	*Shillings.*
Irish:		
Waterford, sizable	50–61	52–65
Waterford, stout and good	46–55	42–61
C. & L. barreled, size	50–58	46–61
Stout and sixes	44–58	40–57
English, lean	58–62	60–68
English, stout	56–58	58–64
Foreign:		
Continental, sizable	48–60	40–65
Continental, sixes	48–58	38–66
Continental, medium	46–56	36–63
American, middles	32–33	30–34
American, Cumberland cut	31–34	28–30
American, singed sides	30–34	34–38
Canadian, singed sides	36–44	....
Canadian, pea fed	46–50	46–52

FRESH BEEF.

The fresh or refrigerated beef from the United States still continues to hold its own against that from every other country in the world. This beef arrives in excellent condition, as a rule, and a large quantity still continues to be sold as "best English," and "Scotch." The following are the prevailing prices of beef in the London market, per stone of 8 pounds, or butcher's stone:

	s. d.	s. d.
Scotch	3 8 to	4 0
English	3 8 to	4 6
American, Birkenhead killed	2 6 to	3 4
American, Deptford killed	2 10 to	3 4
Argentine Republic	2 2 to	2 8
American, chilled, hind quarters	2 10 to	4 8
American, chilled, fore quarters	1 6 to	2 0
Australian, frozen, hind quarters	1 7 to	1 9
New Zealand, frozen, hind quarters		2 0

The prices vary from time to time, according to the supply and demand. The above prices are quite low, especially for "Deptford killed," as the price for that beef will frequently be from 3s. 8d. to 3s. 10d. per stone.

BUTTER.

The shipments of butter for 1897 have generally held their own from all countries except Sweden, Germany, France, and Italy, the trade from these countries having fallen off during 1897 as compared with 1896. All other countries have increased their output, especially the United States and Denmark. The Argentine Republic fell off in her shipments for 1897, but this trade has been of a rapid growth since its commencement. During 1894 only 5 hundredweight were shipped to Great Britain from this latter country.

The British colonies are all increasing their shipments of butter to the mother country; are also doing all they can to increase the trade in all kinds of agricultural produce.

The butter from the United States has undoubtedly a much better reputation in this market than it had two or three years ago, and is giving very good satisfaction to those who purchase it, from the wholesale dealer to the consumer. The better reputation of our butter is undoubtedly due to the efforts and work of the U. S. Department of Agriculture. This work and the samples of butter sent to Great Britain by the Department have successfully convinced the British produce merchant that good butter, and any quantity of it, can be made in the United States; and while there has been much accomplished in the direction indicated, there is yet much more to be done in the way of establishing and maintaining this better reputation for our butter in the English market.

A large quantity of Australian and New Zealand butter has recently been shipped back to those countries on account of the low prices in London at the time and the higher prices prevailing in Australia. The production of butter in Victoria this year is insufficient to meet the local demand.

MARGARINE.

Holland is the largest exporter of this product to Great Britain, while the United States is the smallest. This seems very singular, as the United States surely is capable of producing more fat and oil, from which margarine is manufactured, than Holland. If the different State laws do not interfere with the manufacture of margarine, there is no reason why a large trade should not be built up between the United States and Great Britain. I presume there would be some risk of the margarine interfering with the shipments of butter from the United States if shipped in large quantities.

The following is a copy of the British law for the manufacture and sale of margarine:

The margarine act.

Whereas it is expedient that further provision should be made for protecting the public against the sale, as butter, of substances made in imitation of butter, as well as butter mixed with any such substances:

1. This act may be cited as the margarine act, 1887.

2. This act shall come into operation on the first day of January, one thousand eight hundred and eighty-eight.

3. The word "butter" shall mean the substance usually known as butter made exclusively from milk or cream, or both, with or without salt or other preservative, and with or without the addition of coloring matter.

The word "margarine" shall mean all substances, whether compounds or otherwise, prepared in imitation of butter, and whether mixed with butter or not, and no such substance shall be lawfully sold except under the name of margarine, and under the conditions set forth in this act.

4. Every person dealing in margarine, whether wholesale or retail, whether a manufacturer, importer, or as consignor or consignee, or as commission agent or otherwise, who is found guilty of an offense under this act, shall be liable on summary conviction for the first offense to a fine not exceeding twenty pounds, and for the second offense to a fine not exceeding fifty pounds, and for the third or any subsequent offense to a fine not exceeding one hundred pounds.

5. Where an employer is charged with an offense against this act, he shall be entitled, upon information duly laid by him, to have any other person whom he charges as the actual offender brought before the court at the time appointed for hearing the charge, and if, after the commission of the offense is proved, the employer proves to the satisfaction of the court that he has used due diligence to . enforce the execution of the act, and that the said other person has committed the offense in question without his knowledge, consent, or connivance, the said other person shall be summarily convicted of such offense, and the employer shall be exempt from any penalty.

6. Every person dealing in margarine in the manner described in the preceding section shall conform to the following regulations: Every package, whether opened or closed, and containing margarine, shall be branded or duly marked "margarine" on the top, bottom, and sides, in printed capital letters not less than three-quarters of an inch square ; and if such margarine be exposed for sale by retail there shall be attached to each parcel thereof so exposed, and in such manner as to be clearly visible to the purchaser, a label marked in printed capital letters not less than one and a half inches square, "margarine ;" and every person selling margarine by retail, save in a package duly branded or durably marked as aforesaid, shall in every case deliver the same to the purchaser in or with a paper wrapper, on which shall be printed in capital letters not less than a quarter of an inch square, "margarine."

7. Every person dealing with, selling, or exposing, or offering for sale, or having in his possession for the purpose of sale, any quantity of margarine contrary to the provisions of this act, shall be liable to conviction for an offense against this act, unless he shows to the satisfaction of the court before whom he is charged that he purchased the article in question as butter, and with a written warranty or invoice to that effect, that he had no reason to believe at the time when he sold it that the article was other than butter, and that he sold it in the same state as when he purchased it ; and in such case he shall be discharged from the prosecution, but shall be liable to pay the costs incurred by the prosecutor unless he shall have given due notice to him that he will rely upon the above defense.

8. All margarine imported into the United Kingdom of Great Britain and Ireland, and all margarine whether imported or manufactured within the United Kingdom of Great Britain and Ireland, shall, whenever forwarded by any public conveyance, be duly consigned as margarine ; and it shall be lawful for any officer of Her Majesty's customs or inland revenue, or any medical officer of health, inspector of nuisances, or police constable, authorized under section 13 of the sale of food and drugs act, 1875. to procure samples for analysis if he shall have reasons to believe that the provisions of this act are infringed on this behalf, to examine and take samples from any package, and ascertain, if necessary by submitting the same to be analyzed, whether an offense against this act has been committed.

9. Every manufactory of margarine within the United Kingdom of Great Britain and Ireland shall be registered by the owner or occupier thereof with the local authority from time to time in such manner as the local government boards of England and Ireland and the secretary for Scotland, respectively, may direct,

and every such owner or occupier carrying on such manufacture in a manufactory not duly registered shall be guilty of an offense under this act.

10. Any officer authorized to take samples under the sale of food and drugs act, '1875' may, without going through the form of purchase provided by that act, but otherwise acting in all respects in accordance with the provisions of the said act as to dealing with samples, take for the purposes of analysis samples of any butter, or substances purporting to be butter, which are exposed for sale, and are not marked margarine, as provided by this act, and any such substance not being marked shall be presumed to be exposed for sale as butter.

11. Any part of any penalty recovered under this act may, if the court shall so direct, be paid to the person who proceeds for the same, to reimburse him for the legal costs of obtaining the analysis, and any other reasonable expenses to which the court shall consider him entitled.

12. All proceedings under this act shall, save as expressly varied by this act, be the same as prescribed by sections 12 to 28, inclusive, of the sale of food and drugs act, 1875, and all officers employed under that act are hereby empowered and required to carry out the provisions of this act.

13. The expression "local authority" shall mean any local authority authorized to appoint a public analyst under the sale of food and drugs act, 1875.

NOTES.—It was decided in the case of Smart & Son v. Watts, heard in 1895, that in accordance with section 10 all the formalities necessary under the sale of food and drugs act, 1875, must be carried out; and although the defendant admitted that the substance was margarine, still it was necessary that it should be analyzed.

It was held in the case of Moore v. Pearce's Dining and Refreshment Rooms (limited), decided in 1895, that section 6 of the act did not apply to slices of bread and butter sold in a refreshment room where notices were exhibited stating that the butter supplied was a mixture.

In 1895, in the World's Tea Company v. Gardner, it was held that it is not illegal to sell margarine under another name provided all the provisions of the act are complied with. It is not an offense to put a plain wrapper over the printed wrapper, for the act simply says, "in or with," but of course if the word "margarine" were so placed as to be ineffective or misleading it would not satisfy the requirements of the act, but in the case of Bischof v. Toler, in 1895, it was held that if margarine were put into a box duly labeled, the act is complied with, though costs were not allowed because the box was wrapped up in a plain paper, and it was not clear whether it was done at the request or not of the purchaser.

Margarine will bring from 30 to 50 shillings per hundredweight, and margarine mixtures from 50 to 75 shillings per hundredweight, according to quality.

CHEESE.

The cheese trade with the United Kingdom is a very unsteady one from year to year. Some of the countries which export this product have kept up a fairly even supply during the past five years, notably the United States, Holland, France, and New Zealand. Others have fallen off in their export, as Russia, Germany, Victoria, New South Wales, and Newfoundland; while Italy and Canada have made a steady increase, as follows: Italy, 1893, 143 hundredweights; 1894, 400; 1895, 794; 1896, 1,328; 1897, 1,892. Canada, 1893, 1,046,704 hundredweights; 1894, 1,142,104; 1895, 1,150,018; 1896, 1,234,297; 1897, 1,526,664.

The cause of the short supply is on account of the scarcity of cattle in Germany and Russia and the extreme dry weather throughout Australia. There is a prevailing opinion among the provision mer-. chants of London that the large quantities of frozen and tinned meat that are imported will in time largely interfere with the cheese trade of Great Britain. As this class of meat can now be purchased at a less price per pound than cheese, many poor people who were compelled to eat cheese on account of the high price of meat before the days of refrigerators and the system of preserving in tins came into use will now eat meat from choice and economy. It has been quite a common thing to see a laboring man making a meal of bread (no butter) and cheese and a pint of beer, and many in this country have this only for their breakfast six days in the week.

The prices per hundredweight for the weeks ending August 13, 1897 and 1898, are as follows:

Kind of cheese.	1897.	1898.
	s.	*s.*
English:		
Cheddar	60-66	40-72
Somerset		48-64
Cheshire	60-66	
Wiltshire Loaf	56-62	54-58
Double Gloucester	56-60	35-44
Derby	54	40-42
Foreign:		
United States	44	15-38
Canadian	45	25-39
Gonda	32-44	28-44
Edam	37-47	40-49
Colonial	46-49	36-38

EGGS.

Most of the eggs imported come from Russia, Germany, France, Portugal, and Denmark, some millions of eggs being imported every year. There is an excellent market in London for eggs that are well packed in a neat and attractive package so that they will carry safely.

The following are the wholesale prices of eggs in the London market per great hundred for weeks ending September 3, 1897 and 1898:

Kind of eggs.	1897.	1898.
	s. d. s. d.	*s. d. s. d.*
French, extra	8 6-9 6	9 9-10 3
French, best	7 6-8 0	8 3- 9 0
French, seconds	6 6-7 0	7 0- 7 6
Italian, extra	8 3-0 0	7 6- 7 9
Italian, seconds	6 6-7 6	6 6- 7 3
Hungarian	5 3-6 9	5 3- 6 6
Russian	6 0-6 0	5 6- 6 0
Danish	7 6-9 6	7 0- 9 9

SOME AGRICULTURAL EXPERIMENT STATION WORK.

Many of the State agricultural experiment stations are conducting investigations along the line of work pursued by the Bureau of Animal Industry, and the results are published in bulletin form by the respective States, in accordance with law. The attempt is not made here to present abstracts of all the bulletins relating to the subjects embraced in animal industry which have recently been issued by the experiment stations, but abstracts are given of a few which present new conditions or which have been conducted along new lines. An earnest effort is made not to express an opinion not given in the bulletin abstracted, and consequently the Bureau of Animal Industry does not vouch for any of the opinions expressed.

THE FEEDING OF LAMBS.

[Hon. James Wilson and C. F. Curtiss, M. S. R., Bulletin No. 33, Iowa Experiment Station.]

The fact that the best mutton breeds are handled on the richest lands of Europe suggested that Iowa, with her rich grasses and cheap grain, might become the home of the best breeds of mutton sheep. The consideration led to the experiment detailed in Bulletin No. 33, and comprehended the test of several improved breeds. Ten spring lambs of each of nine pedigreed breeds, 10 crosses between the Shropshire and Merino, 10 range lambs, and 5 yearling Shropshire wethers were used. The following is said of the general characteristics of the breeds:

The several improved breeds are the result of development along special lines. The Merino is the fine-wool sheep, and has been popular for that quality; it was desirable to ascertain its comparative mutton value. The Horned Dorset is famous for its high fecundity, being one of the most prolific of the breeds, and peculiarly valuable when spring lambs are desired from it, its crosses, or its grades; it was desirable to learn of its comparative feeding value at different ages. The Leicesters, Lincolns, and Cotswolds are the heavy, long-wooled mutton breeds developed on the heaviest English pastures. The Down breeds are noted for good mutton qualities. The 10 range lambs were representatives of that extensive locality of our country west of the one hundredth meridian where sheep can be bred in semiwild conditions, but where grains and hay for winter finishing are limited, owing to limited rainfall.

The period of preliminary feeding covered the months of November and December, the test beginning January 1 and continuing ninety

463

days. The following summary of the feeding for the entire period is taken from a complete monthly record:

Feeding record of ninety days with different breeds of lambs.

Breed.	Shelled corn.	Oats.	Bran.	Oil meal.	Turnips.	Mangels.	Clover hay.	Pea hay.
	Pounds.	Pounds.	Pounds.	Pounds.	Pounds	Pounds.	Pounds.	Pounds.
10 Southdown lambs.......	731	753	111	174	99	635	1,385	164
10 Shropshire lambs	808	807	120	189	112	670	1,347	164
10 Oxford lambs	931	933	137	216	115	985	1,613	164
10 Suffolk lambs	950	951	141	223	121	779	1,654	164
10 Lincoln lambs...........	928	930	138	217	115	786	1,660	164
9 Leicester lambs	793	793	122	193	105	806	1,443	164
10 Cotswold lambs	923	930	138	217	127	774	1,665	163
10 Dorset lambs	859	861	127	200 ·	123	847	1,570	164
10 Merino lambs	680	678	101	157	108	635	876	155
10 crossbred lambs........	713	714	107	166	120	623	1,005	153
10 range lambs	572	570	84	133	78	429	1,013	159
5 Shropshire yearlings	464	463	71	107	73	423	570	123

Breed.	Timothy hay.	Total gain.	Average daily gain per head.	Total dry matter.	Amount dry matter per pound of gain.	Total cost of feed.	Cost of feed per pound of gain.
	Pounds.	Pounds.	Pound.	Pounds.	Pounds.	Dollars.	Cents.
10 Southdown lambs	12	405.5	0.45	2,990.2	7.38	11.84	2.93
10 Shropshire lambs........	12	429.5	.48	3,061.7	7.18	12.37	2.88
10 Oxford lambs	14	472.5	.52	3,602.5	7.40	14.31	3.03
10 Suffolk lambs	14	496.5	.55	3,667.8	7.40	14.66	2.95
10 Lincoln lambs	16	499.5	.55	3,639.6	7.29	14.47	2.89
9 Leicester lambs	12	424	.52	3,176.4	7.49	12.55	2.93
10 Cotswold lambs	16	556.5	.62	3,633.5	6.53	14.49	2.60
10 Dorset lambs............	15	436	.48	3,422.8	7.85	13.31	3.05
10 Merino lambs	10	258	.29	2,412.5	9.35	9.76	3.78
10 crossbred lambs	12	370	.41	2,596.4	7.02	10.46	2.83
10 range lambs	11	333	.37	2,277.9	6.84	9.02	2.71
5 Shropshire yearlings	6	149.5	.33	1,638.3	11.00	6.64	4.44

The total gain made by all the lambs was 4,678 pounds from 34,501.5 pounds of dry matter in the feed consumed—a rate of 1 pound of gain for each 7.37 pounds of dry matter. The yearlings required 11 pounds of dry matter per pound of gain, or nearly 50 per cent more feed for a given gain than the lambs.

The average daily gain made by the whole number of lambs is 0.48 pound per head, and the average made by the seven most prominent mutton breeds, grouped separately, is 0.53, or a little over half a pound per head.

The feeds used in the experiments were rated at the following prices, based upon the commercial values prevailing in the local market at that time:

	Cents per cwt.
Bran..	40
Oats	40
Shelled corn...........	28.5
Oil meal	90
Hay...	28
Turnips and mangels	5

At these prices for grain it was found that the total gain of 4,678 pounds made by the 109 lambs was produced at a cost of 2.93 cents per pound for feed consumed. The first seven breeds made a total gain of 3,281 pounds, at a cost of 2.88 cents a pound. The five yearlings made a total gain of 149.5 pounds, at a cost of 4.44 cents a pound.

The first and final weights and gains of the ninety-day test period were as follows:

First and final weights and gain for the ninety-day test.

Breed.	Weight Jan. 1.	Wool sheared (Mar. 16-19).	Weight Mar. 31 (without wool).	Weight Mar. 31 (including wool).	Total gain.
	Pounds.	*Pounds.*	*Pounds.*	*Pounds.*	*Pounds.*
10 Southdown lambs	912	67.5	1,250	1,317.5	405.5
10 Shropshire lambs	1,007	87.5	1,349	1,436.5	429.5
10 Oxford lambs	1,190	109.6	1,553	1,662.5	472.5
10 Suffolk lambs	1,165	76.5	1,585	1,661.5	496.5
10 Lincoln lambs	1,206	128.5	1,577	1,705.5	499.5
9 Leicester lambs	1,186	104	1,506	1,610	424
10 Cotswold lambs	1,183	126.5	1,613	1,739.5	556.5
10 Dorset lambs	1,009	68.25	1,377	1,445.25	436
10 Merino lambs	822	95	985	1,080	258
10 Cross-bred lambs	810	75	1,105	1,180	370
10 Range lambs	707	51.25	989	2,040.25	333.25
5 Shropshire yearlings	840	52.5	937	989.5	149.5
	12,037	1,042	15,826	16,868	a 4,831

a The difference between the total gain here and that in the main feeding table is due to the fact that the decimals were dropped in the latter.

The lambs were sold on the Chicago market twenty-four hours after they were loaded. In comparing the weights in the table below with those in the one above, it will be observed that the shrinkage is considerable. This is due to natural causes incident to travel and, to large extent, to the facts that the home weights were taken on full feed and water, and that the two days on the cars were bitterly cold.

Weights and price per hundredweight in Chicago.

Breed.	Weight.	Price.
	Pounds.	*Dollars.*
10 Southdown lambs	1,150	4.75
10 Shropshire lambs	1,210	4.625
10 Oxford lambs	1,420	4.50
10 Suffolk lambs	1,460	4.25
10 Lincoln lambs	1,420	4.50
9 Leicester lambs	1,380	4.50
10 Cotswold lambs	1,420	4.50
10 Dorset lambs	1,210	3.75
10 Merino lambs	940	4.25
10 Cross-bred lambs	1,010	4.50
10 Range lambs	910	4.50
5 Shropshire yearlings	880	4.25

As these lambs had been sheared before going to market, the value of their fleece should be added to the selling price given in the table above. The value of the wool in the "grease" and "scoured" was fixed by the wool merchants, and the table below shows the results:

Average weight of fleece and its value.

Breed.	Average age of fleece.	Average weight of fleece.	Value per pound in natural condition.	Shrinkage in scouring.	Value per pound in scoured condition.	Value of fleece per head.
	Days.	Pounds.	Cents.	Per cent.	Cents.	Dollars.
10 Southdown lambs	366	6.75	11¼	54¼	25	0.75
10 Shropshire lambs	363	8.75	11	55¼	25	.96
10 Oxford lambs	365	10.95	12¼	47	24	1.44
10 Suffolk lambs	364	7.65	11	54¼	24	.85
10 Lincoln lambs	332	12.85	13¼	40	22	1.79
9 Leicester lambs	348	11.5	14¼	38¼	21	1.76
10 Cotswold lambs	334	12.65	13	43¼	23	1.66
10 Dorset lambs	355	6.825	10¼	55¼	24.	.77
10 Merino lambs	359	9.9	9¼	67¼	30	1.06
10 Cross-bred lambs	364	7.5	11¼	53	25	.86
10 Range lambs	321	5.125	12¼	48	24	.67
10 Shropshire yearlings	313	10.5	12½	40	24	1.36

FURTHER EXPERIMENTS IN FEEDING LAMBS.

[C. F. Curtiss, M. S. R., and James W. Wilson, B. Agr., Bulletin No. 35, Iowa Experiment Station.]

This work is a continuation of the experiment discussed in Bulletin No. 33, which is abstracted above. The authors say:

These experiments were undertaken to determine the relative economy of producing mutton and wool compared with other farm products; their value on the market; the requirements of the markets, and the age at which it is most profitable to feed and sell, rather than point out breed distinctions, though the several breeds present variations that have considerable interest.

The lambs arrived at the station in August, when the preparatory period of feeding was begun and continued to September 16. It was soon discovered that many of the lambs were seriously affected with stomach and intestinal worms, and, while prompt remedial measures were taken, this fact prevented better results from the experiment.

The test covered one hundred and six days, and the first and final weights for that period are recorded in the following table:

First and final weights and the total gain of lambs for one hundred and six days.

Breed.	Weight Sept. 16.	Weight Jan. 1.	Total gain.
	Pounds.	*Pounds.*	*Pounds.*
10 Southdown lambs	646	1,024	378
9 Shropshire lambs	789	1,133	344
9 Oxford lambs	853	1,240	387
9 Suffolk lambs	825	1,210	385
9 Lincoln lambs	848	1,292	444
9 Leicester lambs	772	1,197	425
9 Cotswold lambs	767	1,246	479
9 Dorset lambs	741	1,155	414
8 Merino lambs	595	907	312
10 Shropshire ewes	667	1,600	333
Total	7,503	11,404	3,801

The bulletin contains a tabular statement of the feeding test and also gives a condensed summary of the complete feeding record of the first experiment for the purpose of comparison. The difference in the two feeding tests are not marked. The difference which may be noticed in a summary are due principally to other causes—such as the health of the lambs, the weather, the breeds, poor quality of grain, etc. "The relative rank of the breeds in the comparison and cost of gains is much the same in both tests. The Cotswolds again led, with the Lincolns and Leicesters closely following. The general average for the Southdowns and Shropshires is the same, and their rank is next to the long-wooled breeds for economy of production, and in this way they are closely followed by the Dorsets, and they in turn by the Oxfords and Suffolks. The Merinos have quite materially improved their feeding record in the second experiment. The variation is doubtless largely due to the fact that the Rambouillets are a larger and more growthy sheep than the other Merinos used in the first experiment."

The cost of the feed per hundredweight in this experiment is given below:

	Cents per cwt.
Bran	35
Oats	35
Shelled corn	20
Oil meal	90
Hay	20
Roots	5
Cabbage	10

The lambs were shipped to Chicago, and were sold in about twenty-four hours after being loaded at Ames. The following table shows the weight in Chicago, the price, and the per cent of dressed mutton:

Weight, price per hundredweight, and per cent of dressed mutton.

Breed.	Weight.	Price per cwt.	Dressed mutton.
	Pounds.	Dollars.	Per cent.
10 Southdown lambs	950	5.75	55.26
9 Shropshire lambs	1,040	5.60	52.85
9 Oxford lambs	1,140	5.40	50.08
9 Suffolk lambs	1,110	5.00	52.53
9 Lincoln lambs	1,200	5.25	51.08
9 Leicester lambs	1,120	5.25	51.87
9 Cotswold lambs	1,140	5.25	51.81
9 Dorset lambs	1,070	5.50	54.11
8 Merino lambs	830	5.00	49.27
10 Shropshire ewes	900	5.65	54.55

The average percentage of dressed mutton for all breeds was 52.29. The average in the previous experiment was 62.3. This difference of 10 per cent is "attributed to the facts that the live weights were taken when the lambs were in full fleece, and also that they were younger and perhaps hardly so fat as the first lot. All things considered, the record of the second lot is better than the first."

The wool.—The returns from the wool in this experiment are somewhat lighter than in the previous one, "owing to the fact that the lambs averaged about three months younger, but the comparison between the breeds is quite similar." The table given below shows the total weight of the wool, average weight of the fleece, and the value of each fleece:

Weight of the wool and value per fleece.

Breed.	Total weight of wool.	Average weight of fleece.	Value per fleece.
	Pounds.	Pounds.	Dollars.
10 Southdown lambs	45.9	4.59	0.64
9 Shropshire lambs	70.5	7.83	1.10
9 Oxford lambs	72.3	8.03	1.16
9 Suffolk lambs	46.8	5.20	.75
9 Lincoln lambs	93.9	10.44	1.56
9 Leicester lambs	80	8.88	1.33
9 Cotswold lambs	87.9	9.77	1.46
9 Dorset lambs	53.7	5.97	.83
8 Rambouillet lambs	52.8	6.60	.73

FEEDING RANGE LAMBS.

[C. F. Curtiss, M. S. A., and James W. Wilson, B. Agr., Bulletin No. 35, Iowa Experiment Station.]

It is recited that the territory west of the one-hundredth meridian, known as the range, is becoming the great breeding ground for cattle and sheep, and that bordering on this territory are seven States which produce millions of bushels of oats and corn and an abundance of coarse feed. These conditions, supplemented in Iowa by the short-ened cattle supply and the loss of over 2,000,000 head of hogs from hog cholera, led the Iowa Station to endeavor to determine what opportunities were offered for a profitable market in feeding some of the surplus products of the seven States to range lambs. To this end 252 head were purchased in New Mexico and were fed most of the month of November as a preliminary period. The test, which covered one hundred and ten days, began on December 1. At this time the flock was divided into four lots of 63 head each. The following table shows the feeding in detail:

Character and cost of feed for lambs for one hundred and ten days.

Lot.	Character of lambs.	Oats.	Corn.	Bran.	Oil meal.	Mangels.	Hay.
		Pounds.	*Pounds.*	*Pounds.*	*Pounds.*	*Pounds.*	*Pounds.*
I	63 shorn Merinos	2,785	3,135	514	324	743	14,360
II	63 coarse wool	2,813	3,168	518	327	743	14,360
III	63 Down cross	2,813	3,168	518	327	743	14,360
IV	63 unshorn Merinos	2,728	3,069	533	317	743	14,360
	Total	11,139	12,540	2,083	1,295	2,972	57,440

Lot.	Character of lambs.	Total gains.	Average daily gain per head.	Dry matter.	Dry matter for 1 pound of gain.	Total cost of feed.	Cost of feed for 1 pound of gain.
		Pounds.	*Pounds.*	*Pounds.*	*Pounds.*	*Dollars.*	*Cents.*
I	63 shorn Merinos	1,846	.266	18,253	9.88	49.83	2.7
II	63 coarse wool	1,784	.257	18,314	10.26	50.04	2.8
III	63 Down cross	1,822	.263	18,314	10.05	50.04	2.74
IV	63 unshorn Merinos	1,740	.251	18,153	10.43	49.50	2.84
	Total	7,192	.259	73,034	10.15	199.41	2.77

The figures show that it required more feed (dry matter) to produce a pound of gain with these range lambs than with the pure-bred lambs employed in other experiments. This is due to the fact that the range lambs ate more greedily of hay than the pure-bred lambs, and ate "quite sparingly of grain until they had been on feed for several months."

The following is the record of the weights and gains for each lot during the one hundred and ten days they were on feed:

Weights and gains for one hundred and ten days.

Lot.	Character of lambs.	Weight.		Weight.		Average gain per head.
		Total Mar. 1.	Average Mar. 1.	Total Mar. 1.	Average Mar. 1.	
		Pounds.	*Pounds.*	*Pounds.*	*Pounds.*	*Pounds.*
I	63 shorn Merinos	2,950	46.9	4,796	76.1	29.2
II	63 coarse wool	3,398	52.8	5,114	81.1	28.3
III	63 Down cross	3,390	53.8	5,212	82.7	28.9
IV	63 unshorn Merinos	3,340	53	5,080	80.6	27.6
	Total	13,010	51.6	20,202	80.1	28.5

At the conclusion of the feeding test the lambs were shipped to Chicago, and sold on the market March 23. The price obtained and percentage of dressed mutton were as follows:

Selling price and per cent of dressed mutton.

Lot.	Character of lambs.	Selling price.	Dressed mutton.
		Dollars.	*Per cent.*
I	Shorn Merinos	4.75	55.9
II	Long wools	5.15	53.5
III	Down cross	5.25	52.8
IV	Unshorn Merinos	5.00	52.8

These cost the station, delivered and ready to go into the experiment December 1, about $3.80 per hundredweight. The net profit for Lot I was $26.59; Lot II, $47.53; Lot III, $55.76; Lot IV, $44.09; total, $173.07. To the total should be added $1.90, which was deducted on account of showing effect of scab. The prices per hundredweight paid for feed were: Bran, 35 cents; oats, 35; shelled corn, 20; oil meal, 90; hay, 20; roots, 5. "The above prices are equivalent to 11.2 cents per bushel for the corn and oats. If to these prices be added the net profit in handling this lot of lambs, after deducting the expense of feeding, interest on investment, and taxes, the returns realized for the gain would be equivalent to fully 100 per cent better than the prevailing market value, aside from the advantage of affording a home market for the unfinished products of the farm. While these lambs are not of the class that farmers could afford to raise on high-priced lands, they can nevertheless be fed at a good profit under conditions similar to those reported in this bulletin."

FEEDING FOR MUTTON IN SOUTH DAKOTA.

[E. C. Chilcott and E. A. Burnett, B. S., Bulletin No. 55, South Dakota Experiment Station.]

South Dakota is naturally well adapted for sheep husbandry. The abundance of native grasses and rich pastures, with the additional advantage of location in the zone of cheap food supply, should make sheep husbandry a business of great importance. The great grain fields lie within easy reach of the immense ranges, where sheep may be produced in almost unlimited numbers and at much less cost, evidently, than upon the farms of the East.

The Division of Statistics of this Department gives the number of sheep in South Dakota on January 1, 1897, as 336,250. It is said that this number of sheep could easily be supported in a single county of the State, and that the grass which now annually goes to waste upon unoccupied lands would support enough sheep to consume all the coarse grains and fodder produced on the farms. Another phase of the situation is that "hundreds of thousands of bushels of grain are annually sold at a price that entails an actual loss to the producer."

It is the desire of Messrs. Chilcott and Burnett that the sheep men of South Dakota shall not only produce sheep enough to consume all the grass now going to waste, but to "feed to a finish" on those fodders and grains of the farms which are now produced and disposed of without profit. In order to bring about this condition of things, a series of experiments was begun.

The object of the experiment in hand was to determine the relative value of different food stuffs raised upon the farm in making up a ration for fattening sheep. A "balanced ration," in which the different elements of the food are supposed to be combined so as to produce the most economical results, was selected as the standard of comparison.

Forty-five lambs of ordinary quality were purchased, and from September 30 to November 28 were being prepared for the experiment upon an alfalfa field. In addition they received daily a small quantity of oats and barley. During this period of eight weeks the total gain was 508 pounds, or over 11 pounds per head. This was made at less cost than the gain on the rations after the experiment was begun.

The lambs were divided into five lots of 9 head each. They were fed all the millet hay they would eat, and were confined in sheds with small yards for exercise on pleasant days. They were watered once a day and weighed once a week after feeding, but before watering. Herewith is the ration fed to the lambs of each lot, showing the total amount, the cost, and the nutritive ratio.

Average daily ration for one lamb.

Lot 1:   Pounds.
    Corn 0.359
    Oats .... .359
    Shorts .... .359
    Oil meal .... .359
    Hay .... .875

    Total air-dry matter 2.211
    Nutritive ratio 1:5.2
    Total daily cost for one lamb .... 0.835 cent.
Lot 2:
    Corn 0.717
    Oats .... .717
    Hay .... .851

    Total air-dry matter 2.385
    Nutritive ratio 1:8.6
    Total daily cost for one lamb .... 0.652 cent.
Lot 3:
    Oats 0.718
    Wheat .... .718
    Hay .... .862

    Total air-dry matter 2.298
    Nutritive ratio 1:8.3
    Total daily cost for one lamb .... 1.044 cents.
Lot 4:
    Oats 0.718
    Barley .... .718
    Hay .... .865

    Total air-dry matter 2.301
    Nutritive ratio 1:7.8
    Total daily cost for one lamb .... 0.578 cent.
Lot 5:
    Wheat 0.718
    Barley .... .718
    Hay .... .897

    Total air-dry matter 2.333
    Nutritive ratio 1:7
    Total daily cost for one lamb .... 0.96 cent.

Summary of results of lamb feeding experiments.

	Lot 1.	Lot 2.	Lot 3.	Lot 4.	Lot 5.
Millet hay .... pounds..	379	376	384	382	390
Prairie hay .... do....	496	475	478	483	507
Total hay .... do....	875	851	862	865	897
Corn .... do....	359	717	....	....	....
Oats .... do....	359	717	718	718	....
Wheat .... do....	....	....	718	....	718
Barley .... do....	....	....	....	718	718
Shorts .... do....	359	....	....	....	....
Oil meal .... do....	359	....	....	....	....
Total grain .... do....	1,436	1,434	1,436	1,436	1,436
Weights at beginning .... do....	587	602	600	570	582
Weights at ending .... do....	818	827	795	776	799
Gain .... do....	231	225	195	206	217
Total dry matter .... do....	2,081	2,057	2,068	2,071	2,100
Dry matter for 1 pound of grain .... do....	9	9.14	10.6	10	9.67
Total cost of feed	$8.35	$6.52	$10.44	$5.78	$9.60
Cost of grain per pound .... cents.	3.6	2.45	5.35	.28	4.43
Nutritive ratio	1:5.2	1:8.6	1:8.3	1:7.8	1:7

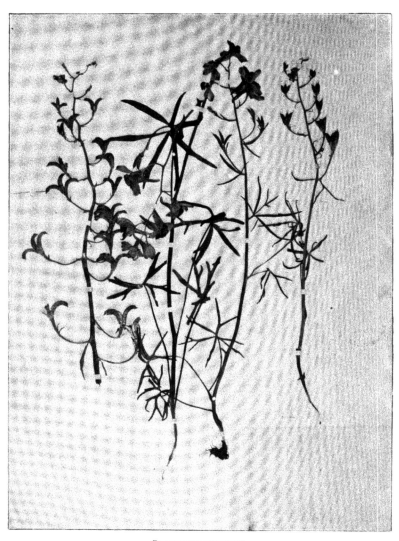

DELPHINIUM MENZIESII.

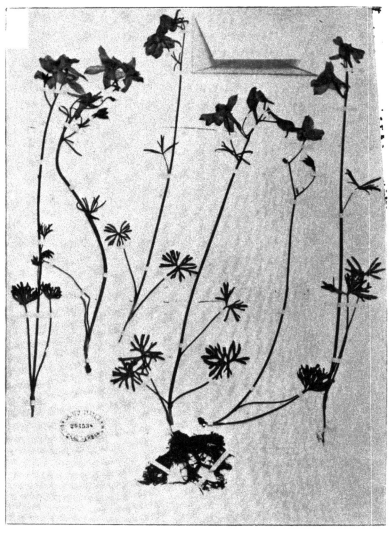

DELPHINIUM MENZIESII.

Delphinium scopulorum.

On January 16 one lamb of Lot 3 died. To equalize this loss one lamb was withdrawn from each of the other four lots, so that there were nine lambs in each lot seven-seventeenths of the time only. This circumstance should be taken into consideration in making deductions from the summary of results.

Three cents per pound was the purchase price of these lambs and the selling price was placed at 4 cents, which was low for the quality of the lambs. A carload would have commanded at least $4\frac{1}{2}$ cents.

The profits on the investment, the finished mutton being reckoned at 4 cents per pound, was as follows:

Lot 1 _____ $6.65
Lot 2 _____ 8.50
Lot 3 _____ 3.86
Lot 4 _____ 8.17
Lot 5 _____ 4.91

In considering the value of the rations the experimenters concluded that all are favorable to good gains, but all are not equally favorable to profits. The rations yielding the highest profits were those fed to Lot 2, which produced gains at 2.45 cents per pound, and Lot 3, which produced gains at 2.8 cents per pound. "In studying the tables we find that the largest gains are not necessarily the cheapest, nor the smallest gains necessarily the most expensive." It was also found that the best and cheapest gains were made in feeding a sheep as nearly as possible to its full capacity. Overfeeding was always attended by loss. The heaviest feeding should be done during the last four or six weeks of the feeding period. Corn and oats, those grains most easily produced in South Dakota, gave the cheapest gains, namely, 2.45 cents per pound.

LARKSPUR POISONING OF SHEEP.

[E. V. Wilcox, Ph. D., Bulletin No. 15, Montana Experiment Station.]

Upon the large western ranges, where sheep are almost entirely dependent upon indigenous plants for subsistence, serious losses from poisoning have been complained of for the last thirty years. The losses are most serious in the springtime, when the animals are tempted to eat any green weed which starts before the grass grows. It is generally conceded in Montana that the losses from plant poisoning exceed those from all other causes combined. The most extensive losses occur in May and June, but frequently occur at other seasons, and sometimes as late as November.

The investigations conducted by Dr. Wilcox, with the assistance of Dr. Traphagen, chemist of the Montana Station, have been produc-

tive of some interesting facts.   The first ranch visited was that of a
Dr. Tudor, whose statement about his sheep is as follows:

On April 30 a band of about 2,000 yearling lambs were moved from the place
where they had been grazing to a new locality about 2 miles distant.   Several
of the sheep were taken sick almost immediately upon arriving at the new feeding grounds.   Three died within two hours after their arrival, and the number of
deaths during the whole day was 10.   On the following day 13 more died and
about 500 to 600 showed signs of sickness.   The band was then moved away
from this locality and during the next day, May 2, the greatest mortality occurred,
the number of deaths being over 50.   Twenty-five died May 3, 1 on May 4, 2 on
May 5, and 1 on May 6.

An examination of one of the sheep immediately after death disclosed no unusual conditions in most respects; but the lungs were
extremely heavy, congested, and full of blood, and this blood was
dark, showing that it had not been thoroughly aerated.   "The only
natural conclusion from the postmortem was that the animal had died
from asphyxia, or oxygen starvation, as the result of some sedative
poison, a poison which had paralyzed the respiratory centers of the
nervous system and had prevented the proper action of the lungs in
the purification of the blood."   In several subsequent postmortems
the conditions were the same.

In the stomach contents were found the stems, leaves, and roots of
a species of larkspur (*Delphinium menziesii*).[1]   These were present in
considerable quantities, and in some cases the leaves were so nearly
complete that identification of the plant was easy.   Further work
showed that this plant was plentiful on the range and that it had a
peculiar and definite distribution.   It was not found on the higher
ground, but was strictly confined to the ravines, or coulees.   Along
these small streams it grew in considerable abundance.

A second severe case of poisoning of a herd of sheep occurred two
weeks later than the one on Dr. Tudor's ranch.   This time 1,900
became sick and 150 died.   An investigation of the matter showed
conclusively that the larkspur was again the cause of the trouble.
Dr. Wilcox's investigations and conclusions are summed up in this
bulletin in a clear and concise manner and are given below:

Symptoms.—The symptoms shown by the sheep poisoned by larkspur have a
general resemblance to those of aconite poisoning, but are sometimes different in
several particulars.   The first signs of the poisoning are a slight general stiffness
and a straddling gait, especially of the hind legs.   The stiffness becomes more
and more pronounced until walking is quite difficult and evidently painful.   Soon
there are manifested various involuntary twitchings of the muscles of the legs
and sides of the body.   There is a loss of control or coordination of the muscles.
There is ordinarily no increase in the quantity of the saliva, no dribbling of saliva

---

[1] In connection with this article it will be interesting to read Prof. S. B. Nelson's
remarks on an experiment in feeding *Delphinium menziesii* to sheep, on page 421.

NOTE.—The plates herewith are from specimens in the United States National
Herbarium.   Dr. Wilcox kindly sent seeds of both species to the Department for
the purpose of growing specimens, but they failed to germinate.

from the mouth, no champing of the jaws or attempts at swallowing. The sheep manifest none of the mental disturbances frequently seen in cases of poisoning from other sources, as for example loco-weed and lupine. There is no impairment of the special senses. The sheep seem to hear and see as well and as correctly as under normal conditions of health.

No indications of any disturbances of the digestive functions are to be seen. The appetite remains good, and the sheep eat up to the very last. They were observed eating industriously during the intervals between the attacks of spasms which they have during the last stages.

At first the frequency of the pulse and of the respiratory movements is lessened and the temperature is lowered. The pulse remains very weak, but in the later stages becomes very rapid, in some cases 130 per minute. Toward the last also the respiration is very shallow and rapid. During the final convulsions the respiration is sometimes 120 per minute, but so shallow that the air is simply pumped up and down the windpipe. The air in the lungs is therefore not renewed and the animal dies by asphyxia or suffocation.

So long as the sheep can stand on his feet, or walk, he keeps up with the herd as nearly as possible. The exercise, however, excites him, makes his respiration more rapid, and he has frequently to lie down for a moment and then get up and hobble along after the herd. The worst cases can thus easily be detected, since they straggle behind the rest of the herd.

The later stages of the poisoning follow rather rapidly. The involuntary movements become more frequent and more severe. All four legs tremble and shake violently. In fact, all the muscles of the body contract spasmodically until the animal totters over on his side and dies in the most violent spasms.

These symptoms, which were very constant in the several hundred sheep affected with the poison, made it evident that the larkspur had the effect of arresting the heart's action and respiration and of paralyzing the spinal cord. Stimulants were therefore necessary.

Treatment.—The herder had tried bleeding the sheep, but, of course, with no success. With an already lowered temperature, bleeding would still further reduce the temperature and weaken the animal. Bleeding may give relief in some cases of poisoning, but not where larkspur is the plant concerned. Lard also has been given internally, and no noticeable effect was produced by it. Lard is especially useful where there is bloating, but in larkspur poisoning there is no bloating.

Where the sheep had eaten but a small quantity of larkspur and were noticed soon afterwards, the administration of ammonia or alcohol was found to give good results. One-half cupful of alcohol in water or one teaspoonful of ammonia in a cup of water was given as a dose. We tried also in the earlier stages "XXX" liniment internally in doses of a teaspoonful. It seemed not to have much value for this purpose.

In the later stages neither alcohol nor ammonia nor "XXX" liniment, when given internally, appeared to have the slightest effect. In fact, during the last violent stages the giving of any medicine by way of the mouth seemed useless and even dangerous, for the sheep were unable to swallow, and choked to death. During the first stages three drams of ether given by the mouth had a good effect, and in the later stages one-half dram of ether given hypodermically stimulated the heart's action and respiration. Squibb's ether was used in both methods.

The most effective remedy which was tried, however, was a hypodermic injection of atropine sulphate. A solution was prepared in camphor water in the proportion of four grains of atropine to one fluid ounce of camphor water. Several sheep were treated by this method, and all but one so treated recovered. Doses of three different sizes were administered—one-third, one-fourth, and one-sixth of a grain of atropine sulphate. This was in solution in camphor water, as just described, so that in order to give the atropine in the quantities mentioned it was necessary to use 40, 30, and 20 minims, respectively, of the solution.

Atropine as a direct stimulant of the heart's action and respiration is perhaps the most powerful drug known to medical science. When used hypodermically its effects are much more immediate than when taken into the stomach, and consequently the doses should be smaller. One-third of a grain is a large dose for an animal of the size of a sheep. In fact, one-twentieth of a grain is quite sufficient in the earlier stages of the poisoning; but the sheep to which these large doses were given were in the very agonies of death. Nothing could be given them by the mouth for the simple reason that the sheep could not swallow. They were lying on their sides and their whole bodies were in spasms. The respiratory movements were extremely rapid, but so weak and shallow that the sheep were getting no pure air into the lungs.

The atropine solution was injected under the skin in the region of the shoulder. The effect of the atropine was shown almost immediately. The pulse at once became stronger, the animal drew a few deep breaths and then began to pant noisily. One minute after the atropine was administered the sheep was lifted upon his feet, when he at once ran away panting loudly. The breathing soon became easier, the involuntary muscular movements ceased, and within five minutes' time the sheep was lying down in a natural position and was almost as quiet as in health.

All sheep, with one exception, which received this treatment reacted in the same way and recovered. This one exception was an interesting case. The sheep had already passed through its last violent spasm, breathing had nearly ceased, and the pulse was so weak as to be almost imperceptible. Atropine (one-third grain) was given as in the other cases. The patient began to breathe deeply and loudly. When placed upon his feet he ran several rods and fell again. The pulse and breathing soon became very irregular and intermittent and at last breathing actually ceased. About one teaspoonful of ammonia was at once dashed into each nostril and the sheep was vigorously shaken. The fumes of the ammonia reached the lungs and caused the sheep to gasp. Breathing was restored. The sheep got up and walked away to a distance of 100 yards. After a few minutes his breathing seemed to be growing weaker and we attempted to give him ammonia in water by the mouth. He could not swallow, however, and as a consequence strangled and died.

In this particular sheep the inability to swallow may have been in part the effect of the atropine. In large doses atropine paralyzes the muscles of the gullet; but sheep which had not been given atropine had a similar difficulty in swallowing.

In our experience we found atropine to be the most prompt and satisfactory remedy, and we would therefore recommend the use of this drug whenever it can be had conveniently. Great precaution should be exercised in its use, since it is a powerful medicine. One should always know exactly how much he is administering. It is only in small doses that atropine has the desired stimulating effect. In large doses it has the opposite effect. We would recommend giving one-sixth to one-fourth grain in the later convulsive stages and in the earlier stages or in mild cases one-twentieth to one-fifteenth of a grain. These doses are for sheep. For cattle we would use four or five times as much, about one grain of atropine, depending somewhat on the size of the animal and the severity of the poisoning.

In the later convulsive stages ammonia fumes in the nostrils act promptly and powerfully. Breathing is stimulated and deepened. If given soon after the sheep have eaten the larkspur ammonia and alcohol are useful stimulants. They may be given together in water. Ether in small doses (2 to 3 drams in water) has also a beneficial effect. It is well to remember that alcohol, ammonia, ether, as well as atropine stimulate the heart's action and respiration only when given in moderate doses. In large doses they all have the opposite effect or act as paralyzers and depressants.

Care in the management of sheep after they are poisoned is quite as important as the giving of medicines. Sheep poisoned with larkspur should be kept as quiet as possible. A trifling fright or excitement may throw them into spasms, and thus result fatally. From the very first the poisoned sheep have considerable difficulty in keeping up with the rest of the herd. They have a stiff and trembling gait. It becomes necessary for them frequently to stop for a moment to rest. In this way they repeatedly fall behind the herd and then run to overtake it again. Thus their excitement is constantly increased until they fall down in spasms.

As soon as the stiffness and straddling gait, which are the first symptoms of larkspur poisoning, are noticed, one or the other of two methods of procedure should be adopted. Either the whole band of sheep should be herded closely and prevented from moving as fast as it usually moves, or, which is perhaps still better, the poisoned sheep should be separated from the others and kept as quiet as may be.

From observation of the action of sheep under the influence of larkspur poisoning, nothing could be more apparent than the advisability of keeping the sheep as quiet as possible. About 5 o'clock in the afternoon the herder began to urge the sheep along toward the corral. Many of the sheep still showed some stiffness in the hind legs. It was five days after the poisoning had occurred and it looked as if all the sheep which were to die from the effects of the larkspur had died. The herder made the band move a trifle faster than usual for about one-half hour. Many of them rapidly became worse during that short time, and some of them had to be taken into a wagon and hauled to the corral. When we reached the corral they were in their last spasms, and could not get upon their feet until treated with atropine, as described above.

Not only is too much exercise dangerous, but any fright is apt to prove fatal. The heart's action is so weakened by the larkspur that at any sudden fright the heart stops beating altogether, and the sheep dies without a struggle. These observations should indicate to any stock raiser the care which is necessary in a case of larkspur poisoning.

There can be no doubt that even in serious poisoning not all of the sheep which have eaten larkspur die. The mortality is increased by driving the sheep too rapidly or by worrying them with dogs or otherwise. Careful management will bring a large proportion safely to recovery, and will prevent the development of the worst symptoms in sheep which have not eaten any large quantity of the larkspur.

In larkspur poisoning, as in other cases, prevention is better than cure, and in order to keep the sheep from being poisoned it is necessary for the herder to know larkspur at sight in all its stages. He should be able to recognize the first leaves which come up in the spring as well as the complete plant in bloom.

Description of the plants.—In Montana, so far as we are aware, there are but two species of larkspur which are common. Larkspur belongs to the genus of plants known as *Delphinium*, and botanists distinguish the two species by the names *Delphinium menziesii* DC., and *Delphinium glaucum* Nuttall. Larkspur belongs to the Crowfoot family, which includes such well-known plants as clematis, buttercup, anemone, columbine, and aconite. Most of the plants of this family have an acrid juice, and at least the larkspur and aconite possess poisonous principles or alkaloids.

The following definitions will, we hope, serve to enable anyone to identify the two species of larkspur which we know to be common in the State.

Delphinium menziesii is the smaller of the two species. It ordinarily attains a height of from 6 to 18 inches. The plant is smooth at its base, but is usually hairy above and upon the flowers. The leaves are five-parted in a palmate manner, and the parts are again cleft two or three times. The ultimate divisions of the leaf are rather narrow. The flowers are of a rich purple color or dark blue, about 1 inch across when fully expanded. Each flower has a backward projecting spur about 1 inch in length. The outer row of flower parts are five in number, and the upper one is prolonged backward into the just-mentioned spur. The inner row of floral parts or petals are four in number, arranged in two pairs. The upper pair is light blue, with darker streaks. All four petals are small as compared with the outer row of floral parts.

Perhaps the only plant whose leaves resemble those of the larkspur, and which is in a condition to be mistaken for larkspur in the early spring, is lupine. Its leaves shoot up in clusters much in the same way as do those of larkspur, but the leaf of the lupine is divided into seven to eleven simple unbranched parts.

This species of larkspur is pretty generally distributed over the State. We have seen specimens from the following counties: Flathead, Teton, Missoula, Ravalli, Deerlodge, Lewis and Clarke, Jefferson, Madison, Gallatin, Meagher, Park, Sweetgrass, Yellowstone, and Carbon. It occurs at all elevations. We have found it from the lowest valley up to a height of 10,500 feet.

The other common species of larkspur in Montana is known to botanists as *Delphinium glaucum* Nuttall. In some localities cattle raisers call it "aconite." But the pure aconite, so far as our observation extends, is found only high up in Gallatin County in the vicinity of the park, and inside of the park. We received specimens of supposed aconite from Big Timber, but they proved to be *Delphinium glaucum*. This species of larkspur often reaches a height of 6 feet. The ordinary specimens are from 3 to 5 feet high. The stem is leafy and considerably branched. The leaves are nearly circular in outline, but are palmately divided into three to five divisions, which are wedge-shaped. The primary divisions are two to three times cleft, and finally these secondary divisions are themselves deeply toothed. The uppermost leaves are much smaller with narrower divisions. The flowers are built on exactly the same plan as are those of the other species of larkspur. They are much smaller and usually of a lighter color. The color varies from dark blue to almost white, but is usually light blue. The flowers are more crowded in a close, compact raceme, and the flowering pedicels are short. The pods, when ripe, are nearly erect and are hairy, as are also all other parts of the plant.

We have found this plant distributed from the lower altitudes up to a height of 9,000 feet. It has a range similar to that of the smaller species, and is usually very abundant in the localities where it occurs.

Besides the two species already mentioned we should perhaps refer to two other species of larkspur found in Montana. Dr. P. A. Rydberg, of Columbia University, informs me that he has collected specimens of *Delphinium scopulorum* Gray at Lima and on Electric Peak. This species differs from *D. glaucum* in its more finely divided leaves, its smaller size, and brighter green colors. It is too rare in the State to be of much economic importance.

Nuttall has described a species under the name of bicolor. In practice, however, it is about impossible to distinguish it from *D. menziesii*, and I believe that these two supposed species belong together as one species.

It will be unnecessary for me to give a description of aconite since it has not been found in Montana, so far as my knowledge goes, except near the edge of the park. Several stock raisers have reported to me cases of deaths from aconite poisoning, but on investigation the plant was found to be in every case the tall larkspur or *Delphinium glaucum*, which is frequently called aconite by ranchers. Aconite and larkspur are two distinct genera of plants and are easily distinguished the one from the other.

Conclusions.—Although the conclusions drawn from our field work and post-mortem examinations were considered well founded, we decided to test the matter further by a direct experiment. From pulverized dried plants of larkspur (*Delphinium menziesii*) extracts were made in water, alcohol, chloroform, and benzole. The alcoholic extract was spoiled by heating too highly while distilling off the alcohol. The extracts in chloroform and benzole, on the other hand, were quite successful. The ordinary chemical tests applied to these extracts showed the presence of alkaloids. No attempt was made to determine just what alkaloids were extracted. As said above, that will be done in the near future. At this time we simply wished to get an extract which would, so far as possible, contain all the active principles of the plant.

An additional experiment.—Mr. James Vestal, of Big Timber, kindly offered us sheep to experiment upon, and on November 6, 1897, we went to the ranch of which Mr. Vestal is manager. Three yearling lambs were selected for experimentation. The first lamb was given the chloroform extract of larkspur. Twenty-five grams of the dried plants had been pulverized and then steeped at a low temperature in chloroform for one-half hour. The extract was poured off and slowly evaporated to dryness and then dissolved in 1 ounce of water. This was given to the first lamb by the mouth. After thirty minutes the lamb showed signs of stiffness, and at the end of two hours the lamb died with convulsions and other symptoms just such as we saw in the sheep previously mentioned. A post-mortem examination made immediately after death disclosed also the same conditions as those recorded above.

The second and third lambs were given larkspur extracts hypodermically. The second was given 1 dram of the chloroform extract made as just described. The third was given 1 dram of a benzole extract of larkspur made in the same way as was the chloroform extract. After fifteen minutes both lambs began to show symptoms of larkspur poisoning, and at the end of one hour the symptoms were so plain and pronounced that it was considered useless to sacrifice the lambs to the experiment. Both were therefore given one-eighth of a grain of atropine, which, with the aid of a small dash of ammonia in the nostrils, counteracted the effects of the poison and the lambs recovered completely.

These experiments are quite in accord with the conclusions reached in the field work, and furnish another strong piece of evidence to the correctness of those conclusions, not only as to the cause of poisoning, but as to remedies to be used.

— —

TUBERCULOSIS IN KANSAS.

[N. S. Mayo, M. S., D. V. M., Bulletin No. 69, Kansas Experiment Station.]

Characteristics.—In this article Dr. Mayo states that tuberculosis is the same disease as tuberculosis in the human family, popularly known as consumption; that it is found more extensively among pure-bred and high-grade cattle than among native Western cattle, "probably on account of inbreeding and the highly artificial state such animals have been subjected to in producing the pure-bred and highly specialized cattle of to-day;" that the disease is contracted from persons or animals affected with the disease, through the sputa and infected food or drink; that there is a tendency for tuberculosis to run through certain families of cattle, due probably to some inherited weakness or to a direct transmission of the germs from parent to offspring; that it can also be transmitted through the medium of the cow's milk.

Insidiousness.—It is stated that this is one of the most insidious animal diseases known. "It is astonishing how badly an animal may be diseased and to all appearance be in good health," says Dr. Mayo, and he gives as an illustration the following:

Several years ago I was called to treat a pure-bred Shorthorn cow that until the day I was called had appeared in excellent health. The disease was diagnosed as tuberculosis and she was destroyed. Postmortem examination showed both lungs badly diseased, a tuberculous abscess in one lung containing a pint of pus (matter). Her heart was a mass of tuberculous tissue, weighing 16.5 pounds, and almost every internal organ more or less diseased. This cow had a sucking calf at her side two months old. The calf was destroyed, and was found to have a tuberculous abscess in one lung as large as a walnut and the bronchial lymphatic glands were also diseased.

Importance.—The importance of tuberculosis is very great, although the resulting deaths are very few, a condition probably due to a large extent to the fact that most cattle are sent to the shambles when quite young.

The chief importance of bovine tuberculosis is its relation to the public health. Tuberculosis, or consumption, is the greatest danger that threatens the human race at present. It is scattered throughout the world, but on account of its insidious nature does not command the attention that its importance deserves. It has been estimated that one-seventh of the total population dies from tuberculosis, and that 125,000 people die annually in the United States from this disease. As tuberculosis of cattle is identical with that of man and the disease can be transmitted to mankind through the milk and flesh, which furnish so large a part of the food of man, the importance of this disease is apparent.

Use of tuberculin.—The tuberculin used was furnished by the Bureau of Animal Industry. Of 81 head tested and reported upon by Dr. Mayo, no bad results from its use appeared except perhaps in one case.

I am led to the opinion that such results, reported by some other experimenters who used the tuberculin prepared by the Bureau of Animal Industry, were due to improper sterilization of instruments or to methods of injection, and not to be attributed to the tuberculin.

With reference to the reliability of tuberculin tests, the author states that from experiment stations, live-stock commissions, and other official sources he had collected reports of 11,313 cattle which had been tested with tuberculin in the United States.

Of this number 5,787 reacted to the test, and postmortem examination revealed tuberculosis in 5,746. Two reacted that did not show tuberculosis, and 9 did not react to the test, but were tuberculous. Adding to this number 81 cattle tested here gives a total of 11,394. Total reacting 5,759; number of errors 12, or about 1 error in 950. When the large number of operators and the varying conditions and circumstances under which the cattle are considered, the results are gratifying, and show that as a means of diagnosing bovine tuberculosis tuberculin is a very reliable test.

Practical application of tuberculin.—It being demonstrated in all experiments that tuberculin is a very reliable means of diagnosing bovine tuberculosis, it is everywhere desirable that measures be taken for the eradication of this disease. The plan followed in Denmark is given:

It consists in testing all animals with tuberculin, separating the tuberculous from the healthy, and keeping the healthy quarters free from infection. It has been demonstrated that tuberculous cows can produce calves free from tuberculosis. As soon as the tuberculous cows drop their calves the latter are taken from the cow at once and fed sterilized milk, to prevent the calves from contracting tuberculosis through the milk. The young calves are tested with tuberculin and all that are affected with hereditary tuberculosis are destroyed. Later the calves are again tested with tuberculin, and any others responding to the test are destroyed. In this manner only healthy animals are raised for breeding and dairy purposes, and bovine tuberculosis is being eradicated from the Danish dairies without the serious loss that would follow the immediate destruction of all tuberculous animals.

TRANSMISSION OF TEXAS FEVER.

[N. S. Mayo, M. S., D. V. M., Bulletin No. 69, Kansas Experiment Station.]

It is generally accepted now that Texas fever is transmitted from one animal to another through the medium of the cattle tick (*Boophilus bovis*). The cattle south of the Texas fever quarantine line, established by the Department of Agriculture, are immune, but they are capable of carrying the ticks to animals north of that line and infecting the cattle there.

Dr. Mayo, desiring to be reassured that the tick is the carrier of the Texas-fever germ, prosecuted an interesting experiment. He obtained from Dr. M. Francis, of the Texas Experiment Station, "eggs of the Southern cattle tick (*Boophilus bovis*). On September 15 [one week after receiving them] these eggs began hatching. * * * On September 22, 300 or 400 of these young ticks were placed on each of two calves, Nos. 1 and 2, and given plenty of time to crawl into the hair." On September 23 a pure-bred Jersey heifer was put in with the calves, and on the 28th "about 200 young ticks (*B. bovis*), that had been received on September 28, were placed upon the heifer." The temperature of the heifer on October 10 was very high, and on the 17th, when she died, reached more than 110°; "the symptoms were those of a typical case of Texas fever." Dr. Mayo says, emphatically:

These experiments prove conclusively that the Southern cattle ticks are the carriers of infection from Southern cattle to Northern cattle. The "tick theory" is no longer a theory; it is a fact, demonstrated beyond a doubt.

10317——31

Treatment.—Medicinal treatment of Texas fever is not satisfactory. A great many remedies have been tried, with no beneficial results apparent. The most satisfactory treatment is good care and surroundings and nourishment to sustain the animal until the fever subsides. The following plan of treatment has given the best results: As soon as an outbreak of Texas fever occurs, remove all susceptible animals to fresh, uninfested ground. Remove all cattle ticks from susceptible animals by greasing with lard or similar oil and scraping the ticks off with a dull knife blade. As Texas fever usually occurs during the summer season, the cattle can be fed green corn fodder. This furnishes a palatable and nutritious food and has a laxative effect upon the bowels.

Sick cattle should be removed to comfortable, shady quarters, and given access to fresh water. Remove ticks as previously described, and feed green corn fodder.

In cases where it is practicable, drenching sick cattle with sweet milk gives good results.

Texas fever is a contagious fever of cattle caused by a microorganism (protozoa). It is carried from Southern cattle to Northern cattle by Southern cattle ticks.

Adult Southern cattle ticks drop off from the Southern cattle, lay eggs, and thus infest the ground with young ticks that carry the germs of Texas fever. Northern cattle passing over this ground get the young Southern cattle ticks and contract Texas fever.

Quarantining against Southern cattle during the summer season is the most effective method of preventing Texas fever.

EXPERIMENTS WITH BLOOD SERUM AS A PREVENTIVE AND CURE FOR TEXAS FEVER.

[J. C. Robert, V. M. D., Bulletin No. 42, Mississippi Experiment Station.]

This bulletin recites that the mild climate, fertile soil, and luxuriant grass crops of Mississippi make stock raising less expensive than in the average Northern State, but that there can be no successful competition with the Northern stockbreeder until the herds are built up with better blood. This might easily be done by importations from the North if the cattle from that section were not almost certain to be attacked by Texas fever. Indeed, it is stated that from 50 to 75 per cent of the cattle imported from the North die of the fever. The South is further hampered by being unable to sell in the markets of the North except under certain quarantine restrictions. All efforts, therefore, looking toward the cure and prevention of Texas fever are laudable; and with this purpose in view Dr. Robert, in the latter part of 1897, conducted some experiments with blood serum in the hope of finding such preventive or cure.

Twenty head of cattle were purchased near Columbia, Mo., a point considerably north of the quarantine line. "The serum used in these experiments was obtained from Southern cows well covered with ticks. The blood was taken from the jugular vein and collected in sterilized glass jars, allowed to set about thirty-six hours on ice, and the blood serum then drawn off into sterilized glass bottles and closed with sealing wax, after adding four-tenths of 1 per cent of carbolic acid."

The quality of the serum given varied between wide ranges, and tests were made to determine the efficiency of inoculation—

(a) Before shipping South.

(b) Inoculation before shipping and after reaching the South.

(c) Inoculation after reaching the South.

(d) Inoculation with serum from cattle with ticks on them and serum from cattle without ticks.

(e) Inoculation with serum from cows sick with Texas fever.

(f) Inoculation with tick juice.

One lot of the cattle was not inoculated and was kept free from ticks by being inclosed on an uninfected lot and oil put on their legs and soft skin.

The results of these experiments indicate unmistakably that the blood serum inoculation, as we practiced it, had no effect either in preventing or curing Texas fever. Our experiments furnished us additional evidence, however, that the cattle tick is the agent for transmitting the disease, and that valuable breeding animals can be brought South at any time with little danger of contracting "acclimation" fever, provided they are kept free from ticks by placing in uninfected inclosures. Such animals should be regularly and carefully examined for ticks, and the legs and soft skin of the body occasionally oiled.

STEER-FEEDING EXPERIMENTS TO ASCERTAIN THE COMPARATIVE VALUE OF CORN AND RED AND WHITE KAFIR CORN.

[C. C. Georgeson, M. S., Bulletin No. 67, Kansas Experiment Station.]

With a view to ascertaining the comparative value of corn and red and white Kafir corn as feed for cattle, 15 steers were purchased on September 23 and October 5, 1896, and divided into three lots of 5 each. Three of the steers were grade Herefords (Nos. 8, 13, and 15), and one went with each lot; the rest were grade Shorthorns. They were 3 years old in the early part of the year 1897.

The preliminary feeding period lasted until November 3, when their weights were as follows:

Weight of steers at beginning of experiment.

Lot.	Feed.	Number of steer.	Weight Nov. 3.
			Pounds.
I	Corn meal	3	1,028
		7	962
		8	956
		9	1,098
		11	1,196
II	Red Kafir corn	1	996
		2	1,029
		4	996
		12	1,014
		13	1,070
III	White Kafir corn	5	1,008
		6	1,011
		10	1,044
		14	1,035
		15	998

Feed and feeding.—Lot I was fed on corn meal, Lot II on ground red Kafir corn, Lot III on ground white Kafir corn, and all were fed equal quantities—not necessarily as much as they would eat. "It was thought that the experiment would afford a better comparison of the feeding value of the three grains if each lot were fed the same quantity, the lots being as nearly equal in all particulars as it was possible to make them." Each lot was started on 80 pounds daily, or 16 pounds for each animal, and was given in two feeds, half in the morning and half in the evening. Any amount above 80 pounds was found to be too much. In addition, each lot was fed daily 100 pounds of Kafir corn fodder of good quality. The heads, of course, had been removed. From one-fifth to one-third of this usually remained uneaten, and was weighed back and proper credit given.

Results.—The results of the test are well shown in detail tables. The following is a summary:

SUMMARY FOR LOT I.

Grain eaten ....pounds..	16,271
Total food eaten ....do....	25,568
Average gain per head ....do....	326.4
Average daily gain per head....................do....	1.86
Total cost of feed......	$60.896
Grain eaten per pound of gain.................pounds..	9.97
Total food eaten per pound of gain ....do....	15.66
Roughness eaten ....do.....	9,297
Total gain, 175 days..........................do.....	1,682
Average daily gain of lot.......................do....	9.32
Average cost per pound of gain.................cents..	3.73
Average cost of feed per head.....................	$12.18
Roughness eaten per pound of gain ....pounds..	5.69

KAFIR CORN COMPARES WELL WITH CORN.

The fact that these lots show so little difference in their gains and the value received for the grain fed is a gratifying proof of the value of Kafir corn. The feeding value of corn has long been known, but this is the first experiment in which Kafir corn has been tested so thoroughly and for so long a period under normal conditions. The steers were fair representatives of the grade cattle raised in the central West. They were neither high-bred cattle nor common scrubs. The conditions of the experiment were those that prevail with the average farmer and feeder. •They were fed in open lots, where they could seek the shelter of a small shed when desired, but they were not pampered or petted in any way. The results obtained in this case can be obtained by any feeder in the State without providing better quarters or giving more attention to their feed and care than can be and is furnished by the average farmer anywhere.

That both the varieties of Kafir corn most popular in the West should have given results which compare so nearly with those of corn under these conditions is a matter of no little interest because of its economic significance. The past half dozen years have developed the fact that Kafir corn can be successfully grown in seasons and in places too dry for corn; that it will grow on poorer soil than corn; and that under equally favorable conditions it will outyield corn both in forage and grain has also been proved. When we now can add to this excellent record the further fact that Kafir corn is nearly equal to corn as a beef producer, the future of beef production in the West seems to me to be assured. Except in unusually disastrous seasons, when everything fails, it is reasonably safe to count on a good crop of Kafir corn. A shortage in the corn crop need not seriously check the procession of fat steers from the pastures and farms of Kansas to the centers of distribution, from whence they go to feed the hungry the world over, and the Kansas farmer and stock raiser who will give his attention to steers and Kafir corn need not dread the hot winds of July, as he is wont to do, because they need no longer rob him of a year's profit, or, at most, do more than slightly diminish his income.

I confess that the results are far more gratifying than I had dared to hope. While I had expected that steers could be fattened on Kafir corn, I had not ventured to hope that it would be so nearly equal to corn as the present experiment proves it to be; for while it is true that corn gave slightly the best returns, it should be borne in mind that the coarse fodder consisted almost wholly of Kafir corn on which the grain had matured before the fodder was cut, with the exception of two weeks in which they were fed on corn stover only. During the last three weeks some alfalfa hay of rather inferior quality was added to all the lots alike, but the Kafir-corn fodder was only partly withdrawn. The two lots fed Kafir corn were thus fattened almost wholly on this plant, while the lot fed on corn meal had a variety, in that their diet was drawn from two classes of plants, both corn and Kafir corn. It is possible that this fact may have something to do with the slightly better gains of this lot.

Future experiments which shall approach the subject from different standpoints will doubtless reveal further qualities in this grain of which we are not now aware, and determine upon the best manner of feeding. But the case as it stands proves conclusively that beeves can be fattened on Kafir corn, and, taken together with the large yields and drought-resisting qualities of this grain, it ought to be coordinate with corn in the economy of the farm.

An effort was made in connection with this experiment to ascertain how much of the feed passed through the animals undigested. The following statement shows the percentage of undigested grain voided by each lot, the figures being obtained by washing out a portion of the manure and weighing it:

Per cent.

Lot I, corn meal... 5.46
Lot II, red Kafir corn....................................... 11.27
Lot III, white Kafir corn 14.13

These figures are favorable to the corn meal, but one reason is that the mill ground the corn finer than the Kafir corn. Professor Georgeson adds this important statement:

The figures further show that there is a large amount of grain expelled in the manure, even when the feed is ground to more than the usual fineness, and if not utilized by having hogs to follow, this waste will represent a money loss, which may make the difference between a profit and a loss on the transaction.

Droppings as hog feed.—Seven shoats were put behind each lot of the above steers on December 15, and a record kept of their gain and the amount of feed given them in addition to what they got from the droppings. "The aim was to keep the hogs growing normally and at the same time feed them as little grain as possible, so that they should always be urged by a good appetite to pick up the droppings clean." The following table shows in condensed form the number of pounds of grain fed to each lot, the number of pounds of feed that was available in the droppings (estimated on the basis of that washed out in the cattle experiment above), the number of pounds of pork made by each lot, and the number of pounds of feed estimated to have been consumed for each pound of gain.

Feed given and available in droppings, and gain.

Item.	Lot I.	Lot II.	Lot III.
	Pounds.	*Pounds.*	*Pounds.*
Grain eaten..	2,520	2,520	2,480
Feed available in manure...............................	705	1,475	1,843
Gain of each lot	635	698	725
Feed available per pound of gain	5.67	5.72	5.96

It will be seen at a glance that, while the hogs following the three sets of steers were fed practically the same amount of grain, the gains vary with the amount of feed that they found in the manure.

It was found, with the hogs following Lot I, that there was feed in the droppings equaling 1.11 pounds for each pound of gain; with Lot II, 2.11 pounds feed in the droppings for each pound of gain; and with Lot III, 2.54 pounds. These results show that the hogs utilized a large percentage, if not quite all, of the undigested food voided by the steers.

FEEDING SHEAF WHEAT TO STEERS.

[H. T. French, Bulletin No. 42, Oregon Experiment Station.]

Four grade Polled Angus steers, nearly 3 years old, were employed for this test. They were kept in their stalls, without exercise except when led out to be weighed, during the experiment, which lasted from November 21 to February 5—a period of seventy-five days.

The steers fed on sheaf wheat were given corn silage and clover hay with the wheat. They consumed an average of 21.9 pounds each of sheaf wheat per day, 20.2 pounds of silage, and 4.9 pounds of clover hay. The sheaf wheat was fed to them in the bundle just as it came from the field, except the bands were cut before placing it in the manger. The sheaf wheat yielded 35 per cent of grain, hence the actual grain consumed by the steers each day was 35 per cent of 21.9, or 7.66 pounds. This is all the animals would eat.

The two steers of Lot 2 were fed on chopped grain, clover hay, corn silage, and oil meal.

Summary of results.

	Lot 1.	Lot 2.
Weight at beginning ....pounds..	1,775	1,715
Weight at ending ....do....	1,922	1,967
Gain ....do....	147	252
Average daily gain ....do....	.98	1.68
Food consumed for 1 pound of gain.......................................do....	7.82	6.01

In the amount of feed consumed, it required 7.82 pounds of grain in the sheaf wheat to make a pound of gain, and 6.01 pounds of grain to make a pound of gain in case of the steers fed with chopped grain. The steers which were fed on sheaf wheat consumed 760 pounds of clover hay and 3,040 pounds of corn silage. Reckoning on the cost of hay at $4 per ton, the silage at $1. and the wheat in the sheaf at $13 per ton, the cost of feed consumed would be $10.50. This divided by the number of pounds gain, 147, would give $7.18 as the cost of feed to produce 100 pounds gain in live weight.

The steers fed on ground grain consumed 1,120 pounds of clover hay, 3,040 pounds of corn silage, 1,212 pounds of chopped wheat and oats, and 804 pounds of oil meal. Reckoning the clover hay and silage as above, chopped grain at $12, and the oil meal at $20 per ton; the total cost of feed would be $11.88. This divided by the total gain, 252 pounds, would give $4.69, the cost of feed for 100 pounds of gain in live weight. Subtract this from $7.18, the cost of 100 pounds gain by steers fed on sheaf wheat, leaves $2.44 per hundred in favor of the ground grain. The cost in either case is too great for profit, but for the sake of comparison the results are valuable.

An important consideration with reference to the lot fed on sheaf wheat was that they were not well fitted for market. They did not fill out well, and their coats were rough. The following observations were made by Professor French:

Observations.—1. Steers will not gain as rapidly on sheaf wheat as when fed on ground grain.

2. The animals do not relish the sheaf wheat.

3. It costs more to make 100 pounds of gain in live weight on sheaf wheat than on ground grain.

4. The difference under all ordinary circumstances is sufficient to pay for thrashing and grinding.

5. The animals can not be as well matured on wheat in the sheaf as when fed ground grain, hence a lower price will be received for the finished product.

*　　　*　　　*　　　*　　　*　　　*　　　*

7. Better results can be obtained by feeding sheaf wheat to steers than to pigs.

8. Much of the grain consumed is not digested. It has a tendency to scour the animals.

TEXAS ITCH IN KANSAS.

[N. S. Mayo, M. S., D. V. M., Bulletin No. 60, Kansas Experiment Station.]

There seems to be no good reason why this disease should be given the name of Texas itch, as it is stated, upon the authority of Dr. M. Francis, of the Texas Experiment Station, that it is never observed among the cattle of that State. It is also known as range itch, cattle itch, and cattle mange. "It is not a dangerous disease so far as the mortality or death losses are concerned, yet it is quite a serious disease considered from a pecuniary point of view. When the disease gets well started among a bunch of cattle it is difficult to eradicate it, and the loss of flesh, general deterioration, and annoyance to cattle which follow result in a considerable loss."

The outbreaks observed in Kansas were introduced by cattle from the ranges of the South and West.

Description of the itch.—Texas itch is a skin disease affecting cattle only, and is caused by a minute animal parasite *Psoroptes communis* var. *bovis*. This disease differs from true mange in that the parasite is of a different nature. In Texas itch the parasite lives upon the surface of the skin; in true mange the parasite (*Sarcoptes*) burrows into the skin.

The Texas itch mite is closely related to the mite which causes scab in sheep; both mites belong to the same genus and species, but are different varieties. The sheep scab mite will not attack cattle, nor will the cattle mite attack sheep or other animals. * * *

These itch mites are very numerous. A very small quantity of débris from an actively infested area of the skin will often reveal a score of parasites.

These mites when removed from an animal retain their activity for a considerable time. Specimens collected in small glass bottles and kept in the laboratory at ordinary temperature of the room during the winter months, which varied from 80° F. during the day to 45° F. during the night, would live and remain active from eight to eleven days. Exposure to bright sunlight will kill most of the mites in a few hours.

The itch does not appear to affect cattle while they are doing well on grass, nor attack any cattle in good condition over three years old. The animals which suffer are calves, yearlings, and two-year-olds, and those in poor condition. The first symptom is the intense itching of the skin about the neck or shoulders. The disease extends along the back and sides and down the outside of the legs, but does not attack the inside of the legs or the thin skin of the abdomen.

There is a scurfy condition of the skin; the scurf becomes mixed with a gummy exudation from the skin and forms a crust in the hair sometimes one-half inch thick. The hair then comes off or is rubbed off the badly affected area. * * * After the hair comes off, the prasites leave that part, the bald area gets well, and the hair starts to grow again.

Remedies.—As remedies Dr. Mayo suggests, first, isolation of the diseased animals; second, thorough disinfection of all posts, mangers, feed racks, etc., against which the animals may have rubbed, "with a moderately strong solution of concentrated lye in water, or by using a solution of 1 part of carbolic acid dissolved in 20 parts of water;" third, the giving internally of sulphur mixed with salt—1 pound of sulphur mixed with 4 pounds of salt, gradually increased from a small handful at first. The external treatment consists in the application to the skin of such remedies as will kill the parasites and destroy their eggs, but not injure the animals. Several such remedies are mentioned by Dr. Mayo, but he says:

The most satisfactory results were obtained by using emulsions of creolin and zenoleum. These remedies are coal-tar derivatives, rendered alkaline, so that, when added to water, they form permanent emulsions without agitation, and are very effective remedies in destroying insect parasites. As zenoleum proved just as effective as creolin, and was much cheaper, it was used in preference to creolin. One part of zenoleum in 75 parts of water was found to be very effective. Sixty head were treated, as follows: 27 head of calves, 21 head of yearlings, and 12 head of mixed calves, yearlings, and two-year-olds. When water was used and the remedy applied with sponges, cloths, and scrubbing brushes. It penetrates scabs and matted hair readily, does not irritate the skin nor the hands, and is easily and quickly applied. No further symptoms of the disease were observed, except in one case; that required a second application. The cost is from 2 to 3 cents per head.

In addition to any treatment it is essential that the affected animal should have good feed, and a careful watch should be made for the appearance of the disease when dry feeding is begun.

DEHORNING CATTLE.

[Gilbert M. Gowell and Fremont L. Russell, Bulletin No. 41, Maine Experiment Station.]

Dehorning has been practiced in this country about ten years and for a longer period in England. Horns are no longer needed by cattle as weapons of defense against natural enemies, and hence serve no good purpose; for this reason the sentiment in favor of dehorning is increasing. The Texas Experiment Station finds "that a drove of the wildest dehorned cattle may run loose together in a building, like a flock of sheep, and they will fatten faster after dehorning than before." Professor Roberts, of the Cornell (New York) Station, is quoted as saying that dehorning is found to be of great practical utility in rendering animals more docile and quiet, in rendering them much less capable of injuring each other or mankind, and in reducing the space necessary for safe housing and shipping.

The Ontario (Canada) government appointed a commission "to obtain the fullest information in reference to the practice recently introduced into this Province of dehorning cattle, and to make full inquiry into and report the reasons for and against the practice." Nearly seventy farmers were interviewed and, with the exception of three or four, all indorsed the practice. The few who opposed it did so on the ground of cruelty. The commission unanimously recommend that the practice of dehorning be permitted and encouraged.

All of the cattle at the Maine Station have been dehorned. The calves are dehorned by the use of caustic potash as soon as the buttons can be felt or not later than twenty days from birth. The method followed is given below:

Dehorning with potash is done by clipping the hair away from around the buttons, moistening the end of the potash slightly, and rubbing one embryo horn for four or five seconds, then moistening the potash again and rubbing the other horn in the same manner. Each horn should be thus treated four or five times. Four or five minutes' time is required in dehorning a calf. Care should be taken not to have too much moisture about the potash, as it might spread and remove the hair from too large a surface. The calf should be kept from getting wet during the next few days for the same reason. Healing soon follows the operation, and smooth polls have resulted in every case except one mentioned as having been done at too late an age.

In dehorning cows, it is said "the operation was evidently painful to the animals" for a few seconds; but after being released went about the paddock as usual, and an hour or two later they ate their dinner as though nothing unusual had taken place. "The milk yield showed no appreciable decrease even on the days immediately following the operation. * * * The dehorning apparently had no effect upon either milk flow or yield of butter fat." Similar experiences are noted by the Minnesota and New York (Cornell) stations, the latter covering seven years.

The authors give the following summary of their conclusions:

1. Dehorning is to be recommended because dehorned cattle are more easily cared for than those with horns, and because dehorned cattle enjoy life better. "A great deal of suffering is prevented by the removal of horns."

2. The best time to dehorn cattle is during cold weather, when there will be no trouble from flies.

3. To dehorn mature animals, clippers should be used that will remove the horn perfectly at a single stroke and in a moment of time.

4. With suitable clippers properly used, the operation is simple and very quickly performed.

5. When it is skillfully performed, animals do not give evidence of great suffering as an effect of dehorning. The tissues injured in dehorning are not very well supplied with nerves, and they are quickly cut through. Good evidence that dehorning is not very painful is the fact that cattle will resume feeding immediately after being operated on, and the yield of milk in cows is not perceptibly affected. Compared with castration of colts and calves, dehorning may be considered painless.

6. Those who are familiar with the operation of dehorning and the results of it are its most enthusiastic advocates.

7. To prevent the growth of horns, calves under three weeks of age can have the embryo horns removed with one stroke of a sharp knife, or they can be treated with a caustic sufficiently powerful to destroy them.

8. In the past, efforts have frequently been made to prevent the practice of dehorning on the ground that it caused needless pain. It would seem to us that efforts can now better be expended by endeavoring to have the last relic of a horn removed from our domestic cattle, who ceased to need them when they came under the protection of man. Horns may sometimes be ornamental, but it is evident that they are usually useless, expensive, and dangerous luxuries.

[F. William Rane, B. Agr., Bulletin No. 50, New Hampshire Experiment Station.]

In April, 1897, the station herd of 33 head of cattle—Jerseys, Ayrshires, Durhams (Shorthorns), and Holsteins—were dehorned. The results corroborate in all essential particulars those given in Bulletin No. 41 of the Maine station. It should be noted that the experience of Professor Rane shows that those breeds having the finer horns suffered most under the clippers. The conclusions are copied below:

It is believed that dehorning eliminates the danger to life, and is therefore of the utmost importance; but it has its economic bearing as well. It is well understood that where milch cows are gently cared for, and not over exercised, other things being equal, more milk is produced. For the same reason it is evident that beef animals will gain more rapidly where hornless, the nourishment exhausted in fighting tendencies being stored up as flesh. Animals are more cheaply transported by live weight when dehorned, as more can be accommodated in less space and with less danger.

I have yet to see the average herd of horned animals without its recognized leaders and masters; it is nothing more than the atavismic tendencies toward the instincts of the wild animal. Domestication has modified these instincts, but will not overcome them until the implements of warfare are laid aside. Even under domestication the horns, therefore, still play an important part in the survival of the fittest.

With our four breeds, it was distinctly shown that such animals as, for example, the Ayrshires, which are noted and bred for their fine horns, suffered the most from dehorning. Next come the Shorthorns, or Durhams, and the Holsteins, the Guernseys and Jerseys coming last. In the case of the two last-mentioned breeds many object to the removal of the well-known crumpled horns, which objection might be sustained. However, in the case of the straighter horns, where any possible danger is involved, it is deemed advisable.

MILKING SCRUB COWS.

[Kansas Experiment Station.]

From January 1 to April 15, 1898, the college bought 30 head of common scrub cows, with the object of testing the value for the dairy of this class of cows when properly handled. These cows were purchased in Lincoln County, cost delivered at Manhattan an average of $34 each, were selected by a farmer who was not a dairyman, and in quality were below the average cows of the State. The cows were shipped from Lincoln County to Manhattan (100 miles) in midwinter, the excitement and weather causing a serious drop in the milk yield of those that had calved. The first week the average daily milk yield per cow was 15¼ pounds, the second week 21 pounds.

At the start the cows were fed alfalfa hay and a mixture of two-thirds bran and one-third old-process linseed meal, a ration rich in protein, designed to stimulate the milk flow and to partially overcome the effects from shipping. As soon as the cows were brought to a fair milk flow they were put on a ration of alfalfa hay and Kafir corn grain. This ration produced the greatest flow of milk with butter fat at least cost, but had to be dropped at the end of seven weeks, so that various feed stuffs could be fed, in order to show our dairy classes the effect of various feeds on the texture of butter. The daily grain ration averaged about 8 pounds per cow while on dry feed. While on pasture the daily grain ration averaged 3 pounds of a mixture of four parts corn meal and one part of bran. Alfalfa hay was also kept in a rack where the cows could eat it at will when they were brought in at milking time. The yield held up well through the fall drought. For a short time green Kafir corn was fed with the pasture, and the cows were pastured on wheat in the fall until the ground became frozen.

Twelve cows were fresh when received January 5, the rest calving in from one to five months. The records here given are for the twelve, for 1898. The butter fat yielded has been credited at the prices paid each month by the Manhattan Creamery, which were as follows: January, 17½ cents; February, 17 cents; March, 16½ cents; April, 15 cents; May, 14½ cents; June, 13 cents; July, 13½ cents; August, 15¼ cents; September, 16 cents; October, 18 cents; November, 18 cents, and December, 17 cents. The feed has been charged at the average retail price in Manhattan for the year: Cost per 100 pounds, corn meal, 55 cents; Kafir corn meal, 55 cents; linseed meal, $1.25; soy bean meal, $1; bran, 55 cents; cottonseed meal, $1; cost per ton, alfalfa hay, $4; corn ensilage, $1; pasture, 75 cents per month. It would pay many Kansas farmers who live distant from market to milk cows if through the milk they could obtain the above prices with no additional profits.

Results.—Average yield of milk per cow, 5,707 pounds; best cow, 9,116 pounds; poorest cow, 3,583 pounds. Average yield of butter fat per cow, 238 pounds; best cow, 383.7 pounds; poorest cow, 135.7 pounds. Average cost of feed per cow, $29.20; best cow, $32.80; poorest cow, $26.75. Average value of butter fat per cow, $37.75; best cow, $60.88; poorest cow, $21.39. Average value per cow of skim milk at 15 cents per 100 pounds, $7.69; best cow, 12.29; poorest cow, $4.83. Average income per cow from butter fat and skim milk, $45.44; best cow, $73.17; poorest cow, $26.22. Average receipts per cow less cost of feed, $16.25; best cow, $40.37; poorest cow, receipts 43 cents less than cost of feed. Average cost of butter fat per pound, 12.2 cents; from best cow, 8.5 cents; from poorest cow, 19.7 cents. The average price received for butter fat for the year was 15.8 cents. To the receipts given above should be added the value of the calf at birth.

This test shows the difference in value between different cows with feed and care alike. The year's record of our best scrub cow (9,116 pounds of milk; 383.7 pounds butter fat, equal to 451 pounds butter; value of products, $73,17; returns, less feed, $40.37) is one that many a pedigree dairy cow would be proud of. This cow is of mongrel breeding, but has a pronounced dairy form. The poorest cow's form is a good beef type, and her yield of 3,583 pounds of milk and 135.7 pounds butter fat was worth 43 cents less than the feed she ate. Is stronger argument needed to induce Kansas dairymen to cull their herds and keep only the best?

This test shows that Kansas cows can be made to give greatly increased yields with proper feed and care. We collected the records of 82 herds owned by creamery patrons in one of the leading dairy sections of the State, finding an average annual yield per cow of milk 3,441 pounds; butter fat, 104.5 pounds; value of butter fat, $19.79. Contrast this with the average for the college scrub herd—milk, 5,707 pounds; butter fat, 238 pounds; value of butter fat, $37.75; and remember that the college herd is much inferior to the average herd of the State.

We attribute the greater yield secured from the college scrub herd to three causes. First, at all times their rations were either balanced or contained an excess of protein—the material which builds blood and milk—while the Kansas cow usually, when on dry feed, has only half enough protein. Second, kindness and shelter. Our scrub cows were petted, comfortably sheltered, never driven faster than a slow walk, and never spoken to in an unkind tone. Third, a full milk yield was secured through the summer drought by giving extra feed.

Record of scrub herd, 1898.

Number of cow.	Products.			Cost of feed.	Value.			Receipts, less cost of feed.		Cost of butter fat, per lb.
	Milk, lbs.	Average test, per ct.	Butter fat, lbs.		Butter fat.	Skim milk, 15c per 100 lbs.	Total.	Gain.	Loss.	
20	9,116	4.21	383.7	$32.80	$60.88	$12.29	$73.17	$40.37	....	$0.085
7	7,015	4.43	310.8	30.61	49.26	9.46	58.72	28.11	....	.098
15	6,509	4.27	277.9	29.20	43.89	8.70	52.59	23.39	....	.105
1	5,904	4.62	272.7	31.06	43.65	7.97	51.62	20.56	....	.114
6	6,269	4.09	256.4	29.95	40.56	8.44	49.00	19.15	....	.113
3	5,864	3.99	233.9	28.93	37.04	7.91	44.95	16.02	....	.123
10	6,580	3.51	230.9	30.79	37.16	8.87	46.03	15.24	....	.133
17	5,236	3.97	207.8	28.83	32.92	7.07	39.99	11.16	....	.138
18	5,023	4.12	206.9	28.97	32.69	6.78	39.47	10.50	....	.139
11	3,475	5.14	178.6	25.24	28.16	4.68	32.84	7.60	....	.134
19	3,913	4.14	161.9	27.27	25.41	5.27	30.68	3.41	....	.168
5	3,583	3.79	135.7	26.75	21.39	4.83	26.22	....	$0.43	.197
Average...	5,707	4.17	238.1	29.20	37.75	7.69	45.44	16.25	....	.122

Price of butter fat per pound: January, 17½ cents; February, 17 cents; March, 16½ cents; April, 15 cents; May, 14½ cents; June, 13 cents; July, 13½ cents; August, 15½ cents; September, 16 cents; October, 18 cents; November, 18 cents; December, 17 cents.

Cost of feed per 100 pounds: Corn meal, 55 cents; Kafir corn meal, 55 cents; linseed meal, $1.25; soy bean meal, $1; cottonseed meal, $1; bran, 55 cents; alfalfa, $4 per ton; ensilage, $1 per ton; pasture, 75 cents per month.

WHEAT IN THE SHEAF AND CHOPPED WHEAT FOR PIGS.

[H. T. French, M. S., Bulletin No. 42, Oregon Experiment Station.]

The object of this experiment was to test the relative feeding value of wheat in the sheaf and chopped wheat. Four crossbred Berkshire-Poland China pigs, four months old, were selected for this trial. The feed used previous to the experiment was shorts and water. They were kept in pens having compartments and fed twice daily. The chopped wheat was soaked from eight to twelve hours. The trial covered the period from August 1 to December 5. Lot 1 was fed sheaf wheat and Lot 2 the chopped wheat.

Summary of results.

	Lot 1.	Lot 2.
Weight August 1...............pounds..	192	197
Weight August 15.......................do	189	223
Weight August 29.......................do	210	242
Weight September 12 ....do	233	307
Weight September 26....................do	230	345
Weight October 10......................do	268	389
Weight October 24......................do	287	436
Weight November 7.....................do	308	492
Weight November 21....................do	332	544
Weight December 5.....................do	346	582
Total gain ....do	154	395
Average daily gain for each pig ....do	.61	1.56
Total amount of grain consumed.........do	1,161.6	1,871
Amount of grain for 1 pound of gain ....do	7.54	4.74
Total cost of food consumed	$7.74	$14.96
Cost 100 pounds gain of live weight	$5.00	$3.80

Sixty pounds of wheat in the sheaf produced 7.95 pounds of gain, while 60 pounds of chopped wheat produced 12.65 pounds of gain. The wheat in the sheaf (the grain) was valued at 40 cents per bushel and the chopped wheat at $16 per ton. The cost of the food consumed by lot 1 was $7.74, and by lot 2 $14.96. At this rate the cost of making 100 pounds of gain in live weight in lot 1 was $5 and in lot 2 $3.80.

There is another consideration in feeding the sheaf wheat, namely, that the pigs are very poorly fitted for market when thus fed. The pigs fed on sheaf wheat in this experiment would not bring as much as those fed on chopped grain by one-half cent per pound. The pigs were not well filled out; they were lank and lean, better fitted for racing than for packing house. The small amount of gain made by them was largely bone, muscle, and sinew rather than adipose tissue.

Observations.—From observations and facts obtained in both of these experiments in feeding sheaf wheat to pigs, we are led to conclude that—

1. Pigs do not like sheaf wheat.
2. The wheat is not well digested.

3. It cost more to put on fat with sheaf wheat than with ground grain.

4. That a proper mixture of grains will give better results than a single grain.

5. The animal can be better matured when fed with ground grain.

6. More rapid gains can be made with ground grain than with grain in the sheaf.

7. The animal product will command a higher price when the animal has been fed on ground grain, because it will be better matured. A fat hog is worth more in the market than a lean hog.

FEEDING SHEAF WHEAT TO HOGS.

[H. T. French, M. S., Bulletin No. 42, Oregon Experiment Station.]

The object of this experiment was to test the merits of sheaf wheat as a feed for hogs as compared with a mixture of grains. Two lots of six hogs each were employed. They were nearly pure-bred Berkshires, and were eight months old. They had been running on stubble since harvest, and were put into this test on September 3. The average weight on this date of those composing Lot 1 was 187 pounds, and those composing Lot 2, 187¼ pounds.

Lot 1 was fed the mixture which was made up of 3 parts chopped wheat, 1 part shorts, and 1 part ground oats. This was soaked in cold water from nine to fifteen hours and fed twice daily. Lot 2 was fed the sheaf wheat, which had been cut and bound in the ordinary way. It was cut as high as the binder could be operated. Samples were thrashed, and it was found that 35 per cent was grain. The wheat was weighed and fed at the same time that Lot 1 was fed.

Both lots were kept in pens of two compartments, with plenty of clean straw for bedding. Charcoal and ashes were in the pens continuously, and salt was mixed with each feed of chopped grain, and was given to the sheaf-wheat lot at regular intervals. The test ended on October 29.

Summary of results.

	Lot 1.	Lot 2.
Total weight at beginning ....pounds..	1,122	1,127
Total weight at ending ....do....	2,033	1,395
Gain ....do....	911	268
Grain consumed for 1 pound of gain..............................do....	3.97	7.44
Average daily gain..do....	2.68	.79
Cost of 1 pound of gain.......................................cents..	2.88	4.96

The hogs were sold at 3 cents live weight, which gave 21 cents in favor of 60 pounds of the mixture as against 60 pounds of the wheat, exclusive of the straw. This 21 cents would pay the cost of thrashing and grinding, even under adverse circumstances.

Observations.—1. It was plainly seen that the pigs fed on sheaf wheat did not relish their food. This interfered very materially in obtaining good results. An animal will not make rapid gains in flesh when it is compelled to work for its food. This is especially true of the pig. The pigs worked from three to four hours daily in getting their food from the straw. In case of other animals this might not be so apparent, for they might require some of the coarse food along with the grain, and hence would not separate the wheat from the straw and chaff. The pigs fed on the mixture would eat their ration in a few minutes, and then lie down; and hence all the food consumed became effective in the production of fat. On the other hand, in Lot 2 rapid assimilation was prevented by length of time employed in securing the food.

2. Much of the grain eaten by the pigs fed on sheaf wheat was found whole in the excreta. It was not masticated. The amount found whole in the excreta was not as great as when pigs are fed on clean thrashed grain, but there was enough to account for considerable of the loss in the weights.

3. The pigs fed on sheaf wheat were not quiet in their pens. Their appetites seemed to never be fully appeased. Hence they were in constant expectancy for something. This unrest prevented the proper digestion and assimilation of the food received.

4. More time is required in caring for animals fed in this way in clearing the straw from the pens.

5. The feed can not be stored in as small quarters as the thrashed grain. Mice, rats, and other vermin will destroy more of the wheat in the straw than when thrashed and properly stored in bins.

These are some of the points noted during the process of the experiment, and while some of them might be obviated, they seem to us to be serious objections to feeding pigs on sheaf wheat.

CORN, COWPEAS, AND WHEAT BRAN FOR FATTENING PIGS.

[J. F. Duggar, M. S., Bulletin No. 82, Alabama Experiment Station.]

The report of the Statistician of this Department shows that the number of swine in Alabama in 1897 was 1,848,158; and, while the same report shows that seven States only had a larger number, it appears from Mr. Duggar's bulletin that Alabama does not produce pork enough for the State consumption. A reason for this apparent discrepancy may be found in the inferior size of the Alabama hogs, the average value per head in 1897 being $2.51, while the average value per head in the United States was $4.39. The reason given for this condition of things is the fear of hog cholera and the high price of corn.

Mr. Duggar states that the counties in which hogs are kept under fence are probably not more frequently and disastrously visited by cholera than are the States where the hog is one of the many sources of farm revenue, and also that "there is no law, save that of custom, that the hog shall live on corn alone." Partial substitutes are abundant and cheap in the South, among which are "almost continuous pasturage, cowpeas grown as a renovating crop, peanuts, sweet potatoes, and several other crops which may be harvested by hogs." He therefore planned this experiment in the hope of aiding the industry of hog raising in Alabama.

The object of the experiment was to learn the relative values of corn, cowpeas, and wheat bran as a food for growing pigs. Comparisons were made between these food stuffs.

(1) As regards the amount of increase in weight made by pigs fed on the different rations.

(2) As regards the cost of the pork produced.

(3) As regards the effects of the several materials on the quality of pork, on the size of the internal organs and general health of the pigs, and on the quality of manure produced.

Twelve Essex pigs, divided into four lots of three each, were employed in the experiment. They were about five months old and averaged in weight 46.8 pounds. When they were divided into lots, the weights of the lots were so nearly equal that the difference between the heaviest and lightest lot was but 6.2 pounds.

For the first twenty-one days, known as Period I, each lot was fed 6 pounds of shelled corn in order to test the evenness of their feeding and fattening qualities, and the results indicated "that the different lots were fairly well matched."

Period II began on September 23, 1896, and from that date until the close of the experiment on January 13, 1897, the pigs were fed as follows: Lot I, corn exclusively; Lot II, cowpeas exclusively; Lot III, equal weights of corn and cowpeas; Lot IV, equal weights of corn and wheat bran.

The following table shows the gain made during Period II, the amount of food eaten, and the number of pounds of feed required to produce 1 pound of increase in live weight:

Amount of feed, total gain, and food required for each pound of gain.

Lot.	Kind of feed.	Total amount eaten.	Total gain.	Amount required for 1 pound of gain.
		Pounds.	Pounds.	Pounds.
I	Corn	844.2	173.3	4.87
II	Cowpeas	954.2	198.0	4.81
III	Corn and cowpeas, half and half	908.7	209.5	4.33
IV	Corn and wheat bran, half and half	1,044.4	203.0	5.21

The lot receiving equal parts of corn and cowpeas made slightly the largest gain, and required least food to produce a pound of increase in weight. Judging by the quantity of food eaten, the ration consisting of corn and wheat bran was most palatable. This last ration, however, was least effective, pound for pound. The figures just given show that a mixture of equal parts of corn and cowpeas was more effective, pound for pound, than an equal weight of either corn or cowpeas.

Not only was a pound of gain made with least weight of food when a mixture of cowpeas and corn was supplied, but also with the least weight of digestible matter. The greater efficiency of a pound of digestible matter in the mixture or balanced rations is shown in the following table:

Digestible matter consumed, pounds of digestible matter for one pound of gain, and nutritive ratio.

Lot.	Kind of food.	Quantity eaten.	Digestible matter.	Digestible matter.	Gain in live weight.	Pounds digestible matter per pound of gain.	Nutritive ratio.
		Pounds.	Per cent.	Pounds.	Pounds.	Pounds.	
I	Corn	844.2	79	667	172.3	3.85	1 to 9.7
II	Cowpeas	954.2	a 77	735	196.0	3.71	1 to 2.6
III	{Corn	454.3	79	706	209.5	3.26	1 to 6.2
	{Cowpeas	454.3	a 77				
IV	{Corn	522.2	79	704	203.0	3.46	1 to 6.8
	{Wheat bran	522.2	56				

a Calculated, using digestion percentages (coefficients) obtained when Canada peas, a closely related food stuff, was fed to swine. Tenn. bul. vol. IX, No. 3, p. 130, and Expt. Sta. Record, vol. VI, No. 1, p. 8.

The above table shows that a pound of digestible matter was most effective in the ration of mixed cowpeas and corn, nearly as valuable in a mixture of wheat bran and corn, decidedly less effective in an exclusive cowpea ration, and least valuable in a pound of corn.

The pigs were sold to a local butcher for 3 cents per pound live weight. The corn fed was worth 40 cents per bushel, the cowpeas 50 cents per bushel, and the wheat bran $15 per ton.

At these prices the cost of 1 pound of gross increase was 3.85 cents when both corn and cowpeas were fed, 3.48 cents when only corn was given, 3.61 cents when cowpeas were fed alone, and also 3.61 cents with a mixture of corn and wheat bran. At the above prices for food stuffs a combination of corn and cowpeas, equal parts of each, afforded the cheapest gain, and this, too, in spite of the fact that cowpeas were priced higher than any other material.

Mr. Duggar also says that this experiment shows that during Period I, when the pigs were on an exclusive feed of corn of 2 pounds each per day, the gain live weight, reckoned at 3 cents per pound, gave the following value per bushel for the corn fed:

                                                                    Cents.
Lot I.. 46
Lot II... 54
Lot III.. 50½
Lot IV... 53½

The average gain of live weight for Period I was 17.3 pounds for each bushel of corn, but in Period II the average was reduced to 11.5 pounds.

Corn (Lot I), per 100 pounds of food, 77 cents; per bushel (56 pounds), 43 cents. Cowpeas (Lot II), per 100 pounds of food, 78 cents; per bushel (60 pounds). 47 cents. Mixture of one-half corn and one-half cowpeas (Lot III), per 100 pounds of food, 86.5 cents. Mixture of one-half corn and one-half wheat bran (Lot IV), per 100 pounds of food, 72 cents.

This mixture of equal parts of corn and cowpeas produced pork to the value of 86.5 cents per 100 pounds of food, or about 8 per cent advance over the value of the same foods fed separately. Assuming that this increased efficiency was shared in equally by both constituents of the mixture, we have a return of 46.4 cents per bushel of corn and 51 cents per bushel of cowpeas when fed in combination.

If we assume a price of only 3 cents per pound gross for pigs, the quotation in Birmingham in January, 1896, the prices obtained for the food consumed are correspondingly lowered. On this basis the returns per 100 pounds of food eaten are 62 cents for corn, 62 cents for cowpeas, 69 cents for a mixture of corn and cowpeas, and 58 cents for a mixture of corn and wheat bran. Only in a year of low prices for foodstuffs would such results be profitable, unless certain indirect benefits of feeding cowpeas instead of selling them be considered. An important indirect benefit of feeding, not taken account of in the above figures, is the value of the manure produced, a subject which will be discussed elsewhere in this bulletin.

In the case of cowpeas an important advantage of feeding instead of selling them is that thereby the heavy cost of picking may be saved, the pigs doing the harvesting. In this locality the custom is to pay half the cowpeas for the picking of the same, which is equivalent to saying that when cowpeas command 50 cents per bushel in the market, they are worth on the vine for purpose of sale only 25 cents per bushel.

On this basis of 25 cents per bushel for cowpeas, the lot fed on cowpeas alone makes a pound of pork at a cost of only 1.8 cents, and the lot fed on a mixture of corn and cowpeas makes its gain at a cost of 2.45 cents per pound.

Twenty-five cents per bushel for unpicked cowpeas will not pay for their culture, whether they are picked for half and sold or pastured off with hogs. However, they are grown for the fertilizing value of their stems, leaves, and roots, and for this main purpose, with the production of seed as an incidental feature, the cultivation of cowpeas can not be too strongly commended.

With reference to the proportion of fat and lean meat, Mr. Duggar says:

This evidence of an increased proportion of lean meat as the result of feeding nitrogenous or narrow rations is reinforced by the figures showing weights and percentages of fat found on the stomach and intestines of the pigs of the different lots. With exclusive corn feeding we find the largest percentage of intestinal fat—an average of 2.3 per cent of the live weight. The lot fed on cowpeas alone showed only about half as much—1.1 per cent; and intermediate percentages were afforded by the two lots fed on part corn along with some more nitrogenous food stuff. A small percentage of fat on the stomach and intestines argues a large proportion of lean meat in the carcass.

In order to ascertain the fertilizing value of the excrement, droppings of forty-eight hours were collected and analyzed, and the result is stated as follows:

The weight of nitrogen excreted in forty-eight hours (and it is nitrogen which is the ingredient that gives to animal manures their chief value) is nearly 70 per cent greater in the manure from cowpeas than in that from corn; it is fully 40 per cent greater in the manure from a ration of half cowpeas and half corn than in that from an exclusive corn ration.

HOG CHOLERA IN IOWA.

[W. B. Niles, D. V. M., Bulletin No. 35, Iowa Experiment Station.]

Dr. Niles does not give the result of any experiments, but rather furnishes a general article on hog cholera for the benefit of the hog raisers of Iowa. He gives the general symptoms of the disease and shows how closely allied it is to swine plague. He emphasizes the statement "that one herd of hogs suffering from cholera may present entirely different symptoms from another herd having the same disease."

Referring to the claim made by some that the virulence of hog cholera—and with some the development of the disease itself from the germ—depends upon secondary causes, Dr. Niles says: "I am firmly of the opinion that virulent cholera will produce an outbreak of cholera without the action of secondary causes." Secondary causes, so called, no doubt render animals more susceptible and enable the disease to become more virulent, but the fact remains that there can be no hog cholera in the absence of the hog cholera germ.

He states that all of the so-called "cures" have proved ineffectual in a series of tests; and he believes that the best treatment for the disease, so far as our knowledge goes at this time, is preventive rather than remedial. On this point he says:

There can be no question but what if a well-organized system of sanitary science and police could be put in force, our swine epizootics would soon cease to cause serious loss. While it may not be possible to completely stamp out these diseases on account of the great extent of territory involved and the length of time the virus lingers about the premises, the loss can be so much reduced as to be of little moment. Such efficient regulations can not be put into force by swine raisers, but must come from the General Government or State, and in the main would consist of destroying some herds, quarantining others, and of a thorough supervision of all swine traffic.

*   *   *   *   *   *   *

If every swine raiser would remember the main facts, namely, that the disease is communicable, occurring only as the result of the presence of the cholera or swine plague germ; that the sick or exposed hog is the usual carrier of the virus, that the disease is incurable, and would then do the best he can to exercise the necessary precaution or prevent disease reaching his premises, the great annual loss would be very greatly reduced. Such work on the part of swine owners in cooperation with sanitary police work on the part of the Government would soon place us in a position where the epizootic diseases of swine would give us little trouble.

PEANUTS, COWPEAS, AND SWEET POTATOES AS FOOD FOR HOGS.

[J. F. Duggar, M. S., Bulletin No. 93, Alabama Experiment Station.]

In the feeding experiment with peanuts, 6 Poland China pigs were employed. At the beginning of the experiment their total weight was 184.3 pounds, and at the conclusion of the experiment at the end of six weeks their total weight was 380.7 pounds—a gain of 196.4 pounds.

A second feature of this experiment was "peanut pasturage v. corn meal," in which 9 Essex pigs were employed, divided into three lots of three pigs each. The first lot was hurdled on peanut pasturage and given daily all the corn meal they would eat, and at the end of four weeks had made a total gain of 38.6 pounds; the second lot was pastured on peanuts, having no other feed, and at the end of four weeks had made a gain of 21.1 pounds; the third lot, confined and given all the ground corn they would eat, lost 5.1 pounds during the four weeks. In connection with this particular test, Mr. Duggar writes as follows concerning the use of peanuts as a hog crop:

The peanut is certainly worthy of a foremost place in the list of hog crops. The Spanish variety can be used for the early crop, and also for planting after oats; the common running variety for the late fall crop. It is highly desirable to arrange a succession of peanut crops rather than to have large areas ripen at the same time, for in wet weather Spanish peanuts will not remain long in the ground after maturity without sprouting.

A third feature of the experiment was with "peanuts v. corn meal," and the same pigs were used as in the test above. This test covered six weeks after the close of the one above. The first lot received equal weights of corn meal and unhulled Spanish peanuts; the second lot, peanuts alone, and the third lot (reduced to two pigs by the removal of an unthrifty one) continued to receive corn meal only. The end of six weeks gave the results shown in the table given:

Peanuts and corn meal v. peanuts alone and corn meal alone.

Lot.	Kind of feed.	Gain.	Amount of food for 1 pound gain.
		Pounds.	*Pounds.*
First	Peanuts and corn meal, half and half............................	84.0	3.7
Second..	Peanuts..	69.5	2.8
Third ...	Corn meal..	8.6	10.7

Six Essex shoats were employed for six weeks in a comparison of cowpea pasturage and shelled corn with corn alone. The shoats were all of the same litter, averaging 50.1 pounds. They were divided into two lots of three each. The result is shown in the tables following.

Cowpea pasturage and corn v. corn alone.

Lot.	Kind of feed.	Gain.	Amount of corn eaten.	Amount of corn for 1 pound of gain.
		Pounds.	*Pounds.*	*Pounds.*
First	Cowpea pasturage and corn.................................	122	374	3.07
Second..	Corn alone...	45.2	263.8	5.85

When corn was fed alone, it took nearly twice as much corn to make a pound of growth as when the pig had access to both corn and cowpeas. The pigs on pasture had a better appetite, ate more corn, made nearly three times as much growth as the pigs on an exclusive corn diet, and made that gain at less cost per pound

Mr. Duggar states that when the pigs were placed in the field the leaves of the peas were all green and about half of the pods were still . green. The pigs ate the green leaves and pods readily as long as they lasted, but during the latter three weeks only the seed were eaten. This green food probably had an important bearing upon the experiment.

At the conclusion of the grazing experiment just noted the same pigs were used in a test of ground cowpeas and corn (equal weights of each) v. ground corn alone. The test covered seventy days, and the results are given below:

Ground cowpeas and corn v. ground corn.

Lot.	Kind of feed.	Gain.	Food eaten.	Amount of food for 1 pound of gain.	Nutritive ratio.
		Pounds.	*Pounds.*	*Pounds.*	
First	Corn and cowpeas, half and half	106.0	569.9	5.28	1 to 6.3
Second..	Corn alone...................................	68.0	548.2	8.06	1 to 9.7

The above table shows that the gain made was much greater with the mixed ration of corn and cowpeas than with corn alone. It required to make 1 pound of growth more than 8 pounds of ground corn fed alone : less than 5¼ pounds of the mixed grain produced the same result.

Sweet potatoes, cowpeas, and corn meal for hogs.—At the conclusion of the first of the experiments noted, the 6 Poland China pigs were divided into two lots of three each and used to test the feeding value of sweet potatoes with cowpeas and corn meal with cowpeas. Lot I received a ration of three parts by weight of sweet potatoes and one part of ground cowpeas. Lot II received a feed of equal weights of ground corn and ground cowpeas. This lasted twenty-eight days, when the rations were exchanged, Lot I receiving for the twenty-eight days of the second period a ration of equal weights of ground corn and ground cowpeas and Lot II the three parts of sweet potatoes and one part of cowpeas. Results are shown in the following table:

Sweet potatoes and ground cowpeas and ground corn and ground cowpeas.

Lot.	Kind of feed.	Gain.	Food consumed.	Amount of food for 1 pound of gain.	Amount of dry matter for 1 pound of gain. a
	First period.	Pounds.	Pounds.	Pounds.	Pounds.
I	Sweet potatoes, three parts; cowpeas, one part.....	36.7	431.0	11.74	5.28
II	Corn and cowpeas, half and half......................	78.5	265.8	3.42	3.08
	Second period.				
I	Sweet potatoes, three parts; cowpeas, one part.....	29.1	446.7	15.35	7.00
II	Corn and cowpeas, half and half......................	51.7	265.0	5.11	4.60
	Totals for two periods.				
	Ration of sweet potatoes, three parts, and cowpeas, one part	65.8	877.7	13.34	6.00
	Ration of corn and cowpeas, half and half	130.2	530.8	4.00	3.60

a Assuming 90 per cent of dry matter in corn and peas and 30 per cent dry matter in sweet potatoes.

In both periods of the experiment the ration containing sweet potatoes was decidedly inferior to that containing corn, a condition that is explained as probably being partly due to the fact that the pigs would not eat a sufficient quantity of the bulky ration to obtain the same amount of dry matter as was furnished by the full rations of the more concentrated mixture.

As to the quality of the pork produced under these experiments, Mr. Duggar concludes that pork resulting from a mixture of corn and cowpeas was scarcely distinguishable in appearance from that produced by exclusive feeding of corn.

Effect of food upon quality of lard.—Fat pigs fed upon each of the feeding stuffs named were rendered into lard in order to test the effects of food upon the quality of the lard. The following table gives the results:

Effects of food on melting point of lard.

Kind of food.	Kind of lard.	Melting point.
		° F.
Cowpeas and corn, half and half	Leaf lard	114.8
	Body lard.............	112.1
Corn	Leaf lard	113.0
	Body lard.............	109.4
Corn...	Leaf and body lard .	109.4
Peanuts and corn, half and half	............do	104.1
Peanuts	............do	76.1

Lard from exclusive peanut feeding solidifies only during the coldest weather of February; at other times in February and March becoming almost a semi-liquid. * * *

It is a common practice among farmers whose hogs depend largely on peanuts, sweet potatoes, and acorns, to feed corn exclusively in the two or four weeks immediately preceding the date of butchering. The aim is to harden the meat.

With the aim of learning to what extent pork can be hardened by this process, one pig from each of the pens receiving peanuts or cowpeas was placed on an exclusive corn diet after the conclusion of the experiments described above. This corn ration was continued for one month. Then the pigs were slaughtered, the fat rendered into lard, and the melting point again determined.

This month of corn feeding had a marked effect in raising the melting point of the peanut lard from 76.1° to 101.3°, a temperature still considerably below that required for corn lard.

Conclusions from all experiments.—From all these tests Mr. Duggar draws the following conclusions:

Spanish peanuts, when harvested by young pigs, were converted into pork, worth, at 3 cents per pound, $18.34 per acre of peanuts, when all conditions were favorable.

In another field, with only half a stand of plants, the value of the pork from an acre of Spanish peanuts was $10.94 and $7.83 in two experiments.

Under favorable conditions, pork (live weight) was produced at the rate of 1,426 pounds per acre of peanuts, supplemented by 37.8 bushels of corn.

With half a stand of plants an acre of Spanish peanuts produced, unaided, pork at the rate of 261 pounds per acre, and at the rate of 840 pounds per acre when the acre of peanuts was supplemented with 35.6 bushels of corn.

When fed to pigs in pens only 2.8 pounds of unhulled Spanish peanuts were required to produce each pound of increase in live weight. This is equal to 9 pounds of increase, worth 27 cents, as a return for each bushel of peanuts eaten.

Shoats pastured on nearly matured cowpeas and supplied with corn made almost three times the gain in live weight made by similar shoats fed exclusively on corn.

The cowpea crop was above the average, and its value in 3-cent pork, after subtracting the cost of the corn fed, was $10.65 per acre.

Shoats fed in pens gained more rapidly in weight on a ration of ground cowpeas and corn than on ground corn alone. In effect, 5.28 pounds of this mixed food was equal to 8.06 pounds of ground corn.

Three pounds of sweet potatoes proved decidedly inferior to 1 pound of corn meal.

Cowpeas fed with corn did not injuriously affect the quality of pork or lard.

Peanuts, when fed with corn, greatly softened the pork and lard.

The softening effect of peanuts was still greater when they constituted the sole food.

This softening effect of peanuts was not [wholly] corrected by feeding exclusively on corn for a month before the date of slaughtering.

GAPE DISEASE OF YOUNG POULTRY IN KENTUCKY.

[H. Garman, Bulletin No. 70, Kentucky Experiment Station.]

Young chickens are much troubled in Kentucky with the gapes. It may be very annoying on one farm, while on another just across the road it does not appear at all. It appears that if once established the disease maintains itself on a place and renders it useless for raising chickens.

Mr. Garman states that when the disease is under way among a brood of chickens it is communicated from one to another through water and food. Upon this theory he conducted an experiment, from which he draws the conclusion that "chicks reared on a plank floor are not attacked by the gapeworm."   .

The chickens hatched by two hens on June 5 and 7 were divided into two lots of 10 each. The coop was divided into two compartments, one of which had a floor, and the other permitting the chicks to run upon the ground. The chicks were thus separated before they were large enough to get out of the nest of their own accord. In all respects, except the floor and feed, the two lots were treated alike. Among other food, the lot on the ground was given a daily ration of earthworms in addition to corn meal and table scraps. These chicks began to die of gapes on June 23, and the last one of the lot died on July 5. Every one had the gapes. "During this time not a single chick kept on the plank floor became affected with the disease."

Conclusions.—"It is evident that the chicks in the compartment without a floor obtained the gapeworms either from the ground or else from the earthworms which were fed to them." The value to the farmer of the result of this experiment is given in Mr. Garman's words:

The result and value to the farmer obtained from this preliminary experiment is that keeping chicks, for several weeks after they hatch, on a plank floor will prevent the gapes. It is my present opinion that the same result would be obtained by simply elevating an earthen floor above the surrounding level so that it would not retain moisture. It must be remembered, though, that after the disease is established in a brood it will be conveyed from one to another through the medium of food and drink, and in such case a plank floor would not alone save them. In case the disease should be introduced by chicks which had contracted it elsewhere, the proper treatment would be to isolate affected individuals as soon as discovered and medicate the drinking water of the rest.

Remedies.—Chicks more than half grown recover without treatment. Young chicks suffer most, and "the only remedial treatment in their case is rubbing the neck from time to time with lard or vaseline thoroughly mixed with a little turpentine (3 parts of lard or vaseline to 1 part of turpentine). This treatment should begin before the disease makes its appearance." Mr. Garman gives the remedy of Mengin, a French naturalist, who asserts that the use of "pounded garlic with the usual food has been made to completely eradicate the disease among pheasants in Europe." He recommends the use of one garlic bulb to ten pheasants each day. This treatment is supplemented with special care in the matter of drinking water.

EXPERIMENTS IN EGG PRODUCTION.

[James Dryden, Bulletin No. 51, Utah Experiment Station.]

In November, 1896, a year's experiments in egg production was begun at the Utah Experiment Station. These experiments were designed to show (1) the relative value of old hens and pullets; (2) the effect of exercise; (3) the relative value of early and late hatched pullets; (4) the effect of crossing; (5) the relative merit of the different breeds; (6) the yearly food cost per hen; (7) the average yearly production of eggs per hen; (8) the food cost per dozen eggs; (9) the relative weight of eggs from different breeds; (10) the relative fertility of eggs under different treatments; (11) the relative fertility of fresh and old eggs; (12) the merits of different incubators.

In this trial there were nine pens of 4 fowls each, except No. 9, which contained 5, and No. 1, which contained but 3 after June 8. They were classified as follows:

Without exercise.

Pen 1. Old hens.
Pen 2. Late-hatched pullets.
Pen 3. Early-hatched pullets.

With exercise.

Pen 4. Early-hatched pullets.
Pen 5. Old hens.
Pen 6. Late-hatched pullets.

} Rose Comb Brown Leghorns.

Pen 7. Brahma-Leghorn cross pullets.
Pen 8. Light Brahma pullets.
Pen 9. Barred Plymouth Rock pullets.

It will be observed that pens 1 and 5, 2 and 6, and 3 and 4 were duplicates, so far as it was possible to make them so, differing only in treatment. All pens were fed alike in regard to variety of food, time of feeding, etc. The exercise was afforded by placing the food in a litter of straw about 6 inches deep, thus compelling the fowls to scratch for it. The fowls without exercise were fed in open boxes. The old hens were 3 and 4 years old; the early-hatched pullets about 7 months old; and the late-hatched pullets about $5\frac{1}{2}$ months old.

The idea kept uppermost in mind in feeding was to so feed as to induce the largest possible consumption of food of the right kind. The theory that the more food an animal will eat and assimilate, the greater will be the product has been proved to be correct in the feeding of other kinds of live stock. A cow, for instance, requires a certain amount of food to maintain existence, and the first use to which food is put is to supply the requirements of the body, and anything beyond that amount which a cow can be induced to eat will go to the production of milk, if she is a good dairy type. A steer requires a certain amount to maintain life. Anything beyond that amount will go to make beef. So it is in feeding for eggs. The hen must be liberally fed; she must consume more than is merely necessary to support life in order to furnish eggs. But one great danger in liberally feeding the hen is that instead of the surplus above maintenance going to the production of eggs, it is very apt to go to the production of fat; at any rate, that is the theory of poultry men. To guard against this result, the question of exercise for the hen has come to be looked upon by successful poultry men as of vital importance. "Make the hen exercise," they say, "and instead of getting a fat hen you will get a fat egg basket." To collect some data in regard to this question was the purpose of the experiment on exercise.

The table herewith shows the total weight for each pen at the beginning and the end of the experiment, the average weight of each pen for the year, and the average weight per fowl.

Weights of pens at beginning and end of experiment, and average weight for the year.

	Pen 1.	Pen 2.	Pen 3.	Pen 4.	Pen 5.	Pen 6.	Pen 7.	Pen 8.	Pen 9.
	Lbs.	*Lbs.*	*Lbs.*	*Lbs.*	*Lbs.*	*Lbs.*	*Lbs.*	*Lbs.*	*Lbs.*
At beginning	15.9	9.5	12.3	13.3	14.1	9.7	17.6	19.3	16.3
At end	13.7	13.2	11.9	12.5	14.4	13.2	17.9	24.4	24.1
Average, 27 weighings ...	17.4	12.2	13.3	13.7	16.1	12.3	20	26.8	23.5
Average per fowl	4.35	3.05	3.32	3.42	4.02	3.07	5	6.7	5.9

As will be seen, the two pens of late hatched pullets averaged 12.25 pounds per pen, or 3.06 pounds per fowl during the year. The early hatched pullets averaged 13.5 pounds for the pen, or 3.4 pounds per pullet. It will be noticed that this difference in weight in favor of the early hatched pullets extended throughout the year, affording evidence, although not conclusive, that early hatching conduces to greater vigor in the stock. The pullets making up the four pens were all hatched by incubator, reared in the same way, and all from the same stock. One important point brought out by the table is that exercise had, apparently, no effect in either increasing or decreasing the weight of the fowls.

The table herewith gives for the year the total food cost per fowl, the number of eggs laid and their value, the food cost per dozen of eggs, and the per cent of profit on food.

Cost of food, number and value of eggs, etc.

Pen.	Fowl.	Cost of food per fowl.	Number of eggs laid per fowl.	Value of eggs per fowl.	Food cost per dozen.	Profit on feed.
		Cents.	*Number.*	*Dollars.*	*Cents.*	*Per cent.*
	Without exercise.					
1	Old hens...........	53¼	64	0.56	9.9	5
2	Late-hatched pullets	56¼	137½	1.32	4.9	135
3	Early-hatched pullets	61¼	157½	1.68	4.6	174
	With exercise.					
4	Early-hatched pullets	62	181½	1.88	4.1	203
5	Old hens............	62	108½	1.00	6.9	61
6	Late-hatched pullets	63	150½	1.51	5.0	124
7	Brahma Leghorn cross pullets............	73¼	145	1.47	6.1	100
8	Light Brahma pullets	81¼	147½	1.40	6.6	73
9	Barred Plymouth Rock pullets	63	79½	.79	9.4	25

It will be observed by consulting the table that with some pens the matter of exercise had little effect on the cost of food consumed. In other cases the difference is marked. With the old hens, for instance, the increased consumption of food, apparently due to exercise, was about 17 per cent.

The table shows some very positive results. Pen 4 is the ideal pen of the lot, or, rather, the only pen under the best conditions for egg production. They consumed during the year, 62 cents worth of food each; they averaged 181¼ eggs each, valued at $1.88 at market prices of eggs. The food cost per dozen of eggs was 4.1 cents, and the profit on feed was 203 per cent. Pen 3 came second; their egg record was two dozen short of pen 4; their value was 20 cents less; the food cost per dozen was half a cent more, and the per cent profit was 174. This result may fairly be attributed to lack of exercise.

Old hens v. pullets as layers—This experiment indicates that there is no profit from egg production from old hens. The profit from the young hens, or pullets, was five or six times greater than that from the old hens. The old hens not only laid considerably fewer eggs, but they were worth less per dozen. "Those of the old hens averaged less than a cent apiece, while those from the pullets, with the exception of Pen 2, averaged more than a cent apiece. This is accounted for by the fact that the pullets laid a larger proportion of their eggs in early winter, when the price was good."

Exercise and food consumption.—The pens without exercise averaged 120 eggs, while the eggs from the exercised pens averaged 146. The average food cost per dozen eggs of the first lot was 6.5 cents; for the second lot, 5.3 cents. This shows that it required 22 per cent more food to make a dozen eggs without exercise than with it. "It was not used in the growth of flesh, for the weights show that the exercised hen was as heavy as the nonexercised. It seems to be a mere question of digestion; the exercise aids digestion and assimilation and prevents a waste of food."

Number and value of eggs produced.—The table herewith gives the number and value of eggs produced each month of the trial.

Number and value of eggs produced per month, with total production and total value.

Month.	Pen 1.		Pen 2.		Pen 3.		Pen 4.		Pen 5.		Pen 6.		Pen 7.		Pen 8.		Pen 9.	
	Number.	Value.	Number.	Value.	Number.	Value.	Number.	Value.	Number.	Value.	Number.	Value.	Number.	Value.	Number.	Value.	Number.	Value.
November ...					15	$0.25	19	$0.32	2			$0.06	1	$0.02			6	$0.12
December					29	.60	28	.54	2	$0.04	3	$0.06	22	.44			6	$0.12
January......			15	$0.22	53	.80	54	.81	11	.17	41	.61	59	.88	25	$0.38	15	.22
February	6	$0.06	28	.29	59	.62	64	.66	19	.20	35	.36	41	.42	50	.52	14	.15
March	38	.32	57	.48	67	.56	76	.63	21	.18	73	.61	77	.64	74	.62	30	.25
April	54	.45	79	.66	80	.67	88	.73	74	.61	72	.60	79	.66	82	.68	46	.38
May	59	.50	80	.66	75	.63	91	.76	73	.61	73	.61	72	.60	72	.60	59	.50
June	27	.23	67	.56	64	.53	78	.65	67	.56	71	.60	58	.48	64	.53	38	.32
July	14	.12	63	.52	57	.48	65	.54	51	.42	72	.60	55	.46	71	.60	27	.23
August	21	.21	76	.76	60	.60	85	.85	49	.49	68	.68	64	.64	79	.79	36	.36
September ...	12	.14	60	.70	44	.51	62	.72	56	.65	52	.61	39	.45	67	.79	30	.36
October			25	.42	28	.47	19	.32	4	.07	a43	.71	18	.20	7	.10	18	.30
Total	231		550		631		727		427		603		580		591		319	
Average..	64		137½		157½		181¾		106¾		150½		145		147¾		79¾	
Total		2.03		5.27		6.72		7.53		4.00		6.06		5.89		5.61		8.17

a Pen 6 laid eight eggs during the last week of the experiment, and they are included in the number for October.

Fertility of eggs.—The tests of fertility did not give data for rational conclusions. They were carried on in two styles of incubators. The results obtained, however, showed that the percentage of fertility for the exercised pens was 31.5, while that from the nonexercised was 47.5.

The percentage of fertility, of course, is low in either case, but it must be remembered that the results are from favorable and unfavorable conditions, from old hens and young, and from old eggs and fresh alike. The exercise apparently did not favor fertility. * * * The results shown would seem to indicate that good results will not be obtained from eggs more than a week old.

Following are some of the conclusions deduced from these experiments by Mr. Dryden:

1. There is little profit in keeping hens 3 or 4 years old at the market prices of food and eggs in Utah. The profit in feeding young hens or pullets was six times greater than in feeding old hens 3 and 4 years old. This conclusion does not apply to 2-year-old hens and hens more than 4 years old.

2. Leghorn pullets hatched in April gave better results than those hatched in late May. The profit was about one and a half times greater from the April-hatched than from the May-hatched.

3. The exercised pens (4, 5, and 6) produced 26 eggs per fowl more than the pens without exercise (1, 2, and 3).

4. The three exercised pens produced eggs at a food cost of 5.3 cents per dozen; the pens without exercise at a food cost of 6.5 cents per dozen.

5. The three exercised pens averaged a profit per fowl during the year of 84 cents; the nonexercised pens, 58 cents.

6. Pen 1, representing egg production under the most unfavorable conditions, except as to ration fed, cleared 2½ cents per fowl during the year on the cost of food. Pen 4, representing egg production under the most favorable conditions, cleared, during the year, $1.26 per fowl; this would have been increased considerably had the eggs laid before the experiment began been counted. In the one case there was a profit on feed of 5 per cent; in the other, 203 per cent.

7. Exercise had no apparent influence on the weight of the fowl. The lack of exercise did not add to the weight of the fowls.

8. The nonexercised pens produced eggs weighing about 3 per cent more than the exercised pens.

9. The eggs produced by the old Leghorn hens weighed about 5½ per cent more than those produced by the Leghorn pullets.

10. The eggs produced by the light Brahma pullets weighed 11¼ per cent more than those produced by the Leghorn pullets.

11. The Barred Plymouth Rock pullets' eggs averaged about the same as those of the Leghorn pullets.

12. In two out of three pens exercise produced a larger consumption of food.

13. The exercised pens made a better use of the food than those without exercise. It required 22 per cent less food to produce a dozen of eggs with exercise than without it. The results are strongly conclusive that exercise aids digestion and assimilation of food. The chief value of exercise, therefore, seems to be in preventing a waste of food.

14. Exercise apparently reduced the percentage of fertility in the eggs.

15. The percentage of fertility was highest with the early hatched pullets and lowest with the old hens, though the results are not conclusive.

16. The fertility of eggs averaging 5 days old was 300 per cent higher than of eggs averaging 22 days old.

17. The results noted above were secured from what was considered a good ration fed alike to all pens. Practically the same ration was fed throughout the year. The conclusions, therefore, must not be accepted if a different ration is used.

18. The results seem to indicate an average capacity for a Leghorn pullet of 200 eggs per year, with intelligent care and feeding.

19. No advantage was discovered in crossing the Brahma and Leghorn.

FOOD VALUE OF CALIFORNIA EGGS.

[M. E. Jaffa, report California experiment stations, 1895-96.]

This investigation, taken at the request of the California State Poultry Association, "was to ascertain if the brown-shelled eggs were of greater value as a food than the white-shelled ones." The number and kind of eggs employed were as follows:

Brown-shelled: Six Partridge Cochin, 6 Dark Brahma, 6 Black Langshan, 6 White Langshan, 6 Wyandotte, and 18 Barred Plymouth Rock.

White-shelled: Twelve Brown Leghorn, 12 Buff Leghorn, 6 White Minorca, and 12 Black Minorca.

The physical analysis showed no essential difference between the brown-shelled and white-shelled eggs, although there was a difference in size of eggs produced by different breeds of fowls. The proximate analysis by parts (white and yolk) also showed no important differences. The following table, showing the composition of the eggs, is interesting:

Composition of eggs.

Variety.	Water.	Protein.	Fat.	Ash.	Shell.	Total.	Calories in 1 pound. a
Brown-shelled eggs:							
Partridge Cochin...........	65.11	12.04	11.04	.70	10.54	99.43	690
Black Langshan............	66.04	11.66	9.89	.61	11.47	99.67	653
White Langshan...........	65.96	11.78	10.62	.66	10.11	99.43	664
White Wyandotte..........	66.21	11.62	10.47	.65	10.70	99.65	646
Dark Brahma..............	64.93	12.34	11.56	.58	10.10	99.51	705
Barred Plymouth Rock....	65.20	11.61	11.02	.63	11.00	99.46	681
Average	65.57	11.84	10.77	.64	10.70	90.52	670
White-shelled eggs:							
Brown Leghorn.............	62.87	11.82	13.12	.73	10.80	99.42	775
Buff Leghorn..............	65.92	11.86	9.83	.68	11.22	99.51	637
White Minorca.............	65.11	11.68	10.52	.66	11.57	99.54	659
Black Minorca.............	65.29	12.31	11.41	.60	10.00	99.61	710
Average	64.79	11.92	11.22	.67	10.92	99.52	695

a The large calorie is the term used to designate the heat required to raise the temperature of a gram of water 1 degree.

In concluding this report, Professor Jaffa says he can "state as a conclusion, both from a chemical and physical point of view, that there are practically no differences, so far as the food value is concerned, between the white-shelled and brown-shelled eggs."

DRAFT UPON HORSES.

Dynamometer tests conducted at the Michigan Station by Mr. M. W. Fulton gave the following results: On good roads the drafts of wide and narrow-tired wagons were about equal; on plowed land a narrow-tired wagon pulled 45 per cent harder than one with wide tires; on a road with sand 2 inches deep, 25 per cent harder, and on sod, 10 per cent harder. A wagon not greased pulled 18 per cent harder than when greased.

FEEDING VALUE OF POTATOES.

The Michigan Experiment Station conducted an experiment in March, 1896, to ascertain whether the addition of mangels or potatoes to a ration affects the digestibility of the other factors of a ration. The experiment covered fifty-two days. Mr. C. D. Smith, the agriculturist, states that "the addition of either beets or potatoes seemed to lessen perceptibly the digestibility of the dry matter (crude protein and crude fat) of the grain and coarse feed."

In another test of the effect of feeding potatoes upon the quality of butter it appeared to give the butter an undue hardness, elevated the melting point, caused the cream to froth and to churn with difficulty, and hence was unsatisfactory.

With pork selling at $3.80, potatoes fed to hogs were worth 7.7 cents per bushel.

EXTRACTS FROM CONSULAR REPORTS.

Animal products in South Africa.—*Eggs.*—The imports of eggs for 1897 through all the ports of South Africa, with the exception of Lourenço Marquez, amounted to 2,650,273 dozen, of which the United States furnished 252,468. The United States should have had a larger share. Eggs are selling to-day in Cape Town at 84 cents per dozen and at higher rates in other parts of South Africa.

The rinderpest, so fatal to the cattle of this country, was supplemented during the past year by diseases among domestic fowls, hence the scarcity and high price of eggs. The fast mail steamers from England bring eggs from Madeira on each trip south. Packed in baskets filled with salt they arrive here fresh, although on the steamers they occupy the upper deck and are protected from the sun's rays only by tarpaulins.

Australia is sending a few in the refrigerator steamers that ply between Australian ports and England.

I can not too strongly urge producers of the United States to give attention to this line. It must be understood that not until steamers with cooling chambers are employed can this trade be captured. If Australia can send eggs here (a voyage of thirty-one days) the United States can surely do the same. Eggs have been imported from our country without cooling chambers and have arrived fresh, and with care in testing and packing can still be imported. Eggs must be what is known as "candle-tested" and packed in clean boxes, with cardboard fillers that have not come into contact with bad eggs or sawdust. A layer of clean straw between fillers would be desirable. Varnishing the eggs has proved the best preservative, but the varnish is at times affected by the damp of the vessel. If requested by buyers here a sample case should be submitted, forwarded by way of fast steamers to England, and then by fast steamer to this port in the cooling chambers. An instance has come to my attention where, if one case had been forwarded for sample (which was refused) and the eggs had arrived in good condition, an order for 3,000,000 eggs would have resulted. Americans do not like the idea of sending samples.

The figures of imports represent the minimum of what should be sent here. Owing to the excessive cost to the consumer, the consumption is small. At half the price, or 40 cents per dozen, the sales would be more than trebled.

The duty on eggs is 10 per cent. If this duty is taken off (see report on meats, further on) a reduction of 4 cents per dozen from the present rates would result. Quite a number of crystallized eggs are imported from the United States for pastry, worth $1.08 per pound in the United States; this pound being equal to 50 fresh eggs.

Butter.—The imports of butter into South Africa for the year 1897, with the exception of the port of Lourenco Marquez, were 4,146,320 pounds, of which about 9,000 pounds came from the United States.

If American producers and shippers had obtained information as to the demands of this country, much loss of trade would have been avoided. Large quantities of butter have been imported from America, but its preparation has been defective, and Danish butter has until recently been the most acceptable.

Butter from America has been colored a too deep yellow, has not been sufficiently worked to extract the milk and water, and has not been packed properly. Both Danish and American butter cross the equator, but the former, imported principally in tin boxes, will arrive sweeter and retain its flavor longer.

Recently Australian butter has found a ready market, owing to its color and purity, and large quantities are imported. Steamers on their way from Australia to England, where they also deliver butter, can perhaps afford to lessen freight rates. Over 50 tons have just been landed from Australia, and it is arriving by every steamer packed in 56-pound boxes (wood). A choice article, for very long distances, is put up in a square glass box holding 1 or 2 pounds; around this box is a layer of asbestos, possibly mixed with plaster, which makes the package impervious to heat or dampness.

This butter sells at 50 to 60 cents per pound; while the butter in 56-pound boxes sells, after paying the duty of 6 cents per pound and the freight of 2 cents per pound, at 30 to 40 cents per pound wholesale. I speak only of the choicest quality. The wooden box is first lined with cheese cloth, then with oiled paper, and the butter is packed tight. The box is fastened closely, with wire around each end.

There is no reason why America should not have a share of this large trade, if the butter is properly prepared, colored a pale yellow (if at all), and shipped in steamers fitted with cooling chambers. Australia is thirty-one days by steamer and New York is about the same, and yet steamers from Australia bring butter, beef, and mutton to South Africa, and continue to England, a distance of 7,000 miles from this port, with the route crossing the equator. It is true that Australian steamers have the advantage of return cargo, which American steamers would not, and liberal concessions are given them by the Government. Owing to the loss of cattle, the demand for butter in this country must continue for years. The shipments from Australia will now fall off and remain few from April to November.

In connection with the importation of butter, eggs, meat, and other perishable products, the local cold-storage facilities should be mentioned. Up to the present, such facilities have been controlled by

10317——33

one company, which owns all the cold-storage plants and refrigerator cars in South Africa, and consequently has been able to control the sale of these products.

If American producers can deliver such products as cheaply as other countries, this company will be their best customer here. I am informed that a company is now being organized for the erection of a large cold-storage plant in this city, and that the Government of the South African Republic has signed a similar contract. This report should be read in connection with that in regard to meats, and American manufacturers of refrigerator and cold storage plants should take notice.

Meats.—It is reported that over 800,000 cattle have died in South Africa from the disease known as the "rinderpest." The wealth of the native tribes was once in cattle. Taxes were paid with cattle; the breed was fair; the condition was good when not on long journeys, and the meat all that could be expected from "range" or grass-fed stock, besides being cheap.

Sheep are easily kept, the bunch grass of the "karoos" affording, except in case of drought, ample food. The weight per head of cattle - when fit for the market ranged from 700 to 900 pounds, dressed. While the disease still exists, it is being rapidly stamped out by the wise and energetic action of the authorities, and inoculation has been the means of saving large numbers. Where once not a pound of beef or mutton was imported, the imports of beef and mutton into South Africa (except through the port of Lourenço Marquez) for the year 1897 were:

Imports of meat products into South Africa.

Description.	Total imports.	From United States.a
	Pounds.	*Pounds.*
Frozen or chilled	1,991,221	....
Tinned or canned	6,806,976	4,847,708
Salted or cured	3,356,147	231,590

a Approximate figures.

One of the issues of the recent election was the elimination of the duties on food products. It is feared, however, that the farmer element in Parliament, which is in the majority, will not consent.

Australia and New Zealand have been the largest shippers, and allow me again to repeat what was stated in the report on eggs, that the distance from Australia and New Zealand to this port is not much less than that from New York; yet steamers with cooling chambers reach this port from these countries weekly, discharge part of their cargo, and then proceed to England. Consideration must be given to the fact that all the steamship lines have concessions from the Government, which is of great assistance. Beef packers in America have been of the opinion that the shipment of meat in refrigerator ships, a journey of thirty-two days, would not be possible. They argue that the meat on arrival, when exposed to the air, would deteriorate and "fall to pieces;" and yet Australia and New Zealand send beef and mutton as great a distance, and add seventeen to twenty-four days to reach England, and it is said the meat arrives there in good condition. I know that when it reaches here it is kept in refrigerators for many days, and I consider the quality excellent. South America has also exported much frozen mutton to this country.

Australia and New Zealand are now sending tinned goods, sheep and beef tongues, boiled and roast mutton, rabbits, and even condensed milk. Packers of the United States should have fast refrigerator ships for this market, build their own cold storage here, and send beef that when dressed will weigh from 700 to 900 pounds, and mutton weighing from 40 to 50 pounds.

If beef, and even mutton and pork, can be landed here at a price not too much in advance over that charged on goods delivered in England the market is ours. But it must be borne in mind that Australia feeds 2,500,000 sheep; Tasmania, 1,500,000; New Zealand, 19,000,000; and that 4 cents per pound for mutton is considered a profitable price. While the United States may not be prepared to compete in mutton at present, it can in beef.

The duty on beef and mutton is 2 cents per 100 pounds. Consumers are paying 18 to 24 cents per pound for mutton and beef, the choicest cuts being very much higher.

The following population is to be supplied:

Population of South Africa.

Colonies and republics.	White.	Colored.
Cape Colony	382,998	1,323,042
Natal	46,788	524,832
Orange Free State	49,950	129,787
South African Republic	118,642	550,000

This does not include the large white and colored population in other parts of South Africa under British, German, and Portuguese protection.

The United States has held the market in tinned meats, but Australia is making rapid encroachments. Imports of tinned and salted or cured meats from England are also of some magnitude, and much of this is of American production, shipped to England and there cured and canned. Bacon and ham are also imported from England.

The English people here prefer the English "cure." The meats consumed in this country must be imported, for many years will pass before meat-producing animals will again exist in sufficient quantities to supply the market. I speak of beef alone. Sheep were not affected by the rinderpest, and there are over 2,000,000 in South Africa. If some of our raisers of cattle would ship cattle and raise them here it would be a profitable enterprise.

Since writing the above, word has reached this office that in the Konigha district sickness is ravaging the sheep. To diseased sheep, grass seems to provide no nourishment. The farmers are powerless to stop mortality, and the Government is asked to investigate. One farmer has lost 800 out of 1,400 sheep.

Lard.—The imports of lard into Cape Colony and Natal for 1896 and 1897 were:

Year.	Total imports.	From United States.
1896	$53,950.64	$45,295.20
1897	92,636.46	72,436.98

The United Kingdom sent the bulk of the remainder, and it is presumed that some portion of those shipments came originally from the United States.

The bulk of the lard from the United States is supplied by only a very few of our producers. It usually comes in tin boxes of from 2 to 20 pounds in weight, and is worth to-day to the consumer 20 cents per pound. I am of the opinion that the substitute known in the United States as cottolene, a product of cotton seed, would find a ready market, provided it could sell at a price slightly lower than that of lard. The duty on lard is 4 cents per pound.—(*James G. Stowe, Consul-General at Cape Colony.*)

Trichinæ: German Inspection of American hog products.— Consul John A. Barnes sends from Cologne, August 3, 1898, a report upon trichinæ, and adds that the health officials of Cologne recently had in their possession two sides of American bacon in which it was claimed evidences of trichinæ were found. This meat came in a shipment of twenty-five cases. The report reads:

Through the medium of a society of German foreign meat importers whose object is the protection and promotion of the German trade in meats and fat products, I learn that for the last fifteen years, beginning with the decree of 1883 prohibiting the importation of American meat, and ending with the close of last year, there were officially confirmed in the Kingdom of Prussia 3,003 reported cases of illness from trichinæ, 207 of which resulted in death. Of these total numbers, there could be traced to the eating of European meat, examined in Germany and found to be free from trichinæ, 1,242 cases of illness and 102 deaths. Thus 41.35 per cent of all the cases of illness and 49.7 per cent of all the deaths were caused by the consumption of European pork, which was examined in Germany and found to be free from trichinæ. The remaining cases could also be traced to importations of European meat, partly examined and partly not examined, and found to contain trichinæ, and yet handled by the trade.

In not one of the above 3,003 cases could it be proved that the illness was caused by the use of American salted, pickled, or tinned meat, nor by smoked sausage (imported under imperial decree of September 3, 1891). This statement holds good for all Germany. In confirmation of this fact, the society hereinbefore mentioned has issued posters wherein a reward of 1,000 marks ($238) is offered to the person who can prove that trichinæ have been transferred to human beings by the consumption of American salted or pickled pork or smoked sausage imported under the imperial decree of September 3, 1891, canceling the edict forbidding the importation.

The inspection of American meats and sausages is much more rigid than the tests for the German home products. The American product is twice inspected. Before the meat leaves the United States, I am informed that from each hog, as a whole, the inspector selects six samples or pieces, and from these pieces are taken eighteen cuts, to which is applied the microscopical test. When this meat reaches Germany it is again cut into eight or ten pieces; from each of these the inspector selects three samples or pieces, and from each of these samples or pieces three are taken for the microscopical test. This results in the inspection of ninety separate pieces from the American hog, while in the inspection of the German hog only eighteen pieces are tested. By this mode of inspection it can be readily seen that opportunities of discovering ten cases of trichinæ are available in the inspection of an American hog, as against two chances in the case of the German hog. When inspected, the German hog is divided into two pieces only, being severed lengthwise, from the head down the back, thus leaving the head still attached to both of the divided parts of the body.

As regards the inspection of American sausage, I learn that in this district (Cologne) three pieces are taken for inspection purposes from 2 pounds of imported sausage. Even if no trichinæ are discovered after this rigid inspection, the sausage is much injured, if not entirely ruined, for selling purposes, inasmuch as this process not only has a tendency to cause the meat to become dry and hard, but it bears plain evidence of having been subjected to an inspection, which is not a very flattering testimonial as to its worth or desirability as food. On the other hand, German sausage is subjected to no such examination since the meat is inspected as hereinbefore stated, thereby escaping the rigid and damaging process followed in the German inspection of the American sausage.

When, in 1891, the edict against sausage and pork products from America was canceled, no inspection of sausage or pickled pork was required until July 1, 1898. Since then both products are subjected to inspection. This will result in the absolute exclusion of sausage and pickled pork or boneless hams from the German market. In the case of boneless hams weighing from 2 to 3 pounds each, the cost of inspection amounts to 15 pfennigs per kilogram, or 15 marks ($3.57) per 100 kilograms of 220 English pounds. Add to this the duty of 20 marks and we will have a total cost of 35 marks, or $8.33 on 220 pounds of meat, which virtually means the prohibition of such products.

Other expedients also appear to be resorted to by self-constituted authorities in order to discourage and prevent the large consumption of American meats. There is now pending before the court at Elberfeld, a town near Cologne, a suit relating to a case of meat from America which was packed in borax. It seems that the municipality of Cologne issued, through the daily papers, a notice or warning to dealers that such meat should not be handled or sold by them, alleging its use to be detrimental to the health of the consumer. Any citizen is permitted under this order to file a complaint regarding this kind of meat. As a consequence, when the bürgermeister (mayor) issues his edict or warning, the dealers in meats are afraid to handle or sell the prohibited products; and this is done in spite of the fact that the Emperor alone has the power to prescribe the manner of packing or preparing human food.

The bürgermeister of Solingen has exercised the same power as claimed by the bürgermeister of Cologne, by indorsing and repeating this edict or warning in his district against the use of boraxed meats, and this action has resulted in bringing the case to the attention of the court of Elberfeld. The society for the protection of German trade and industry in foreign meats and fat products is contesting this question and expects to be able to prove by distinguished German professors that the use of borax for packing meats is not injurious to human life.

I am likewise informed that uninspected American hog products have been introduced into Germany from Belgium in boxes in which other regularly inspected meats had been received from America, bearing the label of microscopic inspection.

The following is a case in point: Originally, in the microscopic inspections in the United States, the certificates thereof were the same as those given for usual antemortem and postmortem inspections, with the addition of a red stamp placed on the certificate, stating that the goods mentioned were microscopically inspected and found free from trichinæ. On one occasion a carload of bacon arrived at the custom-house of Aix la Chapelle, the certificate of which was without the red stamp. The custom-house officers refused to let the car enter Germany and reported the case to the buyer at Düren. This man wrote to the Antwerp firm that he refused to accept said car, because he was entitled to receive the meat regularly inspected, as required by the German laws. The seller at Antwerp replied that, in fact, the meat in question had been regularly inspected microscopically, and it was by mistake that the certificate did not bear the red stamp; that such an error happened sometimes, but that the United States consul in Antwerp would rectify the certificate if the buyer would return it for that purpose. Unfortunately for the Düren merchant, he believed this story, sent the certificate back, and received it again two or three days afterwards bearing now the red stamp. He presented this document at the custom-house at Aix la Chapelle, in order to have the carload entered into Germany, but the custom-house officer had reported first to the American consul at Antwerp, and when he learned that the consul had neither changed the certificate nor had been authorized to do so, the entrance into Germany was refused and the buyer placed under accusation of having falsified a public document. After several years, the suit terminated in the supreme court in Leipzig with a sentence of the Düren merchant to eight days' imprisonment for assisting in the falsification of a public document. The Belgian merchant, of course, could not be prosecuted in Germany.

How many times the Belgian port has sent into Germany uninspected meats it is impossible to say. It is rumored that a regular tariff in empty boxes with proper inspection labels and certificates has existed at Antwerp for some time, with a probability of a like organization in Rotterdam.

American hams in Germany.—Hon. John A. Barnes, United States consul at Cologne, furnished the Department of State an article from the Stadt Anzeiger, of Cologne, bearing upon the sale of American hams in Germany. The article is as follows: "The chief mayor publishes the following notice: American hams have been brought into the market which were painted with boracic acid in order to preserve them. Although they were carefully washed before being offered for sale, the meat was strongly impregnated with boracic acid and crystals of borax had formed on the bone, as was shown by the results of the chemical examination. Now, the court of correction has declared, on the basis of the opinion of experts, that the boracic acid is a poison liable to injure the health of human beings. It is therefore not permitted to keep on sale or sell meat that is preserved with boracic acid, and all those who act against this order will be proceeded against according to the imperial law of May 14, 1879, touching the trade in food."

The consul states that in Germany hams are cured by what is known as the "wet process." The following ingredients are required in this process: Boracic acid, 30 per cent; nitrate of potash, 30 per cent; and common salt 30 per cent. It would seem, therefore, as Mr. Barnes says, that "boracic acid in American meat is 'poison,' while in German products it is, we must infer, palatable and healthy."

Horses, cattle, etc., in Switzerland.—Consul-General Du Bois, writing from St. Gall, on August 5, reports a noticeable increase in the foot-and-mouth disease among Swiss cattle. The disease is quite prevalent in Graubunden, the canton bordering on Austria and Italy. There are more herds affected here than in all the rest of Switzerland. For this reason stringent measures are enforced to prevent the further introduction of this disease from Italy and Austria.

Although there has been an increase of 10 per cent in the importation of horses during the last ten years, the ten cantons of Switzerland have fewer horses to-day than they had thirty years ago. Horse breeding since 1866 has fallen off over 50 per cent. This fact has increased the importation of horses into Switzerland. During the ten years from 1850 to 1860, the average annual importation was 1,000 head, while during the past ten years the average annual importation has amounted to about 7,500 head. There are now about 38 horses for every 1,000 inhabitants in Switzerland.

Of neat cattle there are 1,376,696, or 43 head for every 100 of the population.

Of swine, there are 185 for every 1,000 of the population. In the canton Inner-Rhoden there are 742 head of swine per 1,000 inhabitants, while the canton of Basle has only 9. The importation of these animals has increased 185 per cent in thirty years. Sheep raising has declined greatly in Switzerland during the past thirty years—from 447,001 in 1866 to 271,901 in 1896, or 89 per 1,000 inhabitants. Goat raising has held its own well during this period. In 1866 there were 375,482 goats in Switzerland. There are now 415,875, or about 145 to every 1,000 of the population.

The bee culture has increased during the past twenty years nearly 100 per cent. There are now 275,000 hives in Switzerland. The canton of Lucerne has 187 hives to every 1,000 of the population, which is the highest average in Switzerland.—(*Consular Report,* *November, 1898.*)

Animals and animal products in Malta.—In May, 1898, Hon. John H. Grout, jr., sent a report to the Department of State, from which the following is extracted: "Condensed milk is imported in large quantities, but mostly of inferior quality. This is used mostly by the navy stationed here and by residents who have an aversion to goat's milk. The Maltese are, as a rule, prejudiced against condensed milk. About 30,000 goats and sheep are kept on the islands for milking purposes; also some 900 cows. Cow's milk is not generally used, except by English residents. Fresh cheese, which is also used in a dry form, is made from sheep's milk. The sheep are of a peculiar breed and yield large quantities of milk. There are no pastures on the islands, and the feeding of the goats and sheep has to be done by the best means obtainable. Notwithstanding this drawback, the animals thrive."

Butter in Paraguay.—Appearances would indicate a promising market for American butter in Paraguay. There is very little of this commodity to be found in this country, although everyone likes it and wants it. The scarcity may be due to the small number of dairies and factories. There are no butter factories in the country, and all of the dairies are located in the small town of San Bernardino, whose population is almost exclusively German.

During the year 1897 there were introduced about 2,500 pounds, mostly from Italy, coming in pound cans. The small importation would seem to be due to the fact that no attention is paid to the butter trade. The butter produced in the country is retailed for 35 or 40 cents gold per pound.

The duty on imported butter is 50 per cent ad valorem, and the revenue collected from this source last year amounted to $421 gold.

The best butter to be found comes from the German colony at San Bernardino; that which is imported from Europe is very good, but not equal to what is made by our American butter factories. The superior quality of the American butter would insure its rapid sale. Butter is but little seen on tables generally, and those hotels which use it charge extra for it.

Let any butter manufacturer cater to the whims of the people by placing on their small cans a picture of the President of Paraguay or that of some of the leading statesmen and an old historic house or two, which would catch the eye of the people and cause it to be talked about. This would give popularity to the American brand, and ought to lead to quick and profitable sales. Nothing of this sort exists in the country.—(*John N. Ruffin, Consul at Asuncion.*)

American butter in Japan.—The imports of butter into Japan for the year 1897 amounted to 136,863 catties, or 182,484 pounds, at a declared value of about $37,500 gold. Of this quantity the United States furnished 73,000 pounds, France 32,000 pounds, and Austria, Denmark, Germany, Holland, Italy, and Switzerland the rest. The larger quantity imported from the United States comes from California. The average price is about 70 sen per pound, or some 35 cents gold. A small quantity is imported from Canada, and Danish and Dutch brands are quite popular.

The demand for butter is chiefly confined to the foreign population and vessels touching at Japanese ports, and is, of course, somewhat limited. I have no doubt that United States creamery butter, properly prepared for table use and put up in attractive packages in such a manner as to preserve its sweetness and keep it fresh, would speedily control the market.

We have had no trouble in procuring sweet butter from October to March or April, but during the rest of the year all butter here seems to become more or less strong and rancid. Butter carefully wrapped in cloth and packed in tins and seemingly sweet when first opened, becomes rancid when exposed to the air. The native output is quite limited.—(*John F. Gowey, Consul-General at Yokohama.*)

Sheep and wool in Cape Colony.—Under date of March 15, 1898, Consul Roberts, of Cape Town, sent the following statistics on the sheep and wool industry of Cape Colony to the Department of State, and they are published in the Consular Report for July, 1898:

Sheep area, number of sheep, and amount of wool in Cape Colony in 1856, 1865, 1875, 1891, and 1895.

Year.	Area.	Sheep.	Wool.
	Sq. miles.	*Number.*	*Pounds.*
1850 (estimate)	197,044	6,459,962	8,224,948
1865 (census)	197,044	9,896,065	18,905,036
1875 (census)	199,950	10,976,663	28,316,181
1891 (census)	221,311	16,706,106	56,038,659
1895 (estimate)	276,917	14,409,434	45,521,506

Mr. Roberts adds: "Cape Colony in 1856 and 1865 did not include Kaffraria, Transkeian territories, Pondoland, Griqualand West, and Bechuanaland; in 1875 the Transkeian territories, Pondoland, Griqualand West, and Bechuanaland were not included; and in 1891 Bechuanaland and Pondoland were not included. The territories that have been from time to time absorbed are more noted as cattle than sheep runs."

Somali, or black-head, sheep.—The following interesting statements concerning the black-head, or Somali, sheep were furnished the Department of State by Hon. W. W. Masterson, Consul at Aden, and appeared in the Consular Report for February, 1898:

The principal kind of meat consumed by the people of this country, both native and foreign, is the mutton of the Samoli, or black-head, sheep; and, no matter by whom eaten, all pronounce it the best mutton ever tasted. This sheep, as its name indicates, is from the Somali country, on the African coast; and, singular to say, it thrives better there than anywhere else in the surrounding country.

These sheep are raised in flocks and herds and move from place to place, where food is most plentiful, under the guidance of shepherds, and, generally speaking, a native's wealth is reckoned by the number of sheep he owns.

Somali land is a very barren and sandy country, so the grazing that these sheep get is very limited, but like our American goats, they can subsist on the coarsest and seemingly most unpalatable food, such as the prickly mimosa and a kind of a desert scrub brush, as well as whatever else they can find in such a country.

To the person only accustomed to seeing the different kinds of sheep found in the United States, these sheep, at first sight, present a rather peculiar appearance. As one of their names implies, their heads are perfectly black; this black sometimes extending as far back as the shoulders, the balance of the body and legs being white. They have no wool, as has the ordinary sheep, but a short, fine hair, similar to that of the dog.

The most peculiar thing about them is that they have a large lump of pure fat growing right at the root of the tail, and this fat varies in size and weight according to the condition of the sheep. A medium-sized lump of this fat weighs about 4 pounds, and it varies from 1½ to 6 pounds. People who have studied the nature and habits of these sheep say that, like the camel, which is able to subsist for days without food from the strength derived from the tissues of his hump, this black-head sheep is able to subsist on the strength of this fat at the root of his tail for quite a number of days without any other sustenance.

A black-head sheep in reasonably good order weighs from 35 to 40 pounds, and is worth about 4 or 5 rupees [a rupee is about 21 cents]. This skin when sun-dried weighs about a pound and a half, and sells in the market for a rupee. The principal market for these skins is New York, and commercially they are known as "Mocha skins," but, like the "Mocha coffee" of commerce, this is merely a term and nothing else. In the year 1896–97 there were exported to the United States skins to the value of $653,487.14, and fully one-half of these skins were black-head sheep.

In the first part of this communication I mentioned something about these sheep thriving better in Somali-land than anywhere else in the surrounding country; but I do not mean to imply from this that they would not do well in other parts of the world, for I do not know about their being raised anywhere else, with this exception—that several years ago four of these sheep were taken to the zoological garden at Frankfort, Germany. A person from that place not long ago informed me that these sheep now numbered about thirty from natural increase. So it seems that they are able to stand a considerable change of climate.

If any of the readers of this article would care to investigate this subject further, I would be glad to give any additional information that I may be able to secure.

Prices in Cape Colony.—Hon. James G. Stowe, Consul-General at Cape Colony, furnishes the Department of State with the retail prices of provisions at that place on May 13, 1898, among which are the following:

		Cents.
Bacon	per pound	36
Butter	do	56
Cheese	do	30
Extracts of beef	per tin	24
Hams	per pound	36
Lard	do	25
Milk, condensed	per tin	30
Mince-meat	per pound	36
Tinned tongues	do	22
Tinned hams	per tin	48
Tinned chicken	do	32

Imports of hides and skins from Calcutta.—Hon. R. F. Patterson, Consul-General at Calcutta, is authority for the statement that the United States has imported hides and skins from Calcutta as follows:

1893–94	$1,755,377
1894–95	2,812,400
1895–96	3,857,326
1896–97	2,618,472
1897–98	4,284,072

EXTRACTS FROM CORRESPONDENCE.

The correspondence of the Bureau of Animal Industry covers a range as wide as the subject of animal industry itself. The extracts given herewith touch upon a very small percentage of that part of the correspondence relating to contagious diseases of animals. One letter on a particular disease is considered sufficient for the purpose of this report, although the files show numerous letters on the subject.

It may be of advantage to the public, considered in the light of instruction, to be informed that a majority of the replies to inquiries about diseases of animals bear the statement that sufficient accurate data is not given to enable the Bureau to make a determination of the disease. General symptoms are not sufficient, as they may be characteristic of several different diseases. It often happens, too, that the symptoms given are such that a personal investigation by a veterinarian is evidently necessary in order to make a correct diagnosis. Such investigations the Bureau is unable to make, except in rare cases where a contagious disease is suspicioned.

DISEASES OF CATTLE.

Ergotism.—A disease of cattle has broken out here, new to the farmers and stockmen; and in one instance three shoats had the same disease. I have attended a dozen of the cattle and found the same symptoms in all, as follows: Great stiffness, a drooping of the ears, back roached up, cessation of chewing the cud, an entire loss of milk with the cows, great emaciation, can not eat or graze, driveling at mouth, eyes badly mattered, running at the nostrils like distempered horses, hind legs badly swollen, and a flinching when trying to milk. The disease generally runs its course in fifteen days. I have given only the most prominent points in the cases seen. The loss of flesh is something wonderful. Eight miles east there is a great number of deaths. The hoofs, I am told, came off, and the animals had to be killed. Is not this the foot-and-mouth disease spoken of as in Europe and other countries, as in Switzerland, whose cattle, I see, are debarred from entering the United States? Is it aphthous fever? If so, what is the cause and the best treatment? And will it be worse a year hence? Has cold weather any influence in stopping its ravages? Please give me all the information you can covering the disease.—(*I. S., McComb, Ill., Nov. 26, 1898.*)

REPLY.—Judging from the symptoms you describe, there can be little doubt that the disease in question is ergotism, and is caused by the presence of ergot in the hay which has been fed to the animals. The stiffness and swelling of the limbs, the inflammation of the mucous membrane of the mouth and eye, the remarkable loss of flesh, and sloughing off of the extremities, all indicate a poisoning with ergot.

524

As foot-and-mouth disease has never gained a foothold in this country, and as it is a contagious disease which can not develop spontaneously, its presence in this country would indicate that it had been introduced from Europe or from some other country where it is known to exist. In that case we should most probably have heard of outbreaks between the point of importation and Ohio, as the disease is highly contagious and spreads very rapidly; but as no such reports have reached us, we may safely exclude the diagnosis of foot-and-mouth disease.

Regarding the treatment and prevention of ergotism, the most important point is to make a complete change of food, and especially to see that the hay is free from ergot. A careful examination of the hay fed at the places where the disease has been observed will soon demonstrate whether our diagnosis is correct. Among the varieties of grasses in your section of the country the redtop, spear grass, and wild rye are those which are principally affected. If large quantities of hay are found to be affected with ergot, it should be thrashed before being fed to the cattle, as this will remove the fungoid growth. It is also of importance to see that the animals are warmly housed, as ergot seldom affects cattle except in cold weather. Plenty of fresh water should always be at hand.

The best preventive measure against ergotism is to cut the hay before the seeds are formed, to see that the animals have a sufficient quantity of fresh water, and to protect them as much as possible against inclement weather.

For further particulars regarding the occurrence of this disease in the United States, I will refer you to the First Annual Report of the Bureau of Animal Industry, issued in 1884, where, on pages 175 to 214, you will find a complete description of several outbreaks of the disease in Kansas, Illinois, Ohio, and other States, as well as several illustrations of the lesions caused by ergot and those due to foot-and-mouth disease.

Contagious abortion in cows.—There are a great many cows in this neighborhood that drop their calves prematurely; I should judge that 10 per cent did so last year. Can we do anything to prevent it?—(*W. E. W., Yampa, Colo., Dec. 7, 1898.*)

REPLY.—It is probable that the cows to which you refer are affected with contagious abortion. This is an infectious disease and requires systematic disinfection to prevent its ravages. One of the best disinfectants for use in a cow stable is a 1 per cent solution of commercial sulphuric acid. This acid is poisonous as well as corrosive, and should be put where children and animals can not have access to it, and be kept in wooden or glass vessels. In preparing the solution, add the acid very slowly to the water, being careful that it does not splash upon the face or hands, stir constantly so that the acid will be thoroughly mixed with the water. This solution should be applied freely over the woodwork of the stable, including the floors, and especially to the stalls in which the cows have aborted. A watering can or broom may be used to apply the solution where required. The fetus and membranes should be immediately removed and destroyed, by burning if possible. Place the aborting cows in a stable by themselves with a separate attendant, and do not allow any communication with the stable containing healthy cows. This disinfection should be repeated in both stables every two or three days. In addition, every morning every animal in each stable should be sponged around the vulva, anus, back and hips, and root of the tail with the following solution: 1 dram corrosive sublimate, 1 ounce each alcohol and glycerine, 4 gallons of pure water. Dissolve the corrosive sublimate in alcohol and glycerine and then mix thoroughly with the water. This solution is very poisonous and should be kept in wooden or glass vessels out of the way of animals and children.

When a cow has aborted, her womb should be washed out with 1½ gallons of the solution injected through a rubber tube inserted to the depth of the womb, with a funnel in its outer elevated end. This should be repeated daily for a week. In the case of other cows in the herd which have not aborted, one injection of the same kind should be made into the vagina, after which they need only have their external parts washed daily with the solution.

It is not expected that this disease can be suppressed at once, but by keeping up the treatment the losses may be diminished. In addition to the above measures it is necessary to remove all the manure and contaminated litter, sprinkling the surface of the same with a solution of sulphate of copper—5 ounces to 1 gallon water. Drains should be thoroughly disinfected. Milking stools and other implements may be treated in the same way or with boiling water. Great care should be taken to guard against bulls or cows from another herd in which abortion prevails, and streams even may be suspected if there is an aborting herd higher up the same stream.

Milk fever, or parturient apoplexy, of cows.—We are losing all our cows that calve by a new disease, and we are unable to find a remedy. From one to fifteen days after a cow calves she is suddenly attacked, and lives but a short time. There appears a weakness in the legs, and the animal falls and suffers greatly and soon dies. If you can inform me on this disease, please do so.—(*L. E. McC., Ghent, Ky., June 11, 1897.*)

REPLY.—The disease affecting milch cows in your vicinity is probably that known as milk fever, or parturient apoplexy. This is a disease which is very rapidly fatal, and only a small number of cases recover even after the best medicinal treatment. The cause of the disease is not understood, but there are many indications that the extreme density and richness of the blood at the time of calving is an exciting cause. The object to be sought for, then, in preventing the disease, is to reduce the condition of the animal by allowing only a very limited diet for at least a week before calving, and in very plethoric cows it is often necessary to starve them for four or five days before calving. The animal should have free access to good drinking water and a supply of salt. It is well to give a dose of Epsom salts, 1 to 2 pounds, according to the size of the cow, from twelve to twenty-four hours before calving. The salts should be dissolved in water and given as a drench. Daily exercise is of great importance, except in the heat of summer, when the heat of the sun is injurious; but even in summer the animal is benefited by moving about in an open shed or in a pasture provided with shade trees.

Mad itch, or stomach staggers, etc., of cattle.—A very fatal disease having broken out among our cows in this vicinity, I address you, hoping to learn something of the cause, also the necessary remedies, if there are any, to effect a cure. I was reared on a farm in Iowa, and observe that this disease in some respects resembles the black murrain known with us there, but unknown here. A few cows (always cows) died last year, the first time the disease was noticed here, and this year several have already died and others are now sick. The first symptoms are slabbering and running at the nose, inability to eat, restlessness, turning round and round, the animal sometimes becoming crazy; usually spells of severe straining as though trying to be delivered of a calf, with almost constant moaning as if in great pain. The cow constantly turns her head to her side, sometimes licking it as if the pain were in the lungs or forward part of the body. In most cases it seems impossible to get a passage of either urine or manure. The animal usually dies in from three to five days, although some that had but a slight attack quickly recovered. We opened and examined a cow, and although she had eaten nothing since the preceding Monday yet the stomach and bladder were very full. We first thought the trouble was in the throat and cut out the windpipe, which seemed to be in good condition, but when we cut the esophagus a greenish semifluid, resembling the gall, ran from it in great quantities. The lungs seemed congested and instead of being light and spongy they more nearly resembled the liver, being a dark purple and quite solid and firm. The blood had no sign of clotting, although the animal had been dead three hours. I never saw blood so black and tar-like in character as that was. The right ventricle of the heart appeared nearly worn through and spongy, or porous, while the other side was natural. Nothing about the liver or intestines attracted my attention as being wrong. The kidneys had small kernels through them. If you can throw any light upon this subject you will confer a lasting obligation upon this community.—(*H. S. S., Grand Bay, Ala., July 19, 1897.*)

REPLY.—From your description of the disease in cows in your vicinity I judge that it is a form of indigestion which is known by various names, such as mad itch, stomach staggers, and impaction of the stomach, but the exact pathology of the disease is not known. You do not state the kind of food which is supplied to the animals,

but I would suggest that a change be made in it, and as soon as an
animal is noted with symptoms of the disease that it be given at once
a dose of purgative medicine consisting of 1½ pounds magnesium sulphate dissolved in water and mixed with 1 ounce ground ginger and
a cupful of molasses. After this give 3 ounces of Glauber's salts each
day, either mixed with ground food or dissolved in the drinking
water. I would suggest correspondence with the veterinarian of the
Alabama Experiment Station, at Auburn, who, being familiar with
the locality and the conditions under which the animals are raised,
might give further suggestions as to the cause and methods of prevention.

Ringworm, or mange, of cattle.—My calves are troubled with a
disease unknown here before. It commences by the loss of hair
around the eyes and spots on the neck. The old cows are now
catching it. It looks like mange of some character. There are no
lice on the cattle and all are in good flesh. If you can send me
something to enlighten me, you will confer a favor.—(W. M. P.,
Pratt, Kans., May 11, 1897.)

REPLY.—If the spots that have appeared on your cattle about their
eyes are round or circular in form, it may be that the disease is that
known as "ringworm," the treatment for which consists in the application of grease or oil to soften the scabs. In about twelve hours
after the first application rub the spot with a currycomb or other
instrument to remove these scabs, and then apply an ointment composed of flowers of sulphur and lard mixed together in equal parts.
Should the disease, however, be true cattle mange it will be more
difficult to cure. It is important in the latter case to cleanse the skin
(removing the crusts, etc., which form about the diseased parts) in
order that the remedies can have effect upon the parasites which
cause the disease. For this purpose use soft soap and water, and
give the animal a thorough scrubbing, especially in the regions where
the skin has been rubbed. If the crusts are not all removed by the
first washing apply sweet oil to soften them; then, effectually to
destroy the parasites, apply carefully with a brush the following
mixture: Oil of tar 1 ounce, soft soap one half pint, sulphur one-half
pound, and alcohol 1 pint. After two days wash the parts with soft
soap and water. In three or four days a second application may be
required. It is essential that the stables, stalls, and rubbing posts
where affected cattle have been should be cleansed by whitewashing
them or applying a solution of sulphuric acid, 1 pint of the acid to 3
gallons of water.

"Wolves," or "warbles," in cattle.—Please give me all the information you can about "wolves" in a cow's back, and how they can be
exterminated. On several farms in Henrico County the cattle are
suffering with this disease, and I am requested to write to you for a
possible cure.—(H. V. P., Richmond, Va., Feb. 26, 1897.)

REPLY.—By the term "wolves" in the back of cattle I suppose you refer to the small tumors which are often seen at this time of the year upon cattle which have been pastured during the previous summer. The common name for them is "warbles," and they are caused by an insect, which, it is supposed, deposits its eggs on an animal, and the larvæ develop in the tumors. In most cases these grubs, when they have attained sufficient size, will escape and cause no injury to the cattle. It will aid, however, in the extermination of the insect if the grubs are squeezed out with the fingers and killed by burning or crushing them under the foot. When the opening is too small to permit the removal of the grub it may be enlarged with a sharp knife. Usually, however, it may be pressed out sufficiently to be grasped with a small pair of forceps, and is then easily removed by gentle traction, observing care to prevent breaking. It is seldom that any application is required to the backs of the cattle affected, but in case of suppuration a dilute solution of carbolic acid may be injected into the swellings through the opening.

Lice on cattle.—Some of my cattle have lice on them, caused by a hencoop being near the barn. Have tried to kill them without success.—(*G. B. C., Chepachet, R. I., Dec. 4, 1897.*)

REPLY.—One remedy for the treatment of lice on cattle, which is said to be effective, is a decoction of *Cocculus indicus* (fish berries). Take one-half pound for each animal, pound fine, add 2 quarts of vinegar, and set it on the stove to simmer for an hour. Then apply the solution with a cloth, rubbing well at the points affected. This is said not to injure the skin or sicken the animal. Kerosene emulsion is also used for this purpose. Linseed oil is another remedy; or lard and kerosene; or an infusion of tobacco, 1 ounce tobacco to 1 quart water. The latter should be used cautiously, for when applied too freely it may sicken and kill the animal, especially young calves.

Contagious ophthalmia of cattle.—In our neighborhood are several cases of what is supposed to be contagious ophthalmia of cattle. In many instances the disease is very severe, causing blindness, especially in calves. I think the disease was brought here from Buffalo by a herd of steers, as the 60 head composing it have nearly all had it, and it has not been reported from any other neighborhood.—(*J. T. M., Oramel, N. Y. Sept. 5, 1898.*)

REPLY.—I would advise that the cattle affected with the disease be separated from the healthy cattle, and no communication between the two lots allowed. If it is possible, confine the affected cattle in a darkened stable, and feed them with succulent green food. The eyes should be bathed freely twice a day with a solution containing 30 grains sulphate of zinc, 20 drops fluid extract belladonna leaves, and 1 quart of pure rain water. Another beneficial wash for the eyes is a solution of boracic acid, 1 dram to 4 ounces of water. If there is much fever and constipation give purgative doses of Epsom salts. It

10317——34

has also been recommended to use iodoform vaseline in the proportion of 1 part iodoform to 12 parts vaseline in such cases. A small portion of the mixture is inserted under the eyelids, which are then closed and rubbed for a short time. In most cases one application is sufficient. The mixture should be prepared carefully and have no lumps of iodoform in the mixture.

Osteomalacia, or "creeps."—There is a disease here commonly known as "creeps." The affected animal loses flesh, the eyes sink, hair looks dead, and they walk as if their feet were very sore, bones very rotten and break easily, and the liver is very much atrophied. It comes in some pastures more than others. It is especially bad in dry summers. A heavy rain or cool weather generally relieves the symptoms and they frequently get well, but others linger and die. They can not be handled, as a misstep or stumble will sometimes break a leg or a quick movement will nearly cause a fall. Any information as to the cause and cure will be thankfully received.—(*J. D. M., Victoria, Texas, Dec. 13, 1898.*)

REPLY.—The disease known as "creeps" is more accurately designated "osteomalacia." It is caused by an insufficient supply of certain mineral ingredients in the food, probably phosphates of lime. I presume it has not rained for some time where these cattle are kept, and under these conditions, although there is lime in the soil from the chalky hills, yet the grass does not contain a sufficient amount of lime salts. The disease is especially seen in heifers with their first calf, as these animals require a considerable quantity of mineral salts for their own growth and for the nourishment of their calves. A change of pasture, particularly to regions where there is greater moisture, is beneficial, but when this can not be done the deficiency in the food must be supplied by feeding. Cotton-seed meal is one of the best foods for this purpose, but it should be given carefully, as too large quantities are injurious to cows. Other foods containing mineral salts may be given, such as wheat bran, beans, bean straw, and the like. Phosphate of lime is indicated as the best drug to be administered, but on account of its cost and its slight solubility in water it may not be practicable to use it when a large number of cattle are to be treated. A similar objection exists with reference to pulverized bone meal, which would also supply the lime salts required. Lime water is also beneficial and can often be provided at slight expense by throwing lime into the drinking water. This does not entirely meet the case as it does not provide phosphate of lime, which is probably the ingredient that is lacking in the food.

Disease of eyes of cattle.—There has been considerable complaint here of cows and neat stock going blind. The trouble commences with a whitish film growing over the sight of the eye and in a short time it spreads over the entire eye, producing blindness. Several herds are affected with the disease. One veterinarian says it is caused by a minute insect and another says that is not correct. The latter says that if the affected animal is put in a darkened stable it will recover without medical treatment. The dark stable is a partial success if the animal is not entirely blind before being put there. What is the remedy for this disease?—(*G. R., Belvidere, Ill., Aug. 31, 1898.*)

REPLY.—This eye disease has become prevalent throughout the United States during the past few years and it appears to be of an infectious nature. Cases are reported where one affected animal has been introduced into a herd with the result that in the course of a few weeks a number of animals in the herd became similarly affected. When no attention is given to this lesion a number of the animals will become blind in one or both eyes. The treatment is very simple, and when applied in time will cure most cases. The affected eyes should be well bathed in a solution of boracic acid, and after wiping dry a small amount of iodoform vaseline should be inserted between the eyelids either by means of the finger or a small flat stick with rounded edges. The eyelids should then be rubbed gently, in order to spread the ointment over the whole surface of the eye. It will be found that a few applications made in this way will cure even very progressed cases. When taken at the first appearance, one application is often sufficient to check the development of the lesion. It is important that the ointment, which should be prepared in the strength of 1 part iodoform to 12 parts of vaseline, should be ground very carefully, as small particles of iodoform left undissolved in the vaseline will have an irritating effect on the eye.

Cutting off tails of cattle.—Will you please inform me what causes cattle to lose their tails? I have been called to see a number of cattle, and it seems that the bone in the end dies, one joint after another. I cut the tail off above the affected part, and it seems all right.—(*F. B., Salina, Kans., July 30, 1898.*)

REPLY.—It is not necessary to cut off the tails of cattle in the cases to which you refer, unless there is a severe injury to the lower part of the tail and ordinary treatment does not succeed in healing the wound. The idea that a limp condition of the tail affects the health of cattle is a mistaken one, and the real cause is usually some disorder of the digestive organs. Generally the administration of a dose of purgative medicine will relieve the animal without the necessity of amputating the tail, which disfigures the animal and prevents it from using the switch in keeping away the flies. The purgative medicine may be prepared by taking 1½ pounds Epsom salts, one-half pound common salt, 1 ounce ground ginger, one-half pint molasses, and about 2 quarts of lukewarm water. Mix the ingredients with the water and give to the animal as a drench from a stout long-necked bottle.

Milk sickness.—I have a farm of 1,000 acres here, on several places of which, where cattle or sheep graze, I occasionally lose one from what the old residents call milk sickness, or milk poison. It is claimed that a mineral vapor arises from the ground and settles with the dew on the weeds, grass, or vegetables on which the cattle feed, and within twenty-four to thirty-six hours after eating such food they die. At first their knees seem to weaken, the head shakes from side to side, the teeth (you might say) chatter, and lastly the head is thrown back, as if the neck were broken, and directly death follows. Hogs pasturing on the same land are not affected. The "natives" here contend that there is mineral poison of some kind in the ground that settles on the vegetation, as I have described above. I have two fields of forest land of about 60 acres fenced off and can not allow sheep or cattle in it because of losing quite a number in this way so inexplicable to me. On other parts of the farm I have no trouble whatever, though I understand that years ago, when these older parts were first cleared and used, the same trouble prevailed. Can you inform me from this description as to the nature of the trouble and the proper remedy, if there is one?—(*M. H. C.*, *Blowing Rock*, *N. C.*, *May 3, 1898.*)

REPLY.—The disease known as "milk sickness" is described as a specific infectious disease peculiar to certain unimproved lands, usually occurring in cattle and communicable, through meat, milk, and cheese, to man and animals. The cause of it has been ascribed to certain plants, mineral products, and to bacteria, especially spiral bacteria, which are said to be found in the blood and excretions from human beings suffering from this disease. The disease disappears with the clearing of the forests and the cultivation of the soil. This Bureau has not had an opportunity to investigate it, and no report has been published with reference to it by this Department. But little is known concerning the cause of the disease, and no remedy has been discovered for it. However, it has been found, as you state is your experience, that after the land has been cleared and cultivated for a short time the disease disappears.

Mammitis, or inflammation of the udder, in cows.—I have a cow that has been fresh but a little more than three weeks. I sold the calf about a week ago; a few days after, the cow began to give milk of a decidedly pinkish cast. Since then it has grown worse and now looks almost bloody. I have had her milked three times a day and used some few simple external remedies, but I see no change.—(*M. A. F.*, *Washington*, *D. C.*, *June 16, 1897.*)

REPLY.—It is probable that the cow is affected with mammitis, or inflammation of the udder, which occasions the peculiar appearance of the milk. It would be advisable to foment the udder frequently with water as warm as can be borne without giving pain to the animal. If the inflammation becomes severe, a large poultice may be applied. If treatment of this kind does not cure, I would advise that a competent veterinary surgeon be called in to treat the case according to requirements.

Gummy milk.—I have a cow whose milk becomes gummy and so thick it will not pass through a strainer. Can you tell me how to overcome this and what is the cause?—(*J. V. S.*, *Sligo, Md.*, *May 20, 1898.*)

REPLY.—You have not given facts enough for us to form an opinion, but the Dairy Division suggests that your dairy may be infected with bacteria, which cause milk to become ropy or slimy. A Farmers' Bulletin, entitled "Care of milk on the farm," has been mailed to you, and your attention is called to pages 24 and 25,[1] where a method

[1] From Farmers' Bulletin No. 63: When milk has a strong taint at the time it is drawn, the trouble is usually not due to bacteria, and it can be improved by aeration (see p. 30). But when it is natural at first and gradually becomes more and more tainted the longer it is held bacteria are probably to blame, and if the dairy is badly infected with them energetic measures are often required to get rid of them. If the affected milk is not harmful to health, but only objectionable on account of its smell or taste, its entire loss may be made unnecessary by pasteurizing or sterilizing it as soon as possible after it is drawn and before much of a change has been made, and then using it immediately or keeping where further infection can not take place. But this treatment does not affect the source of the trouble, and if that is not overcome by sterilizing all utensils and practicing scrupulous cleanliness everywhere, the disinfection of the stable or the killing of all the germs must be undertaken. Disinfection is also necessary if cattle have been affected with a contagious disease, and it should be done as soon as the last case is cured or removed and before other cattle are added to the herd. While the germs of some diseases are delicate and can live only a short time outside the body of their host, others are hardy and retain their vitality for months or years. Sunlight is a great purifier and should be admitted in abundance. The same may be said of fresh, pure air. Both of these aid in disinfection.

Whitewash partially serves the purpose of disinfection; it should soon follow other agents which are employed when more thorough work must be done. Before disinfection, the stable should be carefully cleaned as above detailed, and any fodder which may have been stored where it was exposed should be destroyed.

Chemical disinfectants are efficient for thorough work. Most of these are poisonous and must be handled with great care. The cost is an important consideration in the selection of disinfectants for cheap buildings. The following are comparatively inexpensive: Bichloride of mercury or corrosive sublimate, in the proportion of 1 part to 1,000 of water, or 1 ounce to 8 gallons of water, is an effective agent. The poison should first be dissolved in a small amount of hot water and then diluted; it may be applied with a brush or as a spray. One pound of chloride of lime to 8 gallons of water is another effective disinfectant. Carbolic acid is well known; it should be used in the proportion of 1 part to 20 of water.

Sometimes it is best to use a gas as a germicide. In this case no animal nor person can remain in the inclosure being disinfected. It must be tightly closed, so there will be no leaks through cracks or other openings. When sulphur is burned the building is soon filled with its fumes. A considerable quantity should be supplied and fresh air excluded for twenty-four hours, to give full time for the gas to penetrate into every place where germs may be lodged. Chlorine gas is a more powerful disinfectant. It is generated by chloride of lime and muriatic acid. The fumes are very deadly, and great care must be taken not to inhale it. Formaldehyde is an efficient germicide which has recently come into use; it is a gas generated by special apparatus; it may also be applied in a solution.

One of the best and cheapest disinfectants for floors, gutters, waste pipes, etc., is sulphate of iron (copperas). For a floor, as much of this should be dissolved as water will hold; it is then applied with a sprinkler. Lumps of dry copperas are useful for purifying drains.

After a stable has been disinfected it should be allowed to remain empty several days for thorough airing.

of handling milk tainted by bacterial action and the way of over-
coming the difficulty is described. Ropy milk bacteria should be
dealt with in the same manner. If the milk is ropy when it is drawn,
it is probable that the cow is diseased, and a veterinarian should be
consulted.

Ropy appearance of milk.—I have a cow whose milk, when about
twenty-four hours old, becomes slimy and ropy, or stringy. She appears
to be in good health; eats well; in fact, all her functions are in normal
condition except when she urinates. About a quarter or third of the
water at the last of the passage comes in rather easy driblets. I have
given her saltpeter, but there is no improvement. Stable is light and
clean; milking utensils very clean; one horse is in the stable with the
cow; feed pasture grass and 3 quarts of wheat bran in the morning.
Please tell me what to give her. Old cow owners here recommend saltpeter. Is it injurious?—(*D. J. L., Rockland, Mass., Sept. 21, 1891.*)

REPLY.—The ropy or slimy appearance of the milk of your cow
after it has been drawn for twenty-four hours is probably due to the
presence of bacteria which develop in the milk after it is drawn and
not to any disease of the cow. However, if there is any inflammation in the udder of the cow, it might cause a peculiar appearance
of the milk.[1] I would advise that the vessels in which the milk is
drawn be cleaned thoroughly with boiling water and, if possible, be
placed over a jet of steam under pressure; also that the udder and
teats be washed with warm water to which a little carbolic acid has
been added. It may also be necessary to cover with a lime wash the
interior of the stable.

There may be some weeds or plants in the pasture which causes
the coloration of the urine. Saltpeter is not necessarily injurious,
but would probably not be required in the case to which you refer.

Refusing to give down milk.—Will you kindly tell me how to
make a 4-year-old Jersey give down her milk? She now has a second
calf. We milk her as dry as we can, but she gives down only about
a quarter of what she should give. One minute after the calf is at
her side she gives the milk down. She is naturally hard to milk.—
(*J. M., Lawrence Station, N. J., Aug. 19, 1898.*)

REPLY.—It is suggested that you allow the calf to draw milk from
the udder for a few moments before attempting to milk the cow by
hand, as this method in some cases is found to work satisfactorily.
The cow should receive a liberal diet and be handled gently. There
is no method of enlarging the aperture in the teats without placing a
probe in them for a time. This operation, however, should only be
conducted by an expert, as otherwise the animal may be permanently
injured.

White scours in calves.—I wish to know what is the trouble with
my young calves. I have consulted the State veterinary surgeons,

---

[1] See footnote, p. 583.

also those of Colorado, and can find no one who can give me any information as to the best way to treat them. The calves born in the corrals at the ranch are taken with dysentery within one or two days after birth and die in twenty-four hours in great agony. The milk curdles in the first stomach, and the intestines become inflamed, the blood vessels burst, and death ensues. A curious feature is that while deaths of this kind occur in the corrals, there is never a calf affected outside of them, where the larger animals are fed the same hay and have the same water. The corrals are thoroughly cleaned at least once a year and disinfected with lime scattered plentifully all over the ground, and the sheds and fences are whitewashed. We would be greatly pleased to have the opinion of some one who may understand this matter and who can clear up the mystery which has bothered us for five years. It has always acted exactly in the same way, namely, calves put in the corral are taken sick, while outside we have no trouble.—(*H. A. & Co., Cheyenne, Wyo., Apr. 7, 1897.*)

REPLY.—The disease is undoubtedly that known as white scours, or diarrhea, which often affects young animals soon after birth. Some forms of this disease are undoubtedly infectious, though the cause of the infection has not been determined and there are many points relating to it which are still obscure. Since you state that it is confined to the corrals, I would advise, as the first and principal means of combating it, that the corrals be effectively disinfected. You state that this is done each year, but it probably is not done thoroughly enough to accomplish the object. The soil is no doubt impregnated with the disease, and it will be necessary to remove several inches of the surface soil and either supply the place with new soil or mix lime intimately with the first few inches of the remaining soil. Whitewash by itself is not sufficient to destroy the infection of the disease. One of the following disinfecting solutions may be used.

1. Corrosive sublimate (mercuric chloride) 1 ounce in about 8 gallons of water. The water should be put into wooden tubs or barrels and the powdered sublimate added to it. The whole allowed to stand for twenty-four hours to give the sublimate time to become entirely dissolved. Since this solution is poisonous, it should be kept covered and well guarded from animals and children. As it loses its virtue in proportion to the amount of dirt present, all manure and other dirt should be first removed before applying the disinfectant to floors or woodwork.

2. Chloride of lime, 5 ounces to 1 gallon of water. This should be applied to the floor and woodwork with a broom or mop after removal of the dirt.

3. The following disinfectant is very serviceable. It is not poisonous, but quite corrosive, and care must be taken to protect the eyes and hands from accidental splashing: Crude carbolic acid one-half gallon, crude sulphuric acid one-half gallon. These two substances should be mixed in tubs or glass vessels. The sulphuric acid is very slowly added to the carbolic acid. During the mixture a large amount

of heat is developed. The disinfecting power of the mixture is heightened if the amount of heat is kept down by placing the tub or glass demijohn containing the carbolic acid in cold water while the sulphuric acid is being added. The resulting mixture is added to water in the ratio of 1 to 20. One gallon of mixed acids will thus furnish 20 gallons of a strong disinfecting solution having a slightly milky appearance. The treatment of scours is not satisfactory, as the calves succumb so quickly after being attacked that the common remedies do not accomplish good results. Some report favorably the use of creolin, giving one-half dram in a watery solution three times a day so long as the diarrhea continues.

Another remedy that is reported, and by which some French writers obtain excellent results, is tar water used as an injection. For this purpose take pure vegetable tar 4 ounces, boiling water 6 quarts. Let the mixture cool and use about one-third of a quart every half hour as an injection into the rectum.

Another injection recommended is composed of milk and sulphuric ether, using 1 teaspoonful of ether to a pint of milk, gradually increasing to 3 or 4 teaspoonfuls in the same quantity of milk.

Still another remedy that is reported as beneficial is composed of salol 2 drams, oxide of bismuth 4 drams, carbonate of lime 1 ounce. Mix and divide into six doses. Give the first two at intervals of two hours, then give one dose every four hours. Give each dose in a glass of camomile infusion, and if the calf is weak and exhausted add half a glass of good wine.

Diarrhea in calves.—Mr. Bartlett Woods, of Crown Point, Ind., a correspondent of the Division of Statistics, requested information regarding a cure for diarrhea in calves. The following reply was given:

REPLY.—One remedy for diarrhea in calves, which has been used quite effectively in some cases, is as follows: Salol, 2 drams; oxide of bismuth, 4 drams; carbonate of lime, 1 ounce; mix and divide into six doses. Give the first two doses at intervals of three hours, then give one dose every six hours; these doses to be given in 5 ounces of camomile infusion. If the calf is weak give in the intervals between the doses 2 ounces of port wine or 1 ounce of whisky.

Another remedy which is believed to be of special value in cases where disinfection of the intestinal tract is desired.may be prepared as follows: Naphthalin, 5 drams; castor oil, one-half pint. Dissolve the drug in the oil and give a large tablespoonful of the mixture three times a day.

Creolin is another remedy which is of value when administered internally, and is given in doses of from one-half to 1 dram, dissolved in water, every three hours, as required.

This disease, as seen in sucking calves, is infectious and contagious, so that calves affected with it should be separated from healthy animals, and the stalls and utensils used should be disinfected. A good disinfectant for this purpose is a solution of chloride of lime (bleaching powder), 4 ounces to 1 gallon of water. The bowel discharge or droppings from the infected calves should be disinfected by covering with quicklime.

Warts on a calf.—I have a calf affected with what is in this neighborhood called "the warts," and I wish to know if there is any cure for them. The warts are on the nose and mouth and seem to be increasing in number. Kindly let me know if there is any way to get rid of them.—(*P. F. J., Waldrop, Va., Nov. 7, 1898.*) .

REPLY.—One or more applications of a strong solution of creolin, or any of the carbolic sheep dips on the market, will as a rule remove warts of the kind you describe. A solution of 1 to 4 may be used to good effect, applied to the warts with a stiff brush. If proper care is taken to apply the remedy exclusively to the warts without touching the surrounding skin, a solution of 1 to 2, or even the undiluted preparation, may be used.

DISEASES OF HORSES AND MULES.

Cerebro-spinal meningitis in horses.—At the instance of many of our planters and stockmen I write you to say that the horses of this coast country are dying by the thousand with something like the "blind staggers," or, as it is called by the Galveston veterinary surgeon, meningitis. The horses seem to be affected with something like blindness and a turning to one side when they attempt to walk, and seem to be wholly unconscious of where they are going, and will run over anything that may be before them, if possible. They live from one to four days after being attacked, and we are unable to find anything that does them any good; in fact, we have no knowledge of any horse surviving. Our object in writing this letter is to get any information you may be able to give that will help our poor people to save their horses. We will thank you for such information.—(*T. P., Velasco, Tex., Oct. 23, 1897.*)

There is a disease locally known as "sleepy staggers" among the horses here that is killing them off like rats. So far as I know no horse has recovered that has had the disease. We know nothing of the cause of the disease. The principal symptom is that the horse backs up against the side of the stable, and if possible, braces the head against something in front. It is all over this part of the State, and is still spreading.—(*J. A. S., Iowa, La., Sept. 6, 1898.*)

REPLY.—No remedy has been discovered for cerebro-spinal meningitis, which is probably the disease affecting horses in your vicinity. It is a miasmatic, infectious, noncontagious disease, but as yet the specific nature of the infectious agent has not been discovered. Probably the disease is contracted by animals drinking out of stagnant pools which contain decomposing vegetable matter, and one of the first precautions to be taken for prevention is to stop animals from drinking from such pools or streams. Whenever possible only good well water should be provided. With a little observation it can probably be determined which are infected pools. In this particular outbreak only horses seem to be affected, but both cattle and sheep are susceptible to the disease, and preventive measures should include these animals as well. The carcasses of all stock that die from this disease should be destroyed by burying them and covering with lime, or, where it can be done, burning the carcasses. Any stables where infected stock have been should be disinfected, since this is an infectious disease and other animals may contract it from being placed in infected stables or yards.

· The usual mortality from this disease is great, being as high as 90 per cent. The outbreak you report seems especially virulent, so that under these circumstances probably little benefit can result from treatment. Some benefit may be derived from the application of a strong fly blister to the top of the head, extending from between the ears backward for a distance of about six inches. Also give the animal a strong laxative of either Barbados aloes or raw linseed oil.

Azoturia and distemper in horses.—I would like very much to have some advice as to how to prevent and cure the diseases known as distemper and azoturia.—(*M. H. D., Ogden, Iowa.*)

REPLY.—The disease known as distemper, or "strangles," is infectious, and in stables where it is prevalent efforts should be made to disinfect the stalls and utensils used about the infected animals, and such animals should be isolated and put under treatment. In ordinary cases of this disease but little treatment is required beyond keeping the animals comfortable and protecting them from cold. It is often necessary, however, to apply poultices to the swelling which occurs between the branches of the lower jaw, and when an abscess is formed to lance it for the escape of the pus. There are other cases, however, in which the swelling may appear at different parts of the body and require special treatment by a competent veterinary surgeon.

The causes of azoturia are not so well understood, but it is supposed to be connected with high feeding, especially when horses are fed on highly nutritious food, and during a period of rest in the stall under full rations. The disease is never seen at pasture, rarely under constant daily work, even if the feeding be high. Prevention consists in restricting the diet and giving daily exercise when horses are not at work. A horse that is subject to attacks should not be left idle for a single day in the stall; but if required to be kept at rest, should be given only a small amount of food, and also a laxative— one-half to 1 pound of Glauber's salts the first day and one-fourth pound each day thereafter. The treatment required for a horse attacked with this disease varies in different cases and should only be undertaken by a specialist who has had experience with it or has made a study of the disease and the medicines required.

Millet disease of horses.—A year ago I had a mare that was with foal to become lame in one of her hind legs so that at last she was unable to get up. She foaled while she was down, the colt dying the next day. She got up after a few days and seemed to be getting better when she was taken with a swelling of all her legs, with a consequent stiffness of all her limbs, so that she was unable to move. After a few days the swelling subsided in three of her legs, but remained in the fourth one all summer till she died in the fall. This spring I had another mare with foal, and to prevent a recurrence of the same affection in this one I worked her to three weeks before she dropped her colt, the one of last year not having been worked and in good flesh. This mare swelled in all her legs a few days before foaling and could hardly get around; but she became all right apparently two or three days after foaling. At the end of the week she, too, became lame in one of her hind legs, so that when she lies down she is unable to get up without help. The lame leg is not swelled at all, but the other leg is considerably enlarged, especially at the hock. I feed my horses millet, the only hay I have, but they have the range of a stalk field. My neighbors, almost without exception, say that the millet is the cause of my trouble. I have fed this hay for the last eight years and have had no trouble till last year. This year my millet did not do very well, crab grass taking its place, so that fully 75 per cent of the hay is crab grass. Some of my neighbors say that I should not feed millet too green, while others say that it is the seed that affects the horses, so I do not know which to believe. I had a sucking colt get out every day and feed on the ripe seed heads of a patch of this hay. I could not see that it hurt him, and to-day he is as good a horse as there is in the country. If you can enlighten me as to the cause of the trouble among my horses or can tell me the truth as to the effect of millet on a horse's constitution, I shall be greatly obliged.—(*F. F. C., Onaga, Kans., Apr. 26, 1897.*)

REPLY.—The symptoms you describe are very similar to those described for horses affected with "millet disease." This disease has been studied by the veterinarian of the North Dakota Agricultural Experiment Station, Dr. T. D. Hinebaugh, at Fargo, and the conclusion he reached in the bulletin recently published on this subject is that his experiments "have thoroughly demonstrated that millet, when used exclusively as a coarse food, is injurious to horses, first, in producing an increased action of the kidneys; second, in causing lameness and swelling of the joints; third, in producing infusion of blood into the joints, and fourth, in destroying the texture of the bone, rendering it softer and less tenacious, so that traction causes the ligaments and muscles to be torn loose." It has not been determined, to my knowledge, in what stage of growth the millet is most injurious, nor has it been determined whether the injurious substances are contained in the millet seed or in the stalk when green or imperfectly grown. The crab grass, which you state as making up a large percentage of the fodder cut from your field, contains very little nutriment, and it may be that the horses suffered from not being able to obtain nourishment enough from this poor grass, instead of being affected by any substances in the grass itself; but from the investigation and observation of a large number of people who have used millet as a food for horses, it seems to be established that bad effects come from the use of it exclusively as a coarse food.

Osteoporosis.—I write for information with reference to a horse which I have, 6 years of age. In January we noticed that she was not doing well and discovered many little handfuls of hay partly masticated which she had dropped from her mouth and which showed a slight discharge from the head; hair looked rough, no life, and with this condition a swelling of the nostrils was noticeable. A local veterinarian pronounced it a case of "big head," which I have been unable to learn anything about. At this late day she is looking better, her hair commences to brighten, she is eating better and swallows her food, dropping less on the floor, and commences to show some little life, trots about, has shed her hair, but the enlargement of the head is about the same.—(*O. J. W., Amityville, N. Y., June 2, 1898.*)

REPLY.—The horse is probably affected with osteoporosis. The nature of the disease is not well understood, consequently the methods of treatment as a rule are not successful. It is usually advised to give lime salts, especially the phosphates of lime, and in some cases it seems to cause an improvement. It has been recommended and found useful in some cases to give horses suffering from this affection limewater to drink. This can be prepared by placing a bushel of quicklime in a barrel which is water-tight, then fill the barrel with water, and allow the horse to drink out of the barrel as soon as the lime has settled, a new supply of water to be put into the barrel as required. It is necessary to add the water carefully to the quicklime and in small quantities at first.

ADDITIONAL INFORMATION.—Later on a second horse belonging to this gentleman was affected with the same disease. On August 4 the Bureau submitted to its correspondent a series of questions designed to bring out the circumstances surrounding this disease, and the reply follows:

The two horses which were affected with osteoporosis were of Hambletonian stock; on the sire's side of Mambrino Dudley, of General Tracy's stock farm, and on the dam's side Winthrop Morrell. The dam I owned for about eleven years and she was strong and hearty past twenty. I knew of the stock of the sire and dam for some ten years and never heard of any sickness of this nature. The horse was foaled in March, 1890, the mare in 1892. When the horse was 6 and the mare 4 they were strong, active, and full of endurance. The next year, when 7 and 5, there seemed to be a loss of vitality as I recall their condition. They did not stand their drives well, and there was a shifting lameness which we were unable to locate—that is, during the season one year ago—so that I arranged to turn the mare out in the yard for three months, intending to take her up the first of January and turn out the horse. But on the first of January her coat was dead, and when I took her up she had no life, was thin and not eating well, so that after driving her two or three times I again turned her out and called in some home talent to ascertain what was the trouble. He filed her teeth. Along in March a man saw her who recognized enlargement of the head. Although this had been present for many weeks previously, I failed to recognize it, as I had never seen or heard of the disease before. For some time she had been partially chewing her food and dropping it at her feet. The bones of the head, especially the superior and maxillary, continued to enlarge, and she continued to "run down" until about six weeks ago. After hearing from you that there was practically no help for her I shot her. We saved the bones of the skull, in which we found the two bones specified very much enlarged and pliable, and when broken they looked like rotten maple more nearly than anything else I can think of. The other horse's head was noticed to be enlarging after showing the other symptoms for several months, and he was also shot.

I believe that the disease in each case developed in a year and a half to two years, and that the first symptom was a shifting lameness. The horse had been used in light driving only on the road, and very moderate at that. The stable is a wooden building on sandy soil, with ventilation underneath the floors and into the attic of the barn from the box stalls in which the horses were kept. The water supply is from a driven well near the barn in sandy soil. We have an abundance of water only about 10 feet from the surface.

Three other horses have been kept in the same barn with these. Two of them are three or four years older than the affected horses, while one is nearing twenty and has been kept in this barn many years. The other horses are and have been strong and well.

"Wind gall."—I have a fine young mule which has a wind gall on the inside of the hind leg near the large pastern joint. It is large and soft. Will you please give me a remedy for it?—(*S. S. S., Storeville, Ga., August 1, 1898.*)

REPLY.—The so-called "wind-gall" can sometimes be removed in recent cases by the application of a smart blister, and subsequently bandaging very tightly while the animal is in the stable. There is no treatment except a surgical operation which can remove them after they have become chronic. The operation should not be performed by anyone except an expert veterinary surgeon.

Shortening of the tendons.—About a year ago my mule, five or six years old, became lame in her left foot, and since then the disease has caused her to walk more and more on the toe or point of her foot till now she walks that way altogether. No swelling exists to any extent, nor does marked tenderness exist. All other feet are healthy, and otherwise she is in a healthy condition. This year she has plowed. Please advise me as to the usual cause of said trouble and the best plan for effecting a cure. I have been considering the advisability of performing tenotomy, but do not know whether to cut part of the tendon above the ankle joint or the tendons below the joint. The pathology, diagnosis, prognosis, and treatment are desired, and I will thank you for the information.—(*W. A. R., Oakridge, La., July 22, 1898.*)

REPLY.—There are many conditions which shorten the tendons, and it would be quite impossible to make a satisfactory diagnosis of the case to which you refer without an opportunity to examine the animal. This condition often arises from traumatic causes, such as sprain, violent overexertion, lacerations, or contusions of the tendons; or it may arise from lesions in other parts of the limb, as of the foot or digital region proper, such as bad feet, navicular disease, contraction of the heels, corns, quarter or toe cracks, quittors, deep punctured wounds, and quite frequently ringbones or other exostoses. One method of treatment is to place upon the foot a shoe with a long toe. This causes a stretching of the tendons, and may bring the foot into position. As you suggest, the operation known as tenotomy is sometimes performed for the relief of this condition, and in most cases the tendons are cut between the knee and the fetlock. For a description of the operation I would refer you to Professor Liautard's Manual of Operative Veterinary Surgery, which is almost the only work on veterinary surgery published in the English language in which the method is fully described.

Elevations in skin under collar and saddle.—I have a blooded mare that is troubled with a peculiar cutaneous affection. Bumps about the size of chestnuts appear on the point of the shoulders, along the neck under the mane, and on the back where the saddle blanket touches. They are not sore and do not itch, and otherwise the mare has remained in fine health. They resemble the "wolf" so often found in the back of cows. I could not cure the spot under the collar, as it was suppurating, until I stopped using the mare. After she had two and a half months of leisure I find the bumps are still present, and wherever the harness rests they immediately become big, ugly suppurating sores. I use a felt saddlecloth one-half inch thick and very soft, but the bumps continue to come. The mare is not galled or mistreated, and she is in good condition.—(*C. H. P., Warrenton, N. C., Oct. 29, 1898.*)

REPLY.—I am unable, without an opportunity to examine the mare to which you refer, to state the exact nature of the skin disease from which she is suffering. As you state that the elevations in the skin occur where she is chafed by the collar or saddle pad, I would advise that each time after using the animal the skin be washed with either of the following solutions: Salt water (one-half ounce to the quart); extract of witch-hazel; a weak solution of oak bark or camphorated spirits. When the surface is raw it may be beneficial to apply either oxide of zinc, lycopodium, powdered starch, or smear the surface with vaseline, or with 1 ounce of vaseline intimately mixed with one-half dram each of sugar of lead and opium. The mare might also receive twice daily with her feed one-half ounce cream of tartar or a teaspoonful of carbonate of soda.

DISEASES OF SHEEP.

Grub in the head of sheep.—I have some sheep with some disease of the head—running at the nose, difficult of breathing, etc. Have lost several. Will you kindly advise me of some treatment?—(*W. D. D., Rubermont, Va., July 22, 1897.*)

REPLY.—One cause of running at the nose in sheep is from grub in the head, which comes from the larvæ of *Œstrus ovis* that lives in the nasal passages and causes inflammation and discharge from the nose. This parasite develops from eggs which are deposited by the sheep gadfly and hatch into the grub. There are several methods of treating the disease, but none of them are very effective, and most authorities recommend preventive measures instead. Such measures consist in smearing the sheep's nose with a mixture of equal parts of pine tar and grease or of pine tar and fish oil. This may be applied to the nose with a brush or the mixture may be smeared upon the troughs where the sheep will get it upon the nose while feeding. Another mixture which is recommended is to take beeswax 1 pound, linseed oil 1 pint, and carbolic acid 4 ounces; melt the wax and oil together, adding 2 ounces of common rosin, then, as it cools, stir in the carbolic acid. This should be rubbed over the face and nose once in two or three days during the months of July and August. Some sheep breeders use a cover made of canvas, which is tied over the face of the sheep and smeared with the above mixture or with a mixture of asafetida and tallow. This should be hung in such a way that it will not interfere with sight or grazing and yet protect the animal against the fly. Another method of treating affected sheep is by fumigation with tobacco, the process being described as follows: "One person holds the head of the sheep in a convenient position in front of the operator. The latter, having a pipe half filled with tobacco and kindled in the usual manner, places one or two folds of a handkerchief over the opening of the bowl then passes the stem a good way up the nostril, applies his mouth to the covered bowl, and blows vigorously through the handkerchief. When this has continued for a few seconds the pipe is withdrawn and the operation repeated in the other nostril." Another method is by fumigation with sulphur. Confine the sheep in a small room and throw the sulphur upon a bed of coals. A person should remain in the room with the sheep, and when the fumes become painful to the person the door should be opened to prevent suffocation and injury. The fumigation should be repeated at intervals of two or three days.

Flukes in sheep—Intestinal worms of sheep—Grubs in the nose of sheep.—Will you kindly inform me how liver flukes affect sheep and what is the remedy for the disease? I should also like to know what should be given for sheep worms in the intestines, and what length of time elapses after the fly lays the eggs in the sheep's nostril before the worm crawls up into the head and kills the sheep. In several flocks here the bowels of some sheep are very loose and other sheep run at the nose. The bowels of the latter are all right, but they will not fatten, though they eat heartily.—(*W. S., Leesburg, Va., Jan. 1, 1897.*)

REPLY.—Sheep affected with fluke disease first improve in condition. This improvement, however, does not last long, for they soon begin to grow thin again, although they retain their appetites. They finally become very much emaciated, lose part of their wool, and show edematous swellings under the jaw, and distended abdomen. Ewes with lamb frequently abort, and if they carry the lambs to full term the latter usually die from the inability of the mothers to support them. If the fluke disease is suspected, it would be well to have some expert make a microscopical examination of the feces in order to determine the presence of the eggs; or you might kill one of the sheep most affected and examine the liver to find the flukes. This would settle the case.

As regards remedies, the object is to build the animals up in strength against the attack. Consequently food plays a very important part in the treatment. You should remove your animals from the source of infection—namely, swampy land—and then feed them generously with hay and oats. If corn is used it should be crushed. Salt should be given liberally, but as for other remedies none can be given which will reach the flukes in the liver. The only medicines of value therefore are tonics and stimulants, and these can best be given in form of good food.

Regarding the treatment of worms in the intestines of sheep, very satisfactory results have been obtained in South Africa against tapeworms and the twisted strongyles by administering sulphate of copper prepared as follows : Dissolve 1 pound of good commercial bluestone (sulphate of copper), of uniform blue color, in 2 quarts of boiling water. When the bluestone is all dissolved, add 6 gallons of cold water and strain the entire solution. Fast the animals twenty to twenty-four hours before dosing, and then administer the following amount : Lamb 3 months old, 1½ tablespoonfuls ; lamb 6 months old, 2 tablespoonfuls ; sheep 12 to 18 months old, 4 tablespoonfuls ; full-aged sheep, 5 tablespoonfuls. The animals should not be allowed water for some hours after receiving their dose. I would call your attention to the fact that great care is necessary in using this medicine. The doses must be exact, and caution must be taken not to allow the medicine to run into the windpipe of the sheep. If, after treatment, any of the sheep seem to be suffering from an overdose, administer 1 teaspoonful of laudanum in a tumbler of milk to a lamb 4 to 6 months old ; 2 teaspoonfuls of laudanum in a tumbler of milk for sheep 1 year old. Repeat the dose in two to three hours if necessary. While excellent results have been obtained by this treatment, accidents will surely happen if the medicine is carelessly administered. A less dangerous mode of treatment is the administration of turpentine and milk : Add 1 part of spirits of turpentine to 16 parts of milk. Emulsify by shaking well, and give from 2 to 4 ounces to each animal according to age. One dose should be sufficient ; if not, repeat in three to four days.

Referring to the grubs in the nose of sheep, it is exceedingly doubtful whether these were ever fatal. The exact duration of their life in the nose is not definitely known, but it is stated to be about ten months. Your sheep which have the running at the nose may possibly be affected with the grubs. It is impossible at this distance to state the cause of the looseness of the bowels in the other cases. It might be due to any one of numerous different causes, such as tapeworms, round worms, nodular disease, or other troubles.

Nodular disease of the intestines of sheep.—I write you with reference to a complaint among some of the sheep in Logan County, Ohio, and ask your opinion and advice on the same. I have not seen any of the sheep, but the following symptoms have been related to me by the owners: The affected sheep are from 2 to 4 years old and always in lamb. One breeder reported his sheep as being to all appearances in perfect health in the evening and in the morning they would appear unwell, usually being down, but when made to rise or placed on their feet could walk very well; slight mucous discharge from the nose, but this is a condition common to nearly all of the flock; constant grating of the teeth; urine more copious than in health; bowels almost normal, though in some cases there is diarrhea; will take spells of five or ten minutes' duration as if trying to escape from a mortal enemy, during which time the eyes have a staring or strained appearance. This condition lasts from one to three days, when they become stretched out and appear as if death would relieve their sufferings in a few hours. In this condition they last three or four days. An examination was made for grub in the head, but none was found. Another breeder informed me that his sheep had the same symptoms as those described, only suffering more pain; bowels constipated so much that repeated doses of physic failed to overcome it. The bowels of his sheep, after death, showed a nodular appearance, the nodules, or cysts, containing a greenish cheesy deposit. Please let me hear from you as to the cause, treatment, or prevention of the trouble.—(*A. H. L., Bellefontaine, Ohio, Feb. 22, 1897.*)

REPLY.—The nodular appearance you mention as occurring in the intestines of certain sheep is no doubt due to "nodular disease of the intestines" first described by the Bureau in 1890. The disease is caused by a parasite (*Œsophagostoma columbianum*) which develops in cysts in the walls of the intestines. The effect of this parasite is to cause general debility, and in severe cases the diarrhea and emaciation may be excessive. The disease is an insidious one, depending on the rate of infection, the tumors growing slowly from week to week, apparently requiring months for full development. The disturbance of digestion caused by this parasite is mainly due to the derangement of the cecum. For these tumors there is no remedy except the removal and extirpation of the adult worm. These adults are usually very deeply embedded in the mucous secretion and are found in considerable numbers in older sheep. The medical treatment indicated is that for intestinal worms and changing the sheep from pastures which are infected. Pastures known to be permanently infected should be grazed by other stock for a year or two, or on small farms the sheep lots may be plowed and planted to a crop for one or two seasons. Good drinking water should be provided and a plentiful supply of salt.

10317——35

Lung worm disease in sheep.—Relying on a pleasant evening spent with you at the dinner of the New York farmers last winter, I have sent you by express to-day the liver, lungs, and heart of a sheep. Eight sheep in the flock from which the animal came, from which these organs were taken, have been killed, and the lungs found to be affected in much the same way. Nine or ten have been killed in a flock coming from an adjoining farm to the one from which this one came originally. In fact, I am informed that the present owner of the latter flock had lost about thirty head. The animal whose liver and lungs I send you was in fair condition for a breeding ewe. The only symptom of disease was its standing apart from the others and refusing to move unless forced to. What is the matter with the sheep?—(*W. E. D., East Avon, N. Y.*)

REPLY.—After examination of the organs of the sheep which you sent, we find that the lesions are caused by a parasite, the eggs and embryos of which produce the minute tubercles and the lobular centers of broncho-pneumonia.

The lung worm disease is a very common ailment among sheep, especially those which are exposed on wet pastures, and, according to the condition of the animals, the mortality may range from 10 to 70 per cent. Of the various methods of treatment we have found none particularly good. Where the infection is not too severe the animal will fatten tolerably well, and may be marketed; but in the cases where there is great weakness, loss of flesh, and a general anemic condition, a cure can not be hoped for. The disease shows its worst effect as the sheep grow older, and when the disease is once in a flock and the range infected there will be a steady loss until it is in some way exterminated.

To prevent the sheep from becoming infected, they should be kept away from low, wet pastures, and as the lambs may become infected from the older sheep, they should be marketed as soon as possible after they are suspected. Lambs should be weaned as soon as they can be separated from their mothers and pastured where no sheep have been since the previous winter, and never be allowed to pasture, water, or yard after infected animals. Every precaution should be taken to make the surroundings as healthful as possible and grain feeding resorted to in order to improve the condition of those that are losing flesh. It is of the greatest importance that the water supply be good, and if possible the watering should be from tanks alone. Stagnant water should be carefully avoided.

Foot rot in sheep.—The sheep in this section suffer a great deal from foot rot, and we are exceedingly anxious to get hold of a cure for it. If you can inform me where I may obtain such a remedy, I shall very much appreciate it.—(*C. G. D., Mammoth Cave, Ky., July 26, 1898.*)

REPLY.—Foot rot in sheep is considered an infectious disease, and the infected sheep should be separated from the well ones. After this, treatment of those affected should be given daily until cured. The operator should be provided with hoof shears and a sharp knife, and should examine each foot carefully, shortening the toe wherever the hoof is overgrown, and with the knife pare away portions of the horn that are detached from the diseased part of the foot. After the foot has been carefully pared, any of the following mixtures may be applied to the diseased parts: Eight parts of oil of turpentine in 1 part of sulphuric acid is sometimes used. Another favorite application is butter of antimony. Fleming advises application of a mixture of sulphate of copper and Stockholm tar. Another application is sulphate of copper in concentrated solution as warm as can be borne by the hand. It is advisable to provide a wooden trough containing slaked lime and require the sheep to pass through this once a day. Another method is to fill the trough with a hot solution of sulphate of copper, 1 part to 50 parts of water. This disease does not yield readily to treatment in some outbreaks, and whatever remedy is employed it must be applied carefully and persistently to effect a cure.

DISEASE OF FOWLS.

Roup, or diphtheria, in fowls.—In Bulletin No. 8, "Infectious diseases among poultry," you mention remedies, but do not name them. Has the Department any remedy or cure for the disease? My little chickens are dying at the rate of seven or eight a day with a disease very much like the description given for roup. Now and then one of the old fowls dies of the same disease. Please name some remedy.—(*S. F. O., Lynnhaven, Va., Apr. 15, 1897.*)

REPLY.—No particular remedy has been discovered for roup, or diphtheria, in fowls; but as it is an infectious disease, treatment should begin with isolation of the afflicted fowls and thorough disinfection of the poultry houses and yards. The disinfectants which may be used are described on page 26 of Bulletin No. 8. The fowls that die should be burned or deeply buried at a distance from the poultry yards. In the treatment of individual fowls it is important to place them in warm, dry quarters and feed them nutritious food. The use of what is known as the Douglass mixture is said to be of great advantage. This mixture is made by dissolving 1 ounce sulphuric acid and one-half pound sulphate of iron in 2 gallons water. One or two tablespoonfuls of this solution is placed in a pint of the drinking water, and the effect is that of a gentle tonic. The diphtheritic patches may be removed by scraping lightly with a blunt metal or wooden instrument or by rubbing them off with a swab made by wrapping a small pledget of cotton about the end of a toothpick. After they are removed, the raw surface thus exposed should be treated with an antiseptic solution. The best application for this purpose is a 2 per cent solution of creolin or carbolic acid, to be applied cautiously with a camel's-hairbrush. Another solution that may be used is a 10 per cent solution of nitrate of silver. One writer recommends the use of petroleum in this disease, and advises that a drop of this substance be placed in the nasal passage of the diseased fowls and the diseased membranes be treated by light applications with a small brush.

LIME-AND-SULPHUR DIPS—REPLY TO CRITICISM.

In the last annual report of this Bureau there was published an exhaustive article on the subject of "Sheep scab: Its nature and treatment," by Drs. Salmon and Stiles. This was also published as Bulletin No. 21 of the Bureau series. The publication was well received everywhere, except by that class of people who are in some way interested in proprietary dips for killing the mite which causes sheep scab. There has always been a strife between the advocates of proprietary and homemade dips, and this strife will probably continue. Therefore whoever advocates either one of them must expect to bring down upon himself the odium of the advocates of the other. The authors of this article did not court harsh criticism, but expected it when they announced that their experience favored homemade dips, especially if the formula used by the Bureau was the one employed by them. The authors stated that various proprietary dips are recommended by advertisers, some of which were no doubt efficacious; that probably no dip could be named with which failures have not been reported; that the Department can not properly advertise or recommend the use of any dip which is made from a secret formula; that it is important that the farmer be informed of the composition of a ready-made dip if he uses one. The sheep raiser is advised to avoid any dip which irresponsible parties advertise as "the only sure cure for scab," as the advertisers are "either showing gross ignorance of the history and nature of scab, and hence not to be taken as advisers, or they are intentionally misrepresenting established facts." The article further states that "while a dip should not be condemned simply because it is prepared ready for use—it may be frankly admitted that there are some excellent proprietary dips—the value of homemade dips must be insisted upon, and attention is called to the fact that it was almost entirely through homemade dips that scab was eradicated from certain of the Australian colonies," etc. These facts are the results of the experience of the Bureau, and it is due the great sheep industry of our country that they be made known.

The harshest criticism of the position of the Bureau came from the editor of the American Sheep Breeder, Chicago, Ill., who to some extent disarms himself by publishing in his issue of August, 1898—some weeks before the bulletin on sheep scab was issued—the following: "The dip men and sheep men are wondering if Dr. Salmon has the nerve to advocate lime and sulphur in the forthcoming Government bulletin on scab and its treatment." The experience of this Bureau therefore was condemned before it was made public. In the September number of the same journal is a lengthy review of the bulletin, which apparently is dictated solely by prejudice. The value of the entire criticism may be estimated by the following extract read in connection with the reply, which is a letter from the gentleman alluded to in the extract:

We beg to suggest to the distinguished authors of this bulletin that they put the Bureau of Animal Industry in the way of emulating the good work done by the great sheep State of Montana, where scab was stamped out in a year and a half by practical, level-headed sheep men, under the direction of a practical and level-headed State veterinarian, who knew how to use his official prerogative, and, using it, employed the very dips derided and discarded by Dr. Salmon and his scientific lieutenants.   •

CASCADE, MONT., *October 1, 1898.*

DEAR DOCTOR: I chanced to read in the last American Sheep Breeder a criticism on your bulletin regarding scab, etc., which said bulletin reached me at Butte some time ago, and for which please accept my thanks.

There is one part in the Breeder's article which is not true; how much more is of the same character I don't know; but I do know that the following is, to say the least, incorrect: "We beg to suggest * * * in the State of Montana, where scab was stamped out in a year and a half by practical, level-headed sheep men, under the direction of a practical and level-headed State veterinarian, who knew how to use his official prerogative, and, using it, employed the very dips derided and discarded by Dr. Salmon and his scientific lieutenants." Now, as you know, I have been intimately connected with the sheep industry in Montana for years, and was veterinarian at the time when scab was so bad in the State that wool-growers demanded the framing and passage of a law sufficiently strong to wipe the disease out. I had the honor of submitting a few suggestions to the committee who were drafting the law, and when it was passed proceeded to put it into effect. At that time there must have been nearly or quite 100,000 scabby sheep in the State. In three years from that time we could give a clean bill of health. As a matter of fact, I had little to do with this work, which was done by the various county inspectors, and the dip which was used officially by them was, in almost every case, lime and sulphur. Sometimes an owner would wish to use something else, and in many cases had to come to lime and sulphur at last. I know of one case where sheep were dipped seven times in one of the proprietary dips and then had to use lime and sulphur. Every once in a while scab bobs up in the State, and the State officials can not help that, but of late years some of the proprietary dips have found favor with our officials. Now if these dips are so much better than lime and sulphur, how is it that scab has increased so the last two or three years? There must be in Montana to-day 30,000 scab-infected sheep.

Your position on lime and sulphur as a dip I believe to be correct, and if I can do anything to help you sustain it call upon

Yours, very truly,   HERBERT HOLLOWAY.
Dr. D. E. SALMON,
    Washington, D. C.

MOVEMENT OF FARM ANIMALS.

On the following page is a tabular summary of the receipts and shipments of farm animals at the principal stock centers of the United States for the years 1897 and 1898, and following the summary are tables showing the receipts and shipments in detail at the several cities.

The statement has been quite generally current for the last two years that the herds of cattle in the great cattle-growing sections of the country have not increased in the proportion that ought to be expected. The figures here presented tend to confirm the statement. The total receipts of cattle at the stock centers in 1896 were 9,081,070 head, while in 1897, as will be observed, the receipts were 8,982,215, and in 1898, 9,529,430, an increase of only 547,215 over 1897.

It must be remembered, however, that these totals do not indicate the exact number of animals marketed—that is, those which have been marketed but once. For instance, cattle marketed in Lincoln may appear in the receipts and also the shipments at Omaha, and appear again in the receipts at Chicago. The total receipts, therefore, include many duplications and some triplications.

Total receipts and shipments of farm animals at principal stock centers, 1896 to 1898, inclusive.

Animal.	1896.		1897.		1898.	
	Receipts.	Ship-ments.	Receipts.	Ship-ments.	Receipts.	Ship-ments.
Cattle	9,081,070	5,059,131	8,982,215	5,728,435	9,529,430	4,502,216
Calves	515,813	129,347	780,222	240,462	766,864	176,766
Hogs	26,589,353	10,813,649	30,453,688	14,046,765	34,370,109	10,890,858
Sheep	13,903,856	5,655,365	13,074,548	6,674,315	13,100,157	5,679,200
Horses and mules	437,110	411,144	316,992	287,068	549,327	405,707
Total	50,527,202	22,068,681	53,607,665	26,977,045	58,317,887	21,654,747

550

RECEIPTS AND SHIPMENTS OF FARM ANIMALS FOR 1897 AND 1898.

Receipts and shipments of live stock at the principal stock centers for the years 1897 and 1898.

Stock center.	Cattle.		Calves.		Hogs.		Sheep.		Horses and mules.	
	Receipts.	Shipments.	Receipts.	Shipments.	Receipts.	Shipments.	Receipts.	Shipments.	Receipts.	Shipments.
1897.										
Chicago	2,554,924	843,382	122,976	11,217	8,363,724	1,639,984	3,608,640	658,110	111,601	101,006
Kansas City	1,817,525	1,817,053	104,435	104,355	3,350,796	3,345,556	1,134,235	1,134,222	37,006	38,945
Omaha	825,699	382,415		17,905	1,107,698	81,279	612,803	203,054	6,632	2,430
South St. Paul	171,493	154,656	27,199		843,074	154,468	316,210	254,551	52	44
Sioux City	294,181	201,454	7,290	91	353,990	66,678	9,609	6,637	201	178
St. Louis	83,363	18,577			887,397	58,859	40,180	4,709		
East St. Louis	170,010	317,714	62,573	19,794	1,671,406	886,099	562,409	162,174		
Indianapolis	147,740	57,538			1,252,761	464,476	97,399	68,774	25,140	25,140
St. Joseph	49,143	37,114			428,086	108,020	12,915	11,290	2,902	2,379
Milwaukee	29,505	11,594	23,659	2,547	324,430	69,548	33,963	9,876		
Pittsburg	241,336	182,070	33,378	11,594	1,398,990	1,004,187	575,061	335,701	2,256	2,146
Lincoln	98,132	53,780			60,640	3,425	109,422	107,133	2,102	1,871
Cincinnati	178,919	43,614	39,577	968	881,392	306,703	430,868	324,784		
Cleveland	12,705				650,496	203,044	65,729			
Boston	168,932	163,862			244,007	7,373	371,302	100,669	3,973	6,110
Philadelphia	112,500	22,535			532,981	168,646	360,653	66,987	9,211	6,400
Baltimore	100,581	109,671	14,188	3,059	832,981	168,646	360,653	204,073	9,211	6,400
Buffalo	716,859	631,073	22,435	2,525	5,780,679	4,742,390	1,773,400	1,460,730	99,630	95,440
Louisville	128,677	70,734	11,908	1,378	921,110	541,980	291,822	255,775	977	829
Detroit	61,279	19,967	9,200	1,405	324,203	48,076	91,482	45,383	640	634
Jersey City	165,524	131,039	74,245	63,699	778,742		1,099,858	688,703		
New York	250,476		106,128		608,605		637,144			
Weehawken	2,498		39,188		224,054		80,207			
Denver	248,888	248,794			75,086	74,900	308,661	308,661	2,246	2,246
Pueblo	64,810	64,841			20,466	20,466	138,328	138,328	1,558	1,558
Fort Worth	100,514	163,009			122,894	11,227	28,288	20,636	1,885	1,658
Portland (Oregon)	12,480	6,730			15,006	5,870	66,286	20,150	8,700	
San Francisco	74,372		4,963		106,028		139,967			
Total	8,962,215	5,729,435	780,222	240,468	30,453,688	14,046,765	13,074,548	6,674,816	316,992	287,068

Receipts and shipments of live stock at the principal stock centers for the years 1897 and 1898—Continued.

Stock center.	Cattle. Receipts.	Cattle. Shipments.	Calves. Receipts.	Calves. Shipments.	Hogs. Receipts.	Hogs. Shipments.	Sheep. Receipts.	Sheep. Shipments.	Horses and mules. Receipts.	Horses and mules. Shipments.
1898.										
Chicago	2,480,897	895,642	132,783	27,844	8,817,114	1,340,544	3,569,439	543,425	118,754	102,234
Kansas City	1,757,994	851,196	88,299	53,529	3,672,900	373,219	960,803	380,865	17,483	11,285
Omaha	812,244	322,194			2,101,667	172,024	1,095,138	488,171	10,412	7,636
South St. Paul	173,316	134,528	42,677	21,616	399,405	36,374	430,194	317,455	1,322	850
Sioux City	300,903	224,041			474,298	82,985	20,881	12,022	1,079	905
St. Louis	74,354	10,414	11,229		382,317	56,526	29,716	7,328		
East St. Louis	683,707	188,446			1,728,820	488,065	455,863	110,073	110,275	85,557
Indianapolis	118,508	49,078	11,878	1,545	1,675,423	724,638	78,446	51,299	29,357	25,096
St. Joseph	225,994	68,761	6,094	4,987	1,034,125	106,487	121,707	24,138	10,587	7,008
Milwaukee	94,685	10,277	22,857	2,074	597,614	110,547	34,828	9,859	939	303
Pittsburg	228,199	155,756	30,574	5,376	1,428,710	1,054,375	541,469	363,598	63,556	53,653
Lincoln	60,340				74,411		202,897		6,145	
Cincinnati	163,806	53,618	35,701	855	887,524	387,226	399,647	300,072	4,034	1,396
Cleveland	18,288				834,799	275,348	53,701			
Boston	138,840	134,725	38,879	1,414	273,963	11,894	74,628	74,495	3,235	3,235
Philadelphia	137,712	17,371	12,775	2,605	857,991	165,931	414,866	48,857	14,038	5,069
Baltimore	156,998	105,919	16,165	2,360	6,016,616	4,573,138	371,640	240,488	10,307	8,503
Buffalo	638,290	565,087	9,316	973	818,079	336,153	1,562,610	1,459,280	74,290	72,460
Louisville	107,953	46,850	8,662	1,504	400,065	117,729	301,986	243,996	6,065	6,434
Detroit	44,579	14,139	59,311	49,771	794,841		80,177	35,351	881	881
Jersey City	178,705	154,748	202,917		661,195		934,532	615,943		
New York	897,387		37,874		245,970		659,606		59,719	
Weehawken	4,446						101,508			
Denver	287,678	287,007			81,645	81,810	284,305	284,305	4,831	4,831
Pueblo	57,723	57,727			22,109	22,109	79,965	79,965	2,721	2,721
Fort Worth	192,056	191,605			60,415	60,570	13,597	18,357	1,797	1,797
Portland (Oregon)	20,400	12,346			16,486	6,760	88,220	60,445	6,460	2,225
San Francisco	35,316		2,933		67,449		183,879			
Total	9,639,450	4,502,216	768,864	176,766	34,370,109	10,980,856	13,160,157	5,679,200	549,897	405,707

CHICAGO.

Receipts and shipments of live stock at Chicago Stock Yards (Chicago, Ill.) for the years 1897 and 1898.

Year and month	Cattle		Calves		Hogs		Sheep		Horses	
	Receipts	Shipments	Receipts	Shipments	Receipts	Shipments	Receipts	Shipments	Receipts	Shipments
1897.										
January	188,199	63,824	5,349	209	768,904	188,100	272,966	32,905	9,206	8,982
February	180,120	60,972	6,417	225	709,538	164,143	244,877	33,502	10,499	10,178
March	200,510	65,382	10,865	197	576,018	137,291	303,326	74,551	17,782	15,853
April	191,908	62,021	16,901	702	542,987	132,415	277,146	68,251	15,594	14,664
May	200,466	60,382	15,667	1,789	729,748	106,994	288,700	44,017	10,664	9,803
June	203,108	67,429	14,038	1,330	774,987	97,123	270,444	18,706	7,270	6,383
July	202,040	64,901	14,057	787	601,668	140,251	280,671	22,103	4,383	3,977
August	254,240	82,457	11,796	632	643,721	175,781	363,071	76,442	6,756	5,387
September	282,772	90,948	7,473	1,185	601,127	158,251	397,166	92,848	8,253	7,100
October	230,276	80,594	7,648	1,525	729,214	148,306	341,692	81,692	7,733	6,919
November	220,625	70,712	7,159	1,456	817,547	130,489	290,989	42,240	6,494	5,722
December	210,561	74,080	5,576	1,099	873,375	102,938	296,563	50,703	6,767	6,065
Total	2,554,924	843,882	122,976	11,217	8,368,724	1,629,984	3,606,640	638,110	111,601	101,006
1898.										
January	213,987	70,129	5,057	402	757,245	130,283	319,799	49,090	11,373	9,169
February	199,345	77,607	5,220	299	690,066	146,038	297,891	46,004	13,162	11,789
March	217,159	83,109	11,180	445	631,731	127,956	339,230	81,675	16,732	15,499
April	170,852	62,595	16,596	1,269	679,311	96,694	291,857	39,003	12,406	11,639
May	210,903	72,299	18,734	5,847	800,870	98,616	284,791	19,161	11,191	8,239
June	213,361	71,570	18,176	4,721	709,646	122,505	288,571	12,676	11,908	9,706
July	196,555	68,091	14,724	3,278	602,582	114,470	295,818	15,018	5,273	4,655
August	240,000	82,290	11,356	3,417	577,576	140,901	299,516	19,522	7,885	6,038
September	229,156	88,672	10,311	3,365	600,019	135,806	359,906	88,000	7,569	7,444
October	221,091	76,795	8,872	2,706	772,004	114,566	343,991	75,907	8,287	6,573
November	198,163	59,539	6,903	1,228	912,086	60,153	289,276	71,815	6,915	5,698
December	174,265	52,506	5,712	895	1,022,746	51,054	249,061	24,414	5,984	5,802
Total	2,480,897	865,642	132,733	27,844	8,817,114	1,340,644	3,580,439	543,425	118,754	102,324

KANSAS CITY.

Receipts and shipments of live stock at the Kansas City Stock Yards (Kansas City, Kans.) for the years 1897 and 1898.

Year and month.	Cattle. Receipts.	Cattle. Shipments.	Calves. Receipts.	Calves. Shipments.	Hogs. Receipts.	Hogs. Shipments.	Sheep. Receipts.	Sheep. Shipments.	Horses. Receipts.	Horses. Shipments.
1897.										
January	132,412	150,913	9,190	8,653	362,586	363,052	71,556	74,094	5,713	5,579
February	118,242	119,910	7,857	8,364	275,470	274,818	80,307	79,563	4,100	4,015
March	110,506	107,143	7,601	7,525	229,053	229,026	107,800	108,197	4,534	4,548
April	117,368	117,510	2,695	3,057	259,906	259,896	165,833	163,921	3,275	8,379
May	120,165	127,731	2,420	2,400	353,964	353,681	111,046	107,522	2,334	2,408
June	118,215	120,701	6,670	6,032	321,455	318,804	102,751	99,233	1,576	1,807
July	134,422	132,540	7,712	7,412	299,550	271,671	55,882	60,406	1,406	1,016
August	220,717	211,845	12,010	12,256	299,384	229,342	91,874	85,505	2,588	2,677
September	205,246	208,020	13,977	13,604	207,340	207,917	111,670	111,118	8,514	3,325
October	187,816	191,575	14,295	15,368	238,559	227,777	100,105	108,915	2,595	2,987
November	194,814	187,959	18,616	12,063	312,873	312,132	73,098	74,646	2,941	2,490
December	181,901	141,186	6,437	7,606	368,204	359,081	60,734	65,470	2,487	2,773
Total	1,817,526	1,817,033	104,436	104,856	3,350,706	3,846,556	1,134,236	1,134,222	37,006	35,945
1898.										
January	148,366	61,189	4,071	2,330	375,304	12,099	66,850	7,843	2,098	1,177
February	121,298	54,865	3,304	2,263	343,046	17,457	82,707	16,576	1,468	1,056
March	124,968	53,484	5,005	4,723	273,321	18,716	90,877	14,649	1,230	897
April	104,907	47,378	1,640	595	303,599	65,071	84,521	17,803	401	820
May	111,183	40,204	1,555	803	280,774	84,006	66,703	17,976	824	388
June	96,339	35,628	4,853	1,108	338,008	61,685	62,797	24,002	774	466
July	116,318	43,062	7,208	1,820	283,412	35,369	67,473	28,096	906	630
August	165,314	77,000	8,000	2,089	205,071	22,660	91,298	86,988	984	621
September	216,807	129,859	15,100	8,425	186,530	10,841	134,732	68,946	1,050	1,250
October	220,845	131,081	19,129	14,809	239,611	15,410	106,436	49,600	2,063	1,614
November	183,152	99,218	12,929	10,135	363,200	22,924	83,114	40,819	1,756	1,094
December	136,757	79,398	4,270	4,130	381,927	23,822	44,705	10,697	1,899	1,838
Total	1,757,964	851,195	88,260	53,829	3,652,990	373,219	940,908	530,865	17,483	11,325

OMAHA.

Receipts and shipments of live stock at the Union Stock Yards (Omaha, Nebr.) for the years 1897 and 1898.

Year and month.	Cattle.		Calves.		Hogs.		Sheep.		Horses and mules.	
	Receipts.	Shipments.	Receipts.	Shipments.	Receipts.	Shipments.	Receipts.	Shipments.	Receipts.	Shipments.
1897.										
January	48,964	20,382			113,506	2,451	41,094	7,838	569	146
February	47,138	19,878			112,394	2,207	51,049	4,774	553	208
March	52,917	20,173			110,448	3,052	77,300	24,439	739	221
April	51,811	19,942			108,850	250	68,859	38,999	650	127
May	55,804	16,140			109,977	6,121	76,214	35,963	88	81
June	68,185	23,959			176,038	3,636	38,401	11,875	512	129
July	59,863	22,540			151,496	14,239	25,637	1,809	606	141
August	72,013	51,654			148,859	24,340	38,728	7,045	682	352
September	119,557	68,615			93,753	15,988	49,746	13,629	823	321
October	112,102	61,098			105,364	6,873	62,991	81,606	587	295
November	78,362	34,258			121,665	1,571	68,288	17,686	463	254
December	58,966	23,071			150,699	1,071	85,866	18,178	368	185
Total	825,689	382,415			1,197,638	81,270	612,803	203,084	6,632	2,430
1898.										
January	43,406	11,221			159,554	14,029	87,345	19,257	319	239
February	50,141	18,023			134,682	12,060	103,512	40,139	510	293
March	65,236	24,263			139,085	13,138	142,706	64,612	706	277
April	53,065	17,894			147,698	28,997	135,698	69,254	577	252
May	66,134	20,645			181,312	23,864	115,204	60,152	612	322
June	68,386	21,049			183,144	30,356	27,612	5,270	1,302	1,208
July	48,707	15,713			188,498	42,560	43,801	22,024	603	417
August	77,723	28,896			181,242	4,187	67,394	21,811	1,092	943
September	101,560	46,326			159,415	2,253	111,394	52,706	1,871	1,552
October	127,175	68,215			161,400	708	133,167	71,691	1,234	940
November	72,035	85,451			190,953	599	76,877	49,758	884	785
December	43,017	14,498			282,904	945	40,407	5,882	512	418
Total	812,244	322,194			2,101,387	172,024	1,085,136	483,171	10,412	7,636

SOUTH ST. PAUL.

Receipts and shipments of live stock at South St. Paul, Minn., for the years 1897 and 1898.

Year and month.	Cattle.		Calves.		Hogs.		Sheep.		Horses and mules.	
	Receipts.	Shipments.	Receipts.	Shipments.	Receipts.	Shipments.	Receipts.	Shipments.	Receipts.	Shipments.
1897.										
January	7,214	6,251	640	600	23,708	9,381	22,127	20,011		
February	8,880	7,374	1,473	1,473	20,444	9,670	21,788	13,901		
March	7,389	6,965	1,468	1,472	17,977	9,816	17,185	13,681		
April	2,606	5,230	1,054	551	6,962	6,671	758	34,360		
May	6,376	6,399	1,436	914	22,724	22,117	1,703	428		
June	7986	6,782	1,530	1,068	19,622	16,929	2,920	2,401		
July	8,709	9,255	2,048	1,353	12,396	12,399	3,499	3,965	52	44
August	20,273	18,004	2,255	1,165	11,041	8,406	1656	11,179		
September	31,358	31,602	4,365	2,645	14,185	12,007	33,227	16,021		
October	30,157	28,490	4,380	2,647	20,496	17,661	110,618	53,498		
November	28,063	21,229	4,555	2,732	32,856	16,746	64,708	55,082		
December	12,310	7,106	1,955	1,191	40,691	11,979	24,582	31,121		
Total	171,492	154,656	27,139	17,806	243,074	154,463	315,210	254,551	52	44
1898.										
January	11,583	6,085	1,804	865	35,061	6,592	59,067	20,150		
February	10,447	7,147	2,963	1,500	24,300	1,385	8,962	7,091		
March	10,734	8,058	4,308	1,612	35,176	412	5,312	2,005	80	78
April	7,413	6,272	2,653	1,116	29,578	3,846	1,621	12,135	157	118
May	6,234	4,498	2,902	1,208	32,696	7,412	1,388	36,065	55	43
June	7,965	5,080	2,691	1,602	25,476	2,806	11,972	7,583	306	270
July	6,140	4,179	2,365	1,305	13,583	2,846	9,506	9,606	164	124
August	18,784	13,712	3,295	1,240	16,398	1,132	15,137	5,160	40	2
September	31,192	31,110	4,769	2,174	22,408	2,650	83,933	39,359	224	67
October	41,980	31,110	8,954	3,510	31,966	2,728	165,557	92,122	106	84
November	14,903	12,697	4,618	4,086	36,086	2,656	56,019	60,790	73	30
December	5,961	4,710	1,470	1,468	36,236	2,007	11,691	25,797	47	25
Total	173,316	134,628	42,677	21,616	339,405	36,874	430,194	317,455	1,262	850

SIOUX CITY.

Receipts and shipments of live stock at the Sioux City (Iowa) Stock Yards for the years 1897 and 1898.

Year and month	Cattle		Calves		Hogs		Sheep		Horses and mules	
	Receipts.	Shipments.	Receipts.	Shipments.	Receipts.	Shipments.	Receipts.	Shipments.	Receipts.	Shipments.
1897.										
January	16,517	10,538			29,570	6,049	634	304	1	-----
February	24,511	16,404			27,942	3,455	814	585	2	-----
March	25,714	17,642			21,377	2,498	489	289	35	20
April	22,550	16,075			16,440	2,748	127	-----	5	5
May	25,921	17,966			37,505	9,007	399	296	-----	-----
June	23,002	16,587			40,297	7,248	974	162	7	-----
July	11,856	10,254			28,799	8,115	366	129	27	27
August	15,468	9,751			21,733	7,621	363	249	-----	-----
September	38,171	21,220			24,336	5,194	1,624	653	31	30
October	40,745	28,500			23,983	2,574	1,923	2,380	64	52
November	37,595	24,353			37,966	4,841	1,446	1,275	33	33
December	12,121	12,294			47,070	7,228	541	415	6	5
Total	294,161	201,454			363,290	66,578	9,699	6,637	201	172
1898.										
January	19,499	12,556			39,056	10,410	644	413	30	30
February	25,342	19,611			32,999	9,295	635	444	109	107
March	34,577	32,617			36,915	5,885	414	291	64	48
April	22,488	20,438			35,298	7,947	101	96	18	18
May	16,244	13,380			39,025	8,973	137	119	1	-----
June	16,417	13,428			49,612	6,454	275	-----	25	-----
July	11,857	7,559			40,735	10,152	1,665	653	108	99
August	28,897	17,278			29,043	5,063	3,185	2,004	95	69
September	37,516	28,374			25,899	1,085	2,239	1,174	318	255
October	46,472	29,287			30,257	882	5,709	3,295	248	173
November	27,192	19,050			44,630	3,147	4,118	3,036	35	33
December	16,406	12,463			70,069	17,247	1,739	677	43	42
Total	300,908	224,041			474,238	82,905	20,861	12,022	1,079	908

ST. LOUIS.

Receipts and shipments of live stock at St. Louis, Mo., for the years 1897 and 1898.

Year and month	Cattle		Calves		Hogs		Sheep		Horses and mules.	
	Receipts.	Shipments.	Receipts.	Shipments.	Receipts.	Shipments.	Receipts.	Shipments.	Receipts.	Shipments.
1897.										
January	6,848	2,069	471		28,983	4,706	2,450	222		
February	5,450	679	440		24,043	5,451	2,414	60		
March	6,064	547	152		28,094	5,677	2,142	125		
April	5,542	785	578		22,490	4,938	2,157	391		
May	4,376	382	601		24,505	4,887	3,067			
June	8,184	328	653		23,837	5,134	3,088	392		
July	4,871	473	732		18,411	2,906	4,668	739		
August	7,371	688	437		17,417	2,683	3,368	560		
September	15,243	1,715	682	91	29,616	7,425	5,124	976		
October	8,244	1,380	876		26,959	7,319	3,767	71		
November	10,394	3,893	1,009		39,043	4,052	4,194	270		
December	5,806	708	560		38,596	3,466	3,876	455		
Total	88,393	13,577	7,220	91	327,397	58,866	40,180	4,708		
1898.										
January	7,709	2,146	916		33,588	3,680	2,044	224		
February	5,296	561	642		28,910	4,553	1,811	35		
March	5,897	956	1,006		35,602	5,472	1,436	215		
April	5,570	912	2,025		37,676	6,882	1,401	462		
May	5,990	549	1,035		41,568	7,819	1,771	685		
June	4,715	154	1,036		30,209	6,002	2,454	392		
July	5,908	243	909		25,894	3,665	3,716	666		
August	7,063	896	781		25,363	8,410	8,567	1,866		
September	7,295	662	925		27,872	6,279	8,047	737		
October	6,590	1,004	788		29,666	4,254	4,131	1,400		
November	6,877	1,016	873		36,499	3,499	2,181	570		
December	6,019	1,115	440		38,571	3,869	1,554	103		
Total	74,354	10,414	11,229		392,317	68,026	29,716	7,826		

EAST ST. LOUIS.

Receipts and shipments of live stock at the National Stock Yards, (East St. Louis, Ill.) for the years 1897 and 1898.

Year and month	Cattle		Calves		Hogs		Sheep		Horses	
	Receipts.	Shipments.	Receipts.	Shipments.	Receipts.	Shipments.	Receipts.	Shipments.	Receipts.	Shipments.
1897.										
January	73,231	35,234	3,818	2,148	165,291	110,375	23,113	4,396		
February	54,338	25,998	1,593	647	131,024	76,342	30,024	3,696		
March	45,416	18,662	1,804	688	139,940	73,070	37,063	6,955		
April	38,821	12,342	1,505	508	134,681	90,767	65,492	25,290		
May	37,855	15,613	2,722	625	138,008	85,086	79,026	36,368		
June	53,897	19,834	6,396	2,464	115,233	67,238	61,081	27,181		
July	63,891	24,087	5,279	1,997	103,412	58,349	57,445	11,684		
August	87,840	42,421	6,074	2,058	106,161	64,107	45,359	15,612		
September	75,409	31,518	7,753	2,762	101,443	61,617	42,566	10,750		
October	62,056	27,473	6,563	2,632	138,904	70,319	38,704	6,712		
November	76,785	35,394	6,183	2,312	150,288	55,400	29,782	6,810		
December	72,581	28,098	3,883	1,018	140,978	84,060	31,261	7,018		
Total	170,010	317,714	52,572	19,794	1,571,408	866,069	523,409	162,174		
1898.										
January	56,460	30,485			155,977	51,182	20,989	3,708	16,804	14,049
February	52,107	14,843			144,625	53,625	24,406	833	13,710	13,177
March	49,259	10,373			137,032	43,979	24,185	3,144	13,096	11,779
April	32,994	5,046			145,888	52,595	30,228	3,002	9,006	7,001
May	35,599	7,276			144,418	55,063	38,517	6,249	11,767	5,511
June	42,564	7,915			117,778	38,423	61,085	17,173	6,684	3,283
July	46,973	9,320			110,020	29,315	46,941	24,746	4,100	2,194
August	65,654	21,550			98,344	35,477	56,504	22,709	7,835	5,911
September	73,163	24,535			106,537	38,081	42,919	11,759	6,012	4,808
October	78,186	22,163			140,998	33,101	39,714	6,152	7,283	5,347
November	61,310	13,972			133,972	25,814	38,077	5,106	7,079	5,601
December	59,348	18,948			232,686	36,130	17,278	3,398	7,549	6,916
Total	633,707	188,446			1,728,320	488,665	425,893	110,073	110,275	85,657

INDIANAPOLIS.

Receipts and shipments of live stock by Belt Railroad and Stock Yard Company (Indianapolis, Ind.) for the years 1897 and 1898.

Year and month.	Cattle.		Calves.		Hogs.		Sheep.		Horses.	
	Receipts.	Shipments.	Receipts.	Shipments.	Receipts.	Shipments.	Receipts.	Shipments.	Receipts.	Shipments.
1897.										
January	11,577	4,174			114,906	23,906	6,299	5,021	2,176	2,176
February	10,082	3,446			78,743	30,641	5,801	4,482	2,346	2,348
March	9,730	2,905			77,996	48,488	2,253	1,401	3,185	3,185
April	9,015	1,963			84,065	27,052	3,503	2,664	2,805	2,806
May	7,419	1,957			110,709	39,051	2,681	1,299	1,993	1,993
June	11,219	3,782			129,831	47,192	7,758	3,973	1,503	1,503
July	12,849	6,527			110,129	57,813	10,148	5,613	993	993
August	18,903	7,281			81,001	42,771	24,981	18,123	1,464	1,464
September	19,616	8,462			67,580	32,009	13,682	10,140	2,540	2,540
October	12,877	6,146			90,514	29,038	8,442	6,989	2,597	2,597
November	18,199	5,769			128,594	29,472	6,707	6,506	1,944	1,944
December	11,314	4,884			179,960	56,423	4,794	3,023	1,502	1,502
Total	147,740	57,336			1,252,761	464,476	97,369	68,774	25,140	25,140
1898.										
January	12,031	5,837	990	282	132,079	68,128	2,401	1,491	3,381	2,999
February	11,492	6,034	732	35	100,571	39,042	2,688	1,443	2,981	3,017
March	12,745	7,202	972	102	101,975	52,287	1,000	278	4,070	3,822
April	8,300	2,830	1,212	255	127,002	60,015	1,337	89	2,678	2,424
May	6,204	1,615	1,061	81	134,360	63,006	3,014	2,327	3,057	2,700
June	6,776	2,528	1,184	117	144,557	75,645	11,502	8,436	1,709	1,868
July	6,776	2,525	1,184	117	144,557	75,645	11,502	8,436	1,636	1,135
August	9,157	2,832	967	102	124,885	90,382	16,112	9,944	1,951	1,646
September	12,229	3,401	1,069	49	111,977	57,439	10,899	4,915	2,411	1,997
October	12,940	5,847	964	166	181,007	44,219	7,915	5,701	2,243	1,828
November	9,704	3,238	741	97	181,807	37,638	6,665	3,504	1,800	1,818
December	10,158	4,186	702	132	210,146	69,018	3,645	2,646	1,372	1,211
Total	118,508	49,076	11,878	1,545	1,673,423	728,369	78,446	51,250	29,337	28,098

ST. JOSEPH.

Receipts and shipments of live stock at the St. Joseph (Mo.) Stock Yards for the years 1897 and 1898.

Year and month.	Cattle.		Calves.		Hogs.		Sheep.		Horses.	
	Receipts.	Shipments.	Receipts.	Shipments.	Receipts.	Shipments.	Receipts.	Shipments.	Receipts.	Shipments.
1897.										
January	3,223	1,724			18,458	7,077	1,490	603	319	318
February	3,754	2,317			15,839	4,321	438		211	211
March	1,910	1,343			13,761	709	333		209	209
April	3,290	2,576			23,671	3,333	4,982	4,932	105	104
May	6,249	5,166			33,579	4,944	5		164	163
June	6,148	5,197			49,417	9,670	323	265	19	19
July	3,583	2,455			45,029	11,440	a 225		84	84
August	5,552	4,300			40,574	13,014	251	150	252	151
September	5,089	4,658			48,120	17,371	1,230	830	596	404
October	3,824	2,617			33,328	9,218	3,757	3,710	239	237
November	3,975	2,574			44,458	8,427	107	84	338	294
December	2,466	2,187			60,259	18,487	763	695	386	305
Total	49,143	37,114			426,993	108,020	13,915	11,259	2,902	2,379
1898.										
January	2,670	2,198	534	520	61,866	9,128	62		934	652
February	1,575	1,434	10		37,903	7,682	398	254	863	631
March	9,516	3,642	1,072	319	123,899	12,075	1,096	556	2,841	564
April	25,732	7,428	150	294	65,686	6,641	13,808	752	933	660
May	20,838	4,125	248	217	87,233	10,110	16,448	860	1,354	1,140
June	22,300	3,625	155	14	101,663	7,631	4,488	590	1,144	808
July	21,117	5,297	118	57	100,781	16,838	15,572	3,454	570	488
August	24,435	8,777	300	134	104,489	10,059	21,246	4,581	646	509
September	27,372	8,355	409	280	87,640	7,914	19,437	3,640	736	543
October	25,432	9,723	1,257	1,257	91,201	2,907	15,889	5,903	867	520
November	28,080	8,164	1,376	1,139	123,501	11,432	9,553	2,615	774	514
December	21,204	6,195	709	738	138,672	3,097	4,080	1,124	722	730
Total	225,994	69,761	6,094	4,967	1,034,125	106,437	121,707	24,138	10,587	7,908

a In this month 850 goats were received and shipped in addition to the sheep.

MILWAUKEE.

Receipts and shipments of live stock at Milwaukee, Wis., for the years 1897 and 1898.

Year and month.	Cattle.		Calves.		Hogs.		Sheep.		Horses.	
	Receipts.	Shipments.	Receipts.	Shipments.	Receipts.	Shipments.	Receipts.	Shipments.	Receipts.	Shipments.
1897.										
January	3,775	1,694	1,590	190	51,451	14,784	2,824	928		
February	3,228	1,407	1,948	291	40,671	8,117	2,089	1,137		
March	2,883	1,245	2,101	175	30,412	5,787	1,714	434		
April	2,893	1,036	3,320	538	25,157	10,842	1,001	295		
May	1,911	734	3,070	259	30,650	8,938	1,089	344		
June	1,974	819	2,675	124	23,834	5,155	2,412	723		
July	1,663	870	2,980	415	17,099	1,795	4,226	1,104		
August	2,057	961	2,010	254	10,757	1,244	3,901	1,176		
September	2,384	1,011	1,374	85	14,121	1,257	3,528	729		
October	2,754	1,600	1,341	394	28,943	4,969	5,582	2,991		
November	3,043	507	1,250	66	56,849	6,050	4,708	5		
December										
Total	28,565	11,664	23,659	2,547	324,420	69,648	33,953	9,876		
1898.										
January	3,086	794	1,445	85	78,179	11,943	2,548	1,034		48
February	2,846	980	1,561	112	66,217	7,836	2,891	1,406		40
March	2,352	646	1,905	110	55,138	2,570	1,171			43
April	2,719	443	2,804	250	59,682	1,119	1,867	111	244	46
May	2,090	671	2,803	319	73,024	679	1,741	800	148	16
June	2,521	854	2,582	334	46,707	12,280	1,785	382	84	48
July	3,306	449	3,043	540	31,847	3,600	3,637	371	58	46
August	2,997	598	1,821	68	23,897	5,409	2,836		68	16
September	3,425	902	1,240	43	29,001	5,367	5,010	1,777	120	48
October	3,590	1,126	1,000	42	32,438	9,103	4,095	2,166	85	48
November	2,402	1,680	1,107	156	46,178	20,138	4,079	2,032	69	5
December	2,774	1,596	1,490		60,941	30,798	3,008		68	
Total	34,095	10,277	22,857	2,074	597,614	110,547	34,828	9,839	949	303

PITTSBURG.

Receipts and shipments of live stock at East Liberty Stock Yards (Pittsburg, Pa.) for the years 1897 and 1898.

Year and month.	Cattle.		Calves.		Hogs.		Sheep.		Horses and mules.	
	Receipts.	Shipments.	Receipts.	Shipments.	Receipts.	Shipments.	Receipts.	Shipments.	Receipts.	Shipments.
1897.										
January	19,894	14,999	2,306	1,411	128,206	81,127	51,456	14,090	......	......
February	15,165	11,372	2,642	1,596	115,599	83,517	37,704	4,740	......	......
March	16,411	12,349	3,245	784	105,300	67,784	37,348	13,428	......	......
April	20,404	17,380	6,160	2,422	121,472	91,436	48,248	21,606	......	......
May	12,711	9,110	5,717	1,979	100,980	60,500	51,467	7,297	......	......
June	8,616	4,282	4,821	2,100	64,196	24,126	47,599	11,544	......	......
July	27,025	21,537	2,081	427	103,885	73,067	40,391	35,315	......	......
August	28,586	18,997	1,292	146	96,149	83,258	79,356	69,440	......	......
September	28,270	20,005	1,225	178	106,738	93,394	61,987	54,181	......	......
October	23,196	19,992	1,576	288	119,206	104,307	42,104	36,841	......	......
November	19,273	15,060	1,187	125	127,616	111,680	39,563	38,810	......	......
December	21,788	16,166	1,231	134	148,699	180,102	28,643	38,610	......	......
Total	241,398	182,079	33,373	11,584	1,338,950	1,004,187	575,661	336,761	......	......
1898.										
January	21,472	17,176	1,118	98	153,726	113,464	42,822	37,471	5,148	5,148
February	18,778	16,020	1,274	124	112,380	98,749	29,899	25,221	5,744	5,744
March	16,722	13,376	2,840	278	101,604	88,900	28,964	25,354	6,981	6,981
April	14,108	8,460	4,436	408	114,184	71,385	87,000	23,125	5,048	5,048
May	15,136	9,081	5,879	490	109,114	68,195	42,298	28,425	3,794	3,794
June	10,156	6,063	4,090	370	100,502	62,810	97,677	61,046	2,902	2,902
July	19,950	13,300	2,504	517	93,547	59,638	75,731	47,330	2,457	2,457
August	21,620	14,346	2,534	683	96,023	55,364	68,756	38,720	8,720	8,720
September	21,720	14,480	1,727	767	106,996	74,706	40,281	25,175	4,148	4,148
October	23,708	15,894	2,121	1,085	140,298	112,228	32,713	20,446	7,850	7,850
November	20,805	13,930	1,432	398	146,475	117,100	24,251	15,155	2,983	2,983
December	21,949	14,632	1,110	237	163,479	130,780	32,162	20,100	2,906	2,906
Total	226,109	155,768	30,574	5,376	1,429,710	1,054,375	541,469	363,566	53,556	53,553

LINCOLN.

Receipts and shipments of live stock at Lincoln Stock Yards (Lincoln, Nebr.) for the years 1897 and 1898.

Year and month.	Cattle.		Calves.		Hogs.		Sheep.		Horses.	
	Receipts.	Shipments.	Receipts.	Shipments.	Receipts.	Shipments.	Receipts.	Shipments.	Receipts.	Shipments.
1897.										
January	2,411				5,980		752		75	
February	2,199				4,998		11,210		23	
March	1,963				5,065		5,606		45	
April	2,702				7,838		32,848		39	
May	2,738				10,399		6,386		26	
June	4,026				11,658		253		25	
July	4,574				4,161		8,611		384	
August	4,139				1,454		3,086		82	
September	10,000				1,345		5,704		340	
October	11,000				1,309		16,085		217	
November	8,821				1,615		18,777		622	
December	3,829				4,818		4,275		378	
Total	58,132	58,780			60,640	3,425	106,422	107,133	2,256	2,146
1898.										
January	2,490				8,004		6,138		78	
February	3,333				8,717		9,363		98	
March	1,553				7,825		11,798		249	
April	1,784				8,425		10,206		128	
May	6,162				9,061		7,805		135	
June	1,745				8,710		1,822		409	
July	1,256				7,779		17,240		639	
August	4,662				1,782		18,601		1,981	
September	7,548				571		21,455		555	
October	16,835				491		67,910		845	
November	8,717				695		22,366		660	
December	4,235				12,371		9,185		368	
Total	60,340				74,411		202,807		6,145	

CINCINNATI.

Receipts and shipments of live stock at the Cincinnati (Ohio) Union Stock Yards for the years 1897 and 1898.

Year and month.	Cattle.		Calves.		Hogs.		Sheep.		Horses and mules.	
	Receipts.	Shipments.	Receipts.	Shipments.	Receipts.	Shipments.	Receipts.	Shipments.	Receipts.	Shipments.
1897.										
January	12,208	2,293	2,812	3	92,355	45,597	11,637	4,913	135	89
February	10,520	1,418	2,675	58	66,156	27,222	6,633	2,325	62	42
March	12,674	1,463	3,782	34	79,827	34,464	5,806	438	197	146
April	11,196	1,381	4,296	22	73,859	40,023	7,581	1,554	107	79
May	13,927	1,565	4,149	36	72,620	32,759	17,671	8,813	98	80
June	12,882	2,613	3,994	90	71,088	29,639	79,412	61,085	72	57
July	12,374	2,228	3,351	99	48,400	21,799	118,803	106,372	75	54
August	17,149	4,296	3,062	204	45,299	16,735	91,182	76,800	128	110
September	23,133	7,817	3,160	76	52,369	23,652	41,614	29,518	328	291
October	19,668	7,551	3,062	81	72,817	37,408	21,994	12,624	436	453
November	19,863	7,476	2,967	254	98,385	43,240	17,767	12,075	232	196
December	13,325	3,553	2,387	25	106,777	43,665	10,808	6,287	302	274
Total	178,919	43,614	39,677	982	881,382	396,703	430,858	324,784	2,102	1,871
1898.										
January	12,631	2,215	2,632	6	99,205	48,622	8,365	2,583	345	243
February	11,564	1,457	2,678		73,348	39,368	5,687	1,414	199	174
March	11,069	1,241	3,328	55	63,667	27,596	4,002	878	241	55
April	11,528	1,659	4,050	16	74,557	34,194	5,568	791	328	16
May	13,670	2,021	3,820	12	78,381	33,240	14,863	6,708	149	12
June	13,228	2,299	3,815	86	63,851	25,372	105,094	90,995	282	86
July	11,904	2,156	2,837	79	55,370	25,107	107,738	98,175	66	79
August	16,654	3,248	2,960	114	50,271	18,999	74,148	62,474	195	114
September	16,822	5,271	2,683	182	53,386	24,878	27,791	17,652	437	182
October	18,007	4,707	2,363	76	73,741	37,024	16,654	8,356	560	76
November	15,444	4,250	2,299	168	99,232	39,631	11,949	5,131	689	168
December	11,276	3,154	2,267	51	• 102,515	35,282	7,788	4,857	534	51
Total	163,806	33,618	35,701	855	887,524	367,235	389,647	380,072	4,034	1,296

CLEVELAND.

Receipts and shipments of live stock at the Cleveland (Ohio) Stock Yards for the years 1897 and 1898.

Year and month	Cattle		Calves		Hogs		Sheep		Horses and Mules	
	Receipts.	Shipments.	Receipts.	Shipments.	Receipts.	Shipments.	Receipts.	Shipments.	Receipts.	Shipments.
1897.										
January	1,800				67,228	21,249	6,385			
February	1,571				34,564	7,777	5,868			
March	2,046				48,482	14,019	5,541			
April	1,572				49,154	8,481	4,449			
May	1,052				66,538	19,666	4,106			
June	1,075				70,047	25,448	7,053			
July	442				43,873	15,254	8,877			
August	243				81,761	6,867	8,457			
September	373				41,726	15,935	490			
October	561				46,014	17,225	4,875			
November	968				64,268	23,467	4,977			
December	1,069				87,036	27,666	4,096			
Total	12,765				660,486	203,044	65,739			
1898.										
January	1,675				72,017	19,619	4,532			
February	1,974				44,901	14,504	5,170			
March	2,548				55,402	23,506	2,729			
April	2,730				61,482	23,078	3,198			
May	1,891				69,153	27,188	3,383			
June	1,357				66,972	30,069	6,174			
July	1,853				47,800	16,820	5,945			
August	734				43,472	16,274	5,818			
September	568				57,959	19,785	4,283			
October	716				64,207	34,374	3,525			
November	1,360				101,409	23,467	4,896			
December	1,391				120,306	27,666	4,048			
Total	18,295				854,799	273,848	58,701			

BOSTON.

Receipts and shipments of export live stock at the port of Boston, Mass., for the years 1897 and 1898.

Year and month	Cattle		Calves		Hogs		Sheep		Horses	
	Receipts.	Shipments.	Receipts.	Shipments.	Receipts.	Shipments.	Receipts.	Shipments.	Receipts.	Shipments.
1897.										
January	14,120	13,745	......	......	......	......	13,096	13,028	645	......
February	12,911	12,478	......	......	......	......	5,976	5,338	679	......
March	13,538	13,294	......	......	......	......	11,962	12,118	803	......
April	14,822	14,231	......	......	......	......	13,880	11,874	740	......
May	16,316	15,778	......	......	......	......	10,987	12,470	333	......
June	17,745	17,046	......	......	......	......	13,098	13,059	109	......
July	15,428	15,226	......	......	......	......	2,432	2,431	62	......
August	13,354	12,942	......	......	......	......	1,978	1,974	104	......
September	13,490	18,198	......	......	......	......	11,319	10,386	172	......
October	11,090	11,115	......	......	......	......			90	......
November	12,788	11,662	......	......	......	......	11,081	9,868	69	......
December	13,453	13,187	......	......	......	......	8,374	8,152	167	......
Total	108,932	108,862					104,140	100,699	3,973	......
1898.										
January	13,563	13,191	......	......	......	......	8,820	9,734	298	298
February	12,687	12,293	......	......	......	......	7,167	6,617	470	470
March	15,379	15,035	......	......	......	......	10,910	10,901	562	562
April	11,478	11,460	......	......	......	......	13,218	13,096	483	483
May	12,184	11,531	......	......	......	......	11,040	10,689	306	306
June	11,809	11,691	......	......	......	......	4,109	4,396	201	201
July	12,028	11,414	......	......	......	......	2,595	2,596	137	137
August	10,651	10,610	......	......	......	......	544	543	342	342
September	10,116	9,850	......	......	......	......			103	103
October	9,658	9,626	......	......	......	......	603	603	119	119
November	9,220	9,004	......	......	......	......	6,050	5,755	104	104
December	9,637	9,060	......	......	......	......	9,522	9,504	110	110
Total	128,840	124,725					74,628	74,483	3,235	3,235

PHILADELPHIA.

Receipts and shipments of live stock at the Philadelphia (Pa.) Stock Yards for the years 1897 and 1898.

Year and month.	Cattle.		Calves.		Hogs.		Sheep.		Horses and mules.	
	Receipts.	Shipments.	Receipts.	Shipments.	Receipts.	Shipments.	Receipts.	Shipments.	Receipts.	a Shipments.
1897.										
January	9,148	2,307			19,919	888	22,476	2,906		827
February	8,494	1,586			21,990	727	28,294	3,251		435
March	9,747	2,134			22,498	380	28,924	3,360		725
April	9,632	2,225			16,838	620	24,514	2,143		841
May	12,100	2,408			22,040	408	37,063	6,006		853
June	8,890	1,842			17,277	360	30,104	6,989		470
July	8,332	1,853			15,335	531	29,151	6,747		298
August	10,860	1,377			19,730	306	46,983	12,301		270
September	9,019	2,273			19,519	499	35,250	8,082		512
October	8,738	2,273			23,123	804	32,354	6,082		470
November	9,470	1,258			27,708	1,122	37,352	6,008		536
December	7,501	1,384			18,780	862	21,757	3,051		185
Total	112,560	22,695			244,907	7,372	371,302	66,967		6,110
1898.										
January	12,210	1,445	2,492	5	30,180	963	33,541	1,909	1,050	568
February	10,449	1,391	2,782	10	20,540	855	32,096	1,100	2,051	835
March	9,875	1,366	3,145	18	17,906	778	23,227	1,624	2,612	919
April	10,407	1,056	3,685	9	19,765	575	29,811	2,078	1,308	403
May	13,865	1,463	3,871	7	24,067	1,148	39,201	4,519	1,283	388
June	11,828	1,828	3,400	99	17,233	855	39,943	7,400	808	384
July	11,013	1,919	3,019	142	16,323	225	39,708	7,041	544	249
August	13,366	1,773	3,045	321	21,129	568	51,772	9,080	680	177
September	10,337	1,153	3,568	596	21,816	623	37,507	4,705	845	225
October	13,774	1,465	2,787	53	35,032	1,383	41,298	2,495	897	343
November	9,419	1,223	2,580	88	28,649	1,246	31,170	3,908	828	169
December	10,560	1,787	2,450	76	27,753	2,639	24,996	1,680	702	380
Total	137,712	17,871	36,879	1,414	278,963	11,894	414,898	48,357	14,098	5,009

a A record of the receipt of horses for 1897 was not made, except by carloads.

BALTIMORE.

Receipts and shipments of live stock at the Union Stock Yards (Baltimore, Md.) for the years 1897 and 1898.

Year and month.	Cattle.		Calves.		Hogs.		Sheep.		Horses and mules. a	
	Receipts.	Shipments.	Receipts.	Shipments.	Receipts.	Shipments.	Receipts.	Shipments.	Receipts.	Shipments.
1897.										
January	10,624	6,732	1,059	46	81,519	16,438	21,193	7,539	1,054	779
February	8,694	5,499	1,100	96	63,965	14,155	10,557	3,727	548	470
March	11,343	5,668	1,622	171	73,721	14,746	12,652	3,950	1,005	858
April	9,615	6,358	1,463	14	70,290	14,216	18,310	9,658	1,445	653
May	10,259	6,935	2,081	62	72,757	12,900	28,188	12,833	774	616
June	9,884	6,314	1,153	200	60,796	11,687	37,763	28,194	388	298
July	9,804	8,516	932	452	61,587	11,909	60,896	51,036	258	129
August	16,714	11,542	1,165	522	61,046	11,809	65,571	47,940	585	397
September	23,065	15,682	888	556	63,340	13,910	42,807	27,922	813	629
October	21,052	16,431	1,015	298	81,709	18,960	43,961	27,072	1,053	862
November	17,854	10,763	1,008	457	70,861	14,417	31,631	22,713	738	504
December	11,703	9,268	722	230	71,420	13,509	19,119	13,620	488	377
Total	160,581	109,671	14,188	3,089	832,981	168,046	390,638	254,073	9,211	6,460
1898.										
January	10,428	7,023	1,160	363	83,628	17,861	17,217	7,117	984	877
February	11,474	7,232	1,493	276	72,635	13,582	13,578	6,365	2,360	1,198
March	10,532	7,050	1,431	56	71,139	12,193	13,612	6,716	1,776	1,278
April	8,436	5,119	1,295	56	75,204	15,275	17,040	7,336	1,460	1,056
May	9,241	4,515	1,726	21	77,295	16,213	17,464	7,024	714	599
June	7,116	5,225	1,025	314	63,886	10,466	37,960	27,348	514	287
July	11,274	7,539	906	220	63,100	10,072	70,705	53,612	451	355
August	15,028	10,007	570	455	53,363	8,289	58,200	47,311	574	395
September	19,198	14,494	567	219	63,620	11,701	41,667	24,290	779	588
October	22,835	16,307	638	91	83,796	17,253	40,338	25,146	773	698
November	19,185	12,325	977	212	72,189	15,760	28,530	17,342	652	554
December	12,256	9,143	783	322	78,253	17,276	17,359	10,887	750	623
Total	156,998	105,919	12,775	2,605	857,891	165,931	371,640	240,483	10,807	8,503

a 1897.—Horses: Receipts, 8,045; shipments, 5,742. Mules: Receipts, 1,166; shipments, 717. 1898.—Horses: Receipts, 8,876; shipments, 7,017. Mules: Receipts, 1,931; shipments, 1,486.

BUFFALO.

Receipts and shipments of live stock at the East Buffalo (N. Y.) Stock Yards for the years 1897 and 1898.

Year and month.	Cattle.		Calves.		Hogs.		Sheep.		Horses.	
	Receipts.	Shipments.	Receipts.	Shipments.	Receipts.	Shipments.	Receipts.	Shipments.	Receipts.	Shipments.
1897.										
January	60,522	50,390	6,400	670	371,230	320,055	229,700	149,200	6,820	5,900
February	51,194	42,717	1,680	195	440,762	348,902	174,020	157,830	9,380	8,240
March	52,482	46,596	1,675	200	437,960	386,700	164,900	146,670	14,820	14,500
April	58,784	53,218	1,675	150	425,980	383,042	162,600	140,600	14,600	14,160
May	65,834	58,190	1,350	200	405,710	397,170	168,800	143,600	12,960	11,900
June	62,859	54,450	1,050	150	423,320	380,713	107,400	98,380	8,920	8,440
July	60,982	54,334	1,175	165	418,475	354,232	97,600	75,850	4,080	4,400
August	63,525	58,314	1,775	175	470,155	388,055	108,100	87,150	5,500	5,900
September	58,060	51,244	1,440	105	498,896	402,762	181,760	115,870	7,900	7,200
October	60,806	52,006	1,500	180	548,485	443,149	181,700	114,840	7,900	7,120
November	60,154	54,747	1,286	190	588,709	477,726	148,900	118,060	4,690	5,980
December	61,055	56,875	1,430	165	673,517	550,791	164,620	149,200	4,720	4,980
Total	716,850	681,073	22,435	2,625	5,730,679	4,749,969	1,778,400	1,480,730	99,680	95,440
1898.										
January	61,533	59,388	2,080	225	623,687	516,659	173,720	164,590	8,520	8,280
February	54,796	49,783	1,596	190	458,506	381,976	144,130	134,560	10,940	10,680
March	54,516	49,710	1,890	185	467,577	374,889	161,620	150,590	12,600	12,500
April	56,199	50,385	1,070	185	420,228	325,694	173,980	161,090	8,700	8,560
May	56,144	50,452	1,140	185	448,436	364,989	129,560	124,790	6,390	6,100
June	46,304	40,061	1,095	170	429,723	389,473	106,230	86,480	4,780	4,600
July	53,295	45,703	1,150	170	412,016	398,528	125,800	70,690	8,000	8,460
August	50,528	45,836	1,275	220	437,665	350,303	89,050	82,280	4,100	8,480
September	55,941	48,455	1,276	250	505,580	401,660	101,350	105,000	4,720	4,280
October	60,907	50,811	1,490	295	599,431	477,083	127,090	118,730	4,720	4,480
November	44,137	38,280	1,205	160	617,272	505,229	118,370	107,840	8,140	8,280
December	44,000	39,110	1,460	145	605,649	511,423	131,840	123,630	3,180	2,880
Total	638,290	565,057	16,166	2,380	6,016,016	4,878,186	1,582,610	1,429,260	74,290	72,480

LOUISVILLE.

Receipts and shipments of live stock at the Bourbon Stock Yards (Louisville, Ky.) for the years 1897 and 1898.

Year and month.	Cattle.		Calves.		Hogs.		Sheep.		Horses.	
	Receipts.	Shipments.	Receipts.	Shipments.	Receipts.	Shipments.	Receipts.	Shipments.	Receipts.	Shipments.
1897.										
January	11,617	7,521	991	108	113,865	80,391	3,004	1,771	98	96
February	9,553	4,221	802	11	81,884	56,297	1,420	559	82	66
March	7,250	3,064	1,036	64	106,193	80,564	2,052	906	202	181
April	5,180	1,165	929		83,582	66,458	3,810	2,129	110	101
May	5,583	837	1,143	8	94,000	58,912	19,544	12,621	39	23
June	6,905	3,316	966	162	55,240	27,132	53,809	53,770	29	25
July	6,737	4,114	1,078	269	44,360	21,330	98,470	90,438	20	8
August	18,146	12,507	965	244	37,667	18,797	72,678	64,351	80	65
September	20,062	12,662	1,136	79	39,362	14,704	19,383	15,424	20	7
October	12,619	7,861	897	18	74,148	38,141	9,346	7,770	48	34
November	16,986	9,619	1,148	323	98,966	88,808	5,564	8,994	161	155
December	8,299	3,887	789	97	90,000	45,460	2,758	2,172	88	73
Total	128,077	70,734	11,008	1,378	921,110	641,989	291,822	255,775	977	829
1898.										
January	15,944	5,530	903	157	94,925	47,501	2,882	1,164	159	152
February	8,486	5,105	745	110	78,389	45,164	2,290	1,059	154	138
March	7,093	3,408	872	122	67,757	35,568	2,872	1,468	148	137
April	6,051	1,882	833	40	78,069	29,980	4,882	3,046	182	128
May	6,694	2,071	786	22	75,989	31,570	28,045	18,505	224	219
June	6,756	2,688	1,038	96	52,719	16,310	85,176	67,144	663	638
July	5,404	2,090	732	66	37,681	10,794	88,977	80,873	332	319
August	8,560	4,079	692	84	28,246	7,245	63,780	49,613	280	213
September	10,067	4,068	638	70	26,501	8,420	14,241	10,002	2	
October	13,476	5,920	685	67	85,220	23,715	8,717	4,964	4,280	4,253
November	8,987	4,917	538	77	97,673	42,932	4,207	3,560	103	98
December	10,979	4,478	656	56	87,068	32,028	2,836	2,010	162	146
Total	107,953	46,850	9,316	973	818,079	336,153	301,896	243,998	6,696	6,494

DETROIT.

Receipts and shipments of live stock at the Michigan Central Stock Yards (Detroit, Mich.) for the years 1897 and 1898.

Year and month	Cattle		Calves		Hogs		Sheep		Horses	
	Receipts.	Shipments.	Receipts.	Shipments.	Receipts.	Shipments.	Receipts.	Shipments.	Receipts.	Shipments.
1897.										
January	4,039	1,509	552	135	24,059	441	12,725	8,440	......	......
February	3,579	1,450	531	21	19,524	1,682	16,566	12,523	......	......
March	3,635	1,507	734	36	18,011	791	9,889	6,229	......	......
April	5,861	3,773	1,302	457	22,229	3,771	6,209	2,841	162	162
May	4,890	2,118	1,446	229	28,830	2,302	5,435	741	249	243
June	3,363	902	836	96	20,200	360	2,561	125	83	83
July	5,532	2,620	917	10	24,407	903	4,654	194	33	33
August	5,033	2,644	578	31	18,387	1,265	4,891	3,159	42	42
September	4,863	1,665	527	76	21,300	4,028	8,987	5,062	50	50
October	4,547	1,181	735	154	32,461	8,500	7,542	2,520	......	......
November	2,966	432	529	126	38,986	8,827	5,977	2,106	......	......
December	2,961	396	513	64	56,897	14,378	5,936	1,445	21	21
Total	51,279	19,867	9,200	1,405	324,203	48,076	91,422	45,383	640	684
1898.										
January	2,942	......	484	......	31,008	......	7,112	......	......	......
February	3,054	......	467	......	22,590	......	9,595	......	42	......
March	2,910	......	649	......	29,143	......	7,632	......	21	......
April	4,303	......	1,149	......	40,709	......	8,098	......	30	......
May	2,725	......	917	......	30,015	......	3,538	......	47	......
June	3,808	......	850	......	21,800	......	3,487	......	68	......
July	3,381	......	686	......	18,778	......	4,215	......	56	......
August	4,853	......	723	......	30,039	......	7,173	......	172	......
September	3,995	......	607	......	27,516	......	6,162	......	198	......
October	4,938	......	791	......	42,461	......	9,228	......	154	......
November	4,015	......	530	......	48,499	......	5,743	......	88	......
December	3,695	......	839	......	60,267	......	8,384	......	67	......
Total	44,570	14,139	8,062	1,504	400,065	117,729	80,177	36,361	881	801

JERSEY CITY.

Receipts and shipments of live stock at the Jersey City (New Jersey) Stock Yards for the years 1897 and 1898.

Year and month.	Cattle.		Calves.		Hogs.		Sheep.	
	Receipts.	Shipments.	Receipts.	Shipments.	Receipts.	Shipments.	Receipts.	Shipments.
1897.								
January	14,250	12,349	3,165	2,830	69,056	....	89,601	49,088
February	11,106	7,991	4,230	3,935	61,428	....	85,650	54,149
March............	14,560	11,211	7,190	6,543	68,356	....	84,804	56,135
April.............	13,208	9,667	9,426	8,100	62,445	....	92,640	58,057
May..............	12,980	9,590	10,305	8,749	63,728	....	91,320	59,267
June	15,039	11,305	9,640	8,128	62,407	....	94,400	59,207
July.............	15,420	12,483	8,435	7,203	65,750	....	96,650	60,992
August	14,650	11,711	6,485	5,811	61,571	....	98,320	62,444
September........	14,850	12,274	5,134	4,230	63,365	....	96,438	59,238
October..........	13,405	10,633	4,650	3,881	65,410	....	93,200	58,621
November	12,606	10,403	3,265	2,299	66,786	....	84,205	53,349
December	13,450	11,422	2,320	1,980	68,440	....	82,630	58,246
Total........	165,524	131,039	74,245	63,689	778,742	....	1,089,858	688,793
1898.								
January	15,301	13,396	2,257	1,832	70,304	....	76,431	55,248
February	12,460	10,640	3,876	3,520	64,203	....	71,390	54,143
March............	16,320	14,460	6,232	5,399	70,485	....	70,428	53,221
April.............	14,503	12,446	8,490	7,480	60,306	....	80,460	61,741
May..............	13,630	11,388	8,404	6,862	65,501	....	81,301	58,011
June	16,580	14,734	7,805	6,713	60,307	....	86,906	56,394
July.............	16,210	14,452	6,264	5,250	67,254	....	89,204	56,173
August	15,305	13,263	5,123	4,454	64,744	....	82,354	47,234
September........	16,408	14,208	4,106	3,324	62,864	....	80,100	46,253
October..........	14,309	12,150	3,330	2,607	66,507	....	70,104	38,155
November	13,506	11,232	2,154	1,435	70,852	....	74,650	43,993
December	14,258	12,379	1,270	895	71,509	....	71,201	45,377
Total........	178,795	154,748	59,311	49,771	794,841	....	934,532	615,943

NEW YORK.

Receipts of live stock at the New York (New York) Stock Yards for the years 1897 and 1898.

Year and month.	Cattle.	Calves.	Hogs.	Sheep.	Horses.
1897.					
January............................	24,836	6,199	74,558	69,473	....
February	18,659	6,602	59,769	66,008	....
March..............................	18,130	12,116	68,939	58,606	....
April...............................	22,982	34,725	49,525	66,878	....
May	19,293	33,207	65,136	51,477	....
June...............................	18,742	27,977	44,602	21,254	....
July...............................	22,282	23,616	44,138	14,130	....
August.............................	21,335	15,674	53,592	20,637	....
September	20,192	12,182	46,125	57,500	....
October	22,325	11,891	44,795	71,566	....
November	19,374	6,416	63,055	56,716	....
December...........................	22,346	5,523	54,071	73,021	....
Total	250,476	196,128	666,305	627,146	....

Receipts of live stock at the New York (New York) Stock Yards for the years 1897 and 1898—Continued.

Year and month.	Cattle.	Calves.	Hogs.	Sheep.	Horses.
1898.					
January	29,241	4,477	63,841	50,454	5,251
February	29,073	6,585	46,880	52,343	5,842
March	31,490	13,267	43,905	64,567	7,766
April	32,106	32,523	45,157	90,422	5,371
May	33,309	32,314	56,026	56,805	6,493
June	34,023	30,041	42,460	19,991	4,629
July	34,558	16,686	41,876	32,374	2,747
August	32,527	18,195	50,215	24,883	4,282
September	35,025	18,884	54,478	70,947	5,215
October	31,064	12,757	84,551	65,267	5,601
November	38,002	8,141	66,946	58,051	4,645
December	34,969	7,047	63,260	73,502	1,877
Total	397,387	202,917	661,195	659,606	59,719

WEEHAWKEN.

Receipts of live stock at Weehawken, N. J., for the years 1897 and 1898.

Month and year.	Cattle.	Calves.	Hogs.	Sheep.
1897.				
January	133	881	13,579	12,268
February	90	750	17,350	8,306
March		2,348	20,466	9,960
April	19	5,176	17,586	7,035
May	138	6,544	18,857	5,751
June	348	6,530	17,750	735
July	365	4,055	14,930	728
August	383	8,172	18,170	2,658
September	302	1,928	19,157	13,342
October	264	1,423	20,825	7,356
November	326	2,500	21,403	8,903
December	130	866	24,581	3,115
Total	2,498	36,182	224,654	80,207
1898.				
January	353	695	23,156	16,419
February	56	1,180	18,366	9,503
March	511	2,211	20,150	10,447
April	135	4,479	19,321	12,262
May	185	7,572	20,803	11,040
June	908	6,490	16,385	322
July	146	4,020	15,943	1,150
August	1,077	3,807	19,010	5,373
September	320	2,292	18,124	8,439
October	212	1,943	25,685	3,738
November	292	1,996	24,426	8,661
December	251	1,187	24,601	9,448
Total	4,446	37,874	245,970	101,598

DENVER.

Receipts and shipments of live stock at the Denver (Colorado) Union Stock Yards for the years 1897 and 1898.

Year and month.	Cattle.		Hogs.		Sheep.		Horses and mules.	
	Receipts.	Ship-ments.	Receipts.	Ship-ments.	Receipts.	Ship-ments.	Receipts.	Ship-ments.
1897.								
January	7,362	7,155	7,523	7,523	19,763	19,763	66	66
February	7,589	7,754	6,969	6,969	17,330	17,330	10	10
March	10,132	9,723	7,288	7,288	5,296	5,296	2	2
April	10,960	10,399	7,310	7,310	8,656	8,656	47	41
May	51,750	49,988	6,435	6,435	3,709	3,709	162	168
June	37,476	39,452	5,111	5,111	8,226	8,226	137	122
July	21,072	21,738	5,601	5,412	13,072	12,128	80	95
August	12,221	12,326	4,812	5,001	12,497	13,441	243	243
September	24,148	23,671	4,851	4,851	43,118	37,759	597	597
October	32,720	33,102	6,580	6,580	110,610	108,688	377	377
November	23,513	22,602	6,647	6,647	55,798	63,074	272	272
December	9,945	10,794	5,938	5,773	10,591	10,591	253	253
Total	248,888	248,794	75,065	74,900	308,661	308,661	2,246	2,246
1898.								
January	8,296	8,030	6,482	6,647	6,571	6,571	188	185
February	11,274	11,164	5,854	5,854	5,904	5,904	184	187
March	13,306	13,496	8,284	8,284	6,615	6,615	137	137
April	13,181	12,674	5,657	5,657	3,178	3,178	75	75
May	38,244	35,978	6,588	6,588	7,146	7,146	298	298
June	55,380	55,712	7,087	7,087	8,278	8,278	814	814
July	27,653	27,635	4,933	4,933	9,066	9,066	541	541
August	17,609	17,209	5,205	5,205	12,361	11,647	510	510
September	26,480	25,340	5,922	5,922	37,825	34,740	451	377
October	39,866	37,797	7,740	7,740	143,339	145,240	620	694
November	24,722	29,658	8,869	8,869	36,512	38,410	637	637
December	11,577	12,864	9,024	9,024	7,510	7,510	376	376
Total	287,678	287,607	81,645	81,810	284,305	284,305	4,831	4,831

PUEBLO.

Receipts and shipments of live stock at the Pueblo (Colorado) Union Stock Yards for the years 1897 and 1898.

Year and month.	Cattle.		Hogs.		Sheep.		Horses and mules.	
	Re-ceipts.	Ship-ments.	Re-ceipts.	Ship-ments.	Re-ceipts.	Ship-ments.	Re-ceipts.	Ship-ments.
1897.								
January	2,757	2,781	2,687	2,687	1,615	1,615	156	156
February	1,253	1,251	1,868	1,868	3,674	3,674	4	4
March	2,990	2,983	1,906	1,906	3,134	3,134	6	6
April	5,719	5,797	2,185	2,185	1,155	1,155	8	8
May	9,002	9,002	1,695	1,695	2,675	2,675	93	93
June	6,835	6,835	1,306	1,306	1,338	1,338	90	90
July	4,378	4,378	1,396	1,396	3,965	3,965	51	51
August	4,451	4,451	1,528	1,528	5,321	5,321		
September	5,509	5,509	1,970	1,736	9,193	6,033	511	511
October	9,156	8,984	1,373	1,607	86,231	85,721	517	517
November	9,791	9,092	1,171	1,171	17,139	20,809	304	304
December	2,907	3,778	1,381	1,381	2,888	2,888	118	118
Total	64,810	64,841	20,466	20,466	138,328	138,328	1,558	1,558

Receipts and shipments of live stock at the Pueblo (Colorado) Union Stock Yards for the years 1897 and 1898—Continued.

Year and month.	Cattle.		Hogs.		Sheep.		Horses and mules.	
	Re-ceipts.	Ship-ments.	Re-ceipts.	Ship-ments.	Re-ceipts.	Ship-ments.	Re-ceipts.	Ship-ments
1898.								
January	1,736	1,736	1,875	1,875	1	1	57	57
February	2,061	2,061	1,662	1,662	....	....	38	38
March	4,099	4,099	2,307	2,307	....	....	33	33
April	5,335	5,335	2,202	2,202	....	....	258	252
May	7,796	7,796	1,927	1,927	694	694	19	25
June	6,585	5,740	1,593	1,593	3,750	3,750	137	137
July	1,049	1,894	1,486	1,486	2,037	2,037	77	77
August	992	992	1,812	1,812	241	241	156	156
September	5,622	5,234	1,546	1,546	30,402	30,119	862	862
October	14,618	14,104	2,230	2,230	41,033	41,316	398	398
November	5,618	6,520	1,767	1,767	1,325	1,325	573	573
December	2,217	2,216	1,762	1,762	472	472	113	113
Total	57,728	57,727	22,169	22,169	79,955	79,955	2,721	2,721

FORT WORTH.

Receipts and shipments of live stock at the Fort Worth (Texas) Stock Yards for the years 1897 and 1898.

Year and month.	Cattle.		Hogs.		Sheep.		Horses and mules.	
	Re-ceipts.	Ship-ments.	Re-ceipts.	Ship-ments.	Re-ceipts.	Ship-ments.	Re-ceipts.	Ship-ments.
1897.								
January	11,319	5,299	9,114	....	....	....	162	101
February	8,600	5,426	12,137	413	....	....	79	53
March	13,742	12,818	16,494	413	6,165	....	52	77
April	34,420	31,274	10,080	3,053	4,796	4,492	31	31
May	26,064	25,335	11,193	1,773	10,907	10,704	75	53
June	8,438	5,638	12,342	526	1,274	1,020	93	93
July	3,559	2,097	7,961	365	1,360	1,267	74	74
August	4,483	2,514	4,052	....	982	812	144	119
September	8,236	6,587	8,738	442	250	....	340	255
October	9,464	10,123	10,473	163	201	....	160	160
November	42,248	39,063	10,168	1,079	555	543	323	323
December	19,941	16,835	10,142	....	1,798	1,798	352	318
Total	190,514	163,009	122,894	11,227	28,288	20,636	1,885	1,658
1898.								
Total	192,056	191,805	60,415	60,379	13,597	13,357	1,797	1,797

PORTLAND.

Receipts and shipments of live stock at the Union Stock Yards (Portland, Oreg.) for the years 1897 and 1898.

Year and month.	Cattle.		Hogs.		Sheep.		Horses.	
	Receipts.	Shipments.	Receipts.	Shipments.	Receipts.	Shipments.	Receipts.	Shipments.
1897.								
January	1,005	395	605	565	3,220	350	10	
February	440	200	1,215	410	1,785	985		
March	1,055	540	1,355	390	3,045	1,265	20	
April	355	255	950	690	3,690	1,005	20	
May	2,120	1,460	1,415	660	5,320	3,730	55	
June	1,680	970	485	190	7,245	5,305	980	
July	1,125	350	475	90	5,900	4,030	1,010	
August	865	460	560	255	5,875	4,655	1,040	
September	900	540	1,380	640	6,955	4,775	1,110	
October	1,505	850	2,245	1,210	7,045	4,015	1,405	
November	945	380	2,740	290	6,735	5,545	1,600	
December	485	330	1,580	480	9,470	7,490	1,450	
Total	12,480	6,730	15,005	5,870	66,285	43,150	8,700	
1898.								
January	600	265	850	170	6,420	4,690	845	85
February	820	530	945	310	7,065	4,425	1,060	525
March	1,500	590	2,400	665	6,335	2,275	385	195
April	1,290	990	980	515	5,685	3,860	220	305
May	3,920	2,225	735	285	9,145	6,265	170	110
June	4,430	3,670	1,015	740	10,300	8,885	760	510
July	1,150	430	395	465	8,080	5,720	155	140
August	875	410	1,500	845	7,480	6,160	725	140
September	1,815	1,135	1,090	215	7,670	7,190	705	155
October	1,980	1,295	1,440	745	3,985	3,735	660	35
November	1,130	680	3,050	1,040	5,760	3,305	745	
December	950	125	2,135	765	5,315	3,935	50	25
Total	20,460	12,345	16,485	6,760	83,220	60,445	6,480	2,225

NOTE.—In 1897 there was also received at Troutdale the following: Cattle, 8,337 head; hogs, 21,380; sheep, 36,528.

10317——37

SAN FRANCISCO.

Receipts of live stock at San Francisco (California) for the years 1897 and 1898.

Year and month.	Cattle.	Calves.	Hogs.	Sheep.
1897.				
January	9,785	776	14,798	9,643
February	7,818	212	10,632	8,257
March	5,662	89	9,118	10,464
April	5,328	86	10,271	10,684
May	5,654	318	8,621	11,047
June	5,336	405	3,445	11,514
July	6,081	715	6,671	15,377
August	5,510	657	5,354	12,417
September	5,852	487	9,477	12,629
October	5,687	373	8,846	12,196
November	5,889	492	8,942	11,713
December	5,799	373	9,853	11,035
Total	74,572	4,983	106,028	139,977
1898.				
January	2,416	193	7,006	10,332
February	2,005	132	5,078	10,214
March	3,532	32	6,073	9,849
April	2,812	45	4,848	8,300
May	2,658	104	5,059	8,508
June	4,091	272	4,595	12,359
July	3,726	285	4,116	12,880
August	3,577	543	5,832	13,457
September	2,213	236	6,204	10,419
October	2,545	370	4,770	13,325
November	3,753	474	6,360	15,300
December	1,918	287	4,939	8,356
Total	35,316	2,953	67,449	133,379

RANGE OR AVERAGE PRICE OF FARM ANIMALS AT CHICAGO FOR 1897 AND 1898.

Year and month.	Cattle					Hogs		
	Native steers, 1,500 to 1,800 pounds.	Native steers, 1,200 to 1,500 pounds.	Poor to choice cows and heifers.	Native stockers and feeders.	Straight Texans and Westerns.	Heavy packing, 250 to 500 pounds.	Mixed packing, 200 to 250 pounds.	Light bacon, 150 to 200 pounds.
1897.								
January	$4.25 to $5.50	$3.50 to $5.50	$1.35 to $4.80	$2.50 to $4.25	$3.00 to $4.55	$3.00 to $3.55	$3.20 to $3.60	$3.20 to $3.60
February	4.10–5.40	3.60–5.35	1.50–4.25	2.50–4.50	2.75–4.35	3.10–3.67½	3.25–3.70	3.30–3.72¾
March	4.15–5.65	3.60–5.50	1.75–4.75	2.65–4.70	2.80–4.65	3.30–4.25	3.45–4.25	3.50–4.20
April	4.25–5.40	3.75–5.50	1.50–4.80	2.70–4.70	3.00–4.80	3.50–4.22½	3.80–4.22½	3.80–4.25
May	4.35–5.40	3.95–5.40	1.50–5.00	3.00–4.60	3.00–4.65	3.25–4.00	3.40–4.05	3.45–4.05
June	4.40–5.30	3.80–5.20	1.50–4.65	2.80–4.65	2.85–4.70	3.05–3.62½	3.25–3.65	3.25–3.65
July	4.40–5.25	3.65–5.20	1.75–4.40	2.50–4.50	2.75–4.35	3.05–3.95	3.30–3.97½	3.30–4.00
August	4.70–5.50	4.00–5.50	1.75–4.75	2.75–4.75	2.80–4.80	3.45–4.45	3.70–4.45	3.65–4.55
September	4.65–5.75	3.80–6.00	1.50–5.15	2.75–4.60	3.00–4.90	3.55–4.40	3.70–4.50	3.85–4.65
October	4.50–5.40	4.00–5.35	1.75–4.75	2.75–4.55	3.00–4.65	3.20–4.35	3.40–4.35	3.35–4.40
November	4.30–6.00	3.80–5.50	1.00–4.55	2.80–4.45	3.40–4.00	3.15–3.80	3.25–3.80	3.35–3.80
December	4.00–5.65	3.85–5.00	1.00–5.40	2.40–4.35	2.45–4.00	3.10–3.60	3.25–3.60	3.25–3.55
1898.								
January	4.10–5.50	3.80–5.50	2.00–4.00	2.70–4.50	3.50–4.65	3.25–3.97½	3.35–4.00	3.30–3.95
February	4.35–5.85	3.90–5.5	2.25–4.50	3.20–4.80	3.50–4.65	3.60–4.27½	3.65–4.25	3.60–4.20
March	4.40–5.80	3.90–5.75	2.25–4.85	3.10–5.00	3.35–5.40	3.65–4.17½	3.70–4.15	3.65–4.10
April	4.30–5.50	3.90–5.50	2.25–5.05	3.10–5.10	3.65–4.55	3.60–4.15	3.70–4.10	3.60–4.05
May	4.25–5.25	3.95–5.50	2.50–4.85	3.40–5.00	3.50–4.65	3.90–4.80	3.90–4.70	3.70–4.65
June	4.35–5.35	4.00–5.35	2.50–4.85	3.40–5.40	2.45–4.75	3.60–4.50	3.60–4.45	3.60–4.35
July	4.40–5.50	4.25–5.65	2.50–4.85	2.90–4.75	3.00–5.00	3.60–4.17½	3.60–4.12½	3.50–4.10
August	4.70–5.65	4.10–5.75	2.50–5.40	3.00–5.15	3.30–4.50	3.45–4.12½	3.55–4.15	3.50–4.20
September	4.60–5.85	4.00–5.70	2.25–5.15	2.75–4.75	3.25–4.00	3.40–4.15	3.50–4.15	3.40–4.15
October	4.45–5.90	4.00–5.85	2.00–5.00	2.80–4.70	3.15–4.25	3.30–4.00	3.50–4.00	3.30–4.00
November	4.45–5.90	3.90–5.85	2.00–5.15	2.50–4.60	3.15–4.30	3.10–3.85	3.10–3.80	3.10–3.85
December	4.60–6.25	4.00–6.15	2.00–5.40	2.80–4.40	3.25–5.00	3.15–3.75	3.15–3.75	3.15–3.70

Range or average price of farm animals at Chicago for 1897 and 1898—Continued.

Year and month.	Sheep.				Horses.						
	Native sheep, 60 to 150 pounds.	Native lambs, 40 to 100 pounds.	Western sheep, 70 to 150 pounds.	Texas and Mexican sheep.	Draft horses.	Carriage teams.	Drivers.	General use.	Saddlers.	Streeters.	Southern horses.
1897.											
January	$1.75 to $4.50	$3.00 to $5.75	$2.45 to $3.85	$3.00 to $3.85	$110	$350	$85	$70	$100	$90	$35.00
February	2.25	3.00	2.90	3.30	125	360	90	70	100	65	35.00
March	2.25	3.00	3.25	3.25	126	360	95	70	105	65	35.00
April	2.80	3.00	4.00	2.60	130	350	100	75	110	70	35.00
May	2.00	2.60	3.00	2.60	130	340	110	75	140	65	37.00
June	1.50	2.75	2.15	2.50	115	330	90	70	130	70	35.00
July	1.25	2.30	2.15	1.75	115	325	90	70	130	70	30.00
August	2.00	2.75	2.25	2.40	130	325	90	80	120	65	35.00
September	1.75	3.00	3.00	2.50	125	340	85	80	115	65	35.00
October	2.00	2.75	2.25	2.75	125	340	90	70	110	65	30.00
November	2.00	350	2.50	2.80	125	340	75	75	100	70	25.00
December	2.75	3.75	2.80	3.50	120	325	80	80	95	60	25.00
1898.											
January	2.00	4.25	350	2.50	115	340	85	70	100	80	35.00
February	2.50	3.75	350	2.50	130	360	95	75	110	70	35.00
March	2.25	4.00	4.00	4.00	135	360	100	75	115	75	35.00
April	2.75	3.75	3.75	3.50	135	360	110	80	120	80	32.50
May	2.75	3.75	385	3.70	130	360	115	80	145	80	30.00
June	2.75	4.25	4.15	3.00	128	370	95	75	185	80	30.00
July	2.50	3.75	350	3.40	127	360	95	75	185	75	27.50
August	2.25	325	385	3.90	133	365	90	75	125	70	30.00
September	2.50	350	350	3.75	125	358	90	73	125	70	30.00
October	2.50	350	385	3.75	123	360	95	73	115	70	32.50
November	2.00	3.50	45	3.50	123	365	85	70	115	70	27.50
December	2.00	3.75	4.00	3.55	125	360	85	70	105	65	27.50

IMPORTS AND EXPORTS OF ANIMALS AND ANIMAL PRODUCTS.

It is stated officially that the exports of all kinds from the United States last year exceeded those of any previous year. According to the Bureau of Statistics of the Treasury Department, the value of our exports in 1898 was $1,255,494,494. The largest volume of exports of any previous year was in 1897, when the value was $1,099,709,045, an amount less than that for 1898 by $155,785,313. Our foreign trade in animals and animal products has kept pace proportionately with other products. The total value of these exports, as detailed in the tables which follow, was $237,952,127 for 1898, as against $214,-400,463 for 1897; a gain for 1898 of $23,551,764. The trade of 1898 was more nearly equaled by that of 1892 than any subsequent year. In 1892 it amounted to $224,531,279. The accompanying table of the total exports of animals and animal products for the years 1892 to 1898, inclusive, permit a comparison of the several years.

1892	$224,531,279
1893	196,243,366
1894	215,462,956
1895	219,492,191
1896	217,048,412
1897	214,400,463
1898	237,952,127

EXPORTS TO UNITED KINGDOM.

The United Kingdom continues to be our best customer. The value of her purchases from us in 1898 was $159,551,488. All other countries purchased but $78,400,639 worth. A tabular statement of the kinds, amounts, and value of goods purchased by the United Kingdom in 1898 is given below.

Kinds, quantity, and value of goods purchased by the United Kingdom from the United States in 1898.

Kind of goods purchased.	Quantity.	Value.
	Pounds.	*Dollars.*
Butter	6,847,859	1,125,391
Cheese	25,413,146	2,139,905
Canned-beef products	22,322,278	2,055,368
Fresh beef	266,414,299	22,562,155
Salted, pickled, and other cured beef	21,401,576	1,249,507
Tallow	45,060,294	1,759,270
Bacon	449,790,060	34,333,973
Hams	164,389,154	15,215,209
Pork	61,903,739	4,025,464

Kinds, quantity, and value of goods purchased by the United Kingdom from the United States in 1898—Continued.

Kind of goods purchased.	Quantity.	Value
	Pounds.	*Dollars.*
Lard	231,525,366	13,866,718
Lard compounds and substitutes	23,822,956	1,231,253
Oleo and oleomargarine	8,894,144	522,567
Wool, wool manufactures, etc	43,851,362	9,290,422
Hides and skins	180,347	19,319
Leather, and leather manufactures	a 29,902,604	14,342,701
	Number.	
Cattle	342,689	31,668,909
Hogs	930	7,387
Horses	21,819	3,282,115
Sheep	122,784	853,825

a This amount represents the weight of the sole leather only.

EXPORTS TO GERMANY.

Notwithstanding all adverse circumstances, our exports to Germany have increased. Germany took animal products from us in 1898 to the value of $24,853,519, as against $18,017,213 for 1897, the difference in favor of 1898 being $6,836,213. This is a large and gratifying increase, and nothing but legal restrictions in that Empire will prevent still larger increase in the years to come.

Kind, quantity, and value of goods purchased by Germany from the United States in 1898.

Kind of goods purchased.	Quantity.	Value.
	Pounds.	*Dollars.*
Canned beef	3,963,071	342,507
Salted, pickled, and other cured beef	5,936,717	337,738
Tallow	18,450,402	722,616
Bacon	44,212,030	2,983,660
Hams	13,975,056	1,297,710
Pork	12,918,060	710,707
Lard	238,680,471	14,034,380
Butter	671,302	95,043
Oleo and oleomargarine	31,414,750	1,982,102
Hides and skins	5,532,375	454,300
Sole leather	364,811	72,556
Other leather		762,165
Boots and shoes		39,570
Horses ......number	7,185	1,018,465

The tabular statement shows that Germany's principal import from the United States is lard, having taken 238,680,471 pounds, valued at $14,034,380. Bacon holds second place, with 44,212,030 pounds, valued at $2,983,660.

EXPORTS TO FRANCE.

The exports to France likewise increased in 1898. The total value of her imports of our animal products for that year was $2,821,365, as against $2,062,268 in 1897, leaving a balance of $759,097 in favor of 1898. With France, as with Germany, the principal item of import from the United States was lard, having taken during the year 25,599,190 pounds, valued at $1,437,623. In 1897 the value of the lard taken by France was $1,041,932. Tallow occupied second place with 11,480,863 pounds, valued at $453,500, to its credit.

Kind, quantity, and value of goods purchased by France from the United States in 1898.

Kind of goods purchased.	Quantity.	Value.
	Pounds.	*Dollars.*
Canned beef	365,364	31,267
Salted, pickled, and other cured beef	310,175	18,463
Tallow	11,480,863	453,500
Bacon	5,984,342	423,586
Hams	718,017	69,204
Pork	144,875	7,978
Lard	25,599,190	1,437,623
Hides and skins	496,156	49,813
Leather, and leather manufactures		329,981

THE EGG QUESTION.

It would be very difficult indeed to estimate, from the meager data available, the value of the egg product of the United States. There is nothing produced upon the farms that is of more general distribution or which is made a substitute for more kinds of provisions than eggs. A very small percentage of the product finds its way into foreign or interstate commerce, the very much larger percentage being consumed on the farms or in the smaller towns. However, the figures on the foreign trade in eggs show that for several years previous to 1896 we did not produce enough to supply the home demand, inasmuch as we were importers of millions of dozens. The range from 3,179,344 dozens, net imports in 1892, to 1,226,763 dozens, net exports in 1898, is striking. Stated otherwise, the total imports in 1892 were 3,373,086 dozens and the exports 193,742 dozens, while the imports in 1898 were 129,711 dozens and the exports 2,356,474 dozens.

Tabular statement of imports and exports of eggs for the years 1882 to 1898, inclusive.

Year.	Imports.		Exports.	
	Quantity.	Value.	Quantity.	Value.
	Dozens.	*Dollars.*	*Dozens.*	*Dollars.*
1892	3,373,086	379,516	193,742	34,851
1893	2,457,576	284,178	151,311	43,096
1894	1,641,901	190,437	174,523	28,258
1895	1,954,962	219,459	181,754	29,346
1896	677,369	56,004	405,192	63,460
1897	190,674	9,259	2,734,218	2,543,544
1898	129,711	6,531	2,356,474	1,226,768

It will be observed that exports for 1898 were not so great as in 1897 by 377,744 dozens, with a difference in value of $29,837.

BUTTER.

The exports of butter fell greatly in 1898. In 1897 we exported 30,914,783 pounds, valued at $4,497,878, while in 1898 we exported but 15,032,489 pounds, valued at $2,428,143. The falling off occurred principally in the United Kingdom and British North America. During 1897 these countries took from us 22,909,995 pounds, while in 1898 they took from us but 8,658,676 pounds, a difference of 14,251,319 pounds. There was a notable increase of shipments to Brazil, from 465,743 pounds in 1897 to 1,014,866 pounds in 1898.

The imports of butter for 1897 were 37,961 pounds, valued at $6,139, and for 1898 23,944 pounds, valued at $4,055.

Quantity and value of butter exported, and countries to which exported, for the years 1897 and 1898.

Country to which exported.	1897.		1898.	
	Quantity.	Value.	Quantity.	Value.
	Pounds.	*Dollars.*	*Pounds.*	*Dollars.*
United Kingdom	19,312,724	2,906,621	6,847,859	1,125,391
Germany	2,228,799	253,805	671,302	95,043
Other Europe	1,483,228	168,362	754,031	102,207
British North America	3,597,271	532,690	1,810,825	320,439
Central American States and British Honduras	282,558	48,245	262,302	47,861
Mexico	246,478	41,536	259,731	46,520
Santo Domingo	54,451	7,438	75,269	10,531
Cuba	60,245	10,982	157,671	28,653
Porto Rico	49,465	5,918	27,285	4,669
Other West Indies and Bermuda	1,984,157	292,730	1,885,458	300,534
Brazil	465,743	56,188	1,014,866	130,585
Colombia	156,363	21,255	91,982	15,511
Other South America	638,327	84,189	724,330	108,162
China	32,720	6,478	16,496	3,936
Japan	106,289	20,199	120,299	24,055
Other Asia and Oceanica	181,673	35,623	258,763	54,572
Africa	21,194	3,672	19,326	4,151
Other countries	13,078	2,002	34,742	5,273
Total	30,914,783	4,497,878	15,032,489	2,428,143

WOOL AND WOOL MANUFACTURES.

The influence of the tariff is probably not so apparent in any other article of our commerce as it is in its relation to wool and wool manufactures. There can be no proper deduction from statistics on these articles of commerce without taking the tariff rates into consideration. However, nothing more can be given here than the figures for several years as they exist.

It is a gratifying condition that the total imports of wool and wool manufactures in 1898 amounted in value to $25,420,872 only. The previous years showed imports amounting to the enormous sum of $82,762,214. During recent years this sum was exceeded but once, namely, in 1895, when the total imports amounted to $94,089,490.

Tabular statement of value of imports of wool and wool manufactures for the years 1892 to 1898, inclusive.

Year.	Class 1 (clothing wool).	Class 2 (combing wool).	Class 3 (carpet wool).	Manufactures.	Total.
1892	$9,309,640	$1,375,651	$10,505,348	$37,515,445	$58,703,084
1893	5,373,238	895,266	7,485,045	30,238,506	44,182,055
1894	5,315,919	1,166,150	6,780,443	17,342,682	30,605,194
1895	19,657,912	4,092,656	10,019,591	60,319,331	94,089,490
1896	13,077,712	2,032,169	7,311,533	37,109,363	59,530,777
1897	33,953,828	6,946,102	12,532,300	29,330,284	82,762,214
1898	4,639,220	301,337	6,646,019	13,834,296	25,420,872

Our exports of these goods have been small for several years; but it will be observed from the tabular statement that the total has generally been on the increase—from $312,634 in 1892, to $1,035,216 in 1898. The largest exports are credited to 1896, when they amounted to $1,913,969. The wool producers of the United States will have scored a great victory when they produce wool enough to supply the home demand, not to consider the additional victory of increasing the volume of exports.

Tabular statement of value of exports of wool and wool manufactures for the years 1892 to 1898, inclusive.

Year.	Raw wool.	Manufactures.	Total.
1892	$38,799	$273,835	$312,634
1893	36,139	559,379	595,518
1894	232,162	736,360	968,522
1895	689,874	782,855	1,472,729
1896	968,866	945,103	1,913,969
1897	144,608	1,058,956	1,203,564
1898	14,406	1,020,810	1,035,216

ANIMALS.

Number and value of farm animals exported for the years 1870 to 1898, inclusive.

[Compiled from reports of the Bureau of Statistics, Treasury Department.]

Fiscal year.	Cattle.		Hogs.		Horses.		Mules.		Sheep.	
	Number.	Value.	Number.	Value.	Number.	Value.	Number.	Value.	Number.	Value.
1870....	27,530	$439,987	12,058	$189,753	2,121	$177,479	995	$140,350	39,570	$95,193
1871....	20,530	406,491	8,770	61,590	1,186	173,273	1,930	265,827	45,465	86,888
1872....	28,033	505,719	56,110	548,158	1,722	266,475	2,121	294,402	35,218	79,508
1873....	35,455	695,957	99,720	787,402	2,814	255,365	1,659	172,172	66,717	107,698
1874....	56,067	1,150,857	158,581	1,625,837	1,432	169,303	1,252	174,125	124,243	159,735
1875....	57,211	1,103,085	64,979	739,215	3,220	242,081	2,802	356,828	124,416	183,898
1876....	51,593	1,110,708	68,044	670,042	2,030	234,964	1,784	224,860	110,312	171,101
1877....	50,001	1,593,080	65,107	699,180	2,042	301,134	3,441	478,434	179,017	234,480
1878....	80,040	3,896,818	29,284	267,259	4,104	796,723	3,860	501,513	183,995	333,490
1879....	136,720	8,379,200	75,129	700,262	3,915	770,742	4,153	530,989	215,680	1,082,938
1880....	182,756	13,344,195	83,434	421,080	3,060	675,139	5,198	532,362	209,137	892,647
1881...	185,707	14,304,106	77,456	572,138	2,523	390,243	8,207	353,924	179,919	782,902
1882....	108,110	7,800,227	36,368	509,651	2,248	470,183	2,632	320,130	139,676	603,778
1883....	104,444	8,341,431	16,129	272,516	2,800	475,806	4,237	486,560	337,251	1,154,854
1884....	190,518	17,855,495	46,382	627,480	2,721	424,317	3,742	498,809	273,874	850,146
1885....	135,890	12,906,690	55,025	579,188	1,947	377,692	1,028	127,580	234,509	512,596
1886....	119,065	10,966,954	74,187	674,297	1,616	348,323	1,191	148,711	177,594	329,844
1887....	106,459	9,172,136	75,383	504,753	1,611	351,607	1,754	214,734	121,701	254,725
1888....	140,208	11,577,578	23,755	193,017	2,263	412,774	2,971	378,765	143,817	280,490
1889....	205,786	16,616,917	45,128	356,764	3,748	592,469	2,980	356,333	128,852	306,181
1890....	394,836	31,261,131	91,148	909,042	3,501	680,410	3,544	447,108	67,521	243,077
1891....	374,679	30,445,249	95,654	1,146,630	3,110	784,908	2,184	278,658	60,947	261,109
1892....	394,607	35,099,095	42,170	532,136	3,226	611,188	1,896	230,603	46,960	161,105
1893....	287,094	26,032,428	2,029	46,052	2,967	718,607	1,796	216,762	37,260	126,304
1894....	359,278	33,461,922	3,381	31,479	5,246	1,108,995	1,932	201,004	132,370	832,763
1895....	331,722	30,303,796	11,352	116,672	13,984	2,209,298	4,834	321,158	405,748	2,630,636
1896....	272,461	34,560,672	33,785	367,917	25,126	3,530,703	6,534	475,106	491,565	3,076,380
1897....	392,190	36,557,451	16,841	150,814	39,532	4,769,265	7,753	631,904	244,120	1,531,645
1898....	439,255	37,827,500	16,879	117,546	51,150	6,176,569	6,996	514,569	199,690	1,212,886

Number and value of exports of farm animals for the years 1897 and 1898, and countries to which exported.

[Compiled from reports of the Bureau of Statistics, Treasury Department.]

Country to which exported.	1897.		1898.	
	Number.	Value.	Number.	Value.
Cattle:				
United Kingdom..............................	396,371	$37,052,990	342,689	$31,668,909
Other Europe	2,233	215,525	....	....
British North America.......................	17,124	1,198,324	7,187	459,321
Central American States and British Honduras ..	386	15,039	58	4,310
Mexico..	701	36,854	2,500	94,404
West Indies and Bermuda......................	30,513	851,418	44,742	1,209,458
South America................................	30	3,728	484	7,775
Asia and Oceanica	111	5,654	159	8,700
Other countries...............................	....	....	60	9,590
Total.........................	447,469	39,379,532	397,879	33,463,967

Number and value of exports of farm animals for the years 1897 and 1898, and countries to which exported—Continued.

[Compiled from reports of the Bureau of Statistics, Treasury Department.]

Country to which exported.	1897.		1898.	
	Number.	Value.	Number.	Value.
Hogs:				
United Kingdom	101	$700	930	$7,387
British North America	2,105	11,873	4,564	28,301
Mexico	9,494	107,646	3,305	36,014
West Indies and Bermuda	835	6,390	4,043	23,569
South America	14	230	27	521
Asia and Oceanica	4,255	23,494	3,887	19,756
Other countries	37	481	123	1,998
Total	16,841	150,814	16,879	117,546
Horses:				
United Kingdom	21,579	2,980,732	21,819	3,262,115
France	72	9,000		
Germany	6,590	1,015,700	7,185	1,018,465
Other Europe	5,118	541,745	6,964	710,025
British North America	6,105	680,791	9,490	763,943
Central American States and British Honduras	199	13,400	239	11,665
Mexico	1,318	70,672	1,733	99,360
West Indies and Bermuda	4,130	244,520	916	83,788
South America	21	5,950	22	4,289
Asia and Oceanica	436	43,645	438	43,643
Africa	73	10,985	102	14,480
Other countries	1	125		
Total	45,642	5,617,265	48,917	6,010,773
Mules (all countries)	7,753	631,904	6,996	514,569
Sheep:				
United Kingdom	159,646	1,139,709	122,784	883,825
Other Europe			1	50
British North America	49,505	98,832	44,150	99,105
Mexico	2,077	8,275	3,179	12,205
West Indies and Bermuda	5,564	41,295	4,607	34,976
South America	1,356	15,839	1,354	10,653
Other countries	279	27,762	423	30,152
Total	218,427	1,331,712	176,498	1,070,966
All other animals and fowls (all countries)		187,710		226,647

MEAT AND MEAT PRODUCTS.

Quantity and value of exports of meat and meat products for 1897 and 1898.

[Compiled from reports of the Bureau of Statistics, Treasury Department.]

Country to which exported.	1897.		1898.	
	Quantity.	Value.	Quantity.	Value.
Canned beef products:	*Pounds.*	*Dollars.*	*Pounds.*	*Dollars.*
United Kingdom	26,555,988	2,280,994	22,322,278	2,055,366
France	504,538	41,571	365,364	31,267
Germany	5,499,966	478,617	3,963,071	342,507
Other Europe	3,051,968	262,017	2,418,265	207,803
British North America	732,400	55,094	1,511,378	132,049
Central American States and British Honduras	316,105	36,955	213,411	22,499
Mexico	108,267	12,743	111,773	15,006
Santo Domingo	646	55	506	45
Cuba	72,962	5,723	66,846	5,520
Porto Rico	2,688	208	96	8
Other West Indies and Bermuda	412,066	37,054	397,222	38,312
Argentina	4,030	425	5,820	581
Brazil	65,971	5,628	243,977	24,318
Colombia	79,814	6,866	53,798	5,160
Other South America	149,250	13,178	141,761	13,134
China	167,488	23,991	130,125	13,049
British East Indies	8,245	846	4,128	618
Hongkong	212,720	31,192	114,020	16,925
Japan	254,697	37,063	293,240	37,183
British Australasia	182,599	18,280	37,830	4,482
Other Asia and Oceanica	601,369	87,523	407,010	60,450
Africa	4,098,664	323,767	5,084,459	416,636
Other countries	100	9	264	20
Total	42,804,831	3,728,607	37,866,632	3,448,240
Fresh beef:				
United Kingdom	279,515,512	22,271,496	266,414,299	22,562,155
British North America	25,280	1,558	618,792	48,065
West Indies and Bermuda	340,798	25,206	425,236	33,768
Other countries	1,000	66	579	52
Total	279,882,590	22,298,326	267,458,906	22,644,040
Salted, pickled, or other cured beef:				
United Kingdom	17,187,976	947,705	21,401,576	1,249,507
France	158,100	7,531	310,175	18,463
Germany	4,290,470	222,906	5,986,717	337,736
Other Europe	6,127,601	306,008	6,867,045	359,434
British North America	4,025,704	170,361	3,438,637	172,820
Central American States and British Honduras	690,726	34,757	707,024	36,646
Mexico	7,981	505	5,810	291
Santo Domingo	45,350	2,030	65,450	3,478
Cuba	297,969	14,252	316,307	16,111
Porto Rico	125,900	5,049	10,700	532
Other West Indies and Bermuda	5,771,706	281,150	5,162,264	285,166
Brazil	34,700	1,756	34,200	2,082
Colombia	262,933	12,818	242,567	13,146
Other South America	2,422,884	125,475	3,376,896	194,387
Asia and Oceanica	1,661,897	76,599	608,225	33,322
Africa	736,300	35,000	228,500	13,098
Other countries	15,100	681	20,700	1,063
Total	43,865,317	2,244,568	48,732,796	2,737,304

Quantity and value of exports of meat and meat products for 1897 and 1898—Cont'd.

Country to which exported.	1897.		1898.	
	Quantity.	Value.	Quantity.	Value.
Tallow:	*Pounds.*	*Dollars.*	*Pounds.*	*Dollars.*
United Kingdom	21,861,350	802,451	45,060,294	1,759,270
France	9,619,729	331,938	11,480,863	453,500
Germany	6,781,414	247,084	18,450,402	722,616
Other Europe	9,267,049	317,214	24,281,188	960,046
British North America	91,656	2,921	658,666	17,570
Central American States and British Honduras	2,160,512	94,009	2,129,623	98,477
Mexico	742,937	28,743	690,647	27,542
Santo Domingo	602,269	22,096	506,761	20,274
Cuba	323,860	12,331	697,161	24,722
Porto Rico	5,927	309	7,195	404
Other West Indies and Bermuda	2,613,025	106,234	1,473,298	63,972
Brazil	710,544	30,657	483,582	25,730
Colombia	434,436	18,304	191,334	8,563
Other South America	274,734	11,829	577,092	26,124
Asia and Oceanica	32,150	1,173	130,267	5,544
Other countries	4,104	173	817	41
Total	55,524,696	2,027,506	106,819,190	4,209,395
Bacon:				
United Kingdom	434,109,061	30,970,572	449,799,080	34,333,973
France	1,334,096	86,553	5,934,342	423,536
Germany	35,154,312	2,193,807	44,212,080	2,963,660
Other Europe	63,318,749	3,895,976	84,544,352	5,708,096
British North America	14,379,000	826,086	17,209,567	1,140,296
Central American States and British Honduras	284,729	20,852	225,668	16,435
Mexico	95,993	8,974	126,218	12,667
Santo Domingo	36,435	2,236	31,148	2,122
Cuba	10,797,137	650,861	8,550,884	524,717
Porto Rico	617,901	35,566	736,441	49,215
Other West Indies and Bermuda	584,836	44,306	818,524	59,410
Brazil	16,747,886	1,031,141	6,924,513	476,884
Colombia	20,956	1,538	19,287	1,384
Other South America	406,244	30,380	256,825	19,151
China	25,085	3,279	52,720	6,895
Other Asia and Oceanica	113,655	14,592	197,605	24,569
Africa	56,347	3,694	44,031	3,033
Other countries	300	23		
Total	578,082,722	39,820,382	619,683,235	45,786,045
Hams:				
United Kingdom	140,018,122	13,481,301	164,389,154	15,215,209
France	870,118	87,037	718,017	69,204
Germany	4,863,346	434,601	13,975,056	1,297,710
Other Europe	13,946,288	1,376,959	25,232,655	2,358,465
British North America	4,085,321	381,387	8,088,139	689,848
Central American States and British Honduras	311,465	38,118	250,509	24,325
Mexico	200,485	22,191	261,810	29,530
Santo Domingo	58,375	6,758	64,709	7,061
Cuba	3,716,784	372,463	3,562,795	355,622
Porto Rico	978,415	85,208	196,497	16,761

Quantity and value of exports of meat and meat products for 1897 and 1898—Cont'd.

Country to which exported.	1897.		1898.	
	Quantity.	Value.	Quantity.	Value.
Hams—Continued.	*Pounds.*	*Dollars.*	*Pounds.*	*Dollars.*
Other West Indies and Bermuda	1,258,235	120,650	1,680,817	140,557
Brazil	26,042	2,483	40,840	4,207
Colombia	166,162	15,041	158,363	13,798
Other South America	872,719	95,612	752,209	76,972
China	58,464	7,543	83,160	10,819
British Australasia	5,746	766	29,735	3,346
Other Asia and Oceanica	310,029	37,485	490,615	52,522
Africa	172,479	20,251	148,756	16,521
Other countries	8,068	810	25,892	2,178
Total	171,956,663	16,581,659	220,011,750	20,384,650
Pork:				
United Kingdom	23,396,951	1,384,404	61,903,739	4,025,464
France	141,750	7,996	144,875	7,978
Germany	2,858,293	160,477	12,918,060	710,707
Other Europe	5,626,736	331,392	25,317,928	1,483,600
British North America	11,509,114	578,897	19,554,080	1,126,020
Central American States and British Honduras	1,328,644	61,010	1,429,815	72,778
Santo Domingo	71,400	3,455	112,400	6,519
Cuba	219,460	10,766	340,140	17,748
Porto Rico	4,225,300	195,769	2,609,200	138,005
Other West Indies and Bermuda	19,181,730	897,619	17,819,430	958,234
Brazil	284,400	16,077	108,700	7,153
Colombia	145,877	7,749	143,568	8,420
Other South America	3,472,400	167,157	4,410,990	238,290
Asia and Oceanica	237,830	16,525	167,005	11,865
Africa	157,800	9,013	74,400	4,429
Other countries	91,904	4,876	275,735	14,404
Total	72,949,589	3,853,182	147,330,094	8,831,613
Lard:				
United Kingdom	203,293,295	10,751,057	231,525,366	12,866,718
France	20,951,417	1,041,932	25,599,190	1,437,623
Germany	205,240,201	10,414,421	238,680,471	14,034,380
Other Europe	121,095,250	6,253,674	162,218,933	9,350,182
British North America	4,252,008	205,743	10,801,182	585,367
Central American States and British Honduras	2,220,661	117,772	2,828,440	169,895
Mexico	6,102,535	284,585	2,767,292	144,009
Santo Domingo	448,318	24,892	528,439	32,145
Cuba	21,017,677	1,002,426	19,890,106	1,068,055
Porto Rico	4,558,467	234,715	4,042,075	211,379
Other West Indies and Bermuda	6,169,847	365,868	6,231,763	416,246
Argentina	84,796	2,132	54,091	3,655
Brazil	17,801,426	1,014,055	16,701,585	1,146,359
Colombia	4,288,663	137,938	1,552,858	96,274
Other South America	10,799,317	616,585	9,749,404	644,628
Asia and Oceanica	556,629	37,623	922,326	62,201
Africa	1,660,509	113,150	2,400,219	177,063
Other countries	74,595	4,041	45,252	2,713
Total	630,060,611	32,622,409	736,538,992	43,435,922

Quantity and value of exports of meat and meat products for 1897 and 1898—Cont'd.

Country to which exported.	1897. Quantity.	1897. Value.	1898. Quantity.	1898. Value.
	Pounds.	*Dollars.*	*Pounds.*	*Dollars.*
Lard compounds and substitutes (all countries)	15,307,065	788,725	23,822,956	1,231,253
Mutton (all countries)	519,986	41,456	265,527	22,147
Oleo and oleomargarine:				
United Kingdom	7,406,765	453,066	8,894,144	522,567
Germany	27,573,912	1,562,887	31,414,750	1,982,102
Netherlands	73,767,038	4,506,310	84,261,045	4,993,139
Other Europe	9,813,635	558,017	14,319,620	859,215
British North America	891,878	50,835	893,770	51,147
Central American States and British Honduras	4,550	438	14,296	1,695
Mexico	4,410	475	10,713	1,102
Porto Rico			54,530	5,678
Other West Indies and Bermuda	1,927,452	189,025	1,885,783	185,037
Colombia	76,870	6,835	101,598	9,194
Other South America	232,416	24,031	142,222	13,816
Asia and Oceanica	154,958	17,367	192,879	21,295
Other countries	202,027	21,805	87,792	8,734
Total	122,055,911	7,391,091	142,273,139	8,654,721
Cases for sausages		1,677,033		1,762,431
Poultry and game (all countries)		66,316		91,819
All other meat products (all countries)		3,243,189		5,190,547

CHEESE.

Quantity and value of imports and exports of cheese for 1897 and 1898.

[Compiled from reports of the Bureau of Statistics, Treasury Department.]

Year.	Imports. Quantity.	Imports. Value.	Exports. Quantity.	Exports. Value.	Exports over imports. Quantity.	Exports over imports. Value.
	Pounds.	*Dollars.*	*Pounds.*	*Dollars.*	*Pounds.*	*Dollars.*
1897	11,192,754	1,495,837	60,283,755	5,447,036	49,091,001	3,951,199
1898	10,848,082	1,456,934	40,726,542	3,398,059	29,678,460	1,941,125

These exports, omitting the small item of exports of foreign cheese, were sent to the following countries:

Countries to which cheese was exported in 1897 and 1898.

[Compiled from reports of the Bureau of Statistics, Treasury Department.]

Country to which exported.	1897.		1898.	
	Quantity.	Value.	Quantity.	Value.
	Pounds.	*Dollars.*	*Pounds.*	*Dollars.*
United Kingdom	44,350,228	4,080,516	25,413,146	2,139,905
Germany	425	61		
British North America	13,980,688	1,176,381	12,994,969	990,222
Central American States and Honduras	171,295	19,921	155,059	17,553
Mexico	118,546	14,296	135,850	15,419
Santo Domingo	39,011	4,719	38,549	4,631
Cuba	156,841	20,347	376,105	46,898
Porto Rico	21,988	2,601	42,517	5,325
Other West Indies and Bermuda	802,810	100,642	729,485	84,639
Brazil	2,638	314	4,772	521
Colombia	98,212	12,116	74,149	8,974
Other South America	127,285	16,316	134,868	16,484
China	46,669	5,120	96,495	10,535
Japan	30,229	3,303	49,235	5,408
Other Asia and Oceanica	213,485	28,318	265,153	28,836
Other countries	20,301	2,400	13,642	1,464
Total	60,180,651	5,432,371	40,523,994	3,376,818

Countries from which cheese was imported in 1897 and 1898.

[Compiled from reports of the Bureau of Statistics, Treasury Department.]

Country from which imported.	1897.		1898.	
	Quantity.	Value.	Quantity.	Value.
	Pounds.	*Dollars.*	*Pounds.*	*Dollars.*
United Kingdom	120,498	20,717	201,835	32,36
France	864,348	138,089	957,632	159,96
Germany	299,369	38,121	275,092	85,54
Italy	3,378,165	462,479	3,465,284	439,48
Netherlands	919,241	101,385	951,892	101,77
Switzerland	5,299,995	694,522	4,677,461	647,04
Other Europe	280,732	11,773	280,441	33,26
British North America	23,462	3,461	85,212	7,11
Other countries	6,944	25,290	3,233	36
Total	11,192,754	1,495,837	10,848,082	1,456,93

WOOL, WOOL MANUFACTURES, ETC.

Quantity and value of imports and exports of wool and wool manufactures (including hair of goat, camel, etc.) for 1897 and 1898.

IMPORTS.

[Compiled from reports of the Bureau of Statistics, Treasury Department.]

Country from which imported or to which exported.	1897.		1898.	
	Quantity.	Value.	Quantity.	Value.
CLASS 1.—*Clothing wool.*	*Pounds.*	*Dollars.*	*Pounds.*	*Dollars.*
United Kingdom	106,676,127	19,039,491	6,403,793	1,235,365
France	15,534,189	3,870,596	112,111	14,034
South America	37,593,292	4,906,323	4,505,995	513,457
Asia and Oceanica	18,976,425	3,114,322	14,471,220	2,625,479
Other countries	20,046,518	3,023,096	1,650,703	250,885
Total	198,826,551	33,963,828	27,143,822	4,639,220
CLASS 2.—*Combing wool.*				
United Kingdom	21,629,415	4,421,700	968,107	254,253
Other Europe	818,326	172,792	77,494	24,398
British North America	5,929,911	1,150,291	9,943	2,728
South America	8,420,061	1,183,201	143,454	19,126
Asia and Oceanica	22,454	3,639		
Other countries	129,190	14,479	6,524	832
Total	36,949,357	6,946,102	1,205,522	301,337
CLASS 3.—*Carpet wool.*				
United Kingdom	40,994,424	4,942,671	18,067,825	2,011,995
France	9,133,297	1,166,465	2,453,270	249,889
Germany	2,518,137	280,495	788,071	82,219
Other Europe	20,570,393	2,237,187	16,009,405	1,561,773
British North America	54,337	4,108	2,201	135
South America	15,372,042	1,283,684	10,827,312	857,399
China	24,701,012	1,845,290	17,797,059	1,422,858
Other Asia and Oceanica	7,692,817	769,165	4,310,903	428,836
Other countries	27,115	2,935	345,014	30,915
Total	121,063,574	12,532,000	71,501,090	6,646,019
Manufactures of wool (all countries)		40,431,831		15,206,365
Carpets:	*Sq. yards.*		*Sq. yards.*	
United Kingdom	285,448	533,864	239,409	558,405
Other Europe	99,373	276,002	330,511	1,096,174
Japan	10,584	10,576	13,811	17,351
Other Asia and Oceanica	75,875	240,836	84,714	246,367
Other countries	1,567	1,786	31,845	117,539
Total	472,847	1,063,154	700,350	2,035,836
Cloth:	*Pounds.*		*Pounds.*	
United Kingdom	19,013,035	10,667,180	2,873,358	2,677,975
Austria-Hungary	173,376	153,472	76,785	68,804
Belgium	441,321	345,696	104,256	93,303
France	316,488	341,117	192,885	205,243
Germany	2,389,859	2,130,046	878,240	820,493
Other Europe	9,181	8,160	6,655	5,299
Other countries	10,882	9,270	5,478	5,161
Total	22,354,142	13,654,931	4,137,666	3,876,368
Dress goods·	*Sq. yards.*		*Sq. yards.*	
United Kingdom	49,855,080	4,644,135	14,398,110	2,492,359
France	8,358,494	5,666,049	9,270,700	2,104,487
Germany	5,972,701	3,101,953	8,270,007	2,281,056
Other Europe	221,435	140,608	1,293,377	22,654
Other countries	846	498	2,258	726
Total	64,408,556	13,553,243	33,171,452	6,901,282

Quantity and value of imports and exports of wool and wool manufactures (including hair of goat, camel, etc.) for 1887 and 1898—Continued.

EXPORTS.

Country from which imported or to which exported.	1897.		1898.	
	Quantity.	Value.	Quantity.	Value.
Raw wool:	*Pounds.*		*Pounds.*	
United Kingdom	8,608	975	700	100
Other Europe	5,918	789	16,000	1,600
British North America	673,030	112,365	56,839	10,119
Mexico	366,935	30,459	17,000	2,587
Other countries	536	40		
Total	1,055,027	144,608	90,539	14,406
Manufactures of wool (all countries)		1,058,956		1,030,810

NOTE.—This table does not include exports of foreign wool, amounting in value to $776,342 for for 1897, and $760,492 for 1898.

HIDES AND SKINS.

Quantity and value of imports and exports of hides and skins (other than furs) for the years 1897 and 1898.

IMPORTS.

[Compiled from reports of the Bureau of Statistics, Treasury Department.]

Country from which imported or to which exported.	1897.		1898.	
	Quantity.	Value.	Quantity.	Value.
	Pounds.	*Dollars.*	*Pounds.*	*Dollars.*
United Kingdom	45,177,245	5,366,051	52,273,823	7,109,834
France	16,047,973	2,361,877	20,105,264	3,431,753
Germany	8,748,591	1,814,534	15,781,280	2,649,740
Other Europe	16,426,328	2,676,782	26,472,748	4,109,864
British North America	19,694,639	1,494,087	18,555,584	1,154,540
Central American States	1,541,054	210,617	2,310,730	236,676
Mexico	14,335,003	1,859,747	12,341,214	1,771,116
West Indies	10,215,520	855,320	2,285,693	329,517
South America	64,964,158	10,028,755	60,423,155	9,793,530
East Indies	16,529,351	2,522,673	25,425,771	4,480,533
Other Asia and Oceanica	6,901,803	1,384,827	10,371,291	2,109,489
Africa	5,971,738	909,524	7,495,206	1,369,518
Other countries	9,818,690	1,245,945	8,253,761	1,309,197
Total	236,372,088	33,230,749	257,094,920	39,906,307

EXPORTS.

United Kingdom	581,109	56,270	180,347	19,319
France	1,875,025	167,293	496,156	49,813
Germany	6,259,012	491,891	5,532,375	454,300
Other Europe	599,570	82,282	662,181	88,796
British North America	9,232,321	732,820	4,427,905	396,799
Central American States and British Honduras	4,300	543		
Mexico	112,920	13,908	15,174	2,659
West Indies and Bermuda	1,090	107	3,309	376
Japan	4,008	225	20,200	1,205
Other Asia and Oceanica	6,100	925		
Africa	101,280	7,140	56,962	4,910
Other countries	1,296	158	2,500	256
Total	18,778,031	1,553,622	11,397,129	1,018,433

LEATHER AND LEATHER MANUFACTURES.

*Quantity and value of imports and exports of leather and leather manufactures
for the years 1897 and 1898.*

IMPORTS.

[Compiled from reports of the Bureau of Statistics, Treasury Department.]

Country from which imported or to which exported.	1897.		1898.	
	Quantity.	Value.	Quantity.	Value.
	Pounds.	*Dollars.*	*Pounds.*	*Dollars.*
Leather, all kinds.		6,373,726		5,236,171
Gloves:				
Belgium		394,237		264,754
France		2,031,716		2,012,788
Germany		2,820,719		2,635,294
Other Europe		1,090,436		772,900
Other countries		302		728
Total		6,337,410		5,686,464
All other manufactures		452,166		420,792

EXPORTS.

Sole leather:				
United Kingdom	26,421,973	4,461,508	29,992,004	5,109,057
Germany	267,271	51,619	364,811	72,556
Other Europe	4,663,689	885,932	3,779,586	703,809
British North America	767,087	147,940	779,197	146,252
West Indies and Bermuda	44,888	9,190	33,110	7,159
South America	21,005	4,158	34,654	8,113
Japan	1,267,359	266,250	1,295,595	272,966
British Australasia	148,170	30,603	155,012	33,006
Other Asia and Oceanica	227,235	46,500	230,271	49,113
Africa	196,409	38,978	130,008	26,440
Other countries	65,344	12,981	58,095	12,104
Total	34,090,390	5,925,459	36,763,033	6,440,575
Other leather:				
United Kingdom		7,545,351		8,884,614
France		259,242		297,541
Germany		459,065		762,165
Other Europe		1,152,447		1,088,114
British North America		600,290		703,829
Central American States and British Honduras		4,575		8,864
Mexico		12,137		7,586
Santo Domingo		1,236		1,047
Cuba		934		2,638
Porto Rico		895		3,266
Other West Indies and Bermuda		16,084		18,952
Argentina		1,234		18,346
Brazil		30,923		53,088
Colombia		3,039		3,272
Other South America		10,151		20,995
British Australasia		197,108		284,022
Other Asia and Oceanica		14,582		61,028
Africa		25,682		22,406
Other countries		515		495
Total		10,306,390		12,242,268

Quantity and value of imports and exports of leather and leather manufactures for the years 1897 and 1898—Continued.

EXPORTS—Continued.

Country from which imported or to which exported.	1897.		1898.	
	Quantity.	Value.	Quantity.	Value.
Boots and shoes:	*Pounds.*	*Dollars.*	*Pounds.*	*Dollars.*
United Kingdom		323,928		349,030
France		22,175		32,440
Germany		29,515		67,426
Other Europe		32,492		39,570
British North America		237,519		346,112
Central American States and British Honduras		91,823		84,861
Mexico		72,540		116,099
West Indies and Bermuda		259,279		278,561
Colombia		45,690		36,027
Other South America		23,377		40,613
British Australasia		285,944		324,729
Other Asia and Oceanica		165,681		145,856
Africa		95,524		79,864
Other countries		3,162		3,195
Total		1,688,649		1,944,423
Harness and saddles (all countries)		232,634		212,695
All other manufactures (all countries)		984,136		1,076,861

NUMBERS AND VALUES OF FARM ANIMALS, 1897 AND 1898.[1]

HORSES.

State or Territory.	1897.			1898.		
	Number.	Average price.	Value.	Number.	Average price.	Value.
Maine	114,272	$50.50	$5,770,895	111,987	$52.29	$5,855,722
New Hampshire	54,483	47.59	2,592,999	55,028	50.48	2,777,941
Vermont	85,669	44.14	3,781,069	84,812	48.16	4,084,899
Massachusetts	63,162	63.35	4,001,549	63,478	71.95	4,566,926
Rhode Island	10,230	76.54	782,976	10,281	79.84	820,792
Connecticut	43,465	70.19	3,050,873	43,682	71.01	3,101,932
New York	608,916	55.48	33,781,467	596,738	58.04	34,634,083
New Jersey	79,980	64.24	5,137,961	79,180	67.10	5,313,023
Pennsylvania	565,719	49.25	27,862,207	548,747	53.56	29,390,858
Delaware	30,577	52.95	1,619,177	30,883	55.49	1,713,722
Maryland	130,972	47.91	6,274,811	129,662	48.50	6,289,047
Virginia	238,714	37.25	8,891,021	233,940	39.64	9,272,222
North Carolina	146,991	47.16	6,931,728	146,697	47.96	7,035,577
South Carolina	67,113	51.36	3,446,710	66,979	51.45	3,446,020
Georgia	111,380	45.59	5,077,374	110,266	46.09	5,082,333
Florida	37,300	38.95	1,452,853	37,673	39.54	1,489,735
Alabama	130,915	40.52	5,304,161	132,224	39.86	5,270,259
Mississippi	199,482	35.40	7,061,779	201,477	37.25	5,504,111
Louisiana	142,879	29.54	4,220,299	143,593	32.48	4,663,985
Texas	1,148,500	17.30	19,866,178	1,137,015	17.67	20,088,788
Arkansas	237,927	28.40	6,756,888	234,596	29.13	6,833,080
Tennessee	327,424	35.17	11,516,319	317,601	36.35	11,544,013
West Virginia	153,381	35.25	5,406,535	151,847	36.64	5,563,827
Kentucky	380,835	32.46	12,363,042	365,602	34.41	12,581,471
Ohio	666,836	41.37	27,590,332	653,499	45.59	29,791,046
Michigan	418,786	46.44	19,446,741	410,410	51.23	21,023,483
Indiana	613,542	36.13	22,166,072	601,271	39.77	23,909,557
Illinois	1,040,767	36.05	37,519,129	1,003,299	40.30	40,437,954
Wisconsin	412,296	43.07	17,757,998	409,822	49.96	20,473,290
Minnesota	464,410	39.35	18,276,398	455,122	44.75	20,366,015
Iowa	1,022,242	34.01	34,770,027	981,352	38.40	37,686,866
Missouri	802,878	25.28	20,292,746	762,734	28.02	21,371,427
Kansas	749,879	26.12	19,580,832	734,881	29.85	21,935,833
Nebraska	592,985	30.53	18,102,648	652,284	34.69	22,629,031
South Dakota	287,867	28.97	8,339,207	290,746	30.56	8,884,431
North Dakota	170,036	37.94	6,451,838	175,137	42.21	7,392,360
Montana	171,795	18.23	3,131,388	164,923	21.16	3,490,193
Wyoming	73,733	14.93	1,100,948	72,258	18.15	1,311,701
Colorado	151,721	22.86	3,469,095	148,687	24.77	3,682,538
New Mexico	83,854	18.18	1,524,176	83,351	15.55	1,296,524
Arizona	51,973	25.28	1,313,020	50,414	25.56	1,288,464
Utah	67,619	17.21	1,163,489	68,295	20.26	1,383,753
Nevada	50,347	12.82	645,200	44,305	11.94	529,107
Idaho	130,691	13.69	1,788,895	128,077	21.86	2,799,957
Washington	173,157	24.05	4,163,817	169,694	31.03	5,265,775
Oregon	193,588	20.61	3,989,854	185,844	26.51	4,927,567
California	417,396	28.96	12,085,909	342,265	27.54	9,426,483
Oklahoma	42,227	17.34	732,177	42,649	19.86	847,182
Total or general average.	13,960,911	34.26	478,362,407	13,665,307	37.40	511,074,813

[1] These figures are furnished by the Division of Statistics, which dates its returns January 1; but as the figures are really for the previous year, the dates in these tables have been changed accordingly.

*Number, average price, and value of farm animals for 1897 and 1898—*Continued.

MULES.

State or Territory.	1897.			1898.		
	Number.	Average price.	Value.	Number.	Average price.	Value.
Maine						
New Hampshire						
Vermont						
Massachusetts						
Rhode Island						
Connecticut						
New York	4,511	$58.25	$262,746	4,421	$62.87	$277,980
New Jersey	7,342	80.74	592,786	7,289	82.95	602,988
Pennsylvania	36,686	63.32	2,322,825	37,053	66.99	2,482,216
Delaware	5,243	68.91	361,270	4,928	67.95	330,427
Maryland	12,025	70.95	805,684	12,638	64.06	809,577
Virginia	36,733	51.54	1,893,283	35,998	51.34	1,848,026
North Carolina	112,523	53.64	6,036,220	111,308	55.66	6,198,903
South Carolina	98,340	61.27	6,024,889	97,357	60.28	5,869,011
Georgia	165,202	64.72	10,601,811	158,504	61.01	9,676,055
Florida	8,438	63.55	536,274	8,354	57.07	476,792
Alabama	131,086	50.15	6,571,322	129,726	48.72	6,320,059
Mississippi	162,432	49.45	8,029,440	163,082	51.32	8,368,620
Louisiana	90,004	56.28	5,065,747	90,904	57.03	5,184,399
Texas	265,349	30.96	8,214,560	265,880	29.98	7,972,280
Arkansas	146,974	36.52	5,367,264	145,504	37.59	5,469,565
Tennessee	160,920	37.67	6,061,560	151,265	39.36	5,954,253
West Virginia	7,487	43.37	324,727	7,412	45.47	337,055
Kentucky	113,348	35.89	4,067,779	106,547	37.63	4,009,295
Ohio	17,761	43.16	166,482	17,228	47.72	822,196
Michigan	2,756	46.43	127,909	2,646	51.61	136,554
Indiana	44,309	40.54	1,796,173	41,650	44.44	1,851,098
Illinois	86,553	40.09	3,470,287	82,225	44.41	3,651,271
Wisconsin	4,802	45.42	218,092	4,754	49.79	236,713
Minnesota	8,588	44.97	386,231	8,416	49.03	412,663
Iowa	32,861	39.94	1,312,466	31,547	43.12	1,360,209
Missouri	199,306	31.98	6,373,297	183,302	36.03	6,606,802
Kansas	80,212	34.48	2,765,356	79,410	39.25	3,116,611
Nebraska	42,590	37.23	1,585,625	43,016	44.13	1,898,300
South Dakota	6,627	39.59	262,394	6,093	43.82	293,297
North Dakota	7,008	56.04	392,712	7,036	55.44	390,086
Montana	915	32.77	29,984	924	36.45	33,679
Wyoming	1,511	46.08	69,620	1,514	34.17	51,734
Colorado	8,755	43.14	377,687	6,667	44.30	368,941
New Mexico	3,507	32.50	113,978	3,472	30.59	106,198
Arizona	1,031	24.67	25,434	1,041	29.50	30,712
Utah	1,615	26.14	42,218	1,599	32.73	52,329
Nevada	1,408	21.91	30,843	1,394	23.22	32,368
Idaho	936	23.72	22,202	917	33.26	30,501
Washington	1,427	44.09	62,910	1,441	45.16	65,071
Oregon	5,782	28.64	165,606	5,609	29.86	167,488
California	56,898	38.33	2,180,836	52,915	34.15	1,807,174
Oklahoma	7,931	26.60	210,967	8,407	28.41	238,821
Total or general average	2,190,282	43.88	96,109,516	2,134,213	44.96	95,963,261

Number, average price, and value of farm animals for 1897 and 1898—Continued.

MILCH COWS.

State or Territory.	1897.			1898.		
	Number.	Average price.	Value.	Number.	Average price.	Value.
Maine	195,919	$27.55	$5,397,568	197,878	$30.50	$6,085,279
New Hampshire	132,840	29.65	3,938,706	136,825	33.65	4,604,161
Vermont	266,276	27.25	7,256,021	271,602	30.85	8,378,922
Massachusetts	174,554	32.80	5,725,371	179,791	37.75	6,787,110
Rhode Island	25,258	34.00	858,772	25,511	39.90	1,017,889
Connecticut	138,930	32.75	4,549,958	143,098	35.55	5,087,134
New York	1,402,164	32.00	44,869,248	1,458,251	33.55	48,924,321
New Jersey	208,421	36.10	7,523,996	214,674	38.15	8,189,813
Pennsylvania	923,905	29.60	27,495,588	924,260	31.50	29,114,190
Delaware	35,554	26.00	924,404	35,376	28.95	1,024,135
Maryland	151,982	25.60	3,890,739	155,022	26.95	4,177,843
Virginia	252,512	20.55	5,189,122	244,937	22.25	5,449,848
North Carolina	258,607	14.70	3,801,523	248,263	15.90	3,947,332
South Carolina	130,682	16.25	2,123,582	126,762	16.75	2,121,264
Georgia	303,302	21.85	6,629,115	297,324	23.00	6,838,452
Florida	117,785	19.50	2,296,808	114,251	15.60	1,782,316
Alabama	296,194	12.50	3,702,425	254,727	15.45	3,935,532
Mississippi	267,657	14.85	3,974,706	256,951	18.90	4,856,374
Louisiana	138,184	16.70	2,307,673	125,747	19.10	2,401,768
Texas	722,476	20.00	14,449,520	700,802	23.75	16,644,048
Arkansas	223,645	16.10	3,600,684	196,808	19.40	3,818,075
Tennessee	279,863	18.50	5,177,466	254,675	22.05	5,615,584
West Virginia	167,240	25.05	4,189,362	163,895	27.50	4,507,112
Kentucky	264,051	22.15	5,848,730	248,208	25.40	6,304,483
Ohio	729,441	29.35	21,409,093	736,735	31.05	22,875,622
Michigan	454,561	30.85	14,023,207	459,107	31.30	14,370,049
Indiana	605,916	29.20	17,692,747	611,975	31.10	19,032,422
Illinois	1,003,218	32.85	32,955,711	1,001,212	33.60	33,640,723
Wisconsin	814,384	28.70	23,372,821	895,822	31.30	28,039,229
Minnesota	633,993	27.50	17,434,808	646,673	29.45	19,044,520
Iowa	1,214,345	31.95	38,798,323	1,250,775	34.40	43,026,660
Missouri	666,530	26.75	17,829,673	673,195	27.80	18,714,821
Kansas	654,286	29.15	19,072,437	680,437	31.05	21,128,190
Nebraska	571,591	30.65	17,519,264	628,750	33.40	21,000,250
South Dakota	341,579	28.10	9,598,370	372,321	29.20	10,871,773
North Dakota	167,719	27.35	4,587,115	171,073	28.60	4,892,688
Montana	42,713	31.30	1,336,917	43,994	34.40	1,513,394
Wyoming	17,920	31.85	572,026	18,140	38.10	691,134
Colorado	85,669	32.50	2,784,242	91,666	34.95	3,203,727
New Mexico	19,126	26.55	507,795	19,317	31.00	598,827
Arizona	18,222	26.25	478,328	18,404	29.60	544,758
Utah	55,564	23.95	1,330,758	57,787	27.60	1,594,921
Nevada	18,105	27.85	504,224	18,069	29.25	528,518
Idaho	29,167	25.50	743,758	31,500	28.20	888,300
Washington	120,297	25.85	3,109,677	115,485	30.20	3,487,647
Oregon	115,427	23.30	2,689,449	116,581	25.85	3,013,619
California	342,392	28.65	9,809,531	318,425	28.00	8,915,900
Oklahoma	35,590	26.20	932,458	37,014	28.40	1,051,198
Total or general average.	15,840,886	27.45	434,813,826	15,990,115	29.66	474,233,925

Number, average price, and value of farm animals for 1897 and 1898—Continued.

CATTLE OTHER THAN MILCH COWS.

State or Territory.	1897.			1898.		
	Number.	Average price.	Value.	Number.	Average price.	Value.
Maine	107,294	$22.03	$2,363,309	109,440	$25.84	$2,827,763
New Hampshire	76,327	24.59	1,876,685	79,380	29.58	2,347,855
Vermont	135,139	22.07	2,982,522	133,788	24.41	3,265,629
Massachusetts	74,134	25.82	1,914,319	74,875	26.52	1,985,763
Rhode Island	10,676	30.18	322,233	10,356	32.74	339,038
Connecticut	65,282	30.08	1,963,673	66,588	32.09	2,137,078
New York	544,735	26.17	14,256,261	561,077	27.10	15,204,058
New Jersey	42,406	25.14	1,066,254	41,558	26.86	1,116,251
Pennsylvania	550,981	23.64	13,025,756	528,942	25.59	13,538,007
Delaware	23,953	22.90	548,545	22,995	23.63	543,340
Maryland	109,175	22.63	2,470,249	105,900	23.12	2,448,143
Virginia	356,300	19.07	6,795,970	338,542	22.25	7,531,714
North Carolina	321,228	9.92	3,188,029	295,530	10.86	3,210,640
South Carolina	152,160	9.55	1,453,811	141,509	9.45	1,337,399
Georgia	503,593	8.92	4,492,300	423,018	9.07	3,836,978
Florida	350,295	7.50	2,625,811	325,774	7.56	2,462,036
Alabama	442,736	7.02	3,109,998	336,479	8.92	3,001,561
Mississippi	370,876	8.31	3,082,348	304,118	11.38	3,459,645
Louisiana	220,108	9.61	2,115,346	182,690	12.07	2,205,892
Texas	4,823,295	15.27	73,639,656	4,533,897	16.91	76,665,937
Arkansas	305,522	12.03	3,675,886	252,523	13.50	3,381,378
Tennessee	379,168	13.41	5,086,344	322,293	16.43	5,295,279
West Virginia	253,604	20.79	5,273,085	243,460	23.33	5,678,952
Kentucky	392,162	20.65	8,097,948	341,181	23.18	7,908,920
Ohio	606,127	27.16	16,463,012	636,433	27.85	17,725,937
Michigan	348,505	23.13	8,062,319	341,535	24.45	8,352,225
Indiana	675,608	25.25	17,060,685	641,913	29.03	18,636,018
Illinois	1,304,192	27.72	36,150,911	1,285,086	29.04	37,118,303
Wisconsin	607,541	22.76	13,830,060	589,315	25.13	14,811,256
Minnesota	593,922	20.90	12,465,824	570,165	21.97	12,526,243
Iowa	2,207,739	28.71	63,395,211	2,163,584	31.02	67,120,886
Missouri	1,537,523	24.80	38,129,028	1,460,647	25.51	37,256,725
Kansas	2,035,774	26.38	53,705,755	2,076,489	27.10	56,290,123
Nebraska	1,213,764	26.82	32,548,295	1,395,829	27.92	38,974,337
South Dakota	432,079	25.08	10,836,978	449,362	26.69	11,994,588
North Dakota	245,282	23.08	5,660,008	252,640	25.84	6,528,658
Montana	1,082,498	22.00	23,814,965	952,598	25.48	24,272,206
Wyoming	688,092	23.82	16,390,606	694,973	26.10	18,137,398
Colorado	935,820	26.07	24,392,775	973,250	25.73	25,038,538
New Mexico	731,216	16.86	12,329,397	701,967	16.89	11,855,522
Arizona	509,082	15.34	7,807,026	381,812	16.90	6,453,200
Utah	322,464	17.75	5,725,345	302,116	19.33	5,840,137
Nevada	241,201	17.04	4,109,350	224,317	19.80	4,441,143
Idaho	349,142	18.61	6,496,582	384,056	20.26	7,782,125
Washington	294,862	18.44	5,436,952	265,376	20.95	5,560,691
Oregon	667,030	17.93	11,957,188	573,646	19.83	11,377,117
California	810,615	18.91	15,328,334	664,704	18.01	11,970,981
Oklahoma	212,814	22.42	4,771,600	257,505	23.79	6,127,330
Total or general average	29,264,197	20.92	612,296,634	27,994,225	22.79	637,981,135

Number, average price, and value of farm animals for 1897 and 1898—Continued.

SHEEP.

State or Territory.	1897.			1898.		
	Number.	Average price.	Value.	Number.	Average price.	Value.
Maine	232,668	$2.84	$660,196	246,628	$3.07	$758,381
New Hampshire	76,754	2.96	227,959	78,289	3.11	243,068
Vermont	161,107	3.38	543,897	165,940	3.48	576,808
Massachusetts	41,262	3.56	146,997	40,437	4.25	171,857
Rhode Island	10,769	3.23	34,731	10,715	3.49	37,368
Connecticut	30,820	3.52	108,363	31,745	3.77	119,552
New York	825,446	4.04	3,332,739	841,955	4.23	3,557,260
New Jersey	41,067	3.78	155,193	42,299	4.03	170,338
Pennsylvania	782,776	3.41	2,669,266	790,604	3.75	2,963,184
Delaware	12,852	3.59	46,112	12,981	3.69	47,874
Maryland	132,170	3.28	433,452	136,135	3.38	460,008
Virginia	380,956	2.57	980,581	369,527	2.87	1,059,803
North Carolina	290,445	1.47	425,502	261,400	1.52	396,021
South Carolina	70,787	1.58	112,197	66,540	1.50	99,810
Georgia	341,233	1.67	568,494	327,584	1.59	520,203
Florida	89,890	1.77	158,925	83,598	1.58	132,085
Alabama	219,356	1.28	279,896	193,033	1.39	269,281
Mississippi	266,356	1.40	372,898	239,720	1.49	355,985
Louisiana	126,769	1.41	178,808	119,163	1.44	172,190
Texas	2,649,914	1.67	4,409,457	2,543,917	1.75	4,448,009
Arkansas	136,060	1.40	190,688	119,733	1.50	189,777
Tennessee	328,808	1.75	575,907	286,063	2.02	577,418
West Virginia	448,994	2.88	1,292,204	440,014	3.04	1,339,402
Kentucky	649,612	2.46	1,599,995	597,643	2.78	1,660,850
Ohio	2,416,346	3.42	8,274,777	2,730,471	3.55	9,680,885
Michigan	1,355,391	3.46	4,695,075	1,396,053	3.58	4,997,869
Indiana	667,853	3.54	2,361,863	674,532	3.95	2,666,702
Illinois	601,168	3.44	2,065,914	613,191	3.72	2,281,377
Wisconsin	715,809	3.20	2,287,725	722,967	3.43	2,479,778
Minnesota	406,929	2.86	1,164,631	410,998	2.96	1,217,377
Iowa	573,218	3.56	2,044,095	613,343	3.70	2,269,369
Missouri	655,428	2.63	1,727,708	616,102	3.00	1,850,154
Kansas	226,659	2.78	631,586	231,192	2.87	663,522
Nebraska	266,163	2.85	759,362	292,779	3.17	928,256
South Dakota	349,709	2.65	926,029	363,697	3.11	1,139,643
North Dakota	352,668	2.48	876,028	359,721	2.82	1,014,413
Montana	3,247,641	2.40	7,804,081	3,377,547	2.72	9,186,928
Wyoming	1,940,021	2.95	5,714,332	2,328,025	3.08	7,172,645
Colorado	1,623,069	2.38	3,869,445	1,655,551	2.71	4,486,543
New Mexico	2,844,265	1.89	5,364,284	3,128,602	1.99	6,213,583
Arizona	845,239	2.10	1,773,734	1,014,257	2.27	2,299,896
Utah	1,978,457	2.10	4,144,868	2,116,949	2.43	5,139,952
Nevada	549,518	2.20	1,206,467	576,994	2.21	1,275,157
Idaho	1,651,343	2.19	3,612,313	2,311,880	2.65	6,132,262
Washington	744,925	2.18	1,622,446	759,824	2.74	2,084,957
Oregon	2,682,779	1.66	4,451,150	2,575,468	2.49	6,403,901
California	2,589,935	2.23	5,785,915	2,175,545	2.64	5,742,352
Oklahoma	25,536	2.07	52,846	22,982	2.32	53,307
Total or general average	37,656,960	2.46	92,721,133	39,114,453	2.75	107,697,530

Number, average price, and value of farm animals for 1897 and 1898—Continued.

HOGS.

State or Territory.	1897.			1898.		
	Number.	Average price.	Value.	Number.	Average price.	Value.
Maine	76,067	$7.71	$586,474	75,306	$8.20	617,502
New Hampshire	55,825	8.15	454,972	56,104	8.16	457,949
Vermont	75,453	7.88	594,194	76,208	7.50	571,804
Massachusetts	57,131	8.54	488,010	54,846	9.04	495,058
Rhode Island	14,146	7.86	111,187	13,722	8.42	115,377
Connecticut	54,274	9.83	533,514	54,165	10.09	546,525
New York	638,849	7.24	4,636,544	645,237	6.54	4,216,948
New Jersey	150,328	7.25	1,090,545	151,120	8.01	1,210,849
Pennsylvania	1,033,001	6.78	6,999,613	1,043,331	7.61	7,936,027
Delaware	50,055	7.16	358,394	50,556	5.87	296,762
Maryland	328,567	5.69	1,870,368	331,853	5.86	1,944,660
Virginia	955,781	3.45	3,297,444	917,550	3.73	3,422,462
North Carolina	1,426,774	3.03	4,318,844	1,369,703	3.29	4,503,563
South Carolina	1,031,150	3.94	4,062,731	1,041,462	3.44	3,578,483
Georgia	2,073,254	3.66	7,592,255	2,093,087	3.87	8,005,358
Florida	456,519	2.13	972,386	429,128	2.84	877,138
Alabama	1,848,158	2.51	4,648,117	1,866,640	2.84	5,291,925
Mississippi	1,919,019	2.83	5,432,741	1,957,399	2.90	5,672,543
Louisiana	751,413	2.91	2,186,611	796,498	2.94	2,341,704
Texas	2,826,302	3.14	8,874,588	2,684,987	3.47	9,316,906
Arkansas	1,293,051	2.17	2,805,920	1,280,120	2.33	2,982,660
Tennessee	1,688,328	3.23	5,449,956	1,570,154	3.29	5,168,947
West Virginia	352,727	3.93	1,386,217	331,563	3.92	1,298,732
Kentucky	1,475,831	3.36	4,963,219	1,357,765	3.35	4,548,513
Ohio	2,330,365	5.47	12,737,720	2,307,051	5.02	11,572,167
Michigan	727,757	5.70	4,148,943	735,035	5.20	3,824,387
Indiana	1,326,961	5.17	6,857,735	1,340,231	4.92	6,591,257
Illinois	2,159,425	5.57	12,019,300	2,008,295	5.52	11,077,589
Wisconsin	920,557	6.18	5,689,042	929,763	6.24	5,801,721
Minnesota	451,003	5.39	2,331,722	411,353	5.63	2,317,974
Iowa	3,625,851	5.99	21,704,225	3,408,231	5.75	19,590,800
Missouri	3,105,072	3.98	12,358,188	2,949,818	3.90	11,696,028
Kansas	1,682,916	5.10	8,641,489	1,591,341	5.04	8,021,960
Nebraska	1,327,128	5.38	7,146,582	1,353,671	5.32	7,201,529
South Dakota	142,617	5.55	791,524	145,469	5.67	824,068
North Dakota	119,105	5.32	633,045	111,959	6.08	680,712
Montana	46,961	7.26	340,935	42,265	7.22	305,156
Wyoming	22,345	5.84	130,572	22,345	5.98	133,555
Colorado	22,035	5.10	112,379	20,713	4.99	103,305
New Mexico	29,905	6.07	181,524	30,204	4.42	133,503
Arizona	24,772	8.40	208,181	23,286	3.84	89,418
Utah	47,335	6.31	298,471	47,808	6.96	332,596
Nevada	11,349	3.94	44,716	10,441	4.54	47,401
Idaho	71,432	4.61	329,563	75,718	5.83	441,438
Washington	168,546	4.96	835,969	156,748	5.65	886,262
Oregon	220,847	3.63	801,896	216,400	4.02	869,881
California	467,676	4.08	1,906,247	374,141	4.47	1,673,907
Oklahoma	84,010	4.72	396,529	89,891	4.27	383,835
Total or general average	39,759,993	4.39	174,351,409	38,651,631	4.40	170,109,743

STATE LIVE STOCK SANITARY BOARDS, SECRETARIES OF STATE BOARDS OF HEALTH, AND STATE VETERINARIANS HAVING CONTROL OF CONTAGIOUS AND INFECTIOUS DISEASES AMONG DOMESTIC ANIMALS.

ALABAMA—Dr. Jerome Cochran, Secretary State Board of Health, Montgomery.

ARIZONA—Mr. H. Harrison, Secretary Live Stock Sanitary Commission, Phœnix. Dr. J. C. Norton, Territorial Veterinarian, Phœnix.

ARKANSAS—Dr. R. R. Dinwiddie, Veterinarian Experiment Station, Fayetteville.

CALIFORNIA—Mr. Wm. Vanderbilt, Secretary State Dairy Bureau, 114 California street, San Francisco. Dr. J. R. Lane, Secretary State Board of Health, Sacramento.

COLORADO—Mr. B. H. DuBois, President Veterinary Sanitary Board, Denver. Dr. Sol. Bock, Secretary and State Veterinary Surgeon. Seven State Inspectors.

CONNECTICUT—Mr. Wm. B. Sprague, Commissioner on Domestic Animals, Andover.

DELAWARE—Dr. E. B. Frazier, Secretary State Board of Health, Wilmington. Dr. Arthur T. Neale, Consulting Veterinarian to State Board of Health, Newark.

FLORIDA—Dr. Jos. Y. Porter, Secretary State Board of Health, Key West.

GEORGIA—Mr. O. B. Stevens, Commissioner of Agriculture, Atlanta.

IDAHO—Mr. Robert P. Chattin, State Sheep Inspector, Mountainhome.

ILLINOIS—Mr. C. P. Johnson, Secretary State Board of Live Stock Commissioners, Springfield. Dr. C. P. Lovejoy, State Veterinarian, Princeton. Fifty-eight Assistant State Veterinarians.

INDIANA—Mr. M. S. Claypool, President State Live Stock Sanitary Commission, Muncie. Mr. Mortimer Levering, Secretary State Live Stock Sanitary Commission, Lafayette. Dr. F. A. Bolser, State Veterinarian, New Castle.

IOWA—Dr. J. F. Kennedy, Secretary State Board of Health, Des Moines. Dr. J. I. Gibson, State Veterinarian, Denison. Twenty-three Assistant State Veterinarians in the State of Iowa.

KANSAS—Mr. Taylor Riddle, Secretary Live Stock Sanitary Commission, Marion. Dr. Paul Fischer, Consulting Veterinarian to Live Stock Sanitary Commission, Manhattan.

KENTUCKY—Dr. J. N. McCormack, Secretary State Board of Health, Bowling Green. Dr. F. T. Eisenman, State Veterinarian, Louisville.

LOUISIANA—Dr. W. H. Dalrymple, State Veterinarian, Baton Rouge. Mr. Fernando Estopinal, Live Stock Inspector, Arabi.

MAINE—Dr. Geo. H. Bailey, State Veterinarian, Deering. Mr. John M. Deering, Cattle Commissioner, Saco. Mr. F. O. Beal, Cattle Commissioner, Bangor.

MARYLAND—Dr. A. W. Clement, State Veterinarian, 916 Cathedral street, Baltimore. Fourteen Assistant State Veterinarians. Mr. C. W. Melville, Secretary Live Stock Sanitary Board, Westminster.

MASSACHUSETTS—Dr. John M. Parker, Secretary of Board of Cattle Commission, Boston. Mr. Austin Peters, President State Board of Cattle Commissioners, Commonwealth Building, Boston.

MICHIGAN—Dr. Geo. W. Dunphy, State Veterinarian, Quincy. Hon. Henry H. Hinds, President State Live Stock Sanitary Commission, Stanton.

MINNESOTA—Dr. H. M. Bracken, Secretary State Board of Health, Pioneer Press Building, St. Paul. Dr. H. M. Reynolds, Director Veterinary Department, State Board of Health, St. Anthony Park. Six State Field Veterinarians.

MISSISSIPPI—Dr. John F. Hunter, Secretary State Board of Health, Jackson. Dr. J. C. Robert, Consulting Veterinarian to State Board of Health, Agricultural College.

MISSOURI—Dr. Willis P. King, Secretary State Board of Health, No. 1 Fountain place, Kansas City. Dr. T. E. White, State Veterinarian, Sedalia.

MONTANA—Dr. M. E. Knowles, State Veterinarian, Helena. Mr. S. C. Powers, President State Sheep Commissioners, Helena. Mr. Cornelius Hedges, Secretary State Sheep Commissioners, Helena. Five Sheep Inspectors.

NEBRASKA—Mr. H. R. Corbet, Secretary State Board of Health, Lincoln.

NEVADA—Dr. J. A. Lewis, Secretary State Board of Health, Reno.

NEW HAMPSHIRE—Mr. N. J. Bachelder, State Cattle Commissioner, Concord.

NEW JERSEY—Dr. Henry Mitchell, Secretary State Board of Health, Trenton. Mr. Franklin Dye, Secretary Tuberculosis Commission, Trenton.

NEW MEXICO—Mr. Salomon Luna, President Sheep Sanitary Board, Los Lunas. Mr. Harry F. Lee, Secretary Sheep Sanitary Board, Albuquerque. Forty Sheep Inspectors. Mr. J. A. La Rue, Secretary Cattle Sanitary Board, East Las Vegas. Twenty-four Cattle Inspectors.

NEW YORK—Dr. Baxter T. Smelzer, Secretary State Board of Health, Albany. Dr. F. W. Smith, Secretary Tuberculosis Committee of State Board of Health, 700 South West street, Syracuse.

NORTH CAROLINA—Mr. John R. Smith, Commissioner of Agriculture, Raleigh. Dr. Cooper Curtice, Consulting Veterinarian, Raleigh.

NORTH DAKOTA—Dr. W. C. Langdon, Chief State Veterinarian, Fargo. Nine District State Veterinarians in North Dakota.

OHIO—Dr. D. N. Kinsman, Secretary State Live Stock Commission, Columbus. Dr. H. J. Detmers, Veterinarian State College, Columbus.

OKLAHOMA—Mr. R. J. Edwards, Secretary Live Stock Sanitary Commission, Oklahoma City.

OREGON—Dr. Wm. McLean, State Veterinarian, Portland.

PENNSYLVANIA—Dr. Leonard Pearson, State Veterinarian and Secretary State Live Stock Sanitary Board, Harrisburg. One hundred and fifty Consulting Veterinarians.

RHODE ISLAND—Dr. A. L. Parker, State Veterinarian, Providence.

SOUTH CAROLINA—Dr. G. E. Nesom, State Veterinarian, Clemson College.

SOUTH DAKOTA—Dr. J. W. Elliot, State Veterinarian, Aberdeen.

TENNESSEE—Hon. Samuel N. Warren, Live Stock Commissioner, Nashville. Dr. Julius W. Scheibler, State Veterinarian, Memphis. Four State Live Stock Inspectors.

TEXAS—Hon. R. J. Kleberg, Secretary Live Stock and Sanitary Commission, Corpus Christi.

UTAH—Dr. T. B. Beatty, Secretary State Board of Health, Salt Lake City.

VERMONT—Mr. C. J. Bell, Secretary Board of Agriculture and Cattle Commission, East Hardwick.

VIRGINIA—Dr. Chas. McCulloch, State Veterinarian, Blacksburg.

WASHINGTON—Dr. Elmer E. Heg, Secretary State Board of Health, North Yakima. Dr. S. B. Nelson, State Veterinarian and Veterinarian of the Agricultural Experiment Station, Pullman. Four Assistant State Veterinarians.

WEST VIRGINIA—Dr. A. R. Barbee, Secretary State Board of Health, Point Pleasant. Mr. D. M. Sullivan, Secretary State Board of Agriculture, Charleston.

WISCONSIN—Dr. H. P. Clute, State Veterinarian, Marinette.

WYOMING—Dr. Geo. T. Seabury, State Veterinarian, Cheyenne. Three Assistant State Veterinarians. Mr. E. P. Snow, Secretary Board of Sheep Commissioners, Cheyenne.

RULES AND REGULATIONS OF THE BUREAU OF ANIMAL INDUSTRY, ISSUED IN 1897 AND 1898.

[B. A. I. Order No. 6.]

SPECIAL ORDER PLACING CERTAIN COUNTIES IN TEXAS IN QUARANTINE.

U. S. Department of Agriculture,
Office of the Secretary,
Washington, D. C., July 6, 1897.

In consequence of the discovery of splenetic fever infection in the counties of Randall, Swisher, Hale, Lubbock, Lynn, Borden, Howard, Mitchell, Scurry, Fisher, Jones, Knox, Foard, Wilbarger, and Hardeman, in the State of Texas, and the establishment of a quarantine on said counties by the duly constituted authorities of said State:

It is hereby ordered, That the counties above named shall be added to the area quarantined by the special order modifying quarantine line for the State of Texas, dated January 28, 1897.

It is further ordered, That no cattle shall be removed from any of said counties to, or be allowed to pass through, any uninfected area, except in the manner specified in the regulations concerning cattle transportation issued by this Department January 27, 1897, unless satisfactory evidence is given that they are not affected with splenetic fever and have not been exposed to the contagion thereof, in which case a special permit for such movement may be issued by an inspector of the Bureau of Animal Industry, or by the Texas Live Stock Sanitary Commission.

This order will remain in force until November 15, 1897, unless otherwise ordered.

James Wilson, *Secretary.*

[B. A. I. Order No. 6—Amended.]

SPECIAL ORDER PLACING CERTAIN COUNTIES IN TEXAS IN QUARANTINE.

U. S. Department of Agriculture,
Office of the Secretary,
Washington, D. C., July 13, 1897.

In consequence of the discovery of splenetic fever infection in the counties hereinafter named, in the State of Texas, and the establishment of a quarantine on said counties by the duly constituted authorities of said State:

It is hereby ordered, That the counties of Hardeman, Wilbarger, Foard, Knox, Haskell, Jones, Fisher, Scurry, Mitchell, Sterling, Glasscock, Howard, Borden, Garza, Lynn, Lubbock, Hale, Swisher, and Randall shall be added to the area quarantined by the special order modifying quarantine line for the State of Texas, dated January 28, 1897.

It is further ordered, That no cattle shall be removed from the counties, as above specified, to, or be allowed to pass through, any uninfected area, except in the manner prescribed by the Regulations Concerning Cattle Transportation, issued by this Department January 27, 1897, unless satisfactory evidence is given that they are not affected with splenetic fever and have not been exposed to the contagion thereof, in which case a special permit for such movement may be issued by an inspector of the Bureau of Animal Industry or by the Texas Live Stock Sanitary Commission.

This order will remain in force until November 15, 1897, unless otherwise ordered.

JAMES WILSON, *Secretary.*

[B. A. I. ORDER No. 2—AMENDED.[1]]

SPECIAL ORDER MODIFYING QUARANTINE LINE FOR THE STATE OF CALIFORNIA.

U. S. DEPARTMENT OF AGRICULTURE,
OFFICE OF THE SECRETARY,
Washington, D. C., July 17, 1897.

In accordance with the regulations concerning cattle transportation issued by this Department January 27, 1897, the State of California has located a quarantine line described as follows:

Beginning on the Pacific Coast where the southern boundary line of Marin County connects with the Pacific Ocean; thence easterly and northerly along the southern and eastern boundary lines of Marin, Sonoma, Napa, and Lake counties to the southwest corner of Colusa County; thence easterly along the southern boundary of said Colusa County to the southeast corner of said county; thence southerly and easterly along the southern boundaries of Sutter and Placer counties to the intersection with the State boundary line in Lake Tahoe.

And whereas said quarantine line, as above set forth, is satisfactory to this Department, and legislation has been enacted by the State of California to enforce said quarantine line; therefore, in accordance with the regulations of January 27, 1897, the above quarantine line is adopted for the State of California by this Department for the period beginning on this date and ending November 15, 1897, in lieu of the quarantine line described in said order of January 27, 1897, and in the special order of March 19, 1897 (B. A. I. Order No. 2), for said area, unless otherwise ordered.

JAMES WILSON, *Secretary.*

[B. A. I. ORDER No. 7.]

SPECIAL ORDER PLACING CERTAIN COUNTIES IN TENNESSEE IN QUARANTINE.

U. S. DEPARTMENT OF AGRICULTURE,
OFFICE OF THE SECRETARY,
Washington, D. C., August 16. 1897.

In consequence of the existence of Southern, or splenetic, fever among cattle in the counties of Lawrence. Giles, Lincoln, Franklin, Marion, Hamilton. Rhea, James. Bradley, Polk, and Warren in the State of Tennessee:

---

[1] See An. Rpt., 1897, p. 417.

It is hereby ordered, That the counties above named be added to the area quarantined by the special order modifying quarantine line for the State of Tennessee, dated February 10, 1897, and the movement of cattle from said counties to or through any uninfected area shall not be permitted, except in the manner prescribed by the Regulations Concerning Cattle Transportation, issued by this Department January 27, 1897.

This order will remain in force until November 15, 1897, unless otherwise ordered.

J. H. BRIGHAM, Acting Secretary.

[B. A. I. ORDER No. 8.]

REGULATIONS CONCERNING CATTLE TRANSPORTATION.

U. S. DEPARTMENT OF AGRICULTURE,
OFFICE OF THE SECRETARY,
Washington, D. C., December 15, 1897.

To managers and agents of railroads and transportation companies of the United States, stockmen, and others:

In accordance with section 7 of the act of Congress approved May 29, 1884, entitled "An act for the establishment of a Bureau of Animal Industry, to prevent the exportation of diseased cattle, and to provide means for the suppression and extirpation of pleuropneumonia and other contagious diseases among domestic animals," and of the act of Congress approved April 23, 1897, making appropriation for the Department of Agriculture for the fiscal year ending June 30, 1898, you are hereby notified that a contagious and infectious disease known as splenetic, or Southern, fever exists among cattle in the following-described area:

All that country lying south, or below, a line beginning at the northwest corner of the State of California; thence east, south, and southeasterly along the boundary line of said State of California to the southeastern corner of said State; thence southerly along the western boundary line of Arizona to the southwest corner of Arizona; thence along the southern boundary lines of Arizona and New Mexico to the southeastern corner of New Mexico; thence northerly along the eastern boundary of New Mexico to the southern line of the State of Colorado; thence along the southern boundary lines of Colorado and Kansas to the southeastern corner of Kansas; thence southerly along the western boundary line of Missouri to the southwestern corner of Missouri; thence easterly along the southern boundary line of Missouri to the western boundary line of Dunklin County; thence southerly along the said western boundary to the southwestern corner of Dunklin County; thence easterly along the southern boundary line of Missouri to the Mississippi River; thence northerly along the Mississippi River to the northern boundary line of Tennessee at the northwest corner of Lake County; thence easterly along said boundary line to the northeast corner of Henry County; thence in a northerly direction along the boundary of Tennessee to the northwest corner of Stewart County; thence in an easterly direction along the northern boundary of Tennessee to the southwestern corner of Virginia; thence northeasterly along the western boundary line of Virginia to the northernmost point of Virginia; thence southerly along the eastern boundary line of Virginia to the northeast corner of Virginia where it joins the southeastern corner of Maryland, at the Atlantic Ocean.

Whenever any State or Territory located above or below said quarantine line, as above designated, shall duly establish a different quarantine line, and obtain the necessary legislation to enforce said last-mentioned line strictly and completely within the boundaries of said State or Territory, and said last above-mentioned line and the measures taken to enforce it are satisfactory to the Secretary of Agriculture, he may, by a special order, temporarily adopt said State or Territorial line.

Said adoption will apply only to that portion of said line specified, and may cease at any time the Secretary may deem it best for the interest involved, and in no instance shall said modification exist longer than the period specified in said special order, and at the expiration of such time said quarantine line shall revert without further order to the line first above described.

Whenever any State or Territory shall establish a quarantine line for above purposes, differently located from the above-described line, and shall obtain by legislation the necessary laws to enforce same completely and strictly, and shall desire a modification of the Federal quarantine line to agree with such State or Territorial line, the proper authorities of such State or Territory shall forward to the Secretary of Agriculture a true map or description of such line and a copy of the laws for enforcement of same, duly authenticated and certified.

Such States or Territories as now have a line established, as last above mentioned, can immediately forward certified copies of said line and laws for the enforcement thereof, and, if satisfactory to the Secretary of Agriculture, the same may be adopted at once and the Federal line so modified.

From the 15th day of January to the 15th day of November, inclusive, during each year, no cattle are to be transported from said area south or below said Federal quarantine line above described to any portion of the United States above, north, east, or west of the above-described line, except by rail or boat, for immediate slaughter, and when so transported the following regulations must be observed:

1. When any cattle in course of transportation from said area are unloaded above, north, east, or west of this line to be fed or watered, the places where said cattle are to be fed or watered shall be set apart, and no other cattle shall be admitted thereto.

2. On unloading said cattle at their points of destination, pens, sufficiently isolated, shall be set apart to receive them, and no other cattle shall be admitted to said pens; and the regulations relating to the movement of cattle from said area, prescribed by the cattle sanitary officers of the State where unloaded, shall be carefully observed. The cars or boats that have carried said stock shall be cleansed and disinfected as soon as possible after unloading and before they are again used to transport, store, or shelter animals or merchandise.

3. All cars carrying cattle from said area shall bear placards, to be affixed by the railroad company hauling the same, stating that said cars contain Southern cattle, and each of the waybills or bills of lading of said shipments by cars or boats shall have a note upon its face with a similar statement. Whenever any cattle have come from said area and shall be reshipped from any point at which they have been unloaded to other points of destination, the cars carrying said animals shall bear similar placards with like statements, and the waybills or bills of lading be so stamped. At whatever point these cattle are unloaded they must be placed in separate pens, to which no other cattle shall be admitted.

4. (a) No boat having on board cattle from said district shall receive on board cattle from outside of said district.

(b) Cattle from said district shall not be received on board when destined to points outside of said district where proper facilities have not been provided for transferring the said cattle from the landing to the stock yards and slaughterhouses without passing over public highways, unless permission for such passing is first obtained from the local authorities.

5. The cars and boats used to transport such animals, the chutes, alleyways,

and pens used during transportation, and at points of destination, shall be disinfected in the following manner:

(a) Remove all litter and manure. This litter and manure may be disinfected by mixing it with lime or saturating it with a 5 per cent solution of 100 per cent carbolic acid; or, if not disinfected, it may be stored where no cattle can come into contact with it until after November 15.

(b) Wash the cars and the feeding and watering troughs with water until clean.

(c) Saturate the entire interior surface of the cars and the fencing, troughs, and chutes of the pens with a mixture made of 1½ pounds of lime and one-quarter pound 100 per cent straw-colored carbolic acid to each gallon of water; or disinfect the cars with a jet of steam under a pressure of not less than 50 pounds to the square inch.

Cattle from the Republic of Mexico may be admitted into the United States to remain below said Federal quarantine line after inspection, according to law; but said cattle shall not be permitted to cross said quarantine line otherwise than by rail for immediate slaughter, except by special permit from the inspectors of the Bureau of Animal Industry, issued according to the regulations of the said Bureau, and no permit shall be issued except for cattle free from splenetic, or Texas, fever, or from contact therewith during the three months preceding the issuance of said permit, and which have been grazed in a locality free from infection of such fever.

Notice is hereby given that cattle infested with the *Boophilus bovis*, or Southern cattle tick, disseminate the contagion of splenetic, or Southern, fever (Texas, fever); therefore cattle originating outside of the district described by this order, or amendments thereof, and which are infested with the *Boophilus bovis* ticks, shall be considered as infectious cattle and shall be subject to the rules and regulations governing the movement of Southern cattle.

Stock-yard companies receiving cattle infested with said ticks shall place such cattle in the pens set aside for the use of Southern cattle, and transportation companies are required to clean and disinfect all cars and boats which have contained the same, according to the requirements of this Department.

Inspectors are instructed to see that disinfection is properly done, and to report instances of improper disinfection. It is expected that transportation and stock-yard companies will promptly put into operation the above methods.

All prior orders conflicting herewith are hereby revoked.

JAMES WILSON, *Secretary.*

[B. A. I. ORDER NO. 9.]

SPECIAL ORDER MODIFYING QUARANTINE LINE FOR THE STATE OF CALIFORNIA.

U. S. DEPARTMENT OF AGRICULTURE,
OFFICE OF THE SECRETARY,
Washington, D. C., December 16, 1897.

In accordance with the regulations concerning cattle transportation (B. A. I. Order No. 8), issued by this Department December 15, 1897, the State of California has located a quarantine line described as follows:

Beginning on the Pacific Coast, where the southern boundary line of Marin County connects with the Pacific Ocean; thence easterly and northerly, along the southern and eastern boundary lines of Marin, Sonoma, and Solano counties, to the Sacramento River; thence northerly, following the said river, along the

10317——39

southern and eastern boundary lines of Solano County to the southeast corner of Yolo County; thence northerly along the eastern boundary line of Yolo County to its intersection with the boundary line of Sutter County; thence easterly, along the southern boundary lines of Sutter and Placer counties, to the intersection with the western boundary line of Eldorado County; thence southerly and easterly along the southern boundary line of Eldorado County to the intersection with the western boundary line of Alpine County; thence in a southerly direction along the western boundary lines of Alpine, Mono, and Inyo counties, to the southwestern boundary of Inyo County; thence east, along the southern boundary line of Inyo County to its intersection with the eastern boundary line of the State of California.

And whereas said quarantine line, as above set forth, is satisfactory to this Department, and legislation has been enacted by the State of California to enforce said quarantine line, therefore, in accordance with the regulations of December 15, 1897 (B.A.I. Order No. 8), the above quarantine line is adopted for the State of California by this Department for the period beginning on January 15, 1898, and ending November 15, 1898, in lieu of the quarantine line described in said order of December 15, 1897, for said area, unless otherwise ordered.

JAMES WILSON, *Secretary.*

[B. A. I. ORDER No. 10.]

SPECIAL ORDER MODIFYING QUARANTINE LINE FOR THE STATE OF TEXAS.

U. S. DEPARTMENT OF AGRICULTURE,
OFFICE OF THE SECRETARY,
Washington, D. C., December 16, 1897.

In accordance with the regulations concerning cattle transportation issued by this Department December 15, 1897 (B. A. I. Order No. 8), the State of Texas has located a quarantine line as follows:

Beginning at the intersection of the southern boundary of New Mexico with the international boundary line at the Rio Grande River; thence southeasterly along the said international boundary line to the southwest corner of the county of Pecos; thence following the western boundary of Pecos County to the southeast corner of Reeves County; thence following the boundary line between the counties of Pecos and Reeves to the Pecos River; thence southeasterly, following the Pecos River, to the northwest corner of Crockett County; thence east along the northern boundary of Crockett and Schleicher counties to the southeastern corner of Irion County; thence north along the eastern boundary of Irion County to the northeast corner of said county; thence north to the southern boundary of Coke County; thence west to the southwest corner of Coke County; thence north along the western boundary of Coke County to the southern boundary of Mitchell County; thence east to the southeastern corner of Mitchell County; thence north along the eastern boundary of Mitchell County to the northeast corner of said county; thence east along the southern boundaries of Fisher and Jones counties to the southeast corner of Jones County; thence north along the eastern boundary of Jones County to the northeast corner of said county; thence east along the southern boundary of Haskell County to the southeast corner of said county; thence north along the western boundary lines of Throckmorton and Baylor counties to the northwest corner of Baylor County; thence east along the southern boundary of Wilbarger County to the southeast corner of said county; thence north along the eastern boundary of Wilbarger County to the Red River; thence continuing in a northwesterly direction along the course of said river and the northern boundary of Texas to the southeast corner of Greer County.

And whereas said quarantine line, as above set forth, is satisfactory to this Department, and legislation has been enacted by the State of Texas to enforce said quarantine line, therefore, in accordance with the regulations of December 15, 1897 (B. A. I. Order No. 8), the above quarantine line is adopted for the State of Texas by this Department for the period beginning on January 15, 1898, and ending November 15, 1898, in lieu of the quarantine line described in said order of December 15, 1897, for said area, unless otherwise ordered.

JAMES WILSON, *Secretary.*

[B. A. I. ORDER NO. 11.]

SPECIAL ORDER MODIFYING QUARANTINE LINE FOR THE TERRITORY OF OKLAHOMA.

U. S. DEPARTMENT OF AGRICULTURE,
OFFICE OF THE SECRETARY,
Washington, D. C., December 16, 1897.

In accordance with the regulations concerning cattle transportation issued by this Department December 15, 1897 (B. A. I. Order No. 8), the Territory of Oklahoma has located a quarantine line, described as follows:

Beginning on the Red River at the southeast corner of the county of Greer; thence northerly following the course of the North Fork of the Red River to its intersection with the southern boundary line of Roger Mills County along the western boundary lines of the Apache, Comanche, and Kiowa Indian reservations; thence east along the southern boundary lines of Roger Mills and Washita counties to the intersection with the boundary line of the Wichita Indian Reservation on the Washita River; thence north along the western boundary line of said reservation to its northwest corner at its intersection with the Canadian River in the county of G; thence in a southeasterly direction along the course of said river and the northern boundary of the Wichita Indian Reservation to the northeast corner of said reservation: thence easterly along the southern boundary of Canadian County to the southeast corner of said county; thence north along the eastern boundary lines of Canadian and Kingfisher counties to the northeastern corner of Kingfisher County; thence east along the southern boundary of O (Garfield) County to the southeast corner of said county; thence north along the eastern boundary of O (Garfield) County to the northeast corner of said county; thence east along the southern boundary line of K County to the west line of the Ponca Indian Reservation; thence north along the west line of said reservation to the northwest corner of said reservation; thence east along the northern boundary of the Ponca Indian Reservation to the Arkansas River; thence in a northerly direction following the course of the said river to its intersection with the thirty-seventh parallel of north latitude at the southern boundary line of Kansas.

And whereas said quarantine line, as above set forth, is satisfactory to this Department, and legislation has been enacted by the Territory of Oklahoma to enforce said quarantine line, therefore, in accordance with the regulations of December 15, 1897 (B. A. I. Order No. 8), the above quarantine line is adopted for the Territory of Oklahoma by this Department for the period beginning on January 15, 1898, and ending November 15, 1898, in lieu of the quarantine line described in said order of December 15, 1897, for said area, unless otherwise ordered.

JAMES WILSON, *Secretary.*

[B. A. I. ORDER NO. 12.]

SPECIAL ORDER MODIFYING QUARANTINE LINE FOR THE STATE OF TENNESSEE.

U. S. DEPARTMENT OF AGRICULTURE,
OFFICE OF THE SECRETARY,
Washington, D. C., December 16, 1897.

In accordance with the regulations concerning cattle transportation issued by this Department December 15, 1897 (B. A. I. Order No. 8), the State of Tennessee has located a quarantine line, described as follows:

Beginning on the Mississippi River at the southeast corner of the State of Missouri at the western boundary of Tennessee; thence southerly along the western boundaries of the counties of Dyer and Lauderdale to the southwest corner of Lauderdale County, on the Mississippi River; thence easterly along the northern boundary of Tipton County to the northeast corner of said county; thence northerly and easterly along the western and northern boundaries of Haywood County to the northeast corner of said county; thence easterly along the northern boundary lines of Madison, Henderson, and Decatur counties to the northeast corner of Decatur County; thence south along the eastern boundary of Decatur County to the northwest corner of Wayne County; thence easterly along the northern boundary lines of Wayne, Lawrence, Giles, Lincoln, and Moore counties to the northeast corner of Moore County; thence north along the western boundary lines of Coffee and Cannon counties to the northwest corner of Cannon County; thence easterly to the northeast corner of Cannon County;·thence south to the intersection of the eastern boundary line of Cannon County with the boundary of Warren County; thence easterly and northerly along the northern boundary lines of Warren, White, and Cumberland counties to the northeast corner of Cumberland County; thence southerly along the eastern boundary lines of Cumberland, Rhea, •and James counties to the northwest corner of Bradley County; thence northerly and southeasterly along the northern boundary lines of Bradley and Polk counties to the northeast corner of Polk County; thence south along the eastern boundary line of Polk County to the southeast corner thereof at the southwestern corner of North Carolina.

And whereas said quarantine line as above set forth is satisfactory to this Department, and legislation has been enacted by the State of Tennessee to enforce said quarantine line, therefore, in accordance with the regulations of December 15, 1897 (B. A. I. Order No. 8), the above quarantine line is adopted for the State of Tennessee by this Department for the period beginning on January 15, 1898, and ending November 15, 1898, in lieu of the quarantine line described in said order of December 15, 1897, for said area, unless otherwise ordered.

JAMES WILSON, *Secretary.*

[B. A. I. ORDER NO. 13.]

SPECIAL ORDER MODIFYING QUARANTINE LINE FOR THE STATE OF VIRGINIA.   •

U. S. DEPARTMENT OF AGRICULTURE,
OFFICE OF THE SECRETARY,
Washington, D. C., December 16, 1897.

In accordance with the regulations concerning cattle transportation issued by this Department December 15, 1897 (B. A. I. Order No. 8), the State of Virginia has located a quarantine line, described as follows:

· Beginning at the boundary line of Virginia at its southwestern corner (Lee County) ; thence east along the southern boundary of Virginia to the summit of the Blue Ridge Mountains; thence following the summit of said mountains northeasterly to the Blackwater River; thence easterly along the course of said river, through Franklin County, to its intersection with the Staunton River on the eastern boundary of Franklin County; thence in a southerly and northeasterly direction along the southern and eastern boundaries of Bedford County to the James River; thence following the James River to the southeastern corner of Charles City County; thence northerly and easterly along the western and northern boundaries of James City, Gloucester, and Mathews counties to the Chesapeake Bay; thence south to the northern boundary of Elizabeth City County; thence westerly and northerly along the boundaries of Elizabeth City and Warwick counties to the James River; thence southeasterly along the course of the said river to the northwest corner of Norfolk County; thence south along the western boundary of said county to its intersection with the northern boundary of North Carolina; thence east along the southern boundaries of Norfolk and Princess Anne counties to the Atlantic Ocean.

And whereas said quarantine line as above set forth is satisfactory to this Department, and legislation has been enacted by the State of Virginia to enforce said quarantine line, therefore, in accordance with the regulations of December 15. 1897 (B. A. I. Order No. 8), the above quarantine line is adopted for the State of Virginia by this Department for the period beginning on January 15, 1898, and ending November 15, 1898, in lieu of the quarantine line described in said order of December 15, 1897, for said area, unless otherwise ordered.

JAMES WILSON, Secretary.

[B. A. I. ORDER No. 14.]

SPECIAL ORDER MODIFYING QUARANTINE LINE FOR THE STATE OF NORTH CAROLINA.

U. S. DEPARTMENT OF AGRICULTURE,
OFFICE OF THE SECRETARY,
Washington, D. C., December 16, 1897.

In accordance with the regulations concerning cattle transportation issued by this Department December 15, 1897 (B. A. I. Order No. 8), the State of North Carolina has located a quarantine line, described as follows:

Beginning at the southwest corner of the county of Cherokee; thence east along the southern boundary lines of the counties of Cherokee, Clay, Macon, Jackson, and Transylvania to the southeast corner of the county of Transylvania; thence northwesterly along the eastern boundary line of Transylvania County to the southwest corner of the county of Buncombe: thence easterly along the southern boundary line of Buncombe County to the summit of the Blue Ridge Mountains; thence in a northeasterly direction, following the said mountains to their intersection with the northern boundary line of the State of North Carolina.

So much of the quarantine line for the State of Virginia described in the order of December 16, 1897 (B. A. I. Order No. 13), beginning at the southwestern corner of Virginia (Lee County) and extending east along the southern boundary line of Virginia to the summit of the Blue Ridge Mountains, is hereby suspended during the enforcement of the above line for the State of North Carolina.

And whereas said quarantine line as above set forth is satisfactory to this Department, and legislation has been enacted by the State of North Carolina to enforce said quarantine line, therefore, in accordance with the regulations of December 15, 1897 (B. A. I. Order No. 8), the above quarantine line is adopted for the State of North Carolina by this Department for the period beginning on January 15, 1898, and ending November 15, 1898, in lieu of the quarantine line described in said order of December 15. 1897, for said area, unless otherwise ordered.

JAMES WILSON, Secretary.

[B. A. I. ORDER No. 15.—AMENDMENT TO No. 8.[1]]

REGULATIONS CONCERNING CATTLE TRANSPORTATION—FEEDING STATIONS AT FORT WORTH, TEX., AND SALISBURY, N. C.

U. S. DEPARTMENT OF AGRICULTURE,
OFFICE OF THE SECRETARY,
Washington, D. C., January 3, 1898.

It is hereby ordered, That cattle originating outside, north and west, of the quarantine line as defined in Bureau of Animal Industry Order No. 8 (December 15, 1897), or amendments thereto, and which are to be transported by rail through the quarantined district, may be unloaded for rest, feed, and water, into non-infected pens set apart for such cattle at Union Stock Yards, Fort Worth, Tex., and at Salisbury, N. C., providing the cattle are free from Southern cattle ticks and have not been unloaded at any other place within the quarantined district. They may after unloading into said pens be reloaded into the same cars from which unloaded, or into other cleaned and disinfected cars and reshipped as uninfected cattle.

All prior orders conflicting herewith are hereby revoked.

JAMES WILSON, *Secretary.*

[B. A. I. ORDER No. 16.—SPECIAL ORDER SUSPENDING No. 8, ETC.[1]]

REGULATIONS CONCERNING CATTLE TRANSPORTATION.

U. S. DEPARTMENT OF AGRICULTURE,
OFFICE OF THE SECRETARY,
Washington, D. C., January 22, 1898.

Conforming to the State regulations of Kansas, Illinois, Kentucky, and Virginia, it is hereby ordered that B. A. I. Order No. 8 (December 15, 1897), and amendments thereto, be suspended so as to permit the entry of Southern cattle into Kansas, Illinois, and Kentucky until February 1, 1898, and into and through Virginia until February 15, 1898, without restriction.

All prior orders conflicting herewith are hereby suspended.

JAMES WILSON, *Secretary.*

[B. A. I. ORDER No. 17.—AMENDMENT TO No. 8.[1]].

REGULATIONS CONCERNING CATTLE TRANSPORTATION.

U. S. DEPARTMENT OF AGRICULTURE,
OFFICE OF THE SECRETARY,
Washington, D. C., March 4, 1898.

It is hereby ordered, That section c, of rule 5, of the regulations concerning cattle transportation, issued under date of December 15, 1897 (B. A. I. Order No. 8), be, and is hereby, amended to read as follows:

(c.) Saturate the entire interior surface of the cars and the fencing, troughs, and chutes of the pens with a mixture made of 1½ pounds of lime and one-quarter pound 100 per cent straw-colored carbolic acid to each gallon of water; or a solution made by dissolving 4 ounces of chloride of lime to each gallon of water may be used; or disinfect the cars with a jet of steam under a pressure of not less than 50 pounds to the square inch.

JAMES WILSON, *Secretary.*

[1] See p. 607.

[B. A. I. ORDER NO. 18.—SUPERSEDES AND REVOKES NO. 9.[1]]

SPECIAL ORDER MODIFYING QUARANTINE LINE FOR THE STATE OF CALIFORNIA.

U. S. DEPARTMENT OF AGRICULTURE,
OFFICE OF THE SECRETARY,
Washington, D. C., March 25, 1898.

In accordance with the regulations concerning cattle transportation (B. A. I. Order No. 8[2]), issued by this Department December 15, 1897, and on account of the emergency arising from drought in the quarantined area of California and the necessity for allowing cattle to go to other sections of said State for pasture, the order of December 16, 1897 (B. A. I. Order No. 9), is hereby revoked, and the quarantine line will revert to the State boundaries of California, beginning on this date and ending on November 15, 1898, as detailed in the order of December 15, 1897 (B. A. I. Order No. 8), for said area, unless otherwise ordered.

Inspectors of the Bureau of Animal Industry are authorized to grant special permits, in accordance with the instructions of the Chief of that Bureau, for the movement of cattle from the State of California to other States after the said cattle have been inspected and found free from infection. Transportation companies should assure themselves that all cattle shipped from California for purposes other than immediate slaughter are accompanied by special permits signed by an inspector of said Bureau.

JAMES WILSON, *Secretary.*

[B. A. I. ORDER NO. 19.—AMENDMENT TO SECTION 18 OF THE ORDER DATED FEBRUARY 18, 1895.[3]]

REGULATIONS FOR THE SAFE TRANSPORT OF CATTLE FROM THE UNITED STATES TO FOREIGN COUNTRIES.

U. S. DEPARTMENT OF AGRICULTURE,
OFFICE OF THE SECRETARY,
Washington, D. C., May 11, 1898.

It is hereby ordered, That section 18 of the order and regulations of February 18, 1895, be, and the same is hereby, amended to read as follows :

18. No vessel shall be permitted to take on board any cattle or sheep unless the same have been allowed at least twelve hours' actual rest in the yards at the port of embarkation before the vessel sails, nor until the loading of the other cargo has been completed.

JAMES WILSON, *Secretary.*

[B. A. I. ORDER NO. 20.—ADDITIONAL TO NO. 10.[4]]

SPECIAL ORDER PLACING CERTAIN COUNTIES IN TEXAS IN QUARANTINE.

U. S. DEPARTMENT OF AGRICULTURE,
OFFICE OF THE SECRETARY,
Washington, D. C., August 17, 1898.

In consequence of the discovery of splenetic fever infection in the counties hereinafter named in the State of Texas, and the establishment of a quarantine on the said counties by the duly constituted authorities of said State,

It is hereby ordered, That the counties of West [Webb,] Tom Green, Irion, Sterling, Mitchell, Scurry, Fisher, Jones, Haskell, Stonewall, King, Knox, Foard,

---

[1] See p. 609.   [2] See p. 607.   [3] See An. Rpt. 1897, p. 379.   [4] See p. 610.

Cottle, Childress, Hardeman, and Wilbarger shall be added to the area quarantined by the special order modifying quarantine line for the State of-Texas(B. A. I. Order No. 10), December 16, 1897, and the regulations specified in said special order shall apply with equal force to the counties above named.

It is further ordered, That no cattle shall be removed from the counties of Crane, Upton, Midland, Glasscock, Howard, Borden, Kent, Dickens, Motley, Hall, and Donley to, or be allowed to pass through, any uninfected area, except in the manner prescribed by the regulations concerning cattle transportation (B. A. I. Order No. 8) issued by this Department December 15, 1897, unless satisfactory evidence is given that they are not affected with splenetic, or Texas, fever, and have not been exposed to the contagion thereof, in which case a special permit for such movement may be issued by the inspector of the Bureau of Animal Industry or by the Texas Live Stock Sanitary Commission.

This order will remain in force for the period beginning on this date and ending November 15, 1898, for said area, unless otherwise ordered.

JAMES WILSON, *Secretary.*

[B. A. I. ORDER No. 21.]

SPECIAL ORDER RELEASING CATTLE IN THE COUNTIES OF UNION, TOWNS, AND PART OF RABUN, GA., FROM THE RESTRICTIONS IMPOSED BY THE REGULATIONS AND MODIFICATIONS THEREOF CONCERNING CATTLE TRANSPORTATION DURING THE QUARANTINE SEASON OF 1898.

U. S. DEPARTMENT OF AGRICULTURE,
OFFICE OF THE SECRETARY,
Washington, D. C., September 7, 1898.

It is hereby ordered, That cattle now in the territory hereinafter described and which are free from the *Boophilus bovis* (Southern cattle tick) may be moved without restriction to points north of the quarantine line defined in the regulations of December 15, 1897 (B. A. I. Order No. 8), as modified by special orders dated December 16, 1897 (B. A. I. Orders Nos. 9–14);

Provided, That application be first made to the Secretary of Agriculture and permission received for the removal of such cattle; said application to give the name of the owner, the origin and number of the cattle, the place from which they are to be moved, and the destination, with the route to be followed, which must not be through any area infested with Southern cattle ticks.

This order applies only to the following-described territory in the State of Georgia: The whole of the counties of Union and Towns and that part of Rabun County lying north and west of a line drawn from its western corner, near the mouth of Wild Cat Creek, in an easterly direction, through Charlie Mountain, Glassie Mountain, and Tiger Mountain, and along the ridge following Stekoa Creek, to Dick Creek, thence northerly through Rainy Mountain, Hogback Ridge, Pinnacle, Raven Knob, Rock Mountain, and Rabun Bald, to the State boundary.

This order will remain in force until the termination of November 15, 1898, unless otherwise ordered.

JAMES WILSON, *Secretary.*

[B. A. I. Order No. 22—Additional to No. 10.[1]]

SPECIAL ORDER PLACING CERTAIN COUNTIES IN TEXAS IN QUARANTINE.

U. S. Department of Agriculture,
Office of the Secretary,
Washington, D. C., September 30, 1898.

Conforming to the regulations of the State of Texas, made by the duly constituted authorities of that State, it is hereby ordered that B. A. I. Order No. 20 (August 17, 1898) be revoked and that the following be substituted therefor:

It is hereby ordered, That the counties of West, [Webb,] Tom Green, Irion, Sterling, Mitchell, Scurry, Fisher, Jones, Haskell, Knox, and Wilbarger shall be added to the area quarantined by the special order modifying quarantine line for the State of Texas (B. A. I. Order No. 10), December 16, 1897, and the regulations specified in said special order shall apply with equal force to the counties above named.

It is further ordered, That no cattle be removed from the counties of Stonewall, King, Foard, Cottle, Childress, Hardeman, Howard, Glasscock, Kent, Hall, and Donley to, or be allowed to pass through, any uninfected area except in the manner prescribed by the regulations concerning cattle transportation (B. A. I. Order No. 8), issued by this Department December 15, 1897, unless satisfactory evidence is given that they are not affected with splenetic, or Texas, fever and have not been exposed to the contagion thereof, in which case a special permit for such movement may be issued by the inspector of the Bureau of Animal Industry or by the Texas Live Stock Sanitary Commission.

This order will remain in force for the period beginning on this date and ending November 15, 1898, for said area, unless otherwise ordered.

James Wilson, *Secretary.*

[B. A. I. Order No. 23.]

ORDER MODIFYING REGULATIONS CONCERNING CATTLE TRANSPORTATION, ISSUED BY THIS DEPARTMENT DECEMBER 15, 1897. (B. A. I. ORDER NO. 8.)

U. S. Department of Agriculture,
Office of the Secretary,
Washington, D. C., October 12, 1898.

It is hereby ordered, That cattle originating in the district described in the order of December 15, 1897, and amendments thereto, which district is known as the quarantined district, may, after having been properly dipped, under the supervision of an inspector of this Department, in a solution of 86 pounds flowers of sulphur to each 1,000 gallons of extra dynamo oil, be shipped without further restriction : *Provided*, That application be first made to this Department, and permission granted to establish the dipping stations, and that after being dipped the cattle are certified by an inspector of the United States Bureau of Animal Industry, and that the cattle, when dipped within the quarantined district, be shipped in clean cars, without unloading within that district.

J. H. Brigham, *Acting Secretary.*

---

[1] See p. 610.

[B. A. I. Order No. 24.]

REGULATIONS CONCERNING CATTLE TRANSPORTATION.

U. S. Department of Agriculture,
Office of the Secretary,
Washington, D. C., December 19, 1898.

To managers and agents of railroads and transportation companies of the United States, stockmen, and others:

In accordance with section 7 of the act of Congress approved May 29, 1884, entitled "An act for the establishment of a Bureau of Animal Industry, to prevent the exportation of diseased cattle, and to provide means for the suppression and extirpation of pleuropneumonia and other contagious diseases among domestic animals," and of the act of Congress approved March 22, 1898, making appropriation for the Department of Agriculture for the fiscal year ending June 30, 1899, you are hereby notified that a contagious and infectious disease known as splenetic, or Southern, fever exists among cattle in the following-described area:

1. All that country lying south or below a line beginning at the northwest corner of the State of California; thence east, south, and southeasterly along the boundary line of said State of California to the southeastern corner of said State; thence southerly along the western boundary line of Arizona to the southwest corner of Arizona; thence along the southern boundary lines of Arizona and New Mexico to the southeastern corner of New Mexico; thence northerly along the eastern boundary of New Mexico to the southern line of the State of Colorado; thence along the southern boundary lines of Colorado and Kansas to the southeastern corner of Kansas; thence southerly along the western boundary line of Missouri to the southwestern corner of Missouri; thence easterly along the southern boundary line of Missouri to the western boundary line of Dunklin County; thence southerly along the said western boundary to the southwestern corner of Dunklin County; thence easterly along the southern boundary line of Missouri to the Mississippi River; thence northerly along the Mississippi River to the northern boundary line of Tennessee at the northwest corner of Lake County; thence easterly along said boundary line to the northeast corner of Henry County; thence in a northerly direction along the boundary of Tennessee to the northwest corner of Stewart County; thence in an easterly direction along the northern boundary of Tennessee to the southwestern corner of Virginia; thence northeasterly along the western boundary line of Virginia to the northernmost point of Virginia; thence southerly along the eastern boundary line of Virginia to the northeast corner of Virginia where it joins the southeastern corner of Maryland at the Atlantic Ocean.

2. Whenever any State or Territory located above or below said quarantine line, as above designated, shall duly establish a different quarantine line, and obtain the necessary legislation to enforce said last-mentioned line strictly and completely within the boundaries of said State or Territory, and said last above-mentioned line and the measures taken to enforce it are satisfactory to the Secretary of Agriculture, he may, by a special order, temporarily adopt said State or Territorial line.

Said adoption will apply only to that portion of said line specified, and may cease at any time the Secretary may deem it best for the interest involved, and in no instance shall said modification exist longer than the period specified in said special order; and at the expiration of such time said quarantine line shall revert without further order to the line first above described.

Whenever any State or Territory shall establish a quarantine line for above purposes, differently located from the above-described line, and shall obtain by legislation the necessary laws to enforce the same completely and strictly, and shall desire a modification of the Federal quarantine line to agree with such State or Territorial line, the proper authorities of such State or Territory shall forward to the Secretary of Agriculture a true map or description of such line and a copy of the laws for enforcement of same, duly authenticated and certified.

3. From the 1st day of January, 1899, no cattle are to be transported from said area south or below said Federal quarantine line above described to any portion of the United States above, north, east, or west of the above-described line, except as hereinafter provided.

4. Cattle from said area may be transported, by rail or boat, for immediate slaughter, and when so transported the following regulations must be observed:

(a) When any cattle in course of transportation from said area are unloaded above, north, east, or west of this line to be fed or watered, the places where said cattle are to be fed or watered shall be set apart and no other cattle shall be admitted thereto.

(b) On unloading said cattle at their points of destination, pens sufficiently isolated shall be set apart to receive them, and no other cattle shall be admitted to said pens; and the regulations relating to the movement of cattle from said area, prescribed by the cattle sanitary officers of the State where unloaded, shall be carefully observed. The cars or boats that have carried such stock shall be cleansed and disinfected as soon as possible after unloading and before they are again used to transport, store, or shelter animals or merchandise.

(c) All cars carrying cattle from said area shall bear placards, to be affixed by the railroad company hauling the same, stating that said cars contain Southern cattle, and each of the waybills or bills of lading of said shipments by cars or boats shall have a note upon its face with a similar statement. Whenever any cattle have come from said area and shall be reshipped from any point at which they have been unloaded to other points of destination, the cars carrying said animals shall bear similar placards with like statements, and the waybills or bills of lading be so stamped. At whatever point these cattle are unloaded they must be placed in separate pens, to which no other cattle shall be admitted.

(d) No boat having on board cattle from said district shall receive on board cattle from outside of said district. Cattle from said district shall not be received on board when destined to points outside of said district where proper facilities have not been provided for transferring the said cattle from the landing to the stock yards and slaughterhouses without passing over public highways, unless permission for such passing is first obtained from the local authorities.

(e) The cars and boats used to transport such animals, the chutes, alleyways, and pens used during transportation, and at points of destination, shall be disinfected in the following manner :

Remove all litter and manure. This litter and manure may be disinfected by mixing it with lime or saturating it with a 5 per cent solution of 100 per cent carbolic acid ; or, if not disinfected, it may be stored where no cattle can come into contact with it during the period from February 1 to November 15, of each year.

Wash the cars and the feeding and watering troughs with water until clean.

Saturate the entire interior surface of the cars and the fencing, troughs, and chutes of the pens with a mixture made of 1¼ pounds of lime and one-fourth pound 100 per cent straw-colored carbolic acid to each gallon of water ; or a solution made by dissolving 4 ounces of chloride of lime to each gallon of water may be used ; or disinfect the cars with a jet of steam under a pressure of not less than 50 pounds to the square inch.

5. Cattle originating in said area may, after having been properly dipped under the supervision of an inspector of this Department, be shipped without further restriction, excepting such as may be enforced by local authorities at

point of destination: *Provided*, That application be first made to this Department, and permission granted to establish the dipping stations, and that after being dipped the cattle are certified by an inspector of the United States Bureau of Animal Industry, and that the cattle when dipped be shipped in clean cars, and not be driven through the infected district or unloaded therein, except at such point as may be duly designated by an order issued by this Department.

6. From November 1 to December 31, inclusive, cattle from said area which are found free of infection upon inspection by officers of this Department may be moved north of the quarantine line without restriction other than may be enforced by local regulations at destination. If evidence of infection is found upon such inspection the cattle must be dipped in accordance with the provisions of section 5 before being moved north of the quarantine line.

7. Cattle from the Republic of Mexico may be admitted into the United States, after inspection according to law, as follows:

(a) Cattle free from splenetic, or Texas, fever, and from contact therewith during the three months preceding such inspection, and which have been grazed in a locality free from infection of such fever, may be admitted into any part of the United States. If destined to points in the noninfected area a special permit must be obtained from an inspector of the Bureau of Animal Industry, said permit being issued according to the regulations of said Bureau; the cattle for which said permit is issued must not be driven through the infected area nor be unloaded in any part thereof except at such point as may be duly designated by an order issued by this Department; if shipped in infected cars, or unloaded in the infected area, except as above stated, they will be subject to the regulations concerning infectious cattle.

(b) Cattle found upon inspection to be infected or to have been exposed to infection during the preceding three months must be dipped at port of entry under supervision of an inspector of this Department prior to admittance to the United States; after dipping said cattle shall be subject to the conditions specified in the last preceding paragraph.

8. Notice is hereby given that cattle infested with the *Boophilus bovis*, or Southern cattle tick, disseminate the contagion of splenetic, or Southern, fever (Texas fever); therefore cattle originating outside of the district described by this order, or amendments thereof, and which are infested with the *Boophilus bovis* ticks shall be considered as infectious cattle and shall be subject to the rules and regulations governing the movement of Southern cattle.

9. Stock-yard companies receiving cattle infested with said ticks shall place such cattle in the pens set aside for the use of Southern cattle, and transportation companies are required to clean and disinfect all cars and boats which have contained the same, according to the requirements of this Department.

10. Inspectors are instructed to see that disinfection is properly done, and to report instances of improper disinfection. It is expected that transportation and stock-yard companies will promptly put into operation the above methods.

All prior orders conflicting herewith are hereby revoked.

JAMES WILSON, *Secretary.*

[B. A. I. ORDER No. 25.]

SPECIAL ORDER MODIFYING QUARANTINE LINE FOR THE STATE OF TEXAS—1899.

U. S. DEPARTMENT OF AGRICULTURE,
OFFICE OF THE SECRETARY,
Washington, D. C., December 20, 1898.

In accordance with the regulations concerning cattle transportation issued by this Department, the State of Texas has located a quarantine line as follows:

Beginning at the intersection of the southern boundary of New Mexico with the international boundary line at the Rio Grande River; thence southeasterly along the said international boundary line to the southwest corner of the county of Pecos; thence following the western boundary of Pecos County to the southeast corner of Reeves County; thence following the boundary line between the counties of Pecos and Reeves to the Pecos River; thence southeasterly, following the Pecos River, to the northwest corner of Crockett County; thence east along the northern boundary of Crockett and Schleicher counties to the southeastern corner of Irion County; thence north along the eastern boundary of Irion County to the northeast corner of said county; thence north to the southern boundary of Coke County; thence west to the southwest corner of Coke County; thence north along the western boundary of Coke County to the southern boundary of Mitchell County; thence east to the southeastern corner of Mitchell County; thence north along the eastern boundary of Mitchell County to the northeast corner of said county; thence east along the southern boundaries of Fisher and Jones counties to the southeast corner of Jones County; thence north along the eastern boundary of Jones County to the northeast corner of said county; thence east along the southern boundary of Haskell County to the southeast corner of said county; thence north along the western boundary lines of Throckmorton and Baylor counties to the northwest corner of Baylor County; thence east along the southern boundary of Wilbarger County to the southeast corner of said county; thence north along the eastern boundary of Wilbarger County to the Red River; thence continuing in a northwesterly direction along the course of said river and the northern boundary of Texas to the southeast corner of Greer County.

And whereas said quarantine line, as above set forth, is satisfactory to this Department, and legislation has been enacted by the State of Texas to enforce said quarantine line, therefore, the above quarantine line is adopted for the State of Texas by this Department for the period beginning on January 1, 1899, and ending December 81, 1899, in lieu of the quarantine line described in the order of December 19, 1898, for said area, unless otherwise ordered.

JAMES WILSON, *Secretary.*

[B. A. I. ORDER No. 26.]

SPECIAL ORDER MODIFYING QUARANTINE LINE FOR THE TERRITORY OF OKLAHOMA—1899.

U. S. DEPARTMENT OF AGRICULTURE,
OFFICE OF THE SECRETARY,
Washington, D. C., December 20, 1898.

In accordance with the regulations concerning cattle transportation issued by this Department, the Territory of Oklahoma has located a quarantine line, described as follows:

Beginning on the Red River at the southeastern corner of the county of Greer; hence northerly following the course of the North Fork of the Red River to its intersection with the southern boundary line of Roger Mills County along the western boundary lines of the Apache, Comanche, and Kiowa Indian reservations; thence east along the southern boundary lines of Roger Mills and Washita counties to the intersection with the boundary line of the Wichita Indian Reservation on the Washita River; thence north along the western boundary line of said reservation to its northwest corner at its intersection with the Canadian River in the county of G; thence in a southeasterly direction along the course of said river and the northern boundary of the Wichita Indian Reservation to the northeast corner of said reservation; thence easterly along the southern boundary of Canadian County to the southeast corner of said county; thence north along the eastern boundary lines of Canadian and Kingfisher counties to the northeastern corner of Kingfisher County; thence east along the southern boundary of O (Garfield) County to the southeast corner of said county; thence north along the eastern boundary of O (Garfield) County to the northeast corner of said county; thence east along the southern boundary line of K County to the west line of the Ponca Indian Reservation; thence north along the west line of said reservation to the northwest corner of said reservation; thence east along the northern boundary of the Ponca Indian Reservation to the Arkansas River; thence in a northerly direction following the course of the said river to its intersection with the thirty-seventh parallel of north latitude at the southern boundary line of Kansas.

And whereas said quarantine line, as above set forth, is satisfactory to this Department, and legislation has been enacted by the Territory of Oklahoma to enforce said quarantine line; therefore, the above quarantine line is adopted for the Territory of Oklahoma by this Department for the period beginning on January 1, 1899, and ending December 31, 1899, in lieu of the quarantine line described in the order of December 19, 1898, for said area, unless otherwise ordered.

JAMES WILSON, *Secretary.*

[B. A. I. ORDER NO. 27.]

SPECIAL ORDER MODIFYING QUARANTINE LINE FOR THE STATE OF TENNESSEE—1899.

U. S. DEPARTMENT OF AGRICULTURE,
OFFICE OF THE SECRETARY,
Washington, D. C., December 20, 1898.

In accordance with the regulations concerning cattle transportation issued by this Department, the State of Tennessee has located a quarantine line, described as follows:

Beginning on the Mississippi River at the southeast corner of the State of Missouri at the western boundary of Tennessee; thence southerly along the western boundaries of the counties of Dyer and Lauderdale to the southwest corner of Lauderdale County on the Mississippi River; thence easterly along the northern boundary of Tipton County to the northeast corner of said county; thence northerly and easterly along the western and northern boundaries of Haywood County to the northeast corner of said county; thence easterly along the northern boundary lines of Madison, Henderson, and Decatur counties to the northeast corner of Decatur County; thence south along the eastern boundary of Decatur County to the northwest corner of Wayne County; thence easterly along the northern boundary lines of Wayne and Lawrence counties to the northeastern corner of Lawrence County; thence south along the western boundary of Giles County to the southwestern corner of said county; thence east and north along the southern and eastern boundaries of said county to the northwestern corner of Lincoln County; thence easterly along the northern boundaries of Lincoln and Moore counties to the northeast corner of Moore County; thence north along the western boundary lines of Coffee and Cannon counties to the northwest corner of Cannon County; thence easterly to the northeast corner of Cannon County; thence south to the intersection of the eastern boundary line of Cannon County with the boundary of Warren County; thence easterly and northerly along the northern boundary lines of Warren, White, and Cumberland counties to the northeast corner of Cumberland County; thence southerly along the eastern boundary lines of Cumberland, Rhea, and James counties to the northwest corner of Bradley County; thence northerly and southeasterly along the northern boundary lines of Bradley and Polk counties to the northeast corner of Polk County; thence south along the eastern boundary line of Polk County to the southeast corner thereof at the southwestern corner of North Carolina.

So much of the quarantine line for the State of Virginia, described in the order of December 20, 1898 (B.A.I. Order No. 28), beginning at the southwestern corner of Virginia (Lee County) and extending east along the southern boundary line of Virginia to the southwestern corner of Grayson County, is hereby suspended during the enforcement of the above line for the State of Tennessee.

And whereas said quarantine line, as above set forth, is satisfactory to this Department, and legislation has been enacted by the State of Tennessee to enforce said quarantine line, therefore the above quarantine line is adopted for the State of Tennessee by this Department for the period beginning on January 1, 1899, and ending December 31, 1899, in lieu of the quarantine line described in the order of December 19, 1898, for said area, unless otherwise ordered.

JAMES WILSON. Secretary.

[B. A. I. ORDER No. 28.]

SPECIAL ORDER MODIFYING QUARANTINE LINE FOR THE STATE OF VIRGINIA—1899.

U. S. DEPARTMENT OF AGRICULTURE,
OFFICE OF THE SECRETARY,
Washington, D. C., December 20, 1898.

In accordance with the regulations concerning cattle transportation issued by this Department, the State of Virginia has located a quarantine line, described as follows:

Beginning at the boundary line of Virginia at its southwestern corner (Lee County); thence east along the southern boundary of Virginia to the southwestern corner of Patrick County; thence northerly along the western boundaries of Patrick and Franklin counties to the western boundary of Bedford County; thence in a southeasterly and northeasterly direction along the southern and eastern boundaries of Bedford County to the James River; thence following the James River to the southeastern corner of Charles City County; thence northerly and easterly along the western and northern boundaries of James City County to the western boundary of Gloucester County at the York River; thence southerly and northerly along the southern and eastern boundaries of Gloucester County to the northeastern corner of said county; thence easterly and southerly along the northern and eastern boundaries of Mathews County to the southeastern point of said county; thence south to the northern boundary of Elizabeth City County; thence westerly and northerly along the boundaries of Elizabeth City and Warwick counties to the James River; thence southeasterly along the course of the said river to the northwest corner of Norfolk County; thence south along the western boundary of said county to its intersection with the northern boundary of North Carolina; thence east along the southern boundaries of Norfolk and Princess Anne counties to the Atlantic Ocean.

And whereas said quarantine line, as above set forth, is satisfactory to this Department, and legislation has been enacted by the State of Virginia to enforce said quarantine line, therefore the above quarantine line is adopted for the State of Virginia by this Department for the period beginning on January 1, 1899, and ending December 31, 1899, in lieu of the quarantine line described in the order of December 10, 1898, for said area, unless otherwise ordered.

JAMES WILSON, Secretary.

[B. A. I. ORDER No. 29.]

SPECIAL ORDER MODIFYING QUARANTINE LINE FOR THE STATE OF NORTH CAROLINA—1899.

U. S. DEPARTMENT OF AGRICULTURE,
OFFICE OF THE SECRETARY,
Washington, D. C., December 20, 1898.

In accordance with the regulations concerning cattle transportation issued by this Department, the State of North Carolina has located a quarantine line, described as follows:

Beginning at the southwest corner of the county of Cherokee; thence east along the southern boundary lines of the counties of Cherokee, Clay, Macon, Jackson, and Transylvania to the southeast corner of the county of Transylvania; thence northwesterly along the eastern boundary line of Transylvania County to the southwest corner of the county of Buncombe; thence easterly along the southern boundary line of Buncombe County to the summit of the Blue Ridge Mountains; thence in a northeasterly direction, following the said mountains to their intersection with the northern boundary line of the State of North Carolina.

So much of the quarantine line for the State of Virginia, described in the order of December 20, 1898 (B. A. I. Order No. 28), beginning at the southwestern corner of Grayson County and extending east along the southern boundary line of Virginia to the southeastern corner of said county, is hereby suspended during the enforcement of the above line for the State of North Carolina.

And whereas said quarantine line, as above set forth, is satisfactory to this Department, and legislation has been enacted by the State of North Carolina to enforce said quarantine line, therefore the above quarantine line is adopted for the State of North Carolina by this Department for the period beginning on January 1, 1899, and ending December 31, 1899, in lieu of the quarantine line described in the order of December 19, 1898, for said area, unless otherwise ordered.

JAMES WILSON, Secretary.

INDEX.

	Page.
Abattoirs, number in operation in 1897 and 1898	1
Abortion among cows in Scotland, treatment	219
contagious, in cows, inquiry and reply	525
Accounts on dairy farm	222
Aconite, European, poisonous to stock	399
Western, poisonous to stock	399
Aconitum columbianum and *A. napellus*, plants poisonous to stock	399
Actæa alba, plant poisonous to stock	399
spicata, plant poisonous to stock	400
Actinomycosis, method of diagnosing the disease	388
Æsculus californica, A. glabra, A. hippocastanum, A. pavia, plants poisonous to stock	408
Africa, quantity and value of exports of hides and skins to United States in 1897 and 1898	594
imports of hides and skins from United States in 1897 and 1898	594
butter from United States in 1897 and 1898	584
leather from United States in 1897 and 1898	595
Africa, South, animal products	512
population	515
value of imports of boots and shoes from United States in 1897 and 1898	596
Agalactia, infectious, in Italy in 1897 and 1898, statistics	438
Agricultural attaché at Berlin	25
depression in Great Britain, observations	213
practices in Fifeshire, Scotland	216
Agriculture and dairying in Scotland, article by John C. Higgins	213–223
Agrostemma githago, plant poisonous to stock	898
Alabama, number, average price, and value of farm animals in 1897 and 1898	597–602
Alkali grass, poisonous to stock	396
Alvord, H. E., article on breeds of dairy cattle	137–200
experimental exports of butter in 1897	83–136
exports of fresh butter from United States	125–129
American butter in Japan, consular report	521
hams in Germany	519
nightshade, poisonous to stock	398
white hellebore, poisonous to stock	395
Amœba meleagridis, cause of entero-hepatitis	851
Anagallis arvensis, plant poisonous to stock	412
Andromeda polifolia, plant poisonous to stock	410
Anemone quinquefolia, plant poisonous to stock	400
Animal products and animals in Malta	520
in London, prices	458
South Africa	512
Animals and animal products, American, in Great Britain, article by W. H. Wray	440–462
for export, inspection	14
imported, inspection	16
in European countries, report on contagious diseases	428–439
number imported at quarantine stations	17
inspected antemortem in 1891–1898	13
and postmortem	12
to be vaccinated against blackleg	70

Page.
Anise tree, poisonous to stock.. 399
Antenaria luzuloides, experiment in feeding to sheep 424
Anthrax and blackleg in Italy in 1897 and 1898, statistics................. 438
    in Belgium in 1897 and 1898, statistics............................ 433
        Denmark in 1897 and 1898, statistics..................... 435
        France in 1897 and 1898, statistics 433
        Hungary in 1897 and 1898, statistics 435
        Netherlands in 1897 and 1898, statistics................. 434
        Norway in 1897 and 1898, statistics 435
        Switzerland in 1897 and 1898, statistics 439
    method of diagnosing the disease 335
Aphthous fever in France in 1897 and 1898, statistics 423
Apocynum androsœmifolium and *A. cannabium*, plants poisonous to stock. 413
Apple, May, poisonous to stock.. 401
Apoplexy, parturient, or milk fever, of cows, inquiry and reply 526
Aragallus lambertii, plant poisonous to stock 403
Arbutus, trailing, poisonous to stock 410
Argemone mexicana, plant poisonous to stock 402
Argentine Republic, shipment of cattle to England in 1896 441
Arizona, number, average price, and value of farm animals in 1897 and
    1898.. 597–602
Arkansas, number, average price, and value of farm animals in 1897 and
    1898.. 597–602
Arnica fulgens, experiment in feeding to sheep 424
Asclepias eriocarpa, *A. mexicana*, *A. syriaca*, *A. tuberosa*, plants poisonous
    to stock.. 413, 414
Ash, percentage in milk of different breeds............................. 184
Asthenia, bacteriology of the disease.................................. 330
    clinical, history and postmortem appearances................. 329
    etiology 330
    treatment 333
Aspergillus glaucus, poisonous plant 392
Astragalus bigelovii, *A. hornii*, *A. mollisimus*, *A. pattersoni*, plants poison-
    ous to stock... 404
    dorycnioides, *A. palousensis*, *A. spaldingii*, experiment in feed-
    ing to sheep.. 423
Atamosco atamasco, plant poisonous to stock........................... 397
Atamasco lily, poisonous to stock..................................... 397
Autumn sneezeweed, poisonous to stock................................ 417
Ayrshire cattle, average composition of milk............................ 184
    dairy test.. 184
    history, description, and general characteristics............. 189
    number registered and number living 185
    scale of points... 186
Azalea, California, poisonous to stock.................................. 410
    occidentalis, plant poisonous to stock 410
Azoturia and distemper in horses, inquiry and reply..................... 538
Bacon, American, receipts in England in 1897 443
    price in Cape Colony... 523
    prices in London markets..................................... 458
    quantity and value of exports in 1897 and 1898............... 589
        to France in 1898......................... 588
        Germany in 1898 582
        United Kingdom in 1898............... 581
    sizes of packages in London markets 452
Bacteriology of asthenia.. 330
Bacterium asthenix, description 330
Baker, George S., report on cattle tick and tuberculosis in New South
    Wales... 386
Baltimore, receipts and shipments of farm animals in 1897 and 1898, by
    months.. 569
Baneberry, red, poisonous to stock.................................... 399
    white, poisonous to stock.................................... 399
Barnes, John A, report on American hams in Germany................... 519
    trichinæ and German inspection of American
    hog products 516
Bean, coral, poisonous to stock 405
Beaver poison, poisonous to stock..................................... 408

Page.

Beef, canned, quantity and value of exports in 1897 and 1898 588
   to France in 1898 583
   Germany in 1898........... 582
  extracts, prices in Cape Colony 523
  fresh, prices in London markets................................... 458
   quantity and value of exports in 1897 and 1898 588
   to United Kingdom in 1898 581
  products, canned, quantity and value of exports to United Kingdom
   in 1898 581
  salted, pickled, etc., quantity and value of exports in 1897 and 1898.. 588
   to France in 1898. 583
   Germany in 1898.. 582
   United Kingdom
   in 1898......... 581
Belgium, report on contagious diseases in 1897 and 1898 432
  value of exports of gloves to United States in 1897 and 1898 595
Bittersweet, climbing, poisonous to stock 408
  poisonous to stock 415
Bitting, A. W., article on cooperation between station and State veterinarians.. 426, 427
Black greasewood, poisonous to stock................................ 398
  head, or entero-hepatitis, method of diagnosing................... 351
  or Somali, sheep, consular report by W. W. Masterson 523
  henbane, poisonous to stock.................................... 414
  nightshade, poisonous to stock 415
Blackleg, age, class, and sex of cattle most frequently affected 38
  animals to be vaccinated 70
  and anthrax in Italy in 1897 and 1898, statistics 488
  appearance after death 44
  bacillus, description 45
  geographical distribution 86
  historical review of the disease............................... 85
  hygienic measures of prevention 54
  in France in 1897 and 1898, statistics 433
  Norway in 1897 and 1898 435
  Switzerland in 1897 and 1898, statistics 439
  the United States, etc., article by V. A. Nörgaard 27–81
  general remarks............................... 87
  investigations by Pathological Division 20
  in Texas 28
  list of questions 31
  of Bureau, measures of success reached 78
  to be continued by Bureau 77
  manner of infection 47
  method of diagnosing the disease.............................. 342
  number of cattle vaccinated and loss 82
  by States 74
  prophylactic measures of prevention 57
  reports of recoveries 50
  States and Territories affected................................ 37
  symptoms of the disease...................................... 43
  termination and treatment 48
  vaccination, how to operate 71
  vaccine, attitude of Bureau in distributing 34
  directions for using. 67
  extracts from reports of users 78
  its distribution, and results 80
  of the Bureau, how to apply for it 77
  preparation for use 69
  single, necessity 29
Blackwood, W. J., article on meat and milk inspection in Shanghai 205–212
Blood serum as a preventive and cure of Texas fever, by J. C. Robert 482
Blister upon genitals in Hungary in 1897 437
Bolelia, brook, poisonous to stock................................... 417
  plant poisonous to stock.................................... 417
Boophilus bovis carrier of Texas fever, experiments................... 481
Boots and shoes, value of exports in 1897 and 1898, by countries 596
  to Germany in 1898..................... 582

Page.

Boston, receipts and shipments of farm animals in 1897 and 1898, by months.   567
Box, common, poisonous to stock..   407
Bracken fern, poisonous to stock...   394
Branch ivy, poisonous to stock...   411
Bran of wheat, corn, and cowpeas, for fattening pigs, abstract of bulletin
    by J. F. Duggar   496
Braxy in Norway in 1897 and 1898, statistics   435
Brazil, quantity and value of exports of butter from United States in 1897
    and 1898   584
British North America, quantity and value of exports of butter from United
    States in 1897 and 1898   584
Broad cocklebur, poisonous to stock   417
    leaf laurel, poisonous to stock.......................................   411
Brook bolelia, poisonous to stock...   417
Brown Swiss cattle, history, description, and general characteristics   143
            number registered and number living..................   185
            scale of points   187
Buckeye, California, poisonous to stock   408
    fetid, poisonous to stock..   408
    Ohio, poisonous to stock..   408
    red, poisonous to stock...   408
Buffalo cholera in Hungary in 1897 and 1898, report......................   438
    disease in Italy in 1897 and 1898, statistics.........................   438
    N. Y., receipts and shipments of farm animals in 1897 and 1898, by
        months   570
Bulbous crowfoot, poisonous to stock.....................................   401
Burnett, E. A., and E. C. Chilcott, abstract of bulletin on feeding for mut-
    ton in South Dakota...   471
Bush, stagger, poisonous to stock...   412
Butneria fertilis, plant poisonous to stock   402
Butter, American, in Japan, consular report...............................   521
    average amount of annual exports.....................................   83
    amount of exports for selected years from 1790 to 1897   107
        in 1896 and 1897   107
        imports into United Kingdom from countries named in
            1896–1897..   108
    chemical analysis of experimental exports   132
    color preferred in London market.....................................   103
    commission for wholesaling in London.................................   96
    experimental shipments to Great Britain   22
    exports to United Kingdom in 1886–1897   108
        transportation rates in United States.....................   94
    for experimental export, kind of record kept.........................   109
    fresh, exports from United States, article by H. E. Alvord........   125–128
        scoring in New York City..........................   127
    from United States, analysis in United States and London   133
            France, and Denmark, scoring in London   127
    how experimental exports were handled in London......:..........   94
    packed by Department for experimental export   88
    to pack for shipment abroad...................................   87
    imitation, and oleo oil, amount of exports in 1884–1897   108
    in Paraguay, consular report...   521
        South Africa, remarks on receipts and methods of shipment....   513
    kind that brings highest price in London...........................   85
    making, remarks on pasteurization of milk and cream...........   85
    packages, kind preferred in London market......................   105
        size appearing in London market 86, 452
    price in Cape Colony   523
        London in 1897 ....   96, 458
    quantity and value of exports in 1897 and 1898   584
        to Germany in 1898.........................   582
            United Kingdom in 1898   581
    railroad transportation considered..................................   89
    record of scoring of experimental exports.   128
    report upon experimental exports in 1897, article by H. E. Alvord.   83–136
    statements of English consumers regarding experimental exports.   100
    United States and foreign, comparative composition   109

Page.
Butter, use of pasteurized cream, article by John H. Monrad............ 110-125
   value of imports into Great Britain in 1897 84
Butters, foreign made, record of analyses 133
    scorings 131
Butterfly weed, poisonous to stock 414
Buxus sempervirens, plant poisonous to stock 407
Calfkill, poisonous to stock.... 411
California azalea, poisonous to stock.... 410
   buckeye, poisonous to stock................................ 408
   eggs, food value, abstract of article by M. E. Jaffa............ 510
   false hellebore, poisonous to stock.......................... 395
   number, average price, and value of farm animals in 1897 and
    1898.. 597-602
   rhododendron, poisonous to stock 412
Californian Labrador tea, poisonous to stock................... 411
Calf affected with warts, inquiry and reply......................... 537
Calves affected with diarrhea, inquiry and reply..................... 536
   white scours, inquiry and reply 534
  number inspected antemortem in 1892-1898 13
   and postmortem...................... 13
  total receipts and shipments in 1896-1898................. 550
   1897 and 1898................... 551,552
Calycanthus, poisonous to stock.............................. 402
Camas, death, poisonous to stock 396
  poison, experiment in feeding to sheep.................... 424
Canada, amount of exports of butter to United Kingdom in 1886-1897..... 108
Canadian cattle, receipts in England in 1897.................... 441
Cape Colony, number of sheep and amount of wool in 1850-1895 522
  prices, consular report by James G. Stowe 523
Casein, percentage in milk of different breeds 184
Cases for sausages, value of exports in 1897 and 1898.. 591
Castilleja pallescens, experiment in feeding to sheep.................. 423
Castor-oil plant, poisonous to stock 407
Catchfly, sleepy, poisonous to stock 398
Cattle affected with contagious ophthalmia, inquiry and reply.......... 529
   lice, inquiry and reply.......................... 529
   mad itch, or stomach staggers, inquiry and reply 527
   ringworm, or mange, inquiry and reply.............. 528
   "wolves," or "warbles," inquiry and reply 528
  Canadian, receipts in England in 1897 441
  cutting off tails to cure disease, inquiry and reply 531
  dairy breeds, article by H. E. Alvord.................... 187-200
  dehorning, abstract of bulletin by F. William Rane............. 491
   Gilbert M. Gowell and Fremont
    L. Russell 489
  delay in transshipping at London 440
  disease in Marshall County, Kans., description 382-384
   Uruguay, report by Albert W. Swalm.................. 385
   of eyes, inquiry and reply.......................... 530
  diseases and remedies at Kinloch, Scotland..................... 219
   inquiries and replies........................... 524-537
  horses, etc., in Switzerland, numbers................... 520
  in England from Argentine Republic................... 441
  industry in Colorado, Wyoming, and Nevada, and sheep industry in
   Colorado in 1897, article by John T. McNeely................ 377-381
  inspection and export in 1893-1898 16
  number and value of exports in 1870-1898 586
   1897 and 1898 586
   to United Kingdom in 1898 583
   average price and value in 1897 and 1898, by States 600
   having blackleg and percentage of loss after vaccination 32
   inspected antemortem in 1891-1898.................. 13
   and postmortem.. 12
  loss in shipment from United States and Canada in 1898 15
  organizations of breeders, secretaries.................. 200
  range of prices at Chicago in 1897 and 1898, by months 579
  Southern, inspection 16

	Page.
Cattle tick and tuberculosis in New South Wales, report by Geo. S. Baker..	386
total receipts and shipments at leading cities in 1896–1898............	550
1897 and 1898......	551, 552
Celandine, poisonous to stock	402
Celastrus scandens, plant poisonous to stock..............................	408
Celery-leaf crowfoot, poisonous to stock	401
Cerebro-spinal meningitis in Denmark in 1897 and 1898, statistics...........	435
horses, inquiry and reply.....................	537
Chœnactis douglassi, experiment in feeding to sheep....................	424
Cheese, average sizes in London markets....................................	454
price in Cape Colony	523
prices in London markets....................................	463
quantity and value of exports to United Kingdom in 1898	581
imports and exports in 1897 and 1898........	591
Chelidonium majus, plant poisonous to stock	402
Cherry laurel, poisonous to stock	402
wild black, poisonous to stock................................	403
Chesnut, V. K., article on plants poisonous to stock......................	387–420
Chestnut, horse, poisonous to stock...	408
Chicago, range of prices of farm animals in 1897 and 1898, by months ...	579–580
receipts and shipments at leading cities of farm animals in 1897 and 1898, by months	553
Chicken cholera, method of diagnosing the disease	349
tinned, price in Cape Colony	523
Chico, poisonous to stock	398
Chilcott, E. C., and E. A. Burnett, abstract of bulletin on feeding for mutton in South Dakota...	471
China, quantity and value of imports of butter from United States in 1897 and 1898...	584
Chinese umbrella tree, poisonous to stock	406
Chrosperma muscœtoxicum, plant poisonous to stock	395
Cicuta bolanderi and C. vagans, plants poisonous to stock..................	409
maculata plant poisonous to stock	408
Cincinnati, receipts and shipments of farm animals in 1897 and 1898........	565
Clathrus columnatus, fungus poisonous to stock...........................	394
Clematis douglassi, experiment in feeding to sheep	425
Cleveland, receipts and shipments of farm animals in 1897 and 1898, by months..	566
Climbing bittersweet, poisonous to stock..................................	408
nightshade, poisonous to stock....................	415
Clotbur, spiny, poisonous to stock	417
Cockle, corn, poisonous to stock	398
poisonous to stock	398
Cocklebur, broad, poisonous to stock......................................	417
poisonous to stock	417
Colombia, quantity and value of imports of butter from United States in 1897 and 1898..	584
value of imports of boots and shoes from United States in 1897 and 1898	596
Colorado, number, average price, and value of farm animals in 1897 and 1898	597–602
of cattle having blackleg, and percentage of loss after vaccination	82
vaccinated against blackleg, and losses	74
counties affected with blackleg......................	37
Wyoming, and Nevada cattle industry, and sheep industry in Colorado in 1897, article by John T. McNeely	377–381
Common box, poisonous to stock..	407
mandrake, poisonous to stock	401
nightshade, poisonous to stock	415
wind flower, poisonous to stock	400
Conium maculatum, plant poisonous to stock.............................	409
Connecticut, number, average price, and value of farm animals in 1897 and 1898	597–602
Contagious abortion in cows, inquiry and reply	525
diseases of animals in European countries, report	428–439
ophthalmia of cattle, inquiry and reply..........	529

Page.

Contagious pleuropneumonia in France in 1897 and 1898, statistics 433
                         Great Britain, history...................... 428
                                 statistics, 1870–1897....... 429
Convallaria majalis, plant poisonous to stock................................. 397
Coral bean, poisonous to stock 405
Corn and Kafir corn, steer feeding experiments, abstract of bulletin by C.
       C. Georgeson 483
     cockle, poisonous to stock....................................... 398
     cowpeas, and wheat bran for fattening pigs, abstract of bulletin by J.
       F. Duggar... 496
     poppy, poisonous to stock....................................... 402
     supposed poisoning of stock..................................... 395
Cotswold lambs, experiments in feeding 464, 467
Cowbane, poisonous to stock... 408, 409
Cow poison, plant poisonous to stock ....`..`........................... 401
     refusing to give down milk, inquiry and reply 534
Cows affected with mammitis, or inflammation of the udder, inquiry and
     and reply ...`... 532
     contagious abortion, inquiry and reply............................ 525
     feed at Kinloch... 217
     number in Malta 520
     scrub, experiments on milking in Kansas 491
Cowpeas, corn, and wheat bran for fattening pigs, abstract of bulletin by
     J. F. Duggar.. 496
     peanuts, and sweet potatoes for hogs, abstract of bulletin by J.
       F. Duggar.. 501
Cream, pasteurizing for butter, article by John H. Monrad.............. 110–125
Creameries, list cooperating in experimental exports of butter 108
            manufacturing butter for experimental export in 1897........ 84
Creamery at Newton, Kans., description............................... 111
"Creeps," or osteomalacia, inquiry and reply.......................... 530
Crepis barbigera, experiment in feeding to sheep..................... 423
Crotalaria sagittalis, plant poisonous to stock 404
Crow poison, plant poisonous to stock 395, 396
Crowfoot, bulbous, poisonous to stock 401
     celery-leafed, poisonous to stock 401
     cursed, poisonous to stock...................................... 401
     tall, poisonous to stock.. 401
Cuba, quantity and value of imports of butter from the United States in
     1897 and 1898.. 584
Cursed crowfoot, poisonous to stock 401
Curtiss, C. F., and James Wilson, abstract of bulletin on feeding lambs ... 468
            James W. Wilson, abstract of bulletin on feeding lambs.. 466
            abstract of bulletin on feeding range
               lambs 469
Dairies of Shanghai, inspection 211
Dairy breeds of cattle, average composition of milk 184
            comparison of tests 184
            at Columbian Exposition 183
     cattle, breeds, article by H. E. Alvord 137–200
     in United States, number registered and number living...... 185
     points observed in judging................................. 185
     cows, care 202
     Division, outline of work performed 21
     farm, and cost of labor in Scotland 222
     rules, fifty... 201–204
Dairying and agriculture in Scotland, article by John C. Higgins 213–233
Darnel, poisonous to stock.. 395
Datura stramonium and *D. tatula*, plants poisonous to stock 414
Dawson, Charles F., article on asthenia (going light) in fowls........... 329–334
            laboratory methods of diagnosing microor-
            ganismal diseases........................... 335–368
            vitality and virulence of bacteria in milk. 224–228
Death camas, poisonous to stock 396
Dehorning cattle, abstract of bulletin by F. William Rane 491
            Gilbert M. Gowell and Fremont
            L. Russell 489

                                                                            Page.
Delaware, number, average price, and value of farm animals in 1897 and
   1898.. 597–602
Delphinium consolida, D. geyeri, D. menziesii, and *D. tricorne,* plants poi-
               sonous to stock... 400
          glaucum, description.. 477
          menziesii, description.. 478
                   experiments in feeding to sheep....................... 421
                   poisoning sheep... 474
          recurvatum, D. scopulorum, and *D. trolliifolium,* plants poi-
               sonous to stock... 401
          scopulorum, description.. 478
Denmark, amount of exports of butter to United Kingdom in 1886–1897... 108
          report on contagious diseases in 1897 and 1898................... 434
Denver, receipts and shipments of farm animals in 1897 and 1898, by months. 575
Detroit, receipts and shipments of farm animals in 1897 and 1898, by months. 572
Devon cattle, average composition of milk.................................. 184
          dairy test.. 184
          history, description, and general characteristics............... 146
          number registered and number living.......................... 185
          scale of points.. 188
Diarrhea in calves, inquiry and reply....................................... 536
Digitalis purpurea, plant poisonous to stock............................... 416
Diphtheria, method of diagnosing the disease.............................. 352
          or roup, in fowls, inquiry and reply............................... 547
Dipping for Texas fever, remarks.. 19
Dips, lime-and-sulphur, reply to criticism.................................. 548
Diseases, microorganismal, laboratory methods of diagnosing, article by
   Charles F. Dawson.. 335–368
Distemper and azoturia in horses, inquiry and reply......................... 538
Dogbane, spreading, poisonous to stock..................................... 413
Dorset lambs, experiments in feeding...................................... 464–467
Droppings as hog feed... 485
Dryden, James, abstract of bulletin on experiments in egg production.... 506
Duggar, J. F., abstract of bulletin on corn, cowpeas, and wheat bran for fat-
               tening pigs.. 496
          peanuts, cowpeas, and sweet potatoes
               as food for hogs... 501
Dutch Belted cattle, history, description, and general characteristics...... 150
          number registered and number living............ 185
          scale of points.................................... 189
Dwarf larkspur, poisonous to stock... 400
East Indies, quantity and value of exports of hides and skins to United
   States in 1897 and 1898... 594
East St. Louis, receipts and shipments of farm animals in 1897 and 1898, by
   months... 559
Egg production, experiments, abstract of bulletin by James Dryden....... 506
          influence of exercise and food consumption.............. 508
Eggs, California, food value, abstract of article by M. E. Jaffa........... 510
          experiments relative to fertility............................. 509
          how sold in London markets............................... 454
          in South Africa, remarks on receipts and methods of shipment...... 512
          prices in London markets................................. 462
          quantity and value of imports and exports in 1892–1898......... 584
Entero-hepatitis, or blackhead, method of diagnosing the disease.......... 351
Enzootic cerebritis, or staggers, caused by *Aspergillus glaucus*........... 392
Epigæa repens, plant poisonous to stock.................................... 410
Equisetum arvense, plant poisonous to stock............................... 394
Equus burchellii and *E. zebra,* note on domestication..................... 869
Ergotism, inquiries and reply.. 524
Erigonum heracleoides, experiment in feeding to sheep..................... 425
Esophagostoma columbianum, cause of nodular disease in sheep........... 353
Euphorbia bicolor and *E. marginata,* plants poisonous to stock........... 407
          plant poisonous to stock............................... 406
European aconite, poisonous to stock....................................... 399
Eyes of cattle, disease, inquiry and reply.................................. 530
False hellebore, poisonous to stock.. 395
          sunflower, poisonous to stock................................ 417

Page.

Farcy and glanders in Belgium in 1897 and 1898, statistics................... 433
    France in 1897 and 1898, statistics........ 433
    Italy in 1897 and 1898, statistics 438
  or mange, in Netherlands in 1897 and 1898, statistics................. 434
Farm animals, number and value of exports in 1870–1898................. 586
             1897 and 1898............ 586
      average price, and value in 1897 and 1898 by States. 597–602
  of United States and Canada, number of inspections and ex-
    portations in 1897 and 1898............................ 15
  range of prices at Chicago in 1897 and 1898, by months... 579–580
  statistics on movement.................................. 550–578
  lands of Scotland, best use................................... 221
Fat, amount in United States and foreign butters........................... 102
  percentage in milk of different breeds......................... 184
Feed of cows at Kinloch.. 217
Feeding and foods in Scotland.. 214
  of lambs, abstract of bulletin by James Wilson and C. F. Curtiss. 463
  range lambs, abstract of bulletin by James W. Wilson and C. F.
    Curtiss.. 469
Fern, bracken, poisonous to stock.. 394
Fetid buckeye, poisonous to stock 408
Fetter bush, mountain, poisonous to stock 411
Field horsetail, poisonous to stock 394
  larkspur, poisonous to stock................................. 400
  poppy, poisonous to stock................................... 402
Fifeshire, Scotland, agricultural practices 216
Fine-leaf sneezeweed, poisonous to stock................................ 418
Flax, large-flowered, yellow, poisonous to stock......................... 406
Florida, number, average price, and value of farm animals in 1897 and
  1898... 597–602
Flukes in sheep, inquiry and reply....................................... 543
Fly poison, plant poisonous to stock 395
Food, influence on milk 220
  value of California eggs, abstract of article by M. E. Jaffa.......... 510
Foods and feeding in Scotland... 214
  digestible nutrients of different kinds........................ 218
Foot-and-mouth disease in Belgium in 1897 and 1898, statistics 433
    Denmark in 1897 and 1898, statistics.............. 435
    Great Britain in 1897, report 430
    Hungary in 1896 and 1897, report................. 436
    Italy in 1897 and 1898, statistics 438
    Netherlands in 1897 and 1898, statistics.......... 434
    Switzerland in 1897 and 1898, statistics 439
Foot rot in Belgium in 1897 and 1898, statistics........................... 433
  sheep, inquiry and reply 546
  in Netherlands in 1897 and 1898, statistics 434
Foothalt in Hungary in 1897... 437
Fort Worth, receipts and shipments of farm animals in 1897 and 1898...... 576
Fowl cholera, method of diagnosing the disease.. 349
Fowls, diphtheria, or roup, affecting, inquiries and answer............ 547
  nodular tæniasis, methods of diagnosing......................... 353
  inquiries and answers on diseases............................. 547
Foxglove, purple, poisonous to stock 416
France, quantity and value of exports of hides and skins to United States
    in 1897 and 1898................. 594
    wool and wool manufactures to
      United States in 1897 and 1898. 593
    imports of animal products from United
      States in 1898...... 583
    hides and skins from United States
      in 1897 and 1898.............. 594
  report on contagious diseases in 1897 and 1898 433
  value of exports of gloves to United States in 1897 and 1898 595
  imports of boots and shoes from United States in 1897 and
    1898 596
Frasera albicaulis, experiment in feeding to sheep......................... 424

	Page.
French, H. T., abstract of bulletin on feeding sheaf and chopped wheat to pigs	494
feeding sheaf wheat to hogs	495
to steers	486
Frijolillo, poisonous to stock	405
Gape disease in poultry, remedies	505
young poultry, abstract of bulletin by H. Garman	504
Garden nightshade, poisonous to stock	415
poppy, poisonous to stock	402
Garget, poisonous to stock	398
Garlic, yellow false, poisonous to stock	397
Garman, H., abstract of bulletin on gape disease of young poultry	504
Georgeson, C. C., abstract of bulletin on feeding corn and Kafir corn to steers	483
Georgia, number, average price, and value of farm animals in 1897 and 1898	597–602
Geranium, experiment in feeding to sheep	425
Gerardia, slender, poisonous to stock	416
tenuifolia, plant poisonous to stock	416
Germany, military administration and national horse breeding, article	372–376
presence of American hams	519
quantity and value of exports of hides and skins to United States in 1897 and 1898	594
imports of animal products from United States in 1898	583
butter from United States in 1897 and 1898	584
hides and skins from United States in 1897 and 1898	594
sole leather from United States in 1897 and 1898	595
toys, poisonous	18
value of exports of gloves to United States in 1897 and 1898	595
imports of boots and shoes from United States in 1897 and 1898	596
Glanders and farcy in Belgium in 1897 and 1898, statistics	433
France in 1897 and 1898, statistics	428
Great Britain in 1897	431
Italy in 1897 and 1898, statistics	438
in Denmark in 1897 and 1898, statistics	435
Hungary in 1897, report	436
Switzerland in 1897 and 1898, statistics	439
method of diagnosing the disease	344
number of outbreaks in Great Britain in 1877–1898	432
Glaucus zygadenus, plant poisonous to stock	396
Gloves, value of imports in 1897 and 1898	595
Goats, number in Malta	530
Golden rod, poisonous to stock	418
Gowell, Gilbert M., and Fremont L. Russell, abstract of bulletin on dehorning cattle	480
Gowey, John F., report on American butter in Japan	521
Grass, alkali, poisonous to stock	396
poison rye, poisonous to stock	395
sleepy, poisonous to stock	395
Gratiola officinalis, plant poisonous to stock	416
Green hellebore, poisonous to stock	401
Greasewood, black, poisonous to stock	398
Great Britain, consumption of American animals and animal products, article by W. H. Wray	440–463
history of contagious pleuropneumonia	428
report on contagious diseases	428
value of imports of butter in 1897	84
laurel, poisonous to stock	412
lobelia, poisonous to stock	417
Grindelia nana, experiment in feeding to sheep	424
Ground hemlock, poisonous to stock	395
laurel, poisonous to stock	410
Grout, John H., report on animals and animal products in Malta	520

Page.

Grub in head of sheep, inquiry and reply..................................... 542
Guernsey cattle, average composition of milk 184
    dairy test.. 184
    at Columbian Exposition............................... 183
    history, description, and general characteristics............ 152
    number registered and number living 185
    scale of points 190
    herd established at Kinloch............................. 217
Gummy milk, inquiry and reply 532
Gyrotheca capitata, plant poisonous to stock 397
Hams, American, in Germany 519
    price in Cape Colony...................................... 523
    quantity and value of exports in 1897 and 1898.............. 589
    to France in 1898 583
    Germany in 1898 582
    United Kingdom in 1898........... 581
    tinned, price in Cape Colony 523
Health, State boards, list... 603
Hedge hyssop, poisonous to stock.. 416
Helenium autumnale, plant poisonous to stock 417
    tenuifolium, plant poisonous to stock 418
Hellebore, green, poisonous to stock.. 401
    poisonous to stock 395
Helleborus virides, plant poisonous to stock............................. 417
Hemlock, ground and poison, poisonous to stock............................ 395
    poisonous to stock 411
    poison, poisonous to stock.............................. 409
    spotted, poisonous to stock 408, 409
    water parsnip, poisonous to stock 410
    poisonous to stock..................................... 408
Hemp, Indian, poisonous to stock.. 413
Henbane, black, poisonous to stock.. 414
Heuchera glabella, experiment in feeding to sheep 425
Hens, old, v. pullets as layers.. 508
Hides and skins, quantity and value of exports to France in 1898 583
    Germany in 1898 582
    United Kingdom in 1898. 582
    imports and exports in 1897 and 1898. 594
    value of imports from Calcutta in 1894-1898 523
Higgins, John C., article on agriculture and dairying in Scotland 213-223
Hog cholera and swine plague in 1897 and 1898, statistics 488
    methods of diagnosing the disease 345
    in France in 1897 and 1898, statistics............... 488
    Hungary in 1896 and 1897.......................... 487
    Iowa, abstract of bulletin by W. B. Niles................ 500
    Norway in 1897 and 1898, statistics................... 485
    or swine plague in Denmark in 1897 and 1898, statistics 435
    outline of work in Biochemic Division....................... 18
    feed, value of droppings from cattle 485
    products, American, German inspection and trichinæ................ 516
Hogs, number and value of exports in 1870-1898 586
    1897 and 1898 587
    to United Kingdom in 1898 582
    average price, and value in 1897 and 1898................. 602
    inspected antemortem in 1894-1898 13
    and postmortem. 12
    peanuts, cowpeas, and sweet potatoes as food, abstract of bulletin by
    J. F. Duggar.. 501
    range of prices at Chicago in 1897 and 1898, by months 579
    total receipts and shipments at leading cities in 1896-1898 530
    1897 and 1898 ..... 551, 552
Holloway, Herbert, letter relative to lime-and-sulphur dips 549
Holstein-Friesian cattle, average composition of milk 184
    dairy test... 184
    history, description, and general characteristics.... 156
    scale of points 190
    number registered and number living 185
Horse breeding in Germany, relation of national administration, article.. 372-376

                                                                      Page.
Horse chestnut, poisonous to stock 408
Horses affected with azoturia and distemper, inquiry and reply 598
              cerebro-spinal meningitis, inquiry and reply 537
              millet disease, inquiry and reply 539
    and mules, total receipts and shipments at leading cities in 1896–
        1898 550
    and mules, total receipts and shipments at leading cities in 1897
        and 1898 551–552
    cattle, etc., in Switzerland, numbers 520
    for slaughter, work of inspection to be taken up 17
    from United States, receipts in England in 1898 443
    number and value of exports in 1870–1898 586
              1897 and 1898 587
              to Germany in 1898 582
              United Kingdom in 1898 582
        average price, and value in 1897 and 1898, by States 597
    pinkeye affecting, in Italy in 1897 and 1898, statistics 438
    range of prices at Chicago in 1897 and 1898, by months 580
    relation to draft of wagons 511
    requirements for artillery, in Germany 874
              riding, in Germany 874
              medium and light riding, in Germany 875
Horsetail, field, poisonous to stock 394
Hungary, report on contagious diseases in 1897 435
Hydrophobia, method of diagnosing the disease 337
Hyoscyamus niger, plant poisonous to stock 414
Hypericum maculatum and H. perforatum, plants poisonous to stock 406
Hyssop, hedge, poisonous to stock 416
Idaho, number, average price, and value of farm animals in 1897 and 1898 . 597–602
Illicium floridianum, plant poisonous to stock 399
Illinois, number, average price, and value of farm animals in 1897 and 1898 . 597–602
Indiana, number, average price, and value of farm animals in 1897 and 1898 . 597–602
Indianapolis, receipts and shipments of farm animals in 1897 and 1898 560
Indian hemp, poisonous to stock 413
    poke, poisonous to stock 395
    Territory, number of cattle having blackleg and percentage of loss
              after vaccination 82
              vaccinated against blackleg, and losses . 74
              counties affected with blackleg 87
    tobacco, poisonous to stock 417
Infectious agalactia in Italy in 1897 and 1898, statistics 438
    leukæmia, method of diagnosing the disease 350
Influenza among horses in Italy in 1897 and 1898, statistics 438
Intestinal worms of sheep, inquiry and reply 543
Intestines of sheep, nodular disease, inquiry and reply 545
Iowa, average price and value of farm animals in 1897 and 1898 597–602
    presence of hog cholera, abstract of bulletin by W. B. Niles 500
Italy, statistics of contagious diseases 438
Itch, mad, or stomach staggers, of cattle, inquiry and reply 527
    Texas, description and remedies 488
    in Kansas, abstract of bulletin by N. S. Mayo 488
Ivy, branch, poisonous to stock 411
Jaffa, M. E., abstract of article on food value of California eggs 510
Japan and American butter, consular report 521
    quantity and value of imports of butter from United States in 1897
              and 1898 584
              hides and skins from United States
              in 1897 and 1898 594
              leather from United States in 1897
              and 1898 595
Jatropha stimulosa, plant poisonous to stock 407
Jersey cattle, average composition of milk 184
    dairy test 184
    at Columbian Exposition 183
    history, description, and general characteristics 162
    number registered and number living 185
    scale of points 197
City, receipts of farm animals in 1897 and 1898, by months 573

Page.

Jimson weed, poisonous to stock 414
Kafir corn and corn, steer feeding experiments 488
Kansas City, receipts and shipments of farm animals in 1897 and 1898, by
    months 554
Kansas, description of creamery at Newton 111
    Marshall County, cattle disease, description 882–884
    number, average price, and value of farm animals in 1897 and 1898. 597–602
        of cattle having blackleg and percentage of loss after vacci-
           nation 82
           vaccinated against blackleg, and losses 74
           counties affected with blackleg 87
        presence of Texas itch, abstract of bulletin by N.S. Mayo 488
        tuberculosis, abstract of bulletin by N.S. Mayo 479
Kalmia angustifolia, plant poisonous to stock 410
    latifolia, plant poisonous to stock................................. 411
Kentucky, number, average price, and value of farm animals in 1897 and
    1898 597–602
Kinloch, feed of cows.. 217
    Guernsey herd, establishing................................... 217
Labor and cost of dairy farm in Scotland..................................... 222
Laboratory methods for diagnosis of microorganismal diseases, article by
    Charles F. Dawson 835–368
Labrador tea, poisonous to stock... 411
Lambert, poisonous to stock 403
Lambkill, poisonous to stock.... 411
Lambs, crossbred and range, experiments in feeding 464
    experiment in feeding, abstract of bulletin by James W. Wilson
        and C. F. Curtiss...................................... 466
    feeding, abstract of bulletin by James Wilson and C. F. Curtiss.... 463
        James W. Wilson and C. F. Curtiss. 469
Large-flowered yellow flax, poisonous to stock............................... 406
Lard compounds and substitutes, quantity and value of exports to United
        Kingdom in 1898 582
    effect of foods on melting point................................. 503
    exports to Natal in 1896 and 1897............................... 516
    imports into Natal in 1896 and 1897 516
    prices in Cape Colony.. 523
    quantity and value of exports in 1897 and 1898 .... 590, 591
        to France in 1898 583
        Germany in 1898...................... 582
        United Kingdom in 1898 582
Larkspur, dwarf, poisonous to stock.. 400
    experiment in feeding to sheep 421
    field, poisonous to stock 400
    poisoning of sheep, abstract of bulletin by E. V. Wilcox.......... 473
        symptoms....................................... 474
    poisonous to stock 401
    purple, poisonous to stock...................................... 400
    tall mountain, poisonous to stock 401
    Wyoming, poisonous to stock................................... 400
Laurel, cherry, poisonous to stock.. 402
    great, poisonous to stock....................................... 412
    ground, poisonous to stock 410
    mountain, poisonous to stock.................................. 412
    narrow-leaf, poisonous to stock............................... 410
    poisonous to stock... 411
    sheep, poisonous to stock 411
Leather and leather manufactures, quantity and value of exports to France
        in 1898 583
        quantity and value of exports to United
        Kingdom in 1898 582
        quantity and value of imports and
        exports.............................. 595
    sole, quantity and value of exports to Germany in 1898 582
    value of exports to Germany in 1898 582
Ledum glandulosum and *L. groenlandicum,* plants poisonous to stock...... 411
Leicester lambs, experiments in feeding 464, 467
Leptotaenia multifidia, experiments in feeding to sheep.................. 424

                                                                      Page.
Leucocrinum montanum, plant poisonous to stock......................... 396
            poisonous to stock.. 396
Leucothoë catesbœi and *L. racemosa*, plants poisonous to stock........... 411
            swamp, poisonous to stock.................................... 411
Leukæmia, infectious, method of diagnosing the disease................... 350
Lice on cattle, inquiry and reply....................................... 529
Ligustrum vulgare, plant poisonous to stock.......... 413
Lily of the valley, poisonous to stock.................................. 397
Lime-and-sulphur dips, reply to criticism............................... 548
Lincoln lambs, experiments in feeding 464, 467
Lincoln, Nebr., receipts and shipments of farm animals in 1897 and 1898, by
    months 564
Linum rigidum, plant poisonous to stock................................. 406
Lithospermum pilosum, experiment in feeding to sheep.................... 425
Live stock, catalogue of poisonous plants affecting, article by V. K. Ches-
            nut... 387–420
            sanitary boards, list.. 603
Lobelia, great, poisonous to stock...................................... 417
        inflata, *L. kalmii*, *L. spicata*, and *L. syphilitica*, plants poisonous
            to stock 417
        pale-spiked, poisonous to stock.................................. 417
Loco weed, stemless, poisonous to stock................................. 403
        woolly, poisonous to stock....................................... 404
Locust tree, poisonous to stock... 405
Lolium temulentum, plant poisonous to stock............................. 395
London provision trade, average weight of packages..................... 452
            rules governing.. 443
Louisiana, number, average price, and value of farm animals in 1897 and
    1898.. 597–602
Louisville, receipts and shipments of farm animals in 1897 and 1898, by
    months.. 571
Lousewort, poisonous to stock.. 416
Lung-worm disease in sheep, inquiry and reply.......................... 546
Lupines, poisonous to stock... 404
Lupinus albus, notes... 405
            experiment in feeding sheep 424
        leucophyllus, plant poisonous to stock......................... 404
McNeely, John T., article on cattle industry in Colorado, Wyoming, and
    Nevada, etc.. 377–381
Mad itch, or stomach staggers, of cattle, inquiry and reply............. 527
Maine, number, average price, and value of farm animals in 1897 and 1898. 597–602
Maladie du coït in Italy in 1897, statistics............................ 433
Malignant catarrhal fever in Denmark in 1897 and 1898, statistics......... 435
            Norway in 1897 and 1898, statistics.......................... 435
        edema, method of diagnosing the disease......................... 336
Malta, animals and animal products..................................... 520
Mammitis, or inflammation of the udder, inquiry and reply.............. 532
Mandrake, common, poisonous to stock.................................. 401
Mange of cattle in Italy in 1898, statistics............................ 438
    or farcy, in Netherlands in 1897 and 1898, statistics.............. 434
        ringworm, of cattle, inquiry and reply.......................... 529
Manures and manuring in Scotland....................................... 215
Mares, brood, conditions of taking from Government supply depot in Ger-
    many 375
Margarine, prices in London markets.................................... 459
Maryland, number, average price, and value of farm animals in 1897 and
    1898.. 597–602
Massachusetts, number, average price, and value of farm animals in 1897 and
    1898.. 597–602
Masterson, W. W., consular report on Somali, or blackhead, sheep......... 522
May apple, poisonous to stock.. 401
    flower, poisonous to stock.. 410
Mayo, N. S., abstract of bulletin on Texas itch in Kansas............... 488
            transmission of Texas fever................................. 481
            tuberculosis in Kansas....................................... 479
Meat and meat products, quantity and value of exports, 1897 and 1898...... 588
        milk inspection in Shanghai, article by W. J. Blackwood....... 205–212
    canned and cured, exports to South Africa in 1897 514

Page.

Meat imports into South Africa in 1897 ... 514
  inspection in 1898 ... 11
Meats in South Africa, remarks on receipts and methods of shipment ... 514
Melia azedarach, plant poisonous to stock ... 406
Meningitis, cerebro-spinal, in horses, inquiry and reply ... 537
Merino lambs, experiments in feeding ... 464, 467
Mexico, quantity and value of exports of hides and skins to United States in 1897 and 1898 ... 594
  imports of butter from United States in 1897 and 1898 ... 584
  hides and skins from United States in 1897 and 1898 ... 594
  value of imports of boots and shoes from United States in 1897 and 1898 ... 596
Mexican poppy, poisonous to stock ... 402
Michigan, number, average price, and value of farm animals in 1897 and 1898 ... 597-602
Microorganismal diseases, laboratory methods of diagnosis, article by Charles F. Dawson ... 335-368
Milch cows, number, average price, and value in 1897 and 1898 ... 599
Milk and meat inspection in Shanghai, article by W. J. Blackwood ... 205-212
  care in the dairy ... 208
  condensed, in Malta ... 520
    price in Cape Colony ... 523
  cow refusing to give down, inquiry and reply ... 534
  fever, or parturient apoplexy, of cows, inquiry and reply ... 526
  gummy, inquiry and reply ... 532
  influence of food ... 220
  in the dairy ... 208
  of dairy breeds of cattle, average composition ... 184
  ropy appearance, inquiry and reply ... 534
  sickness, inquiry and reply ... 531
  sugar, percentage in milk of different breeds ... 184
  supply in Shanghai, healthfulness ... 210
  yield at Kinloch ... 219
    daily, of different breeds ... 184
Milking scrub cows, experiment in Kansas ... 491
Milkweed, narrow-leaf, poisonous to stock ... 414
  poisonous to stock ... 413, 414
Millet disease of horses, inquiry and reply ... 539
Milwaukee, receipts and shipments of farm animals in 1897 and 1898, by months ... 562
Mince-meat, price in Cape Colony ... 523
Minnesota, number, average price, and value of farm animals in 1897 and 1898 ... 597-602
Mississippi, number, average price, and value of farm animals in 1897 and 1898 ... 597-602
Missouri, number, average price, and value of farm animals in 1897 and 1898 ... 597-602
Mock orange, poisonous to stock ... 402
Mold, woolly, poisonous to stock ... 392
Monkshood, poisonous to stock ... 390
Monrad, John H., article on pasteurizing cream for butter ... 110-125
Montana, number, average price, and value of farm animals in 1897 and 1898 ... 597-602
Moorwort, poisonous to stock ... 410
Mountain fetter bush, poisonous to stock ... 411
  laurel, poisonous to stock ... 412
Mules and horses, receipts and shipments at leading cities in 1896-1898 ... 550
  number and value of exports in 1870-1898 ... 580
    1897 and 1898 ... 587
  number, average price, and value in 1897 and 1898, by States ... 598
Mullein pink, poisonous to stock ... 398
Murrain, red, in swine in Hungary in 1897 ... 437
Mutton, feeding in South Dakota, abstract of bulletin by E. C. Chilcott and E. A. Burnett ... 471
  quantity and value of exports in 1897 and 1898 ... 591
Narrow-leaf laurel, poisonous to stock ... 410

                                                              Page.
Narrow-leaf milkweed, poisonous to stock 414
Nebraska, number, average price, and value of farm animals in 1897 and
           1898 597-602
       of cattle having blackleg, and loss after vaccination... 32
           vaccinated against blackleg, and loss.......... 74
           counties affected with blackleg 37
Nelson, S. B., article on feeding wild plants to sheep..................... 421-425
Nerium oleander, plant poisonous to stock............................... 413
Netherlands, report on contagious diseases in 1897 and 1898.............. 434
Nettle, slender, poisonous to stock....................................... 397
       spurge, poisonous to stock... ˙407
Nevada, Colorado, Wyoming cattle industry, etc., article by John T.
           McNeely... . 377-381
       number, average price, and value of farm animals in 1897 and
           1898.. 597-602
New Hampshire, number, average price, and value of farm animals in 1897
           and 1898... 597-602
New Jersey, number, average price, and value of farm animals in 1897 and
           1898... 597-602
New Mexico, number, average price, and value of farm animals in 1897 and
           1898... 597-602
New South Wales, cattle tick and tuberculosis, report by Geo. S. Baker 386
New York, number, average price, and value of farm animals in 1897 and
           1898... 597-602
Newton, Kans., creamery, description 111
Nicotiana tabacum, plant poisonous to stock 414
Nicotine in sheep dips, estimating by Biochemic Division................. 19
Nitrogen, percentage in milk of different breeds 184
Nightshade, American, poisonous to stock................................ 398
           black, poisonous to stock................................... 415
           climbing, poisonous to stock............................... 415
           common, poisonous to stock............................... 415
           garden, poisonous to stock................................. 415
           spreading, poisonous to stock............................. 416
Niles, W. B., abstract of bulletin on hog cholera in Iowa 500
Nodular disease in sheep, methods of diagnosing...................... 353
       of intestines of sheep, inquiry and reply..................... 545
       tæniasis in fowls, methods of diagnosis...................... 353
Nörgaard, Victor A., article on blackleg and the distribution of vaccine.... 27-81
Normandy cattle, history, description, and general characteristics......... 168-189
           number registered and number living.................... 185
North Carolina, number, average price, and value of farm animals in 1897
           and 1898.. 597-602
North Dakota, number, average price, and value of farm animals in 1897
           and 1898... 597-602
       of cattle having blackleg, and percentage of loss
           after vaccination 32
           cattle vaccinated against blackleg, and losses... 74
           counties affected with blackleg 37
Norway, report on contagious diseases in 1897 and 1898................. 435
Nose of sheep, grub affecting, inquiry and reply 543
Nothoscordum bivalve, plant poisonous to stock 396
Œsophagostoma columbianum, cause of nodular disease in sheep 353
Ohio buckeye, poisonous to stock 408
       number, average price, and value of farm animals in 1897 and 1898. 597-602
Oklahoma Territory, number, average price, and value of farm animals in
           1897 and 1898 597-602
       of cattle having blackleg, and percentage of
           loss after vaccination.................... 32
           cattle vaccinated against blackleg, and
           losses................................... 74
           counties affected with blackleg.......... 37
Oleander, poisonous to stock... 413
Oleo and oleomargarine, quantity and value of exports in 1897 and 1898.... 591
                                   to Germany in 1898. 582
                                   United Kingdom
                                   in 1898 582

Page.

Oleomargarine and oleo, quantity and value of exports in 1897 and 1898.... 591
      to United Kingdom in 1898............ 582
Oleo oil and imitation butter, amounts of exports, 1884–1897............... 108
Omaha, receipts and shipments of farm animals in 1897 and 1898, by months. 555
Ophthalmia, contagious, of cattle, inquiry and reply 529
Opium poppy, poisonous to stock 402
Orange, mock, poisonous to stock 402
Oregon, number, average price, and value of farm animals in 1897 and 1898. 597–602
Osteomalacia, or "creeps," inquiry and reply 530
Osteoporosis, inquiry and reply 440
Oxford lambs, experiments in feeding............................ 464, 467
Oxypolis rigidus, plant poisonous to stock........................... 409
Paint root, poisonous to stock 397
Pale-spiked lobelia, poisonous to stock 417
Papaver rhœas and *P. somniferum*, plants poisonous to stock 402
Paraguay and her butter supply, consular report...................... 521
Parsnip, hemlock water, poisonous to stock 410
Parturient apoplexy, or milk fever, of cows, inquiry and reply 526
Pasteurization in butter making, remarks.............................. 85
Pasteurizing cream for butter, article by John H. Monrad............. 110–125
Patterson, R. F., consular report on value of imports of hides and skins from Calcutta 523
Pea, wild, poisonous to stock 404
Peanuts, cowpeas, and sweet potatoes as food for hogs, abstract of bulletin by J. F. Duggar.. 501
Pedicularis palustris, plant poisonous to stock 416
    plant poisonous to stock.................................. 416
Pennsylvania, number, average price, and value of farm animals in 1897 and 1898... 597–602
Peucedanum grayii, experiments in feeding to sheep................... 425
Philadelphia, receipts and shipments of farm animals in 1897 and 1898, by months... 568
Phytolacca decandra, plant poisonous to stock 398
Pieris floribunda, plant poisonous to stock 411
    mariana, plant poisonous to stock......................... 412
Pigs, corn, cowpeas, and wheat bran for fattening, abstract of bulletin by J. F. Duggar... 496
    experiment in feeding sheaf and chopped wheat, abstract of bulletin by H. F. French.. 494
Pimpernel, poisonous to stock 413
Pinkeye among horses in Italy in 1897 and 1898, statistics............. 438
Pink, mullien, poisonous to stock................................... 398
Pittsburg, receipts and shipments of farm animals in 1897 and 1898, by months.. 563
Plants poisonous to stock, preliminary catalogue, article by V. K. Chesnut... 387–420
    wild, feeding to sheep, experiment, article by S. B. Nelson....... 421–425
Pleurisy root, poisonous to stock.................................... 414
Pleuropneumonia in Hungary in 1897................................ 437
Podophyllum peltatum, plant poisonous to stock..................... 401
Points observed in judging dairy cattle 185
Poison, beaver, poisonous to stock 408
    camas, experiment in feeding to sheep 424
    hemlock, poisonous to stock............................. 395–409
    rye grass, poisonous to stock............................ 395
    weed, poisonous to stock................................ 400–413
Poke, Indian, poisonous to stock 395
    poisonous to stock...................................... 398
Pokeweed, poisonous to stock....................................... 398
Polled Durham cattle, history, description, and general characteristics 170
    number registered and number living............... 185
Poppy, corn, poisonous to stock..................................... 402
    field, poisonous to stock................................. 402
    garden, poisonous to stock............................... 402
    Mexican, poisonous to stock.............................. 402
    opium, poisonous to stock............................... 402

	Page.
Poppy, red, poisonous to stock	402
Pork microscopically inspected, exports, 1892–1898	14
quantity and value of exports, 1897 and 1898	590
to France in 1898	588
Germany in 1898	583
United Kingdom in 1898	581
Portland, Oreg., receipts and shipments of farm animals in 1897 and 1898, by months	577
Porto Rico, quantity and value of imports of butter from United States in 1897 and 1898.	584
Potatoes, notes on feeding value	511
sweet, cowpeas, and peanuts as food for hogs, abstract of bulletin by J. F. Duggar	501
Potentilla, experiment in feeding to sheep	425
Poultry, gape disease in Kentucky, abstract of bulletin by H. Garman	504
value of exports, 1897 and 1898	591
Prairie thermopsis, poisonous to stock	405
Prim, poisonous to stock	413
Privet, poisonous to stock	413
Provision trade of London, average weights of packages	452
rules governing	443
Pteris aquilina, plant poisonous to stock	394
Prunus caroliana, plant poisonous to stock	402
serotina, plant poisonous to stock	403
Pueblo, receipts and shipments of farm animals in 1897 and 1898, by months	575
Pullets, v. old hens as layers	508
Purple foxglove, poisonous to stock	416
larkspur, poisonous to stock	400
Purpurea hæmorrhagica in Italy in 1897, statistics	438
Quamasia quamash, note.	
Quercus, plant poisonous to stock	397
Rabies in Belgium in 1897 and 1898, statistics	433
France in 1897 and 1898, statistics	433
Great Britain in 1897, report	430
Italy in 1897 and 1898, statistics	438
Switzerland in 1897 and 1898, statistics	439
method of diagnosing the disease	837
work of Pathological Division	21
Ragworth, tansy, poisonous to stock	418
Rane, F. William, abstract of bulletin on dehorning cattle	491
Ranunculus acris, R. bulbosus, and *R. sceleratus*, plants poisonous to stock	401
Rattle box, poisonous to stock	404
weed, poisonous to stock	404
Red baneberry, poisonous to stock	399
buckeye, poisonous to stock	408
murrain of swine in Hungary in 1897	437
Polled cattle, history, description, and general characteristics	174
number registered and number living	185
standard description	197
poppy, poisonous to stock	402
root, poisonous to stock	397
Regulations and rules of Bureau issued in 1897 and 1898	605–624
Rhode Island, number, average price, and value of farm animals in 1897 and 1898	597–602
Rhododendron, California, poisonous to stock	412
californicum and *R. maximum*, plants poisonous to stock	413
poisonous to stock	412
Ricinus communis, plant poisonous to stock	407
Ringworm, or mange, of cattle, inquiry and reply	528
Robert, J. C., abstract of bulletin on blood serum as a preventive for Texas fever	482
Robinia pseudacacia, plant poisonous to stock	405
Root, pleurisy, poisonous to stock	414
Ropy appearance of milk, inquiry and reply	534
Rosebay, poisonous to stock	412
Rot, foot, of sheep, inquiry and reply	546
Rouget in France in 1897 and 1898, statistics	438

Page.
Rouget in Netherlands in 1897 and 1898.. 484
           Norway in 1897 and 1898, statistics............................. 435
           Switzerland in 1897 and 1898, statistics......................... 439
Roup, method of diagnosing.. 352
    or diphtheria, in fowls, inquiries and answer.....................·........ 547
Ruffin, John N., report on butter in Paraguay..................................... 521
Rules and regulations of the Bureau issued in 1897 and 1898 605–624
Russell, Fremont L., and Gilbert M. Gowell, abstract of bulletin on dehorn-
    ing cattle 489
Rye grass, poison, poisonous to stock 395
St. John's wort, poisonous to stock.. 408
St. Joseph, receipts and shipments of farm animals in 1897 and 1898, by
    months... 561
St. Louis, receipts and shipments of farm animals in 1897 and 1898, by
    months... 558
San Francisco, receipts of farm animals in 1897 and 1898, by months...... 578
Santo Domingo, quantity and value of imports of butter from United
    States in 1897 and 1898... 584
Sarcobatus vermiculatus, plant poisonous to stock............................ 398
Sausage casings, value of exports in 1897 and 1898 591
Saxifraga integufolia, experiment in feeding to sheep...................... 424
Scab in Hungary in 1897.. 437
    of sheep. (*See* Sheep scab.)
Scours, white, in calves, inquiry and reply...................................... 534
Senecio guadalensis and *S. jacobœa,* plants poisonous to stock........... 418
Serum, blood, as a preventive and cure of Texas fever, abstract of bulletin
    by J. C. Robert... 482
Sesbania vesicaria, plant poisonous to stock.................................. 405
Sheep affected with flukes, inquiry and reply 543
             foot rot, inquiry and reply................................ 546
             grub in the head, inquiry and reply..................... 542
             intestinal worms and grubs in nose, inquiry and reply. 543
             nodular disease of intestines, inquiry and reply....... 545
    and lambs, American, receipts in England in 1896 and 1897........... 441
        wool in Cape Colony, 1850–1895, consular report............. 523
    dips, estimating nicotine by Biochemic Division...................... 19
    diseases, inquiries and replies.. 542
    feeding for mutton in South Dakota, abstract of bulletin by E. C.
        Chilcott and E. A. Burnett....................................... 471
        on wild plants, experiment by S. B. Nelson 421–425
    industry in Colorado and cattle industry in Colorado, Wyoming, and
        Nevada 377–381
    inspection and export in 1893–1898 16
    larkspur poisoning, abstract of bulletin by E. V. Wilcox 473
    laurel, poisonous to stock.. 411
    lungworm disease, inquiry and reply................................. 546
    nodular disease, methods of diagnosing.............................. 353
    number and value of exports in 1870–1898............................ 586
                 1897 and 1898........................... 587
                  to United Kingdom in 1898 582
        average price, and value in 1897 and 1898, by States.......... 601
        inspected antemortem in 1892–1898 13
                 and postmortem............................... 12
        lost in shipment from United States and Canada in 1898 15
    poisoned with larkspur, symptoms and treatment.................... 474
    pox in France in 1897 and 1898, statistics............................ 433
        Hungary in 1897.. 437
    range of prices at Chicago in 1897 and 1898, by months............. 580
    scab, efforts of Bureau to eradicate................................. 24
        in Belgium in 1897 and 1898, statistics........................... 433
           France in 1897 and 1898, statistics........................... 433
           Italy in 1897 and 1898, statistics............................. 438
           Netherlands in 1897 and 1898, statistics...................... 434
           Switzerland in 1897 and 1898, statistics...................... 439
        measures to prevent dissemination............................... 17
Somali, or blackhead, consular report by W. W. Masterson........... 523
    receipts and shipments at leading cities in 1896–1898................. 550

Page.

Sheaf wheat, feeding to hogs, abstract of bulletin by H. T. French............ 495
　　　　steers, abstract of bulletin by H. T. French........ 486
Shoes and boots, value of exports to Germany in 1898................... 583
Shorthorn cattle, dairy test.. 184
　　　　・　at Columbian Exposition........................ 183
　　　　history, description, and general characteristics......... 177
　　　　number registered and number living.................... 185
　　　　scale of points.................................... 198
Shropshire lambs, experiments in feeding............................ 464, 467
Silene antirrhina, plant poisonous to stock............................ 398
Silky sophora, poisonous to stock.................................... 405
Silk weed, poisonous to stock...................................... 414
Simmenthal cattle, history, description, and general characteristics....... 181
　　　　number registered and number living............... 185
Sioux City, receipts and shipments of farm animals in 1897 and 1898, by
　　months.. 557
Sisyrinchium grandiflorum, experiment in feeding to sheep.............. 424
Sium cicutæfolium, plant poisonous to stock......................... 410
Skin, elevations under collar and saddle, inquiry and reply.............. 543
Skins and hides, quantity and value of exports to France in 1898......... 583
　　　　　　　　　　　Germany in 1898........ 583
　　　　　　　　　　　United Kingdom in 1898. 582
　　　　　　　　　　　imports and exports in 1897 and 1898. 594
　　　　value of imports from Calcutta in 1894-1898.............. 523
Sleepy catchfly, poisonous to stock.............................. 398
　　　　grass, poisonous to stock.......................... 395
Slender gerardia, poisonous to stock............................ 416
　　　　nettle, poisonous to stock........................ 397
Sneezeweed, autumn, poisonous to stock........................... 417
　　　　fine-leaf, poisonous to stock....................... 418
　　　　poisonous to stock.............................. 417
Sneezewort, poisonous to stock.................................. 417
Solanum dulcamara and *S. nigrum*, plants poisonous to stock 415
　　triflorum and *S. tuberosum*, plants poisonous to stock 416
Sole leather, quantity and value of exports in 1897 and 1898, by countries.. 595
　　　　　　　　to Germany in 1898 582
Solidago, plant poisonous to stock.................................. 418
Somali, or blackhead, sheep, consular report by W. W. Masterson 523
Sophora secundiflora, plant poisonous to stock 405
　　sercea, plant poisonous to stock............................ 405
South America, quantity and value of exports of hides and skins to United
　　　　　　　　　　States in 1897 and 1898 . 594
　　　　　　　　　　wool and wool manufac-
　　　　　　　　　　tures to United States in
　　　　　　　　　　1897 and 1898 593
　　　　　　　　　　imports of leather from United States
　　　　　　　　　　in 1897 and 1898 595
South Carolina, number, average price, and value of farm animals in 1897
　　and 1898... 597-902
Dakota, feeding for mutton, abstract of bulletin 471
　　number, average price, and value of farm animals in 1897 and
　　1898 597-602
　　　　of cattle having blackleg, and percentage of loss... 32
　　　　vaccinated against blackleg, and losses ... 74
　　　　counties affected with blackleg................. 87
South St. Paul, receipts and shipments of farm animals in 1897 and 1898, by
　　months... 556
Southdown lambs, experiments in feeding..................... 464, 467
Southern cattle inspection 16
Spiny clotbur, poisonous to stock 417
Spotted hemlock, poisonous to stock 408, 409
Spreading dogbane, poisonous to stock 413
　　　　nightshade, poisonous to stock 416
Spurge nettle, poisonous to stock.......................... 407
　　poisonous to stock 406
Stable and dairy house, methods in Scotland 218
　　for dairy cattle and care 201
Staff vine, poisonous to stock 408

Page.

Stagger bush, poisonous to stock 412
Staggers, or enzootic cerebritis, of horses, caused by *Aspergillus glaucus*.... 392
Stagger weed, poisonous to stock.. 400, 417
Staggerwort, poisonous to stock... 418
Steddom, Rice P., report on a cattle disease in Kansas 382–384
Steer-feeding experiments with corn and Kafir corn, abstract of bulletin... 483
Steers, feeding sheaf wheat, abstract of bulletin by H. T. French.......... 486
Stemless loco weed, poisonous to stock... 403
Stiles, Ch. Wardell, agricultural attaché at Berlin 25
Stipa robusta, plant poisonous to stock...................................... 395
Stomach staggers, or mad itch, of cattle, inquiry and reply................... 527
Stowe, James G., consular report on prices of animal products in Cape
               Colony 523
               consular report on prices of animal products in South
               Africa 512
Strangles in Italy in 1890, statistics 438
Suffolk lambs, experiments in feeding 464, 467
Sulphur-and-lime dips, reply and criticism...................................... 548
Sunflower, false, poisonous to stock 417
Swalm, Albert W., report on cattle disease in Uruguay 385
Swamp hellebore poisonous to stock 395
     leucothoë, poisonous to stock 411
Sweet potatoes, peanuts, and cowpeas as food for hogs, abstract of bulletin. 501
     scented shrub, poisonous to stock 402
Swine fever in Great Britain in 1897, report.................................... 430
     plague and hog cholera in Italy in 1897 and 1898, statistics........... 438
           Denmark in 1897 and 1898, statistics 435
           method of diagnosing the disease........... 345
     red murrain affecting in Hungary in 1897 437
Swiss cattle, Brown, history, description, and general characteristics...... 143
Switzerland, number of horses, cattle, etc...................................... 520
     report on contagious diseases in 1897 and 1898................ 439
Synthyris rubra, experiment in feeding to sheep 425
Tæniasis, nodular, in fowls, method of diagnosing 353
Tails of cattle, cutting off to cure disease, inquiry and reply................ 531
Tall crowfoot, poisonous to stock... 401
     mountain larkspur, poisonous to stock 401
Tallow, quantity and value of exports in 1897 and 1898 589
           to France in 1898...................... 583
           Germany in 1898 582
           United Kingdom in 1898 581
Tansy ragwort, poisonous to stock.. 418
Taxus brevifolia, notes 395
     minor, plant poisonous to stock 395
Tea, California Labrador, poisonous to stock................................... 411
     Labrador, poisonous to stock... 411
Tendons, shortening, inquiry and reply... 541
Tennessee, number, average price, and value of farm animals in 1897 and
     1898.. 597–602
Tetanus in Italy in 1897, statistics 438
     method of diagnosing the disease 343
Texas fever, blood serum as a preventive and cure, abstract of bulletin.... 482
     method of diagnosing the disease 339
     remarks on dipping... 19
     transmission, abstract of bulletin....................................... 481
     treatment 482
     itch, description and remedies 488
     in Kansas, abstract of bulletin.. 488
     number, average price, and value of farm animals in 1897 and
     1898 597–602
     of cattle having blackleg and percentage of loss after vac-
        cination... 32
        vaccinated against blackleg, and losses............. 74
        counties affected with blackleg........................... 87
     remarks on blackleg investigations....................................... 28
Thermopsis rhombifolia, plant poisonous to stock 405
Tobacco, Indian, poisonous to stock.. 417
     poisonous to stock 414

Page.

Tongues, tinned, price in Cape Colony 523
Trailing arbutus, poisonous to stock 410
Tree, locust, poisonous to stock 405
Trichinæ and German inspection of American pork products 516
Tuberculosis and cattle tick in New South Wales 386
    in fowls, method of diagnosing the disease 351
    Italy in 1897 and 1898, statistics 438
    Kansas, abstract of bulletin by N.S. Mayo 479
    method of diagnosing the disease 340
    observations by Biochemic Division 19
Udder inflammation, or mammitis, in cows, inquiry and reply 532
United Kingdom, quantity and value of exports of hides and skins to
           United States in
           1897 and 1898.... 594
           wool to United
           States in 1897 and
           1898 593
        imports of animal products from
           United States, 1898. 581
         butter from United
           States, 1897 and
           1898 584
         hides and skins from
           United States, 1897
           and 1898 594
         leather from United
           States, 1897 and
           1898 595
      value of imports of boots and shoes from United States
       in 1897 and 1898 596
Urtica gracilis, plant poisonous to stock 397
Uruguay, cattle disease, report by Albert W. Swalm 385
Utah, number, average price, and value of farm animals in 1897 and
 1898 597-602
Utensils in the dairy, care 203
Vaccination for blackleg, losses due to careless operators 83
Vaccine, blackleg. (See Blackleg vaccine.)
Variolæ in Italy in 1897, statistics 438
Veratrum californicum and V. viride, plants poisonous to stock 395
Vermont, number, average price, and value of farm animals in 1897 and
 1898 597-602
Vessel inspection 14
Veterinarian, Station, cooperation with State veterinarian, article by A. W.
 Bitting 426, 427
Virginia, number, average price, and value of farm animals in 1897 and
 1898 597-602
"Warbles" or "wolves" in cattle, inquiry and reply 528
Warts on calf, inquiry and reply 537
Washington, number, average price, and value of farm animals in 1897 and
 1898 597-602
Water, amount in United States and foreign butters 102
    hemlock, poisonous to stock 408
    percentage in milk of different breeds 184
Weed, butterfly, poisonous to stock 414
    jimson, poisonous to stock 414
    poison, poisonous to stock 400, 413
    rattle, poisonous to stock 404
    stagger, poisonous to stock 400, 417
Weehawken, N.J., receipts of farm animals in 1897 and 1898, by months ... 574
Western aconite, poisonous to stock 399
West Indies and Bermuda, quantity and value of imports of leather from
      United States in 1897 and 1898 595
     quantity and value of exports of hides and skins to United
      States in 1897 and 1898 594
       imports of hides and skins from United
        States in 1897 and 1898 594
    value of imports of boots and shoes from the United States
     in 1897 and 1898 596

Page.

West Virginia, number, average price, and value of farm animals in 1897 and 1898... 597–602
Wharves, foreign animals, increase in Great Britain........................ 440
Wheat bran, corn, and cowpeas for fattening pigs, abstract of bulletin by J. F. Duggar... 496
 in sheaf, feeding to hogs, abstract of bulletin by H. T. French 495
  steers, abstract of bulletin by H. T. French 486
 sheaf and chopped, for pigs, abstract of bulletin by H. T. French.... 494
White baneberry, poisonous to stock 399
 scours in calves, inquiry and reply 514
Wilcox, E. V., abstract of bulletin on larkspur poisoning of sheep 473
Wild black cherry, poisonous to stock..................................... 403
 pea, poisonous to stock... 404
 rosemary, poisonous to stock... 410
Wilson, James, and C. F. Curtiss, abstract of bulletin on feeding of lambs.. 463
 James W., and C. F. Curtiss, abstract of bulletin on feeding of range lambs 469
  abstract of bulletin on feeding of lambs 466
Wind flower, common, poisonous to stock 400
 gall, inquiry and reply 541
Wisconsin, number, average price, and value of farm animals in 1897 and 1898.. 597–602
Wolfsbane, poisonous to stock 399
"Wolves," or "warbles," in cattle, inquiry and reply 528
Wool and sheep in Cape Colony, consular report. 1850–1895 522
 wool manufactures, quantity and value of imports in 1897 and 1898, by countries........................... 593
  value of exports, 1892–1898 585
  imports 1892–1898..................... 585
 manufactures, etc., quantity and value of exports to United Kingdom in 1898... 582
Woolly loco weed, poisonous to stock 404
Worms, lung, disease of sheep, inquiry and reply.......................... 546
 intestinal, of sheep, inquiry and reply 543
Wray, W. H., article on American animals and animal productions in Great Britain... 440–462
Wyoming, Colorado, and Nevada cattle industry, and sheep industry in Colorado in 1897, article by John T. McNeely 377–381
Wyoming larkspur, poisonous to stock 400
 number, average price, and value of farm animals in 1897 and 1898 597–602
Xanthium canadense, *X. spinosum*, and *X. strumarium*, plants poisonous to stock... 417
Yellow false garlic, poisonous to stock 397
Yew, common, poisonous to stock 395
Zea mays, supposed poisoning to stock 395
Zebroid, description of hybrid... 369
Zebroids, article on breeding... 369–371
Zygadenus elegans, plant poisonous to stock.............................. 396
 venenosus, experiment in feeding to sheep........................... 424
  plant poisonous to stock 396

○

Lightning Source UK Ltd.
Milton Keynes UK
UKHW021436160119
335572UK00009B/458/P